THE BEST

of

Alison Holst

First published 1991 by C. J. Publishing and Beckett Sterling
Third printing 1992

ISBN 0-908676-87-5

Copyright © Text: Alison Holst
              Photography: Chanel Publishers Ltd and
Moa Beckett Publishers Ltd

Photographer: Sal Criscillo
Food Styling: Alison Holst
Illustration: Clare Ferguson
Design: Alison Holst and Barbara Nielsen
Cover Design: Russell McKenzie
Produced by Stylus Publishing Services Ltd
Typeset by Typocrafters Ltd
Printed through Communication Arts Ltd

Published in New Zealand for Premier Books
28 Poland Road, Glenfield, Auckland

THE BEST

of

Alison Holst

PREMIER BOOKS

Introduction

For thirty years I have enjoyed cooking and sharing my ideas with many thousands of enthusiastic home cooks.

I have collected recipes and ideas from many places, and brought them home to modify them to suit exciting new kitchen machines, such as food processors and microwave ovens, local ingredients, and our national preferences and way of living.

I have encouraged many cooks to widen their culinary repertoire — in cooking classes and demonstrations on television, through radio and newspaper articles, magazines and cookbooks.

This book is a collection of many of my favourite recipes. I hope that you enjoy them and find them useful.

The Best of Alison Holst contains most of the recipes from
Alison Holst Cooks
Alison Holst's Cooking Class I, II and III

It contains many recipes from
Alison Holst's New Microwave Book

It contains a number of recipes from
Alison Holst's Meals Without Meat

It also includes some recipes from
Here's How
Meals with the Family
Food Without Fuss
Simply Delicious
What's Cooking
Alison Holst's Kitchen Diaries 1–12
Food Processor Book
Let's Cook
Recipes to Remember
Dollars and Sense

About the Author

Alison Holst is New Zealand's best-known and most popular food writer and television cook.

She graduated from the University of Otago with a Bachelor of Home Science degree in 1960, and returned to lecture in the Foods Department. She started cooking on New Zealand national television in 1965, and has appeared regularly ever since. She writes weekly columns for eight newspapers, talks on radio regularly, promotes New Zealand products nationally and internationally, and travels widely.

Alison has written 37 cookbooks, which have sold well over 1 million copies.

Her particular interests are family cooking, and encouraging home cooks to make good use of their kitchen machines. Alison has received a CBE and QSM, and was president of the New Zealand Guild of Food Writers in 1990.

Contents

The following symbols are used in this book to show the cooking method:

C cooked in a conventional oven or on the stove top

M cooked in a microwave oven (see page 7)

B barbecued

U requires no cooking

D made in a dehydrator (see page 250)

Weights & Measures Used In This Book

For best results use standard metric cups and spoons for these recipes.

Wherever possible the ingredients have been measured rather than weighed, and the quantities given in level cup and spoon measures.

A standard metric measuring cup holds 250 millilitres (quarter of a litre). Clear plastic measuring cups with a pouring lip and with the 1 cup mark below the rim are not expensive. These are the best cups to use for measuring liquids. They should be marked with quarter-cup divisions, and also with 50-millilitres divisions.

If you bake a lot, buy two plastic measuring cups — one for liquid and one for dry ingredients. Better still buy a set of single capacity measuring cups to measure dry ingredients quickly and easily.

When you measure the flour, spoon it into the measure lightly, and level it off, without shaking it down or banging the cup. Shaking or banging packs down the flour and means that too much is used in the recipe.

Most butter quantities have been given by weight. Butter packs have 50 g or 100 g markings on them. These are accurate, apart from the markings at each end of the pack. Very small quantities of butter have been measured by spoons — 1 tablespoon of butter weighs 15 g.

Because household spoons vary in size, you should use a set of metric measuring spoons when cooking with metricated recipes. One tablespoon holds 15 millilitres, and 1 teaspoon holds 5 millilitres.

All the cup and spoon measures in this book are level, unless otherwise stated. Remember that a heaped teaspoon can weigh twice as much as a level one, and will upset the balance of the ingredients used in a recipe. The following abbreviations have been used in this book:

cm	centimetre
C	Celsius
F	Fahrenheit
ml	millilitre
l	litre
g	gram
kg	kilogram

Oven Temperatures

Most of the oven-baked recipes in this book were cooked in an oven with a fan. The fan circulates heat so that no parts of the oven are much hotter or colder than other parts.

If you use an oven which does not have a fan, you may find that you need to allow a slightly longer cooking time, or a slightly higher temperature.

To help you judge when your food is cooked, I have given you other indications of readiness to look for, wherever possible, as well as indicating the probable time required.

Glossary

BASMATI RICE: Aromatic long grain rice — addictive!

CREME FRAICHE: A rich, cultured sour cream product, more interesting than sour cream. Replace with sour cream, where not available.

CHOCOLATE: Different varieties of shapes and sizes of cooking chocolate are available at different times. Contact Nestlés about availability of different types, if necessary.

DAIRY CREAM: Ultra-pasteurised (30% fat) multipurpose cream for whipping and pouring.

DAIRY-WIP: Whipped cream in an aerosol can, with a long refrigerator life.

DEHYDRATOR: A dryer consisting of circular trays which fit on top of each other, above a low-wattage electric heater and an efficient fan, and below a lid. For information,

write to Harvest Maid Dehydrators, PO Box 40281, Lower Hutt, N.Z. or Home Food Dehydrators, 3/76 Rushdale St., Knoxfield, Victoria, 3180 Australia.

DOUBLE CREAM: Ultra-pasteurised thickened (40% fat) cream for spooning and whipping.

EVAPORATED MILK: Unsweetened condensed milk.

FISH VARIETIES: See description of fish of different textures, in Fish section. Replace one variety with another of similar texture, if necessary.

FOOD PROCESSOR: A Toshiba Food Processor with a large bowl and a strong motor was used for testing and preparing the recipes in this book. Some food processors would not cope with such large amounts, etc. Follow the instructions given by the maker of individual food processors.

INSTANT STOCK: Concentrated powdered (flavour booster) stocks, in different flavours. Replace with crumbled stock cubes, using similar volumes, if not available. Do not use more than specified, because of saltiness.

MICROCRISP: Film, bought in a roll, which causes surface of food cooking in a microwave oven, in contact with it, to brown, in the same way that a preheated browning dish causes browning.

TEFLON LINERS: Amazingly efficient, re-usable, flexible, non-stick material used to line cake-tins, oven trays, etc. Contact PO Box 1446 Auckland, New Zealand.

TRIM MILK: 0.5% fat milk, with non-fat milk solids added.

TRIM PORK: Known as New-Fashioned Pork in Australia.

Microwave Information

Cooking Levels and Details

The wattage of domestic microwave ovens varies from 500 watts to 740 watts.

In most microwave ovens you can choose one of several different power levels when you cook. Most of the time, you cook at Full power, that is 100% power.

If no power level is specified, cook at Full (or High) power, when using the microwave recipes in this book.

The power levels on various microwave ovens are given different names.

I have used the following names for the different power levels used in the recipes in this book.

```
Full ................. 100% power ... 650 watts
Medium–High .. 70% power ... 450 watts
Medium ............ 50% power ... 350 watts
Defrost ............. 30% power ... 220 watts
```

The percentages and wattages given are approximate only. My recipes were cooked and tested using a Toshiba E.R.7900 A/N 650 watt microwave oven.

Your oven may have different settings. Don't worry! This may be overcome easily, either by using slightly shorter or longer cooking times, or by using your instruction book to find the corresponding settings for your microwave oven.

The recipes in this book have been tested in an oven with a turntable. If you prepare these recipes in an older oven without a turntable you may have to turn the food several times during cooking, to make sure it cooks evenly.

This book, like other microwave recipe books, cannot always give you precise and accurate cooking times because these vary. Watch the food carefully as it nears the end of the cooking time, remembering that it will continue to cook after the oven is turned off.

Be particularly careful, the first time you microwave a new recipe, especially a recipe for a baked product. Occasionally you find that your microwave oven will cook the product in a shorter time than the time specified.

Start checking after half the cooking time has elapsed, then check regularly, especially when you start to smell the food.

Double-check that the wattage, and power level names (and wattages) are similar to those used here, if the food is cooking more quickly than expected.

Make a note of the time required, the dish used, etc., so you have a guide the next time you use the same recipe.

When you can smell the food cooking in the microwave oven you know that it is nearly ready.

You should use Full power in microwave recipes where no power level is specified.

When a particular power level is specified at the start of a recipe you should use it for the rest of the recipe, unless otherwise instructed.

Cooking Times Vary

- Machines with different wattage cook at different rates. The higher the wattage, the faster the food will cook.
- The higher the power level, the quicker the cooking will be. A cake, for example, will take about twice as long to cook at 50% power as it does to cook at 100% power.
- Initial temperature is important. Food from the refrigerator takes longer to cook than food from a warm room.
- Large amounts of food take longer to cook than small amounts of the same food.
- Small pieces of food cook more quickly than large pieces, so finely chopped food will cook faster than large chunks, even though the total weight is the same.
- The shape of the container affects the cooking time, e.g. a cake in a ring-shaped mould will cook faster than a cake in a round pan.
- Food which is covered during cooking usually cooks faster than the same food uncovered.
- Food placed so the densest part is to the outside will cook faster.
- A solid item which is turned over part way through cooking will cook more quickly and evenly than an unturned one.

When the total cooking time is very short, cooking food for a minute longer than necessary will mean it is overcooked.

Because foods continue to cook after they are taken from the oven, you should try to stop cooking them just before they are completely cooked.

Standing Time

Food continues to cook after it is taken out of a microwave oven, e.g. a potato keeps baking for 1–2 minutes.

A roast continues to cook, and its internal temperature rises, for 10–15 minutes after it is taken from the oven.

The appearance and texture of the food change during this time:

- crumble toppings become crisper
- cabbage softens and brightens
- hamburgers and chicken get browner
- cake surfaces dry out

If you wait until food looks and feels cooked before you take it from the oven, you may well find that it is overcooked after standing. If in doubt, undercook. Take food out after the recommended time. You can always put it back in the oven if it is still undercooked after standing. It is much harder to render first aid to overcooked food!

Acknowledgements

The publishers would like to thank Inprint New Zealand for allowing the use of the photographs on pages 35, 125 and 187, and Food Media for allowing the use of the photographs on pages 100 and 260.

Starters and Snacks

The recipes in this section are suitable for use in different ways.

Sometimes I serve one or two of them before a main course when I am having friends to dinner. They may be passed round with drinks, or put on a coffee table. More formally, I may make one recipe only and serve it at the table, in attractively garnished small portions.

For an informal summer buffet lunch for adults, I may prepare several of these recipes and make them a complete meal with bread or crackers and crisp raw vegetables.

The day after a party, if there are leftovers, we eat them very happily as a complete light meal.

The pattern of snacking like this may have shocked our mothers and grandmothers who believed in more structured family meals, served more formally, but it suits the casual life-styles of many people today.

After all, bread and a selection of crisp raw vegetables served with a protein-rich dip makes a meal that is surprisingly balanced from the point of view of colour, texture and nutrients.

Food to be served in small amounts at the start of a meal needs to be carefully seasoned, so you should take particular care to do this.

Hummus

🄲 Hummus

I hope that you will not look at the ingredients for this dip, decide that they are uninteresting, and pass on to the next recipe! This mixture is quite addictive, once you acquire the taste for it, and may, in fact, be served as a complete meal, with dried pita or other bread, and vegetable dipping sticks. Try it made with any white beans. The flavour will change slightly, but the cooking time will be shorter. Black-eyed beans, for example, cook in 20–30 minutes, with no preliminary soaking.

1 cup dried chickpeas or other white
    beans
boiling water
juice of 2–3 lemons
3 cloves garlic
1 tsp salt
2–3 Tbsp tahini (sesame paste)
¹/₂–1 cup oil

Pour boiling water over chickpeas or other beans. Leave to stand for at least an hour, then boil until tender. If using black-eyed beans, boil without soaking for 20–30 minutes, or until tender. Drain cooked peas/beans (2–3 cups) and keep cooking liquid.

Put the cooked peas/beans in a blender with the lemon juice, garlic cloves, salt and tahini. Add half a cup of the cooking liquid and half the oil, then whiz the mixture until it is smooth, stopping the blender and pushing down the mixture several times.

Add more oil slowly to get the texture you like, then add extra seasoning if necessary. Refrigerate until needed (up to a week). Serve piled in a dish. For special occasions, sprinkle the surface with chopped parsley, toasted sesame seeds or a few whole cooked chickpeas, and pour a little extra oil over the surface, so it shines.

Variation:
Use more tahini and more cooking liquid and little or no oil if desired. Use canned chickpeas (garbanzo beans) when time is short.

🄤 Taramasalata

I love turning a combination of unlikely ingredients into something delicious! This is based on a Greek recipe. The resulting 2–3 cups of light, fluffy, mayonnaise-like mixture is wonderful as a dip for fresh vegetables or spread on crusty bread.

Buy smoked cod's roe (tarama) at fish shops or at your delicatessen. You can refrigerate it for weeks, or freeze it for months. Taste a thin slice of it alone before you use the rest in this recipe.

50 g smoked cod's roe
50 g crustless stale white bread
½ cup milk
1 small onion
3 Tbsp lemon juice
about 1 cup corn or soya oil

Cut the roe in six to eight pieces and put in a food processor or blender. Soak the bread (3 toast-thick slices) in the milk before putting this with the roe. Chop and add the onion. Process until smooth, adding the lemon juice gradually. Add the oil in a thin stream, stopping when the mixture becomes too thick to pour. You may use more or less oil.

Use immediately, or refrigerate for up to 3 days.

Eggplant Dip

This popular Middle Eastern dip is traditionally served with dried, crisp pita bread. It is also good on hot toast, however. If you microwave the eggplant rather than grilling or baking it, you get a light green dip instead of a brownish one.

1 small eggplant (about 300 g)
1 large clove garlic, chopped
¼ cup chopped parsley
2 Tbsp lemon juice
2 Tbsp tahini (sesame paste)
salt and pepper

Microwave the eggplant, after puncturing its skin in several places. Allow about 6 minutes per 500 g, and turn after half the estimated cooking time.

Or, roast in an oven heated to 180°C for 45–60 minutes, or turn over a barbecue until soft. However it is cooked, the eggplant should feel evenly soft when ready.

Peel or cut off the skin, and mash or purée the flesh with the remaining ingredients until well blended but not completely smooth. Stand for an hour to blend flavours before using as a spread or dip.

Guacamole

This simple sauce may be used as a dip, or spooned over refried beans for tacos and tostadas.

It is best made to taste rather than by definite quantities of added flavourings, since avocados vary so much in flavour and size.

Halve, stone, and remove the flesh from a ripe avocado. Mash or process the flesh briefly in a food processor, adding the juice from ½–1 lemon.

Add 1 or 2 finely chopped spring onions, a finely chopped tomato for colour, if desired, then season with salt or garlic salt, freshly ground black pepper, and hot pepper sauce. You might like to make other additions, too, such as a little sugar and ground cumin.

Spoon the guacamole into the empty avocado shells, or into a small bowl to serve. Cover until serving.

Avocado Dip

This dip makes an avocado go a long way. It is a beautiful colour, and, rather surprisingly, does not darken on standing, so it can be made hours before it is needed.

1 large avocado
½ cup sour cream
¼ cup oil
3 Tbsp lemon juice
½ tsp sugar
¼ tsp garlic salt
dash of Tabasco sauce
salt to taste

In a food processor or blender, measure and purée the first seven ingredients, then add salt carefully, tasting all the time, until you get a good flavour. The amount of salt depends on the size and ripeness of the avocado. Chill until the flavours blend well and the dip thickens.
Note:
It isn't worth making this if the avocado isn't ripe enough to have a buttery texture. If there are any black, over-ripe bits, remove them or they will spoil the colour of the dip.

Herb Dip

This mixture makes a good dip for raw vegetables or crackers.

2 eggs
3 Tbsp wine vinegar
1 tsp salt
½ tsp sugar
1 tsp mixed mustard
1 large clove garlic, crushed
1 Tbsp chopped dill leaves
1 Tbsp chopped chives
¼ cup chopped parsley
1¾ cups corn or soya oil
2 Tbsp lemon juice
½ cup sour cream

Put first nine ingredients into a food processor fitted with a metal chopping blade. Process till finely chopped. Add oil in a slow stream until mixture heaps in a spoon, adding more or less oil as needed.

Add lemon juice and cream and blend but do not beat. Leave at least an hour before serving.

Refrigerate for up to a week.

Bagna Cauda

I serve this hot dip in a small, thick-sided microwavable bowl in the centre of a large platter of cold crisp vegetables. When the dip cools down, I 'zap' it in the microwave oven, warming it without letting it boil over.

For a party, choose a platter that will fit in your refrigerator. Pile on to it crisp sliced carrot, celery, zucchini, red and green pepper, cauliflower, small whole mushrooms, asparagus tips, young beans, snow peas or sugar snap peas, and radishes, depending on the season. Cover and refrigerate until required.

1½ cups cream
2–3 large cloves garlic, finely chopped
6 flat anchovy fillets, chopped
2 Tbsp butter

Simmer the cream with the chopped garlic until reduced to about a cup. Heat the chopped anchovies with the butter until bubbling, then stir in the reduced cream. Reheat as necessary, and dip the cold vegetables in the hot dip.

Ginger Dipping Sauce

This sauce is particularly good as a dipping sauce for all sorts of fish. Use it to dip mussels, oysters, etc.

It is a good dip for raw vegetables and cooked, unsauced meat, too.

1 Tbsp chopped or grated root ginger
2 small dried chillis
1 clove garlic
2 tsp sugar
2 Tbsp light soya or fish sauce
1 Tbsp water
1 Tbsp lemon or lime juice

Combine all ingredients in a food processor or blender, then pulverise, and strain through a fine strainer.
Note:
If you cannot use a food processor or blender, pulverise the chilli and grate the ginger, shake everything together in a screw-topped jar, and strain before use. For best flavour, make the sauce just before you want to serve it.

Fish sauce is rather like light soya sauce. It is used in Thai and Vietnamese cooking. It keeps for ever, and can be bought at stores selling Oriental ingredients. Do not try to substitute anchovy sauce. Use a light soya sauce instead, but consider buying a bottle of the fish sauce if you want to try Thai cooking. Do not be put off by its name. It tastes savoury, rather than fishy.

U Blue Cheese Dip or Ball

This tasty mixture has the flavour of blue cheese and the texture of cream cheese. With more liquid added, it makes a good dip. Made with a smaller amount of liquid it is firm enough to shape into a ball or cylinder, to coat with sesame seeds, nuts, or chopped parsley. It is a good way to make any of our delicious blue cheeses go further.

1 wrapped wedge NZ blue vein cheese
  or 100 g other blue cheese
1 (250 g) carton cream cheese
1 small onion
1 Tbsp Worcestershire sauce
about ¹/₂ cup (dryish) sherry
flaked almonds, chopped walnuts,
  sesame or sunflower seeds (for the
  ball only)

For the dip:
If you have a good processor, put everything in it. Break or cut the blue vein cheese into small cubes. Put the cream cheese in on top in dessertspoon-sized blobs. Cut the onion into eighths before adding it, then add the Worcestershire sauce and sherry. Process until smooth, using the metal chopping blade and wiping down the sides of the bowl with a rubber spatula when necessary. Thin the mixture with more sherry, cream or milk, if necessary. The mixture always thickens on standing.

Alternatively, mash the blue vein cheese into a large bowl with a fork. Add the cream cheese and beat with a wooden spoon or rubber scraper until smooth. Grate the onion or cut in half and scrape the cut surface with a teaspoon to get onion pulp and onion juice. Add to the cheese with the Worcestershire sauce and sherry. Thin as desired with extra sherry or cream.

For the ball:
Mix as above but use only 2 tablespoons sherry and no extra liquid.

Tip it out of the food processor (or other) bowl on to a piece of plastic on which you have spread toasted sesame seeds, toasted flaked almonds, finely chopped walnuts, or toasted sunflower seeds. Lifting up the edges of the plastic, roll the cheese mixture in its coating until it is the shape you want.

> Use your microwave oven to recrisp softened potato chips, nuts, popcorn, crackers, etc. Lay them on several layers of paper towels (preferably on a ridged roasting pan). Microwave at Full power until food feels warm, starting with 20 seconds. Cool before serving.

Although a ball looks lovely the first time it is served, it is hard to serve attractively a second time. A sausage or log shape is more practical, especially if you can persuade your guests to attack it from one end!

C M Hot Cream Cheese

This cheese mixture makes a delicious hot dip with corn chips, crisp raw vegetables, or slices of French bread.

Leftover dip can be stored in a covered dish in the refrigerator. It is especially nice spread on rolls, crumpets, English muffins, etc. and reheated under a grill.

1 (250 g) carton cream cheese
1 spring onion, chopped
1 clove garlic
1 Tbsp tomato sauce
5 drops or more Tabasco sauce
¹/₄ cup grated Cheddar cheese
1 tomato (optional)
¹/₄ green pepper (optional)

Soften the cream cheese by beating it with a wooden spoon until it is easily workable, or warm it briefly in a microwave oven.

Add the finely sliced spring onion and garlic, then the tomato sauce, Tabasco sauce, and grated cheese. Stir in the finely chopped tomato and pepper, if desired.

Microwave for 2–3 minutes at Full power, stirring after each minute, until the cheese melts, and the mixture is hot and bubbling round the edges. Alternatively put the mixture in a flameproof container and heat under a grill, stirring once or twice as the mixture warms, then leaving it to brown in parts on the surface.

Serve hot with corn chips, raw vegetables or sliced French bread.

U Crudités

Crudités are nothing more than fresh, crisp raw vegetables, cut up, if large, for easy eating.

Arrange several of the following on a plate or platter.

Serve little dishes of coarse salt and freshly ground pepper, and a generous supply of some variety of mayonnaise, e.g. garlic, herb, or chilli mayonnaise. If you are serving radishes, include a small dish of butter, since this is good spread on small cold radishes.

carrots	young beans
celery	tender asparagus
radishes	peppers
cucumber	mushrooms
snow peas	spring onions
califlower	witloof (endive)

C M Tomato Salsa

This easy sauce makes a good dip for corn chips.

1 medium-sized onion
2 cloves garlic, minced
1 (425 g) can whole peeled tomatoes
1 tsp cumin
¹/₂ tsp marjoram or oreganum
1 tsp chilli powder

Put onions and garlic into a blender or food processor, and process until well chopped.

Add the drained tomatoes, and process again until the mixture is evenly combined, but still a little chunky.

Now add the seasonings and heat the mixture to boiling (either in a microwave or on the stove), then simmer for 5 minutes, reducing power level or temperature accordingly.

Serve hot or cold as a dip or sauce. Add hot pepper sauce just before serving, if you want a hotter mixture.

C Green Bean Dip

If you are a guacamole addict but are frightened by the price of off-season avocados, try this recipe. The replacement of avocado with fresh or frozen green beans may seem a little odd but the finished product is surprisingly good!

500 g green beans
3 hard-boiled eggs
¹/₂ cup cream cheese
1 small green pepper
1 large clove garlic
1 tsp (or to taste) hot chilli sauce
1 tsp mustard powder
1 tsp ground cumin
1 tsp sugar
1 tsp salt
juice of 1 lemon
black pepper
3 spring onions

Cook the beans until tender, then drain as much water from them as possible.

Put the beans and hard-boiled eggs into a food processor or blender, and process until smooth.

Add the cream cheese, diced green pepper, seasonings, and sliced spring onions and process again until well mixed.

Refrigerate until you are ready to serve it, with crisp vegetable sticks.

Tomato Salsa and Green Bean Dip

Meat Balls with Indonesian Sauce

up in the oven or under a hot grill whenever you want something tasty, hot, and popular. You can mix the filling ahead of time and keep it in a covered dish in the refrigerator to use whenever you want to turn French bread or any bread roll into something exciting.

4 cloves garlic
100g tasty Cheddar cheese
100 g soft butter
3 Tbsp tomato sauce
1 Tbsp tomato paste (optional)

Chop the garlic finely in a food processor. Add the cheese, in cubes, and chop into small pieces. Add the butter, which has been warmed to easily mixed consistency, then add the tomato sauce, and if you like a definite tomato flavour, the tomato paste. Process until well mixed.

Or chop the garlic very finely. Mix with 4 cups of grated cheese, the soft butter, and the tomato flavourings, and mix well with a rubber spatula, knife, etc.

Spread thickly on any long, thin loaf or roll which has been cut in slices without cutting through the bottom crust, so the bread still holds together in its original shape.

Wrap in foil, sealing joins, and heat through over a barbecue, under a grill, or in a hot oven, turning when necessary. Do not overheat. Fold back the foil so the top part of the loaf can brown and crisp up before serving. Serve hot.

Variations:
Add fresh or dried herbs to the mixture. Replace the tasty cheese with any other type that you have and like.

C M Meat Balls with Indonesian Sauce

This peanutty sauce is delicious with lamb. Use it as a dip for little meat balls (or cubes of barbecued lamb), or thin it for a sauce for bigger meatballs or to serve with roast lamb.

Indonesian sauce
2 cloves garlic, chopped
2 tsp grated root ginger
1 tsp freshly ground coriander seed (optional)
2 Tbsp dark soya sauce
2 Tbsp lemon juice
1 Tbsp oil
3–4 drops hot pepper sauce
$\frac{1}{4}$ cup brown sugar
2 Tbsp peanut butter
$\frac{1}{4}$ cup water

For the sauce, combine ingredients and heat until smooth and thickened. Dilute with water if too thick.

Little meat balls
250 g minced lamb or beef
1 small onion
$1\frac{1}{2}$ thick slices bread
3–4 mint or basil leaves (or $\frac{1}{2}$ tsp dried mint or basil)
$1\frac{1}{2}$ tsp instant chicken stock
1 Tbsp lemon juice

In food processor, chop together quartered onion, bread, leaves, and instant stock. Add lemon juice and minced meat and process until evenly mixed.

With wet hands, shape mixture into 24 small balls. Stand meat balls in a circle round the edge of the microwave turntable, or on a large flat plate, and microwave at Full power for 3–4 minutes until firm, or cook in frypan 5–10 minutes. Brush with a little of the sauce before serving on cocktail skewers alongside dip.

B C Barbecue Bread

Don't save this savoury bread mixture just for barbecues. Warm it

C Crumbed Camembert

This may be served as a meal starter or as dessert. Serve plain with cherries or grapes, with tart fruit jelly, or with a sauce made by heating jam or jelly with lemon or orange juice. Store Camembert (or Brie) in refrigerator. It should be very cold when cooked.

Cut into wedges. Dip in flour, then beaten egg, then in fine wine biscuit crumbs. Repeat egg, and crumb layers to get a firm, fairly thick coating, if desired.

Refrigerate until needed. About 10 minutes before serving, take from refrigerator and, using a fork or slotted spoon, deep fry in a small pot of very hot oil (at about 200°C).

Remove and drain on absorbent paper as soon as crumbed coating is golden brown. If cut immediately, cheese inside crust will be very runny.

If left to stand for 5 minutes before serving, it will thicken slightly.

C M Nachos

Nachos can be made and served in a number of different ways. They can be made from bought corn chips, or if you have the time you can make your own from uncooked tortillas (obtained from some delicatessens or Mexican restaurants).

If you are making your own corn chips, brush both sides of the whole tortillas with oil then cut them into pieces of the desired size.

Traditionally tortillas are fried, but grilling them in the oven, turning once after a few minutes, works well too.

The range of toppings used on nachos can be varied considerably, depending on what you feel like and what you have on hand. Spread the corn chips so they are several layers thick over an oven tray (if you don't mind communal eating) or arrange them in a number of individual plates or bowls.

Top with your choice of:
• refried beans
• sliced mushrooms
• chopped olives
• diced tomatoes
• diced peppers
• tomato salsa
• sliced avocado
• hot pepper sauce
• chopped spring onions
• grated cheese

If you are using refried beans, an alternative arrangement is to place a pile of the heated bean mixture in the centre of a plate or tray and pile the corn chips around this, then arrange additional topping over the top of this. The grated cheese is the only really essential component and should be sprinkled over last.

Place the tray or plates under a grill (or microwave them) until the cheese is well melted, add a dollop of sour cream and/or guacamole if desired, then serve immediately.

The list given above may sound complicated, but once you have tried a few times it's really very simple.

Experiment with the range of toppings you use until you establish your own favourites.

C Filo Triangles

Filo pastry gives the feeling of lightness and crunchiness to savouries.

The traditional filling of spinach and feta cheese is hard to beat. Use cream corn instead of spinach if this suits you better.

Filo filling
½ cup well-squeezed cooked spinach
½ cup crumbed feta cheese
1 egg
½ cup toasted pine nuts (optional)

Bacon Wrapped Cocktail Savouries

Chop the drained spinach finely. Mix with the cheese, egg and nuts, using a fork to combine them.

To make small triangular savouries, sandwich two sheets of filo pastry together with a small amount of melted butter.

Cut the double sheet into six strips, each about 6–7 cm wide. Put a teaspoonful of filling on the end of one strip, about a centimetre from one edge and the bottom. Fold the corner with the filling over, so the bottom edge is against the side, and the filling is enclosed. Keep folding the pastry over and over, until the filling is enclosed by all the pastry in the strip. Fold any ends under, or cut them off. Brush the top surface with melted butter, and place on a lightly buttered baking sheet or sponge roll pan.

Make as many filled triangles as you want, them bake them, uncovered, at 180°C for 10–20 minutes, or until the pastry is crisp and golden brown. Serve immediately, or reheat when required.

C Bacon Wrapped Cocktail Savouries

Next time you want hot savouries to serve with drinks, make bacon wrapped savouries, and watch how quickly they disappear!

Use thinly sliced bacon, and cut each rasher in two or three pieces, depending on its size.

Cut off the rinds and wrap some or all of the following foods fairly tightly in the bacon. Secure with a tooth-pick going in one side and out the other.

Fillings:
button mushrooms
drained pineapple cubes
stoned prunes
raw oysters
drained water chestnuts

You can wrap these in bacon several hours before you need them, then grill them for about ten minutes just before you need them. For a more substantial snack, put each savoury on a slice of French bread when you turn the cooked side away from the heat.

The bread heats and browns slightly and soaks up some bacon drippings.

Remove the toothpicks from bread-based savouries, but leave them in the plain ones.

C Falafel

Falafel are little balls or patties which are made from dried beans. They should be crisp on the outside, and well herbed and spiced when you bite into them. They are a popular street snack in places where Middle Eastern food is eaten.

They make a good eat-in-your-hand meal if you pile them into split pita breads with lettuce, tomatoes, and a sauce made from toasted sesame seeds.

Although falafel are often made from chickpeas, the sky will not fall on your head if you make them from other white beans. Black-eyed beans give a good result, after half an hour's soaking. In Egypt, dried broad beans are used to make falafel.

For 50 walnut-sized balls:
1 cup dried white beans (see above)
boiling water
1 large onion
4–6 cloves garlic
1 cup parsley sprigs
2 spring onions
1/2 cup packed mint or coriander leaves
2 tsp ground cumin
1–1 1/2 tsp salt
black pepper
hot pepper sauce
1/2 tsp baking soda

The beans for this recipe should be soaked so they are soft right through. Different beans take different soaking time. Pour a litre of boiling water over them and leave them to stand. The longest will take overnight, and the shortest, black-eyed beans, will be ready after 30 minutes, if they are fairly fresh. Chew a bean to see if it is ready, crunchy but soft, right through.

Chop the onion finely in a food processor. Squeeze it and remove any liquid, putting this aside, just in case the mixture is dry later. Chop the garlic, parsley, spring onion and mint or coriander leaves in the food processor with the squeezed onion. Remove from food processor.

Drain the soaked but uncooked beans in a sieve. Process them alone until they are as fine as ground almonds. Coarsely ground beans will not stick together during cooking. Add the remaining ingredients, then the chopped herb mixture, and mix well.

Heat about 2 cups of oil in a suitable frying container (an electric wok is good) to about 200°C. The oil should be about 2 cm deep.

Take teaspoon-sized balls of mixture with two spoons. Roll each

Falafel

smooth in your hands or leave them rough if you prefer this. Drop about six balls carefully into the hot oil. Cook for 4–5 minutes, turning once, when the lower part is brown. Drain on kitchen paper. Taste one of these and add more of any seasoning that it needs.

Serve with sesame cream sauce, as pre-meal snacks, or put in split pita breads with chopped tomato and lettuce, for a complete meal.

Sesame Cream Sauce
1 Tbsp tahini (sesame paste)
2 Tbsp lemon juice
2–4 Tbsp water
salt
few drops hot pepper sauce

If possible, make this sauce about half an hour before you want it, since its texture improves on standing.

Measure the tahini into a bowl that holds about a cup. Add the lemon juice and enough water to mix it to a thin, smooth cream. Add salt to taste, and hot sauce until it is as hot as you like it.

C M Roasting Nuts and Seeds

Roasting or toasting nuts and seeds improves their flavour and texture. Uncooked sesame seeds, for example, are virtually tasteless when compared to their toasted counterparts. Sunflower seeds also benefit greatly from roasting, which transforms them into a crisp and delicious snack or topping.

To dry-roast seeds and nuts, cook them over a low heat in a heavy-bottomed pan, or spread them evenly over a baking tray and cook them in an oven heated to 180°C, or about 15 cm away from a preheated grill, until they are golden brown. Don't try to cook too many at once, since a single layer will always cook most evenly. It is also important to shake or stir them frequently as overcooking or burning really spoils the flavour.

If you are going to cook seeds or nuts in a microwave oven, add a little oil or butter, don't use too much or they will be oily and unpleasant. A teaspoon of oil is enough for 1 cup of nuts, which should take about 6 minutes at Full power to cook. You may need more oil for smaller seeds — sesame seeds need about 1 teaspoon per 1/4 cup and will take 4–6 minutes at Full power to cook. Again it is important to stir frequently in order to avoid burning. It also pays to remember that cooking will continue for a few minutes after the seeds/nuts have been removed from the oven.

Allow nuts or seeds to cool, then salt lightly (try a variety of flavoured

salts) if desired. If kept in an airtight container, toasted nuts or seeds should remain fresh for weeks. Try toasting the whole container of sesame or sunflower seeds as soon as you buy them so that they will always be ready on hand when you want them.

Note:
If microwaving, make sure that the container you select is heat resistant. Nuts and seeds get very hot and will melt some plastics.

C Curried Walnuts

Walnuts are particularly nice baked and salted or spiced. Curried walnuts, are really delicious and I notice that a dish of them is always emptied before other nuts are eaten. Walnuts which have been fresh shelled are best.

Boil the halved, shelled walnuts in water for 3 minutes before they are baked. Drain them and bake them in a shallow dish until they start to turn brown at 180°C for 15–30 minutes.

As soon as they come out of the oven, add a little butter and toss them in it, or brush them with melted butter, then sprinkle them with a mixture of 1/2 teaspoon curry powder to 1 teaspoon salt.

Leave to cool on absorbent paper and store in airtight tins when cold.

C Spiced Almonds

These nuts are coated with a sweet, spicy mixture before they are baked.

Wash and drain the almonds to be used, then coat them with a little unbeaten egg white. Use 1–2 teaspoons egg white to 1 cup of almonds, mixing them together with the fingers in a small shallow basin or plate.

When they are coated, sprinkle them with a mixture of 2 tablespoons castor sugar and 2 teaspoons cinnamon or mixed spice.

When they are covered with this, spread them out on an oven slide or shallow pan so that they are not touching, and bake them at 150°C for 20–30 minutes.

Cool, and store in airtight tins.

C Roasted Peanuts

Heat the oven at 180°C. Spread plain (uncooked, unsalted) peanuts one layer thick in a baking tin and bake them for 20–30 minutes or until their colour darkens slightly.

To skin the roasted peanuts, rub them between your hands. Stand outside in a breeze, and the skins will blow away. When the nuts are cold, store in an airtight jar.

C Salted Cashew Nuts

Wash and drain cashews and spread them out thinly, one or two layers thick, in a shallow roasting pan. Sprinkle with salt and add a little butter. For 500 grams of nuts use $^{1}/_{2}$ teaspoon salt and 2 teaspoons butter.

Bake at 180°C for 15–30 minutes shaking the pan or stirring occasionally after the butter melts to make sure the nuts are well coated.

When they turn golden brown remove them and leave them to cool on kitchen or other absorbent paper. They will become crisp as they cool.

Do not put them in tins until they are quite cold.

C Clare's Terrine

This smooth-textured terrine tastes delicious when it is finished, but it looks and smells rather nasty while you are making it. After it is mixed, hold your breath, pour it quickly into the prepared loaf tin and put it in the oven to cook as promptly as possible.

350 g cubed lamb's liver
1 egg
$^{1}/_{4}$ cup sherry
1–2 cloves garlic
1 tsp salt
1 tsp thyme
$^{1}/_{4}$ tsp nutmeg
$^{1}/_{4}$ tsp sage
$^{1}/_{8}$ tsp ground cloves
black pepper
250 g sausage meat
1 or 2 rashers of bacon (or more)

Cut the liver into 12 to 20 cubes. Process with the metal chopping blade until liver is a smooth paste. Drop the egg and sherry through the feed tube. Squash the garlic with the salt, and drop this and the other seasonings through the tube. With wet hands, break the sausage meat into four or five pieces. With the blade rotating, drop the sausage meat down the feed tube, one piece at a time, and process until mixture is combined.

Line the long sides and bottom of a medium-to-large loaf tin with aluminium foil and place the bacon rashers on the bottom (or on the bottom and sides if using extra bacon). Pour the meat mixture into the tin. Stand loaf tin in a larger pan holding water to come halfway up the side of the loaf tin, and bake at 160°C for 1–1$^{1}/_{4}$ hours, until firm in the centre.

While terrine cools, cover it with foil, and stand a board and some fairly heavy jars or cans on it to flatten the bulge. When cold, turn upside down so bacon-covered side is uppermost.

C M Sushi

(See photograph on page 8.)

If you are prepared to take the time to find the ingredients and prepare this, you will be rewarded by a dramatic and inexpensive dish which can be served as a snack or starter at any time of the day.

You can make sushi without using thin sheets of seaweed if you make a large crêpe and use it to roll the rice in.

Don't forget the dips of Japanese horseradish (wasabi) powder, mixed to a paste with water (or sometimes available in tubes), and of Kikkoman soya sauce. These really bring sushi to life!

For about 20 small rolls:
1 cup short-grain rice
1$^{3}/_{4}$ cups water
2 Tbsp dry sherry
2 Tbsp wine vinegar
2 Tbsp sugar
1 tsp salt

Cook the rice and water in a microwave oven at Full power for about 10 minutes, or, if cooking conventionally, in a metal bowl standing in a pot of hot water, until tender.

Add the remaining ingredients and stir together with a fork. Taste, and add more of anything you think it needs.

Assemble the strips of vegetable that you will roll up in the rice. Select colour-contrasting vegetables, choosing from carrot, celery, red or green pepper, avocado, blanched spinach leaves and pickled vegetables. (Pickled oriental turnip is chewy and delicious).

Thin slices of smoked salmon look pretty when sliced and add an interesting flavour to sushi.

If using seaweed sheets as sushi wrappers, hold them over a hot element until they smell toasted, then lie one on a sheet of plastic.

If using a crêpe as a wrapper, make it in a large, preferably square pan, or trim its sides so they are parallel. Place it on plastic, too, for easy rolling.

Place a thin, fairly even covering of warm sushi rice all over the wrapper, then arrange on the end which will be rolled first, lines of your chosen fillings. Lay blanched spinach leaves flat so that you will see a spiral of dark green when the roll is cut, later on.

Using the sheet of plastic to help you, roll up firmly to form a compact cylinder, with the vegetables in the centre. Wrap in plastic film, refrigerate until required (up to 2 days) then cut into short lengths with a sharp or serrated knife.

M Chicken Liver Pâté

This smooth, delicious pâté is poured from the food processor into the container from which it will be served. For formal service, use individual pots. The glaze on top is pretty, but optional.

400 g chicken livers
$^{1}/_{4}$ cup dry or medium sherry
1 Tbsp brandy (optional)
50 g butter
1 clove garlic, chopped
1 Tbsp finely chopped onion
$^{3}/_{4}$ tsp salt
1 Tbsp chopped parsley
$^{1}/_{2}$ tsp dried thyme
$^{1}/_{2}$ tsp dried marjoram

Thaw livers if necessary. Separate the two lobes of the livers, discarding fibrous portion. Halve each lobe. Add sherry and brandy. Leave to stand at least 5 minutes.

Melt butter in fairly large microwave dish. Add remaining ingredients, then chicken livers and liquid. Cover. Microwave at Full power for 3–5 minutes, until livers are pink, not red in centre when cut. Alternatively, heat in frypan on moderate heat.

Using metal chopping blade in food processor, process livers until smooth. Pour into one large or several small individual moulds.

For optional glaze, soak 1 teaspoon gelatine in $^{1}/_{2}$ cup cold water, then heat with $^{1}/_{2}$ teaspoon instant chicken stock and $^{1}/_{2}$ teaspoon dark soya sauce. Pour over surface. Set bay leaves, green peppercorns etc, in glaze if desired.

U Herbed Cream Cheese Pâté

This pâté does not harden on refrigeration. It is good as a dip or spread.

100 g soft butter
2 cloves garlic, chopped
$^{1}/_{8}$ tsp salt
$^{1}/_{4}$ tsp sugar
freshly ground pepper
$^{1}/_{4}$ cup chopped chives
$^{1}/_{4}$ cup chopped parsley
2 tsp thyme leaves
1 (250 g) carton cream cheese
2 Tbsp lemon juice
2 Tbsp milk

Cream soft but not melted butter. Add ingredients one at a time, in the given order, beating after each addition. Use food processor if available. Fill small pots with mixture, or, to unmould later, fill moulds previously lined with plastic film. Refrigerate until required.

Layered Fish Mousse

Ⓜ Layered Fish Mousse

Using a food processor and a microwave oven, you can make this spectacular fish mousse in less than half an hour. What's more, you can make it ahead and reheat it! Serve it plain or with sour cream flavoured with tomato paste and thinned with white wine and lemon juice to suit your own taste.

For 8–10 small servings:

1½ cups fresh breadcrumbs
6 spring onions
750 g cubed, boneless fish fillets
2 small eggs
3 Tbsp lemon juice
2 tsp salt
½ cup cream
½ cup milk
100 g smoked salmon, drained canned salmon, or drained shrimps
1 Tbsp tomato concentrate
½ cup frozen peas
2 Tbsp chopped parsley
1 Tbsp dill or fennel, chopped

Divide first eight ingredients into two equal parts. Mix each part separately in the following way.

Process crumbs with white parts of spring onions. Remove. Purée fish, egg, lemon juice and salt. Add crumbs then cream and milk gradually, processing until fluffy.

Divide first half of mixture into three parts. These will be the three white layers. Spread one-third in a microwave loaf pan, about 20×10×8 cm, which has been lined with baking paper or cling wrap.

Process second half of ingredients. Remove half of this mixture (which will later be coloured green) from the food processor. Add to mixture in food processor the salmon (or shrimps) and tomato concentrate. Process to a smooth purée. Spread over the first white layer in loaf pan.

Cover the orange-coloured layer with the second of the white layers. If difficult to spread evenly, divide it into blobs first, then spread with a wet rubber spatula.

Process unthawed frozen peas with ½ cup chopped green spring onion leaves, parsley and dill leaf if available. When finely chopped, add remaining half of second fish mixture and combine well. Spread over second white layer.

Cover green layer with remaining white fish.

Wrap baking paper or cling wrap over last layer. Microwave on 60% power for 12–15 minutes or until centre springs back and small knife cuts clean in centre. Leave to stand at least 10 minutes. Unmould. Serve hot or cold.

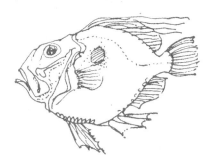

C Mushroom and Walnut Pâté

This pâté makes an elegant and delicious pre-dinner savoury, but is equally good piled on toast or crackers for a quick snack.

For about 2 cups pâté:
1½ cups green beans
2 eggs
1 Tbsp oil
1 medium-sized onion, diced
¼ cup walnuts, chopped
100 g mushrooms, sliced
1 tsp salt
½ tsp ground black pepper
2 Tbsp dry sherry

Cook the beans until tender, then drain well, squeezing out any excess water.

Hard boil, then roughly chop the eggs.

Heat the oil and sauté the onion until it begins to soften. Add the walnuts and mushrooms and cook until the walnuts have darkened and the mushrooms are soft.

Put the beans, eggs and mushroom mixture into a blender or food processor (if using a blender, purée in small amounts). Process until smooth with the metal blade.

Add the seasonings and sherry, mixing in well. Transfer the pâté into a bowl and refrigerate prior to serving.

C M Smoked Fish Pâté

When you make pâté from fish such as mackerel which has been hot-smoked no further cooking is required. When uncooked smoked fish is used the fillets should be cooked first.

Foil-wrap and simmer, or microwave covered, until the flesh flakes. Cool without uncovering, then proceed as below.

Serve the pâté with melba toast or crackers and crisp cold salad vegetables as the main course of a light meal or as a starter course.

200 g smoked mackerel
1 (250 g) carton cream cheese
1 Tbsp capers
1 tsp caper liquid
few drops Tabasco or Worcestershire sauce

Remove skin and bones from fillets of cooked smoked fish (see above). Break into even-sized pieces.

Process pieces in food processor with room-temperature cream cheese. (Soften cheese in microwave at Full power for one minute if necessary). Blend until thick and smooth.

Add capers and liquid, Tabasco or Worcestershire sauce. Process only until capers are finely chopped.

Spoon into one large, or several individual small pots. Seal with melted clarified butter if desired.

Serve within three days.

C Hot Crab Dip

This is a delicious, rich, hot dip, that was often served to me when I lived in California.

Prepare it and put it in a serving dish which can be put under the grill, then refrigerate it until fifteen minutes before you want to serve it.

1 (250 g) carton cream cheese
2–3 tsp Worcestershire sauce
1 Tbsp horseradish sauce
1 Tbsp lemon or lime juice
3–4 spring onions, chopped
few drops Tabasco sauce
1–2 cups (about 250 g) fresh or frozen crabmeat

Cream the first six ingredients together until thoroughly blended. Stir in the crabmeat, carefully but thoroughly, then taste and add salt and more juice and Tabasco if desired. If you like a sweet-sour flavour, add some finely chopped chutney, or cucumber pickles.

Spread in a shallow griller-proof dish, so the dip is no more than 2 cm deep.

When dip is required, put under the grill, so that the surface is about 10 cm from the heat. Grill until it bubbles around the edge, and the peaks brown.

Serve with potato or corn chips, and fresh, crisp vegetable sticks.
Variations:
Replace crabmeat with crayfish flesh, finely chopped mussels, drained salmon, or drained baby clams, if desired.

C Lamb Kidney Pâté

2 Tbsp butter
2–3 slices bacon
1 medium-sized onion
1 clove garlic
½ cup chopped mushrooms
4 lamb kidneys
¼ tsp dried thyme
pepper and salt
1–2 hard-boiled eggs

Melt butter in a large frying pan over medium heat. Add finely chopped bacon, onion and garlic and stir well. Chop mushrooms finely. Halve kidneys, remove outer skin and core, and slice thinly. Add to mixture in pan, season with thyme, plenty of pepper, and a little salt, and cook over medium heat, stirring frequently, for 5 minutes. Remove from heat and add roughly chopped hard-boiled eggs. Put hot mixture into blender, and process until pieces are small and evenly sized, but not completely smooth. Add a little extra butter if mixture is too thick for blender. Or, put mixture through fine blade of mincer, or through a foodmill.

Season carefully to taste, adding extra salt if necessary. Spoon warm mixture into a straight-sided pottery jar in which it can be stored and served, or into a container from which it will be unmoulded before serving. Garnish unmoulded pâté with radishes or tomatoes and parsley.

Pâté should be just firm enough to cut, but soft enough to spread.

Serve it on toast, thin crisp-baked bread, or crackers.

C Chicken Liver Spread

This is a tasty spread on crackers, toast, or bread. It keeps for several days in the refrigerator. You can make it with a mincer or blender. Both are satisfactory, but different, since the blender makes the paste very smooth.

2 eggs
3–4 Tbsp butter
1 medium-sized onion
1 clove garlic
250 g chicken livers
½ tsp salt
¼ tsp pepper
herbs
¼ cup lemon juice
2 Tbsp chopped parsley

Hard boil the eggs. Cook the onion and garlic in the butter until tender but not brown. Remove from the pan. Halve the chicken livers and sauté in the remaining fat until the livers are browned all over. Cook until the livers are no longer pink when cut in half. Season with salt and pepper. Add herbs such as thyme, marjoram or oreganum just before the livers are browned, if desired. While the eggs and liver are still warm, mince or blend them with the onion. Season well with plain or seasoned salt, lemon juice, and the chopped parsley. Pâté or spread may need further seasoning when cold.

Refrigerate until needed.

C Stuffed Eggs with Salmon

Stuff eggs with a filling made by mashing 4 hard-boiled egg yolks with 2 tablespoons sour cream until smooth and creamy. Mix into this 2–3 tablespoons finely chopped smoked salmon, and the white part of 1 spring onion. Add a little anchovy paste or sauce, if desired. If

Squiggles

this mixture is to be piped, the ingredients should be combined in a blender or food processor. Otherwise spoon into halved hard-boiled egg whites.

Garnish with a roll of smoked salmon and fresh herbs.

Squiggles

These are delicious deep-fried pea-flour snacks. Vary the seasonings according to your own taste.

1 cup pea flour
1 Tbsp poppy seeds
1 Tbsp toasted sesame seeds
4 tsp ground cumin
2 tsp ground coriander
2 tsp garam masala
1 tsp paprika
1 tsp turmeric
½–1 tsp chilli powder
½–1 tsp salt
½ cup water

Measure the dry ingredients into a medium-sized bowl, mix together lightly. Add the water and stir to form a dough the consistency of thick paste. If the dough seems too dry, add a little more water.

Preheat 1–2 cm of oil to 200°C. Transfer the dough into a forcer bag fitted with a fine ribbon or fine (2–4

mm) circular nozzle. When the oil is up to heat, begin to squeeze in the dough.

If you like regular shapes, hold the nozzle close to the surface of the oil, this should give you quite good control of the extruded dough. For more random shapes, hold the bag further above the surface (10–15 cm). This will allow the dough to form its own shapes. Be very careful when working around the hot oil as splashes may cause painful burns.

Cook for 3–5 minutes until crisp and brown, turning occasionally to ensure even cooking. Remove from the oil, and stand on paper towels to drain prior to serving.

Poppadoms

These are good substitutes for corn chips or potato crisps. In a microwave oven they wrinkle and cook like magic! Put 1 large or 2 small poppadoms, straight from their packet, on a paper towel, microwave uncovered at Full power for 45 seconds to 1 minute, until whole surface buckles. Remove before it browns and leave 30 seconds. Whole surface should be crisp. Adjust times, if necessary. Serve as snacks with dips or soups.

Popcorn

Don't underestimate popcorn. Apart from the fact that few people can resist it when freshly made, popcorn is cheap, relatively low calorie, and a few dried kernels from your storecupboard make a potful in a short time.

2 Tbsp oil
2 Tbsp popping corn
1–2 Tbsp butter
salt, plain or flavoured

Put oil in frying pan or large saucepan with a lid. Add popping corn, put on the lid, and turn the heat to medium.

Wait patiently until you hear explosions in the pan. Shake frequently. When all the popping has stopped, tip the popped corn on to a tray.

Heat the butter and pour this over the warm popcorn. Sprinkle it with plain salt or with flavoured salt, like celery or onion salt.

Variation:

Candied popcorn; put 2 tablespoons sugar into the pan after the popcorn has cooked. When it turns to caramel, tip popcorn into pan and stir around.

Soup

These days, few of us have the time, desire or lifestyle to keep a soup pot simmering on the back of the stove all winter, as our grandmothers did. This is not to say that we do not enjoy, and make, soup for our families and friends.

Sometimes we simply open a can or a packet, and add a creative garnish! At other times we use instant stocks for speed and flavour, and add vegetables, pasta and cereals. We know that we can make creamy vegetable soups in a remarkably short time.

Some of us remember our mother's stock-based soups so fondly that we are prepared to boil bones on occasions, then strain, chop, grate, stir and taste until we get the same delicious end result.

At times we make economical soups from ingredients that would otherwise have been wasted, and occasionally we splurge on really extravagant ingredients.

We serve our soups as starters and as complete, satisfying meals.

We often speed up our soup-making using food processors, pressure cookers and microwave ovens, and we store the soups we don't want today or tomorrow in our freezers.

Aren't we lucky to have such a choice? We can't help but make wonderful soups.

Corn Chowder

C Corn Chowder

If you move fast, you can sit down to eat this less than 15 minutes after you start to make it.

For 4 large servings:
1 carrot
1 potato
1 onion or leek
1 cup water
2 tsp instant bacon stock
50 g butter
3 Tbsp flour
1 450 g can whole-kernel corn
1 cup milk

Scrub then cube the carrot and potato. Cook with the chopped onion or sliced leek in the water for 10 minutes or until potato is tender. Stir in the bacon stock.

In another pot melt the butter, add the flour and make a sauce using the corn liquid made up to 2 cups with milk.

Stir the sauce into the cooked vegetables. Mash or purée if desired, then add the corn.

Serve with toast or crisp bread rolls as a complete meal. Top with grated cheese if desired.

C Greens Soup

This soup changes with the seasons, and the availability of different green vegetables.

For 4–6 servings:
2 medium-sized potatoes
2 medium-sized onions
2 cups water
2 tsp instant green herb stock
1 tsp instant chicken stock
50 g butter
2–4 cups green vegetables
1/2 cup milk
1/4 cup cream

Chop the unpeeled potatoes and the onions into small cubes and simmer in the water until the potato is cooked, for about 10 minutes. Then stir in the instant stock.

Meantime, melt the butter and add to it enough chopped or grated green vegetables to make about a cup of cooked vegetable. Mixtures make a good soup. Use some of the following: spinach, silverbeet, lettuce and young cabbage leaves, broccoli, watercress, parsley, chickweed, milk thistle, spring onion, cucumber, zucchini. Cover pot tightly and cook with no added liquid until just tender, but still bright green.

Purée with the potato mixture. Sieve if desired, and thin with the milk and cream. Adjust seasonings carefully.

Reheat without boiling.

Ⓒ Curried Kumara Soup

This is a really smooth and soothing soup.

For 4–6 servings:
75 g butter
2 cloves garlic
½–1 tsp curry powder
500 g kumara
1½ cups water
2 tsp instant chicken stock
about 3 cups milk
¼ cup cream (optional)

Add the crushed garlic and curry powder to the butter in a large saucepan.

Peel kumara with a potato peeler and slice 1 cm thick. Cook in the butter, without browning, for 1–2 minutes then add the water. Cover and cook for 10 minutes until tender. Stir in chicken stock, then purée, thinning with milk.

Add the cream and reheat without boiling.
Variation:
Replace kumara with the same weight of parsnip. Different, but equally delicious.

Ⓜ Pumpkin Soup

This soup will brighten the coldest winter night. Use any member of the pumpkin family to make it.

For 6–8 servings:
1 kg pumpkin
1 large onion, quartered
2 cloves garlic, chopped
¼ cup cold water
1½ tsp instant chicken stock
1½ tsp instant green herb stock
1½ tsp sugar
½ tsp nutmeg
3 cups boiling water
¼ cup cream (optional)

Cut pumpkin into several, fairly evenly shaped pieces. Remove seeds but not the skin if it is tough, since it is easy to lift flesh away from skin when cooked. Place the pumpkin, the quartered onion and the garlic with the cold water in a large covered container.

Microwave at Full power for 10 minutes, or until tender. (Smaller pieces cook faster.) Do not overcook.

When cool enough to work with, scrape pumpkin from the skin and purée the flesh, with the cooked onion, garlic and liquid, using a food processor, if available.

Add instant stock, sugar, nutmeg and 1 cup boiling water to make a thick purée. Sieve to remove any lumps. Return mixture to casserole or soup tureen. Add the remaining boiling water. Stir to mix.

Reheat until very hot, stirring every 2 minutes. Add cream before serving, if desired.

Ⓒ Asparagus Soup

A few years ago, in England, I tasted some frozen asparagus soup. It was one of the nicest soups I have ever had, so I experimented making, freezing and thawing a rich asparagus soup.

This is almost as good as the original. You might like to try it. Eat it as soon as the soup is made, or, if you are lucky enough to have access to a lot of cheap fresh asparagus, make extra for your freezer.

For 6–8 servings:
50 g butter
2 cloves garlic, chopped
¼ cup flour
500 g tender asparagus
2 cups water
1¼ cups cream
½ tsp salt
freshly group black pepper

Melt the butter in a saucepan, over moderate heat, add the chopped garlic, and cook for 2 minutes without browning. Stir in the flour, then remove from the heat.

Grate the raw asparagus, using the appropriate blade of a food processor, or a hand grater. (Hold the bunch of asparagus at right angles to the grater.) Bring the asparagus and water to the boil, and boil for 2 minutes. When cooked, the asparagus should be bright green and barely tender.

Drain the asparagus cooking liquid into the butter and flour mixture, and bring to the boil, stirring all the time. Stir in the cream. Bring to the boil, add the cooked asparagus, and return to the boil again.

If serving immediately, thin to desired consistency with milk, vegetable stock, or water. If

freezing, do not thin, but cook the thick soup as soon as possible, so that the asparagus stays bright green. The fastest way to cool it is to stand the saucepan in a large container of cold or iced water, changing the water as it gets warm.

Freeze in covered containers, leaving head space. Use within 6 months. Bring thawed soup to the boil, thin as required, then adjust seasoning.

Serve with croutons or with grated cheese or with toasted cheese sandwiches.

Ⓒ Cheese and Onion Soup

This is a rich, unusual and delicious soup, which may be made in a short time. Served with crusty bread and a salad it makes a satisfying and filling meal.

Do not be too generous with the serving size, since you may overwhelm those with small appetites.

For 6 starter or 4 main course servings:
3 medium-sized onions
2 cloves garlic
2 Tbsp oil or butter
1 tsp mustard powder
1 tsp salt
generous grind of black pepper
2 cups water
2 Tbsp butter
2 Tbsp flour
1½ cups milk
1 cup grated tasty cheese
1 Tbsp sherry
1 tsp dark soya sauce
½ tsp hot pepper sauce

Slice onions finely and chop the garlic. Melt the butter in a large pot, then sauté the onions with the garlic, mustard powder, salt and pepper until soft, without letting them brown. Add the water, bring to the boil, then cover and simmer over a low heat until the onions are tender.

In another pot melt the second measure of butter, then stir in the flour. Continue stirring while the mixture cooks for at least 1 minute. Add the milk and keep stirring until the sauce boils and thickens, allow to boil for a minute or so and then remove from the heat and stir in the grated cheese.

Add the cheese sauce to the onion mixture then stir in the sherry and soya and pepper sauces. Cook over a very low heat (avoiding boiling) for a further 10 minutes.

Serve immediately, or make ahead and reheat as required.

Chilled Tomato Soup

Gazpacho (or chilled tomato soup) is really a cross between a soup and a salad.

The base of this soup consists of well-flavoured tomato juice, or tomato juice with small chunky pieces of tomato in it.

For 4 servings:
1 (420 g) can diced tomatoes in juice
1 (425 g) can savoury tomatoes
1 tsp instant stock
½ cup boiling water
extra water
hot pepper sauce
4–8 iceblocks
1 avocado, cubed
1 green pepper, cubed
1 red pepper, cubed
¼–½ cucumber, cubed
about ½ cup chopped spring onion or mild red onion
1–2 cups small croutons
1 cup cubed tomatoes (optional)

Combine the contents of the two cans. Chop the pieces more finely using a food processor if available, or else mash with a potato masher, or strain off the solids and chop with a knife.

Measure the instant stock* into one of the cans, add boiling water to dissolve it, then rinse out the other can with this liquid. Make the total volume of tomato mixture up to 1 litre. Taste and adjust seasonings if necessary, adding a dash of hot pepper sauce, etc.

Refrigerate until needed, then serve in four fairly large bowls, each containing one or two iceblocks if the weather is hot.

Assemble the other listed ingredients in individual bowls, sprinkling lemon juice over the avocado to stop it browning. Pass these around so that diners can fill up their soup bowls with whatever combination and quantity of these that they want.
*Use any flavour you like, chicken or green herb stock is very good.

Soup Accompaniments
Crisped breads of different types make good soup accompaniments, providing good texture contrast. You can make croutons, crisp bread slices or poppadoms. Buy potato crisps and corn chips for soup accompaniments, too. Serve freshly made toast or warm crusty bread rolls. Make the accompaniments substantial when soup is the main part of the meal. Keep them small and interesting when the soup is served as a meal starter.

Quick Potato Soup

This is a simple, quick and well-flavoured soup. Blending or processing gives it a wonderful smooth texture that is further enhanced by the addition of a little cream.

For 4 servings:
2 onions
3 cloves garlic
3 Tbsp butter or oil
3 medium-sized potatoes (about 500 g)
3 cups of chicken or vegetable stock
1 tsp sugar
a generous grind of pepper and nutmeg
1 sprig each of parsley and mint
1 pinch each of fresh or dried basil and thyme
¼ cup cream (optional)

Chop the onion and garlic. Cook in the butter or oil in a large saucepan over a medium heat for a few minutes, until the onion begins to brown. Scrub and dice the potatoes and add to the onion and garlic. Pour the stock over the vegetables, add the sugar, pepper, nutmeg and herbs, then stir together and cover. Simmer for 10-15 minutes or until the potato is tender.

Blend the soup until smooth. If you don't have a food processor or blender, force vegetables through a sieve. Add the cream and reheat (but do not boil) to serve.

If you find that the colour of this soup is not inspiring, try dressing it up by adding a swirl of cream and a sprinkling of chopped herbs to each bowl.

Yoghurt and Cucumber Soup

The mixture of cucumber and yoghurt is a useful and versatile one. Depending on its seasoning and concentration, it may be used as a soup, a sauce, a dip or a salad dressing.

Although mint, garlic and dill are the herbs usually associated with this, you can please yourself. Allow standing time to allow the flavours to blend well.

For 4 servings:
2–3 long, thin cucumbers
1 tsp salt
2–3 spring onions
2 sprigs mint
1–2 cloves garlic
1 sprig parsley
1 sprig dill (optional)
2 cups plain unsweetened yoghurt
2 Tbsp cream (optional)

Peel cucumbers only if skin is thick. Halve lengthwise. Scoop out and discard seeds. Grate remaining cucumber, sprinkle with salt and leave to stand for 5-10 minutes.

Chop seasonings (in food processor with a little yoghurt). Squeeze cucumber and discard liquid.

Combine with seasonings and remaining yoghurt. Add cream for extra richness, and season. Process again if a smooth mixture is desired. Leave at least 30 minutes before serving.

Curried Cashew and Carrot Soup

This is a delicious and unusual soup. It is filling and substantial. Its flavour and texture will vary with the efficiency of your toasting and grinding of the cashew nuts. For best flavour have the nuts lightly and evenly toasted. The finer the nuts are ground the smoother and thicker the soup will be.

For 4 servings:
3 large carrots (500 g)
2 small onions
1 Tbsp butter
1–2 Tbsp curry powder
3 cups water
3 tsp instant chicken stock
1 cup toasted cashew nuts

Slice the carrots and chop the onions finely.

Melt the butter in a medium-sized saucepan, add the curry powder and chopped onions, and sauté until the onions are soft but not brown.

Add the carrots, water and powdered stock and simmer until the carrots are tender.

In a blender or food processor, process the toasted cashew nuts to the consistency of ground almonds. (Cashew nuts can be toasted under a grill in a sponge roll tin with ½ teaspoon oil.)

Drain the cooked carrots and onion and put into the food processor with the ground nuts. Process, adding the stock as required to get the desired consistency. Taste and adjust seasoning if necessary.

Reheat to serve. Top each serving with a spoonful of yoghurt sauce made with 1 cup unsweetened plain yoghurt mixed with 1 tablespoon finely chopped mint and 1 clove finely crushed garlic.

A covered soup tureen is a really practical investment if you have a microwave oven. You can cook in it, reheat soup in it, and bring it to the table for dramatic presentation. Hunt in your bottom cupboards for a long forgotten tureen or see what you can find in second-hand shops.

Curried Cashew and Carrot Soup

Shrimp Chowder

Ⓜ **Shrimp Chowder**

This is one of the most delicious soups I make — from ingredients I always keep in my store cupboard.

For 4 servings:
2 Tbsp butter
1 onion, chopped
2 cloves garlic, chopped
1 stalk celery, chopped
1 large potato (400 g), cubed
1 cup boiling water
1 tsp instant chicken stock
1 tsp instant green herb stock
1 Tbsp cornflour
1½ cups milk
1 can shrimps (about 200 g)
1 Tbsp chopped parsley

Heat butter, onion, garlic and celery in a covered bowl or casserole dish at Full power for 3 minutes, shaking or stirring after 2 minutes. Add the scrubbed, cubed potato and the boiling water. Cover and cook for 6 minutes or until potato is tender

Stir in instant stock, the cornflour mixed to a paste with some of the milk, the remaining milk, shrimps and shrimp liquid. Heat chowder until it thickens, up to 8 minutes, stirring occasionally. Sprinkle with parsley. The shrimp flavour intensifies on standing.

Ⓜ **Special Fish Chowder**

This soup may be made with any combination of shellfish and fish.

For 4 large servings:
2 Tbsp butter
1 stalk celery, sliced
2 cloves garlic, chopped
2 Tbsp flour
1 cup dry white wine
1 (420 g) can peeled tomatoes in juice
hot water
9–12 oysters
10–12 cooked mussels (optional)
100–200 g scallops
400 g fish fillets

In a large covered bowl or casserole dish heat the butter, celery and garlic at Full power for 3 minutes, stirring after 1 minute. Add the flour and heat for 1 minute. Add the wine and heat for 3 minutes longer. Stir until smooth and thick. Add the juice from the tomatoes and the oyster liquor, made up to 1½ cups with water. Heat until mixture is thick.

If the scallops are large, cut them smaller. Cut the fish into pieces the same size as the scallops and oysters. Add all the seafood and fish to the soup. Heat for 3 minutes or until fish is opaque.

Variations:
Add fresh thyme, grated orange rind or saffron for extra flavour.

C Shellfish Soup

This is a wonderful soup to make from freshly collected shellfish! (Make sure the shellfish have been gathered from a clean, unpolluted seashore.)

For about 6 servings:
2–3 cups shelled clams or tuatuas, pipis, etc.
2 cloves garlic
1 onion
1 bay leaf
¼ tsp thyme
5 cm strip of lemon rind
water or dry white wine
50 g butter
¼ cup flour
¼–½ cup cream
salt and pepper

Open shellfish by heating in a large frying pan in a little liquid, or in a microwave oven, just until the shells open. Save all liquid.

Purée or mince the shellfish with the garlic and onion.

Simmer for 20 minutes the shellfish in their own liquid made up to 4 cups with water, and with the herbs and lemon rind added.

Strain through a cloth in a sieve or colander, squeezing the cloth to extract all liquid. Make liquid up to 5 cups with water or dry white wine if necessary.

In a large saucepan melt the butter and cook gently with the flour for 2–3 minutes. Add the stock, 1 cup at a time, stirring after each addition until it boils again. Watch carefully to prevent burning on bottom of pot.

Remove from heat, add cream and season very carefully to taste. (The more cream added, the blander the flavour will be.)

C Oyster Soup

Use fresh or thawed frozen oysters, for this soup, reserving all oyster liquid to mix with the milk for extra flavour. For best flavour, make ahead and reheat without boiling.

For 4–6 servings:
18 oysters
1–2 cloves garlic
½ tsp grated nutmeg
75 g butter
6 Tbsp flour
4–5 cups milk
juice of 1 lemon
salt and pepper

Drain oysters, reserve liquid. Debeard oysters, put aside fleshy portion. Crush garlic clove(s) and grate nutmeg.

Cook beards, garlic and nutmeg in butter for 3-4 minutes without browning. Stir in flour, cook 2 minutes longer.

Stir in oyster liquid and 1 cup of milk. When thick add next cup of

Oyster Soup

milk. When mixture has boiled, after third cup of milk, food process if possible using metal chopping blade. Add fourth cup of milk to food processor bowl.

Sieve back into pot, discarding beards. Boil again, adding extra milk to reach desired thickness. Add sliced oyster flesh and lemon juice. Season carefully to taste. Reheat but do not boil after adding oysters.
Note:
The beard of an oyster is the frilly part around the 'meaty' eye.

C Fish Stock

Fish stock requires a much shorter cooking time than meat-based stock. When you make it, shut the doors between the kitchen and the rest of the house, and open the window so the odours are confined, and are quickly dispersed.

Fish stock makes a good poaching or baking liquid in which to cook fish. Stirred into a roux with cream, it makes a delicious sauce for plainly cooked fish. Its most important use for me, however, is to make a few

oysters go further when preparing oyster soup, using it to replace part of the milk.

For 3–4 cups:
500–600 g fish skeletons and/or fish heads
1 peeled onion, sliced
1–2 cloves garlic
1 stalk celery, chopped
1 bay leaf
1 sprig parsley
1 sprig thyme
6 peppercorns, or 1 dried chilli
2–3 cm strip lemon rind
4 cups water

Put all the ingredients listed into a fairly large saucepan. Cover loosely and simmer for 30 minutes, then strain through a sieve and wrap and discard the debris. Strain the stock through muslin again, if it is to be used in a light-coloured sauce or soup where no specks are wanted. Refrigerate or freeze in one-cup portions.
Variation:
Add to the fish skeletons crushed crayfish (rock lobster) legs and shells if available.

C Brown Beef Stock

Although you can make stock from any beef bones, bones which contain marrow are generally regarded the best. Make sure the bones have been cut into small sections, otherwise it may be difficult to pack them into a saucepan.

For about 10 cups:
1–2 kg beef soup bones
2–3 onions, chopped
2 carrots, chopped
2 stalks celery (optional)
2 cloves garlic
1–2 bay leaves
10 peppercorns
1 tsp salt
¹/₂ tsp dried thyme
¹/₂ tsp dried marjoram or oreganum
several parsley stalks
about 12 cups cold water

For a good brown colour, and the best flavour, it is important to heat the bones under a grill or in a very hot oven until the edges and rough bits turn dark brown and char slightly. Roughly chopped, unpeeled onions and carrots brown in about the same time as the bones. Turn bones and vegetables so they brown on both sides.

Transfer bones and vegetables to a large saucepan or stock pot, add the water and flavourings, cover and simmer for 4–5 hours.

Pour stock through a sieve or colander and leave to stand in a cool place until the fat rises to the surface and solidifies. Remove fat and refrigerate or freeze the stock in suitable amounts until required.

C Vegetable Stock

Making vegetable stock from scratch is often regarded as being an excessively time-consuming process. This is because of the long periods of time necessary to allow flavours to 'steep' from vegetables as they boil. Finely chopping the vegetables first (either by hand or, better still, in a blender or food processor) eliminates the need for prolonged boiling. This is the principle employed in this recipe, which makes fresh-tasting stock with an attractive colour in less than 20 minutes.

For 4 cups:
1 large onion
2–4 cloves garlic
1 large carrot
2 sticks celery
2 tomatoes or 2 tsp tomato paste
1 stalk parsley
¹/₄ tsp freshly ground black pepper
4 cups (1 litre) cold water
¹/₂ tsp sugar
about 1 tsp salt

Quarter but do not peel the onion. Put in food processor bowl with the unpeeled garlic cloves, the scrubbed but unpeeled carrot cut in chunks, the broken sticks of celery with their leaves removed, the tomatoes and parsley leaves and stalks. Process using the metal chopping blade until very finely chopped.

Transfer the chopped vegetables to a large saucepan, add the pepper then the cold water and bring to the boil.

Simmer for 10–15 minutes, then press through a sieve, extracting as much liquid as possible. Add the sugar and salt to taste.

C Chicken 'Bones' Broth

For 4 cups:

The skeleton and other remains of a roast, barbecued, grilled or baked chicken may be used to make good stock. Use the bones quickly, soon after the original cooking, while drippings, trimmings etc. are still available, and before the bones have dried out.

Crush, break or chop the bones, wingtips, etc. of a large chicken into small pieces. Brown lightly with any reserved giblets, skin, fat etc. in 1–2 tablespoons oil, with 1 or 2 garlic cloves. Add any cooking juices scraped from the original cooking pan, a chopped, unpeeled carrot and onion and a parsley and celery stalk. Add 1 tablespoon light soya sauce, ¹/₂ teaspoon salt, 6 peppercorns or a dried chilli, and 6 cups of water. Add several slices of ginger if you want to use the stock for Oriental recipes, or add a bay leaf and herbs such as thyme, oreganum, tarragon and basil for stock for general use. Cover loosely and simmer for 2 hours. Strain, cool, and skim off fat. Use immediately, refrigerate, or freeze in one-cup portions.

C Chicken Giblet Broth

Chicken hearts, gizzards, backs, necks and feet are sometimes available at meat counters. (Do not use chicken livers, similarly available, for soup.) All of these make good soup. Use them singly, in mixtures, or with poultry bones.

Use a method similar to that given in previous recipe, using 250 g–500 g of giblets or uncooked chicken bones to the quantities suggested. Simmer until the meat is tender, then strain stock. If desired, remove meat from the bones, or trim and slice the giblets and add them to the stock.

Microwaved Crisp Bread Slices
Warm 2 tablespoons butter with ¹/₄ teaspoon garlic salt and ¹/₈ teaspoon paprika to easy-spreading consistency, 20–30 seconds at Full power. Mix well, then spread on 12–16 slices of French bread or on four quartered slices of bread. Arrange on a ridged roasting pan or on paper towels. Microwave for about 15 seconds per slice or piece.

C Chicken Soup

To make soup from chicken stock, add finely sliced or cubed vegetables (e.g. leeks, onions, celery, carrots, turnips, tomatoes, potatoes, kumara, beans, spinach, bean sprouts) rice, noodles or macaroni shapes like alphabet noodles. Cook until tender, then season carefully, adding a little instant chicken stock if necessary. Use chicken 'bones' broth or chicken giblet broth with ginger root added, for wonton soup stock.

C Scotch Broth

(See photograph on page 22.)

Use two lamb shanks or the bones from a forequarter to make this soup.

Although not traditional, it is a good idea to brown the bones under the grill until they have dark patches before boiling them.

Add water to cover bones by 2–3 cm. Add an unskinned carrot, a crushed garlic clove, a roughly chopped unskinned onion, and some thin-stemmed celery tops. Tie ¹/₄ cup barley in a cloth, leaving room for swelling, and boil with bones for 2–3 hours. Strain, discarding everything but barley and stock.

Leave for fat to solidify overnight if possible, then add 1 finely chopped carrot, onion, potato, celery stalk and leek.

Simmer for 30 minutes, season carefully, sprinkle with chopped parsley and serve.

Grilled Croutons
When you make crustless sandwiches, chop the crusts for tiny croutons. For every 3 cups of cubes melt 50 g butter in a roasting pan. Toss cubes to coat then sprinkle with ¹/₄ cup grated Parmesan cheese and 2 teaspoons green herbs stock.

Grill 15 cm from heat until golden and crisp, turning frequently.

C Wonton Soup

For 8 small or 4 main servings:
32 wonton skins

Wonton filling
250 g pork or beef mince
1 Tbsp oil
1 Tbsp dry sherry
1 Tbsp dark soya sauce
1 tsp cornflour
½ tsp sesame oil
¼ tsp salt
4 spring onions, chopped

Broth
4 cups cold chicken stock
2 cups vegetables (see below)
4 cups water
1 Tbsp dark soya sauce
1 Tbsp dry sherry
½ tsp salt

Do not let wonton skins dry out. Mix wonton filling ingredients well, then divide into 32 small portions. Put chicken stock in large saucepan beside stove.

Prepare vegetables, e.g. mushrooms, bean sprouts, spring onions, spinach, for cooking after wontons. Heat water, soya sauce, sherry and salt in large frying pan. Shape wontons as shown. Drop into boiling liquid in pan, jiggling pan to prevent sticking. Cook 4–6 at a time, allowing 5 minutes after liquid returns to the boil. Lift each, with slotted spoon, into cold chicken stock when cooked.

Afterwards briefly cook prepared vegetables in liquid remaining in frying pan. Add vegetables and pan liquid to wontons and stock. Reheat without boiling and serve immediately.

Work quickly, filling and sealing one wonton at a time. Put filling in centre and fold wonton skin diagonally over it. Dampen one folded corner with water as shown.

Hold folded corners between thumbs and forefingers. With one middle finger, press filled area gently so the dampened corner can be brought towards, then under, the other folded corner.

Pinch dampened area firmly against other folded corner. Drop gently into hot liquid after several have been made. Filling will stay enclosed during cooking.

C Lamb Broth with Dumplings

This is quicker than most stock-based soups. If you have any unsalted meat or vegetable stock, use it to replace part of the water.

For 5–6 main servings:
600 g lamb shoulder meat
2 Tbsp oil
4 cloves garlic, crushed
8 cups water
¼ cup barley
2 cups chopped carrot
2 cups chopped celery
1–2 cups chopped beans or frozen peas
1 Tbsp dark soya sauce
½ tsp salt
¾ cup self-raising flour
¼ cup chopped parsley
about ¼ cup water

Cube lamb. Heat oil in a large saucepan and brown meat evenly. Add garlic, then water and barley, and simmer for 45 minutes. Add vegetables, soya sauce and salt, and simmer for 30 minutes longer. Taste and season carefully.

Combine flour, chopped parsley (and other fresh herbs if desired) with enough water to make a stiff scone dough. Cut into 12–16 pieces and drop into simmering broth. Cover and cook about 10 minutes. Serve immediately.

M Dumplings for Soup

½ cup self-raising flour
pinch of celery salt and garlic salt
1 Tbsp chopped parsley
other herbs to taste (optional)
¼ cup milk

Combine ingredients in order given, stirring just enough to dampen flour. Pour ½ cup hot water in a 23 cm flat-bottomed dish. Drop mixture into water in about 12 small amounts, using two teaspoons. Cover. Cook at Full power for 3 minutes, or until firm. Sprinkle with paprika if desired. Add to individual bowls of cooked soup.

Lamb Broth with Dumplings

C Macaroni Soup

When you have made vegetable stock from scratch, you can use it to make lovely, easy soups. Here is one of the simplest.

For 4 servings:
4 cups vegetable stock
2 tsp butter
½ cup macaroni or perciacelli
2 tomatoes, cubed finely
¼ cup chopped parsley

Bring the stock to the boil. Add the butter and macaroni and simmer until the pasta is tender, about 10 minutes.

Cut the tomatoes into small cubes then add them and the chopped parsley to the soup. Bring it back to the boil then serve immediately.

Variations:
Add other quick-cooking vegetables such as sliced mushrooms, frozen peas, or finely chopped spinach.

Add small cubes of tofu as well as quick-cooking vegetables.

Replace the macaroni with fine ribbon noodles, or other small pasta.

C Alphabet Soup

This quickly made favourite family soup is easy enough for children to make for themselves, and takes less than 15 minutes.

The 'alphabets' are fun for children who like to make their initials and names, but you can use any other pasta shapes. Vermicelli or narrow egg noodles are good for people who enjoy sucking up long, thin shapes, while big wavy noodles give the soup a very substantial feel.

The quantities given here may be varied to taste, but the order of additions is important and should be followed.

For 4 servings:
4 cups hot water
2 tsp instant chicken stock
2 tsp instant beef or green herb stock
1 tsp sugar
2 tsp butter
3 Tbsp alphabet noodles (or up to ½ cup larger noodles)
1 small onion
1 stick celery
1 small carrot
1 small potato
1 tomato
1 Tbsp chopped parsley

Put the hot water in a medium-sized saucepan over high heat. Add the stock powder or selected flavourings and the sugar and butter. When this mixture comes to the boil add the noodles. Prepare and add the vegetables in the given order. Chop the onion and celery, grate the carrot and scrubbed potato and chop the tomato. The soup should be cooked about 10 minutes after

noodles are added. Stir in the chopped parsley and serve, or cool and reheat later.

C Brown Onion Soup

My friend next door makes delicious onion soup. In a kitchen conversation recently, we decided that onion soup would be the soup to choose if you decided to make only one soup.
• It is easy to make and requires no expensive or exotic ingredients
• You can eat it 30 minutes after starting to make it
• It is warm and filling in cold weather, yet light enough for warm weather.

However, the fact remains, you can't make onion soup without peeling and chopping onions. Still, what are a few tears? This recipe makes 6–8 servings, but you can 'stretch' it by adding more instant stock and water.

For 8 servings:
4–6 large onions
100 g butter
2 tsp sugar
¼ cup flour
6 cups brown beef stock
2 tsp Worcestershire sauce
¼ cup dry sherry (optional)
seasonings

Cut the onions into 5mm slices. Heat the butter in a large, heavy-bottomed saucepan. Add the onions and cook over moderate heat, stirring frequently, for about 20 minutes, until the onions have softened and browned. Do not hurry this step or the flavour will be spoilt.

Stir in the sugar. Cook for about 5 minutes longer, until the mixture darkens more, then stir in the flour. Add the stock, 2 cups at a time, bringing the soup to the boil after each addition.

Simmer over a very low heat for 30 minutes, then add the Worcestershire sauce and sherry. Taste and add salt (or instant beef stock) as necessary.

Leave to stand for 5 minutes, and serve.

Microwaved Croutons
Melt 2 tablespoons butter in a flat-bottomed dish at Full power for 45 seconds. Toss with 1 cup of small bread cubes. Sprinkle with ¼ teaspoon garlic salt. Add paprika and curry powder if desired. Microwave uncovered, at Full power for 3–4 minutes, stirring after 2 minutes until slightly browned. Stand for 5 minutes on paper towel to crisp.

C Pea Soup

Bacon and vegetables flavour the stock for this main-dish soup. It requires only 2 hours' cooking but will be thicker and even better-flavoured if it is left to stand before reheating to serve.

For 4 main servings:
2 rashers (100 g) bacon
2 Tbsp butter
1 large onion, chopped
2 stalks celery, chopped (optional)
1 large carrot, chopped
½ cup yellow split peas
5 cups water
salt and pepper

Chop bacon into small pieces. Sauté in the butter in a large pan, adding the vegetables as soon as each is finely chopped. (Do not let vegetables brown.)

Add split peas and water, cover loosely, and simmer for 2 hours, stirring to prevent sticking as peas disintegrate.

Taste and season carefully before serving. Top with slices of sautéed precooked sausage if desired.

C Black Bean and Rice Soup

The dark colour of this soup is unusual, to say the least! Sour cream or yoghurt swirled on top, a sprinkling of chopped spring onions, and a few drops of hot red pepper sauce make it look as good as it tastes.

Served with bread and a salad it makes a substantial main meal.

For 4 main servings:
1 cup small black (tiger) beans
3 cups water
3 cups vegetable or chicken or beef stock (from instant stock powders if desired)
2 Tbsp olive or other oil
3 large onions
4 cloves garlic
2 tsp ground cumin
2 tsp dried oreganum
1–2 cups cooked brown rice
2 Tbsp wine vinegar

Simmer the beans in the water until they are very tender, and most of the water is absorbed. Then add the stock, using enough powdered stock with hot water to get a good flavour (about a teaspoonful per cup) and simmer until the beans will break up easily. This should take about an hour.

Measure the oil into a frypan with a lid. Chop the onions and garlic finely, with a food processor if available, and cook in the oil over moderate heat, letting the onions colour lightly, but not browning them. Add the cumin and oreganum after about 5 minutes. Remove from the heat and mix in the cooked rice and vinegar.

When the beans are mushy, purée 1½ cups of them with enough of their cooking stock to make a thick liquid. Then combine the puréed and whole beans and stock, and the onion mixture.

Bring to the boil, and season to taste with hot pepper sauce, ground black pepper and salt. Add extra cumin and oreganum if the soup seems bland. (It should not need these if the cumin is fresh.)

Serve immediately or reheat when required, thinning with more stock if it thickens too much on standing.

Serve each bowl topped with sour cream, yoghurt, or a mixture of the two, chopped spring onion leaves, and a little more hot pepper sauce. Put more of these on the table if you like.

M Red Lentil Soup

Because lentils are the smallest members of the pulse family, they cook fastest, without soaking, to make a good substantial main-course soup. Purée this or leave it plain.

For 4 servings:
½ cup red lentils
1 large carrot, grated
3 cloves garlic, chopped
2 Tbsp butter
½ tsp cumin seed (optional)
3½ cups boiling water
½ tsp grated orange rind (optional)
¾ tsp salt
½ tsp sugar (optional)
3–4 spring onions, chopped

Combine the first four ingredients in a large bowl or casserole. Add whole or ground cumin if you like its flavour, then pour in 2 cups of boiling water. Cover and microwave at Full power for 15 minutes or until the lentils are tender. Add remaining water, and grated orange rind. Cook for 10 minutes longer. Add salt and a little sugar if desired. Purée if desired. Stir in spring onions. Taste and add a little more salt if necessary.
Note:
Leave out the cumin and orange rind if you want a basic lentil soup.

C Creamy Lentil and Vegetable Soup

This is an excellent main-meal soup that you can sit down to eat half an hour after you start to make it.

You can change the ingredients, depending on the bits and pieces you have in the refrigerator, as it is never the same twice.

For 4–6 servings:
1 cup red lentils
1 litre hot water
25–50 g butter
1 or 2 onions
1 or 2 cloves garlic
1 or 2 carrots
1 or 2 stalks celery
1 tsp whole or ground cumin seeds
½ tsp ground coriander (optional)
½ tsp garam masala
½ tsp paprika
2 Tbsp cream
2 Tbsp cornflour
1 cup frozen peas (or other frozen vegetables)
about 1 cup chopped tomato
about ¼ cup chopped fresh herbs (e.g., parsley, spring onions or chives, and small amounts of basil, thyme, oreganum)
1 Tbsp sugar (optional)
1–1½ tsp salt

As soon as you think about making this soup, measure the lentils and hot tap water into a bowl or jug so that the lentils start softening.

Melt the quantity of butter you want in a fairly large saucepan. Add the chopped onions, garlic, carrots and celery. If you intend to purée all or part of the soup, you can leave the vegetables in large pieces. If you want the soup unpuréed and fairly chunky, cut them into small, even pieces.

Add the cumin, coriander, garam masala and paprika to the vegetables. (Leave out any of these which you do not have, or add 1–2 teaspoons curry powder, if you have none of them.)

Cook over moderate heat, stirring occasionally, for 2–3 minutes longer without letting the vegetables brown.

Add the hot water and the lentils, cover, and simmer for about 20 minutes, or until the vegetables and lentils are tender.

Purée all, or part, or none of the mixture, and bring it back to the boil.

Mix the cream and cornflour to a paste with a little extra water, and pour into the soup.

Add the peas or other frozen vegetables and the tomato that has been chopped into pieces the same size as the peas. Add the sugar, then salt to taste. You will need at least a teaspoon, or the soup will be flavourless. Add small amounts, tasting carefully.

Add the fresh herbs. If you have left-over cooked vegetables, cut them into small cubes and add them too.

Serve with hot toast or croutons, French bread or bread rolls, and with a leafy green side salad or coleslaw, if you like.

Creamy Lentil and Vegetable Soup

Eggs and Cheese

Both eggs and cheese are protein-rich foods that require the minimum of preparation and cooking time. What would we do without them when we want quick and easy meals?

Good egg cookery does require some skill, however. The delicate texture and appearance can be ruined by a few seconds carelessness or overcooking, so you should be prepared to practice a little, in order to perfect the skills involved.

Because eggs are used to produce nutritious, quick meals in so many parts of the world, there are numerous recipes using eggs that we, surrounded by ingredients from all parts of the globe, can experiment with and enjoy.

When it comes to producing a quick and easy cheese meal, we are even luckier. Our supermarkets and delicatessens stock a wonderful range of cheeses that can simply be sliced and enjoyed, with no cooking at all.

All the same, it is impossible to forget the wonderful aroma of bubbling hot cheese mixtures, so we cook and enjoy cheese specialties too, especially in cooler weather, more often than not returning to good, basic Cheddar for cooking.

The following pages contain my tried and true egg and cheese family favourites. I hope you enjoy them as much as we do.

French Omelet

C French Omelet

A French omelet for one person cooks in less than a minute! The mixture must be mixed, heated and worked with carefully, for good results.

For a small omelet you need an 18–20 cm pan, preferably with a non-stick finish.

Combine in a bowl: 2 eggs, 2 tablespoons water, milk, or cream, ¼ teaspoon salt, and some finely chopped fresh herbs if desired.

Stir the ingredients together with a fork, only until the whites and yolks are combined. Do not overmix.

Pour the mixture into a hot pan containing 1 teaspoon butter which has been heated until straw-coloured.

Stir mixture for the first 5 seconds only. Tilt pan and lift the set edges to let uncooked egg run underneath.

When egg is set but surface is still moist, omelet is ready to fold, or to fill with a precooked mixture.

Spoon hot filling onto half the omelet. Fold the other half over the filling. Slide or flip onto plate.

C Spanish Omelet

(See photograph on p. 36.)

Although you can make lots of additions to this omelet, it tastes so good when plain that you should try it this way first of all. You can serve it hot, warm or cold.

For two people scrub and cube 3 fairly large potatoes.

Tip cubed potatoes into 3 tablespoons hot oil in a hot pan. Cover pan and cook until potatoes are tender, 5–10 minutes. (Potatoes need not brown.)

Beat 2 eggs with ½ teaspoon salt, using a fork. Tip hot potatoes into beaten egg.

Tip the warm egg and potato mixture back into the pan containing a little oil.

Cook uncovered, tilting pan occasionally, until omelet is nearly set. Slide from pan on to plate, then flip back into pan to brown second side. Serve flat, not folded.

C Cottage Cheese Omelet

Always use small-curd cottage cheese for omelets since larger curd, moister mixtures do not hold together well.

Do not add salt — you will find the flavour good without it.

For 1 omelet:
1 egg
2 Tbsp small-curd cottage cheese
1 tsp chives
1–2 tsp butter, preferably clarified

Stir together the egg, cottage cheese and chives (or other herbs) using a fork. Swirl the butter until it coats a small pan evenly, and is nice and hot, then pour in the omelet mixture. Lift edges of omelet when they set, tilting the pan to let the uncooked mixture run underneath. As soon as surface is set, fold in half and serve immediately.

Variation:
For a sweet omelet, omit the chives. As soon as the omelet is cooked, spread the surface with more cottage cheese and jam or jelly. Fold or roll.

C Swiss Egg

This is an interesting omelet variation.

For 1 large or 2 small servings:
2 thick slices bread
2 Tbsp butter
2 eggs
2 Tbsp milk
1/2 tsp salt
25 g cubed cheese

Cut the bread into small cubes. Heat half the butter in a small frying pan and toss the bread in it. Cook over moderate heat until the croutons are crisp and golden brown. Remove from pan.

Beat the eggs, milk and salt together with a fork. Heat the pan again. Heat the remaining butter in it until straw-coloured. Pour in the egg mixture. Cook, tilting the pan and lifting the edges of the omelet to let the uncooked mixture run underneath.

Sprinkle the croutons and the cheese over half the omelet when it is barely set. Flip the other half of the omelet over the croutons and cheese. Serve immediately. The cheese should be warm but not melted, and the croutons still crunchy.

C M Herbed Scrambled Eggs

Add 1/4–1 teaspoon chopped fresh herbs to each egg to be scrambled. Use one herb at a time until you find your favourite. Use just enough to lightly flavour the mixture.

1 tsp butter
1 egg
2 Tbsp milk
pinch salt
freshly ground pepper
1/3 tsp chopped chives

Microwave method:
Melt butter in a small glass bowl or measuring cup (20 seconds at Full power). Add remaining ingredients, beat with a fork until combined, then microwave for 60–80 seconds or until almost set, stirring after 30 seconds.

Conventional method:
Melt butter in small frying pan. Pour in lightly mixed remaining ingredients. Cook over moderate heat, lifting mixture from pan bottom with a fish slice, as it sets.

Serve before completely set, since cooking continues off stove.

C French Toast

The most uninteresting, stale slices of bread take on new life if they are dipped in an eggy mixture, then browned in a hot pan containing a little butter.

Beat 1 egg with 1 tablespoon milk, orange juice or white wine, until well mixed, but not frothy.

Dip sliced brown or white bread, or diagonally sliced French bread, into this mixture, turning to moisten both sides. Leave coated bread to stand on a flat plate or tray for several minutes before cooking in a moderately hot pan, allowing about 1/2 teaspoon of butter for each side. Cook long enough to brown evenly on both sides.

Serve hot, with honey, maple or golden syrup, jam or jelly, and bananas, if you like sweet accompaniments.

For savoury accompaniments, serve sautéed sliced tomatoes, mushrooms, cream corn, etc. with the French Toast.

C Spaghetti Scramble

For a quick, satisfying meal, cook eggs in a pan with vegetables and spaghetti.

For 4 servings:
1 large onion
1 green pepper
1–2 Tbsp oil or butter
1 (450 g) can spaghetti
herbs, chopped (optional)
3 eggs
2 Tbsp milk
1/4 tsp salt
pepper

Chop the onion and green pepper, and cook in the butter or oil in a large pan until tender but not browned. Add the spaghetti and any herbs you like, and heat until bubbling.

Beat the eggs, milk and seasonings with a fork, and pour over the hot spaghetti. Without stirring, lift the spaghetti with a fish slice so the egg can run underneath.

Serve as soon as the egg has set, garnished with chopped parsley or spring onions. This is nice in split, toasted buns.

SCOTCH EGGS

Scotch Eggs seem to be popular with everybody. They make excellent picnic food, because they can be transported, whole, and cut into halves, when you are serving the picnic meal.

Here are three ways to cook Scotch Eggs.

Microwaved Scotch Eggs are certainly the easiest and quickest, and if you have a microwave oven you should certainly cook them in it.

Baked Scotch Eggs take the longest time to cook, but are less messy to make than the fried version. If you have the oven on for something else, and don't have a microwave oven, try them.

Fried Scotch Eggs cook in about 10 minutes. If you have the oil too hot, they are likely to burst. See if you can choose a saucepan into which all, or half the coated eggs you are cooking, will fit at one time.

M Microwaved Scotch Eggs

4 eggs, hard-boiled
1 cup soft breadcrumbs
1 Tbsp tomato sauce
2 tsp dark soya sauce
1/2 tsp curry powder
500 g sausage meat
1 cup dry breadcrumbs

Shell the hard-boiled eggs. Mix the next five ingredients together thoroughly, then divide in four flat patties, working with wet hands to stop sticking.

Wrap the sausage meat around the eggs, pinching it together well at the joins, and trying to keep the thickness the same all round.

Coat with the dry crumbs, then microwave each egg as it is ready.

Stand the prepared egg on a folded paper towel, in the middle of the oven. Microwave for 1 minute, turn egg over, then cook for 1 minute longer, or until the coating feels firm.

C Baked Scotch Eggs

4 eggs, hard-boiled
500 g sausage meat
1 cup fine, dry breadcrumbs

Shell the hard-boiled eggs, form the sausage meat into four flat patties, and shape as evenly as possible into a coating around each of the eggs, working with wet hands.

Roll each egg in crumbs, then bake uncovered, in a shallow baking tin, at 180°C, for 20–30 minutes, until sausage meat is firm.

C Deep-Fried Scotch Eggs

Use ingredients and shaping method as for Baked Scotch Eggs, above.

Lower the prepared eggs into enough preheated oil to cover the surfaces of the eggs, in a saucepan on the stove. Cooking time should be about 10 minutes for each egg, otherwise the sausage meat will not cook.

Note:
Oil which is too hot causes over-browning and splitting.

C Cottage Cheese Mini-Pancakes

Here is a recipe which was sent to me by the mother of a little girl who loves these pancakes. The pancakes are very tender, and, if made small, are nice rolled up and eaten in your fingers.

For 2 servings:
1/2 cup cottage cheese
2 Tbsp flour, plain or wholemeal
2 eggs
2 tsp sugar
2 tsp wheatgerm (optional)

Combine all the ingredients in the order given, using a food-processor or an egg beater.

Heat a large frying pan, preferably with a non-stick finish, melt about a teaspoon of butter until it bubbles, then pour 2 tablespoon lots of batter on to it.

Cook until bubbles break on the surface, then turn the pancakes carefully, since they are very tender. Brown the second side, and serve while warm.

I like to make a savoury version of these pancakes too.

For these I use wholemeal or rye flour, leave out the sugar, and add the wheatgerm.

These pancakes do not brown as readily as the others, because of the lack of sugar, but they make very nice little pancakes on which to serve savoury fish mixtures, as appetisers.

I serve them a few minutes after they have been cooked, spread with sour cream, (or with quark, if I want a low-calorie version) and topped with smoked salmon, smoked eel, smoked roe, or mussels. A garnish of red or black caviar (or lumpfish roe) and a little sprig of dill make these look beautiful.

C Savoury Spinach Roulade

Roulades are rolls made of a savoury, airy, eggy mixture that enclose a well-seasoned mixture, which usually contrasts in flavour and colour with the outside layer.

They may be made well ahead of the time they are needed, then served sliced, hot or cold.

They look attractive and may be arranged on a plate with a salad or other vegetable garnish, to make an impressive starter or light main course.

Once you have mastered the outer roll mixture, you can have a good time inventing suitable additions and modifications.

Go for contrasting colours, using tomato paste, cheese, curry powder, and bright green vegetables to start you off.

Make vegetarian or fishy fillings, to suit your taste.

Slices of small, well-chilled roulades make good finger food to serve with drinks.

The number of servings from a roulade depends on the way you serve and cut it.

For 4 lunch-sized servings:
50 g butter
1/4 cup flour
3/4 cup milk
3 eggs
1/2 cup grated tasty cheese

Filling
1 cup cooked, well-drained spinach
1 Tbsp horseradish sauce
1 clove garlic, finely chopped
1/2–3/4 cup cream cheese

Melt the butter in a pan, over moderate heat. Add the flour and stir till the flour bubbles, around 30 seconds. Add the milk gradually, stirring continuously, until the sauce boils and thickens. Remove from heat.

Separate the egg yolks and whites. Add the yolk to the hot sauce and quickly stir to combine. Stir in the grated cheese.

Beat the egg whites until soft peaks form. Fold into the cheese mixture. Pour the mixture into a teflon or baking paper-lined medium-sized sponge roll tin (about 20 cm × 30 cm).

Bake at 200°C for 12–15 minutes or until puffed and golden brown. The roulade is cooked as soon as the centre springs back when lightly pressed with a finger. Remove from the oven and turn out on to a rack covered with a teatowel. Carefully remove the lining paper or liner.

Filling
Wash or soak raw spinach in cold water. Remove the stems and cook in a covered saucepan with no added water or seasonings until it has wilted, is tender, and still bright green. Drain, squeezing it to get rid of as much liquid as possible. Chop finely.

Combine the cooked, drained, finely chopped spinach, horseradish sauce, garlic and cream cheese to make a pliable, easily spread mixture. Spread evenly over the room temperature roulade and, holding the teatowel with both hands, gently roll up, starting with the side nearest you.

Wrap the roll in plastic film, and refrigerate until needed, up to 24 hours.

A short time before serving cold, cut in 5 mm–1 cm slices carefully, using a sharp, serrated knife.

If serving warm, microwave carefully on a low power level, or cover in foil and reheat at 180°C.

C Asparagus Roulade

For 4 lunch-sized servings:
50 g butter
1/4 cup flour
3/4 cup milk
3 Tbsp tomato paste
3 eggs
1/2 cup grated tasty cheese

Filling
1 (about 400 g) can asparagus spears
1/4 cup cream cheese
1 clove garlic, finely chopped
1/4 cup finely chopped parsley

Make the soufflé-like roll as in previous recipe.

Make the filling while the roulade cooks. Drain the asparagus liquid into a pan. Chop the asparagus and press gently to remove more liquid. Boil the asparagus liquid and chopped garlic down to 1 tablespoon and stir into the chopped asparagus. Fold together the asparagus, cream cheese and parsley (or other herbs). Taste, and adjust seasoning.

Proceed as in previous recipe.

C Home-Fried Spaghetti

This is a quick, savoury, egg and spaghetti dish, a cross between an omelet, a fritter and a pancake. It tastes good and is filling enough for the hungriest teenagers. I like it with a sauce made of thickened stewed tomatoes. It can also be served with a green salad.

I cook the spaghetti and mix the eggs with the other ingredients earlier in the morning, then combine the spaghetti and egg mixture just before cooking. Although the bacon and onion are added to the egg mixture raw, their final flavour and texture is good, and it is not necessary to sauté them before mixing with the other ingredients.

For 4–6 servings:
225 g uncooked spaghetti
4 eggs
2 tsp salt
1/2 tsp pepper
1 Tbsp finely diced or pulped onion
1 rasher bacon, chopped
1/4 cup grated tasty Cheddar
50 g butter

Place the spaghetti, broken into roughly 5 cm lengths, into rapidly boiling salted water. Cook until just tender.

Beat together the eggs, salt, pepper and add the onion, bacon and cheese.

When the spaghetti is cooked remove from the heat, drain and rinse in cold water. Add the spaghetti to the egg mixture.

Heat the frying pan well, add

Asparagus Roulade

butter, and as soon as it is melted and bubbling pour in the egg-spaghetti mixture. Cook at a medium heat without stirring for 4–5 minutes, or until the bottom is golden brown.

Divide into 4 or 6 portions with an egg slice or spatula, turn and cook the other side for a further 4–5 minutes.

© Macaroni Cheese

Don't forget about macaroni cheese. It is an old-fashioned 'comfort food', enjoyed by all age groups.

For 2–4 servings:
1 cup (125 g) macaroni (or other pasta)
2 Tbsp butter
2 Tbsp flour
1 ½ cups milk
2 cups grated cheese
salt and pepper

Boil macaroni until tender in plenty of boiling salted water, then drain. In another pan melt butter, add flour, and heat until bubbly. Add milk in thirds, stirring and boiling between additions. Stir in the grated cheese. Season to taste. Heat only until cheese melts. Stir macaroni into cheese sauce.

Reheat, browning top in oven for best results, otherwise sprinkle with paprika and serve immediately.

Variations:
Add ¹/₂ cup drained crushed pineapple, and replace ¹/₂ cup milk with pineapple juice.

Add cooked celery, broccoli, etc to the hot cheese sauce with the cooked macaroni.

Ⓜ Macaroni Cheese

This macaroni cheese uses only one microwave-proof dish. If you use pre-grated cheese, you don't even get a dirty grater!

If you like a crisp topping, make it before you cook the macaroni cheese. Microwave a mixture of 2 cups fresh breadcrumbs, 1 tablespoon melted butter and 1 tablespoon chopped parsley until crumbs turn golden, 2–4 minutes.

For 4 servings:
75 g butter
1 tsp garlic salt
2 cups (200 g) macaroni, tortellini or spirals, etc.
2 cups boiling water
1 cup milk
2 cups grated cheese
2 Tbsp flour

Cut butter into nine cubes. Melt in fairly large, flat-bottomed microwave dish, about 1 minute at Full power. Stir in garlic salt and macaroni, or any other shape of pasta that holds a lot of sauce, e.g. tortellini or spirals. Pour boiling water over pasta.

Cover. Cook on medium (50% power) for 10–15 minutes, until pasta is tender, stirring every 5 minutes. Stir in milk immediately.

Mix grated cheese with flour. Stir into hot pasta mixture. Stir gently

Microwaved Macaroni Cheese

for 30–60 seconds until cheese melts.

Microwave for 2 minutes or until mixture bubbles all round edge. Stir again. Leave to stand for 3 minutes.

Sprinkle with prepared crumbs, if desired.

Ⓒ Ⓜ Blue Ribbon Special

While plain macaroni cheese is family fare, this pasta and cheese mixture is definitely for special occasions and candlelight dinners.

It is easy, quick and delicious. Serve it plain, or make decorative and tasty additions, such as toasted pine nuts, slivered almonds or walnuts and/or shreds of smoked salmon or ham. Make it with flat, ribbon-like noodles, for preference.

For 4 servings:
250 g fettucce (or other ribbon noodles)
100 g blue cheese (e.g. Bleu de Montagne)
1 cup sour cream
2 Tbsp chopped chives (or other fresh herbs)

Optional
100 g thinly sliced smoked salmon
¹/₄–¹/₂ cup toasted pine nuts, slivered almonds or finely chopped walnuts.

Boil the noodles in unsalted water until tender. While they cook, mash the crumbled blue cheese with the cream and chives in a microwave dish or a bowl which can be heated over boiling water.

Microwave at Full power for 2 minutes or heat over boiling water until cheese has softened into cream. Drain noodles and stir them into the sauce.

For a special occasion stir in the finely sliced salmon and/or nuts. Sprinkle with fresh herbs and serve within 5 minutes.

Ⓒ Asparagus, Egg and Cheese Casserole

This casserole is always popular, and is good when you are entertaining, since it can be made ahead, and heated through when you want it.

For 4 servings:
2 Tbsp butter
3 Tbsp flour
1 tsp mixed mustard
¹/₂ tsp salt
1¹/₂ cups milk
¹/₂–1 cup grated cheese
1 bunch cooked fresh asparagus or 1 (340 g) can asparagus spears, drained
3 or 4 hard-boiled eggs, chopped
¹/₂ cup crushed potato crisps

Make a cheese sauce by melting the butter, adding the flour, mustard and salt, and stirring until blended. Add the milk ¹/₂ cup at a time, bringing to the boil between each addition, stirring constantly. Stir in the cheese, and remove from the heat.

In a buttered 20 cm casserole, layer the sauce, well-drained chopped asparagus and hard-boiled eggs, starting and finishing with sauce. Top with the crushed potato crisps.

Reheat at 180°C until the sauce bubbles around the edges and the centre is hot.

Serve as is, or on noodles or brown rice if you are cooking for particularly hungry people. A salad is a nice accompaniment.

Ⓒ Macaroni, Pineapple and Cheese

This is a variation of an old favourite. Instead of a milk-based sauce, one made of pineapple juice and chicken stock is used.

I often brown the top of the pineapple and macaroni cheese under the grill for a few minutes before I serve the dish.

For 6–8 servings:
1 (450 g) can crushed pineapple
1 Tbsp instant chicken stock
2 cups boiling water
75 g butter
6 Tbsp flour
1 tsp salt
pepper to taste
350 g macaroni
2 cups grated tasty Cheddar
3 rashers bacon

Drain the pineapple and reserve the juice. Dissolve the chicken stock in boiling water. Melt butter in a saucepan and stir in the flour, salt and pepper.

To make the sauce add the pineapple juice and chicken stock one cup at a time. Heat and stir after each addition.

Cook the macaroni in a large saucepan of rapidly boiling salted water for 15 minutes or until just tender. Drain the cooked macaroni and rinse with cold water.

Spread half the macaroni over the base of a buttered ovenware dish at least 23 cm in diameter. Sprinkle half the grated cheese and spoon half the sauce over the layer of macaroni. Repeat the process, using the remaining macaroni and cheese, then top with crushed pineapple. Cover with the remaining sauce.

Remove the rind from the bacon and cut the rashers in half. Place six slices across the top of the dish. Bake, uncovered, at 180°C for 30 minutes or until thoroughly heated and the bacon is crisp.

PIZZA

Here are several different pizza recipes. Find which base and cooking method suits you best then 'stick with it,' until you can make it with minimum effort! Vary the toppings, depending on what you like and what you have in your store cupboard and refrigerator.

C Traditional Pizza Base

This bread-based pizza doesn't really take long to make. I cook it on a non-stick, 32 cm pizza tray that I recently bought. Until now, I merely rolled it out in a thin, 35 cm circle on an oven slide.

2 tsp dried yeast granules
2 tsp sugar
1/2 cup cold milk
1/2 cup hot tap water
about 2 1/2 cups flour
1/2 tsp salt

Measure the yeast, sugar and milk into a food processor or other bowl. Add hot water, making a lukewarm mixture. Mix well. Leave to stand until bubbling, then add 1 cup of measured flour.

Mix until smooth. Cover and leave to stand in a warm place (or in warm water) while you assemble, mix and slice topping ingredients.

When dough is well risen (after 15–45 minutes) stir in salt and enough flour to make a workable dough. Knead well, until dough feels satiny and springy when poked.

Roll out to 32–35 cm and lay on pan sprinkled with wholemeal flour or cornmeal. Spread with toppings as desired (see list).

Stand in a warm place for 10 minutes. Bake at 200°C for 10–12 minutes, until underside is golden brown.

C Quick Yeast Pizza Base

This recipe seems to break all the bread-making rules.

1 1/4 cups warm water
3 Tbsp sugar
1 Tbsp dried yeast granules
1 Tbsp vegetable oil
1 tsp salt
3 cups wholemeal or white flour (or any combintion of the two)
1/2 tsp baking powder

Dissolve the sugar in the warm (blood temperature) water, then sprinkle in the yeast granules. Add the oil and then stir gently for a few seconds. Leave to stand for at least five minutes to allow the yeast to begin acting.

Once the yeast mixture has begun to bubble and looks a little foamy, add the remaining ingredients. Sprinkle the baking powder in evenly to prevent it forming a single lump. Stir everything together until the dough begins to come away from the sides of the bowl and form one large ball.

Flatten the dough on to a well-oiled baking sheet or sponge roll tin (25 × 35 cm). If you have the time (or the patience) leave to rise for 5–15 minutes, although this is not strictly necessary.

Use this time to assemble and prepare the toppings. Spread your chosen toppings over the unrisen or slightly risen base.

Bake pizza at 230°C for 12–15 minutes, until the underside is brown and the toppings look cooked.

C Easy Pizza Base

1 cup self-raising flour
1/2 cup grated cheese
1/2 tsp dried basil
1/2 tsp dried marjoram
about 1/4 cup + 2 Tbsp milk

Add the grated cheese and dried herbs to the self-raising flour, then add enough milk to make a scone dough slightly firmer than usual.

Roll out on a well-buttered or sprayed oven slide, forming a 25 cm circle.

Dampen the outer edge with 2 tablespoons milk (or water) and fold over about 1 cm to make a neat circle with a slightly raised rim.

Spread with pizza toppings.

Bake at 220°C for about 10 minutes or until the bottom is golden brown.

M Pizza for Two

1/2 cup self-raising flour
2–3 Tbsp milk
2 Tbsp oil

Put browning dish in to heat for 6 minutes. Add enough milk to flour to make a fairly firm dough. Knead dough in bowl until smooth. On a floured board roll to 23 cm round.

Dampen edges with more milk and fold them over about 1 cm, making a neat circular base. Brush top of dough with some of the oil. Prick in several places. Place the oiled side down in the heated browning dish and microwave at Full power for 2 minutes or until firm enough to turn over. Turn and heat for 30 seconds longer. Spread with toppings, then heat in microwave until cheese melts, 2–4 minutes, depending on the amount of topping. Cut into slices and serve.

C Pizza Toppings

Pizza toppings are best if assembled in a defined order. Spread the dough first with a tomato base, followed by the toppings of your choice, and finish with a layer of cheese.

Try spreading the uncooked base with a layer of tomato purée, tomato paste diluted to spreading consistency with water, or canned spaghetti or baked beans. Sprinkle this with fresh or dried basil and marjoram or oreganum.

Follow this with any combination of the following:
leftover refried beans
drained corn
thinly sliced sausage, bacon, ham, or
    salami
red and green peppers
mushrooms
sliced tomatoes
mild onions or sautéed onions
pesto
olives
anchovies

Finally, add a layer of cheese. Grated or sliced Mozzarella is particularly good, but grated mild or tasty Cheddar is just fine if this is what you have on hand.

Bake at 230°C for 12–15 minutes or until the edges and bottom are lightly browned.

C Mini Pizzas

Mini Pizzas can be prepared and cooked in a short time if you start with split hamburger buns as a base.

Spread the split bun with a tomato layer first. Use tomato paste, tomato purée, canned spaghetti and tomato or fresh tomato, depending on your taste. Sprinkle this with basil or marjoram or oreganum.

Next, add a layer of sliced or grated cheese, then sprinkle over this small quantities of salami or bacon or ham, sliced mushrooms and/or peppers, onion rings, olives, anchovies, etc.

Top with a little extra cheese so vegetables do not dry out. Heat at 200°C for 5–8 minutes, or under a hot grill, about 10 cm from the heat. Top with garnishes such as olives which would have dried out during cooking.

C Flying Saucers

At a time when I was experimenting with making pizzas in a frying pan, I made a double-crusted scone pizza with the filling completely enclosed. It was a great success.

Savoury meat filling
1 cup grated cheese
1/2–1 cup chopped luncheon sausage or
    minced cooked roast meat
1/4 cup chutney or relish

Easy Pizza

¹⁄₂ tsp dried marjoram
2 Tbsp chopped parsley

Seafood filling

¹⁄₄ cup cream cheese
¹⁄₂ cup grated Cheddar cheese
3–4 spring onions, chopped
¹⁄₄ tsp garlic salt
100 g can tuna or salmon, drained
¹⁄₂ cup chopped marinated mussels
*   (optional)*
¹⁄₂ cup cooked green peas

Make the Easy Pizza Base, and divide the uncooked dough into two equal parts.

Combine the ingredients for one of the above fillings.

Roll the dough into two 18–20 cm circles, depending on the size of the frying pan to be used. Dampen the edges of one circle and spread one of the above fillings evenly over the rest of it. Top with the other circle, pressing out any trapped air before you press the edges together.

Heat 1 teaspoon butter in the frying pan. Slide in the Flying Saucer and cook over moderate heat for about 4 minutes, jiggling the pan to make sure it does not stick. Adjust the heat so crust is evenly browned in this time. Slide on to a plate.

Melt another teaspoon of butter in the pan and tip the Flying Saucer back into it, uncooked side down.

Cook for another 4–5 minutes, then remove from pan. Eat within 20 minutes of making.

Toasted Cheese Sandwiches

C Toasted Cheese Sandwiches

Although you can make these in any frying pan or under a grill, I find that it is simplest, especially for young children, to use a thermostatically controlled electric frypan.

Preheat the pan to 180°C.

Butter toast-sliced bread on one side. Assemble sandwiches butter side out. Fill with sliced cheese, plain, or with your favourite relish or chutney.

Cook, uncovered, until golden brown, then turn and cook on the second side.

Cut into manageable shapes, and serve while hot.

C M Raclette

Raclette is a cheese which melts easily. Put cubes or slices on halved, boiled or microwaved potatoes and heat in a microwave oven or under a grill until the cheese melts. You can serve these cheese-topped potatoes with pickled gherkins and onions as the main part of a meal.

Some other cheeses that melt easily and quickly are Pyrénées, Saint Paulin, Gouda and Gruyère.

Try different cheeses yourself, until you find your favourite.

C Cheese Spread

This is a 'one stroke' sandwich filling which can be made quickly, keeps well for a week or two, and can be varied if necessary.

By 'one stroke' I mean that it can be spread easily on to bread which does not need to be buttered first.

Creative sandwich-makers can have a good time adding an extra layer of filling for lunch-eaters who like variety.

100 g butter
2 tsp flour
1 tsp mixed mustard
½ cup milk
1½–2 cups grated medium or tasty Cheddar cheese
1½ tsp wine or cider vinegar
1 lightly beaten egg

Have all your ingredients ready before you start cooking this mixture, since it can overcook or curdle if left too long at any stage.

Put some cold water in the sink so that it is ready when you need to cool the pan down quickly.

Melt the butter with the flour and mustard in a frying pan, stirring all the time. Add the milk and stir until the mixture bubbles and is smooth.

Without delay, lift it off the heat and add the grated cheese and vinegar, then stir over the heat until the cheese melts.

Take it off the heat again, and stir or whisk in the egg, which has been beaten just enough to combine the white and yolk, but not to become frothy.

Put it back on the heat for 5–10 seconds, until it becomes noticeably thicker. It is important that it is removed from the heat before the fat in it starts to separate, or the egg to scramble. Stand the pan in a sink of cold water and stir for about a minute, until it cools. This should stop any tendency to separate.

Spoon the spread into a jar, cover, and refrigerate, or keep in a cool place until you use it.

Note:
You may find that you want to alter the amount of flour or milk in this spread, to make it a little thicker or thinner. It may vary a little, depending on the cheese you use.

If you use the filling at room temperature, instead of at refrigerator temperature, it will be softer; make sure it is soft enough to spread easily.

Try it on toast, too, with or without a topping of sliced tomatoes.

C M Cheddar Cheese Fondue

A cheese fondue is a companionable meal for a cold night. Children as well as adults enjoy dipping bread into the communal pot.

Microwave ovens make the cooking and reheating really easy, and do away with the need for table-top burners.

For 2 main or 4 starter servings:
2 cups grated Cheddar cheese
2 Tbsp flour
1 tsp butter (for conventional cooking)
1 clove garlic, chopped finely
½ tsp nutmeg
1 cup flat or fresh beer

Microwave method
Mix the grated cheese and flour in a bowl or flat-bottomed casserole dish. Add the garlic, nutmeg, and beer. Stir to mix. Microwave at Full power for 2 minutes, stir with a whisk, then heat until the whole surface bubbles, stirring each minute.

Serve very hot, with chunks of crusty bread to dip, reheating the bowl of fondue if it cools down.

Conventional method
Mix grated cheese and flour. Melt a teaspoon of butter in a small pot or pan, then add the garlic and nutmeg and cook gently for about a minute,

without browning. Add the beer and heat until hot but not boiling. Stir in the floured cheese gradually, while stirring or whisking the mixture over low heat. Remove from the heat when the cheese has all melted, and the mixture is smooth.

Serve, keeping the fondue warm over a candle or low alcohol burner.
Note:
Although it is not traditional, some people like to dip cubes of raw apple, pear, cauliflower, etc.
Variation:
For special occasions, use other cheese to replace half of the Cheddar (or even all of it!). Try Raclette, Emmentaler or Gruyère.

C Cheese Soufflé

Soufflés are not as complicated or temperamental as they are made out to be — but you would be wise to make one or two in private before serving them to impress guests!

Serve another course before your soufflé, so diners are seated at the table when the soufflé arrives from the oven.

For 3–4 servings:
3 Tbsp butter
½ tsp salt
1 tsp mixed mustard
¼ cup flour
1½ cups milk
1½ cups grated cheese
3 eggs, separated

Melt the butter in a medium-sized pot. Add the salt and mustard, then the flour. Stir over a low heat until the mixture bubbles. Add the milk, half a cup at a time, while stirring continuously and boiling between additions. Add the grated cheese, then remove from the heat and stir until smooth.

Separate eggs, putting the whites in a medium-sized bowl and adding the yolks to the cheese sauce (prepare to this stage in advance if desired).

Beat the whites until the peaks turn over at the tips when the beater is removed. Fold the whites into the sauce. Butter the bottom only of a 6 cup soufflé dish and pour in the mixture.

Run a knife through the mixture in a circle 2 cm inside the edge of the dish (this helps even splitting and rising).

Bake at 190°C for 40–45 minutes, or until a knife inserted in the middle comes out clean. Serve immediately, since soufflés shrink on standing.
Variations:
For vegetable soufflés add 1–2 cups of very well-drained, finely chopped, cooked broccoli, spinach, asparagus, or mushrooms to the cheese sauce after stirring in the egg yolks.

Hot Bubbly Cheese Savouries

C M Hot Bubbly Cheese Savouries

For 3–6 servings:
3 bread rolls, split (and toasted if desired)
2 eggs
1 rasher bacon, finely chopped
1 tomato, chopped
2 spring onions, chopped
1 cup grated cheese
paprika

With a fork, beat together the eggs, bacon pieces, chopped tomato, and onion. Put each of the bread roll halves on a paper towel and spread the cut side with the mixture. Add the cheese and sprinkle with paprika. Heat at Full power for about 2 minutes or until cheese begins to bubble nicely, or brown under a grill.
Variation:
Spread topping on toast, if preferred.

C Cheese Strata

This is a popular recipe. The bread puffs up and browns slightly to produce a product that resembles a soufflé, but which has more body.

For 4–6 servings:
6 slices sandwich bread
sliced cheese
mixed mustard
3 eggs
2 cups milk
1 tsp garlic salt

Make cheese sandwiches, using thick slices of cheese, mustard to taste, and no butter. Cut in quarters and stand, crusts down, on a buttered casserole dish.

Beat eggs, milk and garlic salt together and pour over sandwiches. Leave to stand for 30 minutes or longer, spooning the egg over the exposed bread at intervals.

Bake uncovered, at 190°C for 30–45 minutes, or until the bread is puffed and golden brown, and the centre is firm.

Fish

In the clean and sparkling water around us there are many fish, and many fish varieties.

Don't have fixed or set ideas about the particular type of fish you want to use for a particular recipe. In the recipes that follow you can use many different fish.

The most widely known and used fish are likely to be the most expensive. See if you can find another fish of the same texture and thickness, and try it instead.

Delicate-textured fish flakes readily when cooked. Use it when you *want* flaked fish or when you will be baking or microwaving it, not stirring or breaking up the fish as it cooks. If you are frying this fish cut the pieces fairly small and dip them in a protective coating of egg and crumbs or batter.

Medium-textured fish holds its shape when cooked. It has fairly large flakes and may be cooked in all ways.

Firm-textured fish does not separate into flakes when it is moved around during cooking. It keeps its shape when simmered, steamed and stir-fried.

Some fish have a definite, easily recognisable flavour while others are very mild. Individual preferences vary. To make the most of the fish varieties available, and to save money, experiment using different varieties, recipes, and cooking methods. You will really find it pays!

C Egg-n-Crumbed Fish

It's a good idea to cut fish fillets into fingers before coating them with seasoned egg and breadcrumbs.

• This ensures lots of the popular, crunchy coating.
• It makes the fish go further.
• It stops soft-textured fish from breaking up during cooking.

• It gives you the chance to remove any bones before cooking.
• You can serve the crisp, crunchy 'fingers' in different ways.

1. Lie the fillet skinned side down. Feel where the bones are. Cut out a deep narrow V of flesh, removing the bones.

2. Cut the fillet into fingers the width you want.

3. Cut across the fingers with the knife at 45° to the board so you taper the end of each finger.

4. Coat the fingers with flour if you want a thick crumb coating. Leave out this step if you want a thin coating.

5. Coat fingers with seasoned egg mixture. Mix 1/2 teaspoon each of celery and garlic salt with 1 tablespoon water, then add an egg, stirring to mix.

6. Coat with fine dry crumbs. Leave on a rack for 5 minutes before frying in hot oil 5 mm deep, turning once.

Serve with new potatoes or mashed potatoes, baked or grilled tomatoes, green beans, and/or a side salad. Avoid fried vegetables. Prepare tartare sauce made by stirring into mayonnaise some sliced spring onions, chopped gherkin, capers and parsley. Add a little mustard, lemon juice and cream to thin, if desired.

Serve on rice, with a sweet-sour sauce, with a mixed green salad alongside.

For a sauce mix 2 tablespoons cornflour, $\frac{1}{2}$ cup sugar, 1 tablespoon soy sauce, 1 tablespoon oil, $\frac{1}{4}$ cup milk vinegar and $\frac{3}{4}$ cup water. Add red food colouring if you like.

Serve as 'fast food' in a toasted bread roll or hamburger bun with tartare or tomato sauce, and some lettuce and sliced green pepper for crunch. Put strips of carrot and celery alongside as an instant salad.

Use the same three coatings and cooking method for oysters, mussels, marinated mussels, etc. Remove from hot oil as soon as coating is crisp — do not overcook the shellfish. Try to serve soon after cooking. Coating may break away from shellfish on standing.

C Pan-Fried Fish

When you have small fish, flat fish or fillets less than 15 mm thick, you can pan fry them in butter after coating fillets first in milk, then in flour, or whole fish just in flour. Add the fish to foaming butter in a hot pan. Shake to prevent sticking, and do not crowd the pan, nor cover it during cooking.

Pan fry slightly thicker fillets (15–20 mm) in a mixture of 2 tablespoons oil and 2 tablespoons butter.

The skin should be unbroken, crisp, browned but not burnt, when the flesh is cooked.

C Fish Battercakes

It is hard to stop thin batter falling off shallow-fried fish.

Instead, mix a thicker batter, stir in cubed raw fish, and shallow fry spoonfuls of it. The fish goes further, too!

Add a few sliced oysters, too, if you like them.

For 3–4 servings:
500 g cubed raw fish
1 egg
¼ cup milk
½ tsp each onion salt, paprika and
curry powder
1 cup self-raising flour
oil for cooking

Stir fish into a batter made from the egg, milk, onion salt, paprika, curry powder and self-raising flour.

Drop tablespoonfuls into hot oil, 5 mm deep, and cook for 2–3 minutes per side, until batter is golden brown. When batter is cooked in centre, fish will be cooked.

M 'Fried' Fish Fillets

For crisply coated microwaved fish, use a browning dish.

For 2 servings:
2 100–150 g fish fillets
2 Tbsp flour
¼ tsp each paprika, curry powder,
celery salt and onion salt
milk for dipping
2 Tbsp cooking oil

Combine flour, paprika, curry powder, celery salt and onion salt. Dip fillets first in milk, then in this coating. Stand on rack while preheating browning dish, at Full power for 6 minutes.

Quickly put oil in hot browning dish and microwave fillets for 1½ minutes. Turn and cook for 1½ minutes longer, until flesh flakes.

M Sautéed Fish Steaks

You need a browning dish for this recipe.

For 1 serving:
1 fish steak, about 1 cm thick (250 g)
flour for coating
1 tsp butter or oil

Preheat microwave browning dish at Full power for 6 minutes.

Lightly flour the fish steak. To the browning dish add the butter or oil, then the fish. Microwave for 1 minute. Turn and microwave about 1½ minutes more, or until cooked as desired.

C M Fish Fricadelle

In many parts of the world finely minced fish is used in the same ways that we use finely minced meat. The food processor makes short work of mincing fish. I use any inexpensive fish variety.

Microwaved in small moulds, this mixture makes a good starter course. Pan-fried small patties may be dipped in any well-flavoured sauces as cocktail snacks, while large ones make the main part of the fish meal.

For 3–4 main or 6 starter
courses:
500 g fish fillets
1 egg
1 small onion, sliced
several parsley sprigs
3 slices day-old bread
2 tsp salt
1 cup milk

Cut boneless, skinless fish into 1–2 cm cubes. Process with egg, onion and parsley until finely minced.

Break bread into small pieces, removing crusts if a light-coloured mixture is required. Arrange bread evenly over minced fish mixture. Sprinkle with salt.

Dribble three-quarters of milk over bread. Process until smooth, adding extra milk if needed. Shape into 16 patties, pan cook in clarified butter three minutes each side, until lightly browned.
Or microwave in six small moulds, at 60% power, 8–10 minutes or until centre springs back.

C Curried Fish

In this popular but easy recipe fish is simmered in a rich, well-seasoned coconut sauce. You should use fish with a medium-to-firm texture so the pieces do not fall apart before they are served. Do not use fish with a particularly delicate flavour since it will be overwhelmed by the sauce.

Serve your curried fish on rice or noodles with a salad alongside.

For 4 servings:
2 onions, sliced
2 cloves garlic
25 g butter
2 tsp curry powder
1 (420 g) can coconut cream
600–700 g fish fillets
¼–½ tsp salt

Slice the peeled onion and chop the garlic. Melt the butter in a large pan and cook the onion and garlic over low heat, covered, until tender but not browned.

Stir in the curry powder, cook one minute longer over moderate heat then add the coconut cream using 1–2 cups according to available can size. Cook uncovered for 5–10 minutes until sauce thickens.

Cut fish into pieces about 10 cm long, up to 4 cm wide. Turn pieces in sauce, pack into pan, preferably in one layer. Cover and simmer until centre of fish is opaque and fish will flake fairly easily, 5–10 minutes. Add salt to taste.

C M Fish Ragout

If you have a microwave oven use it to cook this recipe before trying it in a pan.

Use medium-to-firm textured fish for this recipe.

For 4 servings:
50 g butter
2 onions, sliced
2 cloves garlic, chopped
¼ cup water
½ cup white wine
1 cup peeled, cubed tomatoes
1 tsp salt
½ tsp sugar
1 tsp fresh thyme leaves
¼ cup chopped parsley
600 g boneless fish pieces
2–3 tsp cornflour

Microwave cubed butter, onions and garlic in a large, covered dish at Full power for 5–6 minutes, stirring after 1½ minutes, (or cook gently in covered pan until tender).

Add water, wine, tomatoes, seasonings and herbs (in pan, add ¼ cup extra water and simmer for 5 minutes). Replace wine with ½ cup water and 2 tablespoons lemon juice if desired.

Cut fish into fingers 8 cm long and 1–2 cm wide. Add, with cornflour. Mix well. Cover and microwave at Full power for 4–6 minutes until fish is firm, opaque and flakes quite easily. (In pan, cook to same stage, about 4 minutes, then thicken with cornflour.)

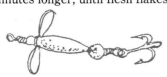

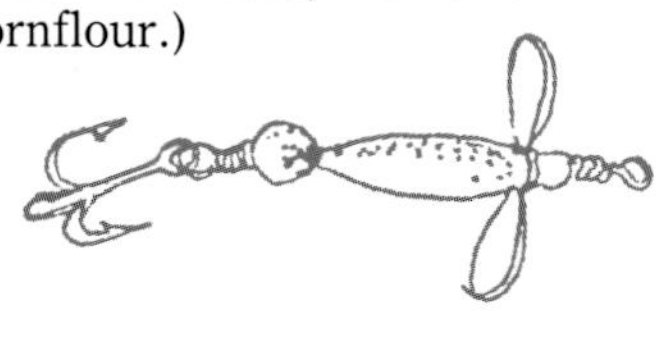

Filo Fish Roll

Filo Fish Roll

I like to roll soft-textured, mild-flavoured fish in sheets of filo pastry, sponge-roll style. Baked then sliced, the roll has a wonderful aroma when cut, an interesting texture and a good flavour. You may like to try your own variations on this theme, adding a variety of seafoods or making individual packages, each wrapped in two sheets of filo and cooked for a shorter time.

For 4 servings:
6 sheets filo pastry
melted butter
¼–½ cup sour cream
400–500 g fish fillets
4 spring onions
1 cup sliced mushrooms
Or 1 cup chopped peppers
fresh herbs, e.g. dill
garlic salt

Slice the fish into fairly thin diagonal slices.

Brush three sheets filo pastry with melted butter. Cover with three more sheets. Spread with sour cream, then fish.

Add seasonings and flavourings as desired, sprinkle with garlic salt and roll up. Brush with melted butter. Bake at 190°C for about 40 minutes. Stand for 15 minutes before serving.

Easy Fish Fillets

M Microwaved Fish

Fish microwaves wonderfully well! Its flavour and texture is excellent and it cooks in next to no time.

Rules for microwaving fish

- Use Full power.
- Allow about 1 minute per 100 g fish, a little more for thicker pieces and less for thinner ones.
- Cook fish until it whitens and turn opaque. Test it to see if it flakes slightly after leaving it to stand for 30–60 seconds per 100 g, after cooking.
- Always allow standing time after microwaving fish.
- Nearly always cover fish with cling wrap during cooking so it cooks more evenly. Remove it after the standing time.
- Put thicker pieces towards the edge of the dish.
- Turn fillets in melted butter or brush with melted plain or garlic butter before cooking.
- Where whole fish is thickest, cut it to the bone in several places for even cooking.
- If you want to cook fish without a recipe, sprinkle the buttered surface with paprika, garlic salt and any chopped fresh herbs you like.
- If you want crunchy fish, sprinkle cooked fish with crisp crumbs before serving it.
- Overcooking dries out, shrinks and toughens fish. Take great care

not to spoil fish by overcooking it.

You may well find that you only ever make 'Easy Fish Fillets' because this recipe is so easy, fast and good, that you can enjoy it time and time again. You can use your mircowave to cook one fish for yourself (in one or two minutes) or present a wonderfully elaborate fish meal for your next lunch or dinner party.

Unless you have a browning dish you will not be able to microwave 'Fried' Fish, but I think that after you have tried other microwave fish recipes, you may feel that you can live without fried fish!

There are several points and techniques which will help you microwave fish to perfection relatively inexpensively. Start with fresh or good quality frozen fish. (This applies to all fish cooking, of course.)

Flatfish have a distinctive shape. Their fillets are thin and roll or fold easily. If they are not available, cut other fine-textured fish in thinner slices and use them instead. You will find it easier to cut frozen fish while it is still partly frozen. You can cook it from this stage, too. Cook one fillet or small whole fish on the plate on which you will serve it.

Don't be frightened of cooking whole fish. They are very easy to work with in the microwave oven. I

have even microwaved small 'just caught' fish without scaling or gutting them.

Immediately after cooking I peel off the skin and scales together and lift the cooked boneless fillets away from the carcase, discarding everything else. (This is a wonderful technique to deal with small fish caught from a jetty!)

If you don't have a suitable cooking dish, use a large oven bag. Lay the fish on it on a concave surface. Add cooking liquid etc., gather up the bag at each end of the fish and secure with a rubber band.

Because fish cooks so fast, you can cook one serving after another on individual plates, if you like.

I don't leave vents when I cover fish with cling wrap. This means that it puffs up a little as the fish cooks, and as soon as it is finished, during the standing time, it sucks down, clinging to the fish and plate. I think the fish is improved and compacted by this method. Try it and see!

Shellfish may be opened and cooked very easily in the microwave. For best flavour and results, put them in a covered container with a little well-flavoured liquid.

Microwave them until the muscle that attaches them to the shell separates from it (1 kg mussels opens in 6–8 minutes).

Overcooking shrinks and toughens shellfish. The liquid from steamed shellfish makes wonderful fish-cooking liquid if saved.

Easy Fish Fillets

Try this very simple, but very good recipe before you experiment with other more complicated mixtures.

For 4 servings:
4 fish fillets (100–150 g each)
1½ Tbsp butter
1 tsp garlic salt
½ tsp paprika
*2 Tbsp chopped parsley (or other fresh
    herbs)*

Melt butter at Full power in a dish large enough to hold fillets in one layer (about 1 minute). Turn fillets in the melted butter. Arrange fish in the dish with thicker parts towards the edges. Sprinkle with garlic salt, paprika and parsley, using more or less seasoning, according to taste. Cover with cling wrap and microwave for 4–5 minutes, until the fish is opaque in the thickest parts. Let stand for 2–3 minutes before uncovering.

Herbed Whole Fish

(See photograph on page 48.)

For this easily prepared dish use any small whole sea or freshwater fish.

For 2 servings:
*2 small salmon, trout or other small
    fish (100–150 g each)*
fresh herbs
lemon slices
2 shallots
2 Tbsp butter
2 cloves garlic

Topping for Fish
2 Tbsp butter
¼ cup slivered almonds

With small pieces of foil, mask the head and tail to prevent overcooking. (The foil must not touch the side of the oven.)

Fill the fish cavity with fresh herbs, slices of lemon and chopped shallots. Heat the butter and garlic at Full power for 1½ minutes or until bubbling. Brush over fish. On a flat plate, arrange the fish with the thicker part towards the outside of the dish.

Cover the fish and plate with cling wrap. Microwave for 4 minutes. In a small bowl microwave the butter and almonds for 2 minutes or until lightly brown.

Spoon on to the fish before serving.

Fish in Parsley Sauce

There are times when plain, old-fashioned food is all you want. Serve this on buttered toast, rice or noodles.

For 4 servings:
2 Tbsp butter
2 Tbsp flour
2 Tbsp chopped parsley
1 cup milk
½ tsp celery, onion, or garlic salt
400–500 g fish fillets

Melt butter at Full power for 30 seconds. Stir in flour and microwave for 30 seconds. Add parsley, milk and seasoned salt. Cook until boiling, about 2 minutes, then beat until smooth. While sauce cooks, cut fish into 2 cm cubes or larger pieces. Stir fish into thick sauce.

Cover and microwave for 4–5 minutes or until fish is opaque. Serve immediately or reheat when required.

Whole Fish with Lemon Sauce

It is much easier to lift pieces of cooked fish off the bone than to bone the fish before cooking. If you prefer to dismember your cooked fish in private, cool fish after microwaving and remove skin and bones. Pour sauce over fish, then reheat, adding garnishes just before serving.

For 4 servings:
1 whole round fish (750 g)
fresh herbs
1 clove garlic (optional)
*1 lemon, halved lengthwise, then
    sliced*
2 Tbsp melted butter
1 egg yolk
1 Tbsp lemon juice
½ tsp cornflour
¼ tsp garlic salt

Place fish on serving platter. (If necessary, remove head and tail so fish fits both the platter and the oven.) Cut several parallel slashes on fish so that the thicker part will cook more evenly and quickly. For extra flavour, insert fresh herbs, garlic and lemon slices in the body cavity and in the cuts. Brush both sides of fish with plain or garlic-flavoured melted butter. Cover with cling wrap. Microwave at Full power for 6–7 minutes. Stand for 2 minutes and then remove wrap, checking to see if flesh at thickest part is opaque and will flake. Pour liquid from the fish into a bowl containing the egg yolk, lemon juice, cornflour and garlic salt. Whisk to mix. Microwave sauce for 1½ minutes, or until it thickens. Do not overheat. Pour sauce over the fish.

Variation:
For a more colourful surface, use the same coating as in Oyster-Stuffed Fillets, sprinkling on the coating before cooking.

Sesame Steamed Fish

You can make this interesting, well-flavoured fish with very little time and trouble in a microwave oven.

Select a microwave-proof platter large enough to hold the fish with its head and tail intact. If the tail extends over the edge of the dish and will not fit in the oven, cut it off, heat it separately at Full power for 30 seconds, and put it in place again for presentation.

For 4 servings:
1 whole fish (600–700 g)
3–4 spring onions
2 cm length root ginger
2 Tbsp soya sauce
1 Tbsp sesame oil

Slash thickest part of fish with several parallel cuts on each side.

Cut spring onions into 2 cm lengths. Peel root ginger. Slice onions and ginger into matchstick strips. Sprinkle half of these on the plate, lay the fish on them, and then sprinkle the rest over it. Sprinkle the soya sauce and sesame oil evenly over the fish. Mask head or eye section with aluminium foil if desired, making sure it will not touch the sides of the oven. Cover with cling wrap. Microwave at Full power, allowing 50 seconds per 100 g of fish. Stand, covered, for 4 minutes. Uncover and check to see if flesh at thickest part is opaque and will flake. If not, microwave for 1–2 minutes longer.

Baste with juices. Serve with unthickened juice, and with parsley or Chinese parsley garnish. To serve, lift fish from bone, starting from back.

Variations:
(a) Just before serving, heat 1 tablespoon sesame oil until it is very hot. Drizzle over the cooked fish, which will sizzle.
(b) Use the same ingredients, replacing whole fish with boned, skinned fillets. Grate ginger and chop spring onions more finely, if desired, Allow same cooking time per 100 g.

Fish flavourings and garnishes include: thyme, marjoram, chervil, spring onions, chillis, root ginger, paprika, dill, bayleaves, lemons, fennel, celery, coriander leaf (Chinese parsley), tarragon, chives, peppercorns, cress, garlic, cucumber and parsley.

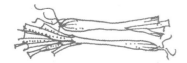 Salmon-Stuffed Rolls

For 4 servings:
*4 large or 8 small flatfish fillets
    (about 400 g)
50 g thinly sliced salmon
¼–½ cup sour cream
2 Tbsp chopped chives or spring onion
    leaves
2 Tbsp white wine
2 Tbsp cream or sour cream
1 tsp mixed mustard*

Lay fillets skin side up. Spread with salmon then sour cream then chives or spring onions.

Roll up, thin end first. After rolling wide fillets, cut into two smaller rolls. Secure each roll with a toothpick. Arrange rolls like pinwheels in dish large enough to hold them in one layer without crowding. Add wine, cover and microwave at Full power for 5 minutes, or until fish is opaque at the thickest part.

Lift fish from dish and remove toothpicks. Add cream and mixed mustard to remaining liquid.

Microwave for 3 minutes or until thick. Replace fillets in sauce and heat if necessary before serving.

Variation:
Replace salmon with herbed puréed fish, as in Stuffed Flatfish.

Quick Kedgeree

You do not need to precook the smoked fish for this recipe.

For 3–4 servings:
*2 eggs
400–500 g smoked fish
2 Tbsp butter
4 spring onions, chopped
2 cups cooked rice*

Add eggs to small, flat-bottomed dish containing ¼ cup boiling water. Pierce yolks. Cover. Microwave at Full power until yolks harden (about 2½ minutes). Skin and bone fish and cut flesh into small pieces.

In dish large enough to cook and serve the kedgeree, melt butter for 1 minute. Toss fish in butter. Add spring onions and cooked (preferably unsalted) rice. Drain eggs, chop and stir into fish mixture. Cover and microwave for 4–6 minutes, stirring after 3 minutes.

Taste and add more seasonings if necessary.

Note:
If using hot smoked fish, flake instead of cutting, if desired.

Orange Fish Steaks

In this recipe, the sauce is cooked before the fish.

For 2 servings:
*2 fish steaks, 200 g each
1 Tbsp butter
1 tsp cornflour
juice and grated rind of 1 orange*

Melt butter in microwave at Full power for about 30 seconds.

Add cornflour, orange juice and grated orange rind. Microwave until sauce bubbles and thickens.

Place the steaks on a plate with the thinner sections near the centre. Spread the sauce over the fish.

Cover with cling wrap. Microwave for 3½ minutes. Allow to stand for 3 minutes before uncovering and serving.

Quick Shrimp Creole

Prepare this ahead, then leave to stand to blend flavours.

For 4 servings:
*250 g shelled shrimp, fresh or frozen
2 Tbsp butter
2 cloves garlic
2 Tbsp flour
10–12 drops hot pepper sauce
1 Tbsp tomato paste
1 green pepper, chopped
1 (420 g) can whole tomatoes in juice,
    chopped*

Thaw shrimp if necessary. In a flat-bottomed microwave dish, melt butter at Full power for 30 seconds. Stir in chopped garlic and flour. Microwave for 2 minutes, until light brown. Add the remaining ingredients. Heat until bubbling and thickened, 4–5 minutes. Add shrimp (and liquid) and reheat until sauce bubbles again. Taste and adjust seasonings, adding salt, sugar and basil, if desired.

Stuffed Flatfish

Smooth-textured stuffing 'dresses up' this fish, making it much more substantial.

For 2 servings:
*1 sole or flounder (200 g)
75 g boneless fish fillets
25 g smoked salmon or shrimp
2 Tbsp cream
1 tsp tomato paste
½ tsp salt
1 Tbsp melted butter*

Cut fish down its midline between head and tail. Run knife along backbone, lifting fillets on each side. If you want a boneless stuffed fish, cut under the backbone and remove it. Otherwise, pack stuffing on top of backbone.

Stuffing:
Mix next five ingredients in food processor until well blended. Pack stuffing into cavity of fish. Brush skin with melted butter. Cover with cling-wrap. Microwave at Full power for 3 minutes. Let stand for 2 minutes.

Uncover. Garnish with sour cream, lump fish roe, etc. or lie a row of lemon slices over stuffing, before serving.

Variation:
For economy, replace salmon or shrimp with extra fish fillet. Appearance will still be good.

Creamy Paprika Fish

Quick, easy, and very good!

For 3–4 servings:
*1 large onion, chopped
1 Tbsp butter
500 g boneless fish fillets, cubed
½ tsp celery salt
2 tsp cornflour
½ cup evaporated milk
½ tsp paprika
2 spring onions, chopped*

Put chopped onion and butter into a 20–22 cm microwave cooking/serving dish. Cover and microwave at Full power for 3 minutes, or until onion is tender, stirring once. Add fish cut into 15 mm cubes. Sprinkle with celery salt and cornflour and turn to mix. Add evaporated milk and mix again.

Sprinkle with paprika and spring onions, cover and cook for 3 minutes or until sauce thickens. Stand for 1 minute before uncovering.

Fish is cooked when the centre is opaque. Cook for 1 minute longer if necessary. Before serving sprinkle with extra paprika if desired.

Variation:
Sprinkle with grated cheese before adding extra paprika, after cooking. Microwave until cheese melts.

Simmered Seafood

To make this delicious fish mixture, microwave all the different ingredients separately so that nothing overcooks. Decide which shellfish you will remove from their shells, strain and then thicken the accumulated cooking liquid, cook the cubed fish, and reheat everything together.

When you buy the shellfish, allow one or two items per serving, rather than buying by weight. Use whatever shellfish is available. If the worst comes to the worst, use only fish, but don't expect the flavour to be the same!

Simmered Seafood

For 4 servings:

½ *cup white wine*
2 cloves garlic, crushed
1 bayleaf
6 peppercorns
herbs or saffron (optional)
8 mussels (400 g)
8 cockles (200 g)
8 pipis, tuatuas or clams (200 g)
8 scallops (100–150 g)
4 green prawns (100 g)
500 g fish fillets
2 Tbsp water and white wine
2 Tbsp butter
2 Tbsp flour

Put wine, crushed garlic, bayleaf, peppercorns (and other herbs or a pinch of saffron threads) in a fairly large microwave casserole with a lid. Add the mussels, microwave at Full power for about 2 minutes, or until shells open. Lift the mussels on to a tray. In same liquid, microwave cockles, then pipis or clams, until they open (1–2 minutes).

Pierce scallop roes. Microwave scallops in liquid 2–3 minutes, until opaque. Remove. Microwave prawns until pink (1½–2 minutes).

Strain liquid into a measuring jug and make up to 1½ cups with water or a water-wine mixture. Melt butter, add flour and microwave for 30 seconds. Add strained liquid and heat to boiling, about 2 minutes.

Whisk until smooth. Taste, adjust seasonings, and add 2–3 tablespoons cream if desired. (This makes the sauce rich but the flavour bland.) Add fish cut into 2 cm cubes. Microwave for about 4 minutes, until opaque. Add cooked shellfish, in or out of their shells, according to your preference. Reheat when required.

Variations:

After cooking fish fillets, divide everything between individual serving plates. Reheat plates separately when required.

Serve with a spoon and fork, crusty bread, and a side salad.

Use whatever combination of seafood appeals to you!

Shellfish Dishes

Shellfish are renowned for their delicate but definite flavour, and their texture. Many of us tend to divide shellfish into two categories — first, rather expensive delicacies in fish shops, and next the shellfish we find at the beach on summer picnics, that we don't really know what to do with! I hope that I can help you to make the most of both, making a little of our seafood specialities go a remarkably long way, and showing you some interesting ways to use the shellfish which we bring home from the seashore, and which are becoming increasingly available commercially.

It is very important to remember that shellfish must never be collected from areas which may be polluted.

OYSTERS: Small rock oysters and faster-growing Pacific oysters are found on rocks, between tide marks. Deep-sea oysters are dredged from the sea bed.

SCALLOPS: Usually bought shelled, fresh or frozen, large scallops have coral-pink roe attached to firm, white flesh. Small queen scallops have no coral.

MUSSELS: Fairly large green-lipped mussels are farmed and sold in their shells, steamed, marinated or smoked. Smaller blue mussels are found on rocks, between tide marks.

TUATUAS: Tuatuas and pipis have hinged shells. These shellfish are found in the sand below the low-water mark, and are cooked and served as clams are.

COCKLES: These hinged shellfish can be collected at low tide in estuaries and harbours. Shells are rounder than tuatuas and pipis, and are usually ridged.

PAUA: A paua has one oval-shaped shell, which is multi-coloured inside. It clings to the rocks, below the low-water mark, with a large muscular foot. It is known as abalone in some countries.

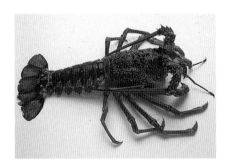

CRAYFISH (Rock lobster): Found in water around rocky coastlines. Most of its firm white flesh is found in the tail. Shell is reddish-brown before it is cooked, when it turns bright red.

CRABS: Found in shallow water on sandy beaches. The flesh is sweet, with a delicate flavour, and is found in the muscles in and above the legs. There is no large tail muscle as in crayfish.

SQUID: Classified as shellfish although they have no visible shell. They have dense white, firm flesh with a delicate flavour, not unlike that of crayfish.

M U Oysters

The classic way to present oysters is to stand the shells on crushed ice, and to serve thinly sliced, lightly buttered brown bread, lemon wedges, freshly ground black pepper, and hot pepper sauce alongside. It is worth trying fresh oysters dipped in a sauce of equal parts of dry white wine and wine vinegar, flavoured with finely chopped shallots and pepper or hot sauce. Oysters which are to be served raw must be very fresh, never thawed from frozen.

Opening Shellfish
To open oysters in the shell you need a strong-bladed oyster knife and considerable skill, or a microwave oven. Put the oysters (or other shellfish to be opened) in a covered dish little bigger than the volume of shellfish.

Microwave at Full power until you see the first shell open.

Remove each shellfish as soon as the shell is ajar. You will need to slip a knife between the shells and cut the muscle holding the shell.

On longer heating, the muscle will separate from the shell by itself, but the flesh will be partly cooked. With prolonged heating, the flesh overcooks, shrinks and toughens.

M Oyster-Stuffed Fillets

You need only a few oysters to flavour these quickly prepared but elegant stuffed fillets.

For 4–6 servings:
500–600 g boneless fish fillets
50 g butter
¼ cup finely chopped onion
1 cup soft breadcrumbs
½ dozen oysters, thinly sliced
¼ cup finely chopped parsley
1 Tbsp Parmesan cheese
½ tsp paprika
½ tsp garlic salt

Select small flatfish fillets or cut thicker round fish fillets diagonally into thinner fillet-shaped slices, making 8–12 pieces altogether. In a dish big enough to hold folded fillets in one layer, melt butter. Tip half of the melted butter into another bowl, add the onion, cover and microwave at Full power for 2 minutes. Stir in the breadcrumbs, the oysters and half of the parsley. Lay fish pieces in a row on the bench, skin side up.

Place equal amounts of stuffing on one end of each. Fold other end over stuffing.

Place stuffed fish into the buttered dish, with rounded sides to edge of dish. Stir together the cheese, paprika, garlic salt and remaining parsley. Sprinkle over fillets. Cover with cling wrap and microwave for 3–4 minutes, or until opaque. Stand for 2–3 minutes before uncovering.

'Stretching' Oysters
To make a few oysters go a long way, make oyster soup based on fish stock, add them to a mixture of other fish in soup, chowder, or fish cocktails, serve them in vol-au-vent cases, or use them to flavour stuffing for whole fish or fillets.

C Scallops

Scallops need gentle cooking, for a longer time than most other shellfish, since they are thicker. If you are in the lucky position of having plenty of scallops, just cook them gently in butter, with chopped garlic, until they are firm, lift them out of the pan and cook the juices with a little wine, lemon juice or pernod, and pepper until syrupy.

Turn the cooked scallops in this, and serve them with fresh crusty bread and butter.

To make a few scallops go a long way, serve them with mushrooms, in a creamy sauce, in a crisp vol-au-vent case (homemade or bought).

C Creamed Scallops with Mushrooms

150–200 g scallops
1–2 cups (200 g) quartered button
*   mushrooms*
1–2 cloves garlic
3 Tbsp butter
½ cup white wine
½ cup sour or plain cream
4 spring onions
⅛ tsp salt
cornflour
4 large or 8 small cooked pastry cases

Cut large scallops into 2–3 smaller pieces. Put scallops aside.

Sauté mushrooms and garlic in butter in a fairly large pan, adding a little water if they look dry before they are cooked.

Add scallops, wine, cream, spring onions and salt, and simmer, stirring often, until scallops are firm, about 5–8 minutes. Add a little more wine or cream if liquid evaporates, or thicken with a little cornflour paste if liquid is too thin.

Adjust seasonings. Spoon hot mixture into warmed pastry cases just before serving.

C Paua (Abalone)

The muscular foot from a fresh paua looks uninviting to the uninitiated. Trim away the mouth area and scrub the remaining hard muscle to remove its black surface. Pound the muscle with a meat hammer, using 50–60 hard blows.

For paua steak, coat with seasoned flour then fry in a little butter over moderate heat, for 30–40 seconds a side.

C Stir-Fried Paua (Abalone)

Very brief cooking is needed for tender results.

For 2 servings:
1 cleaned, beaten paua
1 Tbsp light soya sauce
1 Tbsp sherry
1 Tbsp oil
2 spring onions, chopped
100 g mushrooms, sliced
1 Tbsp butter
½ tsp cornflour
½ tsp sugar
1 Tbsp water

Slice the paua as thinly as possible, using a heavy knife. Mix with next three ingredients. Heat butter in a heavy pan. Stir-fry the vegetables, adding a little water if necessary. Mix cornflour, sugar and water in a small container. Stir the paua into the pan and add the cornflour mixture as soon as the paua has heated through. Paua will toughen if it cooks more than a few seconds.
Note:
This is not so tender if made with unbeaten or frozen paua.

M Cockles

Cockles should be steamed open carefully, or they will be tough. The following method works well with both cockles and mussels.

For 1 serving:
200–300 g mussels or cockles
1 clove garlic, chopped
2 tsp butter
1 bay leaf
¼ cup white wine
1 small tomato (optional)
2 Tbsp chopped parsley

Scrub shellfish. Cook chopped garlic and butter in a serving bowl for 1 minute, at Full power. Add bay leaf, wine, finely chopped tomato and parsley, then shellfish, hinges down. Cover whole dish with cling wrap and microwave for about 2 minutes, or until the shellfish separate from the shells, after they open. Serve with French bread.

Garlic Mussels

M Garlic Mussels

Cook these in individual serving bowls.

For each serving:
mussels (300 g or about 6)
1 clove garlic
2 tsp butter
1–2 bay leaves
¼ cup white wine
2 Tbsp chopped parsley

Scrub the mussels and put aside.
   Chop the garlic, add butter and microwave at Full power for 1 minute in the serving bowl.
   Add bay leaves, wine and chopped parsley. Place the mussels in bowl, hinged end down. Cover with cling wrap. Microwave for 2 minutes or until shells have opened and mussels have separated from the shells. Do not overcook. Lift off wrap, pull off the beards and serve immediately with French bread to soak up cooking liquid.

M Buttered Mussels

Prepare these delicious mussels on their half shells for a few individual servings, or serve them out of their shells for an easy appetiser for larger groups.

For 4–6 servings:
24–26 cooked mussels
50 g butter
2–4 garlic cloves, chopped
2 Tbsp lemon juice
4 drops hot pepper sauce
¼ cup chopped parsley (or mixed fresh
   herbs)

Buy steamed mussels or precook them yourself and arrange them in their half shells. In a loosely covered bowl microwave the butter, garlic, lemon juice and pepper sauce until hot and bubbling, at Full power for about 2½ minutes.
   Then mix all the mussels in butter to coat evenly and microwave for about 2 minutes, until mussels are warm and plump.
   Or brush hot butter over mussels on the half shell. Arrange about six shells on each plate. Cover with cling wrap. When required, heat each plate for about 30 seconds or until you hear the first spatter.
Note:
Do not overcook or mussels will shrink and toughen.

M Crayfish Mornay

Prepare this ahead and reheat individual servings when required.

For 2 servings:
1 cooked crayfish (400 g)
1 Tbsp butter
1 Tbsp flour
¼ cup milk
¼ cup wine or milk
1 cup grated tasty cheese
3–4 drops hot pepper sauce
1 tsp chopped chives
2 tsp chopped spring onion
pinch of paprika

Halve the crayfish and cube the flesh (175–200 g). Remove the legs and save for garnish. Microwave the butter and flour at Full power for 1 minute. Stir in the first measure of milk. Microwave for 1 minute. Add remaining liquid and microwave until sauce thickens.
   Stir in the hot sauce and three-quarters of the cheese, saving the remainder for topping. Reheat sauce to melt cheese. Add the crayfish to the sauce and spoon the mixture into both shells. Place each on a serving plate. Sprinkle with the remaining cheese, chives, spring onions, and paprika. Reheat each plate for 1½ minutes, until flesh is hot and cheese is partially melted. Arrange the legs attractively and serve.

C M Mussels

Mussels may be bought ready to eat, or they may be opened like oysters (see page 59) or steamed like cockles (see page 59). Try cooked mussels dipped in this unusual sauce, or mix them with pasta, using the sauce as a dressing.

U Ginger Dipping Sauce

1 Tbsp chopped root ginger
2 small dried chillis
1 clove garlic
2 tsp sugar
2 Tbsp light soya sauce or fish sauce
1 Tbsp water
1 Tbsp lemon juice or lime juice

Measure all ingredients into a food processor. Mix thoroughly, then strain. Dip cooked mussels into freshly made sauce, before eating.

Seafood Salad

To make dressing, mix sauce with ½ cup oil, and use to moisten cooked seashell pasta, cooked mussels, and chopped parsley, chives or spring onions, or coriander leaf, using amounts of each to suit yourself. Mix with pasta 15–30 minutes before serving.

Which Fish?
Buy fresh fish with care. In general, the price rises with the popularity of the type of fish. You will get much more for your money if you use the lesser-known varieties. Talk to the fish retailer and find what is best value.

ⓒ Squid Rings

Next time you see squid hoods in your fish shop, buy some and experiment with them.

Hoods less than 12 cm long should be tasty and tender, if cooked very briefly.

Cut in rings, dip in milk and flour, or in flour and seasoned egg and crumbs then leave to stand for 15 minutes before shallow frying until lightly browned, 2–4 minutes.

Simmer rings from large squid hoods for 20–30 minutes, until tender, or marinate them in mashed kiwi fruit for 12 hours before coating and frying them.
Or cut hood open flat, cut in very thin whitebait-like slivers and cook them in battercakes batter for mock whitebait fritters.

ⓒ Coconut Squid

For 4 servings:
300–400 g squid tubes
2 Tbsp butter
2 onions, sliced or chopped
1/2 tsp coriander seed
1/2 tsp turmeric
1 can (420 g) coconut cream
salt and pepper

Cut the squid into rings or cubes, place it in a sieve, and pour bath-temperature tap water over it for 30–45 seconds, to tenderise it.

Heat the butter in a large pan. Add the cubed or sliced onion and cook until tender and golden brown. Stir in the freshly ground spices, then the coconut cream. Simmer, uncovered, until the sauce mixture thickens, then stir in the squid.

Simmer for 1–2 minutes, or until the squid is really tender, then serve with rice. Longer cooking toughens the squid, and it may take 45 minutes of simmering to tenderise it again.

Ⓜ Sesame Squid

Cooked briefly, squid is very tender. Its delicate flavour blends well with this sauce.

For 1–2 servings:
200 g squid
1 tsp grated root ginger
2 cloves garlic
2 tsp sesame oil
1 Tbsp corn or soya oil
100 g mushrooms, sliced
1/2 cup chopped spring onions
1/2 tsp instant chicken stock
2 tsp cornflour
2 tsp light soya sauce
1 Tbsp dry sherry
2 Tbsp water

Heat a browning dish at Full power for 6 minutes. Cut squid into 1 cm squares. Mix with grated ginger, crushed garlic, and the two oils. Put aside. Combine chopped mushrooms and spring onions. Mix remaining ingredients to a smooth paste. Add squid to hot browning dish. Stir for 30 seconds.

Add mushroom mixture. Cover and microwave for 1 minute. Stir in paste. Cover again and cook for 2 minutes longer, until thickened. Serve on rice.

ⓒ Squid Salad

Squid rings may be very briefly cooked or else simmered for 30–45 minutes according to the texture you like best. Marinated with an interesting dressing they make a good dinner starter or hot-weather lunch main course.

Marinade:
3 Tbsp lemon juice or wine vinegar
1/4 cup oil
2 cloves garlic, crushed
1/4 cup chopped parsley
1 Tbsp chopped dill (optional)

Dressing:
2 Tbsp lemon juice or wine vinegar
2 anchovy fillets
2 spring onions, chopped
1 clove garlic (optional)
1/4 cup sour cream
1/2 cup mayonnaise

For four servings use 2–3 medium-sized squid tubes. Pull out and discard tough, transparent strip inside each tube. Cut each tube into thin rings or into 1 cm squares.

Boil 1 cup water with a lemon slice, bay leaf, garlic clove and 6 peppercorns for five minutes. Add squid. When water returns to boiling, and squid turns milky, remove.
Or cover and simmer for 30–45 minutes until tender.

Mix marinade (in food processor if available). Leave squid to stand in it until required. Chop first four dressing ingredients in food processor. Add cream and mix again, Stir in mayonnaise. Serve drained squid on mixed salad greens with dressing.

ⓒ Crayfish

The flesh from a cooked crayfish is delicious, hot or cold, with melted butter or mayonnaise, pepper and salt, and lemon juice.

To cook a crayfish, put it in a large pot, pour boiling water over it, and simmer for 8–10 minutes per 500 g, i.e. 12 minutes for a 750 g crayfish.

Lift from water and cool under running water for 1–2 minutes.

Ⓜ Crayfish Terrine

This terrine will serve 6–8 people for the first course of a dinner party.

1 cooked (500–800 g) crayfish
250 g boneless fish fillets
1/2 cup double or other cream
2 eggs
1 cup soft breadcrumbs
1 tsp garlic salt
white part of 4 spring onions
1/4 cup milk
6 spinach leaves
1 Tbsp tomato paste

Remove and chop the flesh from the crayfish. Put aside.

Cut the fillets into 1 cm cubes and purée in a food processor with the cream, eggs, crumbs, garlic salt and chopped spring onions until smooth. Thin with milk only after well blended. Divide into three parts. Spread one-third in a paper-lined microwave loaf pan. Blanch and drain spinach leaves. Cover the fish layer with half the spinach. Stir the chopped crayfish flesh and tomato paste into the second part of the fish, and spread it over the spinach in the loaf pan.

Cover with the remaining spinach, then the rest of the fish. Wrap plastic film tightly over the top of the loaf pan and microwave at Medium-High (70% power) for 15 minutes, or until centre springs back, when pressed, and knife cuts clean in the middle. Serve warm or cold in 6–8 slices.

> **'Stretching' Crayfish**
> It pays to remove the flesh from the body of a crayfish. Using a hammer, pliers, a skewer and perseverance, you can get half as much meat as there is in the tail, from the claws, legs and the body, just above the legs. If you boil the pieces of shell in a cup of water for 30 minutes, you can use the strained liquid as stock. Use the meat from crayfish bodies, and this stock, to make soup, chowder, fried rice, salads and omelets.

ⓒ Crabs

Crabs are cooked in the same way as crayfish, but for a shorter time, about 5–6 minutes for fairly large crabs. Remove the flesh from the legs and the body as you would from a crayfish.

Chicken

What a long way chicken has come in the last 30 years! I remember my excitement when I cooked, for the first time, a chicken which was tender enough to roast uncovered.

This was a revolution, after watching my mother simmer older, rather tough birds for hours, until they were tender, then dressing them up. In those days, chicken was served once or twice a year, as a special treat. These 'chooks' what's more, were bought from the fish shop!

Today we can choose between a frozen, fresh, smoked cooked, or cooked-in-the-store, still warm, whole bird. We can choose from breasts, thighs, legs, drumsticks or wings, without having to first dismember the bird ourselves.

Boneless, skinned chicken cuts are readily available and for the times when we have almost no time to cook, we can take home pre-seasoned kebabs made from the most tender breast meat, or find packs of bigger joints in interesting, well-seasoned marinades.

I am delighted to see that different, exciting, quick chicken recipes are becoming more and more popular as our lives get busier, and cooking time is reduced. In this section I have selected a group of my most used chicken recipes. Some of them have a very short cooking time — especially the microwaved recipes, and the 'flattened' breast and stir-fried recipes.

Some take next to no time to prepare, but a little longer to cook. Others are recipes which 'cut corners', producing chicken that tastes like longer-cooked favourites. I hope you will enjoy them all.

M Whole Chickens

Whole chickens cook well and quickly in microwave ovens.

Defrosting

Defrost chickens at 20% or 30% power levels for about 30 minutes.

Always defrost frozen chickens before cooking them at higher power levels. Remove commercial wrappings and metal clips. Place bird in a bag (unless using automatic function and other instructions). During thawing, turn chicken, pour off accumulating liquid, loosen joints, remove giblets and internal ice, and mask with small pieces of foil any parts that are overcooking. After thawing, centre should be cold but not icy.

Note:
Microwave defrosting is convenient when time is limited.

When possible, however, thaw chicken at room temperature for several hours, or in refrigerator overnight. For chicken which will be marinated before cooking, thaw in marinade, if desired.

Coatings and Marinades

Because chicken skin does not brown much during cooking, it is usually coated with a mixture which will add colour as well as flavour. Use any of the coatings for chicken pieces, on pages 70 and 71 or try the following recipes.

Bags and Covers

Whole chickens cook more quickly, and more evenly, if they are enclosed as they cook.

Oven bags produce excellent results, with the chicken skin losing its 'steamed' appearance soon after it is removed from the bag after cooking. Casseroled chickens cook well, and have the same appearance and texture as those casseroled in conventional ovens. When microwaving chickens uncovered, you should cover them loosely with a tent of baking paper or greaseproof paper, since this helps the bird cook more evenly and quickly.

C Herb-Baked Whole Chicken

Try this variation if you want something that tastes more interesting than plain roast chicken.

1 chicken
2 cloves garlic
¹/₂ tsp rosemary
3-4 Tbsp butter
¹/₄ cup white wine
¹/₂ tsp basil
¹/₂ tsp salt
¹/₄ tsp pepper

Wash and dry the chicken thoroughly, inside and out. Slice the garlic cloves in half and put them with the rosemary inside the body cavity. Mix the remaining ingredients in a small saucepan. Put the chicken in a shallow baking or roasting pan. Brush with butter and wine mixture. Bake at 200°C for 60 minutes. Baste with butter and wine several times during cooking.

Chicken is cooked when the juice in the body cavity is no longer pink, and when the juice from the thickest part of the thigh or drumstick is clear and yellowish rather than pink.

Note:
A stuffed bird cooked this way needs 20-30 minutes more in an oven of the same temperature.

C Roast Lemon Chicken

When I was promoting New Zealand spring lamb in New York I was interviewed by a charming lady, Patricia McCann, on one of the city's highest-rated radio talk shows. Patricia and I really enjoyed our hour's conversation, although I was rather apprehensive before it, since her producer had been very demanding, during planning sessions. He kept asking for 'gimmicks — like the lady a few weeks ago, who put a whole lemon in a chicken, then roasted it'. When I returned home I decided to see what happened when I did the same thing.

After some experimenting I finished up with a delicious lemony chicken — you should try it too.

Start with a fresh or frozen chicken. For best results, thaw a frozen chicken slowly, without removing it from its bag. Just before cooking open the bag and dry the chicken inside and out. Make cuts along a lemon as though you were slicing it, but don't cut right through it, then put the lemon in the body cavity, with one or two squashed garlic cloves.

Put the wing tips behind the chicken's neck, so that it stands firmly on a flat surface. Stand it on a piece of greaseproof paper, then coat lightly with butter or oil for a nicely browned surface.

Sprinkle chicken with lemon pepper or ordinary pepper, and add a sprinkling of your favourite seasoned salt. Put chicken in a roasting bag, on its greaseproof paper bed, and twist the tie, leaving a finger-sized hole so that air and steam can escape freely during cooking. Bake in a low sided dish for about 1 hour, or until the juices run clear when the thigh is pierced with a skewer. (You can do this through the hole if you are careful.)

Pour off and skim the liquid from the bag. Add a little soya sauce and chopped spring onion, and boil until reduced to half its volume or thicken with a little bit of cornflour mixed to a paste. Taste sauce and add a little sugar if you like a sweet lemony flavour, then pour the sauce over the dismembered chicken.

M Roast Chicken

(See photograph on page 62.)

For good colour glaze chicken before (and during) cooking with a mixture of:

2 Tbsp melted butter and
1 Tbsp dark soya sauce

To make sure glaze colours chicken evenly, first scrub the skin with warm water and a soft brush. Pat dry, then brush with butter and soya sauce mixture.

Place chicken, breast side down, on rack in roasting pan or on ridged baking pan. Cover with a tent of greaseproof paper. Microwave at Full power for 10-15 minutes, depending on size of chicken, then at Medium (50% power) for 12 minutes per 500 g.

Turn chicken breast side up after half the estimated cooking time.

Brush with more glaze if desired. Leave to stand for 10 minutes. When cooked, leg should move freely. Flesh between leg and breast should no longer be pink.

M Forcemeat Balls

(See photograph on page 62.)

If you like stuffing, cook these balls during the chicken's standing time and serve alongside the chicken.

450-500 g sausage meat
¹/₂ cup soft breadcrumbs
¹/₂ cup crushed pineapple
1 onion, finely chopped
2 Tbsp chopped parsley
1 tsp fresh thyme
¹/₂ tsp salt
Savoury Crumbs (see page 122)
*   or fine dry crumbs*

Mix first seven ingredients until well blended. Form into 12-16 balls with wet hands. Roll in Savoury or dry crumbs. Arrange in a circle on a flat plate or on the turntable.

Microwave at Full power for 5 minutes, or until firm.

Bagged Roast Chicken

M Bagged Roast Chicken

This chicken gains colour from its marinade.

2 Tbsp dark soya sauce
2 Tbsp sherry
2 Tbsp Worcestershire sauce
1 Tbsp honey
1 clove garlic, crushed or chopped

Mix marinade ingredients in an unpunctured oven bag. If necessary, heat marinade in bag to soften and dissolve honey. Add chicken to bag with marinade.

Remove air from bag so marinade surrounds chicken. Fasten with rubber band. Turn occasionally. Leave to stand for at least an hour, but longer if desired.

Before cooking, loosen rubber band, leaving a finger-sized hole so steam can escape during cooking.

For preference, microwave at 70% power, allowing 10 minutes per 500 g. If necessary, roast at Full power for 8 minutes per 500 g.

After standing for 5 minutes after cooking, the flesh between leg and breast should no longer look pink. When cooking a large chicken, turn it several times during cooking for most even results and best colour.

C Crunchy Chicken

This recipe won an 'Old-Fashioned Recipe' competition. It tastes rather like roast chicken with stuffing and gravy, but eliminates all the last minute mess and fuss that goes along with such a meal.

For 4 servings:
1 chicken
1–2 rashers bacon
1 cup water
1 Tbsp soya sauce
2 cloves garlic, crushed
cornflour to thicken
salt and pepper
2 Tbsp butter
1 onion, finely chopped
1 tsp dried mixed herbs
1 cup fresh breadcrumbs

Place chicken (whole or jointed) in a saucepan with bacon, water, soya sauce and garlic. Cover and simmer over very low heat for about an hour, or until flesh is tender. Bone chicken and place flesh in shallow ovenware dish. Chop bacon and sprinkle over chicken. Strain liquid, thicken with cornflour paste, season and pour over the chicken.

Melt butter and cook chopped onion in it until onion is tender but not browned. Remove from heat and mix well with dried herbs and breadcrumbs. Spread topping evenly over cooled sauce and chicken.

Refrigerate until required. Reheat at 190°C until topping is crisp and sauce and chicken have heated through (about 30–40 minutes).
Variation:
Add chopped sautéed mushrooms to boned chicken and sauce mixture.

Chicken and Vegetable Casserole

C Chicken and Vegetable Casserole

For 4 servings:
8 chicken pieces
butter for frying
4 medium-sized new potatoes
8–12 small whole carrots
12–20 firm button mushrooms
2 tsp chopped fresh tarragon (or ½ tsp
dried tarragon)
1 cup dry white wine
1 cup chicken stock
cornflour to thicken
¼ cup finely chopped parsley

Brown the chicken pieces evenly on all sides, adding just enough butter to the pan to stop them sticking.

Peel the potatoes and carrots. Halve potatoes if large. Arrange potatoes close to the outside of the casserole, so they start to cook quickly, and arrange chicken pieces with the thickest parts close to the bottom or sides.

In the remaining chicken fat sauté the mushrooms until lightly browned. Do not halve or slice. Sprinkle with tarragon (or use thyme if preferred). Add wine and chicken stock. (Make chicken stock from 1 cup water and 2 level teaspoons instant chicken stock if necessary.)

Cover tightly. Bake at 180°C until potatoes and chicken are tender (about 1¼ hours). Thicken juices lightly with cornflour-and-water paste. Stir chopped parsley through the liquid.

C Orange Chicken

For 4 servings:
8 chicken thighs
¼ cup flour
3–4 Tbsp butter
1–2 cloves garlic, sliced
1 Tbsp soya sauce
¼ tsp salt
¼ tsp freshly ground nutmeg
1 cup orange juice
1 Tbsp brown sugar

Shake chicken thighs in a plastic bag with flour. Brown evenly in butter in a large frying pan over high heat. When browned, pour off any extra fat and turn down heat. Add sliced garlic, soya sauce, salt, nutmeg, orange juice and sugar.

Cover and cook for 20 minutes, or until chicken is tender, turning pieces once or twice during this time. There should be just enough liquid left at the end of the cooking time to glaze the pieces of chicken. Remove lid to concentrate glaze if necessary, or add water if mixture dries out too soon.

Taste and adjust seasonings before serving on rice or with noodles.

C Sautéed Chicken in Wine

Follow recipe for Orange Chicken, replacing soya sauce, nutmeg, orange juice and brown sugar with

1 cup fairly dry white wine, ½ teaspoon salt and 2 teaspoons of any fresh chopped herb desired — e.g. thyme, tarragon, marjoram or basil.

Sprinkle with finely chopped parsley before serving.

B C Barbecued Chicken Thighs

Marinade:
2 Tbsp lemon juice
2 Tbsp tomato sauce
1 Tbsp oil
1 tsp paprika
1 tsp garlic salt
2 tsp Worcestershire sauce

Marinate chicken thighs in a mixture of the marinade ingredients for at least 30 minutes.

Barbecue (or grill) 15–20 cm from the heat, until evenly browned on both sides, about 25–30 minutes altogether. Brush with remaining marinade during last 10 minutes of cooking. Chicken is cooked when juices close to bone run clear, not pink.

C Fruity Chicken Casserole

This quick casserole should be cooked in a shallow oven-to-table dish just large enough to hold the chicken in one layer.

For 6 servings:
12 chicken thighs
1½ cups apple and orange juice
1½ tsp dark soya sauce
2 garlic cloves, chopped
1 packet onion soup mix

Spray or butter the ovenware dish. Combine the juice, soya sauce, garlic cloves, and soup mix.

Lay chicken pieces, best side down, in mixture. Cover tightly and bake at 180°C for about 1 hour, until the chicken is nearly cooked. Shake pan several times to make sure chicken does not stick.

Remove from oven, turn over chicken pieces carefully, and replace in oven without lid. Cook 15 minutes longer, until chicken pieces brown and liquid thickens. (If liquid thickens too much in this time, add extra water).

Serve on rice, or with broccoli and mashed potatoes.

Greek Barbecued Chicken

C Paprika-Baked Chicken

This country-style chicken with a tasty coating is good hot or cold, indoors or out.

For 2 servings:
4 pieces chicken, e.g. thighs,
*   drumsticks, or wings.*
1 Tbsp butter, melted
1 Tbsp oil
2 Tbsp flour
1 tsp paprika
½–1 tsp curry powder
1 tsp garlic salt
1 tsp castor sugar

For easiest coating, melt butter with oil in an oven bag, then toss chicken pieces in this to coat evenly. (Wash bag for later use.)

Mix remaining dry ingredients together in a screw-topped jar, then transfer most of this mixture to a small sieve and shake it evenly over the chicken pieces, turning them once. Return any unused coating to jar.

Bake in a foil-lined shallow baking dish at 200°C for 40 minutes, turning after 20 minutes.

Pieces are best cooked with their most attractive side down, for the first 20 minutes.

B C Greek Barbecued Chicken

Cooked outdoors on a barbecue, or inside, under a grill, Greek Barbecued Chicken is easy to prepare and cooks without fuss! Choose chicken legs or quartered chickens for this recipe, or thread wings and small pieces on skewers for easier turning during cooking.

For 4 servings:
4 large or 8 small chicken pieces
juice of 1 lemon
¼ cup olive or other oil
1 tsp paprika (optional)
2 cloves garlic, crushed
1 tsp dried oreganum

If necessary, break joints so chicken pieces lie flat. Combine remaining ingredients into marinade.

For barbecued chicken, cook about 15–20 cm from heat, brushing frequently with marinade.

For grilled chicken, lay the pieces in a shallow, foil-lined pan, e.g. a sponge roll pan. Pour combined ingredients over chicken and ensure the pieces are well coated. Grill 15–20 cm from the heat, turning pieces several times so they are well cooked.

Chicken is cooked in 20–30 minutes, as soon as juices run clear, not pink, when flesh close to bone is pierced.

Serve hot or at room temperature.

C Florentine Chicken

For 2 servings:

For this recipe you can work ahead — the coated, uncooked chicken may be kept for 24 hours in the refrigerator.

Buy two boneless chicken breasts or cut the tender breast meat from each side of a large chicken. Cut along the breastbone, then close to the bony framework, down to the side of the bird. Lift the muscle carefully away from the skin. (Joint the rest of the chicken later.)

Put each boneless, skinless breast between two pieces of plastic (or between two plastic bags). Using a rolling pin, bang evenly and gently until the breast is double its original length and width. Repeat with the second breast.

Life carefully from plastic. Dip first in milk, then in a mixture of 2 tablespoons each grated Parmesan cheese and fine dry breadcrumbs with 1 teaspoon chopped fresh herbs. Cover both sides. (Cut in two if too large to work with easily.) Refrigerate between plastic until required.

Sauté in 1 tablespoon each butter and oil for about 1 minute a side over high heat, until coating is golden. Serve immediately.

Stir-Fry Chicken

▥ Defrosting Chicken Pieces

A piece of chicken will defrost in 2 minutes (at 30% power) and cook in 2 minutes at Full power.

You can eat it 6 minutes after you take it from the freezer — amazing!

To defrost chicken pieces, either put them in a plastic or oven bag in one layer, or wrap them in parcels of greaseproof paper. Defrost at Defrost (30% power). Do not defrost on higher power levels or the chicken may toughen.

▥ Stir-Fry Chicken

A stir-fried taste, but without any spatters.

For 4 servings:
400 g chicken breasts or other boneless chicken meat
3 Tbsp oil
1 Tbsp light soya sauce
1 Tbsp sherry
2 tsp brown sugar
2 tsp instant chicken stock
2 tsp cornflour
1 clove garlic, chopped
1 tsp grated root ginger
400 g quick cooking vegetables, sliced

Cut chicken into 5 mm slices, discarding skin. Place in oven bag with 1 tablespoon oil and all ingredients, except vegetables. Knead to mix and leave to marinate. Slice vegetables into thin slices. Coat with remaining oil. Stir-fry vegetables in covered casserole at Full power for 4 minutes.

Spread bag containing chicken so it is flat. Fasten bag with rubber band, leaving finger-sized hole for steam to escape.

Microwave for 3–4 minutes. Leave to stand for 1 minute. Chicken should be milky white. Stir chicken into vegetables and serve immediately on rice.

M Glazed Chicken Breasts

Chicken breasts toughen if overcooked in a microwave. Cooked for the right time, they should be moist, tender and delicious. Take care!

For 4 servings:
4 chicken breasts
flour
2 Tbsp white wine or apple juice
2 tsp soya sauce
2 tsp Worcestershire sauce
1 clove garlic, chopped
1 Tbsp chives or spring onion leaves

Place chicken breasts between two sheets of plastic. Pound gently with rolling pin until flattened. Sprinkle lightly with flour on both sides.

Measure remaining ingredients into dish large enough to hold chicken in one layer. Turn chicken pieces in liquid. Cover and cook at Full power for 7–8 minutes, turning after 4 minutes.

Stand for 2–3 minutes. Flesh should not be pink or translucent when cooked.

M Crunchy Chicken Rolls

Crunchy chicken rolls cook more evenly in a microwave oven than they could in a conventional oven. The crisp, golden brown crumbs with which the chicken breasts are coated are precooked for good colour and texture.

Savoury Crumbs (see page 122)
4 chicken breasts
50 g butter
1 rasher bacon, chopped
½ cup finely chopped mushrooms
1 Tbsp soft breadcrumbs
¼ cup flour
1 egg, beaten

First make Savoury Crumbs. Next pound chicken breasts between two layers of plastic until thin. To make stuffing, melt butter in a small container. Add 1 tablespoon of the melted butter to the bacon, mushrooms and soft breadcrumbs and mix.

Cover and cook at Full power for 3 minutes, stirring or shaking after 1 minute. Put a pile of stuffing on the inner side of each breast. Roll up and secure with toothpicks. Dust lightly with flour, then turn first in beaten egg to coat, then in the Savoury Crumbs.

Arrange in a circle on a flat dish. Pour remaining melted butter over them and bake, uncovered, for 8 minutes. Stand for 2–3 minutes before serving.

M Chicken Breast for One

This is a very basic, easy way to cook a piece of tender chicken for one person in a very short time. Work at getting it perfect. Because it is a dish you are likely to make often, it is worth investing in a small, shallow-sided dish to cook it in.

1 chicken breast
flour
1 tsp butter
1 tsp Worcestershire sauce
1 tsp white wine or lemon juice
2 tsp chopped parsley
paprika

Dry chicken breast. Pound between two pieces of plastic to flatten, if desired. Coat lightly with flour, patting it in well. In a small dish melt butter for 20 seconds at Full power. Turn chicken in melted butter, then in the sauce and wine or juice. Sprinkle with parsley and paprika. Cover and cook for 1 minute 45 seconds at Full power
Or 2 minutes at Medium-High (70% power)
Or 3 minutes at Medium (50% power)

M Lemon Chicken

A tangy sauce coats chunks of tender breast meat.

For 2 servings:
2 chicken breasts
1 tsp sherry
1 clove garlic (optional)
1 Tbsp oil
½ tsp grated root ginger
1 red pepper
1 green pepper
2–3 spring onions

Sauce
2 tsp cornflour
1 Tbsp sugar
½ tsp instant chicken stock
¼ cup water
1 Tbsp sherry
2 Tbsp lemon juice

Preheat browning dish for 6 minutes. Cut each chicken breast into five or six crosswise slices. Mix with sherry, garlic, oil and ginger.

Cut peppers into pieces about the same size as the chicken. Cut spring onions into 1 cm lengths. Mix sauce ingredients in a cup. Add chicken and vegetables to hot browning dish. Stir briefly. Microwave at Full power for 1 minute.

Add sauce, stir briefly, and cook for 30 second or until sauce thickens and chicken is cooked.
Do not overcook. Serve on rice.
Variation:
Add ½ teaspoon sesame oil to chicken marinade.

M Mushroom Chicken

Chicken breasts in an easy creamy sauce.

For 4 servings:
4 chicken breasts
1 Tbsp butter
½ tsp paprika
6–8 small mushrooms, sliced
1 tsp cornflour
½ tsp garlic salt
¼ cream
2 Tbsp chopped parsley

Pat chicken breasts dry. Melt butter in dish large enough to hold chicken in one layer. Turn in butter. Sprinkle lightly with a little of the paprika. Slice mushrooms thinly over chicken. Cover and microwave at Full power for 6 minutes.

Rearrange chicken if necessary. Mix cornflour, garlic salt, cream and remaining paprika. Pour over chicken. Sprinkle with parsley.

Bake, uncovered for 2–3 minutes, then stand for 2–3 minutes. Meat should not be pink or translucent. Pour juices over chicken again. Serve.
Note:
Use chicken thighs if preferred.

M Curried Pineapple Chicken

This couldn't be easier to prepare and cook!

The sauce that surrounds this bagged chicken as it cooks gives it both colour and flavour. Any leftovers can be refrigerated then reheated in the oven bag in which the chicken cooked.

For 4 servings:
4 chicken legs
1 pkt cream of chicken or onion soup mix
1–2 tsp curry powder
1 can (400 g) pineapple slices or pieces
1–2 tsp dark soya sauce

Halve chicken legs for easier mixing, cooking and serving. Shake in oven bag with the dry soup mix and curry powder. Drain liquid from pineapple. Make up to 1¼ cups with water. Add to chicken with soya sauce, kneading bag gently to mix well. Secure bag with a rubber band, leaving a finger-sized opening to allow steam to escape. Lay bag flat on a dinner plate so chicken pieces are in one layer.

Microwave at Full power for 12 minutes, turning bag after 8 minutes. Add pineapple pieces, circles or half circles. Cook for 2–3 minutes longer.

Test to see that chicken juice is clear, not pink. Serve.

Teriyaki Chicken   *Herbed Crumbed Chicken*   *Paprika Baked Chicken*

Ⓜ Microwaving Chicken Pieces

Chicken pieces microwave wonderfully well, very quickly. They are tender and juicy, with an excellent flavour. If you start with frozen chicken pieces, you should always defrost them first, before coating and cooking them.

Chicken pieces do not brown or become crisp in the short cooking time needed, so you should use coatings which add colour and crispness as well as flavour.

For most even cooking, select one cut, rather than a mixture, e.g. drumsticks or thighs.

To Cook Coated Chicken Pieces

Pat chicken pieces dry with paper towels. Coat chicken pieces with melted butter or oil (or dip in an egg coating). Shake in plastic bag with coating mixture, or turn in shallow bowl of coating. Arrange on a ridged dish or on a flat plate with meatiest side towards edge of dish and the skin side (best-looking side) uppermost. Cover loosely with a paper towel, or leave uncovered. Cook at Full power for 2–3 minutes per piece, allowing about 10 minutes per 500 g.

If dish is crowded, move chicken positions after half the estimated time, but do not turn the pieces over. Leave for 2 minutes before testing to see whether pieces are ready.

When cooked, juices should run clear, not pink, and flesh near bone should not be pink.

Ⓜ Paprika Baked Chicken

For 8–12 pieces:
First coating
melted butter

Second coating
¼ cup flour
2 tsp paprika
1 tsp curry powder
2 tsp garlic salt
2 tsp castor sugar

Brush chicken pieces with butter and lay on plastic or greaseproof paper, skin side down. Combine ingredients for second coating in a jar with an airtight lid.

Tip some of the second coating into a fine sieve. Coat chicken thickly, then turn pieces over and shake coating over skin side. Arrange on baking dish, skin side up. Cook as for coated chicken pieces.
Note:
Keep remaining coating for later use.

Ⓜ Herbed Crumbed Chicken

First coating
1 tsp garlic salt
½ tsp paprika
¼ tsp curry powder
1 Tbsp water
1 egg

Second coating
25 g butter, melted
2 cups soft breadcrumbs
2 Tbsp chopped parsley

Prepare second coating by melting butter at Full power for about 50 seconds. Stir in breadcrumbs and parsley (or other fresh herbs, or small amounts of dried herbs to taste). Heat on a flat dish for about 3 minutes or until golden brown, stirring after every minute.

Mix first coating. Add garlic salt, paprika and curry powder to water. Stir to mix. Add egg and beat with a fork, just enough to combine white, yolk and seasonings.

Turn dried chicken pieces first in the egg dip, then in the crumbs. Place chicken directly on a baking dish, skin side up, thicker pieces near the edge. Cook as for coated chicken pieces.
Note:
Keep leftover crumbs for later use. For thicker coating, dip chicken in flour before other coatings.

Ⓜ Teriyaki Chicken

For 4 chicken pieces:
Marinade
2 Tbsp dark soya sauce
2 Tbsp medium or dry sherry
1 Tbsp brown sugar
1 tsp garlic salt
2 tsp grated root ginger or 1 tsp ground ginger
½ tsp cornflour

Put chicken pieces in an unpunctured oven bag with all marinade ingredients. Remove air from bag and fasten tightly with a rubber band. Leave to stand for 30 minutes to 1 hour if possible, turning occasionally.

Loosen rubber band, leaving a

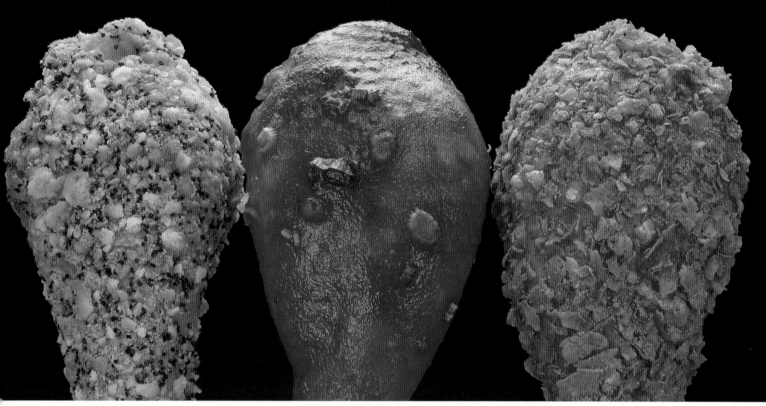

Golden Crusted Chicken   *Barbecued Chicken*   *Cracker-Crusted Chicken*

finger-sized hole to allow steam to escape. Position bag so it is flat, with chicken pieces in one layer, with thicker parts near the outside. Cook as for coated chicken pieces, turning bag once during cooking time, so chicken is evenly coated.

While still very hot, turn pieces in sauce and remove from the bag. Coating dries on standing a few minutes.

M Golden Crusted Chicken

For about 6 chicken pieces:
First coating
1 tsp celery salt
1/2 tsp paprika
1/4 tsp curry powder
1 Tbsp milk
1 egg

Second coating
1 cup crushed cornflakes

Mix first coating. Add celery salt, paprika and curry powder to milk. Stir to mix. Add egg and beat with a fork, just enough to combine. Crush cornflakes in a food processor or in a plastic bag with a rolling pin.

Turn dried chicken pieces, first in the seasoned egg, then in the crushed crumbs. Place on baking dish, skin side up, thicker pieces near the edge. Cook as for coated chicken pieces.
Note:
Keep leftover crumbs for later use.

M Barbecued Chicken

First coating
flour

Second coating
2 Tbsp brown sugar
1 tsp dry mustard
1/2 tsp garlic salt
2 tsp cornflour
1 tsp Worcestershire sauce
1 Tbsp tomato paste
1/2 cup tomato ketchup
basil and marjoram (optional)

Dip chicken pieces first in flour, then brush with second coating made by mixing together the barbecue sauce ingredients in the order given. Add herbs as desired.

Cook as for coated chicken pieces. Coating dries on standing for a few minutes.

M Cracker-Crusted Chicken

For about 6–8 pieces:
First coating
1 tsp onion or garlic salt
1/2 tsp paprika
1/4–1/2 tsp curry powder
1 Tbsp milk
1 egg

Second coating
1/2 cup crushed golden brown coloured crackers
1 Tbsp toasted sesame seeds
1 Tbsp poppy seeds

Mix first coating. Add flavoured salt, paprika and curry powder to milk. Stir to mix. Add egg and beat with a fork, just enough to combine. Mix cracker crumbs with the seeds. Dip dried chicken pieces first in the seasoned egg, then in the cracker crumb mixture. Place on baking dish, skin side up, thicker pieces near the edge. Cook as for coated chicken pieces.
Note:
Keep leftover crumbs for later use if not damp.

M Devilled Drumsticks

For 2 servings:
4 chicken drumsticks
1 Tbsp mixed mustard
1/2 tsp garlic salt
2 tsp Worcestershire sauce
1 Tbsp Parmesan cheese
1/4 tsp paprika

Mix mustard, garlic salt and Worcestershire sauce. Brush on chicken. Sprinkle with mixed Parmesan cheese and paprika. Bake uncovered as for coated chicken pieces, about 8 minutes. Serve hot or cold.

C Curried Roasting Fowl

This is a recipe to use when you have an older bird, such as a 'retired layer' to cook.

A 1.5–2 kg roasting fowl will feed 6–12 people when it's cooked this way — depending on appetites and how and when it is served. Since it improves on standing you can make it one or two days ahead and refrigerate it until you need it.

Put the roasting fowl, breast-side up, in a large saucepan. Add 4–5 cups of water, 2 tablespoons of instant stock and an onion and celery stalk if available. Cover and simmer until the bird is tender. At this stage the skin will be tender and a leg can be broken away from the body easily. The bird will need up to 3½ hours of gentle cooking.

Cool the bird until it can be easily handled, then cut it into small cubes, removing skin and fat, and discarding it.

Strain the liquid and skim off as much fat as possible. Use the stock to make this thickened curry-flavoured sauce.

50 g butter
4 large onions, sliced
2 cups sliced celery
2–4 tsp curry powder
½ tsp ginger
¼ tsp pepper
½ cup flour
4 cups liquid
1 cup crushed pineapple
4–5 cups cooked and diced poultry

Melt the butter in a large saucepan. Add the sliced onions and celery, cover, and cook gently until the onions are tender but not browned. Add the curry, ginger and pepper and cook for 2–3 minutes longer. Stir in the flour. Measure the chicken stock. Add the juice from the pineapple and make up to four cups with water, extra stock, coconut milk or any other desired liquid. Add this liquid to the curry mixture one cup at a time. Boil after each addition.

After the last one simmer for five minutes, taste and adjust seasonings, adding salt and a little sugar if necessary. Add the crushed pineapple and the chicken. Bring to the boil then remove from the heat, cover, cool and refrigerate till needed. Serve reheated on plain boiled rice, noodles or spaghetti.

C M Start with a Rotisseried Chicken

When you are in a hurry and know that you have to produce a dinner within half an hour of stepping in the house, a precooked chicken can set you off to a flying start.

You may choose to add a few final touches, so that it looks as if you have spent all afternoon in the kitchen!
• Try breaking the warm chicken into serving-sized pieces, arranging them, skin side up, in a shallow ovenware dish, and pouring over them a herb-flavoured packaged gravy mix, thinned to a coating consistency. You can take this a step further by putting the pieces on a bed of rice risotto and adding a sprinkling of chopped parsley or spring onion.
• Try crisping up the skin of a bagged cooked chicken by arranging the pieces, skin side up, in a foil-lined sponge roll tin. Heat together in a small saucepan the juice of a lemon, 1 tablespoon melted butter and 1 teaspoon paprika. Brush this mixture over the chicken and heat until bubbly under a preheated grill. Don't overdo it, or the chicken will dry out.
• For variations on this theme, use butter and lemon juice without seasoning, then sprinkle with one of the interesting seasoning mixtures now available commercially, developed for microwave and regular oven use, e.g. Tandoori, Enchilada, Oriental and French chicken seasonings. Such mixtures add interesting flavour quickly and when used with restraint, are a boon for the 'short-order' cook. Of course you can heat these coated chicken pieces in the microwave too.
• For another 'hurry up' treatment, mix in a fairly large, non-stick frying pan, ½ teaspoon cornflour, 1 teaspoon instant green herb stock, ¼ cup white wine, ¼ cup water and 1 teaspoon butter. As soon as this mixture boils and thickens slightly, turn the cooked chicken pieces in it and reheat them with the pan lightly covered. In another pan sauté some sliced mushrooms briefly. Spoon mushrooms over chicken.

C Country Chicken Pie

A casserole of leftovers gets new life when you top it with a scone wreath.

225 g cubed cooked chicken (½ a
*   medium-sized cooked chicken)*
2 cups drained, cooked vegetables
1 packet cream of chicken soup powder
½ cup water
½ cup white wine
2 Tbsp chopped fresh herbs (e.g.
*   marjoram, basil, thyme, rosemary,*
*   parsley)*
2 cups self-raising flour
1 cup grated tasty cheese
about ¾ cup milk

beaten egg
Parmesan cheese

Combine the chicken and vegetables. Heat the soup powder, water and wine until it boils. Remove from heat, add chicken, vegetables and half the herbs.

Turn chicken mixture into a sprayed or buttered casserole (about 25 cm across).

Make scones by combining flour, remaining herbs and cheese, then adding enough milk to make a fairly soft dough. Roll this out on a lightly floured board until about 7 mm thick. Cut into diamonds or rounds. Arrange overlapping scones around the edge of the casserole. Brush with a little beaten egg, then sprinkle with Parmesan cheese.

Bake at 220°C for 15–20 minutes, or until scones brown and centre of casserole is hot.
Variation:
Cut strips of scone dough and arrange in a lattice pattern over the casserole.

M Chicken Fricassee

Smoked chicken is already cooked when you buy it. It reheats deliciously in this sauce. Try this recipe with ordinary cooked chicken too.

Its colour and flavour will not be quite as good, but it is still likely to be popular.

You can make Turkey Fricassee in the same way, to use up small pieces of a Christmas turkey, too.

For 4 servings:
200 g carrots
1 cup sliced celery
4 small onions
50 g butter
¾ cup water
2 Tbsp flour
1 tsp green herb stock
1 cup milk
2 cups smoked chicken or cooked
*   chicken*
½–1 cup peas

Slice carrots thinly. Cook with celery and quartered onions in the butter, with ¼ cup water, in a covered casserole at Full power for 8 minutes, until vegetables are tender. Stir in flour and instant stock, then the milk and remaining water. Cook, uncovered, until sauce boils and thickens, stirring every minute. Add chicken and peas, heat for 2 minutes longer and serve with rice or mashed potatoes.

Chicken Fricassee

C Herbed Chicken Livers

Frozen chicken livers are an excellent buy. They are inexpensive, nutritious, and versatile. They thaw quickly too, so a pack in the freezer is a good standby, for times when you need to produce a meal in a short time.

For 3–4 servings:
500 g chicken livers
3–4 Tbsp butter
1 clove garlic
1 onion
2 Tbsp flour
½ tsp paprika
¼ tsp pepper
½ tsp mixed herbs
1 tsp salt
1 tsp instant chicken stock
½ cup water
2 Tbsp lemon juice

Halve the chicken livers, removing any membrane. Melt the butter in a large frying pan. Slice the garlic and onion finely and cook in the butter until tender but not browned. Mix the flour, paprika and pepper, coat the livers with this and brown, a few at a time. Push browned livers and onion to the side of the pan, then add more. When livers are evenly browned (after 5 minutes), add the herbs, salt and chicken stock, water and lemon juice. Turn livers in this mixture. Leave over low heat for 5 minutes then serve on rice.

Note:
For best results coat livers with flour just before browning. Keep heat high during browning. Do not cut livers in smaller pieces until stock is added.

C Chicken Livers with Bacon

The combination of bacon, onions and chicken livers is very successful, and is likely to be popular, even with 'non-adventurous' diners!

For 4–6 servings:
2 rashers bacon
2 Tbsp butter
1 onion, finely sliced
500 g chicken livers
3 Tbsp flour
1 tsp instant chicken stock
½ cup hot water
1 tsp lemon juice
1–2 Tbsp parsley

Remove the rind from the bacon and chop bacon finely. Melt the butter in a large frying pan and cook the bacon and onion over moderate heat until the onion is tender. Push to side of pan and raise the heat.

Halve the chicken livers, removing any membrane. Coat them with flour and sauté them, a few at a time if necessary, until well browned all over.

Dissolve the instant stock in the hot water. Add the lemon juice and pour over the browned livers. Cook for 1–2 minutes longer, turning livers to coat them with sauce.

Sprinkle them with parsley and serve them in croustade cases (cooked bread cases), on toast, rice or noodles.

C German-Style Chicken Livers

The flavours of apple, onion and thyme go well with chicken livers.

Use fresh thyme if possible. There are many different thymes. All taste good in this recipe.

For 4 servings:
3–4 Tbsp clarified butter
1 onion
2 apples
450–500 g chicken livers
1 Tbsp flour
½ tsp salt
pepper
1–2 tsp chopped fresh thyme
*   or ½ tsp dried thyme*
¼ cup apple juice or wine

Melt half the butter in a large frying pan, on moderate heat. Chop onion, peel and slice apple. Add to the butter, cover and cook until tender and lightly browned. Remove from the pan. Clean the pan and return it to the heat.

Halve chicken livers, removing any membranes.

Combine flour, salt and pepper in a bag or dish. Coat chicken livers with seasoned flour mixture. Melt remaining clarified butter over high heat and add the coated chicken livers.

When they have browned evenly on both sides add the apple, onion and thyme.

Cook over gentle heat for 2–3 minutes then add the liquid. Turn the mixture so it is coated with the sauce. Add a dash of dark soya sauce if colour is pale.

Cook for 1–2 minutes longer. Serve immediately on rice or noodles.

M Chicken Liver Savouries

Fast, tasty and inexpensive!

For 2–3 servings:
2 rashers bacon
2 Tbsp butter
2 cloves garlic, chopped
½ tsp chopped thyme
300 g chicken livers
1 Tbsp flour

1 tsp instant chicken stock
2 tsp dark soya sauce
½ cup hot water
1 Tbsp sherry (optional)

Cook the bacon rashers at Full power for 1½–2 minutes. Remove from dish and chop. To the dish add the butter, chopped garlic and thyme. Cut each chicken liver into four pieces and stir pieces into the butter mixture. Cover and cook for 3–4 minutes, until livers are just firm. Stir in remaining ingredients, including the chopped bacon.

Cover and cook for 3 minutes more, or until liquid thickens. Taste, season and thin with extra liquid if necessary.

Variations:
Add 1 cup chopped mushrooms with chicken livers.

Cook 1 chopped apple in bacon fat before adding butter etc.

C Sweet and Sour Chicken Livers

This dish may be served for lunch or for dinner. It is unusual, quick, colourful and delicious.

For 3–4 servings:
1 large onion
2 stalks celery
25 g butter
1 red pepper
1 green pepper
1 cup pineapple chunks, drained
500 g chicken livers
1 clove garlic, chopped
1 Tbsp cornflour
1 Tbsp tomato ketchup
2 Tbsp wine vinegar
2 tsp instant chicken stock
2 tsp soya sauce
½ cup pineapple juice

Slice onion and celery. Cook in butter in a large covered frying pan for 2–3 minutes. Chop peppers coarsely and add to pan. Cut the pineapple chunks into smaller pieces, if necessary, and brown them lightly with the vegetables. Remove vegetables and pineapple from the pan.

Cut the chicken livers in halves, removing any membrane. Add a little more butter to the pan if necessary and raise the heat. Add garlic and livers and cook until evenly browned, about 5 minutes.

Remove from pan and lower heat. Mix cornflour, tomato ketchup, wine vinegar, instant chicken stock, soya sauce and pineapple juice. Add this to the drippings in the pan.

Bring to the boil, and add the livers and vegetables, stirring to coat with sauce. Taste and add a little sugar if desired. Serve immediately on rice.

Chicken Liver Savouries

Pork

These days, pork has a new, trim image. To show how versatile it is, I have collected a group of pork recipes suitable for many different meals and occasions.

The smell of bacon drifting through the house at breakfast time is one of the few smells that will encourage late risers to roll out of bed! Bacon adds interest to all sorts of snacks, too.

Pork terrines and pâtés are great for summer lunches, for starter courses, for dinner parties, or for sandwiches, or crackers.

For family dinners it is hard to beat a tasty pork stew which will simmer away untended.

When you decide to cook a recipe from another country, you have a wide range of interesting pork dishes to choose from.

For a special party with a festive feeling it's hard to beat a ham. Whether you choose a large, bone-in ham, or a small, meaty 500 g 'mini-ham', you can dress it up and serve it attractively so that it becomes the main attraction on your table.

At the meat counter look to see what new cuts are available, for example:

scotch fillet roasts
fore-loin steaks
shoulder roasts
medallion steaks
rib-loin roasts
butterfly steaks
mid-loin roasts
spare ribs (pork bones)
cubed pork
pork slices and fingers
leg steaks
pork schnitzels
pork leg roasts
pork mince
ham steaks and hocks

And don't forget the 'extremities'. Some of my own favourite pork dishes are made from pig's head, pig's trotters and even pig's tail!

Roast Pork

Roast Pork

Tender pork cuts roast well in microwave ovens at Medium (50% power).

Fairly small, compact roasts cook best. If roast is irregular or tapered, shield thin portions with foil to prevent them overcooking. Roasts of marbled meat are more tender than lean roasts.

Trim fat to an even, thin thickness. Meat close to fat (and close to surface bones) cooks faster. Excess fat can cause uneven cooking. Turn meat at least once (preferably more) during cooking.

Estimate cooking time using weight of meat, but take shape into consideration, too. A long, thin roasts cooks faster than a short, fat one of the same weight. For most accurate meat cookery, use a microwave meat thermometer.

After experimenting, find what internal temperature you like meat cooked to, then always cook to this stage. Meat keeps cooking and its temperature keeps rising after it is taken from the oven. The thicker the meat, the greater the temperature rise, and the longer the standing time should be.

Meat roasted rare or medium is more tender and juicy than meat which is cooked longer, to well done.

Important

Meat thermometer temperatures are often given in °Fahrenheit rather than °Celsius.

Always roast meat on a rack or a raised plate, where it will not sit in a puddle of juice. If you do not have a rack, invert a bread and butter plate on a dinner plate.

Remove meat juices as they accumulate since they slow down the cooking and may make it uneven.

In general, a piece of bone-in meat will cook more quickly than a boneless piece of the same weight.

The microwave energy does not penetrate to the centre of a large roast. Thick pieces of meat cook fairly evenly to 5 cm on all sides. The centre cooks by the transfer of heat, as in conventional roasts.

1–1½ kg rolled shoulder or loin of pork with outer fat and skin removed
dark soya sauce (optional)

Have butcher remove skin and outer fat before rolling pork. Weigh to estimate approximate roasting time.

Rub surface with soya sauce, if desired. Place roast on ridged or raised roasting pan, fat side down. Cover loosely. Cook at Medium (50% power), allowing 15–20 minutes per 500 g. Turn meat after 20–30 minutes.

Internal temperature should be 155°F (68°C). Remove meat and stand it in a warm place for 15 minutes. Temperature will rise to 170°F (77°C).

Skim juices and thicken to make gravy.

M Making Gravy

It's worth taking a little time and effort to make gravy to serve with roast pork. Make the gravy in a measuring jug, or in the jug in which you will serve the gravy.

Make a well-flavoured stock by heating together in a bowl 1 teaspoon instant stock, 1½ cups water, any meat trimmings, and a selection of finely chopped vegetables and herbs. Include onion skins and mushrooms to darken colour, if possible. Microwave at Full power for 10 minutes.

Put 2–3 tablespoons of fat from pan drippings or 2 tablespoons of butter in a measuring jug or gravy boat. Melt if necessary. Stir in 3 tablespoons of flour and mix well.

Microwave at Full power until mixture turns light brown. Add the stock from the vegetables, stirring all the time. Add remaining pan drippings, with fat skimmed off. Microwave at Full power until gravy bubbles, then remove and stir until smooth.

If gravy still looks light, add a few drops of gravy browning. Season to taste.

C Roast Loin of Pork

It is nice to have something that you do not often cook, at one of the special meals you serve over the holiday period.

A roast loin of pork comes into this category, for me.

A roast of Trim pork differs from the pork roasts my mother used to cook, partly because it is so lean, and partly because it is not covered with crackling. I love crackling so I cook it separately, and feel that I get the best of both worlds, since the lean pork cooks quickly, with very little wastage.

In fact, a 2 kg loin of Trim pork, stuffed as below, cooked for 1½ hours at 180°C, weighed 1.74 kg. This means that, from the 2 kg roast you can get:
15 servings of 125 g each
11 servings of 150 g each
 8 servings of 200 g each

I like a pretty stuffing, as well as a tasty one, and find that the following one answers on both counts.

To stuff and roast a loin of pork you need:

a loin of Trim pork, about 2 kg
stuffing (below)
mixed mustard

Stuffing
about 8 prunes
about 8 dried apricot halves
or 8 thick slices bottled or fresh
*   tamarillo*
or 1 red pepper, blanched
2 Tbsp brandy or sherry or fruit juice
1 onion
2 Tbsp butter
½ cup fresh breadcrumbs
2–3 Tbsp finely chopped parsley and
*   any other herb you like*
about 8 spinach leaves

Cut the prunes almost in half, and put on a plate with the apricot halves, if you are using them. Sprinkle with whatever liquid you are using, and leave to stand while you prepare the rest of the stuffing.

Drain the tamarillo halves if using them.

Cut red pepper into strips, and blanch by leaving them to stand in boiling water for 10 minutes.

Chop the onion finely, and cook until tender but not brown in the butter, in a fairly large pan.

Remove from the heat, and add the breadcrumbs (made from stale bread) and the herbs. Add fresh or dried sage or thyme or rosemary to the parsley, for extra flavour, if you like.

Blanch the spinach by pouring boiling water over the leaves, and leaving them to stand for 2–3 minutes, before draining them.

Untie any string that may have been holding the loin of pork in a cylindrical shape, and lie the meat flat. You should have a solid, lean piece of muscle, and a thin strip of meat which was wrapped around it. Your aim is to put the stuffing on the thin strip of meat, close to the big muscle, so that, when you wrap it up again, the stuffing will be completely enclosed, too.

If you have only the muscle, and no thin strip, cut lengthwise down the side of the muscle, in to the centre, and put the stuffing in here. You will not use as much stuffing as is listed.

Spread the upper surface of the meat thinly with mustard. On the thin muscle, close to the large muscle, lie a row of opened prunes.

Beside this lie another row, of apricots or tamarillos, or red pepper strips. Over the top of this, sprinkle the onion and crumb mixture. Overlap the spinach leaves, and lie them in a sheet over the onion, etc.

Now roll the thin part over the main muscle, enclosing the stuffing.

Secure firmly, either with skewers or string, then rub the whole surface evenly but thinly, with more mustard.

Place in an oiled roasting pan, then roast at 180°C for 1½ hours, or until a meat thermometer reads 170°F (75°C). If you like the meat well cooked, allow a little longer, but remember that lean pork, if overcooked, becomes dry.

Leave to stand for 15 minutes, in a warm place, before serving with stewed unsweetened apples, or with tamarillo halves which have been baked, cut side down, in a little honey and vinegar in a covered dish, with crackling and/or with gravy.

Any pickled fruit is good with this pork. Cranberry or any other tart jelly is delicious, too.

C Crackling

These days, you can buy crackling which has been detached from large cuts of Trim pork.

These sheets of crackling cook very quickly, and may be eaten as a snack, or as an accompaniment to roast pork. Either way, they are delicious.

Cut the sheet of pork skin so that it does not have much fat on its under-surface. It should be 1–2 cm thick.

Using a sharp knife, score over the whole surface, with lines about 5 mm apart.

Sprinkle the surface with salt, and rub it into the cuts. Next, rub oil evenly over the whole surface.

Lie the crackling on a rack on a flat pan. You can cut it into strips, about 5–6 cm wide, if this suits you. If you like, tuck the ends under the rungs of the rack, so they do not curl up as they cook.

Grill, 10 cm from the heat, for about 10 minutes, until it bubbles and turns golden brown. Watch it, to take care that it does not burn. Turn, and grill for another 10 minutes, or until cooked on the underside.

Hide it, until you are ready to serve it!

M Tangy Pork Fillet

For 2–3 servings:
1 pork fillet (250–350 g)
1 tsp dark soya sauce
1 tsp sesame oil
1 tsp sherry
1 clove garlic, chopped

Sauce
2 tsp cornflour
1 tsp instant chicken stock
2 tsp dark soya sauce
¼ cup plum jam
¼ cup dry sherry
½ cup water
1 clove garlic, chopped

Cut fillet into pieces about 5 mm thick. Mix with soya sauce, sesame oil, sherry and garlic. Leave to stand for at least 10 minutes. Cover and microwave at Full power for 2–4 minutes, stirring after each minute until meat loses its pinkness. (Fillet can overcook in a very short time.) In another bowl combine sauce ingredients.

Microwave, stirring occasionally, until smooth and clear.

Stir meat into cooked sauce and spoon over rice.

C Chinese Simmered Pork

For this easy but delicious recipe you need a piece of fairly lean belly pork. Choose a piece of meat which will fit in the pot or metal casserole in which you plan to simmer it.

For 4–5 servings:
*500–750 g fresh belly pork, in one
    piece
2 Tbsp dark soya sauce
2 Tbsp sherry
¼ cup water
2 cloves garlic
2 slices ginger root*

Using a very sharp knife, score the skin in parallel lines, about 5 mm apart. Spray the inside of a large heavy pot, frying pan or heavy iron casserole with non-stick spray.

Place the meat, skin side up in the pan, and add the remaining ingredients. Turn meat once or twice so liquid enters cuts. Adjust heat so liquid bubbles gently. Cover tightly using foil inside the lid if necessary.

Simmer, skin side up, for 1 hour, then turn meat and simmer 1–1½ hours longer, until very tender.

Add extra water if liquid evaporates during cooking. You want ¼–½ cup liquid around meat when it is cooked. Lift from liquid, place skin side up on a board and cut into slices, following scoring lines. Pour spoonful of cooking liquid over each serving of sliced meat. Serve with rice or noodles, sprinkled with chopped spring onions or fresh coriander, if desired.

B C 'Barbecued' Pork Bones

Pork spare-ribs or pork bones make a wonderful, if somewhat messy meal.

It is important to buy meaty rib bones (from fresh, not cured or smoked pork) and to cook them gently, until the meat is tender, before brushing them with sauce and browning them, under a grill, or on a barbecue.

Allow about 500 g of pork bones per person. Pork bones are addictive! Once you start eating them it is hard to stop — so buy and cook plenty.

For 4 servings:
*About 2 kg meaty pork bones
    (preferably cut without the
    backbones attached)
pepper and salt
1–2 cups water
1 cup tomato ketchup
2 Tbsp tomato paste
2 Tbsp mixed mustard
1¼ cups brown sugar*

*1 tsp garlic salt
½ tsp celery salt
½ tsp hickory smoked salt (optional)*

Divide the rib bones into strips, so each strip contains 3–6 bones. Place bones in a large, covered roasting pan, sprinkle lightly with pepper and salt, add the water. Cover tightly and bake at 180°C for about 2 hours, until the meat is very tender, adding more water if necessary, (The more bones the longer the cooking time.)

To make sauce, bring the remaining ingredients to the boil. When bones are required, brush them on both sides with the sauce, and heat, turning at least once, until the sauce bubbles.

Eat indoors or out, as finger food with salads, bread rolls, etc.

M Pork Spareribs

Rather messy finger food but deliciously addictive!

For 2–3 servings:
*750 g spareribs, cut into 2-rib strips
1 cup boiling water
1 onion, chopped
1 stick celery, chopped*

Place all ingredients in a covered casserole and microwave at Full power for 5 minutes. Then cook for a further 30–45 minutes at Defrost (30% power) until tender. Cover with Zesty Sauce before further cooking.

Zesty Sauce
*1 Tbsp oil
1 onion, chopped
½ cup tomato ketchup
1 Tbsp brown sugar
1 tsp wine vinegar
1 tsp Worcestershire sauce
dash of hot pepper sauce
¼ tsp garlic salt
½ tsp dry mustard*

Combine the oil and onion in a bowl and microwave at Full power for 2 minutes. Add the rest of the ingredients and cook for 4 minutes or until thick. Lay the spareribs on a flat plate in one layer.

Spread half of the sauce on the ribs and cook, uncovered, for 2 minutes at Medium (50% power). Brush on the rest of the sauce and cook for 2 minutes longer.

Note:
If desired, crisp the surface under a grill just before serving.

C Pork and Paprika Casserole

For 4–5 servings:
*750 g cubed shoulder pork
2 onions, quartered
1 Tbsp instant chicken or green herb
    stock powder
1 Tbsp paprika
1 cup water
about 2 Tbsp cornflour*

This easy casserole has an excellent flavour. Don't reduce the amount of paprika used or you will spoil it!

Paprika is mild, and this recipe is not spicy or hot, but it gives the casserole a richness which makes it special.

Combine the first five ingredients in a fairly deep casserole dish. Place a piece of foil under the lid of the casserole if it does not fit tightly.

Bake at 180°C for 1½–2 hours, tasting a piece of meat after 1½ hours. When meat is tender, thicken with cornflour mixed to a paste with cold water.
Variations:
Add 1 cup sliced celery after 30 minutes.

Add 1 or 2 green or red peppers after 1 hour.

Add ½–1 cup sautéed mushrooms when thickening the casserole.

Sprinkle chopped parsley over surface if desired.

C Pork and Pineapple Bake

The extra vegetables cooked in this mixture make it a complete main course when served with rice, baked potatoes or noodles.

For 3–4 servings:
*600 g pork fingers or slices
flour
1 large onion, sliced
2 stalks celery, sliced
2 green peppers, chopped
1 tsp salt
½ tsp nutmeg
1–2 cups crushed pineapple
1 Tbsp soya sauce*

Coat pork fingers with flour. Brown in a lightly greased pan until meat is golden brown. Put in casserole dish with remaining ingredients, cover tightly and bake at 180°C for 1½ hours or until pork is tender. Turn meat after cooking for 1 hour.

C M Pork Terrine

This terrine makes a good, easy main course for a summer lunch or a starter for a dinner party, and is useful as a sandwich filling.

*500 g belly pork (without skin)
100 g bacon*

Pork and Paprika Casserole

¼ *cup finely chopped onion*
1 *tsp finely chopped fresh sage*
½ *cup white wine*
2 *Tbsp brandy (optional)*
¼ *cup chopped gherkins (optional)*
2 *tsp green peppercorns (optional)*
extra bacon for lining terrine

Remove skin from pork and cut meat into 5 mm cubes. Cut bacon into pieces of similar size. Mix pork, bacon, onion and sage with white wine, and brandy (if used). Leave to stand for 30 minutes.

While it marinates select the optional additions you want. Chop gherkins and mix with peppercorns. Line a small loaf tin or other mould which holds 1 litre (4 cups) with greaseproof paper, then with thinly sliced bacon. Chop up the pork and bacon mixture in three parts using the metal chopping blade of a food processor, cutting to a salami-like texture.

Do not chop too finely. Mix in the optional ingredients. Press mixture firmly into the bacon-lined mould.

Microwave Instructions
Cover with cling film, pressing it tightly round the edges of the mould. Do not vent it. Microwave at Defrost (30% power) for 30 minutes, or until the centre springs back when pressed. Remove from microwave.

As the film sucks down it should press the terrine.

Baking Instructions
Cover top of terrine with another strip of bacon. Bake without any other cover, at 150°C for 1½ hours, or until centre springs back. Cool with a heavy weight on top.

Unmould terrine, removing jelly. Chill Terrine. Warm jelly until liquid. Brush on terrine to give a glazed appearance.

Note:
The flavour of this terrine is best if it is refrigerated for 1–2 days before it is eaten.

C Pig's Head Brawn

Economical and very tasty, this brawn makes wonderful sandwiches and salads. Choose a head which has not had the cheek removed.

For about 12 servings:
½ *a fresh pig's head*
4 *cups hot water*
4 *tsp salt*
2 *Tbsp brown sugar*
4 *halved garlic cloves*
1 *bay leaf*
6 *peppercorns*
1 *Tbsp gelatine*
¼ *cup cold water*
2 *large onions, chopped*
½–1 *tsp dried sage or*
    6 fresh sage leaves, chopped

Place head in a roasting pan, cut side down. Add next six ingredients, cover pan tightly and bake at 150°C for 2–3 hours, until the meat is so tender that the bones may be lifted away from the meat using tongs.

Leave to stand until cool enough to handle.

Strain stock into bowl and remove fat from surface.

With skin side down, lift bones away from head meat. Discard any dark or discoloured pieces of meat, and eye, and any cartilage.

Cut meat into chunks. If discarding some fat take care not to throw out any light-coloured meat.

Taste stock. If very salty, dilute with water to get 2 cups of liquid.

Soften gelatine in second measure of water then mix with stock. Add chopped onion, sage and cubed meat. Bring to boil and simmer for 2 minutes. Pour into loaf tins or bowls and leave to set. Slice and serve with apple sauce.

Variation:
If you start with a salted pig's head, soak in cold water for several hours, discard water, and cook as above in 6 cups of water instead of 4 cups, and without adding any salt.

C Baked Ham

Many people buy a ham to eat over the holiday period. Although the initial cost may seem high, there is a great deal of lean meat on a ham and little bone in proportion to it. A mild-cured ham should keep without trouble for a fortnight after cooking, as long as the meat is covered carefully to stop drying out, and it is stored in a refrigerator.

Although most hams are bought already cooked, you may like to try cooking your own.

Mild-cured hams require 12–24 hours soaking in cold water (e.g. in a bath!) before baking.

Err on the longer soaking side if you are in doubt, as you can always add more salt when you are eating the ham, but it's hard to get rid of any excess.

Scrub the ham after soaking it, put inside two large, unpunctured oven bags and sit the ham in a roasting pan with the outside, fat-covered part of the leg uppermost. Place the pan below the middle of an oven heated to 160°C. Bake for 40–60 minutes per kilo up to 6 kilograms and 15 minutes per kilo over 6 kilograms.

(I bake a 6 kilogram ham for 4½ hours.)

C Glazing Ham

Peel or cut off the brown skin from a cooked ham. Remove as much of the fat as you like or all of it. Either score through the fat, nearly to the meat, making diamond shapes, or if you have removed all fat, leave the surface unscored.

Brush surface with a glaze made by heating ½ cup brown sugar with ¼ cup orange or pineapple juice.

Pat on to it a mixture of equal parts of fine dry breadcrumbs and brown sugar. Put the ham under the grill so that its upper surface is 15–20 cm away from the heat.

Grill until the sugar bubbles and the surface becomes crunchy, turning the ham as necessary.

Take care not to brush off the brown sugar-crumbed surface.

Decorate with pineapple pieces and/or cherries on toothpicks, and/or cloves, and if desired brush again with glaze and brown under the grill again.

Wrap knuckle end in a paper frill if you like.

C Small Hams

If you are cooking for a small number of people, buy and decorate a small cooked boneless leg ham.

You can cut ten 70 g servings or seven 100 g servings from a little meaty ham of 700g.

Mix and boil a glaze, using ½ cup brown sugar and ¼ teaspoon mixed spice and ground cloves. When syrupy, brush over the fatty or meaty surface of the small ham. Score surface, or leave it plain. If you like insert cloves, pineapple, cherries etc — keeping your decorations in scale with the size of the ham.

Brown 12–15 cm from the grill, turning often.

> **Bacon Snacks**
> It's surprising what a little bit of bacon can do to brighten up a slice of toast, piece of bread or a crusty roll.
>
> You can put a little bacon with a variety of foods to make satisfying texture and flavour combinations.
>
> Experiment to see which type of bacon suits you best, how thickly you like it cut, and which is your favourite cooking method.

C Pancooked Bacon

Put bacon into a cold, preferably non-stick, pan.

Have the heat hot enough to keep it 'frizzling' but not so hot that you scorch parts of the bacon before you cook other parts. Save leftover bacon fat to add bacon flavour to other foods.

M Microwaved Bacon

Bacon microwaves superbly in a very short time. You can cook it on its serving plate, if you like. When cooking one or two rashers, lay them flat on a plate with a paper towel loosely over them to stop spatters.

1 rasher of bacon cooks at Full power in about 1 minute — less if very thin — and up to 1½ minutes if large and thick. Bacon browns and crisps on standing. Stop cooking it before it looks cooked.

For more slices, cook bacon on a dish with a ridged surface. Bacon will cook on both sides, out of fat.

Note:
Cook only very fatty bacon between paper towels. Lean bacon sticks to them and cannot curl attractively as it cooks.

Cook bacon on a preheated browning dish if preferred. Preheat browning dish for 5–6 minutes. Immediately add bacon. Cook 30–45 seconds per rasher.

C Grilled Bacon

Grilled bacon cooks evenly and well on a rack quite close to the preheated grill. Fat drips away from the bacon as it cooks.

C Leek and Bacon Flan

(See photograph on page 76.)

For 4–5 servings:
1 cup flour
60 g cold butter
about ¼ cup water
5 thin bacon rashers
2 leeks, sliced
½ cup cottage cheese
2 eggs
½ cup milk

Put flour and cold cubed butter in food processor. Do not chop the butter into the flour before adding the water.

Add water in a slow stream, using the on-off or pulse knob in short bursts to prevent overmixing. Mixture should still look crumbly when enough water has been added.

Stop adding water as soon as you can press dough particles together to form a ball.

Chill dough for 15 minutes then roll out thinly. Ease, do not stretch into a 20 cm flan tin or pie plate.

Run rolling pin over flan tin to cut off excess pastry or fold edges of pie pastry under, and crimp edge.

Chop half bacon and sauté. Slice leek and boil. Put chopped bacon, leek and cottage cheese in uncooked crust. Pour over egg and milk. Top with remaining uncooked bacon. Bake to 200°C for 20 minutes or until centre is set.

C Bacon and Avocado Sandwich

I think that bacon and avocado is one of the world's great combinations! Colour, texture and flavours are complementary — what more could you ask?

For each hearty open sandwich grill one or two thinly sliced bacon rashers.

While they cook, cut a thick slice of crusty bread, or halve a crusty bread roll.

Halve, peel and slice an avocado. Depending on size, allow ¼–½ avocado per sandwich. Sprinkle with lemon juice to prevent browning, and for extra flavour.

As soon as the bacon is cooked put it on the unbuttered bread and top with avocado slices. Add some pepper or some cress, alfalfa or beansprouts if you have them handy.

Bacon Lettuce and Tomato Sandwich

C Bacon Lettuce and Tomato Sandwich

If you have ever eaten a bacon lettuce and tomato sandwich, go out to the kitchen and make yourself one, right now.

Put one or two rashers of thinly cut bacon in a cold frying pan, or under the grill, and make a couple of slices of toast — either under the grill with the bacon, or in a toaster. While they cook, wash one or two lettuce leaves, and slice a tomato. As soon as the bacon has cooked, assemble the sandwich. I like a rasher of bacon next to each slice of toast, and a piece of lettuce between each bacon rasher and the tomato. In other words, my sandwich goes:

Toast–bacon–lettuce–tomato–lettuce–bacon–toast.

You don't need butter or salt or pepper or anything else — just the basic ingredients.

For packed lunches, use bread instead of toast, and wrap tightly.

Lamb

If I was ever told that I had to choose one meat to eat for the rest of my life, I would choose lamb!

We are so lucky to have this tender meat so readily available. It has a mild but distinctive flavour which appeals to young and old, and it is easy to cook. What's more, many lamb cuts are available at a very reasonable price.

Our grandmothers tended to take lamb for granted. They merely divided a side of lamb into three parts, roasted the front and back ends, and cut the middle section into chops which they fried. The only lamb recipes they had were ways to reheat cold meat!

We are much luckier than these cooks. We can take a new look at lamb. We can buy small, well-trimmed cuts which are so lean that they cook in an unbelievably short time. They are marvellously useful for small families and busy life-styles. We can still, however, cook a big lamb roast in the oven, when we want a good, no-fuss family dinner.

What's more, we can season our lamb with ingredients from all parts of the world. So many flavourings complement this versatile meat.

I hope that my lamb recipes will make you really excited! Talk to your butcher if you are not familiar with new lamb cuts, or better still, use a sharp knife, and prepare them for yourself. Whatever you do, do not ignore them!

Boning a Leg

Legs of lamb can be broken down into smaller cuts, more suitable for quick cooking and small families.

1. Have the chump or rump cut from the full leg (in one piece, or in several steaks) leaving the short cut leg, which is easier for a beginner to bone.

2. Skin side down, cut around the H-bone, working slowly and carefully, keeping your knife close to the bone, which is an irregular shape.

3. Wiggle the H-bone so you can see where it is attached to the leg bone at the hip socket, then cut through the space between the joints, lifting the bone out.

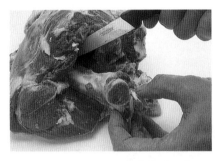

4. Cut around the top of the leg bone then work your knife around it, down towards the knee joint, freeing the bone from all flesh.

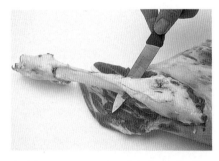

5. Now move to the shank, and cut away the meat from one side of the bone. Cut up and around the knee joint, and up and around the knee cap.

6. Twist the shank, cutting away any pieces of flesh that are attached to the bone. Pull out the shank, knee and leg bones in one piece.

7. You are left with a tunnel-boned leg. The cavity may be filled with stuffing, the shank end tucked under, and the opening secured.

8. The whole boned leg may be sliced thickly into steaks, or thinly into schnitzels. This must be done with a sharp knife.

9. It is easier to cut thin slices from a boneless leg if the meat if partly frozen. The slices vary in size, but each has a central hole where the bone was removed.

10. *Or* prepare a butterflied leg by cutting between the muscles on the inner side of the leg, down to the cavity where the bone was.

11. Open the leg out flat, trimming away any fatty pieces and slashing the thickest muscles. The butterflied leg may be grilled, barbecued or roasted, after marinating.

12. *Or* cut the rump from the full leg, and bone it. Cutting between muscles seams, separate the silverside, topside and thick flank. These four compact lean sections may be roasted whole, sliced thickly into steaks or thinly into schnitzels, or cubed for kebabs etc.

A Lamb Forequarter

A lamb forequarter is good value for money.

You can use it in many ways, once you have removed the bony framework. The meat is lean and tender and full of flavour, and can be cooked deliciously almost any way you like.

1. Cut under the ribs, towards the backbone. Use short strokes, keeping the knife close to the bones.

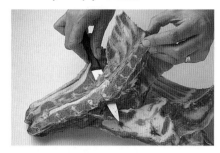

2. Work up to the neck, freeing the bones completely.

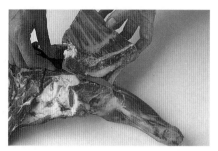

3. Remove the lower rib section, and the fat around it.

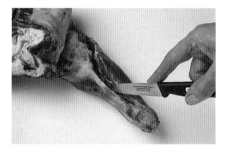

4. Cut a curving line from the knee to the ankle.

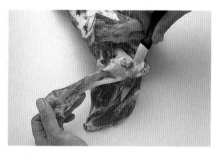

5. Cut the skin meat clear of the knee joint.

6. Cut close to the bone, to the shoulder joint, freeing it.

7. Cut around the blade bone, tunnelling to the shoulder joint.

8. *Or* cut through the meat around the shoulder-blade bone forming a pocket.

9. Lift the bones away completely. Keep the rib and leg bones for soup. Use the boneless forequarter as desired.

10. If the blade bone was tunnelled out, fill the pocket with stuffing and roast it flat.

11. *Or* cut the boned forequarter into two pieces (about 750 g each). Slice then cube the boned meat for kebabs, stews etc.

12. Roll and tie for two 750 g roasts.

Boning a Rack

A lamb loin is made up of the rib end or rack (which can be cut into rib chops) and the shortloin (which can be cut into middle-loin chops).

1. Get rack *chined* by a butcher if possible. Otherwise cut away knobbly bones above top of rib bones.

2. Run your thumb along the natural seam between the muscle and the fat layer outside it. Pull away the yellowish strip of gristle.

3. Where the muscle turns in to meet the bone again, stop following it and cut down to the bone.

4. Keep cutting away the fatty layers above the bones, leaving the bones as clean as possible.

5. *French* the rack by cutting away the thin strip of meat between the rib bones.

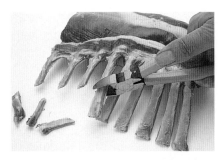

6. If the rib bones are long, snip them off to the desired length using diagonal cutting pliers.

Boning Short Loins

The back end of a lamb loin is called the shortloin. The fillet is the small muscle on one side of the bones. The boneless loin or striploin is the bigger muscle on the other side of the bones. Boneless loins are very popular, especially in restaurants.

You can prepare these yourself, in a few minutes, from untrimmed shortloins.

1. Select a fairly large lamb shortloin. With fat side on working surface cut down, keeping close to the bone to remove the small muscle, the fillet, on the upper side of the bone.

2. Turning the knife blade, cut up and under the bones exposed. Keep cutting close to the bones until the strip of bones can be lifted clear of the large muscle underneath. This muscle may be called the boneless loin, the striploin or the back strap.

3. Separate this muscle from the fat layer beneath it by running your thumb underneath it. Cut away the whitish membrane on one side of this large muscle or the meat will curl as it cooks.

Boning Loin Chops

The shortloin may be cut into six loin chops, each with a small T-shaped bone. Noisettes are made by removing the T-bone and outer fat from middle loin chops. They are held together by a thin strip of side bacon, by string, or by skewers.

1. Cut away the outer fat from middle loin lamb chops and then remove T-bone, cutting as close to the bone as possible using a sharp knife.

2. Wrap the tail of each chop around the large and small eyes of meat so each chop is a compact circle. If desired wrap a thin strip of side bacon around each noisette.

3. Push a short length of bamboo skewer through the middle of the noisette, then another at right angles to the first. (This stops the centres from popping up during cooking.)

C Sautéed Boneless Loin

This exciting, tender, lean lamb cut is very popular in restaurants.

You may not see boneless loins on display in butchers' shops but you should ask for them or prepare them youself, in just a few seconds, from untrimmed shortloins. (Use meat from thin part of shortloin for stir-frying or mincing, if desired.)

To cook a boneless loin, sauté the strip of muscle in 1/2 teaspoon plain or clarified butter with a crushed garlic clove over moderate heat in a medium-sized, preferably non-stick, pan for 6 minutes, turning several times.

Turn off heat, leave to stand for 5 minutes. To carve, slice thinly with a sharp knife held diagonally to both the strip of meat and the board. A 225 g boneless loin makes one or two servings.

C Sesame Lamb Salad

(See photograph on page 95.)

This is a very special lamb salad! It should be served as the main course of a summer meal for two people or with warm bread rolls, or freshly-made scones.

Lamb
1 boneless lamb loin (about 200 g)
1/2 tsp clarified butter
1 clove garlic, crushed
1 Tbsp Japanese soya sauce
1 tsp sesame oil

Salad dressing
1 Tbsp Japanese soya sauce
1 Tbsp wine vinegar
2 tsp sugar
pinch horseradish powder (optional)

1/4 cup oil
1/2 tsp sesame oil

Suggested salad vegetables
red lettuce
nasturtium leaves and flowers
watercress
sliced kiwifruit

Sauté the boneless loin in the clarified butter in a non-stick pan over moderate heat for 6 minutes, turning several times. Remove from heat and add garlic, soya sauce and sesame oil. Turn meat and leave to cool in this marinade for 15 minutes.

Shake dressing ingredients together in a screw-topped jar. Prepare vegetables for two large salads. Dry and chill leaves for best results. Remove garlic from lamb. Slice lamb thinly. Turn slices in marinade, adding 1–2 teaspoons dressing. Toss salad in less than half the dressing and arrange on large, individual plates.

Arrange warm lamb slices on salad greens and serve immediately. (Save remaining dressing for another salad).

B C Glazed Lamb Noisettes

Noisettes are made by removing the T-bones and outer fat from middle-loin chops. Held together by a thin strip of side bacon, they may be sautéed, barbecued or grilled close to the heat until just cooked. After cooking, remove the skewers.

(See Boning Loin Chops for instructions on making noisettes.)

For a glaze and sauce for 8 noisettes:
1/2 cup orange juice
1/4 cup chicken stock
2 Tbsp whisky

1 Tbsp light jam or jelly
2 sprigs tarragon

Boil all ingredients together until thick and syrupy. Brush over noisettes or add to pan juices during last minutes of cooking. Spoon remaining sauce over noisettes when serving.

C Bacon-Wrapped Noisettes

Easy and elegant — bacon-wrapped noisettes taste as good as they look.

Remove the T-bone from middle-loin lamb chops and trim away nearly all visible fat.

Trim a thinly sliced bacon rasher so it is as wide as the noisette is thick. Lie the trimmings on the even strip and wrap this around the noisette, without stretching the bacon. Push two or three bamboo skewers right through each noisette so everything stays flat during cooking. Chop skewers shorter if desired, and refrigerate noisettes, lightly covered, until needed.

Grill, about 10 cm from heat, for 5–6 minutes per side, or until cooked as desired.

Brush with a mixture of softened red currant or crabapple jelly, orange juice and mustard during the last 2–3 minutes if desired.

M Microwaved Loin Chops

Trim chops, removing unwanted fat. Brush lightly on both sides with melted or clarified butter.

Heat browning dish. Add 2 chops, cook at Full power for 1 1/2–2 minutes, depending on size of chops, then quickly turn and cook for 1 1/2 minutes on the second side.

C Roast Lamb and Macaroni

This is an easy but unusual and delicious roasting-pan meal, needing only a green vegetable or salad served with it.

For 5–6 servings:
1 lamb leg
2 cloves garlic
rosemary and thyme (optional)
3 onions, quartered
1 (425 g) can tomato purée
3 cups water
1 green pepper, chopped
1 tsp dried oreganum
1 tsp dried basil
1 tsp salt
1 Tbsp sugar
*2 cups (200 g) macaroni, spirals, or
    other pasta.*

Remove excess fat from lamb leg. Pierce leg in about a dozen places and insert garlic slivers and/or rosemary and thyme sprigs. Put in roasting pan with peeled, quartered onions.

Estimate the total cooking time (from 1½–2½ hours, depending on age, size and personal preference). Cook lamb, uncovered, at 170°C for 45 minutes less than estimated time.

Meantime, mix tomato purée and remaining ingredients except macaroni. Heat to boiling. Drain fat from lamb, leaving only 2 tablespoons. Stir macaroni into pan drippings, then add hot liquid. Cook for 45 minutes longer or until pasta is tender, stirring occasionally, adding extra boiling water if macaroni dries out.

Serve sliced lamb with macaroni and sauce.

C M Stuffed Leg of Lamb

The cavity in a boned leg of lamb may be filled with savoury or sweet stuffing. A boned, stuffed leg is compact and easy to carve. Vary the stuffing to suit your taste and the ingredients on hand. If you like your lamb roasted to the pink stage, make sure all major stuffing ingredients are cooked before the stuffing is mixed.

1 boned leg of lamb
stuffing (see following recipes)

Trim any excess fat from the outer surface of the boned lamb leg. Cut away any fat from the inner surfaces. Prepare any stuffing which suits you.

Spoon stuffing into cavity, packing it loosely rather than tightly. Fold longer ends of leg over shorter ones, and skewer in place.

Push strong toothpicks or short lengths of bamboo skewers across

openings, then zig-zag string or strong thread around skewers, knotting it when all skewers are secured.

Place meat in pan or on rack over pan. Roast, uncovered, at 170°C for 1½–2½ hours, according to the size of the lamb and the desired doneness.

Or read internal temperature of meat by inserting a meat thermometer into the thickest part of the meat.

Lamb is cooked:
pink at   65°C (150°F)
medium at   70°C (160°F)
well done at   80°C (175°F)

Allow roast to stand in a warm place for 5 minutes, remove skewers, then lift away thread. Slice meat fairly thickly.

Microwave Instructions

Brush surface of stuffed leg with a paste of 1 tablespoon dark soya sauce and 1 tablespoon dry mustard. Stand meat in oven bag, on a roasting rack. Leave neck of bag untied. Microwave at Medium (50% power) allowing 15–20 minutes per 500 g, or cook until thermometer reads a little less than temperatures given above.

Allow 20 minutes' standing time before carving.

Savoury Rice Stuffing

1 large onion
2 Tbsp butter
1 cup chopped mushrooms
1 cup cooked rice
¼ cup chopped parsley
1–2 tsp chopped lemon rind
salt and pepper
1 egg yolk

Cook onion in butter until transparent. Add mushrooms. Cook for 1 minute longer. Add rice, parsley, lemon rind, then season to taste. Stir in egg yolk.

Herbed Orange Stuffing

1 medium-sized onion, chopped
1–2 Tbsp butter
½ tsp dried thyme
grated rind of 1 orange
1½ cups soft breadcrumbs
salt and pepper
1 egg yolk

Cook onion in butter until transparent, adding thyme and orange rind when nearly cooked. Stir in soft breadcrumbs. Season to taste, then stir in egg yolk.

Minted Orange Stuffing

Follow the recipe for Herbed Orange Stuffing, replacing thyme with 2 tablespoons chopped mint.

Apricot Rice Stuffing

¼ cup finely chopped dried apricots
¼ cup wine or water or juice
1 Tbsp butter
1–2 rashers bacon
1 medium-sized onion, chopped

¼ cup chopped walnuts
2 cups soft breadcrumbs

Cook chopped apricots and liquid in frying pan until liquid disappears.

Remove apricots.

Over moderate heat cook butter and finely chopped bacon. Add onion when bacon is half cooked. When onion is nearly tender, add walnuts. Cook for 1 minute longer, then stir in breadcrumbs and apricots.

M Bagged Stuffed Lamb

For 4–6 servings:
1 boned, trimmed lamb leg
1 large onion, chopped finely
1 Tbsp oil
¼ cup chopped apricots
½ cup Australian raisins
¼ cup chopped walnuts
¼ cup sherry or orange juice
2–3 Tbsp chopped mint

Marinade
2 Tbsp dark soya sauce
2 Tbsp sherry or orange juice
2 Tbsp lemon juice
1 clove garlic, crushed

In a medium-sized bowl combine the onion and oil. Microwave at Full power for 1 minute. Add the apricots, raisins, walnuts and sherry. Cook, uncovered, for 3 minutes. Stir in the mint. Place this mixture on the meaty surface of the boned leg. Roll up and tie securely with string. (Skewers may puncture oven bag.)

Place stuffed leg in an oven bag with the marinade ingredients, closed loosely with a rubber band, leaving a finger-sized hole to allow steam to escape.

Microwave at Medium (50% power) allowing 15–20 minutes per 500 g. Turn after 15 minutes. For slightly pink lamb the internal temperature of the meat should be 135°F before standing. Pour off liquid, skim off fat and thicken with cornflour paste. Leave meat to stand for 10 minutes. Slice, garnish with fresh herbs and serve.

C Roast Stuffed Forequarter

These is no need to roll a forequarter which has been tunnel-boned. Use stuffings and glazes of your choice, roast at a low temperature for best results, with meat on a rack, so that drippings can coat vegetables underneath.

Don't add extra fat at any stage. Score skin side so fat escapes during cooking. Insert garlic slivers if you like garlic flavour.

Make blade bone cavity a little

Bagged Stuffed Lamb

larger if you want lots of stuffing. Always pack stuffing loosely.

My stuffing is 2 cups fresh breadcrumbs, 2 rashers chopped bacon, grated rind of 1 orange, 1 egg, chopped basil and parsley.

Push toothpicks or skewers through meat each side of pocket opening.

Crisscross string or heavy thread around skewers. Skewer any flaps or openings closed. Knot string.

Roast at 160°C on rack above roasting pan for 1½–2 hours, or to suit individual preference. Put vegetables underneath to roast in drippings for 1–1¼ hours.

Brush with juice of orange and 1 tablespoon honey during last 45 minutes if desired.

Remove skewers with pliers before serving.

Ⓜ Shoulder of Lamb

For 4 servings:

1 shoulder of lamb, boned
2 Tbsp mixed mustard
1 Tbsp dark soya sauce
1 tsp chopped fresh thyme

Trim all excess fat from surface and inner, meaty side of boned lamb shoulder. Score outer skin in a diamond pattern with a sharp knife.

In a small bowl, mix the mustard, soya sauce and thyme to a spreadable paste, and brush over both surfaces of the meat. Roll up, skin side out, and tie securely in several places. Place the lamb on a microwave roasting rack (or substitute). Cover with a tent of greaseproof paper.

Microwave at Medium (50% power) allowing 20–25 minutes per 500 g. Turn lamb, every 10–15 minutes. Allow 10 minutes' standing time. Slice and serve with gravy made by skimming, then reducing or thickening pan juices.

Ⓒ Crown Roast

A crown roast makes a most attractive special occasion roast. Order a two or three rack crown from your butcher (discuss the number of chops you want) or prepare it yourself from two chined, frenched racks, tying them together, meaty side facing out, snipping between meaty ends of rib bones. Fill centre of crown with a ball of foil.

Roast crown uncovered, at 200°C for about 30 minutes or until meat thermometer registers 65°C–70°C for 'medium'. Remove foil, fill with cooked vegetables or rice if desired. Cover bone tips with cutlet frills or grapes. Carve between bones into individual chops.

🄲 Loin Mini-Roasts

One or two-person families can enjoy traditional lamb roasts on a small scale using 'mini-roasts' from the loin cuts from lamb and hogget. Both the rack and shortloin make very tender roasts.

It is a good idea to use a meat thermometer to read the internal temperature of the meat until you get used to cooking small cuts.

Cook at 65°C (about 150°F) for pink meat; 70°C (about 160°F) for medium; 80°C (about 175°F) for well done.

🄲 Sirloin Lamb Roast

This little roasts resembles a miniature rolled sirloin beef roast. For 2 servings select a shortloin weighing about 600 g.

Bone the shortloin following the instructions on page 88. Remove nearly all the visible outer fat using a sharp knife (you should be left with about 400 g lean meat).

Season the inner meaty surface with herbs, spices or stuffing made from cooked rice or fresh breadcrumbs.

Suggested Stuffing
4 dried apricot halves
3 Tbsp orange juice
1/4 cup cooked rice or fresh
*   breadcrumbs*
1 Tbsp pine nuts or chopped almonds
*   (optional)*
1 spring onion, chopped
1 tsp chopped rosemary

Chop apricots, cook in juice until it evaporates. Add remaining ingredients. Spread stuffing down centre of lamb. Roll up meat and tie securely in four places. Lightly flour surface of meat. Roast at 180°C for 40 minutes or 200°C for 25 minutes or until tested with a meat thermometer.

Brush after 20 minutes with Worcestershire sauce for extra colour and flavour, if desired. Add 1/2 cup water and 1/2 teaspoon instant chicken stock to the pan drippings. For extra sweetness and flavour, add 2 tablespoons redcurrant jelly and 1 tablespoon sherry or port, if desired.

Simmer until lightly thickened, strain and serve with meat.

🄼 Microwave Rack Roast

Imagine — a five-minute roast for two or three!

Sirloin Lamb Roast

Mix a thick paste of mustard and dark soya sauce. Use 1 tablespoon mixed or dry mustard and about 2 teaspoons dark soya sauce. Brush this evenly over meaty surfaces of chined, frenched rack.

Chop about 1/4 cup fresh herbs, using a mixture of parsley and thyme or marjoram or tarragon or basil. Pat herbs evenly over mustardy coating. Place rack, meaty side up, on a microwave roasting rack or on a bread and butter plate inverted on a dinner plate.

Microwave rack (weighing 400 g or less after trimming) at Full power for 4 1/2 minutes. Add an extra 30 seconds per extra 50 g. Leave to stand for 5 minutes, then carve into cutlets. Serve with pan juices.

🄱 🄲 Glazed Butterflied Lamb

Trimmed, marinated, barbecued or grilled, and glazed just before serving, this boned and opened flat lamb cooks in half an hour!

1 boned lamb leg
1/4 cup white wine or lemon juice
1 Tbsp Worcestershire sauce
1 Tbsp oil
herbs (optional)
1/2 cup marmalade
2 Tbsp mixed mustard
1 Tbsp dark soya sauce
1/2 tsp hot pepper sauce

Trim outer fat and skin from a boned leg of lamb. (See page 86 for details of boning). Cut between the muscles at the thinnest (inner) part of the leg, opening it out flat. Remove fat from the inner surface.

Place lamb in an unpunctured plastic bag with the wine or lemon juice, Worcestershire sauce and oil. Add rosemary, thyme, oreganum, if desired. Squeeze air from bag, fasten with rubber band and refrigerate overnight. If grilling, lay meat in pan in marinade as it cooks.

Grill or barbecue with surface of meat 17–20 cm from the heat, allowing 15–20 minutes per side, depending on size of lamb and intensity of heat. While lamb cooks, heat marmalade with remaining ingredients. Brush over meat during last 5 minutes of cooking. Serve extra glaze as a sauce with lamb.
Note:
It is important to have lamb far enough from heat to cook the thicker parts of the meat without burning the outside. If you feel that the lamb is not cooking evenly enough, slash the thicker muscles on the side closest to the bone.

Lamb Glazes
Sweet mixtures brushed over roast, barbecued, grilled or pan-cooked lamb near the end of the cooking time give a shiny appearance and an interesting flavour. If a glaze is added too soon, the sugar in it will burn before the lamb is cooked.

Some recipes call for heating glaze ingredients before brushing them over roast, grilled or barbecued meat. This reduces the glaze to a thickish, rather syrupy consistency. Glazes added to meat in a pan seldom need to be cooked ahead, since they reduce in volume quickly, in the hot pan.

Watch carefully, turning the lamb in the pan before the glaze thickens too much. If you do not get your timing right, add a little more wine, juice or water, so glaze is thinned again, and turn the meat in it. Estimate the heat of the pan carefully. It must be hot enough to evaporate the glaze fairly fast, but not instantly. On the other hand, the meat should never 'stew' in a dilute syrup over low heat.

🄱 🄲 Barbecued Lamb Forequarter

A boned forequarter of young lean lamb is delicious cooked under a grill, or on a barbecue. It should be marinated first, then cooked for about 45 minutes, about 20 cm from the heat.

1 boned forequarter (about 1 1/4 kg)
juice of 2 lemons
1/2 cup white wine (optional)
2 Tbsp Worcestershire sauce
2 Tbsp oil
pulp from 2 onions
2 cloves garlic, crushed
1 sprig rosemary, crushed or chopped

Score surface of boned forequarter. Scrape cut surface of onion with a metal spoon for pulp (or grate, or food process all ingredients).

Put all ingredients in a heavy, unpunctured plastic bag.

Squeeze all air from plastic bag. Tie. Refrigerate for 48 hours or leave at room temperature for 24 hours.

Place in roasting pan without rack, in marinade. Grill about 20 cm from heat for about 20 minutes. Turn and grill second side for another 20 minutes.
Note:
For well done lamb, after grilling either microwave for 10 minutes longer at 60% power; or roast for about 20 minutes longer at 180°C, or 'butterfly' forequarter, baste, and grill for 10 minutes longer.

B C Lamb Kebabs

(See photograph on page 84.)

I think that lamb kebabs should be promoted as New Zealand's National Dish, in restaurants, hotels, takeaways and butcher shops. They can be cooked in 5–10 minutes, close to the heat of a barbecue or grill. They look wonderful, taste superb, can be frozen and quickly thawed, are nutritionally well-balanced, and with different marinades, sauces and glazes need never be the same twice. What's more, nearly all the meat from a young lamb can be cut up and skewered.

Cut forequarter or lamb leg meat into 2 cm cubes. Do not trim away all fat. This bastes the meat, dripping away during cooking.

Quarter, skin and separate the 'petals' of onions to make pieces about 2 cm square.

Cut suitable fruit and vegetables into similar pieces if you like. These are not essential additions to kebabs.

Thread alternate pieces of lamb and vegetable (or fruit), or lamb alone, on to bamboo, wood or metal skewers.

Marinate for extra flavour and tenderness. Use these marinades with 1 kg of cubed lamb.

Oriental Marinade

2 Tbsp lemon juice
2 Tbsp dark soya sauce
1 Tbsp brown sugar
1 Tbsp oil
1 clove garlic, crushed
1 tsp grated root ginger (optional)

Mediterranean Marinade

¼ cup red or white wine or 2 Tbsp
* wine vinegar*
2 Tbsp olive or other oil
1 tsp dried basil
1 tsp dried oreganum
¼ tsp dried thyme (optional)
1 Tbsp Worcestershire sauce (optional)

Yoghurt Marinade

¼ cup plain yoghurt
2 tsp honey (optional)
2 Tbsp chopped fresh mint
½–1 tsp ground cumin
½–1 tsp ground coriander
½–1 tsp paprika (optional)

Place trimmed 2–3 cm cubes in an unpunctured plastic bag or covered bowl with your chosen marinade ingredients. Leave to stand for several hours, or overnight if possible. If time is short, leave for 30 minutes. Thread meat on bamboo or metal skewers. If desired, skewer squares of colourful, quick-cooking vegetables between the cubes of marinated meat.

Suitable vegetables include:
onions quartered, separated
mushrooms

quartered or small tomatoes
red and green pepper cubes
zucchini slices
eggplant cubes

Vegetables may be brushed with a little extra marinade before or during cooking.

Cook kebabs close to the heat, on a barbecue or under a preheated grill for 5–10 minutes. Meat should brown on the outside and remain slighly pink in the middle. If meat cubes do not brown quickly enough, brush with a little glaze. The sugar in glazes speeds up browning.

Apricot Glaze

2 Tbsp apricot jam
1 Tbsp mixed mustard
2–3 Tbsp orange or lemon juice
1 Tbsp oil

Tomato Glaze

2 Tbsp tomato sauce
1 Tbsp Worcestershire sauce
1 Tbsp brown sugar
1 Tbsp oil

Oriental Glaze

1 Tbsp soya sauce
1 Tbsp brown sugar
1 Tbsp lemon juice
1 Tbsp oil

Serve kebabs on rice, noodles or in split bread rolls, pulling out the skewers before eating, if desired. (Hold meat in place with fork tines while pulling skewer.)

C Sesame Lamb Schnitzels

Lamb schnitzels are thin slices cut from the leg. They may be cut from any part of a boned leg. To buy a small amount of leg meat for schnitzels, select a chump (see page 86) and bone it yourself, then slice it thinly. For larger quantities, buy a boned leg and cut thin slices from it, or buy an unboned leg, cut each muscle off the bone, then slice thinly.

Using your thumbs more than a knife, remove the fell (skin) and fat close to where you can see a muscle 'seam', i.e. the line between two muscles. Separate the muscles, keeping each in its sheath.

When you reach the bone, cut the muscle free using short strokes of a sharp knife. After a little practice, you will find this easier and less time-consuming. Separate the muscles completely.

This technique is referred to as 'seam-boning'. Some butchers sell a leg already 'seam-boned' into well-trimmed individual muscles.

For easiest slicing, partly freeze meat.

Cut in thin slices, place between sheets of plastic and bang with a rolling pin. Dip slices into 1 egg,

lightly beaten with 1 teaspoon soya sauce and 2 teaspoons sherry. Then dip into 2 tablespoons dry crumbs mixed with 2 tablespoons toasted sesame seeds (or chopped peanuts). Fry in a little clarified butter, in a very hot pan, until golden brown on each side.

C Stir-Fried Lamb

Thinly sliced lamb stir-fries deliciously. Always use a very high heat, and don't crowd the pan or wok, for best results.

about 400 g thinly sliced lamb
1–2 cloves garlic, crushed
2–3 slices root ginger
2 Tbsp soya sauce
2 Tbsp oil
1 Tbsp sherry
2 tsp brown sugar
400 g sliced vegetables
1 Tbsp cornflour

Freeze a chunk of boned forequarter until very firm but not frozen solid. Slice very thinly across grain.

Put in a plastic bag with next six ingredients. Mix and leave for 10–30 minutes.

Slice a selection of quick-cooking vegetables thinly.

Heat a large frying pan or wok with 2 tablespoons oil. Stir-fry vegetables until barely tender. Remove.

Stir-fry marinated lamb on high heat until no longer pink. Add vegetables, mix, and thicken with cornflour paste.

B C Barbecued Shoulder Chops

Brush sauce on shoulder chops during the last few minutes of cooking, or the outside browns and burns before the centre is cooked.

Sauce

½ cup tomato sauce
2 Tbsp soya oil
1 Tbsp brown sugar
1 Tbsp lemon juice
1 Tbsp Worcestershire sauce
1 tsp dry mustard
1 tsp basil
1 tsp marjoram

Mix all ingredients together in a small pan.

Bring to boil then put aside until needed. Refrigerate leftover sauce.

For extra flavour and tenderness marinate chops before cooking, for 1–24 hours, in equal parts soya oil, lemon juice and Worcestershire sauce.

Barbecue or grill about 5 cm from heat, brushing with barbecue sauce when almost cooked.

Sesame Lamb Salad

M Pineapple Lamb Cutlets

For 4 servings:
8 lamb cutlets, well trimmed (about
    350 g)
1 small can pineapple rings
2 Tbsp dark soya sauce
1 Tbsp tomato ketchup
1–2 Tbsp brown sugar
1 clove garlic
1 tsp freshly grated root ginger
2 tsp cornflour
halved circles of pineapple for garnish

Trim the cutlets, removing all outer
fat. In a shallow casserole or dish
large enough to hold the cutlets in
one layer, mix ¼ cup juice from the
pineapple, the sauces, sugar, garlic
and root ginger. Turn cutlets in
liquid. Leave to stand for at least 10
minutes. Turn again. Cover and
microwave at Medium (50% power)
for 12 minutes, turning after 6
minutes. Thicken with cornflour,
mixed to a paste with a little extra
pineapple juice. Stand for 4 minutes.
Test. Cook for 2–3 minutes or
longer if meat is not quite cooked.
Add halved pineapple rings to sauce.
Coat with sauce. Reheat for 1
minute at Full power to heat
pineapple. Serve with rice, noodles
or mashed potatoes and colourful
vegetables.

M Rolled Boneless Lamb Loin

For 4–6 servings:
1 loin of lamb (about 1 kg after
    trimming), about 30 cm long
1–2 tsp dark soya sauce
mixture of herbs and spices, e.g. mint,
    coriander, orange rind
3 kiwifruit, peeled

Bone and carefully trim the lamb,
leaving just enough fat to attach flap
to meaty section. Rub both sides of
meat with soya sauce. Sprinkle with
flavourings to taste. Slice the
kiwifruit and place slices in a line on
top of the lamb, below the meatiest
section. Roll up the lamb and secure
with string. Cook at Medium (50%
power) for 15–20 minutes or to
internal temperature of
135°F–145°F. Remove from oven
and let stand for about 8–10 minutes
while you make the sauce.

Sauce
1 orange, grated rind and juice
¼ cup red currant jelly
¼ cup meat juice (from cooked lamb)
2 tsp cornflour
1 Tbsp water

Blend the orange rind, juice and
jelly by heating at Full power for 2
minutes. Skim fat from meat juices
and add to the mixture with the
cornflour paste. Cook for 3 minutes

until thickened. Serve sauce over
the thickly sliced lamb.

C Lamb Leg Steaks

• Leg steaks cut by a butcher may
contain a small section of bone.
• Steaks cut from a boned leg have
a cavity where the bone was
removed.
• Small steaks or medallions may be
cut from the silverside, topside,
thick flank or boned chump.
• Remove fell (skin) and outer fat
from steaks if this has not been done
already. (Steak curls during cooking
unless this is removed.)
• Steaks from aged and conditioned
lamb may be cooked without
marinating or tenderising.
Otherwise, marinate or tenderise
mechanically.
• To tenderise mechanically, put
steak between sheets of plastic and
bang with a rolling pin or use a
dimpled metal or wooden meat
hammer.

Marinade
2 Tbsp lemon juice or ¼ cup white
    wine
1 Tbsp soya sauce or Worcestershire
    sauce
1 Tbsp oil
herbs as desired

Mix marinade. Turn meat in
marinade, and leave for at least half
an hour. Cook steaks for a short
time in a hot, preheated, heavy pan.
Brown each side over high heat,
then lower heat until cooked to
desired stage. Add a glaze such as
Apricot Ginger Glaze below, when
meat is nearly cooked.
    Other suitable glazes are Tomato
Glaze or Oriental Glaze (see index).
Note:
Overcooked steaks toughen.

Apricot Ginger Glaze
¼ cup syrup from apricot juice
2 Tbsp apricot jam
2 Tbsp lemon juice
2 tsp grated root ginger
1 tsp grated lemon rind

Mix marinade ingredients. Heat
until boiling. Brush on meat,
thinning if desired.

C Hungarian Lamb Stew

Rich, dark and delicious!

750 g cubed shoulder lamb (½ a
    forequarter)
500 g onions
50 g butter
1 Tbsp sugar
1½ Tbsp paprika
1 tsp salt
2 Tbsp flour
2–3 cups water
bunch of fresh herbs

Cube and trim lamb. Put aside.
Chop or slice onions. Cook in half
the butter until soft and golden. Add
sugar and stir over medium heat
until evenly golden brown. Stir in
paprika and salt, cook for 2–3
minutes longer.
    In another pan, brown lamb,
coated with flour, in remaining
butter. Do not crowd pan.
    Combine meat, onions, water and
herbs, cover and simmer on low
heat for 1–1½ hours, until tender.
Add more water if necessary.
    Check seasonings and thickening,
let stand off heat for 5 minutes
before serving.

C Italian Lamb Stew

Light, herbed and tangy.

750 g cubed shoulder lamb
25 g butter
1–2 onions, chopped
2 cloves garlic, sliced
1 Tbsp chopped fresh sage
    or 1 tsp dried sage
½ cup dry white wine
½ cup water
2 tsp instant chicken stock
1 egg yolk
1 Tbsp cornflour
1 large lemon, rind and juice.

Brown lamb in butter. Add onion
and garlic, cook until transparent.
Simmer with next four ingredients
for 1–1½ hours, until tender. Mix
remaining ingredients with a little
liquid from stew. Pour back into
stew, cook until liquid thickens, but
do not boil. Adjust seasoning,
sprinkle with parsley and serve.

C Spiced Lamb with Prunes

For about 6 servings:
1 kg cubed shoulder lamb
3 Tbsp flour
oil for browning
1 cup water
2 Tbsp lemon or orange juice
1 cinnamon stick
1 tsp salt
½–1 cup halved, pitted prunes
2–4 Tbsp brown sugar

Cube lamb, coat with flour, and
brown evenly in a little oil in a very
hot pan.
    Transfer to casserole dish. Add
water, juice, cinnamon stick and
salt. Cover tightly and bake at
150°C for 1 hour, or until lamb is
nearly cooked.
    Add prunes and 2 tablespoons
sugar. Cook for about 20 minutes
longer, then remove from oven,
taste critically and add extra sugar
and salt if necessary.
    Remove cinnamon stick and serve
on rice, with cucumber and tomato
salads.

Creole Lamb Casserole

C Special Lamb Casserole

For 4 servings:
1 kg cubed shoulder lamb
2 Tbsp flour
2 Tbsp butter
4 garlic cloves, chopped
1 tsp salt
1 bay leaf
1 tsp fresh thyme (or ¼ tsp dried thyme)
1 cup white wine
2 egg yolks
1 Tbsp lemon juice
2 Tbsp chopped parsley

Trim lamb well. Coat with flour. Brown until golden, but not dark brown, in butter, a little at a time. Add garlic with last batch, taking care not to let it turn dark brown either.

Transfer to casserole. Add bay leaf, thyme, salt and wine. Cover tightly with foil under lid if necessary, and bake at 150°C for 1½–2 hours, until lamb is tender.

Just before serving, mix egg yolks and lemon juice in bowl. Add 2 tablespoons hot liquid from casserole. Stir into casserole. Do not let mixture boil again or egg will curdle.

Sprinkle with parsley and serve immediately.

C Sweet and Sour Lamb Stew

For 4–6 servings:
1 kg cubed shoulder lamb
450 g pineapple pieces
¼ cup wine vinegar
¼ cup brown sugar
1 tsp salt
2 onions
1 Tbsp oil
cornflour to thicken

Brown lamb cubes evenly in a hot, non-stick pan, in as little oil as possible. Place in heavy saucepan with the liquid from the pineapple, the vinegar, brown sugar and salt. Cover and simmer on very low heat for 30 minutes.

Meanwhile, cut the onions into pieces similar in size to the meat cubes. Brown lightly in a little oil (or in remaining lamb fat) and add to the half-cooked lamb. Simmer for 30 minutes longer, then add pineapple pieces and simmer until lamb is tender, 10–30 minutes.

Just before serving, thicken with cornflour-and-water paste. Serve with rice, peas, and a side salad.

Variation:
Add cubes of red and green pepper with the pineapple pieces, if desired.

C M Creole Lamb Casserole

For 4–6 servings:
750 g cubed shoulder lamb
¼ cup flour
2 tsp instant beef stock
1 tsp dry mustard
1 Tbsp Worcestershire sauce
2 tsp dark soya sauce
1 onion, chopped
1 green pepper, chopped
1 red pepper, chopped
2 cups chopped tomatoes (or 1 cup tomato purée and 1 cup water)

Trim lamb, removing fat, Toss meat with dry ingredients, then add remaining ingredients.

Cook in a large, covered microwave dish at high power for 10 minutes, then stir and cook at Defrost (30% power) for 45 minutes or until meat is tender.

Leave to stand for 10 minutes before serving.

Alternatively, add an extra cup of water and bake at 150°C in a covered casserole for 1½ hours or until tender, stirring every 30 minutes.

Lambs' Tongues with Orange

C M Creamed Sweetbreads

Sweetbreads have a delicate flavour. Serve them with something crisp — on toast, in a croustade case, in a vol-au-vent case or a filo pastry shell.

For 4 servings:
500 g lambs' sweetbreads
³/₄ cup water
1 Tbsp lemon juice
1 bay leaf
2 cloves garlic, chopped
6 peppercorns
sprigs parsley, thyme, tarragon
25 g butter
200 g quartered mushrooms
2 Tbsp flour
¹/₂ cup stock
¹/₂ tsp instant chicken stock
¹/₂ cup milk
2 Tbsp cream (optional)
2 Tbsp chopped chives
2 Tbsp finely chopped parsley

Put sweetbreads into saucepan with next five ingredients. Add fresh herbs or small amounts of dried herbs, cover; and simmer for 15 minutes, or microwave at Full power until firm. Drain, straining and reserving liquid.

Melt butter, sauté mushrooms for 2–3 minutes, then stir in flour and ¹/₂ cup of the strained stock. Stir over low heat until sauce boils then add instant stock, milk, cream (if used), chives and parsley.

Chop and add sweetbreads, warm through in sauce, and adjust seasoning. Add a little more stock if sauce is too thick.

C Lambs' Tongues With Orange

For this recipe you can use fresh or pickled lambs' tongues. With pickled tongues, take care that the sauce is not too salty.

For about 8 servings:
12 lambs' tongues
water to cover
bay leaves
6 allspice berries
6 peppercorns
3 cloves garlic
2 Tbsp butter
2 Tbsp flour
1 orange, rind and juice
salt to taste
2 tsp wine vinegar
1 Tbsp sugar

Trim tongues if necessary. Soak salted tongues in cold water for 3–4 hours, changing water 2–3 times. Discard liquid.

Put tongues in a saucepan with water to cover, add bay leaves, allspice, peppercorns and garlic. Cover and simmer until skin will peel off tongues easily when they are held under cold water. Time will depend on the age of the tongues and will be 1–3 hours. Strain and save 1¹/₂ cups liquid. Peel, trim and halve tongues lengthwise.

Melt butter and stir in flour and finely grated orange rind over low heat. Add orange juice and one cup of stock. If stock is too salty, dilute with water before use. For a sweet and sour sauce, add the wine vinegar, sugar, and more salt. Stir tongues into sauce and reheat when required.

Variations:
Add ¹/₄–¹/₂ cup currants, sultanas or raisins.

C M Brain Puffs

For years I presented these as Lamb Patties, without describing the ingredients in detail! They are great favourites with pre-schoolers.

For 4 servings:
6–8 sets of lambs' brains
¹/₂ cup water
1 Tbsp lemon juice
¹/₂ tsp salt
1 bay leaf
1 clove garlic
sprigs thyme and parsley

1 tsp green herb stock
1 tsp curry powder
1 egg
1/2 cup self-raising flour

Put brains in a small saucepan with next five ingredients, adding sprigs of fresh herbs, or a pinch of these or other dried herbs.

Cover and simmer for 15–20 minutes, or microwave until firm, then cool in cooking liquid. Strain and save liquid.

Chop brains into 1 cm cubes. It is not necessary to remove any 'bits and pieces' since these are not tough, and are not noticed in the final product. Combine 1/4 cup of the cooking liquid in a bowl with the instant stock, curry powder and egg. Stir in the flour, if necessary adding more flour or liquid to form a thick batter. Fold in the brains.

Fry teaspoon-lots in hot oil about 1–2 cm deep, turning when bottom is golden brown. Total cooking time should be about 4 minutes. Drain on kitchen paper.

Serve with egg cup or small dish of tomato sauce on each plate, so diners can dip each puff just before eating it, and puffs stay crisp.

Sesame Liver Strips

This is a good way to introduce liver to people who have not eaten it before.

For 2 servings:
200 g lamb's liver
1 tsp dark soya sauce
1 tsp brown sugar
1 tsp instant beef stock
1 tsp sesame oil
1 clove garlic, finely sliced
1 medium-sized onion, sliced
1 red pepper
1 green pepper
1 stalk celery
1 Tbsp clarified butter
2 tsp cornflour
2 Tbsp water

Cut lamb's liver in 7 mm-thick slices, then cut slices into strips the same width, and 6–7 cm long. Put into a bowl with soya sauce, brown sugar, instant stock, sesame oil and very finely sliced garlic.

Slice onion, peppers and celery in strips fairly similar in size to liver.

Cook onion in clarified butter in covered non-stick pan over low heat for 3–4 minutes until transparent. Meanwhile, mix cornflour and water to a paste, ready to add to cooked liver. Raise heat, add peppers and celery, and stir-fry until tender and crisp.

Remove vegetables from pan using slotted spoon. Still over high heat, add liver (without liquid), and toss until no longer pink, about 2 minutes. Add remaining marinade, then cornflour to thicken the glaze. Stir in cooked vegetables.

Serve immediately, on rice or noodles.

Pan-Fried Liver

Briefly cooked lamb's liver is tender, moist and delicious.

For 4 servings:
400 g lambs' liver (in 5 mm slices)
1/4 cup flour
1/2 tsp garlic salt
1/2 tsp freshly ground pepper
1/2 tsp nutmeg
butter
1/2 cup red or white wine or apple juice (optional)
1–2 tsp Worcestershire sauce or dark soya sauce

Slice lambs' liver thinly, then pat each slice dry. Mix flour, garlic salt, pepper and nutmeg in a fairly flat plate.

Heat a little butter in a large heavy frying pan. Working quickly, turn 3 or 4 slices of liver in the flour mixture, then fry in hot pan, about 30 seconds per side. Remove from pan when no pink juice comes out of a cut in the centre of each slice. Cook remaining liver, adding more butter as needed.

Serve, without sauce or make a sauce by browning 2 teaspoons of the flour mixture in the same amount of butter, then adding the wine or apple juice and Worcestershire or soya sauce.

Season carefully.

Liver and Bacon Kebabs

Cut lambs' liver into 2 cm cubes.

Sprinkle with chopped sage and lemon juice.

De-rind bacon, cut in shorter lengths, spread with mixed mustard. Wrap cubes in bacon and thread on short skewers.

Cook gently in butter in which an onion has been fried, turning to brown all sides. Do not overcook liver.

Kidney Casserole

Slice kidneys if you prefer not to see their anatomical details! Serve unthickened, or thickened over rice.

For 4 servings:
500 g lambs' (or ox) kidneys
2 onions, chopped
2 cloves garlic, chopped
1 tsp grated root ginger
3 Tbsp sherry
2 Tbsp dark soya sauce
1 Tbsp Worcestershire sauce
1/2 tsp sesame oil
1/2 cup water

Halve, chop or slice kidneys as desired.

Mix with remaining ingredients in a double boiler or covered casserole.

Simmer gently or cook at 150°C for 1 hour. Just before serving add finely chopped chives, parsley or fresh coriander. Thicken, if desired, using cornflour stirred to a paste with cold water.

Sherried Kidneys

This is a very quick but delicious recipe, suitable for one as a main course, or for two as a starter.

For 1–2 servings:
2 lambs' kidneys or 100 g calves kidneys
25 g butter
1 clove garlic
1/4 cup finely chopped onion or shallot
1 tsp flour
2 Tbsp sherry
1/4 cup water
fresh or dried herbs

Halve lambs' kidneys lengthwise. Remove fat and membrane and slice very thinly. Rinse with cold water and drain.

Heat half the butter in a medium-sized pan. As soon as it turns straw-coloured, add kidneys, toss over high heat for 30–60 seconds, until all pinkness is gone. Remove from pan. In remaining butter cook finely chopped garlic and onion or shallot for 2–3 minutes. Stir in flour, cook for a few seconds longer, then add dry, medium or sweet sherry and water.

Add thyme, tarragon, parsley to suit your taste, add liquid from cooked kidneys, and let sauce simmer for 2–3 minutes. Stir in kidneys and reheat without boiling.

Serve on toast, noodles or rice.
Variations:
Cook chopped mushrooms with the shallots.

Quick Kidneys

For 2–3 servings:
6 lambs' kidneys (bout 300g)
2 rashers bacon (coarsely chopped)
1 Tbsp flour
1/4 cup water
1 tsp dark soya sauce
1/4 tsp salt
freshly ground black pepper

Halve then slice kidneys, discarding all fat and membrane.

Combine all of the ingredients in a bowl or casserole. Cover and microwave at Full power for 6 minutes. Sprinkle with parsley.

Serve on toast, rice, or noodles.

Beef

How lucky we are that beef, which has become a luxury item in so many parts of the world, is still reasonably priced here. We are lucky to live in a country where grass grows so well, and where our grass-eating cattle thrive.

In the same way that our ideas about lamb have changed, due to demand, and more sophisticated boning and trimming, beef is also getting a new image.

The smaller, lean cuts are becoming popular, and are likely to become more so, as consumers realise that *all* the meat they are buying is edible, and the slightly higher prices are justified.

I hope that you will use the information in this chapter to learn to recognise different beef cuts, and to cook them so that you get the best from each.

Whether you fancy a juicy roast, a sizzling steak, some quick-cooking thin slices, or an aromatic stew or casserole, you will get best value for your money if you know exactly what to buy, and of course, the best way to cook it.

If in doubt, ask your butcher. The more you know, the better are your chances of finishing up with exactly what you want.

Cook 'n' Carve Beef

Roast beef and corned beef are part of our cooking heritage. It is important to know exactly what roast (or pot-roast or corned beef) to choose, and to know how to cook it, to make sure you get maximum enjoyment, and best value for your money. If you are not sure what cut to use, choose a quiet time to ask the butcher at your supermarket or butcher's shop for help. I think it is important to realise that bright red beef is not necessarily the best! Aging and hanging improve both the tenderness and flavour of beef, but the colour of such beef may well be darker.

And last but not least, after you have chosen and cooked your meat carefully — use a sharp carving knife, and cut across the grain of the meat. The cuts shown below are boneless, easy to carve cuts. Learn how to recognise and cook them.

EYE FILLET ROAST: The most tender beef roast. Expensive, but very little wastage. Cooks in a short time, with little shrinkage. Whole fillet weighs about 1.5 kg; halves (pictured) weigh about 750 g each.

RIB-EYE ROAST: Tender with more flavour than fillet. Does not have the fat cover of sirloin, but has a streak of fat running through roast. A good special occasion roast for large or small groups.

SIRLOIN ROAST (UNROLLED): Similar in tenderness and price to rib-eye. Recognisable by fat cover on one side (roast this side up). A special occasion roast for large or small groups.

RUMP ROASTS: Can be cut large or small (from tip of rump).
    Excellent flavour. Not as tender as above cuts from loin. Best cooked pink. Recognisable by heavy fat cover on one side.

TOPSIDE ROAST: Not as tender as rump or loin roasts but good flavour, and tender if cooked pink. Roast corner-cut, choose piece 1.5 kg or more.

FLANK SKIRT: Fairly thin, lean, 'leaf-shaped' beef cut from lower belly area. Barbecue, grill or pan grill. Marinate first, undercook, then carve thinly in diagonal slices across grain. Good flavour.

BOLAR POT-ROAST: Cut from the point end of the blade. Not tender enough to roast. Brown and cook in covered container with added liquid, on stove-top or in oven.

ROLLED CHUCK POT-ROAST: Cut from shoulder. Rolled compactly and tied. Brown and cook in a little liquid in tightly covered container on low heat, on stove-top or in oven.

CORNED SILVERSIDE AND BRISKET: Silverside is lean, usually with fat cover on one side. Brisket is rolled, sometimes streaky. Both require long simmering, immersed in water.

Ⓜ Microwaved Roast Beef

I find that tender roasts of beef up to 1¹/₂ kg microwave very well at Medium (50% power). Large roasts or tougher, rolled roasts I prefer to cook conventionally.

For successful tender roasts for 3–6 people, choose a roast from the rib eye (sometimes called Scotch fillet or Cube Roll) or the boneless loin (or striploin or sirloin). For a small roast for 2–3 people, ask for the triangular tip or the last cut from the rump (less expensive), or the fillet (most tender and most expensive).

Trim any thick pieces of fat from meat, leaving an even coating. Tie meat in several places if you want round, compact slices; otherwise, leave it untied. Weigh meat to estimate approximate cooking time.

Make a paste of equal parts of dry mustard and dark soya sauce and rub the sides (not the ends) of the meat with it, if desired.

Stand meat on a ridged or elevated roasting pan, fat side down. Estimate cooking time, turn after half the time.

Cook at Medium (50% power) allowing:

Rare	10–13 min. per 500 g
Medium	14–16 min. per 500 g
Well done	18–20 min. per 500 g

	Internal temp when cooked	Internal temp after standing
Rare	50°C (125°F)	62°C (145°F)
Medium	60°C (135°–140°F)	65°C (150°F)
Well Done	65°C (145°F–150°F)	70°C (160°F)

Beef will be more tender when cooked rare or medium. Well-done meat will be drier and tougher. If time is short, cook at Medium-High (70% power) and reduce cooking times accordingly.

> **Note:**
> The instructions given here do not apply to 'rolled roasts' of the cheaper type, prepared ahead, skewered, and tied securely. These often include less tender, streaky meat rolled around larger lean muscles and require longer, slower cooking, sometimes in covered pans, to ensure tenderness. These 'roasts' should not be cooked rare or pink but to a 'well-done' stage.

> The best way to find out about the names of cuts in your area, the advantages of each, and their relative prices, is to talk to your butcher at a time when the store or counter is quiet.

Ⓒ Roast Eye Fillet

An eye fillet weighs about 1.5 kg and is a fairly long, tapering muscle. Half of this, i.e. a 750 g roast, yields about 4 servings.

Because it is so tender, this roast can be cooked quickly at a high temperature without toughening or drying out. For preference, roast the thick end of the fillet. If roasting the tapered end, tuck it under, and tie it in place.

1 (750 g) piece of eye fillet
1 Tbsp butter
2 tsp brandy or sherry
1 tsp dark soya sauce

Remove any silvery membrane on surface of fillet, since this causes shape of fillet to distort during cooking.

Tie with string in several places, to keep shape compact and round. Melt butter, add remaining ingredients, and brush over all surfaces of meat. Roast uncovered, preferably on a rack at 200°C for 20–30 minutes, turning several times and basting with remaining butter mixture.

Internal temperature should be about 50°C (125°F) for rare, about 55°C (130°F) for medium.

Leave to stand in a warm place for 10 minutes.

Ⓜ Microwaved Fillet

1 (750 g) eye fillet roast
1 Tbsp dry mustard
2 tsp dark soya sauce
2 tsp oil

Select an evenly shaped piece of eye fillet. Trim and tie as in previous recipe. Brush meat with paste made from mustard, soya sauce and oil.

Shield upper ends of roasts with two strips of foil, each 2 cm × 6 cm. Stand roast on rack or inverted plate on larger plate. Roast uncovered, from room temperature, at Medium (50% power), allowing about 12 minutes per 500 g. Turn meat over, halfway through estimated cooking time, and remove foil shields. Meat thermometer should read 50°C (125°F) for rare, 55°C (130°F) for medium. Cover roast with foil and leave to stand in a warm place for 10 minutes before slicing. (Temperature will rise during this time.)

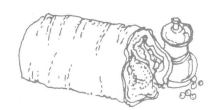

Ⓒ Roast Rib-Eye or Sirloin

These are my favourite 'special occasion' family roasts. Rib-eye and sirloin roasts are similar in tenderness and flavour, and are best roasted uncovered, at a moderate temperature, with fatty surface uppermost, since this helps to baste the meat as it cooks.

1 (1.5–3 kg) rib-eye or sirloin roast
1 Tbsp dry or mixed mustard
2–3 tsp dark soya sauce

Tie the roast at intervals to keep it compactly round. Mix mustard and soya sauce to a paste and brush over meat.

Place the meat on a rack or in an uncovered roasting pan (with no extra fat, water, sugar or flour) and cook in a preheated oven at 160°C–170°C for 1¹/₂ hours. Lift the meat from the roasting pan, leave it to stand in a warm place for 15 minutes before carving it. Make gravy from the pan drippings. Beef cooked according to the above instructions should be brown on the outside and pink in the middle (with an internal temperature of about 60°C (140°F).

For a pinker or well-done roast decrease or increase the cooking time by about 15 minutes.

Ⓜ Microwaved Rib-Eye or Sirloin

Microwave roasts of 1.5 kg or less.

Trim excess fat, leaving an even covering. Prepare as above. Stand meat on ridged or elevated roasting pan, fat side down. Cook at Medium (50% power). (See column 1 for cooking times and power levels.)

Cover with foil. Stand in warm place 10–15 minutes before slicing.
Note:
If meat is long and thin, shield ends for first half of cooking time.

> **How long do stews and casseroles take to cook?**
> Cooking time varies with the amount of meat, the type of meat, the cooking container, and the initial temperature of the meat. Large amounts of meat take a long time to heat through in an oven. If you bring them to simmering point on the top of the stove first, you reduce the oven cooking times considerably. Stews often heat faster, so cook more quickly than casseroles. Cast-iron containers cook both stews and casseroles more quickly than pottery ones.

C Roast Rump or Topside

These roasts are best cooked rare or pink, then cut very thinly across the grain of the meat.

1 (1.5–2 kg) roast of rump or topside
1–2 cloves garlic (optional)
1 Tbsp dry mustard
1 Tbsp dark soya sauce
1 Tbsp cooking oil

If you like a mild garlic flavour in your roast beef, cut the garlic into slivers and push it into small slits in the meat.

Mix the dry mustard, soya sauce and cooking oil to a thick paste and brush evenly over meat. Place the roast, fat side up, in a rack over a roasting pan or directly in the fry pan. Do not add extra fat.

Roast, uncovered, at 160°C for about 1½ hours, or until a meat thermometer registers

from 50°C (125°F) for rare
to 60°C (140°F) for medium.

Leave meat to stand in a warm place for 15 minutes before slicing thinly across the grain.

M Microwaving Small Rump Roasts

The small triangular tip of rump, or the 'last cut from the rump' makes a good small roast. It is usually cut so it weighs 500–700 g. Trim away most of the fat.

Rub meat with a paste made from 1 tablespoon mixed mustard and 2 teaspoons dark soya sauce.

Stand meat on a rack, fat side down. Microwave at medium (50% power) allowing 15 minutes per 500 g. Turn meat once during cooking.

Cover loosely with foil and leave to stand in a warm place for 10 minutes before slicing thinly across the grain.
Note:
I think that large rump and topsides roasts are best cooked conventionally.

C Gravy

Serve thin, dark gravy or unthickened pan juices with roast beef.

When roasting at low temperatures, spread a coating on the meat before cooking, since this helps to produce dark pan drippings.

Pour off most of the fat from pan. Stir in 1 tablespoon flour for four servings, brown if necessary, then add about 1½ cups water and vegetable liquid. Simmer, incorporating pan drippings, strain and season.

C M Special Occasion Sauce

Make a dark, tangy gravy by pouring the fat from the roasting pan, stirring in 1–2 tablespoons of good mixed mustard to the drippings, then adding about 1 cup of liquid, about half of which is dry red (or white) wine. Use vegetable cooking liquid or water for the rest.

Serving Roast Beef

Traditional accompaniments include mustard, horseradish sauce and Yorkshire pudding or popovers. For special occasion dinners I like to offer a selection of accompaniments like these, with several different mustards.

C Beef Pot-Roasts

Bolar and rolled chuck make good pot-roasts. Buy a bigger pot-roast than you think you need since leftovers may be sliced and reheated in gravy most successfully, and pot-roasts always shrink during cooking. Vary the liquids you use until you find your favourites.

For 6–8 servings:
1 (2 kg) bolar or rolled chuck pot-roast
flour
1 Tbsp clarified butter
1–2 onions
1 Tbsp dark soya sauce or
  Worcestershire sauce
2 tsp mixed mustard (optional)
1 cup apple juice, or wine, or flat beer,
  or water

For preference, brown then cook pot-roast in a heavy metal casserole dish or pot. Otherwise, brown meat in large frying pan, then transfer to casserole. Flour meat lightly and turn in heated clarified butter, browning all sides evenly. Do not hurry this step.

Brown quartered onions with meat. Add remaining ingredients, cover very tightly, and simmer on low heat for 1½–2 hours or until meat is tender, turning every 30 minutes.
Or after browning transfer to oven. Cook for same time at 150°C. Strain, skim then thicken juices with cornflour paste, or boil them down until thick. Adjust seasonings.
Variation:
Cook root vegetables with meat during last hour of cooking if desired.

Mustard Sauce
2 Tbsp butter
2 Tbsp flour
1 Tbsp mixed mustard
1 cup beef cooking liquid or ½ cup
  beef liquid and ½ cup water
2 tsp wine vinegar (optional) or
2–3 Tbsp cream or sour cream
  (optional)

Heat butter and flour at Full power for 1 minute. Stir in the mixed mustard, then ½ cup beef cooking liquid. Heat until mixture bubbles and thickens. Stir and taste.

Add another ½ cup more cooking liquid, or water if sauce is too salty. Add wine vinegar if you like a tangy sauce, cream or sour cream if you want to soften the flavours.

Corned Beef

Corned beef is one of my favourite meats. I like it best served steaming and hot, surrounded by boiled vegetables and served with mustard or parsley sauce. For preference, cook in a fairly large piece, 1–2 kg.

Two cuts of beef are usually 'corned' or salted — brisket and silverside. Brisket, which usually costs less per kilogram, has a higher proportion of fat and is rolled and tied to make sure it keeps its shape during cooking. Silverside is lean and is not rolled. It often has an outer layer of fat along one side.

Simmer rather than boil corned beef. If you can keep the heat so the surface of the water is barely moving, the meat will be more tender.

C Simmered Corned Beef

Choose a saucepan into which the meat will just fit. Cover the meat with water. Add flavourings if you like. To a 1–2 kg piece of meat I add 1 onion, 2 cloves garlic, 2 bay leaves, a stalk of celery, a large sprig of parsley and a small sprig of thyme. Cook for 2½ hours. Allow about an hour longer if cooking rolled brisket.

Although it is traditional to boil potatoes, carrots and cabbage in the pot with the corned beef, this is not as simple as it sounds. It is much easier to cook these vegetables in different pots, adding some of the corned beef cooking liquid instead of water.

M Microwaved Silverside

This method saves time and prevents smells and steam in the kitchen.

Microwaved Silverside

1–1.5 kg corned silverside
*Flavourings: bay leaf, garlic clove,
parsley, celery, mustard seeds,
peppercorns, orange rind, coriander
seeds, etc.*
2 cups boiling water

Soak the meat for 1–2 hours in cold water if you think it may be salty.

Place the drained beef in a casserole with whatever seasonings you have and like. Pour the boiling water over the meat. Cook at Defrost (30% power) for 30 minutes per 500 g. Turn twice during cooking.

Leave to stand in cooking liquid for 30–45 minutes before serving hot with mustard sauce.

c Bagged Silverside

This is an excellent way to cook a large piece of silverside.

1 (2–3 kg) piece of silverside
1–2 onions, quartered
2 cloves garlic, halved
1 large stalk parsley
2–4 cloves
1 tsp mustard seeds
½ tsp celery seeds
1 bay leaf
½ tsp dill seed
1 cup water

Put the meat in a large oven bag, without holes punched in it, adding whatever seasonings you like and have. Tie the bag, leaving a finger-sized opening to allow steam to

escape. Stand the bagged meat in a roasting pan, bake at 130°C for 2½–3 hours, turning the bag over two or three times. Leave it to stand in the bag for 20–30 minutes, then pour off the liquid.

Serve hot with chosen vegetables or place the meat in a clean bag with about a cup of strained cooking liquid.

Refrigerate and replace meat in liquid in bag after each use. It will remain moist, juicy and delicious, for a week or more.

Which Steak?

FILLET STEAK: The most tender, and the most expensive.

It has a fine grain and can be reheated or kept warm without toughening.

RIB-EYE STEAK: Cut from the cube roll (or scotch fillet).

Tender, with more flavour than fillet steak.

Marbled meat, often with a curved piece of fat near middle of steak and no fat layer around edge.

SIRLOIN STEAK: Cut from the striploin.

Similar price, flavour and tenderness to rib-eye. There is a strip of fat around one side. Slightly different texture from rib-eye.

T-BONE STEAK: Has a T-shaped bone with a large piece of sirloin on one side and a small eye of fillet on the other.

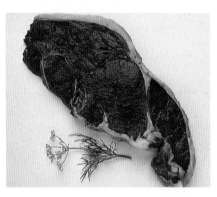

RUMP STEAK: Vary in size, since they are slices cut from a triangular piece of meat.

Have a solid layer of fat along one side.

Not as tender as previous steaks, but excellent flavour.

CROSS-CUT BLADE STEAK: Is cut from beside the shoulder-blade bone. Good flavour, coarser grain, tough if overcooked.

Recognisable by strip of gristle down centre of steak.

**THIN FLANK or
SKIRT FLANK STEAK:**
Excellent flavour.

Needs marinating and undercooking to ensure tenderness. Slice diagonally across grain after cooking in one large piece.

OX-HEART STEAK: An ox-heart can be cut into lots of diagonal slices which need a little trimming to produce a steak-like appearance. Fine, close texture. Tender if cooked rare.

Use meat hammer for texture more like other steaks.

Good flavour — excellent value for money.

HAMBURGERS: Minced fairly lean steak, formed into a patty can be treated like tender steaks. If cooked rare is moist. For New Zealand taste (cooked longer) add soft breadcrumbs with seasoning, for moistness.

C Cooking Tender Steaks

Oven Grilling
Preheat grill, oil steak, cook very close to heat.

It can be difficult to get a domestic oven grill hot enough to brown a steak on the outside before it is overcooked in the middle.

Barbecuing
Produces excellent flavour.

Requires some skill preparing the fire then the ashes, and estimating cooking time, distance from ashes, etc.

Pan Grilling
Reliable and practical. Cast iron pan seems to produce best results. Difficult to brown steaks in pan with non-stick finish.

Best for steaks without bones.

C Pan Grilling Steak

Have steak and marinade at room temperature. Lift steak from marinade.

Place steak in preheated, oiled cast iron or heavy-bottomed pan over high heat. Do not crowd pan. Too many steaks lower the temperature.

Turn after 1–2 minutes or when surface is nicely browned. Cook second side over high heat then lower heat and cook to desired degree. Keep warm.

Add stock, vegetable water and/or remaining marinade to pan.

Scrape bits from bottom of pan. Reduce until 1–2 tablespoons per steak remain.

Swirl a teaspoon of butter per steak into the reduced liquid in the pan.

Pour the butter-thickened glaze over the steak.

Serve immediately.

M Microwaving Steak

Preheat a browning dish for 6 minutes at Full power, or according to manufacturers' instructions.

Add (marinated) steak to hot browning dish. Microwave at Full power for 1 minute.

Turn steak, microwave at Full power for 1 minute longer, or to desired doneness. Do not overcook.

The steak photographed on page 101 is a 3 cm slice of rump, marinated, pan-grilled and thinly sliced, as in the recipe for 'Barbecued' Flank Skirt on page 109.

Tenderise Steaks Before Cooking

Flatten very tender steaks using a rolling pin, with steak between two sheets of plastic.

Heavy pressure may make steak disintegrate.

Stand steaks in marinade for 1–48 hours before cooking, e.g. per steak: 1 teaspoon lemon juice, oil and dark soya sauce, ¼ teaspoon brown sugar, garlic to taste
Or per steak:
1 tablespoon wine, 1 teaspoon oil, herbs and garlic to taste.

Pound tougher steaks using a meat hammer.

Always snip connective tissue at edges to prevent steak curling during cooking.

Testing 'Doneness'

Rare, or underdone steaks feel soft and spongy, as when you relax your hand and press the area between thumb and hand.

Medium steaks feel firmer and springier, as it feels if you flex your fingers and press the same area.

Well done steaks feel very firm (and may be tough) as when you make a tight fist and press the same area.

'Barbecued' Flank Skirt

C Fillet Steak Dinner

When it is important to have a very tender steak, choose fillet.

Because the fillet tapers, one end narrows and is sliced into small steaks. These look bigger if 'butterflied', i.e. cut double thickness, then cut nearly through leaving a hinge, and opened flat.

Plan timing carefully, organising vegetables before you start to cook the steak. Choose vegetables which will not drown the delicate flavour of the steak.

Snip edges then marinate fillet steak for extra flavour rather than tenderness, for a short time. Use a little white or red wine, oil and herbs.

Pan grill as desired, then keep warm. Add sliced mushrooms to the pan with a little butter, then deglaze the pan with vegetable liquid or stock. Add herbs such as thyme, tarragon or parsley. Add a little cream to the syrupy liquid and mushrooms in pan and pour over steak.

C Steak Diane

For this recipe thin slices of tender steak are cooked very quickly in a very hot pan in a simple but delicious sauce. For best results steaks should be pink in the middle.

For 2 servings:
about 200 g thinly sliced tender steak
2 Tbsp butter
2 Tbsp chopped shallots
1–2 Tbsp Worcestershire sauce
2 Tbsp chopped parsley
1–2 Tbsp brandy (optional)

Cut two steaks (each about 7 mm thick) or rib-eye or striploin steak, or four 5 mm slices of fillet steak.

Bang steaks gently between two sheets of plastic, using a rolling pin. Do not let the steaks disintegrate.

Heat butter and cook shallots until tender. Push shallots aside and raise heat in pan.

Brown steaks quickly over high heat. Add sauce to taste, turning steaks. Sprinkle with parsley, add brandy, turn meat, flame carefully.

Serve immediately with pan juices.

C Budget Steak Dinner

Slice ox-heart diagonally into steaks. Trim each to an acceptable shape, (and mince or stew trimmings).

Bang with a meat hammer to modify the fine texture and make it more steak-like.

Marinate for at least 1 hour, using dark soya sauce, and lemon juice with a little oil, garlic, herbs, etc.

Organise vegetables before you start to cook steak. Onion rings take quite a long time to cook — cook them in the pan before the steak, or in another pan.

Pan grill steaks to desired degree. Add remaining marinade and vegetable liquid to deglaze pan, then add onion rings. Spoon over steaks and serve immediately.

Note:
I suggest that you do not tell the diners what cut of steak they are eating, in case you spoil their appetites.

C 'Barbecued' Flank Skirt

If you like steak cooked so that it is still pink you should try this recipe. A relatively inexpensive steak is marinated, cooked briefly in a heavy pan, then sliced thinly across the grain to produce strips of juicy, well-flavoured meat. The steak cut used is called thin flank, or flank skirt.

Ask for the whole steak. It weighs about 500–600 g, and is oval, or leaf-shaped, more pointed at one end, and is about 1–2 cm thick.

Score both flat surfaces into diamond shapes using a sharp knife. The cuts should be only 2–3 mm deep, but will enable the marinade to penetrate better.

Place the meat in a heavy plastic bag, so it lies flat. Add 2 tablespoons each of dark soya sauce, lemon juice (or wine vinegar) and oil.

Add 2 or 3 crushed garlic cloves. Squeeze all air from the bag and secure tightly.

Marinate at room temperature for at least 2 hours. Drain and pan grill in a large, heavy, preheated frying pan, allowing 3–4 minutes per side.

To check whether the meat is cooked to the right stage, cut down to the centre (along the grain of the meat) with a sharp knife.

Leave the cooked steak to stand in a warm place for 5–10 minutes before cutting it into very thin slices, across the grain of the meat, with the knife at a 45° angle to the board.

C Beef Schnitzels

Select thinly cut slices of thick flank silverside or topside allowing about 100 g per serving. Remove fat and connective tissue, cutting each slice into several smaller pieces if desired.

Coat pieces lightly with flour if you want a thick coating.

Mix ½ teaspoon garlic salt or onion salt and ½ teaspoon curry powder or celery salt with 1 tablespoon water, white wine or dry sherry. Add finely chopped fresh herbs if you like, then add an egg. Beat only until white and yolk are combined. Dip the flour-coated or plain schnitzels in the egg, then in fine, dry breadcrumbs.

Let the coated meat stand on a rack, to dry both sides (so the coating sticks) for 5–15 minutes before cooking.

Heat a pan with 5 mm deep clarified butter. When very hot add the meat and cook until the coating is golden brown on both sides. Serve as soon as possible, with a squeeze of lemon juice if desired.

C Barbecued Beef

For 2 servings:
2 hamburger buns or lengths of
    French bread
2 Tbsp tomato ketchup
2 tsp tomato paste
1 Tbsp brown sugar
2 tsp Worcestershire sauce
1 tsp mixed mustard
1 onion, finely chopped
1 Tbsp butter
200 g thinly sliced beef

Split bread and toast cut surfaces. Mix together next five ingredients and put aside.

Chop onion finely.

Melt butter in a frying pan, add onion and cook gently until tender.

Raise heat, cook beef lightly, turning constantly, then add sauce mixture and heat until boiling.

Serve on toasted bread, with salad vegetables.

M Barbecued Beef

For 2 servings:
2 hamburger buns or lengths of
    French bread
1 mild onion, very finely chopped
1 Tbsp oil
2 Tbsp tomato ketchup
2 tsp tomato paste
1 Tbsp brown sugar
2 tsp Worcestershire sauce
1 tsp mixed mustard
200 g thinly sliced raw or cooked beef

Split bread and toast, if desired.

Mix onion and oil in covered microwave dish. Cook at Full power for 3 minutes. Add next five ingredients. Heat for 3 minutes or until sauce bubbles. Stir in beef, coating well with sauce. Cover. If using raw beef, microwave for 3–4 minutes, until beef loses its pink colour. Heat cooked beef for 1–2 minutes or until hot.

Spoon meat and sauce into buns. Reheat if desired. Serve with salad.

M Beef Stroganoff

For 2–3 servings:
250 g rump steak, sliced 5 mm thick
50 g butter
2 onions, sliced
1 cup (100 g) sliced mushrooms
1 Tbsp flour
½ tsp paprika
½ cup white wine
2 tsp tomato paste (optional)
¼ cup sour cream
¾ tsp salt
¼ cup chopped parsley

Slice rump steak into 5mm ribbons, melt butter in large microwave dish.

Add onions, mix, cover and cook at Full power for 4 minutes.

Add mushrooms, the flour-coated meat and paprika. Stir, cover, and

cook for 2–3 minutes until meat loses its pinkness.

Stir in wine, tomato (if used), heat for 1 minute or until liquid thickens. Stir in sour cream and half the parsley. Reheat but do not boil.

Sprinkle with remaining parsley. Serve with noodles.

When you buy beef, undo the packet in which you get it. Add a dash of light soya sauce and a tablespoon or two of lemon juice before you refrigerate it. This simple marinade will keep the refrigerated meat fresh for longer, and will make it more tender. You can use it later, in any way you want, without worrying about the extra ingredients you have added.

B C Peanutty Beefstrips

For 3–4 servings:
400 g thinly sliced beef schnitzels
1 onion, quartered
2 cloves garlic
2 tsp grated root ginger
1 tsp freshly ground coriander
2 Tbsp lemon juice
2 tsp dark soya sauce
¼ cup brown sugar
¼ cup peanut butter

Slice beef into 1 cm strips, as long as possible. Thread strips onto bamboo skewers, in concertina fashion.

Combine remaining ingredients in food processor. Process until smooth. Add water to thin to thick cream consistency if necessary.

Stand skewers, meat-ends down, in a small bowl. Pour marinade over them. Leave to stand for 15–30 minutes.

Drain and grill or barbecue close to heat until meat loses its pinkness.

Heat remaining marinade until boiling. Serve as a dipping sauce with meat.

The most convenient casserole dishes are those in which you can brown the meat etc., add the liquid and bring to simmering point on the stove top, then transfer to the oven. It is an advantage if the dish can be taken to the table for serving, also refrigerated or frozen, and put in the microwave for thawing and reheating. Corningware casserole dishes will fulfil all these functions. They do not brown without some sticking, however, and lids do not fit tightly.

Stir-Fried Beef

C M Stir-Fried Beef

For this recipe choose very thin slices of beef, cut across the grain of the meat, from flank skirt, chuck or blade steak. Each piece of thick steak should be cut so it is about 1 cm × 5 cm.

Use regular stir-frying method or microwave as below.

For 4 servings:
500 g thinly sliced beef
2 cloves garlic
4 Tbsp oil
1 Tbsp sherry
1 Tbsp dark soya sauce
2 tsp cornflour
2 tsp brown sugar
1 tsp instant beef stock
400 g sliced vegetables

Put sliced meat in an oven bag with half the oil and all remaining ingredients except the vegetables. Knead bag thoroughly to mix. Leave to stand for at least 15 minutes.

Select quick-cooking tender vegetables, e.g. mushrooms, snow peas, broccoli, cauliflower, celery, spring onions, young cabbage, bean sprouts, spinach. Slice into strips like meat.

Coat with remaining oil. Cover and microwave at Full power for 3–4 minutes, until just tender.

Microwave meat in oven bag for 3–4 minutes at Full power, until no longer pink. Add to vegetables, stirring to coat.

Serve immediately or add a little extra cornflour paste if vegetables have made liquid, and microwave for 30 second to thicken. Serve on rice.

C Quick Curried Beef

For 4 servings:
400 g thinly sliced beef
1 clove garlic, crushed
1 tsp grated root ginger
2 tsp lemon juice
1 Tbsp butter
1 onion, chopped
2 tsp curry powder
¼ cup tomato relish or other chutney
1 tsp dark soya sauce

Cut thinly sliced beef (from any cut) into pieces about 1–4 cm, trimming away all fat and connective tissue. Mix with garlic, ginger and lemon juice. Leave to stand for at least 15 minutes.

In a fairly large pan melt butter and cook onion gently until tender. Add curry powder, raise heat and add marinated beef. Stir over high heat until no longer pink. Add relish or sauce and soya sauce, and stir to coat.

Serve immediately on rice with sliced kiwifruit, toasted coconut or other curry accompaniments.

M Beef (or Pork) Olives

These cook in an unbelievably short time. Overcooking toughens them so take care!

For 4 servings:
400 g thinly sliced beef or pork schnitzels
Stuffing:
½ cup cooked rice
½ cup chopped pineapple
3 spring onions
2 Tbsp beaten raw egg
¼ tsp curry powder
Coating:
1 Tbsp sherry
1 Tbsp dark soya sauce
1 Tbsp tomato paste
2 tsp cornflour

Trim connective tissue and fat from schnitzels. Cut into eight pieces. If pieces aren't thin enough, place between sheets of plastic and pound with a rolling pin.

Mix stuffing ingredients. Divide among eight schnitzels. Roll each up, making parcels filled with stuffing. Arrange evenly around the edge of a circular dish (in a ring pan) so rolls barely touch.

Mix coating ingredients. Brush over meat. Cover and cook at Full power for 4–6 minutes, turning rolls after 3 minutes. Rolls should be firm when cooked. Stand for 3–4 minutes in a warm place before serving.

> Do not trim away all gristle before stewing, because much of it softens and helps the 'body' of the stew later on.

Quick Curried Beef

M Beef Roulades

For 4 servings beat out 400 g thinly sliced, trimmed topside or silverside schnitzel, using a meat hammer or rolling pin. Cut into eight evenly sized pieces.

Roll up each piece, with small whole, or strips of larger, mild cucumber pickles (or lightly cooked whole green beans), a red pepper strip, and a thin piece of ham if desired.

Mix a paste of 2 tablespoons medium sherry, 1 tablespoon dark soya sauce, 1 tablespoon tomato paste and 2 teaspoons cornflour.

Brush over the beef roulades and arrange in one layer in a microwave dish. Cover and microwave at Full power for 4–5 minutes, until meat is evenly firm. Stand for 3–4 minutes in a warm place before serving.

C Swiss Steak

For 4 servings:
600 g chuck steak, sliced 10 mm thick
¼ cup flour
2–3 Tbsp oil
2 large onions, sliced
2 cloves garlic, chopped
1 packet tomato soup mix
2 cups water
2 tsp Worcestershire sauce

Coat steak thickly with flour. Pound meat on both sides (preferably with a meat hammer) until it is 5 mm thick and has absorbed the flour.

Cut into eight pieces. Brown thoroughly in hot oil.

Lightly brown onions and garlic in extra oil if necessary. Sprinkle half in buttered or sprayed casserole dish, then arrange meat in overlapping slices. Top with remaining onion mixture.

Mix tomato soup, water and Worcestershire sauce. Pour over meat and onions. Cover tightly, using foil under lid if necessary. Bake at 150°C for 1½–2 hours.
Variation:
Replace soup mix and 1 cup water with tomato purée if preferred. Adjust seasoning before serving.

> For stews, use a large, heavy-bottomed saucepan with a well-fitting lid. On a solid-element electric stove, or a smooth-top surface, make sure the saucepan has a bottom which will sit flat.

C M Spicy Steak Casserole

For this casserole, everything is left to stand before cooking, so the meat is tenderised.

For 4–6 servings:
1 kg chuck steak
¼ cup flour
2 Tbsp brown sugar
1 tsp curry powder
½ tsp ground ginger
½ cup water
2 Tbsp vinegar
2 Tbsp tomato sauce
1 tsp Worcestershire sauce
peeled rind of 1 lemon (or orange or tangelo)

Cut the steak into strips 5×40 mm. Toss in the casserole dish with the dry ingredients, then add the liquids and mix thoroughly.

Leave to stand for 1–2 hours (or longer in a refrigerator), then stir again and place the coloured rind peeled from the citrus fruit on top of the meat.

Cover. Bake at 150°C for 1½–2 hours, or until meat is tender.

Alternatively, microwave at Full power for 10 minutes, then at Defrost (30% power) for about an hour, or until tender. Remove peel before serving on rice.

M Beef and Vegetable Casserole

For 4 servings:
750 g chuck or blade steak
¼ cup flour
2 tsp instant beef stock
2 tsp brown sugar
1 tsp paprika
¼ tsp thyme
2 onions, chopped
2 stalks celery, sliced
2 carrots, sliced thinly
1 bay leaf
1½ cups water
1 cup frozen peas
dumplings (optional)
2 Tbsp chopped parsley

Cube steak. Mix with next five ingredients in a large casserole. Add vegetables and bay leaf. Mix again. Add hot tap water and stir well. Cover. Microwave at Full power for 10 minutes, then at Defrost (30% power) for 1¼ hours or until meat is tender. Add peas after 45 minutes.

In another dish make Dumplings if desired (see page 32). Add to stew and sprinkle with parsley.

> The tougher cheaper cuts which come from well-used muscles, and which have an excellent flavour, make very good stews and casseroles.

C Rich Browned Beef Casserole

For 6 servings:
1 kg blade, chuck or skirt steak
about ¼ cup flour
about 2 Tbsp oil
2 large onions
1 cup tomato purée
1 cup beer, wine or water
1 Tbsp fresh herbs (or 1 tsp dried herbs)
2 tsp instant beef stock (or 1 tsp salt)
1 red or green pepper, sliced (optional)
4 fresh tomatoes (optional)

Dry meat with paper towels. Coat lightly with flour. For speed, cut into smaller pieces after browning thoroughly, a few pieces at a time, in a little very hot oil in a heavy pan or casserole dish.

Slice onions and brown well in remaining oil, or extra oil. Do not hurry this step, since it affects flavour and colour. Into casserole put browned onions and meat cut into serving-sized or smaller pieces.

Add purée, liquid, herbs and instant stock powder or salt. Cover and bake at 150°C, allowing about 1½–2 hours after liquid starts to simmer.

Time varies with container, amount, and meat cut used.

About 30 minutes before serving, add red or green pepper and peeled tomatoes.

M Easy Beef Stew

For 4 servings:
600 g cross-cut blade steak, pounded
1 pkt tomato soup
1 Tbsp flour
1 Tbsp Worcestershire sauce
1 tsp dark soya sauce
¼ tsp thyme
1–2 cloves garlic, chopped
1 cup water or beer

Cut pieces of blade steak in half, remove and discard gristle. Pound with a meat hammer until thin.

Place in casserole. Mix soup mix and flour. Sprinkle over meat. Add sauces, thyme and garlic and then the liquid. Cover and microwave at Full power for 5 minutes, then at Defrost (30% power) for 45 minutes, or until meat is tender.

C Oxtail Stew

When my children were small, they called this 'aeroplane stew', because the large bones, when sucked clean of meat, looked like small stubby toy aeroplanes. The gelatinous oxtail meat makes a rich, sticky stew.

For 4–6 servings:
1 large oxtail, sectioned
flour
clarified butter
2 cloves garlic
2 onions, chopped
bouquet garni
2 cups water
1 tsp instant beef stock
pepper
¼ cup chopped parsley

Cut oxtail into small individual vertebrae, coat with flour, then brown in a little clarified butter in a large heavy saucepan or casserole dish, turning often to brown evenly.

Push browned meat aside and add chopped garlic and onions, with a little more butter if necessary. Add bouquet garni, water, instant stock and freshly ground pepper to taste.

Cover tightly and simmer until meat is very tender, 2–3 hours, then leave to stand in a cold place so fat congeals on top.

Skim off fat from surface, remove bouquet garni, add chopped parsley and thicken if necessary with cornflour and water paste.

Reheat. Adjust seasoning to taste.

D Beef Jerky

Beef jerky is a spicy dried meat enjoyed as a snack or back-pack food in North America. It originated as a means of preserving meat, but is now enjoyed for its texture and flavour.

500 g lean beef schnitzels
2 Tbsp light soya sauce
1 Tbsp Worcestershire sauce
1 Tbsp tomato sauce
1 tsp garlic salt
3–4 drops Tabasco sauce

Trim schnitzels, removing all fat and connective tissue. Put in plastic bag with all other ingredients. Squeeze gently to mix.

Refrigerate for 8 hours or stand at room temperature for 4–5 hours.

Lie strips on dehydrator on racks sprayed with non-stick spray.

Dehydrate at 60–70°C for 6–8 hours until strips crack but do not break when bent. Drying time depends on thickness of meat, humidity, etc.

Store in plastic bags in freezer, for up to 6 months, or at room temperature for several weeks.

> If you want to modify a casserole recipe to cook it on top of the stove, add ingredients for thickening towards the end of the cooking time, to minimise the chance of burning.

Herbed Tripe

© **Herbed Tripe**

Tripe is partly cooked before you
buy it. Cook it gently in a well-
flavoured sauce until both tripe and
sauce are the consistency you like
them to be.

For 3–4 servings:

2 large onions, sliced
2 cloves garlic, chopped
2 Tbsp butter
500–600 g tripe
3 cups water
2 tsp instant chicken stock
1 tsp salt
1 tsp sugar
2 sprigs parsley
1–2 bay leaves
1 sprig rosemary
½ tsp thyme leaves
2 cups sliced celery
2–3 carrots, sliced
2 Tbsp tomato paste
¼ cup chopped parsley

In a heavy saucepan, cook the
onions and garlic in butter until
golden brown.

Add tripe, cut in 1 cm × 4 cm
strips, and stir constantly for 2–3
minutes. Add the water, replacing 1
cup with white table wine if
available.

Add next seven flavourings,
cover, and simmer for 1 hour.

Add celery, carrots and tomato
paste, mix well, cover and simmer
for an hour longer. Remove herbs,
and add chopped parsley. Adjust
seasonings if necessary.

Serve in soup bowls, or uncover
and simmer until liquid thickens,
then serve as a stew.

Serve with crusty bread, and a
green salad if desired.

© **Spiced Beef Tongue**

This spiced beef tongue is much
tastier than a plain unseasoned
tongue, but you can use this recipe
without the flavourings if you like.

For 8–12 servings:

1 large corned, beef tongue
water to cover
2 onions
1–2 cloves garlic
1 bay leaf
small cinnamon stick
1 piece root ginger
6 allspice berries
6 peppercorns
½ tsp coriander seeds (optional)
gelatine (see below)

Place tongue in a saucepan just big
enough to hold it. Add remaining
ingredients except gelatine, cover,
and simmer gently for 3 hours, then

pierce with a fork. If tender, remove
from heat, otherwise cook for up to
an hour longer, until tender. Lift
from cooking liquid and plunge into
cold water.

Pull off the skin and trim any
small bones and fatty pieces from
root end.

Arrange in a bowl or any suitable
mould, then pour enough water over
the tongue to cover it. Pour off this
water immediately, measuring it so
you know how much stock will be
needed for the jelly around the
meat.

Strain and skim the cooking
liquid, and save as much stock as
you need. Measure 2 level teaspoons
of gelatine for each cup of stock.
Mix the gelatine with 2–3
tablespoons of cold water or cool
stock, then leave to stand for 2–3
minutes. Pour warm stock over
gelatine. When dissolved, pour
mixture around meat and stand a
small flat plate or saucer on top.
Weigh down with any heavy
container and leave overnight until
gelatine mixture sets.

Unmould by running a knife
between meat and the bowl. The
unmoulded tongue will keep,
covered, in the refrigerator for
about a week.

Mince and Sausage Meat

I love the versatility of these inexpensive meats, and use them in many ways, with a variety of seasonings. You can grill them, barbecue them, stir-fry or roast them, microwave, bake or simmer them as the mood takes you — they should never be boring.

When a carcase is broken down into small cuts, these can generally be divided into two types — the tender ones which can be cooked by dry heat methods and the tougher cuts which need long, slow, moist cooking to make them tender.

Mince has a good flavour because it is made from those hardworking, tougher muscles. It is inexpensive and very versatile.

Different butchers use different grinders, producing fine or coarser mince and sausage meat.

Find your favourite, where the proportion of lean meat to fat and the fineness or coarseness of the grind suit you. Minced lamb is lighter in colour than minced beef, because of the colour of the lamb meat. Minced mutton is darker than lamb, with a more definite flavour. Minced pork is often paler than lamb.

In many recipes you can replace one type of minced meat with another, the flavour will vary with your choice.

These sausage recipes call for ordinary, inexpensive sausages and sausage meat, rather than the more expensive sausage products appearing in recent times. These need little 'dressing up' and should be plainly cooked and served.

Big Burgers

Hamburgers Plus

A good hamburger is delicious.
Experiment with seasonings,
cooking times and cooking methods
until you arrive at your perfect
personal formula.

Unless you like your hamburger
patty rare (red in the middle), don't
leave out the breadcrumbs, because
they keep a longer-cooked
hamburger moist and juicy.

Vary hamburger seasonings as
you would the flavours you add to
roasts, steaks, stews and casseroles.
Use combinations to characterise
the cooking of different countries.
Choose glazes and garnishes
appropriate to these.

Serve interesting and unusual
combinations of raw or cooked
vegetables and fruit with hamburger
patties, whether they are served in
buns, or without bread. Many steak
accompaniments and sauces are just
as delicious with hamburgers.

Especially if you are feeding
children, streamline your production
line. If you make more hamburgers
than you need and freeze them
individually, you have a 'fast food'

bar in your own kitchen.

Hamburger patties thaw fast, or
may be cooked from frozen when
necessary. If you feel you are
competing with fast-food outlets for
your children's custom, make sure
you have the 'trimmings' they want.

Work out the price differences,
and point out that it is often quicker
to make your own hamburgers
rather than stand in a queue waiting
for someone else to make them.

C M Hamburger Patties

For 4–8 patties:
500 g minced beef or lamb
1 slice stale bread, crumbled
2 spring onions, chopped (or 1–2 tsp
*   onion juice)*
2 tsp instant beef stock
1 tsp Worcestershire sauce
1 tsp chopped fresh herbs (optional)
1/2 tsp garlic salt
about 1/4 cup milk

Combine all ingredients except milk.
Mix lightly but thoroughly, then add
milk and mix again until mixture is

moist enough to form into patties
without cracked edges. Shape into
large patties if serving one per
person, in a hamburger bun, or into
small patties if serving two per
person on a plate with vegetables or
salad.

To grill or barbecue
Cook about 20 cm from the heat,
turning when browned.

To cook in a pan
Use a hot pan in which 2 teaspoons
oil have been heated.

Brown patties on both sides, then
lower heat until centre is cooked as
desired. To test, pierce centre with
a small knife. For most tastes, cook
until no pink juice runs out.

To microwave
Before cooking, brush the upper
surface of patty with either dark
soya sauce, Worcestershire sauce,
tomato sauce or barbecue sauce.

Microwave 1 large patty for 1 1/2
minutes. During the 2 minute
standing time, patty centre should
finish cooking and surface will turn
brown.

Variations to patty mixture
• Replace instant stock with
1 teaspoon salt.
• Add ½–1 cup grated Cheddar, or 2
tablespoons Parmesan, or 2–4
tablespoons crumbled blue vein
cheese to basic mixture.
• Replace garlic salt and milk with
finely chopped relish, tomato sauce,
etc. Start with 2 tablespoons; add
more if necessary, or add extra
water.
• Replace Worcestershire sauce
with grated horseradish.
• Replace Worcestershire sauce
with your favourite mixed mustard.
• Replace Worcestershire sauce
with dark soya sauce. Leave out
herbs.
• Add ½ teaspoon sesame oil or
1 tablespoon toasted sesame seeds.
• Press cracked peppercorns into
large hamburgers before cooking.

Big Burgers

Neither my friends nor my family
like rare hamburgers. I add crumbs
to my hamburgers because they
keep the meat moist and juicy when
cooked medium or well done.

For 4 burgers:
500 g minced lamb or beef
1 thick slice bread, crumbled
1 Tbsp tomato ketchup
1 tsp dark soya sauce
2 tsp instant beef stock
2 spring onions, finely chopped

Combine all ingredients in the order
given, until evenly mixed. Add a
little milk if mixture seems firm. Cut
mixture in four. Shape each quarter
into a hamburger. Brush lightly with
soya sauce.

To cook in browning dish
Heat browning dish for 6 minutes.
Place burgers on hot surface. Cook
at Full power.
For 2 burgers, cook for 2
minutes, turn and cook for 1–2
minutes more.
For 4 burgers, cook for 2
minutes, turn and cook for 3–4
minutes more.

Without a browning dish
Cook at Full power.
For 2 burgers, cook for 2
minutes, turn and cook for 2–3
minutes more.
For 4 burgers, cook for 3
minutes, turn, and cook for 3–4
minutes more.

Leave all burgers to stand for 2–3
minutes after cooking.

Hamburger Glazes and Sauces

Patties look and taste better if their
outer surfaces are glazed. Mixtures

which contain sugar in any form
should be added close to the end of
the cooking time, or they will burn
before the patty is cooked.
Suggested glazes:
Use tomato or barbecue sauce, soya
sauce, teriyaki sauce, or
Worcestershire sauce (plain, or
heated with a little butter or oil).

Mixed equal parts of honey, soya
sauce and lemon juice, thin apricot
or plum jam, or tart jelly, with
lemon or orange juice and add
Worcestershire or soya sauce if
desired.

If you cook your hamburgers in a
pan, deglaze the pan, adding a little
water, fruit juice or wine, with or
without some of the glaze, swirling
the mixture around the pan and
turning the hamburgers in it, until it
coats them, and none remains on the
pan itself.

Hamburger Toppings

(See photograph on page 114.)

• Sliced tomato, with basil-flavoured
oil and vinegar dressing.
• Sliced radishes, bean or alfalfa
sprouts, and cucumber in a slightly
sweetened vinegar mixture.
• Chopped red and green peppers
(raw or skinned and roasted) with oil
and vinegar, hot pepper sauce, and
oreganum.
• Lightly sautéed or raw mushrooms
with mustard and sour cream mixed
to a sauce; or, more elegantly, with
bearnaise sauce.
• Sliced gherkins or dill pickles with
fresh dill or spring onions or sour
cream.
• Sliced onions of different colours
and types, crisped by first soaking in
cold water.
• Grilled cheese and pineapple, with
gherkin or preserved cherry garnish.
• Sauerkraut, mild mustard and/or
sour cream with caraway seeds.
• Sliced cucumber with a yoghurt,
mint and garlic sauce.
• Sliced or mashed seasoned
avocado with sour cream, sliced
tomato.

Stuffed Pocket Breads

For 4 servings:
500 g minced lamb or beef
1 onion, chopped finely
1 tsp ground cumin
½ tsp mixed spice
2 Tbsp lemon juice
1 tsp salt
2 Tbsp chopped parsley
1–2 Tbsp chopped mint

Brown the first four ingredients over
a high heat until meat is no longer
pink, breaking it into small pieces.
Stir in next four ingredients.

Spoon mixture onto the middle of
4 large warmed pocket breads. Top
with chopped lettuce, chopped
tomatoes and chopped cucumber.

Spoon unsweetened yoghurt over
mince and vegetable mixture before
eating.
Note:
If pocket breads are not available,
serve mixture in halved bread rolls
or hamburger buns.

Stuffed Vegetables

For about 6 servings:
2 cups cooked rice
400 g minced beef or lamb
2 cloves garlic, chopped
2 onions, chopped
100 g chopped mushrooms (optional)
1 cup chopped drained tomatoes
2 tsp instant stock
herbs as desired
1 cup grated cheese
extra grated cheese for topping

Red and green peppers, large firm
tomatoes, eggplant, scallopini or
large zucchini make good containers
for this rice and minced meat filling.
Serve them alone, with salad. I
precook the filling ingredients so the
vegetables can be served as soon as
they are tender.

Drain the cooked rice if necessary.

Brown the mince with the garlic,
onions and mushrooms if used, until
meat is no longer pink. Add the
fresh or canned tomatoes, then the
instant stock and whatever herbs
you like and have, using fresh in
preference to dried.

Mix all filling ingredients with the
grated cheese.

Remove stem ends of peppers,
tomatoes and scallopini, leaving a
hole large enough to put stuffing in.

Remove seeds and fibrous
material with a teaspoon.

Halve eggplant, large zucchini or
young marrows without peeling
them. Cut and scoop out flesh. Cube
and sauté this in a little butter, then
mix with the other stuffing
ingredients.

Pile mixture firmly into vegetable
cases. Stand in buttered baking dish
in a little vegetable liquid, stock or
water. Cover with lid, foil, etc.

Bake at 200°C for 30–60 minutes,
depending on size, maturity and
thickness of vegetable flesh, until
vegetable case is tender.

Top with Mozarella or extra
grated cheese. Cook for 5 minutes
longer.

Alternatively, microwave
(covered) at Full power for 2–5
minutes per vegetable, or until
tender. Add cheese topping and
cook until melted.

Thicken vegetable juices before
serving if desired.

C M Meat Loaf

For 4 servings:
500 g minced beef
1/2 cup rolled oats
1 onion, finely chopped
1 carrot, grated
1/4 cup tomato sauce
1/4 cup dried milk powder
1/4 cup milk
2 tsp instant beef stock powder
2 tsp Worcestershire sauce
1 tsp dried basil
1 tsp dried oreganum
cheese and extra tomato sauce for
*   topping*

Combine all ingredients until well mixed. Add a little extra oats if mixture is very soft.

Turn into a 20–23 cm-long loaf pan lined with a strip of baking paper or foil along its long sides and bottom. Bake uncovered at 180°C for about an hour or until loaf feels firm in centre.

Alternatively, microwave in microwave pan or small ring pan. Cover and cook at Full power for about 10 minutes, until colour has changed in thickest part.

Turn loaf on to flat ovenproof plate. Top with tomato sauce and overlapping triangles of processed cheese or with grated cheese. Cook a little longer, until cheese melts.

C M Meat Loaf Roll

Make mixture as for meat loaf, but replace milk and dried milk powder with 1 egg. Mix thoroughly. Add milk if mixture seems dry.

Roll out meat mixture between two layers of plastic, until it is 20 × 40 cm. Leaving 1 short end uncovered, spread meat with an even covering of grated cheese, then with spinach leaves which have been blanched then thoroughly dried. Roll up, starting from short, covered end.

Transfer roll to 20 cm strip of greaseproof or baking paper. Lower paper and meat roll into a 20–23 cm loaf pan. Bake as for meat loaf.

M Glazed Meat Loaf

Dress up a basic meat loaf. This cooks faster and more evenly in a ring mould, but you can use a traditional loaf pan if you like.

For 4–5 servings:
500 g minced beef or lamb
1 egg
1 onion, finely chopped
1/4 cup tomato ketchup
1 Tbsp dark soya sauce
1/2 cup rolled oats
2 tsp instant beef stock
1 Tbsp tomato paste
2 Tbsp milk

Mix all of the ingredients above and

pat into a small microwave ring mould. Cover with cling wrap and cook at Medium-high (70% power) for 12 minutes or at Full power for 9 minutes.

Unmould on to serving dish. Drizzle glaze over surface.
Glaze:
1/4 cup tomato sauce
2 tsp golden syrup
1 tsp Worcestershire sauce
1 tsp dry mustard

For glaze, mix all ingredients in a small bowl, microwave at Full power for 1 minute.

M Oaty Meatballs

Meatballs microwave especially well. This basic meatball recipe has a good colour even before it is cooked, so you needn't worry that the colour of the final product will be in the least insipid.

For 4–5 servings:
500 g minced beef or lamb
1/2 cup rolled oats
1 Tbsp instant beef or herb stock
1 1/2 Tbsp dark soya sauce
2 Tbsp tomato ketchup
1 onion, grated or finely chopped
1/2 tsp dried basil
1/2 tsp dried marjoram

Combine all the ingredients in a bowl or food processor. If using a food processor, chop the onion first, then add seasonings, the rolled oats and the meat. If mixture is too soft, add a little extra rolled oats.

Divide mixture in quarters, then divide each quarter into eight walnut-sized balls. Arrange half of the meatballs in a circle round the edge of a large, round, flat dish. Meatballs should not be touching. Microwave, uncovered, at Full power for 3–4 minutes.

While the first meatballs cook, shape the rest of the mixture into balls and cook in the same way.
Variation:
Cook meatballs in a non-stick pan instead of microwaving them, if preferred.

C Fruity Meatballs

For 4 servings:
500 g minced lamb or beef
2 Tbsp onion pulp
1/4 cup fine dry breadcrumbs
1/4 cup currants
1/4 cup chopped toasted almonds or
*   pine nuts*
1 egg
3/4 tsp garlic salt
1/2 tsp curry powder
1/2 tsp mixed spice
2 tsp chopped mint (optional)

To make onion pulp, grate the cut surface of a halved onion.

Combine meat with all other

ingredients, mixing thoroughly. Form into small balls with wet hands.

In a large frying pan brown balls evenly, then lower heat and cook until centres are no longer pink. Remove from pan.

Make a sauce in same pan by adding 1 tablespoon butter and 2 tablespoons flour. Brown flour in butter and pan drippings and then add 1/4 cup water, 1 teaspoon instant chicken stock and 1/4 cup orange juice. When sauce boils and thickens, add meatballs and warm through.

Serve on rice, with salad or vegetables.

M Crumby Meatballs

These microwave very well. Added ingredients give colour, since they do not brown as much as conventionally cooked meatballs. They darken quite a lot in the 5 minutes after cooking, however.

For 4–5 servings:
250 g minced lamb or beef
250 g sausage meat
1 onion, finely chopped
1 cup soft breadcrumbs
1 Tbsp tomato ketchup
1 Tbsp dark soya sauce
1 egg
1 1/2 tsp dried marjoram
1/4 tsp dried thyme

Combine ingredients thoroughly in a bowl or food processor. Working with wet hands, divide mixture into quarters, then each quarter into 8–12 balls.

Arrange half the balls in a circle around the edge of the turntable. Microwave at Full power for 4 minutes or until firm. Remove, with juices. Cook remaining meatballs.

Prepare and cook any suitable sauce, adding cooking juice from meatballs. Turn meatballs in sauce. Reheat and serve on rice, spaghetti, etc.

C M Lazy Lasagne

For this family-style lasagne, nothing is precooked.

For 4–6 servings:
500 g minced beef
2 cloves garlic, chopped
1 tsp dried basil
1 tsp dried oreganum
425 g can tomato purée
2 Tbsp tomato paste
1 packet tomato soup
2 tsp instant beef stock
1 1/2 cups hot water
150 g (1/2 pkt) small lasagne noodles
2 cups grated cheese
2 tsp cornflour
1 egg
3/4 cup milk
paprika

Lazy Lasagne

Mix first nine ingredients thoroughly. Spray or butter a 23 cm square ovenware dish. Pour one-third meat mixture into it. Place half lasagne pieces over meat, then sprinkle with ¹/₂ cup of grated cheese. Layer another third of meat mixture, remaining lasagne and another ¹/₂ cup cheese. Cover with remaining meat.

Bake immediately, uncovered, at 180°C for 50 minutes.

Alternatively, microwave at Full power for 30 minutes, in a covered dish.

Mix remaining cheese, egg, cornflour and milk. Pour over cooked mixture evenly, sprinkle with paprika and bake at 150°C for 10 minutes or until topping sets.

Alternatively, microwave at Medium (50% power) for 10 minutes.

Leave to stand for 15–30 minutes before cutting into squares (or reheat before serving later). Serve with a salad.

Note:
If you have trouble setting the custardy topping in your microwave oven, brown it under a grill until it sets in the middle.

M Mini Lasagne

Microwaved lasagnes are very convenient and quick. It is always convenient to make lasagne in a square or rectangular dish, so that it can be cut into rectangular pieces when serving. A large rectangular dish will not turn around in small microwave ovens.

This recipe makes a small lasagne which will cook in a rectangular 17 × 23 cm or 20 cm square dish with sides 3 cm high. Dishes of this size should rotate in smaller microwave ovens without any trouble.

For 3–4 servings:
250 g minced lamb or beef
1 clove garlic, crushed
¹/₂ tsp basil
¹/₂ tsp oreganum
1 cup tomato purée
1 Tbsp tomato paste
¹/₂ pkt tomato soup
1 tsp instant beef stock
1 cup hot water
100 g lasagne noodles
1¹/₂ cups grated cheese
1 tsp cornflour
1 egg
¹/₂ cup milk
paprika

Follow method for Lazy Lasagne. Microwave at Full power for 25 minutes, add topping and cook at Medium (50% power) for 10 minutes.

Note:
If toppings do not set after specified times, reheat hot lasagne at Full power for 2 minutes, or brown under a grill.

Spaghetti Sauce

C Spaghetti Sauce

For 6 servings:
500 g minced beef
1 onion, chopped
2 cloves garlic, crushed
2 Tbsp flour
1 tsp salt
1 tsp paprika
½ tsp dried basil
½ tsp dried oreganum
¼ tsp cinnamon
¼ tsp allspice
1–2 cups tomato purée
1–2 cups chopped fresh (or canned) tomatoes
1 cup red or white wine
water
1 green pepper (optional)
1 red pepper (optional)

Brown minced beef, onion and garlic together in a large, heavy-bottomed saucepan. When no longer pink add the flour, salt and seasonings.

Measure the cups of available liquid. Make up to 5 cups altogether with water if necessary. Add finely chopped red and green pepper if desired.

Simmer, uncovered, for about 45 minutes, until sauce has thickened. Taste and add extra salt, pepper and a little sugar.

Serve over spaghetti.

M Spaghetti Sauce

For 6 servings:
500 g minced beef
2 onions, chopped
2 cloves garlic, chopped
1 cup water
1 cup chopped or canned tomatoes in their own juice
1 pkt (3 serving size) tomato soup
1–2 red or green peppers, chopped
1 tsp celery or garlic salt
½ tsp dried basil
½ tsp dried marjoram
2 Tbsp tomato paste

Spread the minced beef, onion and garlic in a 23 cm casserole dish and microwave uncovered at Full power for 5–6 minutes, stirring once or twice. Add the water, tomatoes, tomato soup, peppers, flavoured salt and herbs, and tomato paste. Cover and microwave for 15 minutes, stirring once or twice during this time.

Taste, adjust seasonings if necessary, and leave to stand for at least 5 minutes before serving.

M Mushroom Mince

A special occasion, low-priced meat dish.

For 4–6 servings:
500 g mince
2 cloves garlic, chopped
1 pkt mushroom soup
2 tsp mixed mustard
¼ cup water or white wine
1 Tbsp Worcestershire sauce
4 spring onions, chopped
100 g mushrooms, chopped
¼ cup sour cream

In a large microwave casserole mix the mince and garlic and cook at Full power for 5 minutes, stirring after 2 minutes.

Add the soup, mustard, water or wine and the Worcestershire sauce. Cook for another 6 minutes. Then add the spring onions and mushrooms and microwave for 2 minutes.

Stir in the cream and serve over noodles or rice, or spoon onto toasted bread rolls.

C One-Pan Dinner

For 4–5 servings:
500–600 g minced beef
1 large onion, chopped
2 cloves garlic, crushed
1 pkt onion (or mushroom) soup mix
1 Tbsp soya sauce
2 tsp instant beef stock
1 tsp dried oreganum (or ½ tsp dried thyme)
1 cup chopped celery (or carrot)
3 cups hot water
1 cup macaroni or other pasta
2 cups chopped cabbage
grated cheese (optional)

This is a good, easy holiday meal, cooked in a large, heavy-bottomed pan or an electric frypan.

Brown the mince, onion and garlic over high heat, then add all remaining ingredients except the macaroni and cabbage.

Stir in pasta when mixture boils, then cover lightly and cook for 15 minutes, stirring occasionally, until macaroni is barely tender. Add extra liquid if mixture looks dry before pasta is cooked.

Add the cabbage, either stirring it in, or leaving it on top, and cook for 5 minutes longer.

Serve sprinkled with grated cheese if desired.

C Joe's Special

A restaurant in San Francisco once made its name with this recipe. It uses Western ingredients and an Oriental cooking method.

For 4–5 servings:
500 g minced beef
1 onion, chopped
2 cloves garlic, chopped
1 Tbsp oil
250–400 g spinach leaves
1 Tbsp instant beef stock

3 eggs
½ tsp salt

Over high heat brown the mince, onion and garlic, adding the oil only if the mixture looks dry.

Chop the spinach leaves coarsely, discarding stems. Stir into mince, then add the instant beef stock, and a little water if the mixture looks dry. Cover and let spinach cook in steam for 3–4 minutes. Remove lid and stir until any liquid has evaporated.

Beat eggs with salt until combined, then pour over meat mixture in pan.

Lift sides to let uncooked mixture run underneath, but do not stir, and avoid breaking egg into small pieces.

Serve with sautéed or mashed potatoes, or with rice, with tomato ketchup to be traditional!

Variation:
Add 1–2 cups of sliced mushrooms to the mince and onion mixture before the spinach is added.

Mince and Macaroni

For 2–3 servings:
250 g minced beef or lamb
2 cloves garlic
½ cup quick-cooking macaroni (perciacelli)
¼ tsp cinnamon
½ tsp oreganum (optional)
1½ cups hot water
1 pkt tomato soup powder
1 cup cold water
¼ cup chopped parsley

Brown mince and garlic, breaking up lumps. When no longer pink, stir in macaroni, cinnamon and oreganum.

Add hot water, cover and simmer for 10–15 minutes, until macaroni is tender.

Add tomato soup mixed with water. Cover again and cook for 5 minutes longer.

Leave for 5 minutes, then stir in parsley and serve.

Middle-Eastern Mince Casserole

This is a simplified version of Greek Moussaka.

For 4–6 servings:
1 large eggplant
oil and water
1 tsp dried oreganum
500 g minced beef or lamb
2 onions, chopped
2 Tbsp flour
1 cup tomato purée
1 tsp garlic salt
2 cups grated cheese

Chilli Con Carne

Cut eggplant into 1 cm cubes, without peeling it. In a large, heavy frying pan with a lid, heat 2–3 tablespoons oil. Toss eggplant in this, then add about ¼ cup hot water and cover pan. Cook for several minutes, then uncover, turn and add a little extra oil and water and cover again, until eggplant is tender.

Mix with oreganum and spread in a sprayed or buttered ovenware dish.

Brown mince and onion in same pan. When no longer pink, stir in flour, tomato purée, garlic salt and half the cheese.

Spread mince mixture over the eggplant and cover with the remaining grated cheese.

Bake, uncovered, at 180°C for 45–60 minutes.

Serve with salad, and crusty bread.

Variation:
Replace eggplant with same weight of zucchini if desired.

Chilli Con Carne

Serve this on rice with a side salad, for a complete meal. If you want a crunchy accompaniment, add corn chips, crusty bread or crackers, too.

For 4–6 servings:
500 g mince
2 medium-sized onions, chopped
2 large cloves garlic, chopped
¼ tsp chopped dried chillis (or 2 small dried chillis)
2 tsp oreganum
1 tsp cumin
1 tsp paprika
1 can (420 g) tomatoes in juice
1 large can (820 g) baked beans in tomato sauce
1 green pepper, chopped

Combine the first seven ingredients in a large uncovered casserole or bowl and microwave at Full power for 5–7 minutes, stirring after each 2 minutes until meat is no longer pink. Add the tomatoes and juice, beans and green pepper, cover and cook for a further 20 minutes, stirring occasionally. Serve on rice in soup bowls.

Note:
This mixture is fairly hot! Use less chilli, if desired.

Confetti Meat Loaf

1 tsp instant beef stock
1 egg
1 cup fresh breadcrumbs (about 2
  slices bread)
about ¹/₂ cup Savoury Crumbs (see
  below) or fine, dry breadcrumbs.

Mix all except last ingredient. With wet hands, form mixture into a large, sausage-shaped roll. Roll in Savoury or plain crumbs and place on a flat dish. Stand this on an inverted plate so that the meat loaf is raised from the bottom of the oven. Cook at Medium-high (70% power) for 20 minutes. Let stand for 5–8 minutes if serving hot, or leave to cool.

Variation:
Replace peppers with 1¹/₂ cups thawed mixed vegetables and up to 1 cup chopped celery, if desired.

Ⓜ Savoury Crumbs

1 Tbsp butter
1 cup fresh breadcrumbs
1–2 Tbsp chopped parsley (optional)
1–2 tsp finely chopped herbs (optional)

Melt the butter in a fairly large, flat-bottomed microwave dish at Full power for about 30 seconds. Add the breadcrumbs and finely chopped parsley and herbs if you want them for extra colour and flavour.

Spread the crumbs evenly, then cook for 2–4 minutes, until the crumbs turn golden brown. These crumbs make a good coating for any sausage meat mixtures which are to be served without a sauce, e.g. Confetti Meatloaf and Scotch Eggs (see page 39). Clare's Terrine (see page 18) is another good sausage meat recipe.

If you find that your sausage meat mixtures cook unevenly, lower the power level and increase the cooking time. Raise the cooking container by standing it on an inverted plate, or cover the food with a tent of greaseproof paper.

Ⓒ Sausage and Mushroom Patties

This is quick and easy, yet it tastes as if it has had quite a lot of time and trouble spent in its preparation. I made it when my children needed 'instant food'! Serve these patties alone, on rice or noodles, or with mashed potatoes and other vegetables for dinner.

For 3–4 servings:
500 g sausage meat
1 pkt mushroom sauce mix
1 cup hot water
1–2 Tbsp chopped parsley

Hold the packet of sausage meat under the cold tap. With a sharp knife or scissors, cut down the side

Ⓜ Confetti Meat Loaf

This mixture microwaves especially well and is popular hot or cold.

For 8–10 servings:
500 g mince

450 g sausage meat
1 onion, chopped
1 red pepper, chopped
1 green pepper, chopped
1 tsp curry powder
1 tsp instant herb stock

and along the bottom of the plastic bag. No meat should stick to the plastic when it is done this way.

With damp hands, break off small pieces of sausage meat. Flatten these slightly and put them in a frying pan over medium heat. Leave for 2–3 minutes, then turn. Heat should be low so that meat is slightly browned.

Drain off any fat that has accumulated, then sprinkle the contents of the packet of mushroom sauce over the sausages. Add the hot water then turn the patties. Cover and leave over low heat for 3–5 minutes, till the sauce has evaporated, but the patties are nicely coated. Sprinkle with chopped parsley.

Sausage and Mushroom Patties

For 3–4 servings:

With wet hands, shape eight patties from 500 g sausage meat. Arrange in a circle on a large pyrex (or other suitable) round plate. Flatten the patties once they are on the plate, pushing them out with the heel of your hand until each one touches the patties beside it.

Microwave at Full power for 4 minutes, then turn the patties over and pour over them a packet of mushroom sauce mix mixed with 1 cup of hot water and a few drops of gravy browning. Cook for 2 minutes longer.

Press the centre of each patty to see whether it is cooked. The patty will spring back if cooked, and will feel soft in the centre if it is still partly raw. If still uncooked, microwave for 1 minute more, then test again.

When sausages are cooked, turn them in the sauce and leave to stand for several minutes. Sprinkle with chopped parsley and serve.

Browned Sausages

Some skin-on sausages cook very well by this method, others don't. If necessary, brown them under a grill later, or add a topping of grated cheese and tomato ketchup or paprika for more colour.

Heat a browning dish according to manufacturer's instructions, about 6 minutes at Full power. Swirl 1 tablespoon oil around the base. Add sausages (500 g) which have been scored with parallel, diagonal cuts on both sides. Cook at Full power for 3 minutes, then turn sausages and cook for 3 minutes longer, or until firm and cooked.

Saucy Sausages

Crumbed sausages don't brown as well in a microwave as they do in a frying pan, but they cook well. This tasty sauce improves both their colour and flavour.

For 4 servings:
8 crumbed sausages
1 Tbsp oil
2 Tbsp butter
2 medium-sized onions, thinly sliced
2 medium-sized apples, thinly sliced
1 tsp dry mustard
1 tsp instant beef stock
½ tsp celery salt
¼ cup brown sugar
2 tsp cornflour
2 Tbsp dark soya sauce
½ cup tomato ketchup
1 cup boiling water

Heat browning dish according to instructions. Make sure sausages are an even shape. (If crumbing them yourself, use Savoury Crumbs recipe opposite.) Add oil to hot browning dish. Add sausages, side by side. Cook at Full power for 3 minutes, turn and cook for 3 minutes longer. Remove from dish.

If browning dish has sides and a lid, make sauce in it. Otherwise, use another dish. Put butter, onions and apples in a covered dish. Cook until tender, 4–6 minutes, stirring twice.

While they cook, stir together dry ingredients, add sauces and boiling water. Pour over apple and onion and cover. Cook until thick and bubbly. Add sausages and reheat in sauce or serve over sausages.

Devilled Sausages

For 4 servings:
500 g sausage meat
1 cup dry breadcrumbs
1 onion, chopped
1 apple, grated coarsely
¼–½ cup chutney
2 tsp instant beef stock
1½ cups hot water
2 tsp soya sauce
cornflour and water paste

Cut up sausage meat with a wet knife and shape with wet hands. Roll in fine dry breadcrumbs, and fry over a low heat for 10 minutes or until the crumbs are golden brown and the sausage meat cooked through.

Remove excess fat from the pan, leaving about 2 tablespoons, and brown the onion while the sausages finish cooking. Remove the sausages and add the apple. Lower the heat and stir in the chutney. Add the beef stock to the hot water, and stir this into the onion mixture. Pour in the soya sauce and thicken the mixture with cornflour and water paste, until it is of gravy consistency.

Place the sausages back in the sauce to heat through.
Note:
Apple can be chopped instead of grated, or crushed pineapple or pineapple chunks can be used instead.
If chutney is not available, ¼–½ cup jam, or ¼ cup of brown sugar can be mixed with 2 tablespoons of vinegar and used instead.

Sausage and Potato Braid

The plaited pastry coating on this sausage meat really dresses it up! It can be served hot, but I think it is better when cold.

For 4 servings:
500 g short or flaky pastry
450–500 g sausage meat
1 cup onion, finely chopped
1 cup cooked potato, sliced
1 tsp curry powder
½ tsp celery salt
½ tsp onion or vegetable salt
shake pepper
½–1 tsp dried herbs
1 egg, raw

Roll out the pastry to a 45 cm square. Put the square on a baking sheet. Mark it lightly into thirds with the back of a knife. Cut each outside third into 12 strips (so that the pastry looks rather like a stylised fern or tree.)

For the filling, mix in a basin the sausage meat, onion, potato, seasonings and herbs. Beat the egg, keep a teaspoonful aside, then add the rest of the sausage meat.

Mix well by hand until the sausage meat is combined with the other ingredients, then spread the filling down the centre third of the roll. Starting at the far end fold a strip from one side over the filling, at a slight angle, then one from the other side. Continue doing this till the whole of the filling is hidden by the strips which appear to be plaited.

Glaze the top with a little beaten egg and bake in a hot oven at 220°C for 15–20 minutes, until the top and bottom of the pastry case is golden brown, then at 180°C for 10–15 minutes.
Note:
If the sausage meat is very fatty some fat may drip off the oven tray during baking. Either wipe tray with a paper towel at intervals, or bake in a sponge roll tin or a shallow 'tin' made of foil.

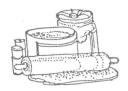

© Curried Pineapple Patties

For 3–4 servings:
450–500 g sausage meat
2 Tbsp butter
1–2 tsp curry powder
1 large onion, chopped
2 tsp flour
1 cup crushed pineapple
1–2 Tbsp pineapple juice

Form sausage meat into 8–10 patties with wet hands. Melt butter in a large frying pan and brown patties over moderate heat. Turn patties and add curry powder and chopped onion. Stir in flour, lower heat then add crushed pineapple, cover and cook gently for 5 minutes. Turn patties, add a little extra liquid (water or pineapple juice) if all liquid has evaporated, and leave over very low heat for 5 minutes longer.

Serve on rice, or with mashed potatoes and any green vegetable.

© Saturday Casserole

This casserole is one that my husband enjoyed as a child. It's good to come home after a winter's outing and know that this casserole is bubbling away in the oven — ready whenever we are.

For 4 servings:
450–500 g sausages or sausage meat
2 apples, sliced
2 onions, sliced
salt, pepper, brown sugar and herbs to taste
1 (425 g) can baked beans
water

Brown the sausages or pieces of sausage meat and arrange them on the bottom of a casserole dish. Cover the sausages with sliced apple and sliced onion.

Sprinkle with salt, pepper, a little brown sugar and herbs if you like them. Spread the baked beans over the apple and onion. Add a measure of water, 1 baked bean can full if the casserole is to bake for 3 or more hours. For 2 hours add ½ can, for 1 hour add ¼ can. Bake for 3 hours at 140°C, 2 hours at 150°C, 1 hour at 180°C.

Remember that sausage meat, bought in a tube, is considerably cheaper, weight for weight, than sausages which have had to be shaped and coated. Save money by using sausage meat where possible.

Remove the plastic tube surrounding the sausage meat in the same way that you take the skin from a sausage.

© Golden Sausage Casserole

I hope that you feel curious enough to try this combination, because it is remarkably good. It is pretty enough to serve any time, the flavour is excellent, it is quick and certainly makes good use of sausage meat.

For 4–6 servings:
750 g sausage meat
flour
250 g mushrooms
2–3 tsp Worcestershire sauce
1 (450 g) can sliced peaches
salt
chopped parsley

Form sausage meat into patties and coat with flour. Brown on both sides in a little fat, add mushrooms (quartered if large) and brown lightly. Add sauce, the peaches and juice from the can, cover, and simmer for 30 minutes, or bake in a casserole dish at 180°C for 30–45 minutes.

Add salt if necessary and sprinkle with chopped parsley just before serving.

© Savoury Sausage Roll with Brown Sauce

This roll looks and tastes good, and any leftovers can be served cold just as successfully. It can be served with vegetables for an economical family dinner or by itself for lunch.

Avoid quick cooking. You may have noticed how sausages or sausage meat shrinks if it is cooked too quickly. Keep the temperature low and turn the roll often while it cooks.

For 4–6 servings:
2–4 Tbsp cooking fat or oil
1 cup sliced onions
1 cup sliced celery
1 cup grated or sliced apple
½ cup soft breadcrumbs
1 Tbsp chopped parsley
½ tsp salt
750 g sausage meat
½ cup dried breadcrumbs

Melt the fat and add to it the onions, celery, and apple in this order. Fry over high heat, stirring occasionally, until the ingredients start to turn golden brown. Remove from the heat, then mix with the soft breadcrumbs, chopped parsley and salt.

Pat out the sausage meat in the dry breadcrumbs to form a 23 cm square. Spread with the cooked mixture, leaving 2–3 cm along one side without any covering. Roll up so that the part without filling is rolled last. Seal this edge with a little cold water.

Bake in a moderate oven at 150°C for 30–45 minutes, turning occasionally.
Note:
If a higher cooking temperature is used, the sausage meat shrinks and the roll will split during cooking.

© Mini Hot Dogs

These are very popular snacks with family members of all ages. They make a few saveloys go a long way — and always seem special.

For 4 servings:
oil
4 saveloys
1 egg
½ cup milk
1 cup self-raising flour
½ tsp curry powder
½ tsp dry mustard
½ tsp paprika

Heat 1 cm oil or fat in a frying pan, or heat an electric frying pan to 200°C.

Run a sharp knife down the saveloys, then peel off the skins. Cut each saveloy diagonally into 5 or 6 slices, and push an iceblock stick into the side of each slice.

Break the egg into a medium-sized bowl. Add the milk, self-raising flour and the seasonings. Stir with a fork. Do not overmix or the hot dogs will be tough. The mixture should look lumpy after you finish mixing.

Hold the bowl on an angle and turn the hot dogs in it, one at a time, so some batter touches the stick and the piece of saveloy is completely covered.

Put each hot dog flat in the hot oil or fat. Turn it over when it is golden brown, using tongs. Cook the other side, then drain on paper and serve straight away, with tomato sauce.

Ⓜ Hot Dogs

When you are serving a number of Hot Dogs, you can prepare them before you need them. Split each roll. Spread thinly with butter, then spread with tomato ketchup and mustard. Put frankfurter or saveloy in roll, adding other relish or a slice of cheese as well, if desired. Wrap each prepared Hot Dog in a paper towel. When required, cook each at Full power for 45 seconds to 1 minute, until frankfurter is hot and roll warm.

(Time the first frankfurter carefully, then heat the rest for the same time.)

Scotch Eggs (See recipe on page 39.)

Peas, Beans, Lentils and Tofu

The recipes in this section are favourites of mine, not because of their low cost and high food value, but because I like the way they taste.

Dried beans, peas and lentils have a much higher protein content that other vegetables. They are also an important source of fibre. They play an important part in vegetarian diets, but they are well worth the consideration of meat-eaters too.

Pulses (beans, peas and lentils) require a considerable amount of love and care as they cook. Undercooked and underseasoned, they are bland and boring. I have used the words 'meltingly tender' in some of the recipes, and I think it describes perfectly the way the beans should finish up.

Beans won't keep forever, even though they are dry. Really old beans will need longer cooking and soaking than those from a recent crop. You can't tell the age of a bean when you buy it, so you should buy amounts you will use fairly quickly, from a supplier with a quick turnover.

One cup of dried beans fills 2 (or more) cups after cooking. This is the amount often allowed for 4 main-dish servings.

I often use the microwave oven to reheat cooked bean mixtures, since there is less danger of a burnt pot.

I seldom microwave beans from their dried state. If you cook pulses frequently, a pressure cooker is a good investment, since it reduces cooking times dramatically.

I hope you will enjoy this 'international' collection of pulse recipes as much as I do.

Bean Basics

The term pulse covers peas, beans, and lentils, all of which are important foods in a vegetarian diet because of their high protein content, especially when they are eaten with other vegetable protein foods.

As well as being a good source of cheap protein, dried beans, peas, and lentils are important for their high fibre content. It is also interesting to note that beans have a much lower fat content than other protein-rich foods.

We are lucky, these days, to have such a variety of pulses to choose from. Try small quantities of a few different beans, to use, one after another, until you find your own favourites. It is best to buy enough pulses to last you for only a couple of months, because pulses *do* deteriorate on long storage, although they look as though they are everlasting.

If you have not cooked dried pulses before, I suggest you start with lentils, cook Lentil and Vegetable Curry (see page 131), then try sprouting some of them following the instructions on page 135. Next, make Hummus, (see page 10) using black-eyed beans, then cook kidney beans for Mexican Beans (see page 131).

If you become a bean enthusiast, invest in a pressure cooker! With a pressure cooker you can use the valuable soya bean regularly. This cooks, without prior soaking, in 45 minutes, in a pressure cooker. It is the cheapest bean, and has the greatest food value, but is often ignored because it takes hours to cook really soft, using conventional methods.

1. BLACK BEANS: Several shapes and sizes of medium to large black beans are available (black beans, turtle beans, tiger beans, black haricots, etc.) but all seem interchangeable. Shiny and attractive when cooked, some have a smoky flavour.

2. SOYA FLOUR: Not the same as pea flour, but made from ground soya beans. Used to boost the protein content of other mixtures, it has a distinctive, slightly bitter soya bean flavour.

3. SOYA BEANS: Smallish, rounded whitish beans. Very high in protein but require very long cooking to soften completely, and have a distinctive 'beany' flavour that bothers some people. Their high protein content is utilised in many other soya products, e.g., soya flour, soya bean sprouts, soya milk, tofu, tempeh, etc. An enormously important crop globally, also used for edible oil production.

4. MOONG DAHL: Mung beans with their outer coat removed. Cook quickly without soaking; good for dahls, curries and soups.

5. MERINO BEANS: Locally produced, these beans have an interesting piebald appearance. Have a rather coarse texture and cook fairly slowly.

6. CHICKPEAS: (Garbanzos, Garbanzo beans). Easily recognised by their distinctive pea shape and their protruding shoot; usually beige (but sometimes brown); cooking times seem to vary considerably. Lovey nutty flavour — traditionally used in hummus, casseroles and falafel.

7. YELLOW SPLIT PEAS: Halved, skinned peas. Similar in flavour and texture to green split peas.

8. ADZUKI (ADUKI) BEANS: Small, rounded dark red beans. Often sweetened in Asian recipes. I have not found these beans to cook as quickly as is sometimes claimed.

9. WHITE LIMA BEANS: (Butter beans in southern USA.) Large, flat white beans. Require soaking and gentle cooking to prevent breaking up. Sweet flavour, make a wonderful creamy purée.

10. BROWN LENTILS: (Green lentils, continental lentils.) Whole lentils with skin. May vary in size and colour (light green to pale red-brown). Very useful as they cook quickly, retaining their shape without soaking. Good in casseroles, salads, spaghetti sauces, lasagne etc. Also good sprouted. After sprouting cook in 2–3 minutes.

11. BABY (GREEN) LIMA BEANS: Small, pale green cousin of the white lima. Don't cook fast and tend to lose their nice green colour, but have a pleasant flavour and nice shape.

12. RED KIDNEY BEANS: Attractive dark red colour, raw and cooked. Cook to a nice mealy texture, good in salads, casseroles,

Mexican bean recipes. Never eat these beans raw, they *must* be boiled rapidly for 10–15 minutes during their cooking to break down a potentially dangerous component. Available canned.

13. MUNG BEANS: Small, roundish dark olive beans. Quick cooking without soaking but usually sprouted (most bought bean sprouts are mung beans).

14. PEA FLOUR: Made by grinding peas (or beans), sometimes called channa or gram flour. I noticed no differences using flour ground from chickpeas or other dried peas. Pea flour mixed with water and flavourings makes a good batter without eggs.

15. SPLIT RED LENTILS: Small halved lentils with their outer skin removed. Cook quickly (in about the same time as white rice) to a lighter beige-orange colour with a slightly mealy texture. Often used in soups or dahls.

16. HARICOT BEANS: Smallish, white oval beans (referred to as Navy beans in the USA). A good all-purpose bean, used in many traditional recipes from England, France and the USA. Probably most commonly seen as the 'baked bean'.

17. GREEN SPLIT PEAS: Skinned, halved bright green peas. Mushy when cooked, commonly used in soups and purées.

18. BLACK-EYED BEANS: (Black-eyed peas, cow peas.) Attractive, creamy rounded beans with a distinctive black 'eye' or spot. Greatest advantage is a short cooking time without soaking. Pleasant, slightly smoky flavour. Use in place of any bean if pressed for time.

19. PINTO BEANS: Attractive beige-pink and red-brown speckled medium-sized beans. Used in much the same way as red kidney beans; pretty in salads or casseroles.

(See photograph on page 126–7.)

1			14
2	7		15
3	8		16
4	9		17
5	10	12	18
6	11	13	19

Soaking Beans

Some types of beans and lentils may be cooked without pre-soaking (see list and table below), however, thicker-skinned beans cook faster if soaked prior to cooking.

There are two soaking methods.
1. The long soak method: Cover beans with about four times their volume of cold water and leave to stand for 8 hours or longer, in refrigerator if longer.
2. The rapid soak method: Cover beans with about four times their volume of boiling water, or bring to boil and boil for 2 minutes, then leave to stand for 1–2 hours before cooking.

Cooking Beans

I usually pour off and discard the soaking liquid. This removes soluble impurities and some of the substances thought to cause flatulence. Replace with about the same quantity of fresh water. Bring to boil, add a tablespoon of oil to prevent excess frothing, and simmer with the lid ajar to prevent boiling over. You can flavour beans with garlic, onion, and herbs during cooking, but you must not add salt, sugar, lemon juice or tomato products until the beans are completely tender, since these toughen the beans. Beans are cooked when they are tender enough to squash with your tongue.

Important:
Beans which are undercooked will put you off recipes which are excellent if made with properly cooked beans.

Approximate cooking times for the beans are given in the table. Use these as a guide only, since times vary with the age and quality of the beans.

Add about $1/2$ teaspoon of salt to 1 cup of dried beans, after cooking. Liquid drained from beans after cooking makes good stock for soups and sauces.

In a hurry?
You can:
• Change bean varieties to use a quick-cooking variety which needs no soaking, e.g., black-eyed beans or brown lentils.
• Use canned beans (this may also mean changing varieties).
• Soak and cook beans in bulk, in advance, then freeze them ready for use.
• Use a pressure cooker.
• Cook beans without soaking, remembering cooking times will be considerably longer.

The resulting recipe may differ from the original recipe, but it will usually be good, nonetheless.

Lima Bean Salad

Type of bean	soak	cook (min)
moong dahl	no	20–30
red lentils	no	25–35
brown lentils	no	40–50
black-eyed beans	no	30–45
split peas	no	40–60
mung beans	no	40–50
lima beans	yes	45–90
pinto beans	yes	60–90
adzuki beans	yes	60–120
red kidney beans*	yes	60–90
haricot beans	yes	75–90
black turtle beans	yes	75–90
merino beans	yes	90–120
chickpeas	yes	90–150
soya beans	yes	120–180

*Need 15 minutes of rapid boiling during cooking.

If preferred, pre-soak first six varieties and reduce cooking time.

Pressure cooking beans:
Pressure cooking dramatically decreases the cooking times of dried beans. The times I recorded with a modern (German) pressure cooker were spectacular.

Unsoaked black-eyed beans cooked in 15 minutes.
Black-eyed beans, rapid-soaked for 1 hour, cooked in 5 minutes.
Unsoaked kidney beans cooked in 35 minutes.
Pinto beans, merino beans and garbanzos rapid-soaked for an hour cooked in 15 minutes to the texture of canned beans.
Unsoaked soya beans cooked to very soft in 45 minutes.

It is obviously worth investing in an efficient pressure cooker if you eat beans often and want to speed up their cooking times. (A borrowed 25-year-old pressure cooker made considerable time savings, although all times were 5–10 minutes longer than those given above.)

For best results you should follow the manufacturer's instructions. If these are not available, use the following as a guide.
• Use 4 cups of water to 1 cup dried beans.
• Do not fill the cooker more than half full, since beans froth as they cook.
• Add 1 tablespoon of oil to lessen frothing.
• Let the pressure fall over 2–3 minutes.
• Cook beans without seasonings, as suggested under cooking instructions here.

Microwaving beans:
Soaked beans may be drained, generously covered with boiling water, then cooked at a low power level (30–50% power) with a lid on. Cooking times are not much shorter, and may vary, but this method may suit you, as the microwave oven turns itself off.

Unsoaked beans or soaked beans cooked at high power levels can burn if they cook dry. A microwave is good for reheating cooked beans.

Yields and costs:
• 1 cup dried beans yields 2–3 cups drained cooked beans.
• 1 can (about 440 g) cooked beans contains about $1^{1}/2$ cups drained beans.
• Canned beans save a lot of time but cost 3–4 times as much as home-cooked beans.

Mexican Tortillas etc.

C Mexican Tortillas etc.

Tortillas are a type of Mexican flat bread.

Uncooked corn tortillas, cut into small wedges and fried, are corn chips or tostaditos.

Taco shells are made by folding and frying corn tortillas until crisp.

Tostadas are tortillas fried flat until they are crisp.

Enchiladas are tortillas which are briefly fried, removed from the pan before they go crisp, spread with sauce, then rolled, folded, or stacked.

If you want to make tostadas, taco shells, corn chips or enchiladas yourself, start with unfried, flexible tortillas, which you can buy fresh or frozen from delicatessens or some Mexican restaurants.

My favourite way to serve tacos and tostadas involves setting out dishes containing the following toppings.

• Mexican or rapid refried beans, hot or warm
• Grated cheese
• Shredded lettuce
• Chopped spring onions (or onion rings)
• Sour cream
• Extra hot pepper sauce (optional)
• Chopped olives (optional)
• Sliced avocado or guacamole (optional)

This allows our family and friends to help themselves to whatever they want. The only suggestion I make is that they start with a layer of beans. If you have guests or family members who may not have eaten this way before, go first yourself, showing the others what to do.

Note:
Don't forget to provide many large paper serviettes as there is no tidy way to eat this type of food.

C Rapid Refried Beans

This recipe takes less than 10 minutes from start to finish, as long as you have a can of beans in the cupboard.

Use it to make delicious nachos or serve the refried beans on rice, with a shredded lettuce or tomato salad to complete the meal.

For 4 servings as nachos or for 2 main course servings:

1 large onion
2 cloves garlic
1 Tbsp oil
1 small green pepper (in season)
½ tsp chilli powder
1 tsp ground cumin
½ tsp oreganum
½ tsp salt
½ tsp sugar
1 (310 g) can kidney beans
1 Tbsp tomato paste

Dice the onion, chop the garlic finely and sauté the oil. When soft, add the chopped green pepper and seasonings. Cook, stirring occasionally to prevent sticking, until the pepper softens, then reduce the heat.

Drain the can of beans, keeping the liquid, and add the beans and the tomato paste to the rest of the ingredients in the pan. Heat through over moderate heat. Mash the mixture with a potato masher or fork, or, for a smoother mixture, process in a blender or food processor. Thin down with a little of the bean liquid if desired. Taste, and adjust seasonings to suit.

For nachos, pile in the middle of a flat plate, top with grated cheese if desired, and surround with corn chips.

c Mexican Beans

This bean mixture can be used as a dip for corn chips or as a spread for fried tortillas. You can make the mixture several days before you want it, as long as you refrigerate it.

It should have the consistency of thick spaghetti sauce.

For 6 cups:
500 g red kidney beans
6 cups hot water
2 large onions, chopped
3–4 cloves garlic, chopped
2–3 medium-sized carrots, chopped
2 tsp whole cumin seeds
¼ cup tomato sauce
2 Tbsp tomato paste
1 Tbsp cider or wine vinegar (or 2 Tbsp lemon juice)
2 tsp salt
2 pickled Jalapeno peppers or enough Tabasco sauce to make the mixture taste hot

Cook the beans in the water until they are tender. Do not drain.

Add the onions, garlic, carrots and cumin seeds and cook for 30 minutes more, or until all vegetables are tender.

Add the tomato sauce, tomato paste, vinegar or lemon juice, salt and the finely chopped pickled peppers or Tabasco sauce.

Simmer for 10–15 minutes longer, then mash or purée roughly in a food processor. Taste, and add extra ground cumin, salt, Tabasco, etc., if the flavour is not as strong as you like it.

Refrigerate until required, or freeze for long storage.

c Lentil and Vegetable Curry

Brown or red lentils, teamed with small amounts of several vegetables, and a well-flavoured sauce make a good meal the day before you go shopping to replenish your food supplies.

Use the last, rather tired vegetables that are hiding in paper or plastic bags, and add any leftover cooked vegetables from little dishes in the refrigerator.

Or, if you have a garden, go out and pick a little bit of this or that.

Take care not to over- or undercook any of the vegetables you use.

For 4 main course servings:
1½ cups red or brown lentils, or moong dahl
2–3 cups water
2 bay leaves
2 Tbsp oil or 25 g butter
2 onions
2 cloves garlic
1 tsp turmeric
1 tsp ground cumin
1 tsp ground ginger
2–3 cups chopped vegetables
1 tsp salt
1 cup hot water
about ½ cup coconut cream (optional)

Cook the lentils or dahl in the water with the bay leaves until tender, adding more water if necessary. Red lentils and dahl should take 20–30 minutes, and brown lentils 40 minutes.

While they cook, prepare the second mixture, preferably in a large non-stick pan with a lid.

Heat the oil or butter, add the chopped onion and garlic, and the spices. Cook without browning for 5 minutes.

Prepare and cut up the vegetables into evenly sized cubes or pieces, starting with those that take longest to cook.

Add each vegetable as it is prepared, tossing it with the onion, and covering the pan between additions. Add the salt and water after the last addition and cook until all vegetables are barely tender. Add the cooked lentils and (optional) coconut cream. Taste, and adjust seasonings, thickness, etc., boiling down or thickening with a little cornflour paste if necessary.

Serve in a bowl or on rice accompanied by a salad of tomatoes and peppers with a yoghurt or French dressing.

c Dahl

This is a mixture of spaghetti-sauce consistency which is nice served with rice and curry side dishes. You can have a wonderful time surrounding the big bowls of dahl and rice with little plates of sweet and savoury, raw and cooked, crunchy and soft foods to provide interesting accents for your meal.

For 4 main course servings or 6–8 side dish servings:
1 cup red or brown lentils or moong dahl
4 cups water
2 Tbsp oil
2 onions, chopped
2 cloves garlic
2 tsp cumin seeds
1 tsp ground turmeric

2 tsp grated root ginger
1 tsp garam masala
1 tsp salt

Boil the lentils or dahl in the water until tender and mushy — about 20 minutes for moong dahl, 30 minutes for red lentils, and 40 minutes for brown lentils.

In another pan heat the oil and cook the next five ingredients over moderate heat until the onion is tender. Stir in the garam masala and the salt and remove from the heat.

Add the onion mixture to the pulses when they are soft, and simmer together for 5 minutes, boiling fast if mixture needs thickening, or adding more water if it is too thick.

c Red Lentil Loaf

This loaf has proved to be popular with vegetarians and meat-eaters alike.

It is good served as a meat loaf would be served, with mashed potatoes, green beans or broccoli, and a fresh tomato sauce to go with the loaf.

For 6–8 servings:
1½ cups red lentils
3 cups water
1 bay leaf
2 cloves garlic, chopped
2 onions, sliced
25 g butter
2 eggs
2 cups grated cheese
1 cup chopped tomatoes
3 slices wholemeal bread, crumbled
2 tsp salt
½ tsp curry powder
½ cup chopped parsley

Simmer the lentils gently with the water, bay leaf and garlic until they are tender and the water is absorbed.

Meanwhile, sauté the onions in the butter until transparent. Remove from the heat and add the eggs, cheese, chopped fresh or canned tomatoes, breadcrumbs, seasonings, and parsley.

Remove the bay leaf from the cooked lentils and drain off any remaining water.

Stir the lentils into the rest of the loaf mixture, then spoon into a well-greased or baking-paper-lined loaf tin (alternatively, pour into a casserole dish and serve from this, without unmoulding).

Bake, uncovered at 180°C for about 45 minutes, or until firm in the middle.

Pea Flour Patties

C Pea Flour Patties

Pea flour is made from finely ground dried peas. It is high in protein and forms a good fritter batter when mixed with water. It does not need the addition of eggs or milk.

In this easy recipe the raw vegetables are surrounded by batter flavoured with Indian spices.

I like to make the patties small, because they cook quickly and have a high proportion of crisp coating. They make excellent finger food, and go very well with beer before a meal, but they are also excellent served with vegetables or salads as the main part of a meal.

Experiment, making them with different vegetables, but don't leave out the onion. To shorten their cooking time you can partly cook dense vegetables before coating them with batter, if you like.

For 4 main course servings or snacks for 8:

1 cup pea flour
about ¹/₂ cup water
1 tsp turmeric
2 tsp ground cumin
2 tsp ground coriander
2 tsp garam masala
2 medium-sized potatoes
1 onion
1 cup frozen peas, or cauliflower
  florets etc.
oil for frying

Mix the pea flour with water and the flavourings to make a fairly stiff paste. Leave to stand for 5 minutes or longer if you can.

Scrub the potatoes, and cut them and the onion into pea-sized cubes. Cut other vegetables into cubes the same size.

Mix all the vegetables into the batter just before you intend to start cooking. They will thin down the mixture. Add extra pea flour or water to make a batter thick enough to hold spoonfuls of the vegetables together.

Heat oil 2 cm deep in a frypan. Drop teaspoonfuls of mixture carefully into it. Adjust heat so patties brown nicely in about 4 minutes, then turn them and cook the other side for the same time. Faster cooking will leave vegetables raw. Drain, and serve as soon as possible, with a sauce made by combining the following in amounts to suit your taste:

  plain, unsweetened yoghurt
  lemon juice
  chopped mint
  salt
  This dip or sauce improves on standing.

C Bean Feast

This is a very useful and tasty bean mixture. It tastes good served hot, warm, or at room temperature. It can be served as soon as it is cooked, but its flavour and texture improves with standing.

You can serve the mixture as the main part of a meal, or include it in a buffet.

Use whatever beans you like. I like haricot beans because they cook relatively fast, are reasonably priced and have a good flavour and texture.

For 8–12 servings:

2 cups haricot or other beans
8 cups water
¹/₄ cup oil
2 large onions
2 scrubbed potatoes
2 cubed carrots
2–3 stalks celery
2 tsp salt
1 tsp paprika
2 tsp sugar
¹/₄ cup tomato paste
1 tsp dried basil
1 tsp dried oreganum
2 cups cauliflower pieces
1 green pepper, sliced (optional)
about ¹/₂ cup chopped parsley

Soak the beans overnight, then boil in the water until tender enough to squash with your tongue on the top of your mouth (see page 129).

Cool the beans in their cooking liquid until you are ready to make the rest of the recipe. Put the oil, onions, potatoes, carrots and celery in a large saucepan.

Stir over moderate heat until vegetables are very hot, then add the next six ingredients, the drained beans and 1¹/₂ cups of their cooking liquid, and simmer, stirring frequently, for 15 minutes. Add the pieces of cauliflower and sliced green pepper and cook for 5 minutes longer. Remove from the heat and add the chopped parsley.

Serve reheated, warm or at room temperature, sprinkled with more parsley. Always taste before serving, and adjust the seasoning if necessary.

C Quick Chilli Con Carne

This quick version of chilli con carne is a cross between a soup and a stew. You save time using beans which have been precooked and flavoured with tomato. Extra seasonings add interest.

I like to serve this in a bowl, with rice, and eat it with a spoon rather than a fork. Team it with a green salad or coleslaw for a complete meal.

For 6–8 servings:

2 Tbsp butter
2 large onions, chopped
2 cloves garlic, chopped
2 small dried chillies
1 tsp freshly ground cumin
1 tsp oreganum
1 tsp paprika
500 g minced beef
2 tsp salt
2 tsp sugar
2 Tbsp flour
1 small can tomato paste

1 green pepper, chopped
1 cup water
1 large can baked beans

In a large saucepan over high heat, lightly brown the onion and garlic in the butter. Grind, crush or finely chop the chillies and cumin, and add with the oreganum, paprika and minced beef.

Stir, breaking up lumps, until the mince is no longer pink.

Stir in the salt, sugar and flour. Add the tomato paste, chopped green pepper and water, and simmer for 15 minutes. Add more water for a more liquid mixture, if this is what you prefer.

Serve immediately, over rice, or reheat when required.

Red Beans and Rice

Don't be put off by the name of this recipe, thinking that it sounds boring. It appears on hundreds of New Orleans menus, and is eaten by visitors and locals at all hours.

For 4–6 servings:
2 cups red beans
6 cups water
50 g butter
3 onions, chopped
4–6 cloves garlic, chopped
1 green pepper, chopped
½ cup chopped parsley
2–3 bay leaves
1 tsp dried thyme
12 drops Tabasco sauce, or chilli
    powder to taste
1 tsp salt
2 cups brown rice

Put everything except salt and rice into a large saucepan. Boil vigorously for 15 minutes, then turn down and simmer for 3–4 hours, until the beans are meltingly soft and quite mushy, forming a thick sauce.

Remove the bay leaves, add the salt, and adjust the seasonings, adding more herbs and chilli sauce if you like.

Cook the rice so that it will be ready when the beans are cooked (rice seasonings are not given here, see page 142).

Serve the beans on the rice, with or without a knob of butter on each serving.

If you think it needs more colour and texture, depart from tradition and serve cubes of brightly coloured peppers to sprinkle over the top, or stir them into the beans a few minutes before serving.

Red Beans and Rice

Lima Bean Salad

(See photograph on page 129.)

Large white lima beans make an unusual but elegant salad. Serve with cheese or hard-boiled eggs, a salad, and crusty bread.

For 6 servings:
2–3 cups cooked lima beans
¼ cup olive or corn oil
¼ cup white wine vinegar
1 clove garlic, chopped
1 tsp sugar
½ tsp salt
½ tsp grated nutmeg
6–10 drops hot pepper sauce
¼ cup chopped parsley
2 Tbsp chopped spring onion

To prepare the beans, cover 500 g lima beans with plenty of boiling water. Leave for 3–4 hours or overnight, then simmer, or microwave at Medium (50% power) for about 1½ hours until meltingly tender, with 1 onion, garlic clove, bay leaf and carrot. Lift out 2–3 cups of cooked beans with a slotted spoon. (Make sure beans do not boil dry and burn).

To make the salad, shake, process or blend together the remaining ingredients. Pour this dressing over drained beans and leave to stand for at least 2 hours, or up to 24 hours in a refrigerator.

Serve at room temperature.

Chickpea and Pumpkin Casserole

This is an interesting and unusual main course for vegetarians. Children love it, too. It can be served as a side dish, with sausages or barbecued or grilled meat — and is one of those recipes which is much nicer than it sounds.

For 8 servings:
3 cups cooked chickpeas
750 g pumpkin
1 large onion, chopped
2 cloves garlic, crushed
50 g butter
6–8 drops hot pepper sauce
2 cups grated tasty cheese
salt and pepper

Drain canned or precooked chickpeas.

Cut pumpkin into cubes and simmer in a little water until tender.

Sauté onion and garlic in butter until transparent, then mash with the pumpkin, keeping mixture slightly chunky.

Mix in the pepper sauce and cheese. Taste after adding cheese, adding salt as necessary.

Spread in a large (23 cm), well sprayed or buttered baking dish and heat until bubbly at edges and hot in centre.
Note:
Replace chickpeas with haricot beans if desired.

C Bean Burgers

Most recipes using dried beans require long cooking. This is an exception to the rule. It seems unbelievable that dried beans can be soaked and cooked so quickly, but it works!

Keep a jar of this mixture on hand, since you can use it to produce very fast food when you are caught out.

Burger Mix
½ cup chickpeas
½ cup soybeans
½ cup peanuts (raw) or sunflower
    kernels
¼ cup toasted sesame seeds
½ cup rolled oats
¼ cup pea flour
1 Tbsp parsley
1 tsp salt
¼ cup wheat germ (optional)
1 Tbsp nutritional yeast (optional)

Measure the first four ingredients into a bowl and mix together. Using a blender or food processor (the coffee-grinder attachment of a food processor is most effective) grind half a cup of this mixture at a time until it is the consistency of dry breadcrumbs.

This process makes a terrible noise, but the convenience of the completed product makes it all worthwhile!

Combine the freshly ground bean mixture with the remaining ingredients. Store in an air-tight jar until desired.

C Making Burgers

For 2 x 10 cm burgers:
1 cup burger mix (from above)
½ cup water
2 tsp dark soya sauce
1–2 Tbsp oil to cook

Mix everything except the cooking oil together and allow to stand for at least 15 minutes. For extra flavour add a clove of chopped garlic, or a few garlic granules, if desired.

Cook over a moderate heat for at least 5 minutes on each side, covering the pan with a suitable lid to collect steam and speed up the cooking.
Note:
Other bean varieties may be used in place of chick peas and soyabeans, but kidney beans should be avoided.

C Lentil Spaghetti Sauce

This lentil sauce for pasta is well flavoured and cheap, with an interesting texture.

For 4–6 servings:
1 cup brown lentils

1 bay leaf
3 medium-sized onions
3 cloves garlic
2 Tbsp oil
100 g mushrooms (optional)
1 green pepper (optional)
1 (425 g) can tomato purée
1 tsp basil
1 gtsp marjoram
1 tsp oreganum
¼ tsp thyme
½ tsp sugar
½ tsp salt
black pepper
350–500 g spaghetti, wholemeal or
    plain, or other pasta

Rinse the lentils, and then cover with plenty of water and boil with the bay leaf until tender.

While the lentils are cooking, finely chop the onions and sauté with the crushed, chopped garlic in the oil until tender. Add the sliced mushrooms and diced green pepper (if desired) and continue to cook until the onion is soft and clear.

Pour in the tomato purée, then add the herbs, sugar, salt and pepper. Simmer for a few minutes over a low heat to allow the flavours to blend.

Stir in the cooked lentils and reheat to serve as desired. This mixture may be eaten immediately if you are in a hurry, but its flavour improves if it is allowed to stand for a while.

Serve over spaghetti, or other pasta.

C Brown Lentil Burgers

These burgers have a definite firm texture, much like that of burgers made from meat.

For 8–10 burgers, to serve 4–5:
½ cup brown lentils
1 bay leaf
2 medium-sized onions
2 cloves garlic
2 Tbsp oil or butter
1 Tbsp parsley
½ tsp basil
½ tsp marjoram
¼ tsp (a large pinch) thyme
1 tsp salt
black pepper to taste
½ cup fresh wholemeal breadcrumbs
2 eggs
2 Tbsp tomato paste
2 tsp dark soya sauce
½ cup flour

Cook the lentils with the bay leaf until they are tender. Remove them from the heat, drain, and remove the bay leaf.

Finely chop the onions and garlic and sauté in the oil or butter until the onion is soft and clear. Add the herbs, salt and pepper.

Tip the cooked, drained lentils into a large bowl, add the onions and garlic, then mix in the remaining ingredients.

Divide the mixture into 8–10 evenly sized portions. Shape each portion into a 10–12 cm pattie, wetting your hands with cold water to prevent the mixture sticking. If the mixture won't hold its shape, add a few more breadcrumbs or a little more flour until it does.

Cook in a little oil until lightly browned on each side and firm when pressed in the middle.

C Bulgar and Bean 'Chilli Con Carne'

The bulgar in this sauce thickens it and gives it body in the same way that minced beef gives substance to spaghetti sauce, while the beans add extra interest. The final combination of chopped wheat, beans and rice is not only interesting to eat, but nutritionally well balanced too! Try it if you want a quick-cooking dinner — although you may find, as I do, that leftovers taste even better.

For 4–6 main course servings:
¼ cup bulgar
1½ cups boiling water
2 large onions
2 cloves of garlic
2 Tbsp oil or butter
2 tsp ground cumin
2 tsp oreganum
½–1 tsp chilli powder (to taste)
1 Tbsp dark soya sauce
3 Tbsp tomato paste
2 tsp sugar
½ cup hot water
juice of 1 lemon
black pepper
1 (425 g) can kidney beans, drained

Pour the boiling water over the bulgar and then leave to stand, stirring occasionally while preparing the rest of the recipe.

Dice the onions and finely chop the garlic, heat the oil or butter in a large pot or frypan and sauté these until the onion is soft and beginning to turn clear. Stir in the cumin, oreganum and chilli powder and continue to cook for a few minutes. Add remaining ingredients.

Add the bulgar and combine everything well. The mixture should be about the consistency of a thick spaghetti sauce. If you think that it is still too thick, add a little more water (some batches of bulgar seem to absorb much more water than others). Allow to simmer over a low heat for 5–10 minutes, stirring occasionally to prevent sticking on the bottom.

Serve over brown or white rice, topped with sour cream and spring onions or chives, accompanied by a

Bean Sprout Eggs

lettuce salad or coleslaw.
Note:
Bulgar is sometimes called Burghul.

How to Sprout Beans and Lentils

Some beans and lentils will sprout and grow easily in a warm kitchen. They grow fastest in summer, protected from the light. Start with small, oval, olive-green mung beans before attempting to grow other varieties.

Put 2 tablespoons mung beans in a large coffee jar. Cover the top with a 20 cm square of muslin or other thin, coarsley woven material, and screw on, over it, a preserving jar band.

Half fill the jar with cold tap water and leave for 8–12 hours, then drain off all the water.

Surround the jar with a collar of brown paper to keep out most of the light and rinse the sprouting beans twice or 3 times each day. Make sure all water is removed after each rinse.

The sprouts are normally used when the stems are 2–4 cm long and small leaves are forming, but they may be used earlier.

For greatest food value, remove the paper collar and stand the jar of sprouts in sunlight the day before use.

Sprouting Brown Lentils

Put enough brown lentils to come more than a third, but less than half way up a jar. Fill the jar with water a little cooler than body temperature and leave for 24 hours. After an hour or so the lentils will fill the jar. After 24 hours drain off the water. Rinse once every morning and once every evening.

The lentils will split their brown skins and sprout. The actual sprouts are small, and the volume of the soaked lentils will not increase very much more.

Any time after the first hour of soaking, you can eat them by the spoonful, exactly as they are, or you can add them to anything you are cooking — they will be cooked after 3 or 4 minutes.

Using Sprouts

Bean sprouts may be added to other salad vegetables, stir-fried by themselves, or stir-fried in egg, meat and/or vegetable mixtures. To keep the sprouts for a few days, cover them with cold water in the refrigerator, and change the water daily.

Bean-Sprout Eggs

For 4 servings:
Sauce
1 Tbsp cornflour
2 tsp dark soya sauce
1 tsp instant chicken stock
1 tsp sugar
1 cup water

Omelette
2 cups bean sprouts
1–2 cups sliced mushrooms
3–4 spring onions, chopped
cooking oil
3–4 eggs
2 Tbsp water
¹/₂ tsp salt

Make the sauce by mixing the ingredients, in the order given, in a saucepan. Simmer for 2–3 minutes, then remove from heat.

Sauté first the bean sprouts, then the mushrooms and spring onions in about 1 tablespoon of oil in a hot pan. Cook just enough to wilt the vegetables. Remove to a flattish dish, mix, then divide into four piles.

Beat together the eggs, water and salt to combine. Pour into a measuring cup. Heat a medium-sized frying pan, add 1 teaspoon oil, then a quarter of the egg mixture. Before this sets sprinkle one quarter of the vegetables over it. Lift edges and let uncooked egg from surface run under the edges to cook. Roll loosely, or fold in quarters, as soon as egg in centre is no longer liquid.

Serve with some of the sauce. Repeat for other three servings.

C Tofu Burgers

Many people would like to try tofu but don't know what to make with this bland, white high-protein food made from soyabeans. This recipe serves as a good way to introduce tofu to your diet.

For 8 burgers, to serve 4:
250 g tofu
1 medium-sized onion
2–3 cloves garlic
1 Tbsp dark soya sauce
1 Tbsp sherry
¼ tsp ground ginger
1 Tbsp nutritional yeast (optional)
¼ cup sunflower seeds
¼ cup wholemeal flour
black pepper to taste

Remove the tofu from its package and stand it on a sloping board for a few minutes, allowing any excess liquid to drain away.

Dice the onion and garlic very finely. Crumble the tofu into a bowl, add the onion and garlic, then the remaining ingredients. (If you don't have any sherry, add a little water and a dash of lemon juice instead).

Mix together well, then, working with wet hands, divide the mixture into quarters, then eighths. Shape each portion into a 7–10 cm pattie (so you have a total of 8 burgers).

Cook for 5 minutes per side, or until the burgers are golden brown.
Note:
If you have a choice, buy firm tofu for this recipe.

C Sweet and Sour Tofu

Fast and colourful, this sweet-sour mixture is ready in less than the time it takes rice to cook.

For 2 servings:
200–300 g firm or very firm tofu, cubed
2 Tbsp oil
1 large onion
1 green and/or red pepper
1 Tbsp oil
1 Tbsp cornflour
¼ cup brown sugar
2 Tbsp wine vinegar
1½ tsp light soya sauce
½ cup water
red food colouring (optional)

Cut the tofu into 1 cm cubes (approx.) and brown evenly on all sides, in the first measure of oil, in a non-stick pan. This should take about 5 minutes.

In another pan, or after the tofu has cooked and been removed, sauté the onion and pepper, cut into pieces about the same size as the tofu, in the remaining measure of oil. When tender, but not browned (about 5 minutes), stir in the cornflour and brown sugar, then add the vinegar, soya sauce and water and bring to the boil, stirring constantly. Colour red with food colouring if desired.

Stir the tofu into the sauce and serve over rice or noodles.
Variation:
Replace the water and half the sugar with pineapple juice. Stir pineapple cubes into the hot sauce before adding the tofu.

C Tomato Tofu Tortilla Stack

This is a colourful and very popular casserole with a Mexican flavour. It contains uncooked tortillas, which are available from some delicatessens and Mexican restaurants.

Make the sauce first.

Tomato and Chilli Sauce
1 (425 g) can tomato purée
½ tsp chilli powder
1 tsp ground cumin
½ tsp oreganum
½ tsp ground coriander
½ tsp salt
1 tsp sugar
½–1 tsp hot pepper sauce to taste
juice of ½ lemon

Combine all the ingredients in a medium-sized pot and simmer gently while preparing the remaining components of the stack as described below:

For 6 servings:
1 large onion
1 green pepper
2 Tbsp oil or butter
500 g (approx.) firm tofu
½ tsp chilli powder
1 tsp cumin
½ tsp oreganum
1 tsp salt
black pepper
6 uncooked corn tortillas
1 (425 g) can whole kernel corn
Tomato and Chilli Sauce (above)
½ cup grated cheese

Chop the onion and green pepper. In a large pan or pot sauté these in the oil or butter over a medium heat. While this cooks, drain and crumble the tofu. Tofu comes in a variety of different-sized blocks. Don't worry if you have 100 g more or less than the suggested amount.

Add the tofu and seasonings to the onion-and-pepper mixture, and continue to cook until they dry out a little.

To assemble the whole stack, lay two of the flat tortillas on the bottom of a medium-sized casserole dish so that they overlap as little as possible (an oval dish is probably the best shape if you have one). Spread one-third of the tofu mixture over these, then one-third of the drained corn over this. Complete the layer by pouring over one-third of the Tomato and Chilli Sauce. Repeat this process twice so that there are three layers of everything.

Sprinkle the grated cheese evenly over the top and bake, uncovered at 180°C, for 30–40 minutes, until hot right through.
Note:
Replace tortillas with barely cooked lasagne noodles or with corn chips, if you cannot get uncooked tortillas.

C Eggy Tofu

In this recipe tofu is sautéed until crusted, mixed first with quick-cooking vegetables, then with an egg to hold it together, and finally coated with an interesting sauce. You finish up with a substantial meal for one person.

For 1 serving:
2 tsp oil
about 100 g tofu, drained and cubed
¼–½ cup sliced mushroom
1–2 spring onions
1 egg
¼ cup water
2 tsp Kikkoman soya sauce
¼ tsp sesame oil
hot pepper sauce to taste
1 tsp cornflour

Buy firm or very firm tofu if you have a choice. Heat the oil in a non-stick frying pan. Cut tofu into cubes. Cook in the hot oil until all sides are golden brown. Add the mushrooms and spring onions. Stir-fry from 1–2 minutes until wilted.

Now prepare two separate mixtures. Beat the egg with a fork to combine the white and yolk, and mix the remaining ingredients in another container. Add the egg to the tofu mixture in the pan, stirring until the egg sets. Add the remaining ingredients which have been stirred together, and heat until this mixture thickens and turns transparent.

Sprinkle with chopped parsley or chives, and serve immediately on rice, toast or noodles.

Double or triple the recipe for 2 or 3 servings.

C Marinated Tofu (for Burgers and Kebabs)

When left to stand in a well-flavoured marinade, tofu absorbs its flavour.

Square slabs of the marinated tofu, sautéed in a teaspoon or so of oil, make good burgers or toasted sandwiches.

Cubes, sautéed for a few minutes on all sides, may be threaded on

Marinated Tofu Kebabs and Grilled Polenta Kebabs

sticks with vegetables to make kebabs, which are then carefully grilled or barbecued.

Although the outside will be quite firm and crusty, the inside will keep its original soft texture. Start with tofu which is firm, or extra-firm, or the tofu may fall apart when skewered.

about 500 g extra-firm tofu
¼ cup corn or soya oil
¼ cup lemon juice
¼ cup dark soya sauce
2 large cloves garlic, chopped
1 Tbsp sesame oil
1 tsp dried oreganum
hot pepper sauce to taste

Drain the tofu, cut into 15 mm thick, 10 cm square slices, or 2 cm cubes (approx.), and leave to stand while you prepare the marinade.

Measure the remaining ingredients into an unpunctured plastic bag, using enough hot pepper sauce to give the hotness you like.

Stand the bag in a shallow baking pan and place the tofu in it so that the slices or cubes lie flat. Suck out the air, so that the tofu is surrounded by the marinade, and fasten with a rubber band. Leave for at least 4 hours, or up to 48 hours, turning occasionally.

Brown the drained tofu in a non-stick pan with a few drops of oil, over moderate to high heat. Give cubes 30–40 seconds per side, and give slices several minutes per side at lower heat, since the slices will not be grilled later.

For kebabs, thread the lightly sautéed cubes on skewers with mushrooms, little tomatoes, red and green pepper squares and cubes of zucchini or eggplant, all of which have been turned in the marinade. Grill about 5 cm from the heat, for about 5 minutes per side, turning once, and brushing with mayonnaise or with extra marinade if desired.

Serve the slices in toasted rolls or between slices of toasted bread, with tomato relish and other burger accompaniments. Serve the kebabs on rice, noodles, bulgar, etc. They taste good with tomato sauce.

Rice and Other Grains

Grains, the seeds of grasses, are the most important staple foods in the world. Rice, wheat and corn are the most used grains, but many others are grown in different parts of the world, according to climate.

Half the world lives on rice — or at least on a rice-based diet. Particularly now, when nutritionists are telling us to include more starches or complex carbohydrates in our diets, it is sensible to include a variety of interesting rice dishes as we increase our consumption of grains in general.

Grains are processed in many ways; they may be left whole, flaked, chopped (kibbled), or ground coarsely or to fine powders. The outer layers of the grain are often removed during processing. As these layers contain valuable nutrients as well as dietary fibre, it is very important to include unprocessed or whole grains in your diet. Many grain products are now widely available and are worth trying for their interesting flavours and textures as well as their nutritional content.

How Many of These Grains Do You Know and Use?

1. WHOLE GRAIN RYE: Requires long cooking. Serve like brown rice. Sauté in butter or oil before cooking.

2. FLAKED RYE: If stirred during cooking, forms a chewy porridge-like mixture. If lightly browned in butter or oil, before cooking without stirring, the grains stay separate.

3. KIBBLED RYE: Chopped rye grains. Boil or microwave, and serve instead of rice.

4. COARSE CORN MEAL and

5. FINE CORN MEAL: Corn kernels ground to different particle sizes. The finer types are usually used in baking, while the coarser types may be boiled with water to make a porridge-like mixture (polenta).

6. POPPING CORN: Whole kernels of a special variety of corn. When heated with a little oil, the grains expand and pop violently. Without additions popcorn is a low-calorie, low-fat snack.

7. SEMOLINA: The coarsely ground heart of wheat kernels. In Indian cookery it is lightly browned before cooking, with interesting results.

8. FLAKED WHEAT: Steamed and crushed wheat. If stirred as cooked, the flakes produce a porridgey mixture. If cooked without stirring, with a little oil or butter, they keep their shape. Use in place of rice, or in muesli mixtures.

9. WHEAT BRAN: Made from the outer layers of wheat grains. Does not contain the wheat germ. High in fibre. Sometimes sold as baking bran. May be added to baking, porridge, etc.

10. WHEAT GRAINS (wheat berries): Use as rice etc. Requires longer cooking than kibbled or flaked wheat.

11. WHEAT GERM: A small part of the wheat grain, from which the new wheat plant grows. A concentrated food, especially high in protein, vitamins and minerals. Add it to baking, porridge, and other foods, to enrich them. Excellent value for money, nutritionally.

12. KIBBLED WHEAT: Chopped wheat grains. Not cooked during manufacture, it needs more cooking than bulgar. Cook and serve as rice, include in porridge mixtures, or use in coarse-textured bread, after heating to boiling point in water, then draining.

13. WHOLEMEAL FLOUR: Made by milling the whole wheat grain. It contains the outer bran layer and the germ, which are high in fibre, vitamins and minerals, as well as the inner white part (or endosperm) of the grain. It gives a solid texture to baked products. To include more in your diet, try replacing half, rather than all the flour in an existing recipe with wholemeal flour, and be prepared to add a slightly different amount of liquid to reach the usual consistency.

14. BULGAR OR BURGHUL: Heat-treated, precooked chopped wheat which needs soaking or brief cooking in water, before being used in salads and savoury mixtures. Soaks up flavours of accompanying foods.

15. PEARL BARLEY: Polished to remove the outside layers. Use in soups, or as rice, or in salads etc.

16. BUCKWHEAT: Often toasted before sale to improve flavour. Cook in place of rice and in porridge mixtures. Ground for use in pancakes.

17. FLAKED BARLEY: Made from steamed, rolled barley grains. Use as you would other flaked grains.

18. OAT BRAN: Made from outer layers of oat grain; cooks with water to a much softer mixture than bran. Acclaimed as soluble fibre. If used to replace flour in baking, texture becomes drier.

19. FLAKED MILLET: Flaked for quicker cooking in porridgey mixtures. Millet is gluten-free.

20. MILLET: Small, round grain (also sold for birdseed) which will grow in very hot and dry places.

21. WHOLE GRAIN ROLLED OATS: Oat grains which are steamed then flattened. Widely used in muesli etc. Cook, without stirring, in mixtures to replace rice.

22. SHORT-GRAIN WHITE RICE: The short, plump grains tend to break down during cooking, becoming sticky and thickening surrounding liquid. This is desirable in rice puddings, soups, and in sushi.

23. BASMATI RICE: Aromatic rice, with appearance and nutritive value of long-grain white rice. Cooking smells are startling and unusual. Flavour outstanding, stronger in some brands than others. More highly priced, understandably, than white rice.

24. WILD RICE: Formerly expensive and rare because it was not cultivated, but is now grown commercially, so price has decreased, and availability increased. Nutty flavour; cooking time similar to that of brown rice. Sold in rice mixtures. A luxury item.

25. HEAT-TREATED RICE: Easily recognisable by its yellowish colour. Is heat-treated before outer layers are removed and is said to contain more nutrients that white rice because of this. Costs more than plain long-grain rice but cooks more easily and produces greater volume. Microwaves very well. When cooked, loses most of its yellowish colour. Usually sold under brand names, e.g. Uncle Ben.

26. MIXED RICE: Mixed long-grain rices, mainly brown and glutinous rices. Need long cooking time, as for brown rice. Looks attractive, and may be used to replace other cooked rice, in recipes.

27. SHORT-GRAIN BROWN and

30. LONG-GRAIN BROWN RICE: Retains its bran layers and germ, thus more vitamins, minerals and protein. Needs longer cooking, and often more water than white rice. It has firmer, more chewy texture and nutty flavour. Microwave or pressure cook to reduce cooking time. Little difference in behaviour of long and short grains. Serve in same way as cooked long-grain white rice. Pressure cooks in less than 10 minutes.

28. BLACK GLUTINOUS RICE: Novelty value. Cooking water is dark red, and cooked grains reddish-brown. When mixed with plain cooked rice, it looks interesting. Available in Asian food stores.

29. LONG-GRAIN WHITE RICE: Grain shape and length vary slightly, but cooking and nutritional qualities are similar. The usual choice for plainly cooked rice to accompany other foods. Many different cooking methods are used. Methods where all water is absorbed give slightly more flavour. Overcooking causes stickiness. Microwaves well.

See photograph on page 138–9.

1		8	15	23
				24
2		9	16	25
		10		26
3	5	11	17	27
4	6	12	18	28
7		13	19	21	29
		14	20	22	30

B C Grilled Polenta

(See photograph on page 137.)

Polenta is a type of corn porridge. This thick, well-flavoured porridge is left to set, then cut into cubes and browned lightly in a non-stick pan.

The browned cubes, threaded on skewers with vegetables, make good barbecue food for vegetarians, or can be re-heated on a tabletop grill.

For 4 servings:
2 cups water
about 1 tsp salt
fresh or dried thyme, basil and oreganum
1 cup coarse yellow corn meal
¹/₂–1 cup grated cheese

Bring the water and salt to the boil. Add about ¹/₂ teaspoon each of dried herbs, or more fresh herbs.

Sprinkle the corn meal into the water while stirring thoroughly. Keep stirring, over low to moderate heat, for about 5 minutes, until very thick. Remove from the heat and stir in the grated cheese. (Polenta may seem salty at first, but saltiness diminishes on standing.)

Pour into a buttered or oiled 20 cm square pan, and leave to cool for about 30 minutes, then turn out and cut into 2 cm cubes.

Brown on all sides in a non-stick pan with a little butter or oil, then thread on skewers, alternated with vegetables, and barbecue or grill when required.

Variation:
Pour into a round pan, then cut in wedges, brown and serve with fried eggs, mushrooms, tomatoes, etc.

Make without cheese for vegan diets.

C M Muesli

This is, without a doubt, the easiest muesli I make.

¹/₂ cup honey
¹/₄ cup brown sugar
¹/₄ cup oil
1 tsp cinnamon
1 tsp vanilla
¹/₂ tsp salt
3 cups whole grain oats
¹/₂ cup oat or wheat bran
¹/₂ cup coconut
¹/₂ cup wheatgerm
¹/₂ cup chopped nuts

Mix the first six ingredients in a bowl. Heat at Full power until mixture bubbles, about 2 minutes.

Meantime, combine remaining ingredients in a large, wide, shallow microwave dish. Stir in hot mixture.

Cook at Full power, stirring every minute after 4 minutes, until mixture turns golden brown and starts to firm up, from 6–10 minutes.

Or heat syrup until it bubbles, in a pan on the stove. Combine with dry ingredients and bake in a roasting pan at 150°C, stirring frequently until it browns lightly, in about 30 minutes, or brown in a large shallow dish under a grill, turning frequently.

Cool. Break up if necessary. Store in airtight jars when cold.

Variation:
Add chopped dried fruit to the cooked muesli.

C M Hot Cereal Mix

Although you may not be particularly excited by porridge or boiled rice, you may find that you really enjoy mixtures of flaked and/or kibbled cereals which are simmered together in a bowl in the microwave oven, or in a pot on the stove.

It is easy to cook a different combination every day if you keep different cereals in jars near your cooking area.

Use one or more level measuring tablespoon(s) of each, and keep a count of the total number of tablespoons used. If you are going to microwave your cereal, add twice as many tablespoons of water. For stovetop cooking allow three times as many tablespoons of water.

Four tablespoons cereal will need 8 tablespoons water if microwaved, and 12 tablespoons water if boiled. This should be about one serving. Add a pinch of salt per serving.

Microwave one serving for about 5 minutes, and a two-serving container for about 10 minutes, both at 50% power.

Or simmer in a pot for about 15 minutes. Alter times and amounts of liquid if necessary.

Top with sesame sugar, brown sugar, maple syrup, etc., add toasted sunflower seeds if you like and serve with plenty of milk, yoghurt, soya milk or fromage frais.

Suitable cereals include
• flaked barley, oats, wheat, rye and millet
• kibbled wheat, rye and bulgar
• corn meal and oatmeal
• wheatgerm, oat bran and wheat bran

Sesame Sugar
Grind together in a pestle and mortar or in an electric grinder,

more or less equal volumes of toasted sesame seeds and sugar, and a pinch of salt. Store in an airtight container.

C Super Muesli Bars

These bars are solid-packed with goodies. Their texture, chewy or firm, depends on the stage to which you cook the toffee-like mixture into which you stir the solids.

For 20 bars (2 × 2 × 10 cm):
50 g butter or ¹/₄ cup oil
¹/₂ cup honey
¹/₄ cup peanut butter
1 cup rolled oats, toasted
¹/₂ cup wheatgerm, toasted
¹/₂ cup roasted sesame seeds
¹/₂ cup roasted sunflower seeds
¹/₄ cup dried apricots, chopped, (optional)

Measure the butter or oil, the honey and peanut butter into a large frying pan. Bring to the boil, stirring to blend the ingredients, then turn the heat to very low, and lightly toast the rolled oats, then the wheatgerm, about 10 cm from a grill, stirring frequently, and watching carefully so neither burns.

Mix these in a bowl with the previously roasted sesame seeds and sunflower seeds. Next chop the dried apricots finely, in a food processor if available, and mix with the other dry ingredients.

Cook the honey mixture gently until it forms a firm ball when a little is dropped into cold water and left for about 1 minute, then stir in the dry ingredients thoroughly.

Press into a lightly buttered or oiled 20 cm square, loose-bottomed pan, and leave to cool until it is firm but still flexible. This is the time to turn it out and cut, with a serrated knife, into two pieces, then cut each piece into ten fingers. Wrap individually in cling wrap, or store in a completely airtight container.

Serving Cooked Cereals
These cereals have such a good flavour that you may find you like them best without any added sweetener.

If not, sweeten them with white or brown sugar, plain, dark or fruit flavoured honey or golden syrup.

Vary the liquid you pour on to porridge. Use milk, plain or flavoured yoghurt, evaporated milk, condensed milk, cream or sour cream.

C M Cooking Rice

FOOLPROOF WHITE RICE

If you coat rice grains with oil or butter before you cook them, there is much less chance that they will stick together.

Heat 1 tablespoon oil or butter in a heavy-bottomed saucepan with a tight-fitting lid. Add ½ teaspoon salt.

Stir in 1 cup long-grain white rice. Add 2 cups boiling water. Put on a tight-fitting lid and cook gently, without lifting the lid or stirring, for about 15 minutes. Lift out a few grains of rice and test by squeezing them. (See Butterless White Rice below.) If it is not cooked, check if there is any water left in the pan. If not, add about ¼ cup more, cover again and cook for 3–4 minutes longer. Transfer to serving dish, forking it lightly to get a fluffy appearance.

FOOLPROOF HEAT-TREATED RICE

Cook as above, adding 2¼ cups water of any temperature to 1 cup of rice. Allow a little longer cooking time.

Note:

For softer-textured rice, add ¼–½ cup more water, and cook for about 5 minutes longer.

BUTTERLESS WHITE RICE

This is a good way to cook rice when you don't have a heavy pot with a tight-fitting lid, or when you don't want to add oil or butter.

Bring 8 cups water and 1 tablespoon salt to the boil in a large saucepan. Slowly shake 1 cup long-grain rice into the bubbling water, making sure water doesn't stop boiling. Boil gently with the pot lid ajar, or without a lid, for about 15 minutes.

Squeeze a grain of rice btween your finger and thumb. If you can squeeze it completely in half, without having a hard core left, it is cooked.

Drain, using a large sieve.

If serving within an hour, rinsing is not necessary. If serving later, rinse with hot (or cold) water, leave to drain again, then store in a container in which the rice will not dry out.

MICROWAVED WHITE RICE

The microwave oven cooks rice very well. Use heat-treated or plain long-grain rice. You do not need to attend to it at all during or after cooking so you can put in the rice, turn on the oven, and go away. When you come back later (any time after the cooking time plus the standing time), all you need to do is reheat the rice at Full power, allowing 1–2 minutes per cup. It needs no draining, no stirring. It will not have stuck to the container, and will have a good flavour.

In a large microwave bowl, turn 1 cup long-grained or heat-treated rice in 1–2 teaspoons oil (or melted butter). Add 2¼ cups (preferably hot) water, and cover, folding back the edge 5mm if you use plastic cling wrap.

For 1 cup, cook at Full power for 12–15 minutes. Allow 10 minutes standing time.

For 2 cups allow 20–25 minutes, with 15 minutes standing time.

If rice boils over, use a larger container, keep lid ajar, or lower power level (to 50% power) and increase cooking time by 5 minutes.

To reheat cook at Full power, allowing 1–2 minutes per cup. It needs no draining, no stirring. It will not have stuck to the container, and will have a good flavour.

BROWN RICE

Brown rice has a nutty flavour, an interesting, slightly chewy texture, and is nutritionally better than white rice. It is available in long- and short-grained varieties. Both may be cooked and served as long-grain white rice is served. All types of brown rice take longer to cook than white rice. Some brown rices absorb more liquid than others, and take longer to cook. You should always be prepared to add some extra water, and cook for longer, if the grains seem dry and hard.

Undercooked brown rice may put your friends and family off it forever. Brown rice is easier to cook than white rice, because the outer coating on the grains stops them sticking together as they cook.

Make sure that you allow plenty of cooking time.

SIMMERED BROWN RICE

Turn 1 cup brown rice in 1 teaspoon oil or melted butter

Add 2½ cups water and ½ teaspoon salt. Cover tightly and simmer for about 45 minutes, adding extra water if rice dries out before it is tender.

MICROWAVED BROWN RICE

Microwave for 25 minutes, using same proportions as for simmered brown rice and general method as for white rice. Allow 15 minutes standing time.

PRESSURE-COOKED BROWN RICE

A pressure cooker revolutionises the cooking of brown rice. My modern German pressure cooker cooks 1 cup of brown rice in 3 cups of water, with ½ teaspoon salt, at high pressure, in 9–10 minutes. I leave it to stand for 3–5 minutes after the pressure is lowered, before draining off any remaining water and serving it.

Allow a little longer if pressure cooker is old, or is not working efficiently.

BUTTERLESS HEAT-TREATED RICE

Proceed as above for quantities, adding the rice to hot or cold water, but stirring until the water boils again, if necessary. Rice may be removed from heat, then heated again, if necessary, before cooking is completed. Cooking time is unlikely to be shorter than that of plain long-grain rice.

ADDING FLAVOUR TO RICE

Add butter, or chopped fresh herbs, or Parmesan cheese, or soya sauce, or sesame oil, or chopped, sautéed sesame or sunflower seeds or nuts (or a combination of several of these) to cooked rice.

Replace salt with instant stock powder when cooking. Use 1–2 level teaspoons to 1 cup rice. When using little butter, use the larger quantity.

Sauté onion, celery, peppers, or mushrooms in extra butter before stirring in uncooked rice. Add curry powder, paprika, etc., before water. Add raisins, sultanas, currants, orange or lemon rind to rice when it is about half cooked.

It is important to season rice carefully. Add extra salt with herbs, butter, etc., *after* cooking, if rice tastes too bland.

STORING AND REHEATING RICE

Cooked rice should be covered to prevent drying out, and refrigerated to prevent spoilage. Tough, heatproof plastic oven bags (without holes) make excellent containers for refrigerating and reheating rice. Stir with fork or toss in bag once or twice during reheating. Sprinkle with extra water if rice looks dry before or during heating.

• Reheat rice in microwave oven at Full power for 1–2 minutes per cup, in its serving dish or in an oven bag (without a metal twist tie).

• In conventional oven, spread oven bag flat on a flat, shallow dish, e.g. a sponge-roll pan. Tie loosely. Reheat at whatever temperature oven is already heated to. Flip bag over once during reheating, so both sides heat.

• Reheat in a sieve or colander over a saucepan of boiling water. Cover with a lid so that the steam from the boiling water is prevented from escaping.

• For fastest reheating (without a microwave oven) but with some flavour loss, pour boiling water through cooked rice in colander or sieve or add boiling water to rice in saucepan, then strain.

• Add rice to hot oil, or melted butter, or sautéed, finely chopped ingredients, in a preheated, preferably non-stick pan. Stir to heat evenly.

Flavour and store other cooked grains in the same way as you would rice.

☐ Egg Fried Rice

This is a useful and delicious way to use up small quantities of vegetables that you may have sitting around in your refrigerator.

For 4 servings:
4 cups cooked long-grain white rice, or cooked brown rice
2–3 eggs
1/2 tsp salt
6 spring onions
3–4 Tbsp oil or butter
1 cup sliced mushrooms
1–2 cups beansprouts, chopped peppers, celery, etc.
1/2–1 cup shredded lettuce
soya sauce
sesame oil

Use rice that has been cooked and left to cool for several hours (overcooked or soggy rice cannot be used for this dish). Put the rice in a large bowl, break in the eggs and add the salt. Add the chopped spring onions and stir until the eggs evenly coat the rice.

Heat a large, non-stick frypan or wok. Heat the oil or butter and lightly cook the mushrooms and vegetables (but not the lettuce). Add the rice, then lift the mixture with a fish slice as it heats. The grains should separate as the mixture cooks.

When thoroughly heated through, add the shredded lettuce, stir briefly, and remove from the heat (the lettuce should still be slightly crisp when the rice is served). Taste, and add a little soya sauce if desired. Sprinkle with extra soya sauce and sesame oil just before eating.

☐ Coconut Rice

This rice has an interesting coconut flavour and is especially good with curries. Try leftovers, reheated with sultanas and served with cinnamon sugar, as a breakfast cereal!

For 4 servings:
1 cup long-grain rice (preferably heat-treated)
1/2 tsp salt
1 1/4 cups hot water
1 cup coconut cream

Measure rice, salt and hot water into a 2 litre casserole. Cover and cook at Full power for 10 minutes. Uncover, add coconut cream, and cook for 5 minutes longer, covered loosely with a paper towel or greaseproof paper. Leave to stand for 5–10 minutes before serving
Variation:
Add a finely chopped garlic clove, and 1/2 teaspoon turmeric to the uncooked rice. Proceed as above.

Curried Rice and Tomato Casserole

☐ Curried Rice and Tomato Casserole

Any leftovers from this casserole are good piled on toast, sprinkled with grated cheese, and browned under a grill.

For 4–6 servings:
1 cup long-grain rice (preferably heat-treated)
2 medium-sized onions, finely chopped
1 tsp salt
1 tsp curry powder
1 cup tomato purée
1 1/2 cups water
25–50 g butter or 3 Tbsp oil
2 firm tomatoes, cubed
1 green pepper, if available
1 red pepper, if available

Put the first six ingredients together in a medium-sized casserole. Cube the butter, using the smaller amount if the larger amount bothers you, and add it, or the oil, too. Leave until required.

Bake, tightly covered, at 180°C for 45 minutes, or until rice is tender and all liquid absorbed, stirring once after about 20 minutes if possible.

Add the tomato and cubed peppers and fold through the hot rice. Bake for 5 minutes longer, then leave to stand for 10 minutes, before sprinkling with parsley and serving with a selection of vegetables and/or salads.

Variation:
Replace white rice with brown rice, add an extra 1/2 cup of water, and cook for 1 1/2 hours, or until rice is tender, making sure mixture does not dry out.

☐ Takefumi Rice

Spiced rice and eggs make an interesting quick meal.

For 4 servings:
3 cups water
1 1/2 tsp salt
1/2 tsp cinnamon
8 whole cloves
3–4 drops hot chilli sauce
1 1/2 cups long-grain rice
50 g butter
1 onion, sliced
1/4 cup chopped celery
1–2 cloves garlic, chopped
3–4 eggs, lightly beaten

Heat the first five ingredients until boiling, in a tightly lidded pot. Add the rice and simmer gently for 15 minutes, or until the rice is tender and the water absorbed.

Melt the butter in a large frying pan. Sauté the onion, celery and garlic until tender but not browned. Add the beaten eggs, stir for 30 seconds, then add the hot spiced rice. Mix carefully but thoroughly, then serve with a salad.

C Fried Rice

When fried rice is served as a side dish, smaller amounts of flavouring ingredients may be used. When it is the main part of the meal, use larger quantities. Change or add ingredients, according to what is available. Before starting to cook, cut all solid additions into pieces similar in size to the cooked rice grains. Cook rice ahead of time if possible. Make sure it has been well drained, with the grains separate.

For 2 main or 4 small servings:
1 egg
1 tsp light soya sauce
2–3 Tbsp oil
2–3 rashers bacon
½–1 cup sliced mushrooms
½ cup thawed frozen peas
1 cup bean sprouts
½–1 cup chopped red or green peppers (or celery)
2 cups cooked long-grain rice
2–3 spring onions, chopped
seasonings

Mix egg and soya sauce until evenly combined. In enough of the oil to coat a large pan or wok, cook the egg lightly without stirring, to form a thin omelette.

Roll or fold egg when set, then remove from pan. Slice thinly.

Add remaining oil, then bacon. When nearly cooked, add vegetables one at a time, the ones requiring shortest cooking last. Stir frequently.

Add the rice and mix with other ingredients. Lift mixture away from hot surface of pan or wok as it heats. When heated through, add chopped spring onions (or other quick-cooking leafy vegetables, e.g. chopped raw lettuce).

Add sliced egg mixture. Season carefully with ¼–1 teaspoon sesame oil (optional), light soya sauce, oyster sauce, hot pepper oil or sauce, and fresh coriander leaf or parsley if desired.

Serve immediately.
Variations:
Replace bacon with small pieces of raw chicken breast or pork or lamb fillet meat, or tender steak.

C Risotto with Mushrooms and Peas

This is not the type of risotto where the liquid is added at intervals to the rice mixture which is stirred frequently. Here you finish up with a mixture with separate grains.

For 2–4 servings:
50 g butter
2 onions, chopped
2 rashers bacon, chopped
1 cup long-grain rice
150–200 g mushrooms, sliced
2 tsp instant chicken stock
½ tsp dried thyme
2 cups frozen peas
¼ cup parsley, chopped

Heat three-quarters of the butter in a large frying pan or saucepan with a tight-fitting lid. Add the onions and bacon and cook until the onions are transparent and golden brown.

Add the rice and heat until it turns just milky white, then slightly golden brown.

Add half the sliced mushrooms, stir until wilted, then add the hot water, instant stock and thyme.

Cover tightly, lower heat until mixture is just simmering, and cook for about 12 minutes, or until the rice is just tender. Check and add extra water if it looks dry before the rice is cooked.

Stir the frozen peas through the rice, cover again and cook for about 5 minutes longer.

While the rice cooks, sauté the remaining mushrooms in another pan with the remaining butter, until lightly cooked. Add the parsley. Just before serving, stir the mushroom mixture into the rice. Adjust seasonings carefully.

C Basic Pilaf

Try this recipe with kibbled or flaked wheat, rye, oats or barley. You will wonder why we so often ignore these grains in favour of rice!

For 4 servings:
2 Tbsp butter or oil
1 medium-sized onion
2 cloves garlic
¼ cup kibbled grain (or long-grain white rice), or 1 cup flaked grain
1 cup chopped celery
3 cups water
½ tsp salt
¼ cup chopped parsley (2 Tbsp dried)
freshly ground black pepper to taste

Melt the butter in a large non-stick frying pan with a close-fitting lid. Add the chopped onion and garlic and cook gently for 3–4 minutes without browning.

Stir in the flaked or kibbled grain, or long-grain rice. Continue to stir until all the grains are evenly coated with the oil or butter and have browned lightly.

Add the finely chopped celery, water and salt. Cover and cook for 20–30 minutes, or until the water is absorbed and the grains tender. Add a little more water (½ cup) if you think the mixture looks too dry and the grains are not tender. Stir in the chopped parsley, pepper, and add a little more salt if desired, then serve.

C Curried Rice Salad

For 4 servings:
¼ cup oil
1 onion, chopped
2 cloves garlic, chopped
½–1 tsp curry powder
½ cup sultanas
¼ cup pineapple juice
1 small carrot, grated
2 cups cooked long-grain rice
about ½ cup drained, finely chopped pineapple
2–3 Tbsp lemon juice (or wine vinegar)
salt to taste
3–4 spring onions, finely sliced

Heat oil in a medium-to-large, preferably non-stick frying pan.

Add chopped onion and finely chopped garlic and cook until transparent but not browned. Add curry powder, then sultanas. Sauté lightly.

Add pineapple juice, then carrot, then cooked rice. Toss to mix ingredients evenly, then remove from heat.

Stir in pineapple and add lemon juice or wine vinegar and salt, a little at a time, to taste.

Stir in finely sliced spring onions.

Serve at room temperature, with or without mayonnaise. Check seasoning before serving.

C M Special Spiced Rice

When you cook rice with spices, you raise it from 'every day accompaniment' level to 'special treat' status.

With two additions the rice made by this recipe may be transformed into an interesting 'comfort-food' dessert. If you don't have saffron or pine nuts, leave them out. The spiced rice will still be fairly special.

For 4–6 servings:
¼ tsp saffron strands
½ cup boiling water
1 Tbsp clarified butter
4 cardamom pods
4 whole cloves
1 small cinnamon stick
1 cup Basmati rice
1 bay leaf
a strip (20 cm) orange peel
a strip)10 cm) lime or lemon peel
1 tsp salt
2 cups boiling water
¼ cup currants
¼ cup pine nuts
1 Tbsp clarified butter

Soak saffron strands in first measure of boiling water. Melt clarified butter in microwave at Full power or in frypan. Add crushed cardamom pods, cloves and a broken cinnamon stick. Heat for 2

Layered Fluffy Rice and Fruit

minutes. Stir in rice and heat for 1 minute longer, then add bay leaf, orange and lemon peel, salt, the second measure of boiling water and the soaked saffron and liquid.

Cover and microwave at Medium (50% power) for 15 minutes or simmer for 20 minutes. Leave to stand for 10 minutes. Meantime stir currants, pine nuts and second measure of clarified butter in a small pan until pine nuts turn golden brown.

Sprinkle over, or stir into cooked rice and serve.

M Special Spiced Rice Pudding

For about 6 servings:
Reserve half the mixture above, after cooking. Add ½ can coconut cream and 2–4 Tbsp white or brown sugar. Microwave at Full power, uncovered, for 5–10 minutes. Serve warm.

C M Fluffy Rice Pudding

For 4–6 servings:
½ cup short-grain rice
3 cups milk
¼ tsp salt
2 eggs
½ cup sugar
1 tsp vanilla

Cook rice in salted milk until tender, in a covered bowl above a pot of boiling water for an hour, or in a large, uncovered microwave bowl for 30 minutes at Full power. Stir every 10 minutes.

Separate eggs. Beat whites with sugar until they form peaks which turn over. (Use less sugar if desired.)

Stir egg yolks and vanilla into hot cooked rice. Reheat briefly until yolks thicken.

Fold beaten whites into hot thickened rice.

Serve immediately, or cover and serve at room temperature or chilled.

Variations:
Do not separate eggs. Use less sugar. Add sugar, then eggs, to hot cooked rice. Heat briefly. Serve like this, or cool to room temperature and fold about 1 cup whipped cream into rice mixture.

C Layered Fluffy Rice and Fruit

For 4–6 servings:
Make fluffy rice or whipped cream variation.

Drain juice from stewed or canned fruit. Add half its volume of white wine or orange juice. (For raw fruit, e.g. raspberries, use white wine and/or orange juice alone.)

Simmer for 3–4 minutes to concentrate liquid, then thicken to medium-sauce consistency with custard powder and water paste. Sweeten to taste. Remove from heat.

Stir in fruit carefully. Cool to room temperature, then layer with rice.

Noodles

Noodles, spaghetti and macaroni are three well-known members of the pasta family but there are many more! Increasingly popular nutritionally as a good source of complex carbohydrates, pasta comes in many interesting shapes and sizes.

Although you can often substitute one type for another, you should try to keep several shapes in your store cupboard so that you can fully exploit the different characteristics of each one. When you substitute one pasta shape for another, you should think carefully. By using the same weight rather than the same volume, you achieve a more uniform result.

When you cook pasta, always add it to rapidly boiling water, slowly enough for the water to remain boiling. Pasta made from hard flour has more 'bounce' when cooked, and is more satisfying to eat than pasta made of ordinary flour.

Overcooked pasta loses its shape and is floppy and soft. Just-cooked pasta is springier, firmer and has more 'bite'.

These recipes use pasta of different shapes and sizes, with a variety of ingredients and sauces. Try them for quick, tasty, nutritious and economical meals.

So that you can always produce a meal for unexpected guests, make a point of keeping a few packets of different pasta shapes in your store cupboard.

© Pasta with 'Instant' Sauce

This is sauce which can be prepared while the pasta cooks. Choose a pasta shape with lots of convolutions and crevices since these hold more of the sauce, which is stirred in so that it coats and flavours each individual piece.

For 4–6 servings:
350–500 g uncooked pasta
75 g butter
¼ cup hot water
1 Tbsp instant vegetable stock
1 Tbsp pesto (or chopped fresh basil or
*   1 tsp dried basil)*
1 tsp sugar
½ tsp salt (to taste)
¼ tsp garlic powder
black pepper to taste
dash of hot pepper sauce
¼ cup grated Parmesan cheese
½ cup grated tasty cheese (optional)
3–4 tomatoes, diced (optional)
1–2 Tbsp chopped fresh herbs if
*   available, such as basil, parsley or*
*   chives (optional)*

Cook the pasta, following packet instructions.

Melt the butter, and add the next eight ingredients, stirring to make sure no lumps remain.

Pour this mixture over the hot, cooked pasta. Add the grated Parmesan and any of the optional additions if desired.

Stir together, reheating over a low heat if necessary, and serve.

© Peanut and Sesame Pasta Sauce

This sauce has a nice nutty flavour and can be made from ingredients which you are likely to have in your cupboard.

For 4 servings:
1 large onion
1 Tbsp oil
¼ cup peanut butter
1 Tbsp tahini (optional)
2 Tbsp sweet hot pepper sauce
1½ cups water
light soya sauce or salt
2 Tbsp toasted sesame seeds
about 350 g of your favourite pasta

Cut the onion in half from top to bottom, then cut in thin slices, to form half-rings. Cook these in the oil in a covered pan for about 5 minutes, stirring and turning several times until evenly and lightly browned.

Add the peanut butter, tahini, sweet chilli sauce and water, and stir over moderate heat until the lumps have dissolved. Add extra water, or cook for a little longer until sauce is of thin coating consistency, then season carefully, adding extra chilli sauce for extra sweetness or hotness, and enough light soya sauce or salt to bring out the flavour.

Stir sauce into the freshly cooked, drained pasta, sprinkle with toasted sesame seeds, and serve hot or warm with a cucumber salad, marinated green beans or a crisp green salad.

Variation:
For extra richness, add cream cheese or sour cream to taste.

© Peanutty Pasta Salad

This is an interesting and different pasta recipe for peanut butter fans. It is good served warm, not hot, in summer.

For 2 servings:
100 g spaghetti
200 g of a mixture of carrots, celery
*   and beans, sliced thinly*
100 g bean sprouts (optional)
2 Tbsp crunchy peanut butter
1 Tbsp Kikkoman soya sauce
1 Tbsp wine vinegar
2 tsp sugar
1 tsp sesame oil

Break the spaghetti into 10 cm lengths. Cook in a litre of boiling salted water with a teaspoon of added oil.

Trim the vegetables and cut them into long, thin matchsticks. Rinse the beansprouts.

Measure the remaining ingredients into a cup, and mix well until smooth. Thin down by adding 1 tablespoon each of water and oil, then repeat if necessary, until sauce is of pouring consistency.

When the spaghetti is almost cooked, add the vegetable matchsticks and cook for 2 minutes longer. Add the beansprouts and cook for 30 seconds more.

Drain, pour the peanut sauce over spaghetti and turn gently to coat everything with it. Serve warm, with cucumber and lettuce salads.

© Fresh Tomato Sauce

If you have ripe red, flavourful tomatoes on hand, by all means use them to make sauces for pasta.

You will be wasting your time, however, if the tomatoes are pale, or watery, or out of season. If this is the case, open a can instead, and save yourself disappointment.

I make a light, fresh-tasting sauce with the tomatoes from our garden.

For 4 servings (2–3 cups):
1 kg ripe red tomatoes
1 or 2 onions
2 Tbsp butter
basil, oreganum, thyme
1 tsp sugar
½ tsp salt
freshly ground pepper
hot pepper sauce

Pour hot water over the tomatoes, leave to stand for 20–30 seconds, or till you see the skins split, then drain and peel.

Chop the onion(s) finely and cook gently in the butter in a large non-stick pan, for 5 minutes, without browning. Add chopped tomatoes, herbs to taste, and remaining seasonings, and cook, uncovered, for 10–20 minutes, stirring often. Let mixture evaporate or thicken with about a tablespoon of cornflour mixed to a paste with cold water.

Serve over freshly cooked pasta.

© One Pan Dinner for Two

(See photograph on page 146.)

Although you can use any shaped pasta for this recipe, large macaroni shapes are best because they get filled up with savoury sauce. I like to finish up with a fairly 'sloppy' mixture but you can modify its thickness depending on the heat and whether the lid is on or off during the last part of the cooking.

250 g minced beef
1 clove garlic
1 large onion
thyme or basil
1 pkt tomato soup
3 cups boiling water
250 g fresh vegetables
1 cup (75 g) large macaroni shapes
½ cup grated Cheddar or Mozzarella
*   cheese*

Brown the mince, garlic and onion in a large pan over high heat, breaking up meat as it loses its pinkness. Add fresh or dried herbs to taste, if required.

Sprinkle dry soup mix into pan, stir well, then add the boiling water and the vegetables. Use fairly large pieces of broccoli, cauliflower, celery, peppers, etc.

Stir macaroni into boiling mixture. Cover pan and cook until macaroni is tender, about 15 minutes. Remove lid, raise heat for a drier mixture. Serve in bowls, sprinkled with cheese.

© Savoury Noodles

For 2–4 servings:
1–2 cups large macaroni shapes
water for cooking
2 Tbsp butter
2 tsp instant chicken stock

Spinach and Cottage Cheese Cannelloni

1 tsp instant green herb stock
1 tsp sugar
¼ cup chopped parsley
other chopped fresh herbs (optional)
Parmesan cheese (optional)
about 2 tsp cornflour

Boil pasta in lightly salted water until tender. Drain, leaving ½ cup liquid in pan with pasta.

Add butter, toss to coat, then sprinkle instant stocks, sugar, parsley and other herbs through noodles. Add a sprinkling of Parmesan cheese if desired.

Mix cornflour to a paste with a little extra water. Add gradually, using just enough to thicken liquid to coat pasta.

C Spinach and Cottage Cheese Cannelloni

This is an exceedingly popular and delicious mixture, as suitable for dinner parties as it is for a family meal. You can cook the whole casserole ahead, and reheat it when you want to eat, or you can prepare the sauce and the filling ahead, *but* once the filling is put into the cannelloni tubes the casserole should be cooked promptly, or the pasta will disintegrate.

For 4—6 servings:
1 pkt cannelloni tubes (about 16)

Sauce
2 medium-sized onions
4 cloves garlic
2 Tbsp oil
1 small green pepper
1 tsp basil
½ tsp thyme
½ tsp sugar
½ tsp salt
1 (300 g) can tomato purée
1 Tbsp wine vinegar
¼ cup water

Filling
about 1 kg fresh spinach (2 cups when
    lightly cooked)
1 cup cottage cheese
1 tsp dried oreganum
½ tsp salt
½ tsp sugar
¼ tsp grated nutmeg
black pepper to taste

Topping
1 cup cream cheese
1 cup grated cheese

Chop the onions finely and peel and chop the garlic. Sauté in the oil, stirring occasionally. Stir in the chopped green pepper and continue to cook until everything has softened and the onion turns clear.

Add the seasonings, then the can of tomato purée, vinegar and water. Bring to the boil, then reduce the heat and leave to simmer while you prepare the filling.

Bring a large pot of water to the boil, then add the fresh spinach. Cook for a minute or two, just until the spinach has softened and wilted, then remove from the heat and drain well.

Coarsely chop the spinach, then return to the pot or a medium-sized bowl. Add the cottage cheese and remaining filling ingredients to the spinach, and mix everything together until evenly combined.

Select a shallow casserole dish that will hold all the cannelloni tubes comfortably, then butter it lightly.

Fill each cannelloni tube, then place in the casserole dish. (There is no neat and tidy way to do this — just use your hands. Don't stuff the tubes too full or they may break, or you might run out of filling. Look for 'instant' cannelloni tubes when shopping — these make life much easier as you don't have to cook them first.)

Once all the tubes are full and arranged in the casserole, pour over the sauce. (This should be no thicker than tomato sauce — if it is, add a little more water to thin it down.) Shake the casserole gently to ensure the sauce is evenly distributed and has reached all the little nooks and crannies.

Soften the cream cheese (microwave for about 30 seconds or stand the unopened container in hot water for a few minutes) and spread over the sauce-covered tubes. Sprinkle the grated cheese evenly over this, then bake at 180°C for 40 minutes, or until the top is nicely browned and the pasta is tender.

Serve with your favourite vegetables and/or a salad.

Two Minute Noodle Soup

Leave to stand

Leave to stand for at least 5 minutes before serving, but preferably for longer. Reheat if necessary.

C Zucchini and Yoghurt Pasta

This is a lovely light, summery pasta dish.

For 4 servings:
500 g zucchini
250 g pasta, ribbons or your favourite shape
3 cloves garlic, crushed
1 Tbsp butter
1¹/₂ cups yoghurt
¹/₂ cup sour cream
¹/₂–1 tsp salt to taste
¹/₂ tsp sugar
1 tsp paprika
2–3 Tbsp freshly chopped parsley
1 Tbsp lemon juice
freshly ground black pepper

Cut the zucchini into slices (or chunks depending on size), not more than 1 cm thick.

Put the pasta on to cook, using instructions on the packet.

Sauté the zucchini with the crushed and chopped garlic, until it has softened and is beginning to turn golden.

Remove from the heat and add the yoghurt, sour cream and seasonings. Stir gently until everything is well combined.

Stir into the cooked pasta and serve while hot. Sprinkle individual servings with grated Parmesan if desired.

C Pasta and Tomato Bake

This is a good recipe for a hungry family or flat.

For 4–6 servings:
500 g pasta shells, macaroni, crests or spirals
3 medium-sized onions
2–3 cloves garlic
1 Tbsp butter or oil
1 (425 g) can tomato purée
1 tsp sugar
¹/₂ tsp salt
1 tsp basil
¹/₂ tsp marjoram
¹/₄ tsp thyme
2 Tbsp chopped fresh parsley (or 1 Tbsp dried parsley)
black pepper
2 cups grated cheese
paprika

Cook the pasta in a large pot of lightly salted water.

While the pasta cooks, dice and sauté the onion and garlic in the butter or oil. When the onion is soft and beginning to turn clear, reduce the heat and add the remaining ingredients, except for the cheese and paprika. Simmer gently over a low heat for a few minutes.

Drain the pasta, then combine with the tomato mixture in a large shallow casserole or soufflé dish. Sprinkle the remaining cheese evenly over the top, then dust lightly with paprika.

At this stage you may either brown the top briefly under the grill for a few minutes to form a light crust, or, for a more solid product that can be sliced into squares and served more like a loaf, bake, uncovered, at 180°C for 40 minutes.

M Two Minute Noodle Soup

For 4 servings:
1 carrot
1 stalk celery
¹/₂ cup frozen peas
2 tsp butter
1 tsp light soya sauce
¹/₂ tsp sesame oil
1 pkt of 2-minute noodles (with stock sachet)
3 cups boiling water
¹/₂–1 cup shredded cooked chicken (optional)
2 Tbsp dry sherry (optional)
2 spring onions

Cut the carrot and celery into strips the size of matches. Put into a bowl or casserole dish with the next four ingredients, the stock sachet, and the block of noodles, broken up.

Pour 2 cups of the boiling water over all this. Cover and cook at Full power for 5 minutes, stirring twice. Add the remaining boiling water, cooked chicken, the sherry, and the spring onions, sliced or cut into matchstick strips.

M Creamy Noodles

For 2–3 servings:
2 cups cooked noodles
about ¹/₄ cup sour cream
about ¹/₄ cup milk, or more sour cream
¹/₂ tsp onion, celery or garlic salt or instant stock
¹/₄ cup chopped parsley or spring onion
1–3 tsp chopped fresh herbs

Put the cooked noodles in an unpunctured oven bag or casserole dish.

Add the liquid, seasoning, and herbs. If the noodles can be separated, mix together lightly, otherwise fasten bag with a rubber band, leaving a finger-sized hole to allow steam to escape, or cover casserole and heat for 3–4 minutes at Full power, stirring once, when noodles are hot enough to be separated. When noodles are hot right through, shake in bag (with air in the bag) or stir gently.

Adjust seasoning and quantity of liquid if necessary.

Cream will be absorbed if noodles are left to stand.

Variations:
Replace herbs with poppy or
caraway seeds.

C Chunky Vegetable and Tomato Sauce on Pasta

This sauce has a good rich flavour and seems more substantial than it actually is.

For 4–6 servings:
2 large onions, chopped
2 cloves garlic, chopped
2 tsp oil
1–2 cups dark-gilled mushrooms
1–2 red peppers
1–2 green peppers
basil, oreganum, thyme
freshly ground pepper
¼–½ cup water
1 (400 g) can whole peeled tomatoes
2–3 Tbsp tomato paste
about 500 g fettucine or spaghetti
(plain, spinach or wholemeal)

In a large non-stick frypan with a lid, cook the chopped onion and garlic in the oil until browned. Add a little water to soften the vegetables during the first few minutes of cooking, if desired, then turn up the heat until it evaporates. Add the chopped mushrooms after the onions have started browning, and cook until the mushrooms have browned.

Stir in the chopped peppers, add herbs according to your taste (about 1 teaspoon each of basil and oreganum, and ¼ teaspoon dried thyme) then add the water, cover, and cook over high heat until the water evaporates.

Stir over lower heat for 2–3 minutes, then add the chopped canned tomatoes and their liquid, and enough tomato paste to give a good colour and flavour. Simmer for about 10 minutes, adjusting the thickness by boiling it down, adding a little cornflour paste, or thinning it with extra water. Taste, and adjust seasonings if necessary.

Cook and drain the pasta, adding chopped herbs and Parmesan cheese as well as butter or oil if desired. Arrange in nests on the required number of plates, and pour the sauce over it.

C Sea Shell Salad

For 4 servings:
1 cup sea shell pasta
1 can (about 200 g) salmon
or
1 cup thawed cooked shrimps or prawns
½–1 cup thinly sliced celery and/or cubed cucumber
2 Tbsp wine vinegar
2 Tbsp oil

Fresh Pasta in Savoury Tomato Sauce

1 tsp sugar
6–8 drops Tabasco sauce
3–4 chopped spring onions

At least 2 hours before serving, cook the pasta in plenty of boiling salted water until tender. Drain and rinse with cold water.

While pasta cooks, drain fish. Reserve salmon liquid but discard liquid from canned shrimps. Retain liquid from frozen shrimps.

In serving bowl, break up salmon, chop prawns if large, and mix with celery, cucumber and remaining seasonings. Add rinsed pasta and mix well. Cover tightly, stirring occasionally. If pasta absorbs all dressing, add extra, using the same proportions, with some fish liquid if desired. Add extra fresh herbs, if desired. Serve with thinned mayonnaise.

C Fresh Pasta in Savoury Tomato Sauce

Look in delicatessens' specialty food cabinets to see whether they stock

fresh pasta, stuffed or unstuffed. To cook, follow the instructions on the packets.

For 3–4 servings:
1 large red pepper
2 Tbsp butter
2 cloves garlic
1½ cups peeled canned tomatoes or 750 g fresh tomatoes, peeled
1 tsp sugar
2 tsp cornflour
¼ cup water or wine
fresh basil (if available)

Cut pepper into small cubes. Cook gently in butter, with garlic, without browning, for 10–15 minutes, in a covered pan.

Add chopped tomatoes and liquid from can, and simmer, uncovered, for 10 minutes. Stir in mixed sugar, cornflour and water or wine.

If necessary, add more water or wine so sauce is lightly thickened.

Add fresh basil, taste, and adjust seasoning carefully. Serve over ravoili etc. as a first or main course.

Potatoes

Three cheers for the potato! It is nutritionally important, high in complex carbohydrates, and provides us with many nutrients per calorie. In fact, it is one of the foods that nutritionalists tell us to eat more of. What's more, potatoes are usually cheaper, per kilogram, than other vegetables or fruit.

There are a number of ways that you can cook the potatoes that you serve with your main meal of the day. Many of these interesting recipes actually cook more quickly than plain boiled potatoes, and are sure to become popular with your family.

Your microwave oven is a wonderful help with potato cookery. It takes only a few minutes to precook potatoes for some of the interesting recipes that call for cooked potatoes.

Tasty potato dishes are likely to be so popular that you may well find that you can serve smaller amounts of other foods alongside them, often at considerable savings.

The potato is a good mixer. It may be combined with many other foods, making exciting dishes suitable for the main part of the meal.

I have many favourites, which I serve for breakfasts, brunches, lunches, picnics, buffet meals, as well as dinners.

M Potato Microwave Shortcuts

Many recipes call for precooked potatoes. The easiest way to do this is to halve (or quarter) potatoes, put them in a covered container that they nearly fill, add a little liquid (about a tablespoon per potato) and microwave them. This is even faster than 'microbaking' potatoes.

One kilogram of halved potatoes, in a covered casserole dish with 4–6 tablespoons of water, will cook in about 10 minutes. You get best results and most even cooking if you use a ring pan.

If you want to precook only one or two potatoes, halve or quarter them and put them in an oven bag with 1–2 tablespoons water. Secure the bag with a rubber band, moving it down so the body of the bag is just big enough to hold the potatoes, and leaving a finger-sized hole, so hot air and steam can escape. The cooking time is usually about 2½–5 minutes for 1–2 potatoes.

Use your microwave oven when you want to speed up the cooking of potatoes which are to be fried, roasted, etc.

Fried Potatoes
Some recipes call for raw potatoes to be sliced or cubed, then cooked in a frying pan, covered, (to cook them) then uncovered until they are browned and crisp. With very little modification of flavour and texture, you can cut the potatoes as required, half cook them in the microwave, then finish cooking them until they are crisp in an uncovered frying pan.

'Roast' Potatoes
When you want roast potatoes, but are short of time, place them in an oven bag, and cook them until nearly tender. Transfer them to the pan, turning them in the pan drippings frequently, while they brown.

Or microwave till just cooked then roughen their surfaces with a fork, brush them with a little butter and brown under a grill, turning as required.

Or microwave potatoes after cutting so each large piece of potato has two flat surfaces, then brown in a heavy, hot frypan containing a thin film of clarified or plain butter.

M New Potatoes

New potatoes cook beautifully in a microwave oven!

Scrub potatoes, scraping them if desired, halve or quarter large potatoes, or peel a ring of skin from around the middle of small whole potatoes. Drop into cold water as

they are prepared, to stop them browning.

Just before cooking, transfer to a microwave casserole, or oven bag. Add 1 tablespoon water per serving and a mint sprig and ½ teaspoon butter per serving. Cover or close bag loosely.

Approximate cooking times at Full power:
1 serving (100–125 g) 2½ minutes
2 servings (200–250 g)
    3½–4 minutes
4 servings (400–500 g)
    5½–6 minutes

Shake casserole or turn bag halfway through cooking time. Potatoes are cooked when barely tender. Allow standing time of 3–4 minutes.

M Cubed Potatoes

Additions before cooking mean no fuss when serving.

These are good used in salads and cooked potato recipes, too.

For each serving:
100 g cubed raw potatoes
½ tsp butter or oil
2 tsp water
½ clove garlic, chopped
    or 1–2 tsp chopped parsley
    or spring onion

Scrub or peel potatoes. Cut in 15 mm cubes, dropping these into a bowl of cold water, as prepared. Drain and put in oven bag or casserole. Add remaining ingredients, using oil if potatoes will be used for a salad. Cover.

Estimate cooking time as for new potatoes. Shake container to coat evenly with thin film of butter and seasonings as soon as butter melts. Allow standing time of 3–4 minutes after cooking.

C Skillet Potatoes

These take no longer than boiled potatoes, but they turn any meal into something special.

For 4 servings:
2 Tbsp butter
2 onions, sliced
4 potatoes, scrubbed
½ tsp salt
2–3 Tbsp parsley

Melt the butter and cook the onions in it in a heavy pan, without browning, while you scrub and slice

the potatoes. Rinse potatoes under a cold tap, then mix with the onions, cover and cook over low heat for 15 minutes, or until potatoes are tender, turning every 4 or 5 minutes.

Uncover, raise heat slightly and cook for 15 minutes longer, turning at intervals so potatoes brown evenly. Sprinkle with parsley and serve.

Variation:
Leave out onions, cut potatoes in 1 cm cubes, and cook the same way, letting them brown on all sides.

M Golden Potatoes

These are cooked in a preheated browning dish for a crispy surface.

For 2 servings:
2 medium-sized potatoes
1 Tbsp flour
1 tsp salt
1 tsp paprika
½ tsp curry powder
1 Tbsp butter or oil

Preheat browning dish for 6 minutes. Scrub or peel potatoes. Cut into small (1 cm) cubes. Shake in plastic bag with the next four ingredients, to coat evenly.

Add butter to heated browning dish. Quickly spread coated potatoes on hot buttered surface. Microwave at Full power for 3 minutes. Turn. Cook for 2–3 minutes longer, or until tender.

M Mashed Potato

Make sure potatoes are not overcooked or undercooked when you prepare these.

For 4 servings:
4 medium–large potatoes
¼ cup water
1 Tbsp butter
milk
salt and pepper

Select a bowl in which potatoes can be cooked, mashed and served.

Half fill bowl with cold water. Peel potatoes, halve each lengthwise, then cut each half into 4–6 fairly even, fairly square pieces. When all are prepared, drain off water.

Add butter and water. Cover. Microwave at Full power for 7–10 minutes. Shake after 4–5 minutes, to coat with melted butter and reposition.

Test with sharp knife. Cook until centre cubes are tender.

Leave to stand for 4–5 minutes, or until potatoes are required, then mash (without draining), adding milk, salt and pepper to taste. Beat mashed potatoes with a fork, after mashing.

Hash Browns

▢ Hash Browns

Cold cooked shredded potato, browned in butter. It doesn't sound special, but it tastes great. Try it for a weekend brunch and see for yourself. It's worth buying a non-stick pan, if you become addicted to hash browns!

Grate potato which has been baked ahead and refrigerated overnight.

Spoon into preheated pan with butter heated to straw colour. Pat lightly down to form a cake. Brown over moderate heat. Use lid if time is short.

Slide out of pan on to a plate when first side has a crisp brown crust. Flip back into pan, uncooked side down. Slip extra butter down sides of pan. Cook uncovered until crust forms on this side.

Note:
Use undercooked rather than overcooked potatoes.

▢ Potato Cakes

(See photograph on page 152.)

Enormously popular, these potato cakes don't need to be made in any precise formula — vary the seasoning each time, using what is available.

Use potatoes which have been boiled or microwaved (preferably the day before) or leftover mashed potato.

Do not mix the flour and potatoes until you are ready to cook them, as the mixture sometimes turns sticky with prolonged standing.

For 4 servings:
*2 cups of grated cooked potato or 2
  cups mashed potato*
1 cup self-raising flour
1 tsp celery salt
1 tsp garlic salt or onion salt
¹/₂ tsp curry powder
4 spring onions, chopped
¹/₄ cup chopped parsley

*up to 1 cup cooked cold carrots, peas or
  mixed vegetables (optional)*

Mix the cold grated (or mashed) potato with the remaining ingredients, adding other fresh or dried herbs and spices if desired.

If the dough is too dry to mould into a 10-cm-wide cylinder, add a little milk. If it is too moist, add a little extra flour.

Cut into 1-cm-thick slices with a sharp serrated knife. Turn in a little extra flour and cook in a preheated (preferably non-stick) pan in a small amount of oil or butter. Allow about 3 minutes per side.

Serve with a salad or cooked vegetables.

A microwaved dinner which includes Scalloped Potatoes

▣ Scalloped Potatoes

For 2 servings:
2–3 medium-sized potatoes
1 small–medium-sized onion
1 clove garlic
2 tsp butter
1 Tbsp water
1 Tbsp flour
¹/₂ cup milk
flavoured salt
¹/₂ cup grated cheese
parsley and paprika

Scrub potatoes. Slice thinly into a shallow casserole dish (about 20 cm across) with thinly sliced onion and finely chopped garlic between layers of potato. Add butter and water, cover, and cook at Full power for 5 minutes until barely tender, shaking dish after 2–3 minutes. Sprinkle potatoes with flour then add milk.

Sprinkle with a little celery, onion, or garlic salt. Cover and cook again until sauce thickens.

Sprinkle surface with grated cheese, chopped parsley and

paprika. Microwave, uncovered, until cheese melts, about 1 minute.

▣ Savoury Potatoes

This is a quick way to make a plain dinner more interesting.

For 4 servings:
3 fairly large potatoes (500 g)
2 onions, sliced
1 clove garlic
25 g butter
100 g mushrooms, sliced
¹/₂ tsp salt
2 spring onions, chopped
paprika

Scrub or peel and slice potatoes.
Combine onions, finely chopped garlic and butter in a shallow casserole dish. Cover and microwave at Full power for 2 minutes.

Add potatoes and mix evenly. Cover and cook for 6–7 minutes, until barely tender.

Add mushrooms, cover and cook for 2 minutes longer. Stand for 2 minutes, then toss gently with the salt, spring onions and paprika.

▣ Grated Potato Ring

This cake sometimes looks slightly grey, but it tastes wonderful and looks fine after it has been hidden under a colourful topping.

You may well find that it becomes a family favourite.

4 potatoes
25 g butter
1 or 2 cloves garlic
2 tsp instant stock
¹/₄ cup chopped spring onion
Or finely chopped parsley
¹/₂–1 cup grated cheese
parsley and paprika

Scrub potatoes and grate coarsely. Heat butter and finely chopped garlic in small ring pan.

Rinse potatoes with cold water and drain throughly in sieve.

Mix with melted butter, green herb or chicken stock granules and spring onion or parsley in a large mixing bowl.

Press evenly and lightly into ring pan. Cover with vented plastic film. Microwave at Full power for 10 minutes, or until potato is tender.

Leave for 2 minutes, then turn on to flat plate. Sprinkle evenly with cheese, parsley and paprika. Reheat before serving if necessary. Cut into slices.

> Do not ever peel potatoes and leave them to stand, covered with water, since they lose important nutrients.

C M Baked Potatoes

Scrub fairly large potatoes, rub with a little oil, and stand on oven racks, not a solid surface. Bake at 200°C for 45–60 minutes, until flesh 'gives' when pressed. Split or cut a cross in the top, press down between cuts to open them attractively.

Top with butter, sour cream, yoghurt, cream, hard or soft cheese, blue cheese, mustard pickle, mayonnaise or chilli mayonnaise. Melt or heat topping briefly, if desired.

Garnish with parsley and/or paprika and serve.

Checkerboard Potatoes
Scrub, and cut in half. Cut lines lengthwise then crosswise in checkerboard design on cut side. Cut deeply, without piercing skin.

Blot cut surface on paper towel then dip in melted butter or oil. Sprinkle with paprika, and bake, cut side up, as above.

The cuts should open during cooking. No last minute attention is required for these attractively scored potatoes, nor is butter needed at the table.

Half-Baked Potatoes
Scrub potatoes as for baking. Cut in half, and place cut surface down on a buttered or greased baking tray. Bake at 200°C for about 35–45 minutes until potatoes 'give' slightly when pressed.

The cut surface of the cooked potato resembles that of a roast potato, while the rest is the same as a baked potato.

Microwaved Baked Potatoes
Scrub potatoes, pierce in several places, arrange in a circle and microwave at Full power, for 3–5 minutes per potato, until potato feels evenly cooked when pressed. Time required will depend on size. Turn potatoes over halfway through cooking.

Baking times at Full power:
1 small potato (100 g) 3 minutes
2 med. potatoes (300 g) 7–8 minutes
3 med. potatoes (400 g) 10 minutes
4 large potatoes (600–800 g) 12–14 minutes

Remember that potato finishes cooking during the standing time.

C M Stuffed Baked Potatoes

Everybody likes potatoes which have been baked, emptied of their cooked insides, filled again with mashed potato and exciting additions, and reheated.

Scrub large potatoes, bake or microwave. Potatoes are cooked when they 'give' when pressed.

Remove a slice from the top, or halve the cooked potatoes. Scoop out the flesh with a small spoon, and mash it with one or more of the following:

- butter/quark
- grated cheese
- cubed cheese
- tofu
- mayonnaise
- milk
- sour cream
- cream cheese
- yoghurt
- cottage cheese

Season with:
- chopped spring onion or chives
- chopped parsley
- finely chopped thyme, basil, marjoram, dill, mint, etc.
- pepper
- chutney, pickle, or relish
- garlic or garlic spreads
- mustard
- chilli sauce
- chopped gherkins
- chopped red or green peppers

Stir in:
- sautéed mushrooms
- sautéed onions
- chopped avocado
- chopped nuts
- chopped bacon or ham
- cooked mince mixtures
- sliced salami
- finely chopped cooked meat
- smoked fish
- shrimps
- smoked salmon
- sardines
- corn
- asparagus
- baked beans
- Mexican beans
- salmon or tuna

Taste and season if necessary. Pile the filling back into the potato shells. Reheat at 200°C until heated through and browned, for about 15 minutes, or microwave until heated through, for about 2–3 minutes per potato. Brown under a grill if desired.

Serve alone, or with a salad as the main part of a light meal.

C Potato Savouries

These may be served with soup for lunch or dinner, or served as small hot savouries with tea or coffee, between main meals. They freeze well, and may be thawed in a microwave oven, but are best reheated in a conventional oven, to retain their crispness.

For 12 savouries:
3 large slices thin-cut bread
butter for spreading
1 cup mashed potato
1 cup grated tasty cheese
1 egg
2 spring onions, finely chopped
Or 1–2 Tbsp onion pulp
1 rasher bacon, chopped
paprika

Butter the sliced bread thinly but evenly, then cut away the crusts and cut each slice into four small squares. Press into pattie tins, buttered side down.

Mix together potato, cheese and egg. Add chopped white and green leaves of spring onions. If these are not available, scrape the cut surface of an onion with a teaspoon to get onion pulp and juice. Add this to potato mixture with finely chopped bacon.

Put rounded, rough spoonfuls of mixture in each unbaked bread case and bake at 190°C for 20–30 minutes, until bread cases are evenly and lightly browned.

Note:
You will find filling may be used for more or fewer bread cases, depending on the amount of filling you want in each.

Watch when eating hot Potato Savouries. The filling gets very hot, and can burn your mouth!

U Potato Salads

You can make 101 versions of potato salad, all of which are likely to be popular!

Slice or cube cooked waxy or new potatoes, making sure that you allow up to twice as many as you allow for a normal serving.

Mix with chopped chives or spring onions, chopped parsley, basil and/or oreganum, or chopped dill leaf. Add chopped or sliced hard-boiled egg if you like.

For dressing, thin down mayonnaise with more mild vinegar, or with French Dressing, or another thin dressing. *Or* use French Herb, Cumin or Tomato Dressing.

Fold the dressing through the sliced potato, trying not to break up the pieces. Arrange in serving dish and leave to stand for at least 15 minutes. Garnish with more herbs, or egg, etc. Serve with extra dressing, if desired.

Note:
Never leave potato and pasta salads standing at room temperature in hot weather since they spoil easily.

ⓒ Potato Pancakes

Potato pancakes seem especially popular with children — they enjoy their texture and mild flavour.

Because the potato browns on prolonged standing, do not mix the batter before you plan to cook it. If you like, you can mix the first six ingredients in a bowl and add the potato and flour just before cooking. In this recipe the potato is grated straight into the bowl, and is not squeezed first. If the mixture seems a little wet, add 2–3 tablespoons of extra flour. This will depend on the potatoes.

For 6 servings:
2 eggs, unbeaten
2 Tbsp milk
1 onion, very finely chopped
1 tsp curry powder
1 tsp salt
½ tsp celery salt
500 g raw potatoes
¼ cup flour
oil

In a basin mix the eggs, milk, onion and seasonings. Stir with a fork until mixed. Just before cooking, grate the scrubbed (or thinly peeled) potatoes into the mixture and add the flour. Fry spoonfuls of the mixture in hot corn or soya oil, about 5 mm deep, for 3 minutes per side, until golden brown. If the cooking time is too short, the potato will not be cooked in the centre.

Serve alone, or with tomatoes, mushrooms or bacon.

ⓒ Self-Crusting Potato and Asparagus Quiche

This quiche forms its own crust as it cooks. (It is important not to overmix, or crust may not form.) Bake in a 23 cm solid-bottomed flan tin or pie plate with a non-stick finish.

For 4–6 servings:
1 large onion, chopped
2 cloves garlic
1 Tbsp butter
3 eggs
½ tsp salt
1 cup milk
½ cup self-raising flour
2 cooked potatoes
1 cup drained cooked asparagus or
*   spinach, mushrooms, broccoli*
1 cup grated tasty cheese

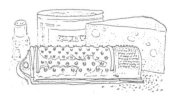

Cook the chopped onion and garlic in butter until tender. Cool. Stir in eggs, salt and milk and beat with fork until mixed. Pour this into a large bowl, containing flour, and stir with the fork until just combined. Add the potatoes cut in 1 cm cubes, and chopped, well-drained vegetables and cheese.

Pour mixture into a well-sprayed pan (see above). Bake at 200°C for 25–30 minutes, until lightly browned and set in the centre. Leave to stand for 10–15 minutes before unmoulding or serving from pan.

ⓒ Neptune's Pie

This pie crust is made from a rich, homemade pastry. The filling utilises inexpensive canned smoked fish fillets to advantage. You can use other canned fish if you like, but you may find you need more seasoning or some of the liquid from the can, if a very mild fish is used.

For about 6 servings:
Pastry
1¼ cups flour
125 g cold butter, cubed
½ cup cold milk
1 tsp wine vinegar

Filling
2–3 (500 g) large cooked potatoes
1 (300–425 g) can smoked fish fillets
3 eggs
½ cup chopped spring onions
1 cup grated tasty cheese

Make the pastry in a food processor.

Put the flour and the refrigerated butter, cut in nine cubes, into the food processor bowl, fitted with the metal cutting blade. Sour the milk by stirring the vinegar into it. Process in bursts, adding liquid in a steady steam while the butter is being chopped into the flour. Do not overmix.

Stop before last 2 tablespoons milk is added, and feel if pastry is damp enough. It should be a little wetter than normal short pastry. Add liquid until this stage is reached. Discard any remaining milk.

Refrigerate pastry for 5–10 minutes. Roll out in two circles, one larger, to fit a 20 cm cake tin with sides at least 5 cm high. Spray cake tin with non-stick spray and line bottom with a circle of baking paper. Line tin with large piece of pastry.

Combine filling ingredients. Chop potatoes into 1-cm-thick slices, in a mixing bowl. Add drained fillets, broken into fairly small pieces, the unbeaten eggs, the onions and cheese. Mix carefully, stirring eggs through mixture without breaking up potatoes too much. Tip into uncooked crust. Cover with

remaining pastry. Seal edges by folding them over. Cut vent in middle.

Bake at 200°C for 30–40 minutes, or until pastry is evenly browned and centre of pie is set. Leave to cool for 15–30 minutes before turning out of the pan, and removing paper. Finish cooling upside down on rack.

Serve cold or warm.

ⓒ Potato Frittata

Make a variation of this recipe at weekends when you want something quick and easy, and at times when you haven't bought any special ingredients, but want to use up leftovers.

You will also find this a useful recipe if you want to take something substantial for a picnic and don't have time to make a pie.

For 4–6 servings:
50 g butter
3 onions, sliced
3–4 medium-sized
*   potatoes (500–600 g)*
2 zucchini, sliced (or other vegetables)
4 eggs
2 Tbsp water
½ cup grated Parmesan cheese

Melt the butter in a large heavy pan. Cook the sliced onions in the butter, over moderate heat, until they are evenly browned. Add the sliced, unpeeled potatoes, stir well, cover pan and cook for 15–20 minutes, stirring occasionally. After 10–15 minutes add the zucchini or other vegetables, so they will be cooked when the potatoes are.

Beat the eggs with the water and half the cheese. Pour over the pressed-down vegetable mixture, and cook over gentle heat for 10 minutes or until the sides and bottom are cooked. Sprinkle remaining Parmesan cheese over the top, then brown under a grill, until the top puffs up and browns lightly. Serve hot, warm or at room temperature, with a salad if desired.
Variations:
Add chopped garlic with the potatoes, and fresh or dried herbs with the egg mixture.

Potato Frittata

Spiced Potatoes and Peas

C Spiced Potatoes and Peas

When you use several spices to flavour a coconut-cream-flavoured sauce, you can turn potatoes and peas into a whole meal — and an interesting one at that. The mixture will not be 'hot' unless you add the chilli powder.

For 4 large servings:
1 large onion, chopped
2 cloves garlic, chopped
2 Tbsp oil or butter
½ tsp ground cumin
½ tsp ground cardamom
½ tsp ground coriander
¼ tsp ground celery seed
¼ tsp ground cloves
⅛ tsp chilli powder (optional)
¾–1 tsp turmeric
1 (410 g) can coconut cream
600–700 g small potatoes, preferably new
3 cups frozen peas
1 Tbsp sugar
¼ tsp salt

Put the chopped onion and garlic into a large frying pan with the oil or butter. Cook gently for 4–5 minutes, until transparent. Add the next seven spices. Stir over low heat for 2–3 minutes longer. Add the coconut cream and bring to the boil.

Scrub, scrape or peel the potatoes, and halve or quarter if large. Add to pan, cover and simmer, turning potatoes occasionally, until they are just tender, usually 15–20 minutes. Add the peas, sugar and salt and cook for a few minutes longer until peas are tender.

Adjust thickness of sauce by boiling briskly for a few minutes if too thin, or adding a little water if it is too thick.

Taste, adjust seasonings if necessary, and serve.

C Curried New Potatoes

This is a simple version of the previous recipe. It is a good way to cook and serve two vegetables in a sauce, to serve with, say barbecued chops or sausages.

Use mild or hot curry powder, and vary the amount used to suit your taste.

For 4 servings:
25 g butter
1–1½ tsp curry powder
1 onion, chopped
4 medium–large new potatoes
1 tsp instant chicken stock.
1 tsp sugar
1 cup hot water
½ cup frozen peas

Melt butter in a medium-sized frying pan. Add curry powder and chopped onion. Cook gently while you scrape the new potatoes. Cut each potato in half lengthwise, then cut each half into four quarters.

Add the potato pieces to the curry mixture, then add the instant chicken stock and sugar dissolved in 1 cup of hot water.

Cover pan and simmer gently for 15 minutes or until potatoes are tender and liquid is thick. (Watch liquid and add extra or raise heat, so you finish up with the correct consistency.)

Add the peas and keep cooking until they are tender.

Variation:
Add ¼ cup sour cream after the peas are tender. Stir in 4–6 quartered hard-boiled eggs. Serve with rice, as a complete meal.

C M Egmont Potatoes

Remember those wonderful potato casseroles that your grandmother pulled out from her big black stove for Saturday lunches? The ones that filled the house with aromas that made everybody ravenous?

We have eaten casseroles like this for years. Everybody loves them. Whenever one is served as part of a buffet meal, people seem to bypass exotic and expensive foods to take second helpings!

For 4 servings:
800 g potatoes
2–4 rashers of bacon, finely chopped
¼ cup water
2 Tbsp butter
4 onions
1 (250 g) carton sour cream
about 2 cups grated tasty cheese

Scrub or thinly peel the potatoes, and slice them 5 mm thick. Put them in an oven bag or small lidded microwave casserole with the water and all but 1 rasher of the chopped bacon. Close the bag with a rubberband, leaving a finger-sized hole to allow steam to escape, or cover the casserole, and microwave at Full power for 10 minutes, or until tender, shaking the container once, after about 4 minutes.

While the potatoes cook, slice the onions, and cook them in the butter, in a covered frying pan, with the heat high enough to brown them lightly. Stir them several times as they cook.

Thin down the sour cream (or low-fat sour cream) with enough milk to make it pourable, then pour this over the cooked potato, and mix well. Add chopped herbs to this, if you like, then spoon half the creamy potatoes into a buttered dish, about 20 × 30 cm. Sprinkle with half the cheese, and half the onions, then arrange the remaining potato on top. Cover with the rest of the onions and cheese, then sprinkle the uncooked bacon on top.

Grill for about 5 minutes, until the bacon and cheese are brown. For most even browning, have dish 18–20 cm from the heat.

If potatoes on the bottom have not heated through completely, microwave at Full power until bubbling.

This is nicest if left to stand for 5 minutes before serving.

C M Potato-Egg Casserole

This is one of the most useful casseroles I make. Serve it for lunch or dinner with a salad and bread rolls.

If you use less bacon, cheese and eggs, you can serve this as a potato side dish, or as one of the dishes at a buffet dinner.

For a vegetarian version, leave out the bacon, adding more seasonings as necessary.

For 4–6 servings:
4 (800 g) large cooked potatoes
4 hard-boiled eggs
3–4 rashers bacon
50 g butter
2 large onions, chopped
$\frac{1}{4}$ cup flour
1 tsp dry mustard
$\frac{1}{2}$ tsp salt
$2\frac{1}{4}$ cups milk
1 cup grated cheese

Topping
1 Tbsp butter, melted
1 cup fresh breadcrumbs

Slice cooked potatoes into a fairly large, shallow casserole dish which has been sprayed with non-stick spray.

Add eggs which have been quartered, sliced or chopped.

Chop bacon into small pieces and cook for 2–3 minutes. Sprinkle over potatoes, leaving bacon fat in cooking container. Add butter to it, then cook chopped onions until tender, but not brown.

Stir in flour, mustard and salt, add 1 cup of milk and bring to the boil, stirring frequently. Stir in remaining milk, and boil again.

Add cheese, stir until smooth, then pour over potato mixture, after stirring it to make sure ingredients are well distributed.

Cover with topping made by tossing melted butter and breadcrumbs together. Refrigerate until required, then bake uncovered at 180°C for 30–45 minutes until crumbs are golden brown, and filling has heated through.

Microwave Instructions
Arrange potatoes and eggs in microwave casserole. Cook bacon, butter and onion in a large covered measuring jug or bowl for about 4 minutes, then add flour, mustard and salt. Add all the milk and stir sauce at intervals for 4–5 minutes or until it is thick. Stir in cheese and pour sauce over potato mixture.

Potato Egg Casserole

For topping, melt butter in a flat-bottomed dish. Stir in crumbs then microwave until crumbs are evenly browned. Reheat covered casserole in microwave oven until hot right through, then sprinkle with browned crumbs and a little paprika, just before serving.

C Cheesy Potato Bake

This layered potato and cheese 'cake' is much more interesting than it sounds from its contents. It can be made from any cream soup that you like, remembering only to select a flavour that goes well with potatoes and cheese.

If you find a suitable packet cream soup, this will do just as well as the can when made up with 2 cups of liquid.

This 'cake' firms up on standing after cooking, and is just as nice reheated a day or two later when it can be cut in wedges and served like a pie.

For 4–6 servings:
5–6 large potatoes (1 kg)
1 (440 g) can cream of vegetable soup
$\frac{1}{4}$–$\frac{1}{2}$ cup milk, cream or cherry (or any combination of these)
2 cups (200 g) grated tasty (or Raclette) cheese
paprika

Cook the potatoes, then cut them into slices no more than 1 cm thick. Open the can of soup and measure the contents into a small bowl, add enough milk, cream, sherry or a mixture of these to make the soup up to 2 cups.

Grease a large, shallow ovenware dish, then cover its bottom with half of the potato slices. Sprinkle over half the cheese, then pour over half the soup. Repeat this process using the other half of the potato, cheese and soup mixture. Sprinkle the top with paprika and bake, uncovered, at 200°C for 45 minutes.

Leave to stand for 30 minutes or so prior to serving. This will allow the flavours to blend and the potatoes to absorb all the remaining liquid. Serve with a green or tomato salad and crusty bread rolls.

Vegetables and Salads

Nowadays we can choose, all year round, from a tempting array of vegetables. We cook these vegetables carefully to retain as much flavour, food value, crunch and colour as possible, and we find the diners around our tables not only enjoy the vegetables, which are an important part of the meal, but ask for more.

I have always tried to cook vegetables for a short time, in as little water as possible. Now I use non-stick pans with lids for much of my basic vegetable cookery. I often turn the vegetables in a little butter or oil first, and add so little water that it has evaporated by the time the vegetables are cooked. Using this method I add little or no salt, and I find the vegetables have a wonderful flavour.

Many vegetables are at their best when microwaved for a very short time. Experiment until you perfect your microwave cooking techniques, for maximum flavour, colour and texture.

Interesting salads made from raw or cooked vegetables appear regularly on our tables, right through the year.

Our tastes in dressings have changed. We enjoy lighter dressings with stronger, more definite seasonings which are readily available in the stores where we shop regularly.

Our magic kitchen machines enable us to chop, shred, mix and blend with ease and unbelievable speed.

Those of us who have gardens can experiment with new varieties, as well as reviving old favourites, and most important, can harvest our crops earlier than a commercial grower does.

My collection of vegetable recipes is not comprehensive, but may add new ideas to your repertoire.

Ways to Cook Vegetables

Here are some of the different ways you can cook vegetables. Don't drown them! You are throwing away a lot of flavour and vitamins when you boil vegetables in water to cover, or leave them to soak before cooking, or boil them until they discolour, or throw out lots of cooking liquid! Try to vary your cooking techniques, giving emphasis to methods using very little liquid.

BLANCHING:
Vegetables are immersed for a short time in a large pan of boiling water. They are often then dipped into cold water to halt the cooking process. This produces a very bright colour and is one of the steps in freezing. Opinions vary about flavour and nutrient losses by this method.

BOILING:
Add vegetables to boiling water in a saucepan which is then usually covered to keep in the steam formed. With this method it is best to use only a small amount of water.

STEAMING:
Place vegetables in steamer with perforated bottom, or in a basket resting above the water-level in a saucepan. The vegetables cook in steam instead of water, and lose fewer nutrients. Neither their flavour nor their food value is as good as that of stir-fried vegetables, however.

SAUTÉING:
This method is good for conserving flavour and nutrients. Cook sliced or chopped vegetables in a little oil, butter, margarine, etc., in a pan over a a a high heat, stirring at intervals. With a non-stick pan very little oil etc, is required. Many vegetables can be sautéed before being cooked by another method.

STIR-FRYING:
One vegetable or a mixture may be cooked this way. Vegetables are usually sliced in varying sizes so they all take the same time to cook. Heat a little oil, sometimes with garlic and/or ginger, in a large pan or wok. Add the vegetables and toss and stir them to keep them moving, and to coat them. Pour in a little liquid and cover, so the steam formed cooks the vegetables until tender-crisp. Evaporate remaining liquid, or add extra flavourings mixed with cornflour to thicken juices. Toss so this coats the vegetables. Excellent for conserving flavour, texture and nutrients.

BARBECUING AND GRILLING:
Food is turned above hot embers or under a hot element. Pieces of pepper, eggplant, onion, tomato, mushroom, zucchini, etc. may be threaded on skewers with other food. They require brushing with oil, butter, mayonnaise, French dressing, etc. to prevent them burning before they cook.

DEEP-FRYING:
Tender vegetables may be coated in a light batter, then cooked briefly in hot oil, as in Japanese tempura.

PRESSURE COOKING:
Vegetables are cooked in super-heated steam, resulting in a considerably shortened cooking time, and saved nutrients. Take care not to overcook green vegetables with this method, or colour and texture suffer.

BRAISING:
Turn the vegetable in hot butter or oil, then add flavoured liquid and cook slowly in a saucepan or in a covered ovenproof dish. Cooking liquid is often eaten with vegetables.

MICROWAVING
The microwave oven cooks many vegetables very well in a short time, conserving colour, flavour and food value. In most cases green vegetables need very little or no added liquid. All vegetables should be cooked in a covered container which they nearly fill, and seasoned very lightly after cooking, if necessary.

STIR-FRY-STEAMING:
This very good way of cooking vegetables falls into none of the foregoing categories, but is best described as the 'stir-fry-steam' method. Turn the prepared vegetable in a non-stick pan containing a little butter, and sometimes garlic. Soon afterwards add a small amount of water, cover the pan tightly and cook over a fairly high heat, turning or stirring occasionally. By the time the vegetable is cooked tender-crisp, the water should have disappeared completely. The vegetable is lightly glazed with the butter, and usually needs no other seasoning. The heat used is lower than that required for a real stir-fry, but hotter than that used in braising.

EASY ON THE SALT!
It is easy to add salt by habit rather than by taste. We now season most vegetables very lightly, after cooking. Vegetables cooked so that no liquid remains (in pan or microwave) require little or no salt. If a little salted butter is added at any stage, it is probable that no salt will be needed at all.

KEEP COOKING LIQUID:
Keep any vegetable cooking liquid that remains when vegetables are served. Refrigerate for up to 2 days. Use this as liquid for sauces, soups and stocks.

Microwaved Vegetables

Microwaved vegetables have excellent colour, flavour, texture and vitamin content. Salt is not added before cooking.

Experiment with small additions of water, oil or butter, and different vegetable combinations, to find your favourites.

For most vegetables (and mixtures) use the following general method.

Allow about 100 g prepared vegetable per serving. Wash, then slice or cut as you would for stir-frying. Cut quick-cooking vegetables in larger pieces than slow-cooking ones.

For each serving heat ½–1 teaspoon butter or oil with ½ finely sliced garlic clove in the cooking container. Add prepared vegetable and toss to coat evenly.

Add 1 teaspoon water per serving to cook vegetables to fairly soft texture. Add no water for tender-crisp

vegetables.
Cover tightly. Microwave at Full Power.

Allow 1–2 minutes for 1 serving
1½–3 minutes for 2 servings
2½–4 minutes for 3 servings
3–5 minutes for 4 servings

Allow 2 minutes' standing time.

Some vegetables need no wrapping because their skin holds in moisture.

Always puncture or cut skins before cooking.

Cut, sliced or chopped vegetables should be covered during cooking so that they cook in steam. Add salt and pepper after cooking, only if necessary.

Oven bags are very useful for cooking vegetables. Close bags loosely with rubber bands, leaving an unobstructed finger-sized hole for steam and air to escape.

When cooking vegetables in dishes that have no lids, cover with plastic cling

wrap, folding back one edge or piercing plastic so that steam can escape during cooking.

Vegetables for one serving may be cooked in a double-layered parcel of greaseproof paper. Paper cannot be used for large quantities or long cooking.

Small quantities of frozen vegetables can be cooked in the sealed plastic bags in which they are bought. Always pierce bag before cooking.

Cut vegetables into small, even pieces before microwaving. Large pieces of hard vegetable require much longer cooking than small pieces.

Stir or shake containers of vegetables, especially larger quantities, several times during cooking, so food in the centre will cook more quickly and evenly.

Vegetables may not appear ready after cooking but finish cooking during standing time.

Ⓒ Marinated Artichokes

Serve one cold artichoke per person as a starter course, or as a light lunch.

Place artichokes in a large saucepan and cover with lightly salted water. Add the juice of 1 or 2 lemons, several crushed garlic cloves, a few peppercorns, a bay leaf, some basil and oreganum, and a few tablespoons of oil.

Cover the saucepan and simmer the artichokes for 30 minutes or more, until the outer petals pull away from the base easily. Leave to cool in the cooking liquid.

Serve each drained artichoke on a flat plate big enough to hold mayonnaise for dipping and a pile of discarded petals. To eat, pull off a petal at a time. Dip the stem end into the mayonnaise, then bite off the fleshy part of the petal and discard the fibrous core. You will find the inner petals are more fleshy and less fibrous. Eventually only the fleshy base, holding immature seeds, remains. Discard these if they are stringy, cut the base into quarters, and eat each piece with mayonnaise.

Ⓜ Jerusalem Artichokes

Peel, slice thinly. Use general cooking method on opposite page. Allow 1 teaspoon water per serving, 1–2 minutes per serving, depending on desired texture. Toss with chopped parsley and add pepper.

Use in stir-fries, or in julienne vegetable mixtures.

Ⓤ Avocados with Tomato Dressing

Avocados come in different shapes, sizes, colours and prices, at different times of the year. It isn't worth eating any avocado until it is soft enough to 'give' when you hold it in your hand and squeeze it gently. At this stage you can refrigerate it for several days, if necessary, to slow down further ripening. Don't buy soft avocados with blotchy skins, for their flesh may be soft and dark in patches too.

Although avocado halves are often used as containers for other food, serving them this way sometimes loses the avocado flavour. Try avocado halves alone with this tomato dressing. Either fill the stone cavity with dressing or, more elegantly, lie the halved, peeled, stoned avocado on its cut surface,

Asparagus with Hollandaise Sauce

cut down in slices, then flatten and fan the slices slightly. Brush a little lemon juice over the avocado cut surfaces so they don't brown before the dressing is added. Garnish as desired. Serve dressing separately.

Tomato dressing
1–2 Tbsp onion pulp
¹⁄₄ cup tomato purée
3 Tbsp wine vinegar
1–2 Tbsp sugar
¹⁄₂ tsp salt
¹⁄₂ tsp celery salt
1 tsp mixed mustard
³⁄₄ cup corn or soya oil

Combine all ingredients in a blender, food processor or screw-topped jar, using the smaller quantities given. Taste and increase optional quantities if desired. (For onion pulp, scrape a halved onion, cut crosswise, with the tip of a teaspoon.)
Note:
To prepare avocados, run knife lengthwise through the skin and flesh to the centre stone, then twist the halves in opposite directions to separate them. Lift out the stone by cutting a sharp knife into it with an abrupt chopping motion, then

twisting the knife so the stone is lifted free of the flesh.

Ⓜ Asparagus

Choose good quality spears of even thickness. Fat spears cook better than very thin ones. Snap off bottom of stems. Peel bottom 5–6 cm of stems with a potato peeler or sharp knife for best results and most even cooking.

Use an oven bag for a few servings, and a covered casserole for more.

Melt 1–2 teaspoons butter per serving. Add prepared asparagus turning to coat. Add 1–2 teaspoons water per serving. Fold bag, excluding air. Cover casserole. Microwave at Full power. Ten medium stalks take about 2 minutes. 500 g asparagus takes 4–5 minutes. Allow about 2 minutes' standing time.

Do not overcook. Asparagus should be bright green and slightly crunchy. Serve plain, or with hollandaise or cheese sauce.

With frozen asparagus, cook 250 g in 2 tablespoons water for 6–8 minutes.

Beans à la Grecque

Beans à la Grecque

Use this recipe to prepare a number of other vegetables in this way, too, if you find that you like it as much as I do! It is usual to cut vegetables lengthwise into strips.

For 4 servings:
1 large onion
2 cloves garlic
¼ cup oil
½ tsp crushed coriander seeds
¼ cup wine vinegar
¼ cup water
1 tsp sugar
½ tsp salt
freshly ground pepper
300–500 g green beans
4 tomatoes, peeled, seeded and cubed
½ cup chopped parsley
1 Tbsp lemon juice

Chop onion and garlic. Cook in oil until transparent but not browned.

Add coriander, vinegar, water, sugar, salt and pepper to taste. Add topped and tailed beans (with strings removed if necessary). Simmer for 2–3 minutes, then add the tomatoes, Cook until beans are tender-crisp. Cover and cool.

Just before serving (at room temperature) add the chopped parsley and lemon juice.

Variation:
Replace beans with celery, fennel, leeks, chokos, peppers, scallopini or zucchini.

Cumin Bean Salad

Use canned or freshly cooked dried beans for this salad. A combination of white haricot, pink pinto, tiger beans and red kidney beans with the addition of some lightly cooked fresh beans makes a most attractive salad.

This salad may be kept in a covered container in the refrigerator for a week, and served whenever you want something quick and easy.

For 6 servings:
4 cups cooked, drained dried beans
1 cup chopped, cooked green beans
½–1 cup diced green peppers
1 cup diced celery
about 1 cup diced tomato
Cumin Dressing (see page 201)

Put the drained beans, peppers and celery in a large, covered container. Add the dressing and mix to coat. Cover and refrigerate for at least 2 hours before serving. When

required, bring to room temperature, add tomato to the amount you want to serve, and toss to mix.

Note:
Cook dried beans until you can squash them on the top of your mouth, following the guidelines on page 131.

Sweet-Sour Bean Salad

This recipe has stood the test of time.

For 8–10 servings:
2 cups cooked green beans, in chunks, not thin slices
1–2 cups cooked kidney beans
1 onion, chopped
1 red or green pepper, chopped
¼ cup sugar
¼ cup wine vinegar
¼ cup bean liquid
¼ cup oil
1 tsp salt

Put the prepared vegetables in a bowl. Add the remaining ingredients stir gently to mix, cover, and refrigerate for at least 24 hours before serving.

C Shredded Beetroot

Beetroot does not have to be boiled whole before it is used in other ways. Cooked in this way it is an interesting accompaniment to lamb.

For 4 servings:
300–400 g beetroot
1 clove garlic
2 tsp butter
¼ cup water
1 Tbsp orange or lemon juice
pepper and salt
fresh herbs (optional)

Thinly peel the beetroot, then shred using a blade that produces long thin shreds if possible. Do not worry if beetroot is not dark red right through.

Finely chop the garlic and cook in the butter without browning.

Add the beetroot, water and juice, cover and cook over moderate heat for 5–15 minutes, depending on the age of the beetroot. Try to have all liquid evaporated by the time the beetroot is tender.

Season, tasting to judge quantities required. Add a little sugar if the beetroot is not young, or if you feel that the flavour is too bland. Add any fresh herbs you like, finely chopped.

Serve hot, reheated if desired, plain or with sour cream.

M Brussels Sprouts

Select small tight Brussels sprouts, allowing 75–100 g per serving. Wash thoroughly. Remove outer leaves. Cut a deep cross in stem for even cooking.

Add 1–2 teaspoons water per serving.

Microwave at Full power.
150–200 g about 3 minutes
300–400 g about 5 minutes
Toss with butter and grated nutmeg.

M Broccoli

Broccoli microwaves beautifully. Allow 125–150 g per serving. Cut off heads, then peel stalks, pulling tough skin from base of stem towards tips. Cut peeled stalks into short lengths.

Add 2 teaspoons water per serving.

Cook at Full power.
1 serving 1½ minutes
2 servings 2½ minutes
4 servings 4 minutes
Allow 2 minutes' standing time.
Toss with butter.
Or use general method, page 164.

Unpeeled broccoli overcooks before stems become tender.

With frozen broccoli, cook 250 g for 5–9 minutes, depending on size of frozen pieces.

Serve with cheese sauce if desired.

M Cabbage

Very good in microwave, keeping good colour and slight crunchiness. Add a little water for a softer texture. Allow 75–100 g per serving.

Slice thinly, removing thick ribs. Add 1 teaspoon water per serving if desired. Cook at Full power for 1–1½ minutes per serving.

C Joanna's Cabbage

This is a good way to make late summer cabbage interesting.

For 4 servings:
12 Tbsp butter or oil
1 medium-sized onion, sliced thinly
½ medium-sized cabbage, shredded
2 Tbsp wine vinegar
1 Tbsp sugar
1 tsp salt
black pepper to taste
1 cup tomatoes, skinned and chopped

Heat the butter or oil in a medium-to-large frying pan. Add the onion and cabbage, toss to coat, then add remaining ingredients.

Mix well, cover pan and cook over fairly high heat for 5–10 minutes, then remove the lid. Cook, turning mixture frequently for 5 minutes more, or until the cooking liquid has evaporated and the cabbage is tender but still crisp.

C M Sweet-Sour Red Cabbage

Red cabbage doesn't always have to be simmered for hours. For four servings slice an onion, a clove of garlic and two large apples (or tamarillos).

Sauté in a large saucepan containing 3 or 4 tablespoons of butter until lightly coloured.

Add about 500 g shredded red cabbage (with central stem and outer leaves removed before slicing,) ¼ cup wine vinegar and ½ cup water. Cover and boil briskly over fairly high heat for 15–20 minutes, tossing occasionally.

Uncover and boil fast until only 2–3 tablespoons of liquid remain, then add enough cornflour paste to thicken this so it coats the leaves.

Serve immediately or reheat.

To microwave, cook at Full power for 10–15 minutes, or until tender. Stir in salt and brown sugar after 5 minutes' standing time.

U Coleslaw

Coleslaw is based on drumhead cabbage, which is available all year round, at a reasonable price.

Add one or more extra vegetables such as shredded carrot, sliced celery, chopped cauliflower.

Added toasted sunflower seeds, chopped peanuts, sultanas, etc. for extra flavour and texture.

Coleslaw dressings are usually sweeter and more acid than most other dressings. Modify any of the dressings on pages 200 and 201. One of my favourites is made by stirring together:

½ cup mayonnaise
1–2 Tbsp tomato ketchup
1 Tbsp lemon juice

C Lamb-Stuffed Cabbage Leaves

For 4–6 servings:
1 medium-sized cabbage
400 g minced lamb
1 large onion, chopped
1 cup cooked rice
2 tsp instant chicken stock
¼–½ cup currants (or raisins)
¼ cup pine nuts (or chopped almonds)
1 tsp chopped rosemary (or oreganum)
1 Tbsp lemon juice
3 chopped tomatoes
1 Tbsp butter
¼ cup water

Cut the core out of the cabbage so the leaves are detached. Plunge cabbage into a large container of boiling water. Lift off outer leaves as they soften. Select 10–12 leaves and cut away part of the main rib if this is thick.

Combine lamb with next seven ingredients, reserving half the onion. Divide lamb mixture between the leaves. First fold stem end, then sides, over filling, then roll up.

Line a flat baking dish with a layer of cut cabbage leaves, and sprinkle with remaining onion.

Lay cabbage-leaf rolls, join sides down, over this, in one layer. Top with peeled, chopped, seeded tomatoes, and dots of butter, then lay more cabbage leaves over the top. Add ¼ cup water and cover with foil or lid.

Bake at 180°C for about 30 minutes (longer if previously refrigerated). Discard upper and lower cabbage leaves from the dish. Serve tomato-onion sauce over rolls. Provide sour cream as extra sauce if desired.

Ⓜ Carrots

Young early-season carrots microwave well. Mid-season carrots cook well if they are cut into thin slices or thin strips. Old carrots are best avoided. If necessary, slice very thinly, or shred. Longer cooking shrivels old carrots, rather than making them more tender.

The cooking time varies with the maturity of the carrot and the size of the pieces. The amount of liquid needed increases with the maturity of the carrot. All pieces should be same size, thickness etc. Fruit juice, sugar, honey etc. are best added after the carrots are cooked.

Cut carrots into 5 mm slices or long thin strips, allowing about 75 g per serving.

Add 1–4 teaspoons water per serving depending on age.

Add finely chopped herbs or poppy seeds or caraway seeds if desired.

Cover and cook for 2–4 minutes per serving, depending on age. Allow 2 minutes' standing time.

Add butter, brown sugar or honey, orange juice and rind, nutmeg, or whatever flavourings you like. Add a little cornflour if desired. Reheat to glaze and thicken.

Ⓒ Cooked Carrot Salad

Cooked carrots, cooled in a well-flavoured tomato dressing, make a good addition to a salad table. Add leeks, green pepper or celery two minutes before the carrots are cooked, for contrasting colours, textures and flavours.

For 4 servings:
400–500 g carrots
1 pkt tomato soup
1 cup water
½ cup wine vinegar
½ cup oil
¼–½ cup sugar

Scrub or thinly peel carrots and slice crossways so they are about 5 mm thick.

Cover and cook without seasonings in a small amount of water until barely tender, adding small amounts of other vegetables (as above), if desired. Drain off any remaining water.

While carrots cook, simmer soup and water for 3 minutes. Add vinegar, oil and half the sugar, and simmer for 2 minutes longer. Taste and add extra sugar, if necessary. Pour half this dressing over the hot drained carrot. Cover and leave in the dressing to cool.

Stir just before serving, adding herbs to garnish if desired.

Ⓤ Raw Carrot Salad

If possible shred the carrot for this recipe using a blade that will produce long, thin strips.

If the carrot is laid so that its long side is against the shredding blade, longer, more attractive strips result.

For 4 servings:
300 g carrots
2 Tbsp oil
1 Tbsp orange or lemon juice
salt, pepper and sugar
1–2 Tbsp chopped parsley, dill, chives,
    spring onions, etc.

Just before the salad is needed, or up to 3 hours ahead, shred thinly peeled (or scrubbed) carrots. (If using a food processor, lie the lengths of carrots flat in the feed-tube.)

Put in a serving dish and add the oil and juice. Sprinkle with salt, then pepper, then sugar, adding just enough of each to accentuate the carrot flavour.

Chop whatever herb you use very finely and sprinkle over the salad. Mix lightly.

Cover tightly and refrigerate if not using immediately.

Ⓤ Sweet-Sour Carrot Salad

This salad has definite character, and will 'lift' other bland foods.

For 4 servings:
1½ cups shredded raw carrot
1 Tbsp Dijon-type mustard
1 Tbsp honey
1 Tbsp lemon juice
1 tsp grated root ginger

Grate the carrot into long, even shreds, in a food processor if available.

Measure the mustard and honey into a shallow serving bowl. Mix in the lemon juice. Grate the root ginger finely into a little pile, then pick this up and squeeze it, so its juice runs into the mustard mixture. Discard the fibres.

Turn the grated carrot in the dressing until it is evenly coated. Taste and season only if necessary.

Garnish with a few watercress leaves, or with chopped parsley.
Variation:
Mix ½–1 cup of chopped roasted peanuts through the salad a few minutes before serving it.

Do not peel vegetables unless really necessary. You get more fibre, more nutrients and more value for your money, if you simply scrub root vegetables thoroughly, then use skin and all.

Ⓒ Carrot and Mushroom Loaf

Everybody likes this loaf! It is a good choice when you want to present a meal to rather conservative people. Team it with mashed potatoes, green beans or broccoli, and cubed pumpkin or baked tomatoes.

For 4 servings:
1 medium-sized onion
1–2 cloves garlic
2 Tbsp oil or butter
200 g mushrooms
1 tsp basil
¼ tsp thyme
½ tsp salt
black pepper
3 cups grated carrot (400 g)
½ cup dry breadcrumbs
½ cup grated cheese
½ cup milk
2 eggs
2 Tbsp dry breadcrumbs
2 Tbsp grated cheese
paprika

Finely chop the onion and garlic, then cook in the oil or butter until the onion is soft. Add the sliced mushrooms and continue to cook until these have softened.

Transfer the cooked onion-and-mushroom mixture to a medium-sized bowl and then add the next nine ingredients. Mix together well, then pour into a well-greased loaf tin. (Line long sides and bottom with a strip of baking paper, if you think it could stick.) Sprinkle with the remaining measures of breadcrumbs and cheese and dust lightly with paprika.

Cover pan with foil, and bake at 180°C for 30 minutes, then uncover and cook for a further 30 minutes or until the centre is firm when pressed.

Ⓤ Carrot and Apple Salad

These two flavours and textures complement each other to make a good winter salad.

For 2 servings:
1 carrot, grated
2 tart (preferably Sturmer) apples
2 Tbsp mayonnaise (see page 200)
lettuce cups

Grate the carrot and unpeeled apple into long shreds. Coat with mayonnaise immediately to stop apple browning. Spoon into lettuce cups if available.

Serve within 30 minutes, if possible.

Carrot and Mushroom Loaf

Microwaved Corn Cobs

M Corn

Microwaved corn cooks fast and very easily in its husk, exactly as it grows.

Choose corn with green husks and plump kernels which puncture easily, and contain milky liquid.

To cook one, two or three cobs of corn, lie cobs directly on floor or turntable of microwave oven, with spaces between two, or to form a triangle.

Microwave at Full power, allowing 2–4 minutes per cob. Stand for 3–5 minutes before serving.

If you have more than three corn cobs, or if you have peeled corn cobs, put them in an oven bag with 1 tablespoon of water per corn cob. Microwave for 2–5 minutes per corn cob, depending on size and variety. Turn over and rearrange cobs several times during cooking.

Serve with Chilli Mayonnaise (see page 200).

B Barbecued Corn Cobs

Use small cobs of young tender corn.

Soak in a bucket of water for 10 minutes, then barbecue over low heat, turning frequently, until the husks char.

Cut bases from cobs, and peel off husks and silk. Eat with Chilli Mayonnaise (see page 200).

C Corn Fritters

Keep a can of corn in your storecupboard so that you can make corn fritters whenever you need a quick meal at short notice.

The size of the can you use in this recipe does not matter, so use a large can if you want fritters for a lot of people, or a small can if it is only for two or three.

For 2 large or 6 small servings:
1 egg
3–4 Tbsp liquid from corn
1 can whole kernel corn, drained
1 cup self-raising flour

Put the egg into a mixing bowl. Drain the liquid from the can of corn. Put 3 tablespoonfuls of corn liquid in with the egg, and keep the rest aside in case you need to thin the batter later. Tip the drained corn into the bowl, add the flour, and stir with a fork, just until the mixture is dampened. Do not over-mix or the fritters won't be so nice. The dry ingredients should be just dampened.

Drop teaspoonfuls of fritter batter into a pan with hot oil about 5 mm deep. (Heat an electric pan to 190°C.)

Turn the fritters with tongs as soon as they are brown on the bottom. Lift them from the pan as soon as the second side is cooked,

and keep them warm in a plate lined with paper towels.
Note:
A large pile of little fritters is much nicer than a small pile of large fritters.

M Cauliflower

Cauliflower microwaves well. Cut or break into evenly sized florets. Peel and chop stems as for broccoli if desired.

Allow 1–2 teaspoons water per 100 g serving or add garlic and butter as in general method, page 164. Cook at Full power, allowing 1–2 minutes per serving.

Drain if necessary. Pile in serving dish. Sprinkle with grated cheese, paprika and parsley. If cheese does not melt straight away, reheat.

Cauliflower cooks well in vegetable mixtures. For 'stir-fried', cut florets into 5 mm slices.

U Celery and Apple Salad

This makes a good winter salad.

For 1 or 2 servings:
1 stalk tender celery
1 firm apple
2 Tbsp Mayonnaise (see page 200)
1 Tbsp chopped walnuts

Cut the celery and unpeeled apple into cubes. Mix immediately with the mayonnaise, and sprinkle with chopped walnuts. Serve in a lettuce cup if available.

ⒸⓂ Braised Celery

This recipe needs little attention while it cooks in the oven, or on the stovetop.

For 4 servings:
3 cups sliced celery
2 Tbsp butter
2 cloves garlic, finely chopped
1 cup water
1 tsp vegetable bouillon powder
1 tsp sugar
¼ tsp salt
cornflour
chopped parsley

Remove strings from celery and slice crosswise or diagonally.

Melt butter in a pan. Add garlic, then celery. Transfer to ovenware dish if desired, or leave in pan. Add next four ingredients.

Either cover and bake at 180°C for 45–60 minutes, or simmer in covered pan for 20–30 minutes. Thicken liquid with cornflour paste and sprinkle with chopped parsley.

To microwave, combine all ingredients in a small covered casserole. Cook at Full power for 5–6 minutes, stirring after 2 minutes.

Ⓜ Eggplant

Eggplant microwaves well. Eggplant which is to be puréed for other recipes may be baked whole. The baked flesh is pale green, rather than beige.

Puncture skin in several places. Bake at Full power, allowing about 6 minutes per 500 g. Eggplant is cooked as soon as it feels soft all over.

Allow 5 minutes' standing time. Halve, and scoop out flesh, discarding skin.

Ⓒ Grilled Eggplant

Cut eggplant in 1 cm slices or in 2 cm cubes. Thread cubes loosely on skewers. Brush generously with Tomato Dressing, (see recipe on page 165) and cook about 12 cm from the heat, turning frequently, until tender, about 15 minutes.

Ⓜ Savoury Eggplant

For 4–6 servings:
1 eggplant (about 500 g)
25 g butter
2 cloves garlic, chopped
2 Tbsp chopped parsley

Just before cooking, cut unpeeled eggplant into 1 cm cubes.

Heat butter and chopped garlic in a medium-sized casserole for 1 minute, then add the cubed eggplant and parsley. Cover and microwave at Full power for 5–8 minutes or until tender, shaking or stirring twice.

Stand for 3 minutes then sprinkle with grated Parmesan cheese, basil and oreganum.

Ⓒ Eggplant Casserole

My daughter Kirsten sent this recipe with the note 'Absolutely delicious — even the most suspicious people ask for more.' This says it all, really. Eggplant has a very meaty texture and colour, and is often used in casseroles where a meaty appearance is an advantage.

This is a casserole which can be served as part of a buffet meal for a group of people which includes meat-eaters and vegetarians. It is great when served as the main part of a dinner, with other vegetables.

For about 4 main servings:
1 large eggplant (about 750 g)
1 egg
1 Tbsp water
½ cup dry breadcrumbs
2 Tbsp oil
2 onions, quartered and sliced
1 Tbsp oil
8 large tomatoes, sliced
fresh basil or 1 tsp dried basil
½ cup water
1 tsp salt
2 tsp sugar
freshly ground pepper
1 cup grated tasty cheese

In this recipe you prepare two mixtures. For speed, brown the eggplant slices while the tomato mixture simmers.

Cut the eggplant into slices about 1 cm thick. In a shallow dish big enough to hold the slices, beat the egg with the water, just enough to combine. Dip the eggplant slices first in the egg, then in the crumbs, coating both sides.

Fry slices in a little hot oil until brown on both sides. Leave to drain on paper towels.

In another pan, sauté the sliced onions in 1 tablespoon of oil until lightly browned. Add the tomatoes, basil, water, salt, sugar and pepper, and simmer until the onion is tender.

Coat a large, shallow casserole dish (about 23×30 cm) with non-stick spray or butter, then put half the browned eggplant slices into the dish, cutting them to fit, if necessary. Pour half the tomato mixture over this layer, top with remaining eggplant, then spread the remaining tomato mixture on top. Top with the grated cheese.

Bake, uncovered, at 180°C for 45 minutes, or until the top browns and the eggplant is very tender. Do not hurry the cooking. Leave to stand for at least 10 minutes before serving, or reheat later, preferably in a microwave oven.

Varitions:
Put a layer of grated cheese between the two layers of eggplant, as well as above the top layer.

Ⓜ Baked Kumara

Scrub evenly shaped kumara well. Cut off any stringy ends. Prick in several places.

Microwave at Full power, allowing 3 minutes per 100 g, turning over after half the estimated cooking time. Cook until kumara gives when pressed. Leave to stand for 3–4 minutes.

Cut a cross in the top and press between cuts.

Serve with sour cream and chives, or with 2 tablespoons sour cream mixed with 1 teaspoon brown sugar.

ⒸⓂ Kumara Purée with Coriander

Coriander gives kumara a lovely aromatic flavour.

Scrub kumara thoroughly. Microwave at Full power for 6–8 minutes per 250 g kumara or bake in a conventional oven, in an oven bag for 45–60 minutes.

Kumara is cooked when the flesh 'gives' when squeezed. Peel the cooked kumara without removing the coloured flesh under the skin.

Chop roughly and mash with a potato masher or purée in a food processor, adding a little butter and milk in equal quantities. Add pepper and salt to taste, then add freshly crushed coriander seed until the flavour suits you.

Ⓒ Kumara or Parsnip Patties

For 3–4 servings:
1½–2 cups mashed cooked kumara or parsnip
1 egg
1 Tbsp brown sugar
¼ cup self-raising flour
pinch of ginger, cinnamon or mixed spice

Measure all ingredients into a mixing bowl, combine with a fork and add a little extra self-raising flour to make a mixture firm enough to drop in spoonfuls into a pan containing 3 mm hot oil or melted butter.

Brown until evenly coloured on both sides, then serve immediately.

Green salads are usually served as side dishes to provide texture and flavour contrast.

Use a variety of green leafy salad vegetables, with small amounts of thinly sliced spring onion, cucumber, bean sprouts, etc.

Make sure that leaves are washed, then dried and chilled before they are coated with a thin, tangy dressing before serving. (To dry and chill them, spread washed leaves on a clean teatowel or paper towel, then roll up like a sponge roll, and store in the refrigerator, for up to 24 hours.)

Choose a thin dressing from page 201, sprinkle it over the prepared leaves, and toss gently to coat leaves.

C Mushroom Burgers

These burgers are very popular with mushroom lovers. The recipe is especially good made with older mushrooms with dark gills, as these have a stronger flavour.

Double the quantities for larger groups.

For 4 burgers, to serve 2:
1 medium-sized onion
1 clove garlic
1 Tbsp oil
150 g mushrooms
1 cup fresh wholemeal breadcrumbs
1 tsp cornflour
1 Tbsp fresh chopped parsley (or 1 tsp dried parsley)
1 tsp nutritional yeast
1 egg
1 Tbsp lemon juice (juice of ¹/₂ lemon)
1 tsp dark soya sauce

Chop the onion and garlic, then sauté in the oil until the onion begins to soften. Add the mushrooms and continue cooking until they turn soft and dark.

Tip the onion-and-mushroom mixture into a medium-sized bowl, and add the remaining ingredients. Mix well, using your hands if necessary. Add a few more breadcrumbs if the mixture seems too wet. Divide into four equal portions and then shape each quarter into a 10 cm patty.

Cook in a little oil or butter, using a non-stick pan if you have one, until lightly browned on each side and firm when pressed in the middle.
Note:
A little fresh thyme is a nice addition to these burgers.

U Mushroom Salad

Firm, small button mushrooms make wonderful salads. Make this salad about 15 mintues before serving, if possible.

Slice or quarter cleaned mushrooms, and turn gently in any of the following dressings (see page 201), using quantities to suit yourself.

French Dressing
Herb Dressing
Tomato Dressing
Herbed Creamy Vinaigrette
Cumin Dressing

U Mushroom, Leek and Cashew Salad

Wipe the caps of firm, white button mushrooms with a damp cloth and slice thinly. Mix with French Dressing (see page 201), before cut surfaces discolour.

Slice a short section of raw leek very thinly, separate rings and mix with mushrooms. Cover, and leave to stand for 30 minutes before serving. Sprinkle with lightly browned fried cashew nuts just before serving over wedges of lettuce.

M Garlic Mushrooms

This is a very fast and easy mushroom recipe which is good as a side dish or as the main part of a light meal.

For 4 servings:
400 g mushrooms
2 cloves garlic, chopped
1 Tbsp butter
1 tsp light soya sauce
1 tsp cornflour
2 Tbsp chopped parsley or spring onion

Wipe mushrooms. Halve or slice if large. Chop garlic finely, and place with butter in a microwave casserole dish just large enough to hold mushrooms. Heat at Full power for 30 seconds or until butter has melted. Stir in soya sauce and cornflour, then toss mushrooms in this mixture, coating them evenly and lightly. Sprinkle with parsley or spring onion.

Cover loosely and microwave for 3–4 minutes or until mushrooms have softened to the desired amount and are coated with lightly thickened sauce. Sprinkle with pepper. Serve on noodles, rice or toast.

C M Sweet and Sour Onions

These small onions are cooked in a tomato sauce with sultanas. Serve hot or at room temperature.

For 4–6 servings:
500 g small onions
2 Tbsp tomato paste
2 Tbsp wine vinegar
1 Tbsp olive or other oil
1 Tbsp sugar
1 tsp salt
1 cup water
¹/₄ cup sultanas
1 bay leaf

Pour boiling water over the onions and leave to stand for 1 minute. Drain and cut off root and top sections, then lift off skins.

Combine next five ingredients in a microwave dish or saucepan big enough to hold the onions in one layer. Add water, sultanas and bay leaf then the onions.

Cover and microwave at Full power for 6 minutes or until onions are tender, or simmer on the stovetop for 20–30 minutes.

Serve immediately, reheat later or serve warm.

M Baked Onions

Peel small onions, cutting a thick slice from the top and bottom, so the centres do not pop out during cooking.

Put in a small covered casserole, allowing ¹/₂ teaspoon each of water and butter per serving.

Cook at Full power, allowing 1–2 minutes per onion.

M Stuffed Onions

Slice tops and bottoms from large onions. Add ¹/₂ teaspoon each of butter and water per onion. Cover and cook at Full power for 3 minutes per onion.

Lift out and chop the central portion of each onion. Mix with chopped parsley or other fresh herbs, fresh breadcrumbs, grated cheese, chopped nuts or minced meat etc. When required, cover and bake for about 3 minutes per onion.

M Caramelised Onion Rings

For 3–4 servings:
1 Tbsp sugar
1 tsp water
25 g butter
2–3 large onions
1 Tbsp water
¹/₂ tsp dark soya sauce
1 tsp wine vinegar

Combine sugar and water in a high-heat resistant dish. Microwave at Full power until evenly golden brown. Add butter, sliced onions, water, dark soya sauce and vinegar.

Cover and cook for 3–6 minutes, or until onion is cooked to the

Garlic Mushrooms

desired degree. To thicken the sauce, uncover and cook for about 1 minute more.

Spoon over sausages, steak, etc.

Variation:
Add 2 sliced apples and ½ teaspoon fresh sage to the onions after they have cooked for 3 minutes. Cook for about 5 minutes longer, until apples are tender.

Parsnip-Carrot Mix

For 4 servings:
2 cups grated carrot
2 cups grated parsnip
25 g butter
¼ tsp salt
¼ cup water

Microwave all ingredients in a covered casserole for 8 minutes. Leave to stand for 3–4 minutes then mash, or purée in food processor.

Add pepper to taste.

Glazed Parsnips

For 2 servings:
1 medium-sized parsnip (200 g)
2 tsp butter
2 Tbsp brown sugar
1 Tbsp orange juice

Cut parsnip into pencil-thickness strips. Combine all ingredients in a small casserole. Cover and bake at Full power for 6–8 minutes, or until barely tender. Leave to stand for 2–3 minutes, turning to coat with glaze.

Peas

Frozen peas are at their best when microwaved, since none of their flavour is lost in cooking liquid.

For 1 serving:
½ cup frozen peas
½ tsp butter
1 tsp water
1 sprig mint (optional)
pinch sugar

Put everything together in a small casserole, oven bag or double-layered packet of greaseproof paper.

Cook at Full power for 1–1½ minutes.

For larger quantities allow 1–2 minutes per ½ cup serving, and stir several times during cooking.

Parsnip Crisps

The natural sweetness of parsnips is emphasised in this recipe which is popular with those who think they do not like this vegetable!

For 4 servings:
Thinly peel about 400 g parsnips. Cut into 5 cm lengths, then lengthwise into sticks, cutting the larger top portions into twice as many pieces as the smaller bottoms. Remove the central core only if the parsnips are old and woody.

Microwave at Full power in a covered dish with 2 tablespoons water until barely tender, about 4 minutes.

Add 1 tablespoon butter and shake to coat. Shake buttered strips in a paper or plastic bag containing flour. Shake off excess.

Heat enough clarified butter to cover the bottom of a large frying pan. When very hot, add floured parsnips and cook, turning several times, until evenly browned.

Serve immediately as a vegetable or warm as finger food.

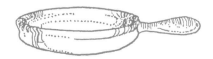

Creamy Pumpkin Cubes

C Stuffed Peppers

No particular ethnic group would want to claim these stuffed peppers. I like all the flavourings added to stuffed vegetables by different countries in the Middle East, so I put them all in, without restraint.

Do not make this recipe unless you can get fleshy, plump peppers. Choose red rather than green, since they are sweeter, if you have the choice. If golden-yellow peppers are available try them too. A mixture of different coloured peppers is prettiest of all.

For 4 servings:
4 large or 8 small peppers (see above)
3 onions
2 cloves garlic
3 Tbsp oil
1 cup brown or white long-grain rice
½ cup pine nuts or chopped almonds
½ cup currants
¼ cup chopped mint
¼ cup chopped parsley
½ tsp ground allspice
½ tsp ground nutmeg
½ tsp cinnamon
1 tsp salt
1 (425 g) can savoury tomatoes or tomatoes in juice

First prepare the peppers. Cut across the tops, removing the stem portion, or cut large peppers in half lengthwise. Remove and discard seeds and pith, but chop trimmings from around the stem.

Chop two of the onions, and the garlic, finely. Heat in 1 tablespoon of the oil, in a large pan with a cover, until transparent. Add any chopped pepper, then the rice, and cook for a minute or two longer, then add 2 cups water, cover, and simmer until the rice is tender, about half an hour for brown rice, or about 15 minutes for white rice.

Soften the prepared peppers by putting them in a bowl, pouring boiling water over them, and leaving them to stand for 5 minutes. Drain, and discard the water.

Put the second tablespoon of oil in another pan and lightly brown the pine nuts or chopped almonds in it. Watch carefully so they do not darken. When evenly coloured, add the currants, and cook a little longer, until they have plumped up. Turn off the heat and remove from pan, mixing with the chopped mint and parsley.

Stir the allspice, nutmeg, cinnamon and salt into the almost-cooked rice. Add extra water if necessary. It should be tender and dry by the time it finishes. Stir most of the currant mixture into the cooked rice.

Lightly brown the last onion in the last tablespoon of oil, in the pot or pan in which the peppers will cook. Add the tomatoes, chopping them into smaller pieces.

Pack the rice into the peppers, so that the tops are rounded, and all or most of the filling is used. Arrange peppers on the tomato, then cover pan and simmer very gently for 20–30 minutes, until the peppers are tender and the tomato mixture has thickened.

Serve two peppers or half peppers per serving, standing each on a spoonful of tomato mixture. Top with reserved currant mixture.

M Pumpkin

This is easy and good.
Whole:
When you have a whole pumpkin and want purée for pies and soups, put it in the oven just as it is and microwave at Full power, turning over every now and then, until the flesh 'gives' all over when pressed. A 1½ kg pumpkin will take 15–20 minutes.

Halve, discard seeds, then scoop out and sieve the flesh to use as you like.
Wedges:
Remove and discard seeds from wedge, place in an unsealed oven bag, cook until it feels tender through the bag;
5–7 minutes per 500 g.

M Creamy Pumpkin Cubes

For about 4 servings:
400 g cubed pumpkin
2 tsp flour
1 clove garlic, chopped
½ tsp curry powder (optional)
¼ tsp salt
¼ cup cream, creamy milk or coconut cream
1 spring onion, chopped

Cut pumpkin in 1 cm cubes. Toss to coat with flour.

Add remaining ingredients except spring onion. Cover and cook at Full power until pumpkin is tender, stirring several times, for 5–8 minutes.
Variations:
Leave out curry powder. Sprinkle cooked pumpkin with cinnamon sugar.

C M Pumpkin in Cream

Rich and particularly good when made with floury pumpkin. For four servings cut 400–500 g pumpkin into slices or cubes.

Pack pieces tightly into an ovenproof dish, sprinkle with salt and pepper then pour about ½ cup cream over and around the pumpkin.

Sprinkle with about ¼ cup brown sugar mixed with ½ teaspoon ginger or cinnamon if desired.

Cover and bake at 180°C for about an hour, or until pumpkin is tender (or microwave at Full power for 6–10 minutes). Floury pumpkin needs no thickening. Coat early season pumpkin with flour before adding other ingredients.

U Orange and Radish Salad

Cut the peel from oranges (or tangelos) very carefully, removing all white pith. Slice thinly and arrange slices in a shallow dish with thinly sliced red-skinned radishes. Use proportions to suit individual preference.

Cover dish and chill until required.

Sprinkle with French Dressing (see page 201) just before serving with cold roast pork, turkey or chicken.

C Spinach and Cheese Crêpes

For really successful spinach crêpes, you need to thicken the spinach and season it very carefully.

For 4–6 servings:
1 recipe crêpe batter
1–2 cups cooked, drained, chopped spinach
3 Tbsp butter
3 Tbsp flour
½ tsp salt
1 tsp grated nutmeg
1½ cups milk
1½ cups grated cheese
paprika or Parmesan cheese

Prepare batter and make crêpes, using a small pan.

Cook, drain, squeeze and chop spinach.

Make the sauce. Melt the butter, add the flour, salt and nutmeg. Add the milk, ½ cup at a time, boiling and stirring between additions. After last boiling, add the cheese.

Mix a third of the cheese sauce with the spinach. Spread spinach mixture over the crêpes and roll up. Place the filled crêpes in a well-sprayed ovenware pan. Pour sauce (thinned a little if necessary) over crêpes. Sprinkle with paprika or Parmesan cheese. Bake at 200°C for 20 minutes or until bubbly. Brown surface under grill before serving, if desired.

C Spinach and Bacon Salad

Wash dry and crisp the leaves from 500 g fresh spinach. Discard the stems.

Fry 4 bacon rashers until crisp, then crumble them. Mix with the bacon fat ¼ cup oil, 2 teaspoons mixed mustard and 2 tablespoons lemon juice. Warm slightly to combine.

Just before serving, toss spinach leaves in this dressing. Sprinkle with crumbled bacon and ¼ cup small croutons.

Serve as a first course or side salad.

Shredded Swede

C Spanish Spinach

Interesting enough to stand alone as a light lunch dish.

For four servings fry 2–3 rashers of bacon in 3 tablespoons oil. When crisp, remove bacon and crumble or chop in small pieces.

Add to the bacon fat in the pan 2–3 tablespoons pine nuts and ¼ cup Australian raisins. Cook gently until nuts are golden and raisins plumped. Put aside with bacon.

Add 500 g stemmed spinach to the remaining oil. Turn to coat then cover tightly, and cook until tender, but still bright green. Uncover, chop roughly, heat to evaporate cooking liquids then mix with bacon, pine nuts and raisins.

C Silverbeet

Cook young silverbeet (Swiss Chard) or spinach beet (perpetual spinach) as you would spinach, with stems sliced very thinly.

Young silverbeet or spinach beet may be used as a substitute for spinach in many spinach recipes.

C Shredded Swede

High in vitamin C, bacon-flavoured shredded swede is full of flavour!

Chop 1–2 rashers of bacon into small pieces and fry until crisp. Remove half bacon from pan.

To the remaining bacon add a tablespoon of butter and enough grated swede for four servings. Add about ¼ cup water, cover tightly and cook over high heat for about 5 minutes, until just tender.

Remove lid and cook until liquid has evaporated, adding ¼ cup chopped parsley, freshly ground pepper, and salt and sugar to taste.

Serve sprinkled with the remaining bacon.

M Swede

Although swede cooks conventionally in the same time, it can be microwaved. For 4 servings cube 250 g peeled swede. Add 1 tablespoon bacon fat or butter and 1 tablespoon each water and parsley. Cover and cook until tender, 6–8 minutes. Serve as is, or mash.

C Summer Squash Savoury

Here the term 'summer squash' is used to cover zucchini, scallopini, young marrows, crook-necked squash, etc. Choko may be cooked by this method, too.

For 2 main or 4 side servings:
1 Tbsp butter
2 cloves garlic, chopped
400–500 g prepared squash (see above
    for suggested types)
½ cup water
1 tsp instant chicken stock
1 tsp instant green herb stock
basil and oreganum
½ tsp sugar (optional)
1 cup chopped skinned tomatoes
    (optional)
cornflour
water
chopped parsley

Heat the butter in a large pan. Add garlic and cook gently.

Slice vegetables crosswise, or cube, or cut in sticks 5 cm long, 5 mm thick. Toss in garlic butter, add water, cover and cook over high heat until vegetables are barely tender-crisp.

Sprinkle with instant stocks, fresh or dry herbs, sugar and the tomato (from which the seeds have been squeezed). Toss or stir to combine and cook for 2–3 minutes longer.

If any liquid remains, thicken it with a small amount of cornflour paste. Sprinkle with parsley before serving.

U Marinated Tomato Salad

It's hard to beat a tomato salad, especially when you can pick ripe red tomatoes from your own garden.

For 4 servings:
5–6 medium-sized tomatoes
1 tsp sugar
¼–½ tsp salt
black pepper to taste
few drops hot pepper sauce
1 Tbsp wine vinegar (optional)
1 Tbsp chopped fresh basil, marjoram
    or parsley
1–2 Tbsp oil (optional)

Slice, quarter or cube the tomatoes into their serving dish.

About 10–15 minutes before serving sprinkle the remaining ingredients, in the order given, over the tomatoes. Toss lightly and leave to stand at room temperature.

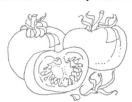

M Stuffed Tomatoes

For 4 servings:
4 large tomatoes
2 spring onions, chopped
2–4 mushrooms, chopped
2 tsp butter
¼ cup herbed crumbs
salt, pepper, sugar
fresh herbs, chopped

Cut tops off tomatoes or halve tomatoes and scoop out pulp. Cook onions, mushrooms and butter at Full power in a small covered container for 2 minutes.

Add tomato pulp, herbed crumbs and more fresh herbs if desired. Taste and adjust seasoning.

Pile filling into or on to tomatoes. Cover lightly in a shallow dish. Bake until tomatoes have heated through.

Herbed Crumbs
25 g butter
1½ cups fresh breadcrumbs
1 Tbsp chopped parsley
2 tsp chopped basil (optional)
1 Tbsp Parmesan cheese (optional)

Melt butter in shallow casserole. Stir in crumbs and herbs and cheese, if used. Microwave for about 2 minutes, until golden brown.

M Baked Tomatoes

Halve or thickly slice tomatoes and season to taste or cut a deep cross in the top of whole tomatoes to prevent steam build up. Cook uncovered until soft at Full power allowing 30–60 seconds per tomato.

M Sweet-Sour Yams

For 2 servings:
200–250 g scrubbed yams
1 Tbsp butter
1 Tbsp brown sugar
1 Tbsp wine vinegar
1 tsp cornflour
2 Tbsp water

Slice yams crosswise into 1 cm slices. Heat butter, brown sugar and wine vinegar in a medium-sized casserole dish at Full power for 2 minutes. Sprinkle cornflour over sliced yams. Add these, with water, to sugar mixture. Cover and cook for 5 minutes, or to desired tenderness.

Season to taste with salt and pepper. Add a little extra water if sauce is not smooth when yams are cooked. Stir to coat with sauce.

C Zucchini and Mushroom Loaf

This loaf has an excellent texture and an interesting flavour. It also provides a great way to disguise zucchini should you be cooking for those who would not otherwise enjoy such a treat!

For 4–6 servings:
1 medium-sized onion, diced
2 cloves garlic, crushed
2 Tbsp oil
200 g mushrooms, sliced
500 g zucchini, grated
2 cups fresh wholemeal breadcrumbs
2 eggs
1 cup grated cheese
1 tsp salt
1 tsp basil
¼ tsp thyme
black pepper
2 Tbsp dried breadcrumbs

Dice the onion and garlic, then sauté until soft in the oil. Add the sliced mushrooms and cook until soft and beginning to darken.

Grate the zucchini coarsely, and squeeze to remove as much liquid as possible.

Put the zucchini in a large bowl, and add the onion-mushroom mixture then add the remaining ingredients, except ¼ cup of grated cheese and the dried breadcrumbs.

Transfer the mixture to a well-greased loaf tin, and top with the remaining cheese and the dried crumbs.

Bake at 180°C for 1 hour, or until the middle feels firm to touch, covering with foil during the first half of the cooking.

Unmould and leave for 5 minutes before slicing.

C Easy Zucchini Pie

If you grow zucchini, or if you can buy 'teenage' zucchini at a reasonable price, I think you will find this recipe very useful!

It is a variation of an American recipe, and it makes a very good weekend main meal or lunch, any time during the warmer months. It makes a good addition to an outdoor buffet, too.

If you like this sort of easy, crustless pie, spend the time and money to find and buy some fairly heavy, non-stick, dark coloured metal pieplates, flan tins, cake tins or roasting pans. I make this recipe in a heavy, non-stick 23 × 25 cm roasting pan, but it looks more elegant when made in two 23 cm cake or flan tins.

For 6–8 servings:
3 cups (500 g) grated zucchini
1 onion, grated
4 eggs
1½ cups grated cheese
½ tsp salt
¾ cup self-raising flour
pepper
herbs and tomato slices (optional)

Zucchini with Cream

Grate the zucchini and onion, and place in a fairly large mixing bowl, with the egg, cheese and salt. Mix well with a fork.

Add the flour and as much pepper as you like, and chop in any fresh herbs you have and like.

Pour the mixture into a pan or pans which have been well sprayed or buttered. Because it rises quite a lot as it cooks, do not fill any pan more than two-thirds full. Even though it may look skimpy, it does not matter if a pan is only filled to half its depth.

If you like, and if you have them, top the pies with sliced tomatoes.

Again, if you like, sprinkle the top of the pie or tomatoes with more grated cheese, or with grated Parmesan cheese.

Bake at 200°C for 25–40 minutes, until the centre feels firm, and the top has browned slightly.

Leave to stand for at least 5 minutes before cutting into pieces.

C Zucchini Pancakes

(See photograph on page 179.)

These little pancakes with red pepper purée will convert the staunchest zucchini-hater!

For 4 main servings:
2 eggs
½ tsp salt
1 large clove garlic
3 cups shredded zucchini (unpeeled)
¼ cup grated Parmesan cheese
about ½ cup self-raising flour
oil

In a medium-sized bowl beat the eggs to combine white and yolks. Crush the garlic clove into the salt, and add the paste to the eggs. Mix again.

Add the fairly firmly packed, shredded zucchini and the Parmesan cheese, then stir in enough flour to make a batter of fritter consistency.

Drop batter into hot oil, 5 mm deep, a tablespoon at a time to make small pancakes. Turn when golden brown. Lower heat if necessary and cook until centres are firm. Serve with the following sauce.

Red pepper purée

Sauté 1 chopped onion, 1 chopped garlic clove and 1 chopped red pepper in 1 tablespoon butter, until onion is transparent but not brown. Add ¾ cup chicken stock (or water). Cover and simmer for 10 minutes, then purée. Season, and if necessary cook a little longer to thicken, then serve over pancakes.

C M Zucchini with Cream

This is a really interesting way to serve zucchini.

For 4 servings:
500 g sliced zucchini
½ cup water
1 Tbsp butter
¼ cup cream
1 tsp chopped rosemary or thyme or sage or marjoram

Slice the young zucchini 5 mm thick. Cook in a covered frying pan over high heat, with the water and butter. When the liquid has evaporated, add the cream and herbs and cook uncovered, over high heat, until the cream thickens and coats the zucchini.

To microwave, combine all ingredients in a shallow covered casserole . Microwave at Full power for 3 minutes, until zucchini are tender-crisp, shaking casserole to mix after 1½ minutes.

Uncover and cook for 2–3 minutes longer, until cream sauce thickens. Stir to coat zucchini and serve immediately.

Julienne Vegetable Strips

C Ratatouille

This vegetable stew is tasty and substantial.

For 8 servings:
2 large onions, sliced
2 cloves garlic
2 Tbsp cooking oil
2–3 cups sliced zucchini
1–2 green peppers, seeded and sliced
2–3 cups diced eggplant
¼ cup cooking oil
3 cups chopped and peeled tomatoes
fresh or dried basil or oreganum to taste
salt, pepper and sugar
cornflour
chopped parsley

In a large frying pan fry the onions and sliced garlic in the oil, allowing them to colour very slightly. Add the zucchini and peppers. Cook over moderate heat, turning vegetables occasionally, for 5–10 minutes.

Remove vegetables from pan and brown the eggplant in the second amount of oil. Add the partly cooked vegetable mixture and the tomatoes. Cover and add a little basil and oreganum. Cook over low heat for about 30 minutes, then season carefully with salt, pepper and sugar to taste.

Adjust heat and lid of pan so that vegetables cook in a small amount of liquid (from the vegetables). If too much liquid forms, remove lid and raise heat. If mixture dries out, lower heat and add a little water. If serving hot, thicken with a little cornflour paste and sprinkle with chopped parsley. If serving at room temperature, do not thicken.

M Julienne Vegetable Strips

Long thin strips of vegetables look attractive and cook quickly together in the microwave oven. The strips should be thicker than matches but thinner than pencils.

For 2 servings:
50 g carrots
50 g zucchini
50 g celery
1 tsp butter
2 Tbsp water
1 finely chopped clove garlic (optional)
1–4 tsp chopped fresh herbs

Cut carrots, zucchini and celery into thin strips, making the carrot strips the thinnest, if carrots are fairly mature.

Put vegetable strips with butter, water and garlic into a small microwave casserole.

Cover and cook at Full power for 3–4 minutes, until barely tender, shaking vegetables to coat with butter after 2 minutes. Leave to stand for 2 minutes, then sprinkle with finely chopped parsley or other fresh herbs.

Other suitable vegetables to replace or add to the above vegetables include white turnips, swede, long white radish, green peppers, red peppers, yellow peppers, yellow zucchini.

C Vegetable Combo

This recipe makes a very pretty vegetable mixture. It isn't a stir-fried mixture, nor a long and slowly simmered one, nor is it a sauce — but it is somewhere between the three!

It is liquid enough to serve alongside any other food which needs a sauce, and it may be served on rice or on flat egg noodles, topped with grated cheese, as a complete meal.

You need a large frypan and a high heat to make this successful. If you have a non-stick pan, use it! You can alter proportions and seasonings to suit yourself. Keep tasting, adjusting the salt and sugar to get an interesting flavour.

For 4 servings:
1 small-to-medium-sized (about 200 g) eggplant
¼ cup oil
1 medium-sized onion
2 cloves garlic
1 green pepper
1 red pepper
1 cup chopped marrow, zucchini or butternut
1 cup cauliflower pieces or 1 cup green beans
1 cup water
freshly ground pepper
1–2 tsp sugar
salt to taste
fresh herbs, chopped (optional)
2 tsp cornflour
¼–½ cup chopped parsley

For this recipe all the vegetables should be cut into 1 cm cubes.

Cut up the eggplant first, without peeling or salting it. Heat the pan, add the oil, and when hot, drop in the eggplant. Cook it on high heat, turning frequently, until it is golden brown on some surfaces. While it cooks add the chopped onion and garlic.

Chop the remaining vegetables while the first three cook. When the eggplant is evenly coloured, add the remaining vegetables, and stir to coat with oil. Keep the heat high, and put the lid on the pan. Cook for 3–4 minutes until all vegetables are wilted and brightly coloured, then add the water, cover, and cook on high heat for 3–4 minutes longer. By this stage the vegetables should be tender-crisp, and quite a lot of the added water should have evaporated.

Remove the lid and add the seasonings in the order given. Keep tasting. After adding the sugar, add enough salt to bring out all the other flavours. Add fresh herbs at this stage, too. Mix the cornflour to a paste with cold water. Add enough of this to thicken the mixture. Sprinkle generously with parsley, stir it through briefly, then serve immediately.

C Pakora Vegetables

These are best eaten very soon after they are cooked. If you have an electric wok or deep frier, try cooking them at the table.

For 4–6 servings:
500 g assorted vegetable pieces, such as cauliflower florets, thinly sliced potato, kumara and/or pumpkin, broccoli, small whole mushrooms, strips of peppers, etc.
1¹/₂ cups pea flour
1 tsp salt
¹/₂ tsp chilli powder
1 tsp turmeric
1 tsp ground cumin
1 tsp ground coriander
1 tsp garam masala
1 cup water
1–1¹/₂ cups water
oil to deep fry

Cut the vegetables into thin slices.

In a bowl, mix together the dry ingredients. Add half the water, and whisk, getting rid of as many lumps as you can. Add the remaining water, plus a little more if necessary, to form a thin coating batter.

Heat oil about 2 cm deep in a suitable container to about 200°C. Dip the vegetable pieces one at a time into the batter to coat them completely, then drop gently into the oil. At first they will sink, but they will rise to the surface again as they cook. Fry for about 5 minutes or until brown.

These coated vegetables are delicious served with Chilli Mayonnaise (see page 200) or minted yoghurt for dipping. Serve with an interesting rice mixture, a tomato salad, and other curry-style side dishes.

C M Stir-Fried Vegetables

(See photograph on page 162.)

Slice a selection of quick-cooking vegetables such as cabbage, celery, cauliflower, broccoli, green beans, bean sprouts, mushrooms, pea pods, peppers, and zucchini, allowing about 200 g per serving.

For two servings heat 1 tablespoon oil in a large pan or wok. Add a finely chopped garlic clove, then the prepared vegetables. Toss over high heat, then add 2 tablespoons water, cover, and leave to steam for 1–2 minutes, or until tender-crisp.

Stir together in a small container:

1 tsp cornflour
1 tsp brown sugar
1 tsp light soya sauce
¹/₄ tsp salt
1 Tbsp sherry
¹/₂ tsp sesame oil (optional)

Zucchini Pancakes

Stir liquid into vegetable mixture to coat vegetables, and serve immediately over rice or noodles.

To microwave, toss prepared vegetables in the preheated garlic and oil in a microwave dish, then cover and microwave at Full power for about 3 minutes, or until tender-crisp. Stir in mixed liquid, then cook for about 30 seconds longer, or until glaze thickens.
Note:
Alter proportions to taste.

B C Vegetable Kebabs

(See photo on page 137.)

Thread 2 cm cubes of eggplant, red and green peppers and zucchini with squares of onion, blanched button mushrooms and quartered or whole small tomatoes. Brush liberally with Tomato or Cumin Dressing (see page 201), or Chilli Mayonnaise (see page 200) before and during cooking, and cook on a barbecue or under a grill, about 12 cm from the heat, turning frequently until tender.

Thread only one type of vegetable on each skewer for more even cooking, if desired.
Variations:
Thread Marinated Tofu (see page 136) or pan-browned cubes of Polenta (see page 141) between the vegetables, if desired.

C Glazed Root Vegetables

Coat cooked kumara, parsnips, carrots or yams with this glaze.

For 4 servings:
cooked root vegetables for 4 servings
¹/₄ cup brown sugar
25 g butter
¹/₄ cup orange juice

Drain the cooked vegetables. Heat the sugar, butter and orange juice until blended and bubbling. Add vegetables, turn to coat, and heat uncovered, stirring frequently, until glaze darkens slightly. Serve immediately.

C Peanut-Sauced Vegetable Plate

A plate of vegetables can be turned into an interesting, filling and delicious main course when you serve peanut sauce to pour over all or some of the vegetables.

This platter is a modification of Gado-Gado Salad, where the vegetables are served at room temperature. Decide for yourself whether you want your vegetables hot, warm, or somewhere in between.

Choose from this vegetable selection:

• Boiled or microwaved potatoes
• Green beans, whole or halved, lightly cooked
• Carrots, halved or quartered lengthwise, cooked until tender-crisp
• Cauliflower florets, cooked
• Cabbage, thickly sliced, lightly cooked
• Red and green peppers, raw or blanched
• Bean sprouts, raw or blanched
• Jerusalem artichokes, lightly cooked in thick slices
• Celery, raw or blanched
• Zucchini sticks, raw or lightly cooked
• Brussels sprouts, halved and lightly cooked
• Cucumber strips
• Radishes
• Kumara, cooked and sliced
• Mushrooms, raw or lightly sautéed
• Spring onions, in 4 cm lengths
• Red onion rings
• Witloof leaves
• Yams, boiled and halved
• Shredded lettuce

Arrange the vegetables you have chosen, prepared and cooked, on individual plates, on shredded lettuce or lettuce leaves if you like, in a sunburst pattern, or serve a large central platter and let everybody help themselves.

Serve jugs of thinned, or bowls of thicker peanut sauce, and let your friends pour it over their vegetables.

Make sure that you have extra seasonings such as:

• lemon wedges
• black pepper (in grinder)
• salt (in grinder)
• hot pepper sauce
• Kikkoman soya sauce

Peanut Sauce
2 Tbsp oil
1 large onion, chopped
2 tsp chopped garlic
¼ tsp chilli powder
1 Tbsp dark soya sauce
1 Tbsp lemon juice
½ cup peanut butter
1–2 Tbsp soft brown sugar
¼ tsp salt

about 1 cup (or ½ can) coconut cream water

Heat the oil in a small pan, add the finely chopped onion, garlic and chilli powder, cover and cook gently without browning, until the onion is tender.

Add the soya sauce, lemon juice and smooth or chunky peanut butter, then 1 tablespoon of brown sugar. Add the salt and coconut cream, and bring to the boil, stirring constantly.

Taste, and add the extra sugar if required, (most people like it sweeter) more coconut cream if you like it bland, or water if you want it thinner. Add other seasonings as desired.

Bring to the boil again, purée in a food processor if you want it smooth, and serve immediately, or reheat when needed.

Note:
Don't worry about leftover sauce. You can refrigerate it, freeze it, spread it on crackers or serve it on spaghetti or rice.

Variation:
Add quartered hard-boiled eggs to your vegetable platter, if you like.

C Confetti Salad

This is a very pretty salad! I make it to serve as part of a buffet meal, or when I want an interesting filling for pita bread.

For 4 servings:
½ cup uncooked red or brown lentils
1½ cups hot water
about 1 cup cooked rice
1 cup chopped celery
about ½ cup chopped red pepper
¼–½ cup chopped spring onions
2 Tbsp wine vinegar
¼ cup oil
½ tsp salt
½ tsp sugar
¼ cup chopped parsley
black pepper

Cook the lentils in the water until very tender (see page 129), then drain.

Add to the hot lentils the rice, celery, chopped pepper and onions. Mix the dressing ingredients (vinegar, oil, salt and sugar), sprinkle over the mixed salad, and mix again.

Stir in the parsley and as much black pepper as you like.

Cover the salad and leave it to stand from 30–60 minutes before tasting it again, adjusting seasonings if necessary, and serving.

Note:
Vary the proportions of ingredients, or make additions or replacements. Suitable extras include cooked corn, barely cooked carrots or peas, firm cubed tomatoes, sunflower seeds or

pine nuts, currants, chopped mint or other herbs, cubed cucumber, bean sprouts, Do not include too great a mixture, since this can spoil the flavour.

C Tabbouleh

Make this salad when fresh, ripe tomatoes and fresh mint and parsley are plentiful.

For about 4 servings:
1 cup bulgar or kibbled wheat
2–3 cups water
¼ cup chopped spring onions
or ¼ cup chopped onion
¼ cup lemon juice
¼ cup olive or salad oil
½–1 cup chopped parsley
½ cup chopped mint
1–2 cups finely cubed tomato
salt and pepper to taste

Bring bulgar or kibbled wheat to the boil with the water. Simmer for 2–3 minutes then remove from heat and leave to stand for about an hour.

Line a sieve with a clean tea towel, add bulgar and squeeze the water out. Put the drained wheat mixture in a bowl with the remaining ingredients, toss to mix, and season carefully using enough salt to bring out the flavours. Serve in a bowl lined with lettuce leaves.

Note:
If you are making this salad several hours before it is to be eaten, stir the tomato into it in the last half hour so the tomato does not make the wheat soggy. You can also make the salad with precooked brown rice.

C Tempura Vegetables

It is always interesting to sit around a communal cooking container, and to let your friends prepare and cook their own food.

Try this using an electric wok or deep frier. If you do not have a suitably presentable cooking container, someone should resign him or herself to cooking in the kitchen while the rest of the party eats, as these vegetables are best eaten as soon as they are cooked!

For 4–6 servings:
500g assorted vegetables pieces such as cauliflower florets, thinly sliced potato, kumara and/or pumpkin, broccoli, small whole mushrooms, strips of peppers, zucchini, etc.
1 egg
1 cup cold water
1 cup plain white flour
¼ tsp baking soda
¼ tsp salt
oil for deep frying

Tempura Vegetables

Prepare the vegetables cutting them into pieces about 5 mm thick, and arrange attractively on plates. Using a fork, lightly beat the egg and the cold water. Sift the dry ingredients into this mixture while you stir. Mix enough to combine everything. Thin batter with extra water so that it lightly coats a piece of prepared vegetable.

Heat the oil to about 200°C. Dip the vegetables in the batter, and fry, a few pieces at a time, until golden brown and puffed up. Raise heat if necessary.

Serve with commercially made tempura sauce or make the following dipping sauce:

¹/₄ cup water
¹/₄ cup Kikkoman soya sauce
1 Tbsp dry sherry
2 tsp brown sugar
2 tsp grated fresh ginger
juice of ¹/₂ lemon
1 clove garlic, crushed and chopped
1 tsp dark sesame oil

Mix together all the ingredients and allow to stand for about 10 minutes.

Serve with brown or white rice.
Note:
Use leftover sauce as a marinade for tofu or other vegetables, at a later time.

Savoury Pies

Pies always seem to be popular!

From the cook's point of view, pies are very useful. A completed pie always looks so much more impressive than its components!

The crust of a pie is very important. You have a good choice, here. You can make a basic short pastry from plain or wholemeal flour, or you can make a richer flakier pastry if you like. You may choose a light filo pastry crust if you do not want to make your own pastry, or you may decide to make a scone-dough crust for a low-fat, substantial family pie.

I find that ready-made pastry is often too fatty for my liking, and makes a crust that does not brown easily on the bottom, but you may feel that it is worth trying, if you are short of time or energy.

A food processor makes pastry-making very easy, quick, and inexpensive. It doesn't take too long to pay for itself in pastry savings, if you make pies often!

Mix and match the pastry and filling recipes here, to make a wide variety of popular pies.

Mushroom Strudel

Short Pastry

Home-made short pastry contains less fat than bought flaky pastry. It is particularly good for flans and quiches (single-crust pies) and it is less likely to become soggy, and shrinks less during cooking.

One cup of flour makes enough pastry for a large single-crust pie. Double these amounts for a pie with filling enclosed in pastry (a double-crust pie).

Traditional Method

Measure 1 cup plain or wholemeal flour into a mixing bowl. Cut or rub in 60–75 g cold butter using a pastry blender, fingertips or two knives, until the butter is cut in small pieces and the mixture resembles rolled oats.

Add about ¼ cup cold water, a few drops at a time, tossing the mixture with a fork until it will form a ball when pressed with fingers. Chill for 5–10 minutes before rolling out.

Food Processor Method

Fit the food processor with its metal cutting blade. Add 1 cup plain or wholemeal flour and add 60–70 g cold butter, cut into about nine cubes. Do not process.

Acidify ¼ cup cold water with 1–2 teaspoons lemon juice for extra tenderness if desired. Using the pulse button, add water in a thin stream while chopping butter through flour.

Test at intervals to see if the particles are moist enough to press together to form a ball. The mixture will still look crumbly at this stage. (If a ball of dough forms in the processor, the mixture is too wet.)
Note:
Overmixing or too much water makes tough pastry.

Quick Flaky Pastry

This is an easy recipe for a pastry which is flakier and richer than the Short Pastry above.

For 1 thinly rolled double-crust 20 cm pie:
1¼ cups flour
1 tsp baking powder
125 g cold butter
about ½ cup milk
1 tsp wine vinegar

Mix the flour and baking powder. Grate butter or cut it into about 25 small cubes, and rub or cut into the flour, by hand or with a food processor. (Pieces of butter should be visible when pastry is rolled out.) Mix liquids, and add slowly to flour mixture until it forms a fairly stiff dough. Roll out thinly, and use as required.

Filo Pastry

Filo is fun! Although it costs more than regular bought pastry, it may be used for several different filo-wrapped foods which will disintegrate in your mouth in a very satisfying way.

When you buy them, the sheets of filo should be quite soft and flexible, and you should be able to roll and fold them without any cracking and breaking.

Always rewrap, seal, and refrigerate unused filo promptly, to stop it drying out.

Use filo pastry to replace bought pastry or home-made short pastry in other recipes in this or other books, if you like, following the cooking instructions for filo pies given here.

Don't be heavy-handed with butter when brushing melted butter between layers of filo. A few dabs over a sheet will do. You can try

layering filo without any butter between the sheets, if you like. The sheets will brown more quickly and be very crisp and light-textured.

Scone Dough

Scone dough makes a low-fat, substantial pie crust.

2 cups self-raising plain or wholemeal flour
25 g butter
about ¾ cup milk

Measure the flour into the bowl of a food processor. Add the butter, cut into cubes, and process until chopped into small pieces.

Tip into a bowl, and add the measured milk, all at once. Cut and stir the liquid into the dry ingredients. Add a little more milk or flour if the mixture seems too dry or too wet. The dough should be as soft as you can handle, to roll out on a floured bench. The dough will rise better if the mixture has been lightly kneaded with your fingertips before it is rolled out into two rounds.

Scone dough which is used for a pie crust should be a little firmer than dough which is used to shape individual scones.

Brush top of scone dough crust with beaten egg before baking, for best appearance.

Mushroom Strudel

This recipe makes two long rolls of strudel. The completed rolls are not only delicious, but very attractive.

For 4–8 servings:
2 medium-sized onions
250 g mushrooms
2 Tbsp butter or oil
250–500 g cottage cheese
2 Tbsp fresh (or 1 Tbsp dried) parsley
½ tsp dried tarragon
½ tsp thyme
½ tsp salt
black pepper to taste
juice of 1 lemon
10 sheets filo pastry
25 g melted butter

Chop the onions and slice mushrooms 5 mm thick. Sauté the onion in the oil or butter over medium heat until tender then add the sliced mushrooms. Continue to cook until the mushrooms have heated through.

In a large bowl mix together the cottage cheese, seasonings and lemon juice. Add the mushroom-and-onion mixture and stir to combine.

Lay the first sheet of filo on a dry surface and dot or brush very lightly with melted butter. Lay the next sheet directly on top. Repeat this process until you have a stack five

sheets thick.

Spoon half the filling in a band across the pastry, about 5 cm from one of the short edges, then roll up loosely. Using a sharp (serrated) knife make diagonal slashes through several layers, 3 cm apart, across the top of the roll (to prevent the roll bursting during cooking).

Repeat this process with the remaining filo and the rest of the filling. Stand the rolls on a buttered sponge roll tin. Bake at 225°C for 20–25 minutes or until the pastry is golden brown and crisp. Leave to stand for 5–10 minutes before serving.

Slice diagonally and serve with colourful vegetables and/or a mixed green salad.
Note:
Smaller amounts of cheese will make fewer servings.

If rolls split during cooking, slice them in the kitchen and serve, after reshaping them.

Vegetable Flan

You can use this recipe to make a flan from any cooked vegetable that you have on hand. It will make a deep 17 cm flan or a thin 23 cm flan with a shorter cooking time. Make it in a pie plate if you do not have a flan tin.

For a 17 or 23 cm flan:
1 uncooked pastry pie crust
3 eggs
½ cup cream, sour cream or cream cheese
¼ cup milk
1½ cups grated cheese
1–1½ cups well-drained, cooked vegetables

Roll out home-made or bought pastry thinly, to line a pie plate or flan tin.

Combine the eggs, cream or cream cheese, milk and a cup of the grated cheese, using a fork, beater, or food processor.

Put the well-drained, chopped cooked vegetable (or vegetable mixture) into the prepared, unbaked pastry shell, pour over the egg mixture, then top with the remaining grated cheese.

Bake at 200°C for 20 minutes, then at 180°C until the filling sets in the middle, about 10 minutes.
Note:
Suitable vegetables include asparagus, broccoli, corn, mushrooms, spinach, zucchini, etc.

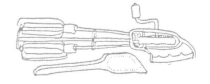

C Mushroom-Topped Spinach Flan

For a 20 cm flan:
1 uncooked 20 cm pie crust
½ cup cream cheese
2 eggs
½ tsp salt
½ tsp grated nutmeg
black pepper
2 cups cooked spinach

Roll bought or home-made pastry (see page 185) thinly to line a 20 cm flan or pie dish.

In a large bowl mix together the cream cheese, eggs and seasonings. Fold in the chopped, drained spinach, then gently pour the filling mixture into the uncooked pie crust.

Bake at 220°C for 20 minutes or until the centre is firm. While the flan cooks, prepare the mushroom toppping below.

200–300 g button mushrooms
2 Tbsp oil
1–2 cloves garlic, chopped
½ tsp cornflour
2 tsp light soya sauce
1 Tbsp water
2 Tbsp chopped parsley

Slice the mushrooms and sauté in the oil with the crushed garlic. As soon as the mushrooms soften, stir in the cornflour dissolved in the soya sauce and water, then the chopped parsley.

Pile the mushroom mixture on top of the cooked flan. Leave to stand for about 5 minutes before serving.

C Cheese and Mushroom Quiche

This makes good lunch or dinner fare. Because it tastes almost as good cold as it does warm, a quiche like this is ideal if you want to turn a picnic into something really special.

For a 20–25 cm quiche:
1 uncooked 20–25 cm pastry pie crust
1 medium-sized onion
125 g mushrooms, sliced
pinch of thyme
2 Tbsp butter
1½ cups grated Cheddar or Gruyère cheese
2 large eggs
½ cup sour cream
¼ cup milk
1 Tbsp flour
¼ tsp salt
½ tsp mustard powder
black pepper
paprika

Make pastry (see page 185), and roll out to line a 20–25 cm flan tin or pie plate.

Sauté the onions, mushrooms and thyme in the butter until soft.

Cover the bottom of the uncooked crust with the grated cheese, then cover this layer with the onion-and-mushroom mixture.

Beat the remaining ingredients except paprika together, and pour into the crust.

Sprinkle with paprika, and bake at 200°C for about 30 minutes, or until the filling is set in the centre.

Serve with your favourite green vegetables and a potato salad.

C Tuna Luncheon Pie

A pie with only a bottom crust may be called an open-face pie, a quiche, a flan or a tart. Often these 'open' pies contain fillings which are liquid when poured in and which set during cooking. Because the side of the dish slopes out, the pastry is supported as it cooks. The folded pastry edge may be decorated as desired.

For a 23 cm pie:
1 uncooked short pastry crust
4 eggs, beaten
4 spring onions, chopped
½ tsp salt
1 cup grated tasty cheese
1½ cups cream or unsweetened condensed milk
175–200 g can tuna, drained

Make short pastry following instructions on page 185. Roll thinly, about 25 cm round. Use to line a 23 cm pie plate previously sprayed with non-stick spray.

Trim edge 15 mm beyond edge of pie plate and brush with water. Fold edge of pastry inwards, a little more than 1 cm. Press evenly and firmly. Combine all filling ingredients using food processor if available.

Decorate edge of pie. For scalloped edge pinch firmly at intervals, push pinched section down against pastry sides. Pour in mixed filling. Sprinkle with paprika if desired.

Bake at 220°C for 15 minutes then at 180°C until centre is set. Serve warm, reheated if necessary.

C Salmon Flan

A flan like this makes a good main course for lunch or a starter for a dinner party, whether it is cut into little pieces to be eaten as finger food or served at the table.

For a 23 cm flan:
1 uncooked short pastry crust
3 eggs
50 g tasty cheese
3–4 spring onions
1 cup cream
¼ tsp salt
1 can (approx 120 g) salmon
paprika

Make the short pastry according to instructions on page 185, using 1 cup flour, and roll it out thinly to fit a 23 cm flan tin or pie plate. Break eggs into food processor bowl.

Add the cheese, cut into eight smaller cubes. (50 g is equivalent to a 4 cm or 1½ inch cube.) Add the spring onions, chopped into 2 cm lengths, Process to chop cheese and spring onions, then add the cream, salt and the fish and liquid from the can of salmon. Process briefly to break up fish but not to purée it.

Pour this mixture into the uncooked crust, sprinkle with paprika, and bake at 220°C for 15–20 minutes, then at 180°C for 15 minutes or until the flan has set in the centre. Serve hot, warm or reheated.

C Spinach Quiche

For a 20–23 cm quiche:
1 uncooked short pastry crust
500 g spinach
2 large eggs
½ cup sour cream
½ tsp salt
1 cup grated cheese
1 tsp grated nutmeg

To make short pastry, follow instructions on page 185, using 1 cup flour and adding ½ teaspoon salt. Roll out and use to line a loose-bottomed 20 or 23 cm flat tin.

Cook spinach in a little or no added liquid until barely tender, then squeeze away all liquid. Chop block of squeezed spinach into 5 mm slices.

Beat eggs, sour cream and salt to combine.

Add chopped spinach, grated cheese and grated nutmeg. Turn into uncooked flan case. Sprinkle with a little extra cheese if desired.

Bake at 200°C for 20 minutes, or until filling is set. Remove sides of flan tin so pastry cools crisp. Serve warm.

M Salmon Flan

For 4–6 servings:
60–70 g cold butter
1 cup flour
¼ tsp microwave browning liquid
4 Tbsp milk

Filling
1 cup cream
1 can (220 g) salmon
paprika
¼ tsp salt
4 spring onions
4 eggs
1 cup grated cheese

Cut the cold butter into the flour until it resembles rolled oats. Add

Cheese and Onion Flan

browning liquid to milk until medium-brown. Add this, a few drops at a time, to flour to form a stiff dough. Roll out very thinly. Drape over a 20–23 cm inverted glass pie plate or casserole. Trim edges, moistening edge and folding it back if desired. Prick thoroughly.

Microwave at Full power for 5 minutes. If case tilts during cooking, reposition it. Cook until dry in centre. Turn right side up on serving plate.

Pour prepared filling into cooked flan case. Cook at Medium (50% power) until just firm in centre, about 25 minutes. Remove from oven.

In a medium-sized bowl, combine cream, undrained salmon, paprika, salt and spring onions. Heat until mixture bubbles around edge. Add eggs and grated cheese and beat with a fork until mixed. Spoon into cooked shell.

C Cheese and Onion Flan

For a 20 cm flan:
2 onions, sliced
25 g butter
2 cups grated cheese
2 eggs
³/₄ cup milk
¹/₂ tsp salt

Make short pastry with 1¹/₂ cups flour, using recipe and method on page 185. Roll out and use to line a 20 cm flan tin or pie plate. Slice the onions and cook for 5 minutes in the butter in a covered pan over low heat. Leave to cool.

Put half the grated cheese in the uncooked shell, then half the onions, then repeat layers. Beat eggs with the milk, add the salt, and pour over the cheese and onion. Arrange slices of tomato around the edge of the pie if desired.

Bake at 220°C for 15 minutes or until pastry browns, then at 180°C for 15 minutes longer, or until filling is set in centre.

Mushroom Mounds

🄲 Mushroom Mounds

For 9 individual pies:
Pastry
2 cups flour
125 g cold butter
1 cup grated cheese
about ½ cup cold water
milk
toasted sesame seeds (optional)

Filling
400 g minced beef
100 g finely chopped mushrooms
1 Tbsp butter
1 Tbsp lemon juice
1 pkt mushroom soup mix
1 Tbsp flour
1 Tbsp dark soya sauce
1 egg, beaten

Make short pastry following directions on page 185. Roll thinly into two 30 cm squares.

Sauté mushrooms in butter with lemon juice, then combine with other filling ingredients, reserving half the egg. Form into nine balls.

Arrange balls on pastry in rows of three. Brush between balls with milk. Cover with other square of pastry. Press between mounds with a rolling pin and cut air vents in top of each mound. Press pastry around outer edges of mounds. Cut with a knife or serrated cutting wheel. Reroll and cut pastry scraps in long strips. Arrange strips on mounds.

Brush with remaining egg. Sprinkle with toasted sesame seeds if desired. Bake at 200°C for 30 minutes or until golden brown.

🄲 Double-Crust Sausage Pie

(See photograph on page 182.)

Double-crust pies are especially good when baked in deep cake tins instead of pie plates. If it suits you better, however, use a 23 cm pie plate instead of a 20 cm round cake tin. Serve warm or at room temperature.

For a 20–23 cm pie:
1½ cups flour
75 g cold butter
5–6 Tbsp water
2 onions, chopped
1 apple, chopped
2 tsp curry powder
1 tsp garlic salt
about 800 g sausage meat
4 firm tomatoes, sliced
2 Tbsp chopped parsley
1 tsp fresh thyme or sage
3 eggs, lightly beaten

Make short pastry from flour, butter and water (see page 185). Roll two-thirds to form a 30 cm circle. Ease into 20 cm cake tin with bottom lined with paper.

Chop onions and apple finely in food processor. Add curry, seasoned salt and sausage meat and mix well.

Put half tomatoes, herbs and egg in the uncooked crust. Cover with half the sausage mixture. Repeat these layers, reserving a little egg. Trim crust 1 cm beyond filling. Brush with water.

Roll out remaining pastry. Lift pastry over rolling pin to avoid stretching it, and lay on pie. Press it against the dampened bottom crust.

Trim upper crust 2 cm beyond edge of filling. Fold outer centimetre of top crust around rim of bottom crust, pressing evenly and firmly. Cut one or two holes in centre of crust. Flute edge.

Brush with reserved egg. Bake at 220°C for 20 minutes or until brown, then at 180°C for 30 minutes. Cool for at least 30 minutes before serving.

Picnic Pie

For a 20 cm pie:
short pastry using 1½ cups flour
4 medium-sized potatoes
25 g butter
1 large onion, sliced
1 (450 g) can cream-style corn
4 eggs
2 tsp instant green herb stock
¼ cup chopped parsley

Make short pastry following instructions on page 185. Roll two-thirds pastry in a 30 cm circle, and use it to line a buttered 20 cm round cake tin with sides about 4 cm high. Roll remaining pastry to a 22 cm circle.

Scrub potatoes and boil until tender. Cool and slice or cube. Melt butter in a medium-sized saucepan. Add onion and cook gently until transparent and barely tender. Remove from heat. Add corn, eggs, instant stock and chopped parsley, and stir with a fork until combined. Add cold cooked potato and stir again.

Spoon filling into uncooked crust. Dampen edges. Top with smaller circle of pastry. Seal edges, fold excess down sides of cake tin. Glaze with a little reserved egg or milk, cut a steam vent.

Bake at 220°C for 30 minutes or until brown, then at 180°C for 30 minutes more. Cool for 5 minutes before removing from tin.

Blue Cheese and Mushroom Packages

These little packages make very elegant dinner party food.

Shape them into small triangular, or more conventional rectangular packages.

For 6–8 packages:
1 medium-sized onion
2 cloves garlic
2 Tbsp butter
200 g mushrooms, chopped
250 g cream cheese
50 g blue cheese
½ tsp sugar
¼ tsp thyme
1 spring onion, chopped
1 Tbsp sherry (optional)

6–8 sheets filo pastry
100 g butter, melted

Sauté the finely chopped onion and crushed garlic in the butter. When soft add the mushrooms, and cook until they begin to soften.

Reduce the heat to very low, and then stir in the cream cheese. (If the cream cheese is cold or very firm, it may pay to soften it by stirring or mashing first.) Crumble in the blue cheese while stirring, and add the remaining seasonings.

Remove the filo sheets from the package. Lay one sheet on a dry surface, lightly brush with melted butter and then fold in half, lengthwise for triangles or crosswise for packages.

Place about ¼ cup of filling on the pastry and roll or fold it into the shape desired, completely enclosing the filling. Do not roll too tightly or packages may burst during cooking. Cut a slash on top as a further precaution against splitting. Repeat until you have used all the filling.

Place on a buttered oven tray, and bake for 15–20 minutes at 200°C or until golden brown.

One package per person is usually enough because of the rich filling.

Leek in Filo Quiche

If you can't buy fresh, easily-worked-with filo, use home-made short pastry or flaky pastry to make the crust instead.

For a 20 cm quiche:
4 sheets filo pastry
50 g butter
3 small leeks (approx 450 g)
½ cup water
1 clove garlic, chopped
3 eggs
1 cup grated tasty cheese
1 (150 g) tub reduced cream
¼ cup milk
¼ tsp salt

Take 4 sheets of filo pastry out of the packet, then return the rest and seal it so that it is airtight, straight away.

Melt the butter, and brush a little of it over half of each sheet. Then fold the unbuttered half over the buttered part, so each piece is almost square.

Arrange the sheets on top of each other so that the corners are not overlapping, in a 20 cm pie plate. The edges of the pastry should form a frilly edging.

Slice and wash the leeks carefully. Use only the inner parts of the upper leaves. Cup the slices about 5 mm thick. Put the leeks, and the finely chopped garlic to cook in the remaining butter for 2–3 minutes,

without letting them brown, then add the water, cover, and cook for about 5 minutes, until the leek is tender. At the end of this time, raise the heat and evaporate the rest of the liquid.

Remove from the heat then stir in the eggs, cheese, reduced cream, milk and salt. Stir with a fork until mixed. Add a little fresh dill, chervil, or tarragon if you have and like these herbs, then pour the mixture carefully into the prepared crust.

Bake at 180°C for about 30 minutes or until the filling is set in the centre, and the pastry edging is light brown. If the centre has not browned much, sprinkle with chopped herbs and/or paprika before serving, if desired.

Serve warm, from the pie plate.

Silver Beet and Cheese Pie

This is a delicious way to serve silver beet from your garden.

For 6–8 servings:
about 20 large silver beet leaves
500 g cottage cheese
1 cup grated tasty cheese
1 onion
3 eggs
1 tsp salt
½ tsp freshly grated nutmeg
freshly ground black pepper
10 sheets filo pastry
2 Tbsp melted butter

Discard the silver beet stalks, Wash the leaves carefully, then chop finely and cook until tender but still bright green (about 5 minutes) in a large pan with little or no added water. Press in a sieve to remove any surplus liquid. Mix the cottage cheese, grated cheese, diced onion, eggs and seasonings together in a large bowl. Add the silver beet and stir until well combined.

Remove 10 sheets of filo from the package then return the rest and seal it. Lightly brush half of each sheet with melted butter then fold in half. Arrange five folded sheets in the bottom of a 23 × 30 cm (or 25-cm-square) roasting pan. The sheets should cover the bottom completely, although they need not cover each other exactly.

Spread the filling over the base, then top with the remaining folded filo sheets. Brush the top with any remaining butter and bake at 180°C for 35–40 minutes, until the top is lightly browned and the filling set.

Cut in squares and serve hot or warm with cooked vegetables or a tomato salad.

C Self-Crusting Quiches

Self-crusting quiches are made without pastry crusts but form their own fairly firm outer layers as they cook.

For best results you should remember these points:
• Use a metal pie plate or flan tin with a solid (not push-out) base.
• Use a non-stick finish if possible.
• Lightly oil or butter the dish before use, regardless of the finish.
• Take care not to overmix the egg mixture when you add the flour, or it may not form two layers as it cooks.
• Bake at a high temperature so the crust browns well.
• Leave to stand for 5 minutes after removing from oven, before turning out.

C Self-Crusting Herbed Mushroom Quiche

For 4–6 servings:
2 medium-sized onions
2 Tbsp oil or butter
200 g mushrooms
½ tsp dried basil
¼ tsp dried thyme
black pepper to taste
2 eggs
½ cup sour cream
¾ cup milk
½ tsp salt
½ cup self-raising flour
½ cup grated tasty cheese

Slice onions finely. Sauté in the oil or butter, and when soft add the mushrooms and cook until these soften too. Add the basil, thyme and black pepper, then remove from the heat and leave to stand while preparing the egg mixture.

In a medium-sized bowl lightly beat together the eggs, sour cream, milk and salt. Sprinkle the flour over this mixture and stir just enough to combine, then add the grated cheese, again stirring just enough to mix.

Butter a 25–30 cm flan or pie dish (see above). Tip in the onion-and-mushroom mixture, and spread it evenly over the bottom, then pour the batter evenly over this.

Bake at 220°C for 20–30 minutes, until light brown and firm in the centre. Cool for 10–15 minutes before turning out.

Serve with baked potatoes or pasta, fresh tomatoes and a mixed green salad.

Two different versions of Self-Crusting Potato and Vegetable Quiche

C Self-Crusting Lentil and Tomato Quiche

This is a good way to introduce brown lentils to those who may have doubts about their virtues! The lentils give the quiche an interesting texture and make it quite substantial.

For 4–6 servings:
½ cup dry brown lentils
1 bay leaf
2 medium-sized onions
2 cloves garlic
1 Tbsp oil or butter
1 Tbsp lemon juice
black pepper
3 eggs
1 cup milk
½ tsp salt
½ tsp basil
½ tsp oreganum
½ cup self-raising flour
½ cup grated tasty cheese
3 tomatoes, thinly sliced
2 Tbsp grated Parmesan

Cook the lentils with the bay leaf until they are tender (see page 129).

Sauté sliced onions in the oil with the chopped garlic. When soft and clear, remove from the heat and add lemon juice and black pepper to taste.

In a large bowl, beat together the eggs, milk, salt and herbs. Stir in the flour and grated cheese, but do not overmix.

Combine drained lentils with the cooked onions, Stir into the batter. Pour into a prepared 23–30 cm flan tin or pie plate. Top with tomato slices, then sprinkle with the grated Parmesan.

Bake for 25–30 minutes at 220°C, or until the centre is firm when pressed. Serve with salad or cooked vegetables.

C Self-Crusting Potato and Vegetable Quiche

This quiche contains cooked potato for bulk and another vegetable for flavour.

For 4–6 servings;
1 large onion, chopped
2 garlic cloves
1 Tbsp butter
3 eggs
¾ tsp salt
1 cup milk
½ cup self-raising flour
2 cooked potatoes
1 cup drained cooked asparagus or spinach or mushrooms or broccoli
1 cup grated tasty cheese

Cook the chopped onion and garlic in butter until tender. Cool. Stir in

the eggs, salt and milk, and beat with fork until mixed. Pour this into a large bowl containing the flour, and stir with the fork until just combined. Add the potatoes cut in 1 cm cubes, the chopped, well-drained vegetables and cheese.

Pour into a prepared 20–23 cm pan. Garnish with sliced tomato, or thinly sliced red and green peppers if desired. Bake at 220°C for 20–30 minutes, until lightly browned and set in the centre.

C Low-Cal Self-Crusting Quiche

This is lower in fat and calories than most other quiches, but it still tastes good!

For 4 servings:
1 (450 g) can whole-kernel corn, drained
2–4 spring onions, chopped
½ cup self-raising flour
¾ cup non-fat milk
2 eggs
2 Tbsp grated Parmesan cheese
black pepper to taste
3 firm tomatoes, sliced
paprika

Lightly oil or butter a 20–23 cm pie plate or flan tin. Arrange the drained corn and chopped spring onions in it.

In another bowl, mixing with a fork, combine the self-raising flour, milk, eggs, half of the cheese and black pepper.

Pour the egg mixture over the corn and spring onions, then slice the tomatoes, and arrange these over the surface of the quiche.

Sprinkle the remaining grated Parmesan and a little paprika over the surface. Bake at 220°C for 20–30 minutes or until the centre is set and the top is golden brown.
Variations:
Replace the corn with 1 cup well-drained cooked spinach, 1½ cups cooked zucchini, 2 cups sliced mushrooms, or 2 cups chopped cooked broccoli.

• Pastry browns best in a dark coloured metal pie plate or flan tin.
• Pastry made in glass or ceramic dishes does not brown well, and tends to stick badly.
• Using a high temperature, like 220°C, for the start of the cooking, means that the crust will brown better.
• Short pastry (made with less fat) bases brown better than richer pastry bases.
• Pastry made in cast-iron fry pans (not those with wooden handles) browns very well.

ᴄ Onion-Cream Pie

This pie can be made with a scone dough crust or a short pastry crust, depending on appetites. The scone dough crust is good for a family meal when you are not planning to serve bread as well.

The pastry pie is suitable for a dinner party starter course, or a main lunch course for friends. Use 1 cup of flour for a scone dough crust (see page 185) and make the pie in a 23 cm pie plate, or use 1 cup of flour for a short pastry crust (see page 185) and make it in a flan tin or pie plate of the same diameter.

For a 23 cm pie:
Filling
2–3 large onions, sliced
25 g butter
2 eggs
1 carton (250 g) sour cream
1 tsp salt
caraway seeds or paprika

Prepare the crust and line the pie plate or flan tin with it.

Cook the sliced onions in the melted butter in a large frying pan, until transparent and golden, but not brown. This should take about 10 minutes.

While they cook, mix the eggs, sour cream and salt until smooth.

Cool the pan containing the partly cooked onions, then pour in the egg-cream mixture and mix gently. Pour filling into the uncooked pie crust and sprinkle with caraway seeds or paprika.

Bake at 220°C until crust starts to brown, then lower the heat and cook at 180°C for 20 minutes, or until the filling has set.

Some pies call for a cooked pie crust. Save yourself the trouble of 'baking blind'.

Turn a pie plate upside down. Lay the rolled-out pastry over the top of the inverted pie plate, taking care not to stretch it.

Cut off excess pastry about 2 cm beyond the rim.

Dampen the outer 2 cm with cold water, then fold the excess pastry back against the pastry which is touching the slanting sides of the inverted pie plate. Press firmly in place, decorating doubled pastry with fork marks or pinch marks, if you like.

Prick the surface which covers the flat base evenly, in many places.

Slide inverted pie plate on to oven rack. Bake at 200–210°C until golden brown.

When shell is cold and crisp, carefully turn upside down, on a flat plate, or in a bigger pie plate, and fill as desired.

ᴄ Empanadas

If you like Spanish and/or Mexican food, you should really enjoy these cheesy savouries. They may be baked or deep fried, as you like.

Try halving the size and making twice as many 'empanaditas' (little empanadas) to serve as pre-dinner starters or snacks.

Although this is an unusual pastry, it is made in the same way as normal pastry (see page 185). Be very careful not to add too much water or the pastry will be sticky and difficult to work with.

For 6 empanadas or 12 empanaditas:
Pastry
3 cups plain white flour
½ tsp salt
75 g melted butter
½ cup yoghurt
2–3 Tbsp water

Filling
2 cups (200 g) grated cheese
2 hard-boiled eggs, chopped
*1 large green or red pepper, or 1 small
   (130 g) can diced peppers*
10–12 olives, chopped
1 Tbsp capers (optional)
½ tsp chilli powder
1 tsp ground cumin
½ tsp oreganum

Once the pastry has been made, knead for a few minutes, then divide it into six (or 12) equal-sized balls. Cover these and leave to stand while preparing the filling.

In a bowl combine all filling ingredients using liquid from canned peppers, if used.

Roll out the first ball of pastry until it is about 15–20 cm across. Place about ½ cup of filling just to one side of the middle, and then fold over until the edges meet (you should have a D-shape). Seal the seam using a little water, then press around the edge with a fork. Repeat to make six (or 12) empanadas.

Deep fry in oil heated to 180°C for 5 minutes or until golden brown, *or* bake for 30 minutes at 180°C. Brush liberally with oil before putting in the oven, and again once or twice during cooking.

For a light meal or lunch, serve the empanadas alone or with a salad (they are surprisingly substantial), or, for a main meal, serve with brown rice and a salad.

Variation:
If you can't be bothered hard-boiling the eggs, just break the eggs straight in, and stir until combined.

ᴄ Samosas

These little savouries are traditional Indian 'fast foods'.

It is nice to shape samosas in the traditional way, but you can made them into small turnovers if you find this easier. The spiciness of the filling may be varied by adding more or less of the various seasonings.

For 16 samosas (4–8 servings):
Pastry
1 cup wholemeal flour
1 cup plain white flour
¼ cup oil
4–6 Tbsp water
1 tsp salt

Filling
2 Tbsp oil
1 medium-sized onion, diced
*4 medium-sized potatoes (500 g total),
   boiled and peeled*
1 cup peas, fresh or frozen
2–3 tsp curry powder
1 tsp garam masala
1 tsp ground coriander
1 tsp ground cumin
1–2 tsp salt, to taste
1 tsp sugar
¼ cup water
juice of 1 lemon

Make the pastry as usual (see page 185), using oil instead of butter. Be careful to add only enough water to form the 'crumbs' into one large ball.

Knead on a lightly floured surface for a few minutes, then oil the surface and allow the dough to stand while you prepare the filling.

In a large frypan, sauté the onion in the oil until soft. Add the potatoes (cut into 1.5 cm cubes), peas and seasonings. Cook together for a few minutes, until the peas are soft.

Stir in the water and lemon juice. There should be enough liquid to form everything into a very thick, lumpy paste.

Taste and add more curry powder and/or salt if you wish.

Divide the pastry into eight balls. Keep one of these to work with but cover the rest. Roll the ball into a 20 cm circle. Cut this in half. Take one half and form it into a cone by overlapping the cut edges, using a little water to seal the join.

Place 1–2 tablespoons (or as much as you can fit) of the filling into the cone, then, as before, seal this edge with a little water. You may wish to decorate this edge by folding again and squashing with a fork.

Repeat with the other half of the circle, then with the other balls of pastry.

Cook three or four at a time, in oil heated to about 180°C, for about 5 minutes, or until golden brown.

Serve warm, reheating in a microwave or conventional oven if necessary.

Empanadas and Samosas

Sauces and Dressings

Sauces and dressings are used to coat foods. In general, the thinner the sauce, the more thinly it coats whatever it is poured over.

Some sauces and dressings are highly flavoured and give a boost to the blander foods they cover. Other sauces have little flavour, but have a richness that alters the way the coated food feels and tastes in our mouths.

Sauces do not have to be complicated, very rich mixtures to be successful. Some of the simplest sauces that I use, you may not even classify as sauces at all.

A thin coating of melted butter on vegetables acts as a sauce. A mixture of melted butter and lemon juice is another. Lemon juice mixed with seasonings and chopped herbs, and lemon juice and mixed mustard are other successful, simple sauces.

Cream, thin, thickened, or lightly whipped, is a sauce. When the yolk of a poached egg runs over the spinach the egg sits on, it is acting as a sauce too.

In general it is a mistake to have sauces too thick and stodgy, but on the other hand, a sauce that is too thin will sometimes run straight off food. When you are dealing with very small quantities, you can reduce a sauce by boiling to thicken it. At other times, a little cornflour or arrowroot will thicken it enough.

Use the following recipes to start you off, to make interesting savoury and sweet sauces, and dressings.

Gravy

🄲 Gravy

A well-coloured gravy with a good flavour can make all the difference to a roast dinner. A light coating of soya sauce and mustard, brushed over beef or lamb before cooking, ensures dripping with good colour and flavour — a good start to gravy making.

Lift meat from roasting pan and pour away nearly all the fat from the pan. Leave only 1–2 tablespoons as well as the pan drippings.

Stir in about 2 tablespoons flour, over a moderate heat. Mix thoroughly, browning flour lightly. (For a rich, tangy gravy replace flour with a tablespoon mixed mustard.)

Add about 1¹⁄₂ cups liquid. Use lightly salted vegetable liquid, stock, water, wine or a mixture of these. (Add ¹⁄₂–1 cup wine to the mustard-based gravy.) Stir during cooking. Season and strain.

Variation:
Sometimes the roasting pan contains several spoonfuls of syrupy sediment. In this case, pour about two tablespoons of fat from the pan into a saucepan, brown the flour in this, then add the sediment later with the liquid, after discarding all other fatty drippings.

🄲 Special Occasion Sauce

Make a dark, tangy gravy by pouring the fat from the roasting pan, stirring in 1–2 tablespoons of good mixed mustard to the drippings, then adding about 1 cup of liquid, about half of which is dry red (or white) wine. Use vegetable cooking liquid or water for the rest.

🄲 🄼 Redcurrant and Orange Sauce

(See photograph on page 194.)

Combine in a sauce pan or microwave dish the grated rind and juice of 1 orange, 1 tablespoon finely chopped shallot or 1 finely chopped garlic clove, ¹⁄₂ cup redcurrant jelly and ¹⁄₄ cup sherry. Cook until evenly mixed and syrupy. Use as glaze near end of cooking time or in small quantities as a sauce on grilled or roast lamb, duck, pork.

Variations:
Use other citrus fruit. Replace jelly with plum or apricot jam.

Add mustard, grated root ginger, etc. to vary the flavour.

🄲 Vegetarian Gravy

To many of us, gravy is 'comfort food'. Serve this gravy in a jug, and let your family and friends pour it over their main course, mashed potatoes, or whatever they like. You will probably be surprised by their pleasure!

2 medium-sized onions
2–3 cloves garlic
2 Tbsp oil or butter
1 tsp sugar
2 Tbsp flour
2 cups water
2 Tbsp dark soya sauce
black pepper to taste
¹⁄₄–¹⁄₂ tsp salt

Finely chop or mince the onions and garlic. Heat the oil or butter in a large frypan or pot, add the onions and garlic, and cook, stirring occasionally until they brown. Stir in the sugar and flour and cook for about a minute longer.

Add half the water, stirring to remove any lumps, bring to the boil and allow to thicken before adding the remaining water and soya sauce. Bring to the boil again, season with black pepper and salt to taste, then serve!

C White Sauce

White sauce is the base of many other sauces. Learn how to make a smooth, creamy sauce.

2 Tbsp butter
2 Tbsp flour
1 cup milk
1/2 tsp salt

Melt the butter in a medium-sized saucepan. Add the flour and stir until bubbly. Do not brown flour. Add a third of the milk, stir well and heat until thick. Add next third of milk, stir well and heat again until thick. Add remaining milk, stir until sauce has boiled and bubbled gently for 1–2 minutes. Add salt.

M White Sauce

Measure 2 tablespoons butter into a 2 cup measuring jug. Using Full power, microwave until melted, about 40 seconds. Stir in 2 tablespoons flour. Microwave until mixture bubbles. Add 1 cup milk and mix thoroughly. Microwave for 2–3 minutes, stirring after each minute, until sauce is smooth and thick. Season, adding less than 1/4 teaspoon salt, and pepper to taste.
Note:
For a sauce with more flavour, heat the milk with a bayleaf and a sliced onion for 10–30 minutes at a low power level before making the sauce, so milk is flavoured.

C M Cheese Sauce

Melt 2 tablespoons butter, stir in 2 tablespoons flour and a pinch of mustard and heat until bubbly. Stir in 3/4 cup milk. Heat until boiling, stirring often. Add 1/2 cup extra milk. Boil again, still stirring.

Stir in 1–1 1/2 cups grated tasty cheese, a little freshly grated nutmeg and 1–2 tablespoons Parmesan cheese if available. Add pepper and salt if necessary.

Serve with vegetables, pasta, etc. Cook in a microwave in preference to cooking on stovetop.

C M Parsley Sauce

(See photograph on page 195.)

Melt 2 tablespoons butter, stir in 2 tablespoons flour and heat until bubbly. Stir in 1/2 cup milk and heat until boiling, stirring often. Add 1/2 cup stock (or 1/2 cup water and 1/2 teaspoon instant stock) or 1/2 cup extra milk and 1/4 cup finely chopped parsley. Heat again until boiling, stirring constantly, then season carefully.

Serve with corned meat, plainly cooked chicken, vegetables or fish.

C M Caper Sauce

Melt 2 tablespoons butter, stir in 2 tablespoons flour and heat until bubbly. Stir in 1 teaspoon mixed mustard and 1 cup of stock from the food with which sauce is to be served, diluted if very salty. Bring to boil, stirring frequently.

Add 2–3 teaspoons capers, 1–2 teaspoons caper vinegar and 2 tablespoons cream. Bring back to boiling.

Season as necessary with salt, pepper and sugar. Serve with boiled meat, plain cooked fish, etc.
Note:
Use 1 teaspoon instant stock and 1 cup water if no other stock is available. Make sauce in microwave oven, if available.

C M Mustard Sauce

(See photograph on page 194.)

Melt 2 tablespoons butter, stir in 2 tablespoons flour and heat until bubbly. Stir in 1/2 cup of chicken, lamb or beef stock and heat to boiling. Add another 1/2 cup stock, 2 tablespoons mild mixed mustard and 1 teaspoon sugar. Boil again, stirring constantly. Add 2 tablespoons cream, then taste and season.

When serving this sauce with boiled meat, use the meat-cooking liquid as stock. Always check its saltiness. If too salty, dilute it with water.
Note:
Mixed mustard can be replaced with 2 teaspoons dry mustard and 1 tablespoon wine vinegar.

Make sauce in microwave oven, if available.

C Red Pepper Coulis

A coulis is a purée of vegetables (or fruit) which is not thickened with flour.

Chop a large red pepper. Add 1 tablespoon finely chopped shallot or onion and 1 clove garlic. Melt 1 tablespoon butter in a small saucepan and add vegetables. Stir, cover and cook gently, without browning, for 4–5 minutes.

Add 1 cup meat, fish or vegetable stock (or use 1/2 teaspoon instant stock, 1/2 cup water and 1/2 cup dry white wine). Choose liquid after considering how coulis will be served.

Simmer until tender then purée in food processor, sieve and adjust seasonings.
Variations:
For different colours and flavours replace red pepper with green or yellow peppers, zucchini or tomatoes.

C Sage and Apple Sauce

Melt 2 tablespoons butter in a medium-sized saucepan. Add 2 large cooking apples, peeled and sliced, and 2 teaspoons chopped fresh sage. Cover and cook in 2 tablespoons apple juice, white wine or water until apples are tender.

Taste, add up to 1 tablespoon sugar and salt and pepper to bring out the flavour. Mash or purée.

Serve warm with sausages, hot or cold roast pork, etc.

M Fresh Tomato Sauce with Basil

Measure into a food processor bowl 2 cups quartered tomatoes, 2 teaspoons tomato paste, 2 basil leaves, 1 sprig parsley, 1 teaspoon sugar, 1/2 teaspoon salt and 3 teaspoons cornflour. Process until finely chopped but not puréed.

Microwave at Full power in bowl containing 2 teaspoons butter, until bubbling and clear, about 3 minutes.

Serve with pasta, over poached eggs on toast, etc.

C Wine Butter Sauce

Remove sautéed chicken, fish, lamb or veal from pan. Tip out any fat or oil but leave pan drippings. Add 1/2 cup white wine and the juice of 1/2 lemon. Heat until reduced to half original volume.

Remove from heat and tilt and shake pan to incorporate 25 g butter, cut in small pieces. Sauce should thicken with the addition of the butter.
Variations:
Add chopped herbs to wine. Replace wine with good quality chicken stock.

C Mushroom Cream Sauce

Slice 1 cup mushrooms and chop 1 clove garlic finely. Cook in small pan in 1 tablespoon butter and 1 tablespoon sherry until mushrooms are wilted. Add a pinch of tarragon if available.

Stir in 1 tablespoon flour then 1/2 cup chicken stock (or 1/2 teaspoon instant stock and 1/2 cup water). Keep stirring until sauce boils and thickens.

Remove from heat, stir in about 1/2 cup sour cream to get a sauce of the thickness you want. Do not reheat after sour cream has been added. Serve warm over chicken or fish, on baked potatoes or pasta, etc.

Ⓜ Anchovy Cream

Microwave 1 tablespoon butter, 2 finely chopped garlic cloves and 4 crushed anchovy fillets in a glass bowl or jug at Full power, for 1 minute.

Add 1 carton (150 g) double cream and mix well. Microwave at Full Power for 2 minutes.

Ⓤ Seafood Cocktail Sauce

¼ cup tomato sauce
½ cup mayonnaise
2 Tbsp brandy or sherry or lemon juice
2 tsp Worcestershire sauce
3–4 drops Tabasco sauce or sprinkle of chilli powder
½ cup cream
paprika

Combine tomato sauce, mayonnaise, brandy, sherry or lemon juice, Worcestershire sauce and Tabasco sauce. This mixture can be stored until required in a covered container in the refrigerator. Lightly whip cream and add to previously prepared mixture.

Add paprika to sauce or sprinkle over seafood cocktail. This sauce is suitable served over shellfish, shrimps or soused, marinated, poached, baked or tinned fish arranged in lettuce cups or on shredded lettuce. (See fish section for fish salad suggestions.)

Ⓤ Tartare Sauce

1 tsp onion, chopped
1 tsp gherkin or other pickle, chopped
1 tsp parsley, chopped
1 tsp capers or green pepper, chopped
¼ cup mayonnaise
lemon juice (optional)

Finely chop vegetables and add to the mayonnaise. Leave to stand for at least an hour before serving for flavour to develop. Thin with lemon juice if desired. Serve with fried seafood or use as a dip.

Ⓤ Ginger Dipping Sauce

1 Tbsp chopped root ginger
2 small dried chillis
1 clove garlic
2 tsp sugar
2 Tbsp light soya sauce or fish sauce
1 Tbsp water
1 Tbsp lemon juice or lime juice

Measure all ingredients into a food processor. Mix thoroughly, then strain. Dip cooked mussels into freshly made sauce, before eating.

Ⓜ Spicy Indonesian Sauce

2 cloves garlic, chopped
2 tsp grated root ginger
1 tsp freshly ground coriander seed (optional)
2 Tbsp dark soya sauce
2 Tbsp lemon juice
1 Tbsp oil
3–4 drops hot pepper sauce
¼ cup brown sugar
2 Tbsp peanut butter
¼ cup water

Combine all the ingredients in a bowl and microwave, uncovered, at Full power until smooth and thickened, about 4–5 minutes. Thin sauce with more water if necessary.

Ⓜ Hot Barbecue Sauce

1 tsp chopped garlic
1 onion, chopped
1 Tbsp oil
2 Tbsp tomato ketchup
2 tsp tomato paste
1 Tbsp brown sugar
2 tsp Worcestershire sauce
1 tsp mixed mustard

In a medium-sized bowl microwave garlic, onion and oil at Full power for 3 minutes. Add the remaining ingredients and heat until mixture is bubbling (about 2 minutes). This sauce is especially good served on meatballs or frankfurters.

Ⓜ Hollandaise Sauce

This is traditionally served with fish, asparagus, broccoli, on poached eggs, etc.

For 4 servings:
100 g butter
2 egg yolks
1 Tbsp lemon juice

Heat the butter in a 2 cup measuring cup, covered with a saucer to stop spatters, for 3 minutes at Full power.

In a fairly small bowl with a rounded bottom, beat the egg yolks with a whisk until well mixed.

Add the hot butter to the egg yolks in a thin stream, whisking all the time. Do not add the butter sediment — i.e. stop after about three-quarters of the butter is added.

The sauce should thicken as the hot butter is added. Whisk the lemon juice into the thickened sauce. This may thin the sauce considerably. If sauce needs further thickening microwave at Defrost (30% power) for 1–1½ minutes, whisking after each 30 seconds. Stop as soon as sauce thickens

round edge. Whisk to make sauce smooth.

Serve sauce warm, not hot, warming carefully at Defrost (30% power) for short intervals if necessary.
Variation:
Replace lemon juice with orange juice if desired.

Ⓜ Bearnaise Sauce

This very rich, buttery sauce has a wonderful flavour and texture, and is served with choice steaks.

Made with a food processor and microwave oven, this sauce is easy. Try it using clarified butter, too. It takes longer to heat but it doesn't spit and splatter at all!

To reheat the sauce or to thicken it more, microwave at Medium (50% power) for 10 second bursts, stirring after each.

Place 2 large egg yolks in food processor bowl with a few fresh tarragon leaves, if available.

Microwave 2 tablespoons wine vinegar with 1 tablespoon chopped shallot and a tarragon sprig (or ½ teaspoon dried tarragon) at Full power for 2½ minutes or until 1 tablespoon liquid remains. Pour liquid on to egg yolks. Mix on low speed until thick.

Heat 100 g butter in a glass measuring jug or bowl, covered with a saucer to stop splatters, for 2 minutes or until very hot. Add to mixture in a slow stream, processing at slow speed.

Serve warm not hot, preferably soon after making.

It is important to stir sauces efficiently as they cook on a stove top.

A wire whisk does a good job, because you can hold the saucepan handle with one hand while you whisk with the other.

Make sure you whisk the sauce at the edges of the pot as well as the sauce near the middle.

A whisk, although it works well, does not reach into the corners as well as a square-cornered wooden spoon or spurtle.

When you are making delicate sauces which must not overcook, fill the sink, or a large bowl, with cold water, or a mixture of ice and cold water, so that you can cool the saucepan of sauce very quickly, by taking it straight from the heat, and standing it in the cold water. Stir all the time, while heating, then cooling the sauce.

Bearnaise Sauce

Herb Mayonnaise

U Mayonnaise

This is an extremely useful and delicious sauce which is easy and quick to make in a food processor or blender.

1 egg
½ tsp salt
½ tsp sugar
1 tsp Dijon mustard
2 Tbsp wine vinegar
about 1 cup corn or olive oil

Measure the first five ingredients into a blender or food processor. Turn on, and pour in the oil in a thin stream until the mayonnaise is as thick as you like.

Store in a covered container in the refrigerator for up to 2–3 weeks.

Garlic Mayonnaise
Add one or two cloves of garlic before adding the oil. Leave to stand for an hour to soften the flavour, before using.

Herb Mayonnaise
Add about ¼ cup roughly chopped parsley, and 1–2 teaspoons each of one or more fresh or dried herbs such as basil, oreganum, thyme, dill, etc. before adding the oil.

Chilli Mayonnaise
This is a particularly delicious variation. Add ½–1 teaspoon chilli powder, 1 teaspoon dried oreganum, 1–2 teaspoons ground cumin, and 1 clove garlic before adding the oil. The flavour improves and becomes hotter after it stands for several hours.

U Tofu 'Mayonnaise' Dressing

This low-fat, high-protein mayonnaise tastes remarkably good, due to careful seasoning. It contains no eggs and very little oil, and can be used in place of regular mayonnaise, where necessary.

For about 1 cup:
2 small cloves garlic
2 Tbsp roughly chopped parsley
1 Tbsp roughly chopped chives
1 cup (300 g) crumbled firm tofu
¼ cup vegetable oil
1 Tbsp white wine vinegar
*½ tsp mustard powder or 1 tsp Dijon
   mustard*
½ tsp salt
¼ tsp sugar
juice of ½ lemon
black pepper to taste

Chop the garlic and herbs in a blender or food processor. Don't be over-generous with the garlic or the dressing will taste of little else. Add the remaining ingredients and blend until the mixture is smooth and creamy.

Refrigerate in a screw-topped jar for several weeks, if desired.

U Herbed Creamy Vinaigrette

There are times when you want a dressing which is sharper than mayonnaise but more solid than an oil and vinegar dressing. This dressing provides the answer.

It is particularly good on vegetables which have been lightly cooked, cooled and well drained, e.g. carrots, beans and cauliflower. It makes a good potato salad too.

1 egg yolk
1 Tbsp Dijon-type mustard
¼ cup wine vinegar
1–1½ cups oil
2 spring onions, finely chopped
2 Tbsp finely chopped parsley
2 tsp finely chopped tarragon
  (optional)
salt and pepper

Beat the egg yolk, mustard and vinegar together with a wire whisk, then add the oil in a thin stream, beating all the time. Stop adding the oil when it gets to the thickness you want.

Stir in the very finely chopped herbs, and add extra seasonings if you think they are needed.

If you have a blender or food processor, use it to make the dressing, following the same order.

Refrigerate in a covered container, for up to a week.

Green Sauce

This substantial sauce turns many warm or room-temperature vegetables into a light meal.

1 egg yolk
1 Tbsp mild mixed mustard
1 tsp sugar
¼ tsp salt
2 cloves garlic
2 spring onions
3 Tbsp wine vinegar
½–1 cup mixed fresh herb leaves (e.g. parsley, chives, dill, tarragon)
½–¾ cup corn or soya oil
2 hard-boiled eggs, chopped

Combine first seven ingredients in food processor with metal chopping blade. Add herbs. (Use small amounts of strongly flavoured tarragon.)

Process while adding oil, stopping when thick. Add 1 hard-boiled egg. Chop remaining egg fairly finely and use to sprinkle over sauce when serving. Spoon over cooked cauliflower, asparagus, beans, new potatoes or raw halved avocados, tomatoes, etc. just before serving.

Cumin Dressing

½ cup corn or soya oil
¼ cup wine or cider vinegar
2 tsp ground cumin
1–2 tsp onion powder
¾ tsp salt
2 tsp dried oreganum
½–1 tsp garlic powder
black pepper and hot pepper sauce to taste

Place all the ingredients in a screw-topped jar. Shake well.
Note:
It is very important that the cumin is fresh and has a pungent, definite flavour.

French Dressing

The name of this dressing is loosely given to dressings of oil and vinegar in proportions of two or three parts of oil shaken with one part of mild vinegar. Mustard is added for extra flavour and to stop the two main ingredients from separating immediately.

I like to season this dressing fairly strongly, since I use it in very small amounts to coat salad greens. If you use a lot of dressing, reduce the amount of seasoning.

You can mix small amounts of this dressing, by guesswork, in the bottom of a salad bowl, and combine it with a whisk or fork, before tossing it with the salad ingredients, or you can mix larger amounts and keep it in a jar, to be shaken and applied over a period of several days.

You can change the character of the dressing by adding one or more of the optional ingredients. It is worth experimenting with one at a time.

2 Tbsp olive or corn or soya oil
2 Tbsp corn or soya oil
2 Tbsp wine or cider vinegar
1–2 tsp Dijon mustard
¼–½ tsp salt
freshly ground pepper
hot pepper sauce

Optional
chopped capers
chopped fresh herbs
chopped spring onions
finely chopped garlic
about 1 Tbsp cream
1–2 tsp tomato paste
½–1 tsp sugar

Combine the ingredients of your choice in a screw-topped jar, or a blender or food processor. Shake or process, and use as requried.

Herb Dressing

Toss with leafy salads just before serving, or pour over cooked vegetables and leave to cool to room temperature.

Vary the herbs to suit the vegetable. Try new potatoes, young carrots, whole beans, sliced zucchini or cauliflower.

¼ cup corn, soya or olive oil
2 Tbsp wine vinegar
1–2 cloves garlic (optional)
½ tsp salt
½ tsp sugar
¼ cup finely chopped parsley
small amounts of other fresh herbs, finely chopped

Combine all dressing ingredients in a food processor, blender, or screw-topped jar. Mix thoroughly.

Pesto

Fresh basil has a wonderful flavour but a short season. Make pesto so you can enjoy it all year, adding it to pasta, dressings, sauces, and many other dishes, as required.

3–4 cups lightly packed basil leaves
1 cup parsley
4 cloves garlic
¼–½ cup Parmesan cheese
¼ cup pine nuts, almonds, or walnuts
½–1 cup olive and/or corn oil
about 1 tsp salt

Put the basil and parsley leaves into a food processor with the peeled garlic cloves, the Parmesan cheese and the nuts.

Using olive oil for preference, or some olive and some corn oil, process the leaves, adding up to half a cup of oil until they are finely chopped. Keep adding oil until you have a dark green paste, just liquid enough to pour.

Add salt to taste. Store in the refrigerator, in a lidded glass or plastic container, for use within 3 months. Freeze pesto for longer storage.
Note:
Pesto may darken at the top of jars where it is exposed to the air. Make sure there is a layer of oil at the top of each jar.

Leave out cheese and nuts if you like, if you will add pesto to other mixtures.

Sesame Dressing

Sprinkle this on cucumber, avocado, or any salad you want to serve with Oriental food.

1 Tbsp Kikkoman soya sauce
1 Tbsp sesame oil
1 Tbsp lemon juice
1 tsp sugar

Shake all ingredients together in a small jar, and sprinkle over food in its serving dish or plate.

Tomato Dressing

This dressing is especially good with sliced or halved avocado, or with pasta salads.

1 Tbsp onion pulp
¼ cup tomato purée
3 Tbsp wine vinegar
1 Tbsp sugar
½ tsp salt
½ tsp celery salt
1 tsp mixed mustard
¾ cup corn or soya oil

Combine all ingredients in a blender, food processor or screw-topped jar. (For onion pulp, scrape a halved onion, cut crosswise, with the tip of a teaspoon.)

Refrigerate in a screw-topped jar for up to a week.

C Trifle Topping Custard

This eggy custard is also popular with young children.

2 Tbsp cornflour
1 Tbsp sugar
2 cups milk
2 egg yolks
1 Tbsp butter

Stir the cornflour and sugar together in a saucepan. Mix to a smooth paste with ¼ cup milk and the egg yolks. Add the remaining milk and butter. Stir over moderate heat until mixture thickens.

As soon as it bubbles, transfer the pot quickly to a sink of cold water. Stir until cool. Pour over trifle or store in jug or bowl with plastic film touching the surface of the custard.

M Raspberry Sauce

½ cup sugar
1 Tbsp custard powder
½ cup water or white wine
2 cups frozen raspberries
2–3 Tbsp rum or brandy (optional)

In a small bowl or jug microwave the sugar, custard powder and liquid at Full power until bubbling. Stir, then boil for 1–2 minutes. Stir in the thawed raspberries, mashing if desired. Add flavouring, if used. Serve warm or cold, with ice-cream, cream or plain pudding or cake.

M Orange Sauce

½ cup sugar
1 Tbsp cornflour or custard powder
50 g butter
1 orange, grated rind and juice
juice of ½ lemon
½ cup water

Stir together sugar and custard powder in a bowl or 2-cup measure. Add remaining ingredients.

Microwave at Full power for 5–6 minutes, stirring every minute after 3 minutes.

Serve warm on ice-cream, with or without sliced bananas.
Variation:
Replace orange with a tangelo.

M Sour Cream Sauce

½ cup brown sugar
½ cup sour cream
½ tsp vanilla

In a small jug or bowl mix the sugar, sour cream and vanilla.

Microwave at Full power for 30–60 seconds, or until sugar melts. Do not boil. Stir until smooth and cool to room temperature. Serve with ice-cream, raw or cooked fruit, plain puddings, etc.

Variation:
To make Sour Cream Coffee Sauce add 1 teaspoon instant coffee mixed with 1 teaspoon water. Serve with ice-cream and bananas.

M Peanut Chocolate Sauce

¾ cup (½ pkt) chocolate chips
¼ cup peanut butter
¼ cup milk

In a small bowl or jug microwave all the ingredients at Medium (50% power) for 2 minutes. Stir until smooth. Thin with extra milk. The sauce will thicken on cooling.

Reheat before use. Extra milk may be needed to thin the sauce after reheating it. Serve over ice-cream, with or without bananas.
Note:
Use smooth or crunchy peanut butter.

M Lemon Sauce

1½ Tbsp custard powder or cornflour
2 Tbsp sugar
1 Tbsp golden syrup
¾ cup water
1 lemon, grated rind and juice
1 Tbsp butter

Stir dry ingredients together in a 2 cup measuring jug or bowl. Add syrup, then remaining ingredients.

Microwave at Full power for 5 minutes, stirring every minute after 3 minutes. Serve warm with ice-cream, steamed pudding or gingerbread.

C Spiced Fruit Sauce

Spices turn a can of fruit into something exciting.

2 Tbsp butter
¼ cup brown sugar
½ tsp cinnamon
½ tsp mixed spice
½ tsp ginger
1 can (500 g) apricot halves or sliced peaches
2 Tbsp sherry
1 banana, sliced
6 glacé cherries (optional)

In a large frypan, over a fairly high heat, melt the butter and add brown sugar and spices. Cook mixture without stirring, tilting the pan to mix, until the sugar becomes liquid. Tip in fruit and syrup, add sherry and cook rapidly until the liquid has become very thick, and coats the fruit.

Remove from the heat and add the sliced banana and quartered cherries. Serve warm over ice-cream.

M Baked Apple Sauce

When you have a lot of apples, make this simple apple sauce. Put the uncored whole apples in a suitable large casserole dish. Cover and microwave at Full power, allowing 2–4 minutes for each apple, depending on variety. When apples are soft and cool enough to handle, push or bang them through a sieve, discarding skin and cores. Add a little sugar to the puréed mixture.

Apple Fool
Fold 1 cup whipped cream into 2 cups of cold, sweetened apple purée.
Variation:
Purée in food processor before sieving.

M Caramel Nut Sauce

½ cup brown sugar
75 g butter, cubed
2 Tbsp water
¼ cup chopped walnuts
½ tsp vanilla or rum flavouring

Combine the sugar, butter and water in a 2 cup glass measuring cup. Microwave at Full power for 4 minutes, stirring after 2 minutes. (Sauce should bubble rapidly for 1½ minutes.) Stir in chopped walnuts and vanilla or rum flavouring.

Serve warm, reheating if necessary. Serve with ice-cream, and/or peaches or with plain cake.

C M Christmas Sauce

This recipe combines spices and dried fruits that we associate with Christmas in a warm sauce which is delicious over ice-cream.

¾ cup mixed dried fruit
½ tsp cinnamon
½ tsp mixed spice
¼ tsp ground cloves
½ cup sugar
1 Tbsp custard powder
1 cup apple (or other) juice
1 Tbsp wine vinegar
25 g butter
1–2 Tbsp brandy or ½ tsp brandy essence

Make a dried fruit mixture, including halved or quartered red and green cherries.

Mix this in a saucepan or microwave dish with the spices, sugar and custard powder, then add the apple juice and vinegar. Add the butter, cut in 4–6 cubes. Bring sauce to the boil, then simmer for 2–3 minutes. Stir until boiling (or use Full power in microwave). Stir in flavouring.

Cool to room temperature before serving over ice-cream.

Trifle Topping Custard

Desserts

Although food fashions come and go, just as clothing fashions change, many family recipes remain virtually unchanged bcause they are so popular.

Many adults remember, with special fondness, the desserts, sweet pies and homely puddings which they enjoyed as children. These are seldom exotic or expensive, but they often require more time than the cook of today has. Many of us must fit a lot of meal preparation into a short time, so I have given many golden oldies a new look, using modern kitchen machines, ingredients, and methods.

Why, for example, peel an apple, when you can grate it, skin and all? It tastes better, you get more apple for your money, and you get extra fibre, as well as saving time.

As well as these short-cut favourites, you will find many new ideas here, too.

I am sure that you will find some good ideas here, whether you make desserts regularly, or serve them only on special occasions.

Short Pastry

Traditional Method

Measure 1 cup plain or wholemeal flour into a mixing bowl. Cut or rub in 60–75 g cold butter using a pastry blender, fingertips or two knives, until the butter is cut in small pieces.

Add about ¼ cup cold water, a few drops at a time, tossing the mixture with a fork until it will form a ball when pressed with fingers. Chill for 5–10 minutes before rolling out.

Food Processor Method

Fit the food processor with its metal cutting blade. Add 1 cup plain or wholemeal flour and add 60–70 g cold butter, cut into about nine cubes. Do not process.

Acidify ¼ cup cold water with 1–2 teaspoons lemon juice for extra tenderness if desired. Using the pulse button, add water in a thin stream while chopping butter through flour.

Test at intervals to see if the particles are moist enough to press together to form a ball. The mixture will still look crumbly at this stage. (If a ball of dough forms in the processor, the mixture is too wet.)
Note:
Overmixing or too much water makes tough pastry.

Quick Flaky Pastry

This is an easy recipe for pastry which is flakier and richer than short pastry.

For 1 thinly rolled double crust 20 cm pie:
1¼ cups flour
1 tsp baking powder
125 g cold butter
about ½ cup milk
1 tsp wine vinegar

Mix the flour and baking powder. Grate butter or cut it into about 25 small cubes, and rub or cut into the flour, by hand or with a food processor. (Pieces of butter should be visible when pastry is rolled out.) Mix liquids, and add slowly to flour mixture until it forms a fairly stiff dough. Roll out thinly, and use as required.

ⓒ Sweet Shortcrust

This pastry is rich and buttery with a texture more like that of shortbread. It may be used for sweet double crust pies (e.g. mince pies), for sweet flan shells (baked blind) or for small unfilled tart shells.

200 g butter
½ cup icing sugar
½ tsp vanilla
2 cups flour

Warm the butter to room temperature. Cream until easily worked in food processor with metal cutting blade. Add icing sugar and vanilla and mix to a light, smooth consistency. Add flour and mix well. If mixture is too crumbly to stick together, add milk, using as little as possible. Chill until firm.

Roll out thinly. Cut as desired. Bake at 150°C. Small 6 cm tart shells cook in about 10 minutes; baked blind flan shells in 20–30 minutes.

ⓒ Apple Pie

Everybody likes an apple pie!

For a 20–23 cm pie:
Quick Flaky Pastry
½ cup sugar
2 Tbsp flour
4–6 apples
25 g butter, melted
6 cloves or ¼ tsp ground cloves

Make once the recipe of the pastry. Cut the pastry in half, then roll it out thinly and evenly on a lightly floured board, turning it often to form two rounds a little bigger than a 20 or 23 cm pie plate. Put one piece in the plate, with its edges overhanging, stretching it as little as possible.

Put the sugar and flour in a bowl. Coarsely shred or slice the peeled or unpeeled apples, and toss them in the sugar and flour. Pour the melted butter over the apple, add the cloves if you like them, and toss to mix. Put the prepared apple into the pastry-lined pan, dampen the surface of the remaining pastry, and place on the apple, dampened side down. Press the two layers of pastry together, trim about 1 cm beyond the edge of the pie plate, then fold the overhanging pastry under, pinching the layers together. Flute or fork the edges if desired, make one central hole or several holes for steam to escape, and brush with lightly beaten egg if you want a glazed surface. Bake at 220°C until golden brown and the apple is tender when tested with a skewer, lowering the heat to 180°C if the pastry browns before the apple is cooked.

Serve warm, with cream, ice-cream, yoghurt, or fromage frais.

ⓒ Fruited Cream Flan

(See photograph on page 204.)

Flans, cooked in tins with straight, low sides, are sometimes baked blind then filled. For this cream cheese filling the cream cheese is softened, beaten with icing sugar until smooth, then combined with the gelatine which has been softened in, then heated with, the orange juice.

For a 32 cm flan:
Pastry
1½ cups flour
75 g cold butter
about 6 Tbsp cold water

Filling
2 (250 g) cartons cream cheese
1 cup icing sugar
2–3 tsp gelatine
½ cup orange juice
fruit for topping

Make pastry. Roll thinly to a 36 cm circle. Spray a 32 cm flan tin (with removable base) with non-stick spray. Ease pastry into tin. Press firmly against sides. Cut off edges with rolling pin.

Line pastry with paper or an opened oven bag then fill with macaroni, beans, etc. kept for this purpose.

Bake crust at 200°C until golden brown. Remove beans and liner, bake until base browns. Mix cream filling (see above). Fill with cream cheese filling and refrigerate until firm. Arrange sliced fruit on cream filling. Brush with warmed jam if desired.

Ⓜ Tamarillo-Apple Pie

This pie cooks in four easy stages. Make topping and filling before pastry.

For a 20 cm pie:
Topping
½ cup rolled oats
¼ cup flour
¼ cup sugar
50 g cold butter

Filling
4 cups sliced apple
1 cup chopped peeled tamarillo
¾ cup sugar
¼ cup flour
½ tsp cinnamon

Crust
1 cup flour
60 g cold butter
about ¼ cup milk
4–6 drops gravy browning (optional)

Make pastry using milk mixed with gravy browning to replace water. Add just enough liquid to make a very firm dough. Roll out and place in a 20 cm pie plate, fluting pastry *above* top rim of pie plate.

Prick base all over. Microwave at Full power for 4–6 minutes, until bottom is dry. Sides will subside a little on cooking. Pour cooked fruit filling into cooked pie shell.

Mix filling ingredients in a large covered microwave dish. Microwave at Full power for 7–8 minutes or until tender and thick.

Sprinkle precooked topping over pie. Microwave at Full power for about 2 minutes, until edges start bubbling.

To mix topping, cut butter finely through other ingredients. Microwave in a 23 cm pie plate at Full power for 3 minutes. Transfer to another container.

C Lattice-Topped Peach Pie

A lattice topping looks elaborate but does not take long to make. Here the pie is made in a flan tin but it can also be made in a pie plate where, to hide the ends of the lattice strips, an extra strip is run right around the edge of the pie, or the bottom crust is folded inwards.

For a 23 cm pie:
2 cups flour
75 g cold butter
about ¹/₂ cup cold water
3 cups drained cooked peaches
2 Tbsp sugar
1 Tbsp cornflour or custard powder
2 Tbsp orange liqueur (optional)

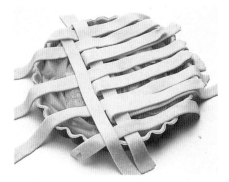

Make short pastry (see page 206). Roll in two 25 cm circles. Line a 23 cm flan tin. Mix drained peaches with remaining ingredients. Fill flan.

Cut remaining circle in 1 cm strips. Drape half strips across flan in one direction. Fold every second strip back, as shown.

Lie a strip crosswise, over half the strips. Unfold the folded strips again. Fold the previously unfolded strips back over the crosswise strip. Continue, forming a lattice design, then repeat on other side of pie.

Press lattice ends off at edge of flan tin. Bake at 220°C for 20 minutes, then at 180°C for 15 minutes. Then glaze while hot with hot apricot jam, if desired. Serve warm.

C Blackberry Pie

Although I enjoy picking and eating cultivated blackberries, there is something even better about scrambling through prickles to get wild blackberries.

Three cups of blackberries will make a pie for four people — if you don't have as many berries as this you can use a mixture of chopped or grated apple and blackberries. The resulting pie is nearly as good as a 'straight' blackberry pie.

Blackberries produce an enormous amount of liquid as they cook inside their pastry case. For this reason I mix the berries, just before they are put into the pastry, with a large amount of custard powder. If you replace some of the blackberries with apples, reduce the amount of custard powder accordingly. If you don't have custard powder, use cornflour instead.

For a 23 cm double-crust pie:
3 cups blackberries
¼ cup custard powder
¼–½ cup sugar
½–1 tsp cinnamon (optional)

Make short pastry for a double crust 23 cm pie (see page 206).

Refrigerate dough for 5–10 minutes, then roll it out thinly to form two rounds big enough to cover the pie plate. Line plate with one round of pastry, and leave edges untrimmed.

Do not mix the fruit, custard powder, sugar and cinnamon together until the oven is up to heat, and all the pastry has been rolled out. Toss fruit with dry ingredients, breaking up the berries as little as possible. The larger amount of sugar makes a sweeter pie.

Transfer this floury-looking mixture to the pastry-lined pie plate and cover with the remaining pastry. Press edges of pastry together, trim and decorate as desired.

Cut several steam holes in the upper crust, brush pastry with beaten egg or milk and sugar if you like a shiny-topped pie, and put pie into a very hot oven, 200–250°C for 15 minutes. Lower heat to 180°C and cook for 10–15 minutes longer.

Serve pie warm, but not straight from the oven, with cream or ice-cream.

C Feijoa Pie

Feijoas are an interesting fruit with a distinctive flavour, intensified by cooking.

For a 20 cm pie:
Filling
500 g feijoas
2 Tbsp cornflour or custard powder
½ cup sugar

Make Quick Flaky Pastry (see page 206) for a 20 cm pie. Cut the dough in half and refrigerate for 5–10 minutes then roll each piece out thinly to form two 23 cm circles.

Line the pie plate with one circle of pastry. When the pastry is rolled out, and the oven hot, peel the feijoas thinly, and chop the flesh into the bowl in which the pastry was mixed. Sprinkle the cornflour (or custard powder) and the sugar over the fruit, and mix gently to mix it through the pieces of feijoa. Spoon this mixture into the lined pie plate, dampen the edges of the pastry and put the other circle of pastry over the fruit. Press the edges together and trim the outer edges about 1 cm beyond the edge of the pie plate, then tuck the cut edges underneath the edge of the lower crust. Pinch or flute the folded edge attractively. Cut several steam vents in the top of the pie.

Bake at 220°C for 20 minutes, or until the edges and top of the pie are brown. Lower the heat to 180°C and bake for 10 minutes longer, or if the pie has not browned, cook it 10 minutes longer at the higher temperature.

C Sliced Apple Flan

This is an impressive apple flan. It takes a little longer to slice the apples, then to arrange them attractively, but it is worth doing if you want something that looks special.

For a 23 cm flan:
Pastry
¾ cup flour
¼ cup chopped walnuts
60 g cold butter
about 2 Tbsp cold water

Filling
2–3 apples
2 eggs
½ cup cream
¼–½ cup sugar

Measure the flour and walnuts into the bowl of a food processor. Process until very finely chopped, then add the butter, cut in cubes. Add the cold water, in a slow stream, while chopping in the butter, using the pulse button. Stop adding the water as soon as the dough is soft enough to press together to form a ball. Refrigerate this while you peel and quarter the apples, and leave them to stand in cold, salted water, to stop them browning.

Roll out the pastry to line a 23 cm flan tin.

Without washing the food processor bowl, mix together the eggs, cream, and sugar.

Cut the core out of each piece of apple, then slice each quarter into 5

to 6 pieces, crosswise. Place the apple quarters so they radiate out from the centre, arranging them neatly, close together. Pour the creamy mixture over them, then bake at 200°C for 30 minutes, or until the apples are just tender. Leave to stand for 15 to 30 minutes, then serve just like this, or brush with apricot jam.

C Apple and Walnut Flan

For a 23 cm flan:
Filling
1 can apple pie filling (or 2 cups well-drained, chunky stewed apple)
½ cup walnut pieces
2 eggs
¾ cup cream or sour cream
¼–½ cup brown sugar
1 tsp cinnamon
½ tsp mixed spice
1 Tbsp wine vinegar

Make short pastry using recipe on page 206. Form into a ball, leave to stand in a cool place for 5 minutes if possible, then roll out to line a 23 cm pie plate. Fold edges double. Pinch or flute decoratively.

Spread the chopped apple fairly evenly over the uncooked pastry. Leave surface rough so the custardy mixture can fill hollows.

Into the unwashed food processor bowl measure the remaining ingredients. (Use whatever cream is available, or replace it with yoghurt.) Use more sugar for a sweeter flan.

If without a food processor; chop nuts, combine other ingredients, beat to combine, then add nuts. Pour custard mixture over apple. Do not overmix.

Bake at 220°C for about 30 minutes, until the custard has set and browned lightly.

Serve warm or reheated.

C Cherry Pies

Use imported bottled cherries to make delicious small pies or tarts, varying the sugar with the tartness of the fruit.

For 4–6 servings:
1–1½ cups (200 g) sour cherries
¼ cup sugar
1 Tbsp cornflour
¼ tsp cinnamon
¼ cup hot water
4 sheets filo pastry
2 Tbsp melted butter

Drain juice from bottled cherries. Combine ¼ cup sugar, 1 tablespoon cornflour, ¼ tsp cinnamon with ½ cup juice. Heat until thick, then stir in cooked fruit.

Lay two sheets of pastry on a dry surface. Working fast, brush sheets

Cherry Pies

lightly with butter. Cover each with remaining sheet of pastry. Cut into squares big enough to fit patty tins, muffin tins, small pie plates or ramekins. Press two (doubled) squares into each container, so corners do not overlap. Prick bottoms. Bake at 180°C for 5–10 minutes or until evenly browned. Remove from tins. Just before serving, fill each cooked filo case with a spoonful of warm pie filling. Dredge with icing sugar.

Variations:
Replace water with white wine. Add 2–3 teaspoon Kirsch or other liqueur to thickened filling.

ⓒ Rhubarb Cream Flan

Rhubarb in party dress!

For 4–5 servings:
Quick Flaky Pastry (see page 206)
3–4 cups thinly sliced rhubarb
3 eggs
$^1\!/_2$ cup sugar
$^1\!/_2$ cup sour cream

Make once the recipe of the pastry. Roll out pastry thinly and use to line a 20 cm pie plate or loose-bottomed flan tin. (There will be some pastry left over.) Fold pastry edges back for a pie, and cut pastry level with edge for a flan.

Cut rhubarb thinly, and arrange in uncooked crust. Combine eggs, sugar, and sour cream until well mixed, then pour over fruit.

Bake at 220°C for 20 minutes, or until golden brown, then at 180°C until filling is set in the middle. Serve warm.

ⓒ Individual Fruit Tarts

Small pre-cooked pastry shells look pretty when piled with sparkling, thickened fruit mixtures.

2 cups flour
125 g cold butter
about $^1\!/_2$ cup cold water

Cooked filling
$^1\!/_4$ cup sugar
1$^1\!/_2$ Tbsp custard powder
$^1\!/_4$ cup fruit juice
$^1\!/_4$ cup white wine or extra juice
about 2 cups drained fruit

Uncooked filling
1 cup cold milk
1 cup cold cream
1 pkt butterscotch instant pudding
2–3 bananas

Make pastry (see page 206). Roll thinly. Ease over inverted individual pie plates.

Cut pastry 1 cm beyond edge. Brush outer edge with cold water.

Fold up dampened edge. Pinch with fingers or press with fork. Prick bases all over. Bake (without turning over) until evenly golden. Cool on rack. Fill about 30 minutes before required.

For cooked filling:
Stir ingredients (except fruit) in order given, over low heat until thick. Remove from heat. Add fruit. Spoon into shells.

For uncooked filling:
Measure milk then cream then pudding mix into bowl. Beat until thick. Fold in sliced bananas. Spoon in shells.

Sweet Carrot Pie

C Sweet Carrot Pie

You may not have thought of using carrots to flavour a pie! Their mild, sweet flavour is combined with that of an orange, producing a pie with a very interesting texture and flavour.

For a 25 cm pie:
25 cm uncooked flan shell
2 cups finely grated carrot
1 cup fresh breadcrumbs
3 eggs
1 orange or tangelo, grated rind and juice
1/2 cup sugar
pinch of salt
3/4 cup unsweetened condensed milk (or cream)
3 Tbsp orange-flavoured liqueur (optional)
grated nutmeg

Line a 25 cm flan tin with short pastry. Grate and measure carrot and crumbs. Combine eggs, rind and juice, sugar and salt. Add carrots and crumbs.

Process again to chop these even more finely through the egg mixture. Then add milk or cream. Process again to mix thoroughly.

Place flan shell on oven rack. Immediately pour in the filling almost to the rim of the pastry. Grate nutmeg over the surface. Bake at 220°C for 15 minutes, then at 180°C for about 30 minutes, until set.

C Apple Crumble

It's much quicker to make a crumbled topping than to make pastry, and in our house the crumble rates nearly as high as a pie. Leftovers, warmed in the microwave oven, and eaten with yoghurt, make a good breakfast.

I grate the apples, skin and all, instead of peeling then slicing the fruit. It gives a 'fresher' flavour to the crumble.

For 4 servings:
1/2 cup flour
1/2 tsp cinnamon
1/2 tsp mixed spice
3/4 cup sugar
75 g butter
1/2 cup rolled oats
4 medium-sized apples

Measure the flour, spices and sugar into a medium-sized bowl or food processor. Cut or rub in the butter until crumbly, then add the rolled oats.

Grate the unpeeled apples into a shallow medium-sized ovenware dish.

Sprinkle the crumbly topping evenly over them.

Bake at 190°C for 45 minutes, until the topping is golden brown. Serve hot or warm with cream or ice-cream.

M Fruit Crumble

Microwaved fruit crumble does not turn golden brown, but it is very quick and easy.

For 4–6 servings:
4 cups sliced raw apples, peaches or rhubarb
1/2 cup rolled oats
1/2 cup white or brown sugar
1/2 cup wholemeal or plain flour
1 tsp mixed spice
50 g cold butter
ground cloves

Put the prepared raw fruit in a microwave-proof 23 cm pie plate or another shallow dish.

Combine the remaining ingredients except the ground cloves.

Cut in butter until crumbly. Sprinkle topping evenly over fruit, then sprinkle with the cloves.

Microwave at Full power for 8–12 minutes (or until fruit is tender). Leave for 15–20 minutes and serve warm.

M Apple Layer Cake

For 6 servings:
Pastry
1/4 cup sugar
2 tsp cinnamon
3 cups flour
200 g cold butter
1 egg
1/4 cup cream
1/2 tsp microwave browning

Combine sugar and cinnamon. Put aside half of this mixture for topping. In a food processor, combine remaining sugar mixture and flour. Cut in the butter until it resembles coarse crumbs. Combine egg, cream and browning and add to the flour mixture. Blend until mixture holds together. Chill for 20 minutes. Divide into four parts.

On floured baking paper roll out four 23 cm circles. Cut out and remove a 6 cm circle from the centre. Sprinkle each ring with 1 teaspoon of the sugar and cinnamon mixture. Place each ring of mixture on its paper on the turntable and microwave at Full power for 2 1/2–3 minutes or until lightly browned. Watch carefully to prevent burning.

Filling
6 large apples, peeled and sliced
3/4 cup sugar
1/4 cup flour
1 tsp cinnamon

Mix ingredients in a large covered dish. Microwave at Full power for 10–12 minutes or until tender and thickened.

To serve
Layer pastry rings and warm apple mixture on serving plate, starting and finishing with pastry. Cut carefully. Top each serving with whipped cream.
Variation:
Cook pastry in small squares. Layer three or four squares with apple for one serving.

C M Bread Pudding

This old-fashioned American dessert is rich and sinfully delicious!

For 4 servings:
25 g butter
75 g very dry bread (2 bread rolls)
3/4 cup milk
1/4 cup cream
1/2 cup sugar
1 egg
1 egg white
1 tsp vanilla
1/4 cup sultanas or currants
1/4 cup walnuts or almonds
1/4 tsp cinnamon
1/4 tsp mixed spice
1/4 tsp grated nutmeg

In a large bowl melt the butter at Full power for 1–2 minutes. Add bread, broken into small pieces. Stir in milk and cream, sugar, egg, egg white and vanilla. Press mixture to soften bread, then beat with fork to combine. Add the fruit, nuts and spices. The mixture should be firm enough to keep a rounded shape in four individual dishes. Microwave the dishes uncovered at Medium (50% power) for 8–10 minutes or until firm. Serve with rum or whisky sauce.

Sauce
50 g butter
3/4 cup icing sugar
1 egg yolk
2–3 Tbsp rum or whisky

In a medium-sized bowl melt the butter at Full power for 1 minute. Beat in the icing sugar and egg yolk. Microwave for 30 seconds or until the liquid bubbles around the edges. Cool, then stir in whisky or rum.

To cook this pudding in a conventional oven make these changes in the method:

Melt the butter in a saucepan. Remove from heat and add other ingredients as above.

Stand the individual dishes in a large pan of hot water and bake them, uncovered, for about 30 minutes, at 180°C, or until the centre feels firm.

Make the sauce in a small saucepan. Heat the butter until it bubbles, add the icing sugar and egg yolk and remove from heat immediately. Beat until smooth. Cool, and stir in the whisky or rum.

C M Chocolate Fudge Pudding

This is a real 'comfort' pudding. Nearly all my friends remember making it in their youth. I haven't met a child who doesn't like it, either.

I have worked out the simplest version I could think of. Hopefully, you won't be left with a kitchen full of dirty dishes, whatever the age of the cook.

For about 4 servings:
1 cup self-raising flour
2 Tbsp cocoa
1/4–1/2 cup sugar
1/2 cup milk
1/4 cup brown sugar
2 Tbsp cocoa
1 tsp instant coffee
1 Tbsp butter
1/4–1/2 cup chopped walnuts
1 tsp vanilla
1–1 1/2 cups boiling water

In a 20–23 cm flat-bottomed microwave casserole dish, fork together the flour, first measure of cocoa, and sugar, using the larger amount for a sweeter pudding. Stir in the milk to make a fairly stiff dough. Still using the fork, arrange the dough fairly evenly in a ring around the edge of the casserole dish, if microwaving, and stand a central tube insert or inverted glass in the middle.

If baking conventionally, spread the dough evenly over the bottom of the dish.

Rinse out and dry the cup measure. Use it to measure the brown sugar, then add to it the second measure of cocoa, and the instant coffee. Stir to mix, then sprinkle over the dough. Dot the butter evenly over the surface. Spread the nuts over this. Measure the vanilla into the cup. Pour the water on top of it then pour this carefully and evenly over everything. Add the extra water if the pudding will not be eaten immediately after cooking.

Cover and microwave at Full power for 8 minutes, or until springy all over the surface, or bake, uncovered at 180°C, for 20–30 minutes, or until dough has risen and is springy, too.

Serve hot or warm, with ice-cream.

C American Strawberry Shortcakes

Although you can use plain scones for these strawberry shortcakes, a richer, sweeter mixture is even nicer.

Add 3 tablespoons castor sugar to the plain scone recipe on page 231. Replace 1/4 cup milk with 1/4 cup cream (or sour cream if possible).

Pat mixture out to a rectangle 20 × 30 cm. Cut into 6 squares. Brush tops with melted butter. Bake at 220°C for about 10 minutes, until golden brown underneath.

Split and serve scones while warm. Spread each with strawberry jam, then fill and top each with sliced strawberries and whipped cream.

C M Steamed Carrot Pudding

Most steamed puddings microwave well though I have found a few of my low-fat recipes do not.

Experiment for yourself, remembering that a dry pudding is usually the result of overcooking. Use these instructions as a guide when you want to speed up the cooking of your own favourite steamed puddings.

For 6 servings:
Optional Topping
1 Tbsp butter, melted
1 Tbsp golden syrup
1/4 cup chopped walnuts

Pudding
100 g butter, melted
2 cups (200 g) grated carrot
1 egg
1 cup brown sugar
1 cup flour
3/4 tsp baking soda
1 tsp cinnamon

If using topping, combine ingredients in bottom of chosen container.

To mix pudding, melt butter in bowl or saucepan. Add finely grated carrot, egg, and brown sugar, and mix thoroughly with a fork. Fold in sifted dry ingredients. Mixture should be just thin enough to pour. Add extra flour or milk if necessary.

Cooking options
• Steam in a buttered 4–5 cup-capacity bowl, covered with lid, string-tied greaseproof paper, or foil with sides pressed down, for 2–2½ hours.
• Steam in a buttered metal or plastic ring mould covered with foil for 1–1½ hours.
• Steam as above, but uncovered, for 45–60 minutes, in a covered saucepan. (Pudding texture will be heavier and stickier.)
• Microwave in a plastic ring mould, covered with vented plastic film and elevated on an inverted plate, at Full power for 6 minutes, or until centre is cooked.

C M Apple Roly-Poly

This pudding never loses its popularity. This version is easy enough to make often.

For 4–6 servings:
1/4 cup sugar
2 Tbsp golden syrup
25 g butter
1 cup boiling water
1 1/4 cups self-raising flour
1/2 cup milk
2–3 apples, grated
2 Tbsp melted butter
2 Tbsp sugar

1 Tbsp flour
1 tsp cinnamon

In a 23 cm round or square baking dish, put the first measure of sugar, syrup, and cubed butter. Stir boiling water into this and put aside.

In a bowl, stir the flour and milk to a fairly stiff dough, using a little more flour or milk if needed. Roll out to about 25 × 30 cm.

Grate unpeeled apples and mix with remaining ingredients, in the same bowl, or in a food processor bowl.

Spread the apple mixture over the dough, leaving a strip on the far long side uncovered. Dampen strip with a little water. Roll up so damp strip seals the 'sausage'. Cut in 6–9 pieces, and place, cut side down, in the syrup.

Bake at 180°C for 45 minutes or until firm and golden-brown, basting with the syrup occasionally. Serve warm or hot.
Variations:
Cook without cutting into slices.

Microwave in a large covered ring pan at Full power for 5–6 minutes, or until firm near centre. Turn upside down to serve.

M 'Encore' Steamed Pudding

The colour, texture and flavour of the pudding will vary, depending on the cake being 'recycled'.

For 4–6 servings:
2 cups (200 g) crumbled, stale cake
1/2 cup flour
1/2 tsp baking soda
1/4 cup white or brown sugar
50 g cold butter
1/4–1/2 cup sultanas or currants (optional)
3/4–1 cup milk, juice, etc

In a food processor or mixing bowl, crumble the cake finely. Add flour, soda and sugar. Mix thoroughly. Cut or rub in butter. Add dried fruit, if desired. Stir in enough liquid to make a batter wet enough to pour into a lightly sprayed or buttered small ring mould. Cover with cling wrap. Place the mould on an inverted dinner plate and microwave at Full power for 5 minutes, or until firm.

Leave to stand for 2–3 minutes, then unmould.

C M Golden Queen Pudding

For 4–6 servings:
2 Tbsp butter
1 Tbsp custard powder
2 Tbsp peach syrup
1/4 cup golden syrup
2–3 cooked peach halves

1/4 cup walnut halves or pieces
2 cups self-raising flour
2 Tbsp custard powder
1 cup milk
2 Tbsp melted butter

In a small microwave ring pan melt the butter, then add the first measure of custard powder, peach syrup and golden syrup. Microwave at Full power for 1½ minutes, then place the peach halves (halved again), rounded side down, in the sauce. Sprinkle the walnuts between the peaches.

With a fork, toss the flour and custard powder together in a mixing bowl, then stir in the milk and melted butter to form a drop-scone dough.

Drop dough evenly, in spoonfuls, on top of the peaches and sauce, putting each second spoonful on the opposite side of the pan. Cover with a lid or vented plastic film.

Microwave at Full power for 4½–5 minutes, until dough feels firm. Leave for 2 minutes before turning out on to a serving plate.

Alternatively, place mixture in ring pan as described, and steam this, uncovered, on a rack over boiling water in a covered saucepan for 45 minutes or until centre feels firm.

C M Mini Peach Puddings

You can modify the preceding recipe to produce 1 large or 2 small servings. Use 2 teacups (without metal trim) or 1 large, wide breakfast cup, or a wide Pyrex measuring cup, as a pudding mould.

In 1 cup melt 2 teaspoons butter. Add 1 teaspoon custard powder, peach syrup and 1 tablespoon golden syrup and microwave at Full power for 45 seconds. (Divide between 2 cups.)

Cut a peach half into smaller pieces if desired. Arrange in syrup with chopped walnuts. Mix ½ cup self-raising flour, 2 teaspoons custard powder and milk to a drop-scone consistency. Place on top of peaches.

Microwave at Full power (equidistant from middle of oven if in 2 cups) for 1½ minutes. Leave 1 minute before unmoulding.

Alternatively, steam, uncovered, in boiling water in a covered saucepan for 20 minutes or until centre feels firm.

Golden Queen Pudding

ᴄ Sultana Dumplings

For 4 servings:
2 cups water
¼ cup golden syrup
2 Tbsp butter
½ tsp vanilla
½ tsp rum essence (optional)
1¼ cups self-raising flour
½ cup sultanas
½ cup milk
2 Tbsp melted butter

Measure the first five ingredients into a frying pan with a lid, and make a syrup by bringing this mixture to the boil.

Put the flour into a bowl, then add sultanas, milk and melted butter, using a little more or less milk if necessary, to make a soft scone dough. Pat mixture into a square, then cut into nine pieces.

Drop dumplings gently into the syrup. Cover frying pan tightly, adjust heat so mixture is boiling gently, but does not boil over, and cook for about 15 minutes. Do not lift the lid to look at dumplings until they have cooked for 10 minutes.

Variation:
Replace 1 cup water with apple or orange juice.

Ice-Cream Custard

Creamy Custards

Don't forget about custards!

Creamy and smooth, custards are 'comfort foods' many of us associate with our childhood.

Custards may be thickened by different means: flour, cornflour, eggs, or combinations of these ingredients.

Microwaving Custard

Stirred microwaved custard doesn't cook any more quickly than custard cooked in a pot, but you benefit in other ways.
1. You won't have a sticky-bottomed pot to clean.
2. You set the cooking time, so your custard will stop cooking even if you get called away.
3. You don't have to stir the custard all the time.
4. Microwaved custards are as smooth as velvet!

Custard Sauce

Mix together 2 tablespoons brown sugar and 2 tablespoons custard powder before adding 1–1½ cups milk and 1 tablespoon butter.

Microwave at Full power for 2–3 minutes until mixture bubbles or rises all round the sides of the 2–3 cup bowl or jug.

Stir thoroughly with a wooden spoon or whisk. Mixture will seem unevenly lumpy at first, but will thicken to a beautifully smooth sauce after about a minute of stirring.

Simon's Custard

For twenty years the mothers of young children have told me how useful they have found this recipe.

For 3–4 servings:
1–1½ Tbsp cornflour
2 tsp white or brown sugar
1½ cups milk
2 egg yolks
1–2 tsp butter

Mix the cornflour and sugar together in a 1 litre measuring bowl/cup. Add enough milk to blend them to a smooth paste, then break in the egg yolks. Mix well. Add the rest of the milk, then the pieces of butter.

Microwave at Full power for 5–6 minutes, stirring after 3, 4 and 5 minutes. When it is cooked, the whole surface of the custard should have bubbled up. Take it out of the oven and stir well.

Or cook in a saucepan over moderate heat stirring constantly. As soon as custard boils around the edge, cool pot quickly, by standing in cold water.

Note:
Use the smaller quantity of cornflour if you want a custard thin enough to pour.

Variations:
Replace the cornflour with vanilla custard powder.

Use one whole egg instead of two egg yolks for children old enough to eat whole egg.

Ice-Cream Custard

Serve this old-fashioned custard with stewed fruit or give it a new look with raw fruit salad.

For 4–6 servings:
3 Tbsp butter
3 Tbsp flour
2½ cups milk
2 eggs
3 Tbsp brown sugar
½ tsp vanilla

Melt butter, add flour and cook gently for 2 minutes. Add three half cup portions of milk, stirring and boiling between additions. In a bowl beat together with a fork the last half cup of milk, the eggs, brown (or white) sugar and vanilla.

Add hot sauce to bowl, stirring constantly. When mixed, pour back into saucepan and bring to boil.

Remove from heat. Cover surface with plastic film until ready to use.

Chocolate Pudding

For 4 servings:
¼ cup cocoa
¼ cup sugar
3 Tbsp cornflour or custard powder
2 cups milk
½ tsp vanilla
1 Tbsp butter
1 egg

Stir together the cocoa, sugar and cornflour. Using a whisk, gradually stir in the milk. Add vanilla.

Microwave at Full power for 6 minutes, stirring after 3, 4 and 5 minutes. After whole surface of custard has bubbled, add butter and stir until it is melted. Break egg on top of pudding, then quickly whisk it into the mixture.

Microwave for 1 minute or until custard bubbles again. Beat thoroughly with a whisk. Cover surface with cling wrap to prevent skin forming.

'Baked' Custard

For successful baked custards preheat the milk, using individual dishes and low power levels.

For 4 servings:
2 cups milk
¼ cup sugar
pinch salt
3 eggs, beaten
1 tsp vanilla
ground nutmeg

Microwave milk at Full power for about 5 minutes or until hot. Stir in sugar, salt, eggs and vanilla. Beat briefly. Pour through sieve into 4 individual serving dishes and sprinkle with nutmeg.

Stand in baking dish with hot water 1 cm deep. Microwave at Medium (50% power) for about 8–15 minutes or until centres are just set. (Cooking time varies.)

Ⓜ Caramel Custard

Serve with peaches, or over sherry-sprinkled sponge to make trifle.

For 4 servings:
¼ cup brown sugar
¼ cup custard powder
2 cups milk
1 tsp vanilla
2 Tbsp butter

Mix the brown sugar and custard powder thoroughly in a fairly large bowl. Stir in milk and vanilla. Add butter and microwave at Full power for 6 minutes, stirring after 3, 4 and 5 minutes. Custard should bubble over whole surface. Cover.

Serve warm or at room temperature. Add an egg or egg yolk with the milk, if desired.
Variations:
For Banana Custard, stir in 1–2 thinly sliced ripe bananas when custard is bath temperature.

Ⓜ Moulded Caramel Custard

For 2 servings:
Caramel layer
2 Tbsp sugar
2 tsp water

Custard
¾ cup milk
1 Tbsp sugar
1 large egg
¼ tsp vanilla

Put 1 tablespoon of sugar and 1 teaspoon of water in two heat-resistant glass custard cups. Microwave at Full power for 2–3 minutes, until light brown. (As soon as you smell caramel, stop cooking it!) Tilt custard cups to line with caramel.

In a litre-sized measuring jug heat milk and sugar until very hot but not boiling (1–1½ minutes). Add egg and vanilla and beat until thoroughly mixed. Pour through a sieve into custard cups.

Microwave at Defrost (30% power) for 4 minutes, or until custards have barely set. Reposition them once or twice, so they cook evenly.

Refrigerate for 1 hour or longer. Unmould.
Note:
At lower power levels waterbath is not necessary.

Instant Banana Nut Custard

Ⓤ Instant Banana-Nut Custard

It is worth experimenting with 'instant' concoctions when time is short. Here is one of my favourites.

For 4 servings:
1 tsp instant coffee
2 tsp hot water
1½ cups milk
½ cup cream
1 pkt chocolate or butterscotch or vanilla instant pudding
¼–½ cup cream, whipped
1–2 bananas sliced
2 Tbsp finely chopped nuts

Put the first four ingredients, in the order given, into a bowl. Add the instant pudding and beat until thick.

Beat the second measure of cream using whichever quantity you like.

Fold the whipped cream, sliced bananas and chopped nuts into the pudding as it is thickening. Pile into individual dishes.

Serve chilled or at room temperature, within an hour.

Ⓜ Curds and Whey

I was fascinated when, as a small child, I realised that 'curds and whey' was another name for junket. Don't forget this old-fashioned pudding, loved by many children.

For 4 servings:
2 cups milk
2 Tbsp brown sugar
½ tsp vanilla
¼ tsp almond essence
1 tsp rennet

Heat milk, sugar, and flavourings to blood heat (about 2 minutes in microwave for refrigerated milk). Junket will not set if milk is too hot or cold.

Add rennet and stir for 5–10 seconds, then pour into individual dishes and leave to stand at room temperature to set. Refrigerate only when firm.

Decorate with thick or whipped cream, sliced bananas, and freshly grated nutmeg.
Variations:
Flavour and sweeten milk to taste, with instant coffee, Milo, etc. before adding rennet. The best-known brand of rennet is Renco.

▣ Tamarillo Cream

For 4 servings:
4 tamarillos, halved
½ cup brown sugar
¼ cup sugar
2 tsp gelatine
1 cup cream
½ tsp vanilla

Cut the stem end of each unpeeled tamarillo. Cut each lengthwise. Place halves in a flat-bottomed casserole, cut surface down. Cover and microwave at Full power for 2–4 minutes or until skins lift. Remove skins.

Sprinkle the sugars over the tamarillos. Purée with potato masher. Heat briefly until sugar dissolves, if necessary. Cool.

Sprinkle with gelatine, leave for 2–3 minutes, then stir. Microwave for 1 minute, stirring until gelatine melts. Cool over ice and water until cold and beginning to thicken.

In another bowl beat the cream and vanilla until thick. Fold the cream into the tamarillos. Pile into stemmed glasses or individual dessert dishes and serve. Garnish with slices of fresh tamarillo.

Variations:
Stir in 2 cups plain yoghurt instead of cream.

Place more cold, cooked tamarillos in serving dishes, underneath the tamarillo cream.

▣ Fruit Salad Sago

For 4 servings:
¼ cup sago
1 cup water
1 cup fruit juice, made up with a little water or sherry if necessary
½ cup sugar
1 cup drained pineapple pieces
1 cup drained peach slices
2 passionfruit (optional)
1–2 bananas, sliced

In a medium-sized bowl, add the water to the sago and leave to stand for 15 minutes. Microwave at Full power for 3 minutes. Add the other liquid, stir and cook for 5 minutes longer. Add the fruit and allow to stand for 10–15 minutes, then spoon into individual serving dishes.

Serve with cream. This pudding is best served warm, within 2 hours. Longer standing makes it rather tough, and spoils the flavour.

Variation:
Replace sago with quick-cooking tapioca.

Clockwise from left: Fruit Salad Sago, Tamarillo Cream and Tapioca Cream

▣ Sago or Tapioca Cream

For 4 servings:
¼ cup sago or quick-cooking tapioca
2 cups milk
¼ tsp vanilla
⅛ tsp salt
¼ cup sugar
1 egg, separated

Mix the sago and milk in a large bowl or casserole. Cook uncovered at Full power for 10–12 minutes, stirring every 2–3 minutes until sago is tender. (Note: bowl must be large and uncovered or the mixture will boil over.)

Stir in vanilla, salt, 3 tablespoons of the sugar, and the egg yolk, putting aside the egg white in another bowl. Microwave sago mixture for 3 minutes, stirring each minute, until bubbling.

Beat egg white until foamy. Add remaining tablespoon of sugar. Beat until peaks turn over.

Fold the beaten egg white into the hot sago and serve warm, plain or layered with whipped cream, mashed kiwifruit, strawberries, etc.

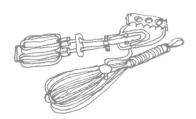

▣ Rhubarb Sago

For 4 servings:
¼ cup sago
1½ cups hot tap water
500 g (4 cups) chopped rhubarb
½ cup sugar

Put the sago and hot tap water into a covered dish about 23 cm in diameter. Cover and microwave at Full power for 3–4 minutes or until sago mixture has thickened and nearly all the grains of sago have gone clear.

Stir in the rhubarb, chopped into short (1 cm) lengths, and the sugar. Cover again and microwave for 3 minutes, then stir well. Microwave for 3–4 minutes longer until all rhubarb pieces are hot. Leave to stand for 5 minutes — rhubarb should finish cooking in this time.

▣ Caramel Bananas

For 4 servings:
3–4 medium firm bananas
2 Tbsp butter
¼ cup packed brown sugar
½ tsp cinnamon
2 Tbsp cream
¼ tsp rum essence or 2 Tbsp rum
¼ cup chopped walnuts

Slice bananas in half, both lengthwise and crosswise.

Place butter in a casserole and microwave at Full power for 30 seconds or until melted. Add the sugar, spice and cream, stir and heat for 1½–2 minutes, or until slightly thickened. Stir in rum or essence.

Add the bananas, turning each to coat with sauce. Microwave again for 30 seconds and serve sprinkled with nuts.

▣ Gooseberry Fool

Tart fruit loses its sharpness when it is thickened and mixed with thick cream. You can alter the proportions of sugar and cream to suit your own taste.

For 6 servings:
500 g young green gooseberries
½ cup sugar
1 Tbsp cornflour or custard powder
2 Tbsp water or wine
1 (150 g) bottle double cream

Microwave gooseberries and sugar at Full power until mushy. Gooseberries may be frozen or fresh, and need not be 'topped and tailed'.

Stir in cornflour and water paste immediately, so mixture thickens. Purée briefly in food processor, then bang or press through sieve, back into cooking container and leave to cool.

Tip cream into food processor bowl. Process briefly, add purée and process until the two mixtures are combined.

Spoon mixture into six stemmed glass dishes and serve at room temperature.

▣ Stewed Fruit

Fruit stews well in a microwave oven, with very good flavour and texture.

For preference, use a flat-bottomed round casserole dish with a lid. For small quantities, stew fruit in a ring pan. This gives even results.

You will find that soft fruits with a high water content will cook well with no added water. Add sugar to taste afterwards, stirring gently until it dissolves. Or, cook a small amount of syrup first, then cook the fruit in this until it is tender.

If you want fruit to keep its shape, stew it at a lower power level for a longer time.

For a thickened fruit mixture, mix fruit, sugar and thickening together (e.g. fruit pie filling) or prepare the sweetened, thickened sauce, then cook the fruit in it as in Rhubarb Sago.

Coconut Ice-Cream

Most of the old ice-cream recipes I have are based on a rich custard and are churned as they freeze.

I have modified both the custard and the mixing in this recipe, and use a food processor instead of a churn, to produce a rich, coconut ice-cream which makes a delicious finish to a formal or special family meal.

For 4–6 servings:
1 tsp gelatine
1 Tbsp water
2 eggs
¼ cup brown or white sugar
1 (410 g) can coconut cream
about ¼ cup double cream
¼–½ tsp almond or other essence

Mix the gelatine and water in a small container. Mix the eggs and sugar together in a medium to large saucepan. Add the coconut cream made up to 2 cups with cream.

Fill the sink with cold water.

Heat the egg mixture very carefully over moderate heat (or stand it in a frying pan of hot water), stirring all the time with a whisk. As soon as the mixture thickens and starts to bubble around the edges, lift it off the heat and stand it in the cold water, still stirring.

Add the soaked gelatine and the essence, using the flavour you like best with coconut (e.g. rum, pineapple, or almond) tasting the custard to judge the strength of flavour.

Pour into a metal cake tin, cover and freeze until solid. When solid, turn out on to a board, cut quickly into 2 cm chunks, and food process (using the metal chopping blade) until smooth and creamy, adding extra chilled cream or coconut cream if mixture does not turn creamy when processed. Cover.

Refreeze until firm enough to keep its shape when scooped. Serve in small scoops, topped with toasted coconut, passionfruit pulp, fresh or canned pineapple, etc.

Easy Ice-Cream

This ice-cream is so rich that it doesn't need to be mixed in any way after freezing, because it never freezes rock hard.

For 4–6 servings:
2 eggs, separated
½ cup sugar
1 Tbsp warm water
1 (300 ml) bottle cream
½ tsp vanilla

Beat egg whites in a large bowl until peaks turn over. Add half the sugar and beat again.

Beat yolks and water in a small bowl until frothy. Add remaining sugar and beat until thick and light.

Whip the cream in the container you will freeze the ice-cream in. Add vanilla, then fold the three mixtures together. Cover and freeze.

Variation:
Replace vanilla with other essence, puréed fruit, passionfruit pulp, dissolved instant coffee, small pieces of chocolate, brandy or rum, etc. using amounts to suit yourself.

Instant Ice-Cream

This ice-cream is ready to eat 1 minute after you start making it.

Either freeze the fruit or berry of your choice in packets containing 2 cups, or buy frozen berries.

Start with strawberry ice-cream, then experiment with cubed peaches and other berries.

For 3–4 servings:
2 cups frozen strawberries, etc.
½ cup icing sugar
about ½ cup chilled cream, milk, yoghurt, or soya milk

Chop frozen berries into smaller pieces if necessary. Fruit must be frozen hard, free-flow and in 1–2 cm cubes. Tip into food processor bowl. Work quickly to keep fruit very cold.

Process with metal chopping blade until fruit is finely chopped (10–20 seconds). This is a noisy operation. Add icing sugar and process until mixed. Gradually add the chilled liquid of your choice through the feed-tube, using just enough to form a smooth cream. Stop as soon as mixture is evenly textured and creamy, cleaning the sides of the processor bowl once or twice.

Serve immediately.

Tofu-Fruit Whip

When you mix puréed fruit and tofu, you get a thick, amazingly smooth and delicious, pudding-like mixture.

Adjust the flavouring carefully, top with some toasted flaked almonds, and you have a popular, cholesterol-free, almost instant dessert.

For 2–4 servings:
175–250 g fresh apricots, strawberries, bananas or drained canned fruit
250–300 g tofu
about 1 cup orange juice or white wine/water mixture
2 Tbsp brown sugar
¼–½ tsp vanilla

Chop the fruit into a food processor

or blender. Process until it forms a fairly smooth purée. Crumble in the tofu and process for about a minute, until very smooth, before gradually adding enough orange juice or wine and water to thin the mixture to the consistency you want. Add sugar to taste. Add the vanilla.

Serve immediately, or refrigerate.

Marshmallow Pavlova

This doesn't have a crisp crust, but it has a lovely marshmallow texture.

For 4–6 servings:
4 egg whites
¼ tsp salt
1 cup castor sugar
1 tsp wine vinegar
1 tsp vanilla

In an electric mixer, beat whites with salt until soft peaks form. Add sugar gradually, over 2–3 minutes, then vinegar and vanilla.

Pile meringue on to a flat plate. Stand this on an inverted plate. Microwave at Full power for 3 minutes. Leave to stand in oven to cool or transfer to conventional oven and brown top under the grill. Leave to cool in the oven with the door ajar. When cold, decorate as desired.

Note:
Pavlova may split while baking. Splits close on standing. Some syrup will leak from pavlova on standing.

Variation:
Slide pavlova on top of a cooked pie.

Fruit Toppings

Not long ago, when you saw a thick, creamy liquid being poured over fruit, you could be fairly sure it was lightly whipped cream.

Not any longer! With the wide range of creamy products now available, it is possible to use convenience products exactly as you buy them, so you don't have to use an egg beater.

You can choose very low-fat toppings (e.g. low-fat yoghurt), enjoy interestingly soured products (such as sour cream) or spoon on really thick cream, enjoying its richness.

You can make many variations of your own by combining two or more of these products.

For example, try beating cream cheese, quark or ricotta with yoghurt or milk, adding flavourings to suit yourself.

Stop when the texture and flavour is exactly as you want it.

Double cream mixed with fruit-flavoured yoghurt makes a thick topping with a good flavour.

Coconut Ice-Cream

C **Citrus Syllabub**

For 8 servings:
1 lemon
1 orange
¹/₂–³/₄ cup sugar
2 cups cream

Grate the citrus rinds. Place in a saucepan with the squeezed juice of both fruit, and the sugar (according to desired sweetness).

Heat until the sugar is dissolved, then cool to room temperature.

Mix cream and cooled syrup and beat until soft peaks form. Pour into serving dish and chill in a freezer for about 2 hours. If mixture freezes solid transfer to the refrigerator 30–45 minutes before serving.

c Crêpes

These thin, delicate, tender pancakes are made in a small pan. As long as they are kept from drying out, they may be made ahead and refrigerated or frozen until required.

For about 12 small crêpes
2 eggs
¾ cup milk
½ cup flour
½ tsp salt

Combine ingredients in order given, in a food processor or blender. If mixing in a bowl, add egg then milk to dry ingredients and beat until smooth. Pour a measured quantity (e.g. 2 tablespoons) into a smooth, sprayed or buttered, preheated pan.

Immediately tilt pan so batter covers bottom in a thin film. If batter does not spread thinly, add more milk to thin batter before making the next crêpe. Do not worry if pancakes are not evenly shaped circles.

When batter no longer looks wet in the centre, ease edges of crêpe from pan. Lift carefully with fingers, over wooden stirrer if desired. Dry second side, without necessarily browning it. Remove from pan. Stack crêpes until required. Place them on a plate in plastic bag to prevent drying out.

Sweet Fillings and Filling Suggestions

Cooked apples, peaches, pears, feijoas in thickened juices, with or without spices, with or without toasted nuts. Roll and sprinkle with sugar and brown under grill, or fold into parcels, fry until crisp, serve with sour cream, or with concentrated apple juice.

• Sprinkle with lemon juice and castor sugar. Roll and serve while still warm, or sprinkle with sugar, and brown under grill.

• Fill freshly made pancakes with lightly sugared fresh fruit such as strawberries, raspberries, blueberries, kiwifruit, peaches, pineapple, or add honey to fruit. Roll and serve sprinkled with icing sugar, with whipped cream and ice-cream.

• Fill with bananas, whole, sliced lengthways or crosswise, sautéed in brown sugar, orange juice (and a little rum if desired). Roll and serve plain, or sprinkle with sugar and brown under grill.

• Spread with jam or ice-cream or whipped cream. Roll. Soak chopped dried apricots. Sweeten, purée, mix with whipped cream or cream cheese and spread on pancakes, then roll up.

• Mix cream cheese, cottage cheese, quark or ricotta cheese with chopped cherries, toasted nuts, ginger, candied pineapple, etc. Spread on pancakes, then roll, or fold pancake round filling and sauté in butter. Serve with sour cream or thinned jam sauce.

• Sauté raisins or sultanas in butter. Add toasted nuts and orange juice and thicken slightly. Roll or fold pancakes and sauté in this sauce. Serve with sour cream.

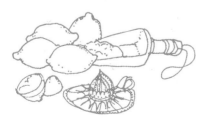

• Fill with lemon or passionfruit honey and ice-cream. Roll up. Dust with icing sugar.

• Fill with mincemeat, plain or mixed with stewed apple. Roll or fold and sauté. Serve with whipped cream or ice-cream and use concentrated apple juice as sauce.

• Spread pancakes with thick coconut syrup mixed with shredded or flaked toasted coconut. Roll up. Serve with ice-cream.

• Spread with hazelnut-chocolate mixture. Sprinkle with toasted almonds or hazelnuts. Roll. Serve warm.

• Fill with whipped cream, ricotta or quark mixed with grated dark chocolate. Serve with a coffee sauce or concentrated apple juice.

• Add liqueurs, brandy or rum to previous fillings, or pour a little over pancakes instead of sauces.

• Spoon on cherry pie filling (or other pie fillings). Roll up. Use almond-flavoured liqueur as sauce.

• Drop folded pancakes into hot concentrated fruit syrups. Turn. Serve hot with cream or ice-cream.

The first few times you make crêpes, you may find that you use up a lot of crêpe batter before your crêpes are acceptable.

You will improve with practice, and will soon notice whether your mixture is too thick or too thin.

Even when crêpes are rather oddly shaped, you can still use them to roll, fold in quarters, or as a folded wrapping. Their imperfections are unlikely to be noticed in situations like this.

Pancake First-Aid

Pancakes sticking
Clean pan thoroughly. Rub with dry salt on paper towel. Spray, butter or oil the surface, heat pan, polish with paper towel, spray etc. again, heat again, add more batter.

Batter doesn't set
Pan not hot enough. Batter too thick. Not enough eggs in batter.

Batter burns on bottom
Pan too hot. Too much sugar in batter.

Pancake stodgy and thick
Batter too thick. Add 1–2 teaspoons milk, mix again, and try another pancake.

Pancakes too thin, breaking when lifted
Batter too thin. Add another egg to it.

Pancakes of uneven thickness
Tilt and swirl pan fast to spread evenly. Thin down the batter.

Crisp-edged pancakes
Overcooked or cooked in too much oil, butter, etc. Don't add extra oil, etc. between pancakes unless they stick.

Variations to Pancake Batter

• Use 1 egg instead of 2. Add milk to reach desired batter consistency.

• For economy, use only 1 egg, and add an extra ¼ cup flour. Thin mixture with extra milk.

• Replace all, or part of the milk in the original recipe with yoghurt, cream, water, beer, orange juice etc., to vary the flavour. Milk produces a slightly firmer pancake, and water a more tender one.

• Add 1–2 teaspoons sugar to sweeten the batter for sweet fillings, if desired. Sugar makes the pancakes brown more quickly.

• Flavour the batter by adding chopped fresh herbs, Parmesan cheese, grated lemon or orange rind, almond or vanilla essence, etc.

C Easy Crêpes Suzette

If you make the crêpes ahead and freeze them, and make and cook the sauce ingredients whenever it suits you on the day of a special dinner, you can produce this elegant dessert with the minimum last-minute effort.

Sauce for about 12 cooked crêpes:
75 g butter, melted
grated rind and juice of 1 orange
juice of ½ lemon
½ cup sugar
1 Tbsp orange liqueur (optional)

Combine all the sauce ingredients in the order given, in a fairly large, heavy pan.

Heat, stirring frequently, until the sugar has dissolved and the sauce is quite thick.

Fold each crêpe in half. Drop, one at a time, into the syrup, and once coated, fold in half again and push to the side of the pan. Repeat with remaining pancakes.

When pan looks crowded, remove the first two or three, putting them on a plate for serving. Garnish with a twist of orange rind if desired.

M Cheesecake Tarts

For about 20 tarts:
1 Tbsp butter
½ cup malt biscuit crumbs
*1 can (400 g) sweetened condensed
    milk*
2 eggs, lightly beaten
6 Tbsp lemon juice
grated rind of 1 lemon
about 20 paper cupcake liners

In a small bowl melt butter at Full power for 30 seconds. Stir in crumbs. (Mixture will be fairly dry.) In another, bigger bowl, mix together the condensed milk, eggs, lemon juice and finely grated lemon rind.

Place 1 rounded household teaspoon of crumbs in each of 15 cupcake liners. Put 5 or 6 of these into microwave cupcake pans. Press crumbs evenly, then top with 2–3 tablespoons of the filling.

Microwave at Medium (50% power) until filling is firm in centre, about 2–3 minutes. Lift from pan and cool. Cook other tarts as above.

Refrigerate or keep in cool place up to 48 hours. Serve topped with whipped cream and a cherry, strawberry, sliced kiwifruit or other fresh berries.
Note:
6 tablespoons equals ³/₈ cup.

M Upside-Down Cake

Upside-down cakes cook best in lined ring pans with straight sides.

For 6 servings:
Topping
2 Tbsp butter
2–3 Tbsp golden syrup
6–8 pineapple rings
6–8 cherries

Line a 23-cm-round pan with a cut-open oven bag so topping will not stick to the pan. Place a glass in the centre. Melt butter in the pan at Full power for about 30 seconds, then dribble the golden syrup evenly over the butter. Arrange the pineapple in a circle. Halve the cherries and place in and around pineapple rings.

Cake
50 g butter
½ cup brown sugar
1 tsp vanilla
½ tsp cinnamon
1 egg
1¼ cups flour
2 tsp baking powder
pineapple juice or milk

In a mixing bowl, melt the butter. Add the brown sugar, vanilla, cinnamon and egg and beat until light. Sift the flour and baking powder into the mixture with nearly ½ cup of juice from the pineapple. Add extra juice and/or milk to make a soft drop batter. Do not overmix.

Spoon batter over pineapple rings. Cover pan lightly with cling wrap. Stand pan on an inverted dinner plate. Microwave at Full power for about 6 minutes, until batter has set, or for more even cooking, microwave at Medium (50% power) for about 12 minutes. Leave for 5 minutes, remove the glass and invert on to serving plate.

C Apple Cheesecake

This isn't the quickest of recipes, but it is worth a little effort. Make it several hours ahead, if you like, and reheat to serve warm, but not hot.

For a 23 cm cake:
1½ cups flour
100 g butter
4–5 apples
¼ cup sugar
1 tsp cinnamon
¼ cup sultanas
125 g cream cheese
125 g sour cream
2 eggs
2 Tbsp sugar
½ cup orange juice.

Cut the butter finely into the flour. Press into a loose-bottomed 23-cm-square pan.

Cut each peeled apple into 16–20 wedges. Stand in lightly salted water to prevent browning. Arrange overlapping wedges on crumb mixture.

Sprinkle with first measure of sugar, the cinnamon and sultanas. Cover with foil and bake at 200°C for 15–30 minutes, until apples are tender.

Soften cream cheese, blend thoroughly with remaining ingredients. Pour over hot apple mixture. Sprinkle with extra sugar and cinnamon if desired.

Bake at 150°C for 15 minutes or until custard sets.

C Passionfruit Cream Pie

This rich passionfruit cream pie is one of the nicest desserts I have ever made. It can be made and refrigerated 8–24 hours before it is needed.

For 8 servings:
Filling
½ cup fresh passionfruit pulp
¾ cup sugar
¾ cup water
1 lemon jelly
1 (250 g) carton cream cheese
1 cup cream, whipped

Crust
*1 cup wine biscuit crumbs (about ½
    pkt biscuts, crumbled)*
50 g butter

Measure the passionfruit pulp, sugar and water into a medium-sized saucepan and bring to the boil. Add the jelly crystals, remove the pan from the heat and stir until crystals dissolve. If necessary warm the saucepan gently to dissolve all crystals, but do not heat more than necessary. Cool to room temperature.

Soften the cream cheese by beating with a fork or wooden spoon in a mixing bowl. Sieve jelly mixture into the cream cheese, pressing through all the pulp from around the seeds, but leaving seeds themselves. Beat until smooth, then chill until quite cold, and partly set.

Whip cream and fold into the partly set jelly. Pour into prepared crust, and leave to set in the refrigerator. Cover with plastic film as soon as filling is firm enough.

To make crust, crush the biscuits, and soften the butter. Stir crumbs and butter together then press the mixture on to the bottom of a pie plate or loose-bottomed cake tin about 23 cm in diameter.

Decorate just before serving with stiffly whipped cream.
Variation:
Serve the filling (without extra gelatine) in small individual dishes instead of pouring it into a pie shell, if desired. Used like this, the filling will make six rather than eight servings.

C Spiced Apple Shortcake

For about 9 servings:

First make the filling.

Mix in a frying pan ½ cup brown sugar, 2 teaspoons mixed spice and ½ teaspoon ground cloves. Add ½ cup orange juice (or orange juice substitute) then add three large apples, peeled, cored, and cut in small cubes. As soon as mixture boils, thicken with 1 tablespoon custard powder mixed with a little water. Remove from heat and cool to room temperature.

To make shortcake, cream 125 g butter with ½ cup sugar. Add 1 egg, beat briefly, then stir in 1 cup of self-raising flour and 1 cup plain flour.

Halve dough and chill one piece in the freezer. Press the remaining dough into a 23-cm-square tin lined with greaseproof paper (if you have a loose-bottomed tin, use it, without a paper lining).

Spiced Apple Shortcake

Spread the cold apple mixture over the shortcake. Grate the remaining, chilled shortcake mixture over the apple filling.

Bake at 180°C for about 45 minutes, until shortcake is cooked in the middle.

Cut in 9–12 pieces, freezing pieces which are not required for immediate use.

Serve warm.
Variation:
Add ¼–½ cup sultanas with the cubed apple.

Bread and Baking

There is nothing quite so welcoming as opening the front door and being greeted by the warm and friendly aroma of baking.

At times, all you want is something that you can make faster than your family can eat it — a recipe as easy as possible, that you can mix in a saucepan, and drop quickly on oven trays, and bake with little fuss.

At other times, however, you may decide to make something very special, to impress your friends.

You may feel in the mood to cook very traditionally, the way your mother did, or you may want to use all the machines in your kitchen to help you streamline the whole procedure.

Whatever situation applies to you, a good recipe is important. For baking you need to measure carefully, and follow the instructions precisely, if you want consistent results.

I'm sure that you will find that the pleasure of the recipients of your baking makes your effort worthwhile!

Ⓒ Basic Bread Rolls

When you ask friends to dinner, bake hot rolls to turn a simple meal into something exciting!

Breadmaking does take a while from start to finish but you can do many other things while the bread is rising and cooking.

For 12–16 rolls:
2 tsp dried yeast granules
1 Tbsp sugar
½ cup warm water
50 g butter
1 cup milk
1–1½ tsp salt
about 3 cups white or 1½ cups white and 1½ cups wholemeal flour

As soon as you think about making bread, mix the yeast, sugar and lukewarm water in a large mixing bowl. Leave in a warm place until frothy and bubbly, from 5–15 minutes.

Meantime, melt the butter, add the milk and salt, and warm to the same temperature as the yeast mixture. Add the milk mixture and 2½ cups of flour to the bubbly yeast, and beat well with a wooden spoon for about 30 seconds. Cover the bowl with plastic film or a plastic bag, and put it in a warm place until it rises to twice its original size.

Stir the mixture, then add just enough flour to make a dough which is soft enough to turn out on to the bench or a table to knead.

To knead, push the dough away from you with the heel of one hand, then collect it, and bring it back towards you with your other hand. Make sure you push the dough really hard.

Sprinkle just enough flour on the bench to stop the dough sticking. The longer you knead the dough the easier it will be to handle. It will become smooth and satiny, but should not stick to the bench.

Cut the kneaded dough into 12–16 pieces. Shape each piece as you like, making balls, or long pencil shapes which you can knot or twist or plait.

Place the shaped rolls on a lightly greased or sprayed oven tray or cake tin, leaving room for them to rise. Cover them loosely with oiled plastic, stand the tray over a sink of warm water if it is cold, and leave the rolls until they are 1½ times the size they were when you shaped them.

To make them shine, brush them very lightly with beaten egg. Sprinkle with poppy seeds, sesame seeds, or grated cheese, if you like, then bake in a hot oven, at 230°C for about 10 minutes, or until golden brown.

Eat warm, or reheat, or freeze as soon as they are cold.

Ⓒ Pita Bread (Pocket Bread)

This bread is fun to cook, since each flat circle of dough puffs up like a balloon, in 1–2 minutes.

The cooled, deflated balls of bread are cut in half to form pockets which can be filled with anything you like. They may also be frozen for later use.

1½ tsp dried yeast granules
2 tsp sugar
1 cup warm water
1 Tbsp corn or soya oil
2–3 cups flour
1 tsp salt

Mix the yeast, sugar and water and leave in a warm place to bubble.

Stir in the oil then enough flour to form a dough firm enough to knead. Use all white or 1½ cups wholemeal flour, with ½–1½ cups white flour.

Knead until smooth and springy then place in an oiled plastic bag, and leave to rise to about 1½ times its original size.

While the dough rises, turn the oven on to heat to its highest temperature. Put the oven-slide, on which the bread will cook, in the middle of the oven, and, if you have a cast-iron pan with a heat-resistant handle, put it on the rack underneath. Each circle of bread must be slid quickly on to a hot oven-slide to cook. A heavy-weight hot pan just underneath the oven-slide helps to keep it hot.

When the dough has risen, add the salt to it. Knead it again, then cut into pieces of golf ball size. Using just enough flour to prevent sticking, roll each piece out to form a circle the thickness of a 50-cent piece. By the time the last piece has been rolled out, the oven should be very hot, and the first bread ready to be cooked.

Slip the bottom of a loose-bottomed pan or a piece of cardboard, under the bread which was rolled out first, and, opening the oven for as short a time as possible, slide it on to the pre-heated tray. Within a minute the bread should puff up, and within another minute the crust should be set. Remove it from the oven, and slide in another bread circle. Put the cooked bread into an ovenbag or plastic bag so it will not dry out. Cut each circle to make a pocket when cool.

Note:
If the first pita breads cooked do not puff, leave the rest to stand for 5 or 10 minutes longer, before cooking them. Cook two or three pita breads together if you want to.
Pita breads should be light in colour. If you leave them to brown, they become crisp, and lose their flexibility.

Ⓒ Ⓜ Fruit Braid

It is fun to plait strips of yeast dough to enclose a fruit filling. The end result looks both professional and beautiful.

1 tsp dried yeast granules
1 tsp sugar
¼ cup warm water
25 g butter
½ cup milk
½ tsp salt
about 2 cups flour

Filling
½ cup chopped dates
¼ cup walnuts
¼ cup sultanas
2 Tbsp brown sugar
¼ cup orange juice
1 tsp orange rind
2 tsp wine vinegar
¼ tsp salt

Process yeast, sugar and warm water in food processor bowl. When bubbly melt butter (microwave at Full power for 30 seconds) add milk and salt and heat (microwave at Full power for 30 seconds) until lukewarm.

Add to yeast with 1 cup flour. Process for 10 seconds then leave to rise until double bulk, about 30 minutes. Add enough extra flour (about 1 cup) to form ball of dough in processor. Turn dough on to work-top. Knead until smooth and satiny, adding just enough flour to stop sticking.

Roll out to 20 × 30 cm. Mark in thirds lengthwise. Cut the outer thirds in about 10 strips.

Mix and microwave all filling ingredients while dough rises in food processor. Heat until dates soften and liquid is absorbed. Cool to lukewarm. Spread the lukewarm filling down the centre section evenly. Tuck the end over then fold alternate strips over filling.

Plaited braid should have an even shape. Transfer to oven slide sprayed with non-stick spray. Brush with beaten egg if desired. Leave about 15 minutes until slightly risen then bake at 190°C for 15–20 minutes, until lightly browned. Drizzle with icing sugar and lemon juice glaze while warm. Sprinkle with nuts, cherries etc. Serve warm, with or without butter.

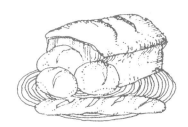

Fruit Braid

ⓒ Brown Bread

This well-flavoured nutritious bread requires no kneading.

For 2 or 3 loaves:
1 Tbsp dried yeast granules
1 cup warm water
2 tsp sugar
1 rounded household Tbsp malt
1 rounded household Tbsp treacle
2 cups hot water
3 Tbsp oil
2 tsp salt
1 cup wheatgerm
1 cup wheat bran (optional)
4–6 cups wholemeal flour
toasted sesame seeds (optional)

Mix the yeast, lukewarm water, and sugar together in a food processor or bowl. (Yeast starts to work fast when food-processed.) Make sure the water is not too hot, or the yeast wil be killed. Leave it to stand in a warm place while you prepare the rest of the mixture.

In a large bowl stir together the malt, treacle, hot water, oil and salt. The water should be as hot as a hot bath, to dissolve the (generous) spoonfuls of malt and treacle. Let the liquid cool to lukewarm.

Measure the wheatgerm and bran (if used) into the bowl of warm, malty liquid, and stir well. Measure 4 cups of the wholemeal flour on to this, make sure that the malty liquid is not too hot for the yeast, then tip in the yeast mixture, which by this time should be showing some signs of activity by bubbling or by fizzing when stirred.

Stir everything together thoroughly, using a large wooden spoon if possible. The mixture should be too thick to pour, but soft enough to spoon into pans and smooth the top surface with the back of a wet spoon. Add more flour as necessary. This amount of dough should rise to fill loaf tins which hold 12–15 cups altogether (depending on the amount of flour used).

Butter the tins well, or spray thoroughly with non-stick spray. Spoon the mixture evenly into the tins, half filling each, sprinkle with toasted sesame seeds if desired, cover with plastic film and leave in a warm place to rise, e.g., a warming oven which has been preheated then turned off, a sunny windowsill or a sink of warm water.

When the dough has risen to the tops of the tins or to twice its original volume, remove plastic film. Bake uncovered at 200°C for 30 minutes, or until the loaves sound hollow when tapped, or until a skewer comes out clean.

Turn out of the tins immediately, if they will fall out cleanly, otherwise leave to stand for 5 minutes, then remove, with the help of a knife if necessary.
Note:
Replace the malt with golden syrup, if desired. The colour and flavour will be good, but not malty.

ⓒ Hot Cross Buns

For 30 buns:
1 cup milk
½ cup hot water
2 Tbsp sugar
1–2 Tbsp dried yeast granules
2 cups flour
100 g butter
½ cup brown sugar
1 egg
1 tsp salt
1½ Tbsp mixed spice
1 tsp grated nutmeg
1 tsp vanilla
¼–1 cup mixed fruit
2–3 cups flour

Measure milk, hot water and sugar into a large bowl or saucepan.

Warm or cool to body temperature, then sprinkle on yeast granules. Stir after 1–2 minutes to remove lumps of yeast.

Mix in first measure of flour, cover and leave mixture to rise in the sun or in a sink of warm water while preparing other mixture. In another bowl, cream butter and brown sugar, then beat in egg, salt, spices, vanilla and dried fruit.

When the yeast mixture is nearly three times its original volume add it to the creamed mixture with 2 cups of the second measure of flour. Add enough extra flour to make a dough firm enough to turn on to a dry benchtop to knead.

Knead, adding just enough flour to stop dough sticking, until it is satiny and springs back when poked. Cut dough into four pieces, then each piece into seven or eight pieces.

Shape each into a round ball and arrange in greased cake tins in rows, allowing room for rising.

Leave to rise covered with plastic film or large plastic bags.

Make short pastry crosses. Rub 60 g cold butter into 1 cup flour then add water to form a stiff dough. Roll very thinly, then cut into strips.

Dip strips in beaten egg and place gently on buns when risen to twice original size.

Bake at 225°C for 10–12 minutes, until lightly browned.

Glaze immediately with syrup made by boiling 2 tablespoons golden syrup with 1 tablespoon water for 1 minute.

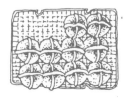

ⓒ Cheese Muffins

To make these savoury muffins easily and quickly, buy pre-grated tasty cheese.

For about 12 muffins:
2 cups (200 g) grated tasty cheese
1½ cup self-raising flour
½ tsp salt
1 Tbsp sugar
pinch of cayenne pepper
1 egg
1 cup milk

Measure the grated cheese, self-raising flour, salt, sugar and cayenne pepper into a large bowl. Mix lightly with your fingertips to combine.

In a small container beat the egg and milk until evenly combined. Pour all the liquid on to the dry ingredients, then fold the two mixtures together, taking care not to overmix.

Spoon mixture carefully off a tablespoon, helping it off with another spoon, into well-sprayed or buttered deep muffin pans. Sprinkle with paprika if desired. Bake at 210°C for about 12 minutes, until muffins spring back when pressed in the middle and are golden brown. Cool before removing from pan.

ⓒ Corn Muffins

These muffins make a good summer lunch when served with salads. If you like, replace the cornmeal with extra flour.

For 12–15 muffins:
50g butter, melted
1 egg
½ cup creamed corn
½ cup yoghurt or milk
½ cup grated tasty cheese
¼ cup sugar
¼ tsp salt
½ cup yellow cornmeal (or flour)
1 cup white or wholemeal flour
3 tsp baking powder

Melt the butter in a fairly large mixing bowl. Add the egg and creamed corn and mix with a fork. Add plain yoghurt in preference to milk — it makes muffins more tender.

Add the cheese, sugar and salt and mix again. Stir in the cornmeal, if using it; otherwise sift, or fork lightly together, the flour and baking powder.

Fold the flour mixture into the wet ingredients, taking great care not to overmix.

Spoon into well-sprayed, deep muffin pans, half filling them. Bake at 210°C for 10–15 minutes, until quite crusty and nicely browned. Stand for 5 minutes before removing from pans. Serve warm.

Bran Muffins

C M Bran Muffins

These bran muffins are full of fibre!
They taste especially good topped
with whipped quark or large-curd,
creamy cottage cheese, then with a
light tart jelly.

For about 12 muffins:
2 cups wheat bran
¹/₂ cup flour
1 tsp baking powder
1 tsp baking soda
¹/₂ cup golden syrup or treacle
1 egg
1 cup milk

Put the bran in a fairly large mixing
bowl.

Measure the next three
ingredients into a fine sieve or sifter
on top of the bowl. Shake on to
bran, then stir flour and bran
together.

Warm the golden syrup (or
treacle) if making microwaved
muffins in a saucepan or microwave
bowl until runny. Remove from
heat, then add the egg and milk and
mix well until combined. Pour all
the liquid into the dry ingredients.
Fold together until dry ingredients
are barely damp.

Spoon mixture into well-sprayed
baking pans, or unsprayed
microwave muffin containers. Each
cup should be about two-thirds full.
Bake at 200°C until firm in the
middle (10–15 minutes) or
microwave 5–6 muffins at Full
power for about 1¹/₂ minutes. Stand
for several minutes before removing
from pans.

C M Oaty Muffins

Make muffins all at once and freeze
them, or refrigerate the uncooked
mixture for up to two weeks,
cooking them as required.

For 36 large muffins:
¹/₂ cup treacle
2 cups rolled oats
1 cup baking bran
1 cup boiling water
1 cup brown sugar
2 Tbsp wine vinegar
1 tsp salt
2 eggs
2 cups milk
2 cups flour
1 cup oat bran
1¹/₂ tsp baking soda

Measure the treacle, rolled oats and
baking bran in a large bowl.

Pour over boiling water and mix
until treacle and oats are mixed.
Leave to cool for 5 minutes, then
add the next four ingredients and
beat with a fork to combine eggs.

Add milk and then the last three
ingredients, previously forked
together. Stir only enough to
combine. Spoon into well-buttered
(or sprayed) muffin tins, filling each
one half to three-quarters full. Bake
at 220°C for 10 minutes or until firm
or microwave half-filled microwave
muffin moulds for 2 minutes at Full
power for 5 muffins. Always leave
to stand for a few minutes before
removing muffins from pans.

C Ginger Gems

Gems are made by cooking muffin
mixture in special, heavy gem irons.
If you do not have these, cook the
mixture in muffin tins.

For 36 small gems:
1 cup sugar
1 heaped household Tbsp golden syrup
2 tsp ground ginger
2 eggs
100 g butter
1 cup milk
2 cups flour
1¹/₂ tsp baking soda

Measure sugar, golden syrup which
has been warmed, if necessary, until
liquid, ground ginger and eggs into a
food processor bowl. Add the butter
which has been warmed until it is
very soft, but not liquid. Process to
mix.

Add milk and process to blend in.

Sift or sieve flour and baking soda
into a fairly large bowl. Add all the
mixture from the food processor at
once, and fold into dry ingredients,
taking great care not to overmix.
Mixture should look lumpy.

Heat gem irons at 200°C until
very hot. Spray well with non-stick
spray. Spoon mixture from side of a
tablespoon into hot irons so each is
about two-thirds full. Bake at 200°C
for 12 minutes or until centres
spring back. Leave for 2–3 minutes,
then remove gems. Respray and
refill with more mixture without
heating irons.

Oaty Pancakes

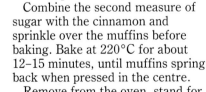 Fruity Muffins

These muffins may be made right through the year, using different fruits and berries in season. Blueberries make especially good muffins because they are not sour when cooked. Use currants or sultanas in these muffins if fresh fruit is not available.

For about 12 muffins:
2 cups flour
4 tsp baking powder
½ tsp salt
½ cup castor sugar
100 g butter
1 cup milk
1 egg
1–1½ cups blackberries, blueberries, chopped banana, etc. or ¾ cup sultanas or ½ cup currants
about ¼ cup chopped walnuts (optional)

1 Tbsp sugar
½ tsp cinnamon

Sieve the first three dry ingredients into a fairly large bowl. Add the castor sugar. In another container melt the butter, remove from the heat and then add the milk and egg, and beat to combine these three.

Prepare the fruit then tip the liquid, fruit, and nuts if used, into the bowl with the dry ingredients. Fold everything together, taking great care not to overmix. The flour should be dampened, but the mixture should not be smooth.

Butter or oil 12 deep muffin pans thoroughly. Without stirring or extra mixing, place spoonfuls of mixture into pans, filling each half to three-quarters full.

Combine the second measure of sugar with the cinnamon and sprinkle over the muffins before baking. Bake at 220°C for about 12–15 minutes, until muffins spring back when pressed in the centre.

Remove from the oven, stand for 2–3 minutes, then twist muffins carefully to loosen before lifting them from their pans.

Pikelets

25 g butter
1 household tablespoon golden syrup
½ cup sugar
2 eggs
¼ cup milk
1½ cups flour
1 tsp baking soda
1 tsp cream of tartar

Melt the butter in the bowl in which you will mix the pikelets. Add a rounded spoon of golden syrup, and warm until this is softened too. Add the sugar and eggs and beat until mixed, with a rotary beater. Add the milk, then shake in the sifted flour, baking soda, and cream of tartar.

Beat very briefly with the beater, until there are no floury lumps, but stopping before the mixture is smooth. It is important not to overmix at this stage.

Heat a large pan, preferably with a non-stick surface. If it has a thermostat, heat to 180°C. If not, heat until a drop of water on the surface breaks into several smaller drops, and these run around the pan.

Spray lightly with non-stick spray, or rub with a little butter on a paper towel.

Drop spoonfuls from the end of a dessertspoon or tablespoon, twisting the spoon around as you drop off the mixture, for an evenly round shape. Leave room for some spreading. Turn carefully when you see the first bubbles on the top of the first pikelet burst. The second side is cooked when it springs back when lightly touched in the middle. Place cooked pikelets between the layers of a folded teatowel.

☐ Oaty Pancakes

Serve oaty pancakes (or American pancakes) for breakfast or brunch, with juice and coffee. Pour syrup over the pile of buttered pancakes, and serve bacon or sausages alongside if you like.

3/4 cup milk
3/4 cup rolled oats
1 egg
1/2 tsp salt
2–3 Tbsp sugar
1/2 cup flour
2 tsp baking powder
25 g butter, melted

Pour milk over rolled oats. Add remaining ingredients. Mix with fork (or in a food processor) just enough to combine ingredients. Put spoonfuls on to preheated, greased or sprayed griddle or frypan. Turn spoon for round pancakes.

Turn pancakes as soon as bubbles form and burst in the middle. Slide thin metal blade under pancake and flip it over.

Second side is cooked when centre springs back. Put a dab of butter on cooked surface of several pancakes. Pile up so butter is between pancakes. Pour syrup over just before serving.

☐ American Pancakes

Makes about 8 pancakes:
50 g butter, melted
2 eggs
1 cup milk
1 1/2 cups self-raising flour
3 Tbsp sugar

Measure ingredients into a fairly large bowl, in the order listed. Beat with a rotary beater just until no longer lumpy, but do not overbeat, or pancakes will be tough.

Heat a smooth metal surface (frypan or griddle) until a drop of water dances around the pan (to 190°C), then spray or butter it lightly. Tip about 1/4 cup batter into the pan, spreading it into an even circle.

Turn pancake when bubbles break in the middle of the pancake. Cook second side until the middle springs back when pressed with a finger.

Pile hot pancakes, with a little butter between each, on a warm plate. Serve with syrup, etc.

Fruity Pancakes

Stir raw fruit into the uncooked batter. Try grated apple, chopped peaches, nectarines or pears, blackberries, blueberries, slivered strawberries, sliced banana, etc. Do not use fruit which is especially tart or tangy, as its tartness is usually more marked after cooking.

Pancake Toppings

Top pancakes with golden syrup, maple syrup, or with mock maple syrup made by boiling 3/4 cup brown sugar with 1/4 cup water for 1–2 minutes, then adding 1/2–1 tsp vanilla.

Concentrated apple juice makes a delicious, interesting, thick but less sweet topping.

Use jams which have not thickened as they should have, or which have been thinned by heating with orange juice.

☐ Plain Scones

You can do many interesting things with scone dough. Learn how to make it from scratch. It is important to select a good flour. Read information on side of packet. Flour used should be good for bread-making, rather than good for light cakes.

2 cups all-purpose flour
4 tsp baking powder
1/2 tsp salt
25–50 g cold butter
about 3/4 cup milk

Sift dry ingredients into a medium-sized bowl. Add cold butter, cut in 6–10 small cubes, or grated if preferred. Cut or rub it into the flour using a pastry blender, or two knives, or your fingertips, to the consistency of rolled oats.

Alternatively, measure dry ingredients into food-processor bowl without sifting them. Cut in cubes of butter to the same stage, using the metal chopping blade. Transfer mixture to bowl for easiest addition of milk.

Pour about 3/4 cup of the measured milk into a well in the middle of the dry mixture, all at once.

Mix dough with a knife, adding more milk if it is needed to make a soft dough. Collect mixture from sides of bowl and turn dough out on to a floured board.

Knead dough lightly 6–10 times, pushing it with fingertips of one hand and collecting it towards you

with the other hand. Do not overknead or underknead.

Pat or roll out lightly until about 1 cm thick. Cut into 9 squares or rounds with sharp knife or cutter. Place close together on ungreased oven slide for soft-sided scones. Bake at 220–230°C for 8–10 minutes until bottom and tops are golden.

☐ Girdle Scones

Girdle scones are cooked on a hot metal surface (like pikelets) instead of in an oven. Always eat girdle scones soon after making them.

Make scone dough using 1 cup flour. Pat or roll into a 20 cm circle.

For traditional girdle scones, cut circle in 6–8 wedges. Cook on preheated solid element, griddle or frying pan, turn when lightly browned and cooked half-way through (about 2–3 minutes).

For a non-traditional golden surface, brush top of dough with butter before inverting on to hot surface. Brush second surface while bottom cooks.

For lighter girdle scones, cover pan, etc. while first side cooks.

☐ Cinnamon Scone Ring

Both the topping and the filling used here provide the colour and texture lacking in plain microwaved scone dough. First mix topping.

Topping
1 Tbsp butter
2 Tbsp golden syrup
2 Tbsp chopped walnuts

In a small ring pan melt butter, for 30–40 seconds at Full power. Tilt the pan to coat the bottom evenly. Drizzle golden syrup over bottom and sides. Add chopped walnuts. Next mix scone dough, using 2 cups of flour and about 3/4 cup milk.

Make a soft dough. Knead lightly 5–6 times, then roll out to form a rectangle 30 cm × 20 cm.

Filling
2 Tbsp butter, melted
2 Tbsp chopped walnuts
1 tsp cinnamon
2 Tbsp brown sugar

Brush dough evenly with melted butter. Combine walnuts, cinnamon and brown sugar and sprinkle evenly over the dough. Roll up, starting with a long side. Cut roll into eight slices. Arrange, cut side down, on the prepared topping in the pan. Cover pan with cling wrap.

Cook for 6–7 minutes, or until dough nearest the ring insert feels firm. Leave to stand in pan for 2 minutes, then turn out on plate and serve immediately, buttered or plain.

C Pumpkin Loaf

This recipe makes a sweet, spicy loaf. It can be served warm with sauce or whipped cream as dessert the day it is baked.

1 cup pumpkin purée
100 g butter
1½ cups soft brown sugar
2 eggs
2 cups self-raising flour
½ tsp baking soda
1 tsp cinnamon
½ tsp grated nutmeg
½ tsp ginger
¼ tsp ground cloves

To make the pumpkin purée, microwave or boil the pumpkin pieces in lightly salted water, then purée in a food processor or press through a sieve.

Cream the butter and sugar, add the eggs and beat well, then stir in the cold puréed pumpkin. Sift the dry ingredients together. Fold in half of this sifted mixture to the pumpkin mixture, then mix in the remaining half until evenly combined, but do not beat.

Spoon the mixture into a lined 23 × 10 cm loaf tin. Bake at 180°C for 1 hour, or until a skewer poked into the middle of the loaf comes out clean.

Store in a loosely covered container or refrigerate in a plastic bag.

C Brown Banana Bread

This bread has a good banana flavour, and may be sliced like a cake when fresh. For special occasions it is good spread with cream cheese flavoured with finely grated orange rind.

100 g butter
¾ cup sugar
1 egg
1 cup mashed ripe banana
1 cup wholemeal flour
¼ cup orange juice
¼–½ cup chopped walnuts (or
*   sunflower seeds)*
1 cup plain flour
1 tsp baking powder
1 tsp baking soda

Cream the butter and sugar together until light and fluffy. Add the egg and beat again. Mash the bananas (about 2 medium-sized bananas make one cup), and add them to the creamed mixture with the wholemeal flour, orange juice and walnuts (or sunflower seeds). Stir together until just combined. Sift in the plain flour, baking powder and baking soda. Mix until all the ingredients are just combined.

Line a 23 × 10 cm loaf tin with greaseproof paper, so that the paper covers the bottom and long sides, and spoon in the mixture.

Bake at 180°C for about an hour. When the loaf is cooked, the centre will spring back when pressed, and a skewer poked into the middle will come out clean. Stand for 5–10 minutes before removing from the tin. Store as for Pumpkin Loaf.

C Boiled Fruit Loaf

This low-fat, no egg, fruity loaf tastes so good that you do not even need to butter the slices.

1 cup hot water
¾ cup sugar
1 cup sultanas
25 g butter
1 tsp cinnamon
1 tsp mixed spice
½ tsp ground cloves
1½ cups flour
1 tsp baking powder
½ tsp baking soda
½ tsp salt

Place water, sugar, sultanas, and butter in a medium-sized saucepan. Bring to the boil, stirring occasionally, then simmer (uncovered) for 5 minutes. Stand the pot in cold water to cool contents to room temperature. Line a loaf tin with greaseproof paper while you wait.

Sift remaining ingredients into the cooled fruit mixture. Stir only enough to blend ingredients, as overmixing causes toughening and uneven rising.

Bake at 180°C for 45–60 minutes, until a skewer pushed into the centre comes out clean. This loaf is best left for 24 hours before eating.

C Gingerbread

Gingerbread is always popular. I flavour it with equal amounts of cinnamon and ginger, and like the resulting flavour.

Serve this gingerbread warm for dessert, cold as a cake on the day it is cooked, and after that, butter the slices. This recipe makes two loaves or 20-cm-square cakes. Freeze one of these if you like.

100 g butter
¾ cup sugar
2 eggs
1 cup golden syrup
1 cup milk
3 cups flour
2 tsp ginger
2 tsp cinnamon
1½ tsp baking soda

Soften but do not melt the butter. In a large bowl, cream it with the sugar until light-coloured. Add the eggs and beat again. Warm the golden syrup just enough to make it runny. Remove from heat and stir in the milk. Sift or sieve the dry ingredients together several time.

Fold the syrup mixture and dry ingredients alternately into the butter mixture. Take care not to overmix. Fold together only until no more dry flour remains. Turn into two loaf pans or two 20-cm-square cake pans, or one of each size, each lined with a strip of baking paper. Bake at 150°C, until a skewer comes out clean from the centre of the gingerbread, about 30–40 minutes for the square pan, 40–45 minutes for the loaf pan.

C Steamed High-Protein Loaf

I worked out this recipe for children who were refusing to eat other protein-rich foods. Try it!

For 2–4 cylindrical loaves:
1½ cups wholemeal flour
½ cup wheatgerm
1 cup soya flour
3 tsp baking powder
1 tsp salt
½ cup milk powder
½ cup chopped walnuts
3 Tbsp butter or oil
1 orange, grated rind and juice
½–¾ cup golden syrup
2 eggs
1 cup milk

Mix the first seven ingredients in a large bowl. Grate orange rind into a saucepan with the butter or oil. Warm to melt butter. Add the juice and syrup (the larger amount makes a sweeter, more orangey loaf), warm until liquid, then beat in the eggs. Tip this slightly warm liquid, and the milk, into the bowl with the dry ingredients, and stir just enough to moisten.

Spoon into well-buttered empty fruit cans, filling each no more than two-thirds full. Cover cans with buttered foil, leaving plenty of foil folded down the sides in case loaves rise more than estimated. Stand in a pot containing about 5 cm boiling water, cover pot, and simmer for about 3 hours. Remove foil, cool for 5 minutes, then turn out on to a rack to finish cooling.

Slice and spread with butter or cream cheese. Freeze for long storage.

From top: Pumpkin Loaf, Brown Banana Bread; sliced: Pumpkin Loaf, Boiled Fruit Loaf, Brown Banana Bread

ⓒ Spicy Butter Biscuits

If you have time, roll these out and cut into shapes, decorating each with beaten egg and an almond before cooking, or with white icing afterwards. If you don't, cut thin slices from a chilled cylinder of dough and cook them plain. Whatever way, they taste quite delicious.

225 g soft butter
1 cup brown sugar
1 egg
2 cups flour
2 Tbsp cinnamon
1 Tbsp mixed spice

Cream softened but not melted butter in the food processor. Add remaining ingredients, mix to combine, then form into a roll 70 mm thick. Roll in plastic and refrigerate until firm.

Cut in very thin slices with a sharp knife. Bake at 180°C for 8–10 minutes or until biscuits darken slightly.

When cool, transfer from tray to an airtight container.
Note:
These contain no baking powder — use tablespoons not teaspoons of spices.

ⓒ Oaty Fingers

I mix these in seconds, then roll them out directly on to the baking sheet, under plastic to stop the mixture sticking to the rolling pin.

Serve plain or buttered, whichever you prefer.

100 g soft butter
½ cup brown sugar
½ cup flour
½ cup rolled oats
½ cup oat bran
¼ cup toasted sesame seeds (optional)

Soften but do not melt the butter. Mix with remaining ingredients in food processor bowl, adding 1–2 tablespoons water if dough will not stick together.

Roll out, under plastic, on the baking sheet, to 5 mm thickness. Mark into 25 mm × 100 mm rectangles. Bake at 170°C–180°C for 10–15 minutes, until golden brown.

Spicy Butter Biscuits

ⓒ Shortbread

This mixture is so rich and buttery it is hard to decorate. Patterns pressed into the raw mixture lose their firm outlines during cooking.

200 g soft butter
½ cup castor sugar
1½ cups flour
½ cup ground almonds
1 cup cornflour

Cream butter in food processor. Add sugar, process for 30 seconds then stir in remaining ingredients. Mix together, chilling if too soft to handle.

Roll out 1 cm thick. Cut in squares or rectangles. Prick or decorate with fork handle.

Bake at 200°C for 12–15 minutes. Remove from oven as soon as edges brown slightly.

ⓒ Birdseed Bar

Deliciously crisp and crunchy, but resist the temptation to eat too much at once, or you will not enjoy it again!

1 cup sesame seeds
1 cup sunflower seeds
1 cup coconut
1 cup chopped cashew nuts
1 cup sultanas
100 g butter
¼ cup honey
½ cup brown sugar

Heat the first four ingredients, one after another in a large frying pan, until toasted and lightly browned. Mix with sultanas in a large bowl.

Heat butter, honey and brown sugar to the soft ball stage, then pour over mixture in bowl. Mix well.

Press into pan so it is 2 cm thick. When nearly cold, cut into bars. Store in airtight container.

ⓒ Almond Crisps

Flecked with toasted almonds, these buttery, crisp biscuits are irresistible!

100 g soft butter
½ cup sugar
1 cup flour
1 tsp baking powder
½–1 tsp almond essence
¼–½ cup toasted slivered almonds

Soften but do not melt the butter. Cream butter and sugar in food processor then add remaining ingredients without sifting. Process briefly to mix. Form into a cylinder and chill.

When cold and firm cut in thin slices. Bake on buttered oven slide, at 170°C for about 10 minutes until edges colour slightly. Cool slightly on oven slide. Store in airtight container.
Note:
If butter is too liquid, and mixture crumbly to handle, add milk until dough sticks together. Cream conventionally, omit toasted almonds, roll into balls, flatten and top with almonds or cherries, if preferred.

ⓒ Cheesy Snacks

I cut these into long sticks on the baking sheet, but you can use biscuit cutters and make fancy shapes if you have more time.

1 cup flour
100 g cold butter, cubed
1 cup grated cheese
1 pkt onion soup mix
2 Tbsp poppy seeds
1 tsp celery salt
½ tsp baking powder
½ tsp paprika
about 2 Tbsp water

Put all ingredients except water in food processor with metal chopping blade. Mix, adding just enough water to make a firm dough.

Roll out thinly on a floured board, transfer to baking tray then mark into long fingers with a sharp knife.

Bake at 180°C for 10–15 minutes until browning at edges. Slide on to board while hot, cut to separate sticks, cool on rack then store in airtight container.

ⓒ Gingernuts

Homemade gingernuts can be made almost as quickly as they can be eaten!

100 g butter
1 Tbsp golden syrup
1 cup sugar
1 egg
1¾ cups flour
2 tsp ginger
1 tsp baking soda

Melt butter in saucepan. Stir in a rounded household tablespoon of syrup. Soften then remove from heat.

Add the sugar and egg and beat with a wooden spoon to mix. Measure dry ingredients into pot through a sieve. Stir to mix.

Spoon warm mixture on to greased or sprayed trays, allowing space for spreading. Cool mixture may be shaped into balls if preferred. Preheat oven to 190°C between tray loads, bake at 180°C for about 10 minutes, until lightly browned.

Lift off tray when cool. Store in airtight containers.

Citrus Slice

C Citrus Slice

This is one of our family favourites. I flavour it with finely grated rind and juice from lemons, oranges, mandarins and tangelos in season.

Base
100 g butter
³/₄ cup (¹/₂ can) sweetened condensed milk
1 cup coconut
grated rind of 1 or 2 citrus fruit
1 (200 g) pkt wine biscuits

Icing
1 cup icing sugar
2 Tbsp soft butter
citrus fruit juice

Melt the butter. Add condensed milk, coconut, finely grated rind of one large or two small lemons, oranges, mandarins or tangelos, and the crumbs made from biscuits.

Mix well, then press into a lightly buttered or sprayed square or rectangular dish. Mixture need not fill dish but may be pressed to desired depth.

Mix icing sugar with soft butter, then add juice, a few drops at a time, to icing consistency. Spread with a knife and decorate with fork if desired. Refrigerate until firm. Cut in squares or rectangles and store in the refrigerator.

C Brownies

I find brownies most useful. They are quick to mix and need no icing. They keep well, freeze well and can be served with a cup of tea or coffee, or at the side of a plate of stewed fruit or ice-cream as dessert — American style.

125 g butter
5 Tbsp cocoa
200 g sugar
2 eggs
¹/₄ tsp salt
1 tsp vanilla
100 g sifted flour
1 tsp baking powder
¹/₂ cup walnuts, chopped

Mix the brownies in a medium-sized saucepan. Melt the butter. (Work with it liquid but not hot.) Add to it the cocoa, sugar and eggs, salt and vanilla. Beat thoroughly. Sift together the flour and baking powder. Stir these in with the chopped nuts.

Pour mixture into greased 20–23-cm-square tin (with removable base for preference). Bake at 180°C for 30 minutes or until firm in the centre. When cold cut into rectangles.

Ⓜ Peanut Butter Squares

100 g butter
½ cup peanut butter
1 cup biscuit crumbs
1 cup icing sugar
about 6 drops almond essence
¼ tsp vanilla
½ cup small pieces of chocolate
2 tsp butter

In a large bowl microwave at Full power the butter (cut into cubes), and the peanut butter (in 4–5 blobs) for 2 minutes. Mix and blend thoroughly. Stir in crumbs, icing sugar and essences. Mix well. Press into loaf pan lined with baking paper.

In another dish, melt chocolate and second measure of butter in the microwave for 1–2 minutes, or until the two can be mixed together smoothly. Add vanilla and spread on top of peanut butter mixture.

Leave to set in a cool place before cutting into small squares.

Ⓒ Quark Pastry Cheesecakes

Quark is a type of 'fresh cheese'. It has a similar fat content to cottage cheese but has a texture more like cream cheese.

Used in this pastry, quark gives a very nice texture.

1 cup flour
1 tsp baking powder
100 g cold butter
½ cup (125 g) quark
1–2 Tbsp cold water

Use a food processor to make the pastry if you have one.

Cut the butter and quark into the flour and baking powder. Add just enough liquid to dampen the dough. Roll out to 30 cm square and cut into 16 smaller squares. Spray patty tins with non-stick spray. Gently ease a pastry square into each.

Filling
½ cup (125 g) cream cheese
½ egg
1 Tbsp sugar
a few drops of almond essence
apricot jam

Without washing the food processor, mix together cream cheese, egg, sugar and almond essence.

Spoon this filling evenly into the squares. Top with a little apricot jam (or brush with microwaved apricot jam when cooked).

Fold corners into middle and pinch newly formed corners.

Brush with some of the remaining egg. Bake at 190°C for about 20 minutes until pastry is an even golden brown. Glaze with heated apricot jam if desired.

Ⓒ Ⓜ Lemon Cheesecake Slice

Cook this rich, lemony slice in the microwave oven for speed.

Crust
1 cup flour
1 cup rolled oats
½ cup brown sugar
125 g butter, cubed

Filling
1 package (250 g) cream cheese
¼ cup sugar
2 Tbsp brown sugar
1 egg
2 Tbsp lemon juice
1 tsp lemon rind

Crust
Measure ingredients into food processor. Mix until crumbly. Reserve 1 cup and press the rest into a 20 cm square or round baking-paper-lined pan. Microwave at Medium (50% power) for 8 minutes on an inverted plate or rack.

Filling
Microwave cream cheese for 1 minute at Medium (50% power). Mix with remaining filling ingredients. Pour over base and cover with remaining crumbly topping.

Microwave at Full power for about 8 minutes longer until firm in centre. Cool, then refrigerate until quite cold and hard, then cut into rectangles or wedges.

Alternatively, bake base at 190°C for 10 minutes then whole slice for 30 minutes.

Ⓒ Brandy Snaps

Crunchy, fragile, but quick to mix and make.

2 Tbsp golden syrup
100 g butter
½ cup brown sugar
2 tsp ginger
½ cup flour

Use rounded household tablespoons of syrup. Heat with butter and brown sugar in saucepan until butter melts. Remove from heat and add

ginger and flour.

Drop four heaped teaspoon lots on a greased oven slide. Spread each flat with the back of a spoon.

Bake at 180°C for 5–10 minutes, until mixture darkens slightly. Cool until firm enough to roll around a wooden spoon handle etc. Reheat if too firm to roll.

Store in airtight container immediately. Fill with cream flavoured with brandy essence just before serving.

Note:
If brandy snaps spread too much, add a little extra flour.

Ⓒ Fruit Square

1½ cups flour
100 g butter
about 6 Tbsp cold water
3 cups cake crumbs
1 cup currants
1 cup sultanas
½ cup brown sugar
1 tsp mixed spice
1 cup drained stewed apple
½ tsp vanilla
¼ tsp rum essence

Make short pastry (see page 206) using flour, butter and water. Roll out to a 50 cm circle.

Mix cake crumbs with remaining ingredients. Place in a 20 cm square in the middle of pastry. Dampen edges then fold over filling.

Turn over carefully onto a 20 cm strip of baking paper. Lower into a 20 cm tin. Prick top evenly. Brush top with beaten egg if desired.

Bake at 200°C for 45–50 minutes. Cool in tin for up to 12 hours, pressing top with a weight if possible. When cold and firm, cut in rectangles with sharp serrated knife.

Ⓤ Christmas Mincemeat

2 small apples
1 cup sultanas
1 cup mixed fruit
½ lemon, rind and juice
grated rind of ½ orange
½ cup brown sugar
½ tsp each mixed spice, cinnamon and salt
¼ tsp ground cloves
¼ cup spirits

Mince apple, dried fruit and rinds then mix with other ingredients or use food processor to chop unpeeled apple and thinly peeled rinds, then combine them with remaining ingredients. Spoon into sterilised jars, top with extra spirits, cover and refrigerate.

For mincemeat pies make sweet shortcrust (see page 206), cut and fill and bake for 160°C for about 20 minutes.

Spicy Fruit Spread

75 g–100 g butter
1 cup brown sugar
1 tsp mixed spice
1/2 tsp cinnamon
1/4 tsp ground cloves
2 eggs, beaten slightly
2 cups currants
1/4–1/2 cup mixed peel
1/2 orange, rind and juice
2 apples, finely chopped
    or 1 cup drained canned apple
2 Tbsp sherry
2–3 Tbsp spirits

Melt butter in microwave dish or double boiler. Mix in next eight ingredients.

Chop apple small but not mushy. Stir in with sherry.

Microwave at Full power for about 8 minutes or simmer over boiling water for 20–30 minutes. Stir regularly. Mixture thickens when cooked.

Cook, add brandy, store in refrigerator.

Serve warm in tart shells made of sweet shortcrust (see page 206).

Family Carrot Cake

This recipe makes a good, large family cake. I sometimes make it in a small, straight-sided roasting pan, 23 × 30 cm, but it is more usually cooked in a 25-cm-square pan.

3 eggs
3/4 cup oil
2 cups raw sugar
2 tsp vanilla
1/2 tsp salt
3 cups (350 g) grated carrot
2 cups wholemeal flour
1 cup coconut
2 tsp baking soda
2 tsp baking powder
2 tsp cinnamon
3/4 cup apple juice

Put eggs, oil, sugar, vanilla and salt in a large bowl. Beat to mix thoroughly, then fold in the grated carrots.

Toss all the dry ingredients together. Tip them on top of the wet mixture and fold in carefully, adding the apple juice while you mix. If mixture seems too wet, do not add the last 2–3 tablespoons of apple juice.

Turn into a large, square or rectangular paper-lined tin (see above) and bake at 180°C for 45–60 minutes or until a skewer comes out clean. Ice with double the recipe of Cream Cheese Icing or Lemon Butter Icing (see this page).

Carrot Cake

(See photograph on page 224.)

This is one of my favourite microwave cakes. When it is cooked in a good quality, smooth pan with a lid, no lining is necessary.

2 cups finely grated carrot
2 eggs
1 cup sugar
3/4 cup oil
1 tsp vanilla
1 1/4 cups flour
2–3 tsp cinnamon
2–3 tsp mixed spice
1 tsp baking soda
1/2 tsp salt

Grate carrots finely and put aside. Mix eggs, sugar, oil and vanilla in a food processor until smooth. Add carrot and remaining ingredients. (Add larger amounts of spices for a darker, spicier cake.) Process enough to combine everything thoroughly, but do not overmix.

Turn mixture into a 10 cup capacity ring pan. If pan has a tendency to stick, line it first with strips of plastic cling film. Cover pan with a lid or plate.

Microwave at Full power for about 8 minutes or until top and bottom look just dry and centre springs back. Turn out and cool.

Ice with Lemon Butter Icing and garnish with chopped walnuts.

Lemon Butter Icing

1 Tbsp butter
1 1/2 Tbsp lemon juice
1 1/2 cups sifted icing sugar
1/2 tsp finely grated lemon rind
    (optional)

Put butter, lemon rind and juice in a medium-sized bowl. Microwave at Full power for 20 seconds, or until butter is soft. Add icing sugar and mix with a knife until smooth and creamy. Spread on slightly warm cake.

Cream Cheese Icing

2 Tbsp cream cheese
1 Tbsp butter
1/2 tsp vanilla
1 1/2 cups sifted icing sugar

Put cream cheese, butter and vanilla in a medium-sized bowl. Microwave at Full power for 20–30 seconds until cream cheese and butter are very soft.

Add icing sugar and mix with a knife until smooth and creamy. Add a little milk or icing sugar if mixture is too thick or thin. Spread on slightly warm cake.

Crazy Cake

1 1/2 cups flour
2 Tbsp cocoa
1 tsp cinnamon
1 tsp ginger
1 tsp baking soda
1 tsp salt
1 cup sugar
1/2 cup corn or soya oil
3/4 cup water
2 Tbsp vinegar
1 tsp vanilla

Sift first six ingredients into a medium-sized bowl.

Add sugar and mix with a fork. Then add corn or soya oil, water, vinegar and vanilla. Do not stir between additions. Stir with a fork until mixed (but do not overmix) then pour mixture into a 23 cm tin lined with greaseproof paper and sprayed with non-stick spray, or well greased and floured.

Bake at 200°C for 15–20 minutes or until the centre springs back when touched. Turn out on rack and remove paper. (If you use a smaller pan reduce temperature and increase cooking time.)

Serve warm for dessert. Top each slice with a swirl of cream as you serve.

Note:
If desired, split cake before serving and fill with raspberry or blackcurrant jam.

Walnut Torte

In this cake, ground nuts and biscuit crumbs replace flour. The resulting cake is rich and popular. It makes a wonderful snack or dinner party finale, served alone or with fresh berries. It is easy to chop the nuts and crumb the biscuits if you have a food processor.

1/2 cup biscuit crumbs
125 g freshly shelled walnuts
1 cup sugar
3 large eggs

Thoroughly butter, or line, a round or square 23 cm cake tin, so it is ready as soon as the cake mixture is prepared. Heat the oven to 160°C.

Crumb maltmeal wafers or other biscuits, using a food processor or a plastic bag and rolling pin. Sieve crumbs to make sure they are evenly fine, before measuring them.

Chop the walnuts with half the sugar, in a food processor if possible, otherwise chop very finely, then mix with half the sugar. The nuts should be nearly as fine as ground almonds.

Beat the room-temperature eggs until thick, then add the remaining sugar and beat until very thick. (Beat yolks, then whites and sugar separately if you have trouble

Walnut Torte

getting really thick egg mixtures.)
Fold the three mixtures carefully together, pour into the prepared tin, and bake at 160°C for 30–40 minutes, or until the centre springs back when gently pressed. Leave for 10 minutes before removing carefully from pan.

Serve squares or wedges lightly dusted with icing sugar. Accompany with whipped cream with extra nuts or berries.

C Zucchini Chocolate Cake

When you pick up a slice of this delicious, moist, rich, chocolate-flavoured cake, you may be surprised to notice green flecks through it. The combination of ingredients is unusual, but most successful.

125 g butter
1 cup brown sugar
½ cup white sugar
3 eggs
2½ cups flour
1 tsp vanilla
½ cup yoghurt
¼ cup cocoa
2 tsp baking soda
1 tsp cinnamon
½ tsp mixed spice
½ tsp salt
3 cups (350 g) grated zucchini
½–1 cup small pieces of chocolate (optional)

Prepare a 25-cm-square pan or roasting pan by lining it with two crosswise strips of baking paper. Beat the butter with the sugars until light and creamy. Do not hurry this step. Use a mixer or food processor.

Add the eggs one at a time, with a spoonful of the measured flour to prevent the mixture curdling. Add the vanilla and yoghurt and mix well.

Sift the dry ingredients together. Stir in, with the grated zucchini. Turn into the prepared pan. Sprinkle surface with the small pieces of chocolate if desired. Bake at 170°C for 45 minutes, or until centre feels firm and a skewer comes out clean.

M Chocolate Cake

50 g butter, melted
2 eggs
1 cup brown sugar
½ cup milk
1 cup flour
3 Tbsp cocoa
½ tsp baking soda
½ tsp cream of tartar

Melt butter in a medium-sized bowl at Full power for about 1 minute. Add eggs and sugar and beat with a rotary beater until thick and creamy. Add milk and sifted dry ingredients. Beat again briefly, stopping as soon as ingredients are combined.

Pour into a small ring pan which has been lightly sprayed or buttered. Cover pan with vented cling wrap. Microwave at Medium-High (70% power) for about 6–10 minutes or until firm near ring. Leave to stand for 3–4 minutes, then unmould on to flat plate. Ice when cold.
Variations:
Make cake in a loaf pan or in a 20 cm square pan. Cover during cooking, or shield corners.

M Chocolate Icing

1 Tbsp cocoa
2 Tbsp water
2 tsp butter
1½ cups sifted icing sugar

Mix cocoa and water to a smooth paste. Heat cocoa at Full power for 1–1½ minutes, until dark brown and thick. Add the butter, then stir in the sifted icing sugar. Add extra liquid only after the icing sugar is mixed, if necessary.

M Banana Cake

125 g butter, melted
1 cup brown sugar
1 Tbsp wine vinegar
2 eggs
2–3 very ripe bananas, mashed
1 cup wholemeal flour
¾ cup flour
1 tsp baking soda
¼ cup milk

In a fairly large mixing bowl melt the butter at Full power for 1½ minutes. Add the sugar, vinegar and eggs, then beat with a fork or rotary beater until well mixed. Stir in the mashed bananas. Sprinkle the wholemeal flour over the surface. Add the flour and baking soda, sifted together, and the milk. Fold everything together, using a rubber scraper.

Turn into a paper-lined or lightly buttered ring pan. Microwave at Medium-High (70% power) for 10–12 minutes, or until centre is firm.

Ice with Lemon Butter Icing or with Cream Cheese Icing (see page 238) and sprinkle with walnuts if desired.

C Apple Yoghurt Cake

This is a popular, low-fat, low-sugar family cake that you can easily make richer by using the larger options. Please yourself!

¼–½ cup corn oil
¼–½ cup brown sugar
2 eggs
1½ cups (firmly packed) grated apple
½ cup plain yoghurt
½ cup milk
1 cup rolled oats
½ cup wheatgerm
½ sultanas
1 cup self-raising flour
½ tsp baking soda
2 Tbsp cocoa
2 tsp cinnamon
½ tsp salt

Measure the oil, brown sugar and eggs into a food processor bowl. Mix well, then add the unpeeled grated apple, yoghurt, and milk, and mix again.

Measure the oats, wheatgerm and sultanas into a large mixing bowl, and sift on top of them the other dry ingredients. Toss together, then pour on the liquid mixture. Mix only enough to combine, and turn into a paper-lined 23-cm-square pan. Bake at 180°C for 30 minutes, or until firm in the centre.

Sprinkle with icing sugar before serving. Eat within two days.

C Apple and Walnut Cake

This is a lovey moist, dense cake which is unlikely to sit around for long!

Its generous size makes it useful when serving coffee and cake to a large group.

¾ cup corn or soya oil
1¾ cups soft brown sugar
2 eggs
1 tsp vanilla
1¾ cups wholemeal flour
1 tsp baking soda
2 tsp cinnamon
1 tsp grated nutmeg
1 tsp salt
½ cup chopped walnuts or lightly toasted sunflower seeds
4 cups grated apple (6 medium-sized apples)

In a smallish bowl or food processor combine the oil, sugar, eggs and vanilla until light coloured and creamy.

In a large bowl, toss together all the dry ingredients and nuts or seeds with a fork until they are lightly and evenly mixed.

Grate the unpeeled apples using a sharp grater (or food processor) so they are not too mushy and wet, press them lightly into a four-cup measure, then combine the three mixtures in the big bowl, stirring only until the dry ingredients are moistened.

Pour into a well-buttered roasting pan about 25 cm square, and bake at 180°C for 30–45 minutes, or until the centre springs back when pressed.

Cool in the tin, sprinkle with icing sugar, and cut into generous pieces,

C Date and Walnut Cake

You can't actually see the fruit and nuts in this delicious cake because they are so finely chopped. Serve it for dessert or for a special occasion, with coffee.

Date and Walnut Cake

1 cup (150 g) chopped dates
1 cup (90 g) fresh walnuts
¹/₂ cup sugar
2 Tbsp flour
1 tsp baking powder
2 large eggs
1 tsp vanilla

Line the bottom of a 23 cm cake tin with baking paper. Spray sides with non-stick spray.

Chop the dates, nuts, half the measured sugar, the flour and baking powder in a food processor. Chop until dates and nuts are as fine as coarse breadcrumbs.

In separate bowls beat egg whites with half remaining sugar until peaks turn over, beat yolks with rest of sugar and vanilla until thick and creamy.

Combine three mixtures, folding together lightly. Turn into prepared tin. Bake at 180°C for about 30 minutes, until centre springs back.

Leave for 10 minutes then turn on to rack to cool. Top with whipped cream, quark or ricotta, and garnish with chopped dried fruit and nuts.

Orange Snacking Cake

Although this may be cooked in a loaf tin, I like it best as a flatter, thin cake, cut in pieces and served straight from its baking pan.

1 orange, grated rind and juice
water
1 egg
¹/₄ cup sour cream
50 g very soft butter
¹/₂ cup brown sugar
1 cup plus 2 Tbsp cake or plain flour
¹/₂ tsp baking soda

Grate rind from orange. Reserve ¹/₂ teaspoon for the icing and put the rest in a bowl. Squeeze juice. Reserve 1 tablespoon for the icing. Make the rest of the juice up to ¹/₂ cup with water. Combine with the rind and the remaining ingredients. Mix only until blended (about 10 seconds in a food processor).

Turn into a 20-cm-square pan. Cover with a lid, greaseproof paper or cling wrap. Elevate on an inverted plate. Cook at Medium-High (70% power) for 7 minutes or until just firm in centre. Uncover. Leave to stand for about 5 minutes, then ice.

Icing
reserved rind and juice
2 tsp butter
1 cup icing sugar

Heat butter, reserved rind and juice for 10 seconds in the microwave. Add icing sugar. Beat until smooth. Spread over the warm or cooled cake.

Coffee Cake

This special occasion rich, yet light, cake is quite different from most made with wholemeal flour.

150 g soft butter
1 cup brown sugar
2 Tbsp instant coffee
2 eggs
2 tsp vanilla
2 cups wholemeal flour
1 tsp baking powder
1¹/₂ tsp baking soda
2 tsp ground cinnamon
1 tsp ground cardomom
¹/₂ tsp salt
250 g sour cream
¹/₄ cup walnuts, chopped
juice of one lemon (2 Tbsp)

Cream the butter and sugar, then add the powdered or granular coffee and mix in well. Break in the eggs and add the vanilla, beat well, then transfer to a large bowl.

In another bowl, toss together the sifted dry ingredients. Add half of this to the creamed mixture, then mix in half the sour cream. Repeat with the other half of the dry ingredients and sour cream.

Stir in the walnuts and lemon juice, then tip into a large, well-oiled ring tin or a 23 cm paper-lined pan.

Bake at 180°C for 40–50 minutes, until a skewer poked into the middle comes out clean. Leave to stand in tin for a few minutes before turning out.

Pineapple Christmas Cake

C Pineapple Christmas Cake

This is my favourite Christmas cake. It has proved popular in thousands of households over twenty-five years!

225 g butter
1 cup sugar
½ tsp vanilla
½ tsp lemon essence
1 tsp cinnamon
1 tsp ground ginger
1 tsp mixed spice
¼ tsp nutmeg
3 cups flour
6 eggs
500 g sultanas, washed & dried
500 g currants, washed & dried
500 g mixed fruit, washed & dried
1 cup drained crushed pineapple

blanched almonds and cherries
¼ cup brandy (optional)

Line a 23 cm tin with one or two layers of greaseproof or baking paper. Measure spices and flour into any suitable container and put aside. Cream butter, sugar and essences until light and fluffy.

Add eggs, one at a time, with a spoonful of flour mixture after each, to prevent curdling. Add prepared fruit and pineapple to remaining flour.

Add flour and fruit to creamed mixture and mix thoroughly by hand.

Press evenly into prepared tin. Use almonds and cherries to decorate top. Bake at 150°C for 1½ hours, then at 130°C for about 2 hours, until a skewer comes out

clean. Sprinkle hot cake with brandy if desired.

C Two-Egg Christmas Cake

125 g butter
½ cup brown sugar
¼ tsp baking soda
½ tsp each mixed spice, cinnamon and ginger
1 cup all-purpose flour
2 large eggs
¼ tsp each vanilla, almond and lemon essence
2 cups sultanas
1 cup currants
½–1 cup any dried fruit
2 Tbsp sherry or spirits

Cream butter and brown sugar in

food processor. Mix soda, spices and flour. Add eggs with a tablespoon of flour mixture with each, to prevent curdling.

Add half the flour and essences. Add remaining flour mixed with prepared fruit, and liquid. Turn into prepared tin 18 cm round or 15 cm square.

Bake at 150°C for 1½–2 hours, until a skewer comes out clean.

Sprinkle extra sherry or spirits over hot cake, if desired. Leave 2 days or longer, before cutting.

C Dark Spicy Christmas Cake

This is a lovely, dark, moist, fruity cake. It is flavoured by small amounts of six spices, which give the cake a wonderful flavour. I make a fairly shallow cake in a 23 cm pan but you may prefer to cook it in a smaller, deeper pan. This takes longer to cook.

500 g currants, washed & dried
500 g raisins, washed & dried
500 g sultanas, washed & dried
1½ cups packed brown sugar
rind of 1 lemon
rind of 1 orange
250 g soft butter
1 Tbsp treacle
5 eggs
2 cups flour
½ tsp each ground allspice,
* cardamom, cinnamon, cloves,*
* coriander and nutmeg*

Weigh, separate and wash the dried fruit several hours before you plan to make the cake. Spread fruit out thinly to dry in the sun or in a low oven. Fruit should be cool and dry before you start mixing.

Remove citrus peel with a potato peeler and chop with the sugar in a food processor or grate the peel and mix with the sugar. Cream the sugar and butter, than add the treacle and cream again.

Add the eggs, one at a time, with a tablespoon of the measured flour between each. Mix the rest of the flour and the spices with the fruit, in a very large bowl.

Tip the creamed mixture into the floured fruit, and mix until soft enough to drop from your hand. If mixture is too dry, add up to ¼ cup of spirits, or sherry.

Put the mixture into a 20–23 cm round or square tin that has been lined with one or two layers of paper. Decorate top with almonds or cherries if you like. Bake at 150°C for 1 hour, then at 140°C for about 3 hours, until a skewer in the centre comes out clean. Dribble ¼ cup of any spirit over it while it is very hot, if you like. Leave an hour before removing from the tin.

C Cathedral Window Cake

This cake is mainly nuts and glacé fruit, held together by a small amount of cake batter.

When sliced thinly and held up to the light, it resembles a stained glass window.

3 cups Brazil nuts
1 cup almonds
1 cup cashew nuts
1 cup red cherries
1 cup mixed cherries
3 cups glacé fruit, e.g. pineapple,
* mangoes, peaches, apricots*
1 cup sultanas
1 cup sticky raisins
1½ cups flour
1 cup brown sugar
1 tsp baking powder
½ tsp salt
4 small eggs
1 tsp vanilla

Measure the nuts, fruit and dry ingredients into a large bowl, reserving some for decoration. Cut up large pieces of fruit, but leave some long thin pieces if desired, especially if using mango.

Mix eggs and vanilla until thoroughly combined and add to other ingredients. Mix thoroughly by hand.

Line metal ring pan with baking paper. Spray with non-stick spray. Press mixture firmly into pan, lying long pieces of glacé fruit in the middle of the mixture. Decorate top with reserved cherries etc.

Bake ring cake at 130°C for 2½–3 hours until cake feels firm. If top browns too quickly, cover loosely with baking paper.

The recipe as given makes one 20 cm ring cake 8 cm high. Use half the recipe to make a loaf-shaped cake. Cooking time should be about the same as the cake in the ring pan.
Note:
Glacé fruit is sweeter than, and more transparent than plain dried fruit. Dried fruit will not do for this cake.

Decorating Christmas Cakes

Decorating the Christmas cake used to be one of the highlights of my Christmas holidays when I was at school. I thought that a layer of almond icing and a coat of royal icing were necessities, and I can remember that both needed a great deal of sampling!

Another way of decorating Christmas cakes is to brush the cake with a thick layer of golden syrup or ordinary sugar syrup about half an hour before the end of cooking time, press on the halved almonds and cherries which have been similarly coated, and leave to finish cooking.

A thinned down syrup can be brushed over once or twice more during the last half hour to get a really shiny surface.

These decorations can look most attractive on the top of a cake, with the addition of a cake frill, a candle, a sprig of holly, or small tinselled decoration.

U Marzipan, or Almond Icing

Marzipan or almond paste can be made very quickly and although ground almonds are not cheap, I think you will find the icing cheaper than the bought variety which usually contains only almond flavouring, not the almonds themselves. This quantity is enough for one medium-sized cake.

75–100 g ground almonds
1 cup icing sugar
½ cup castor sugar
1 egg yolk
2 Tbsp lemon juice
¼–½ tsp almond essence

Mix the ground almonds with the icing and castor sugar. Make a well in the center of the mixture and add the egg yolk mixed with the strained lemon juice and a little of the essence. Mix together, then turn out on a board dusted with icing sugar and knead until smooth. Taste, and add more almond essence if it is needed.

Brush the top of the cake with a little apricot or plum jam which has been warmed to thin it down a little. Roll out the marzipan on the sugared board until it is the desired size, then place it on the jam-coated surface.

U Royal Icing

1 egg white
1 tsp lemon juice (strained)
½ tsp glycerine (optional)
250 g icing sugar

Beat the egg white and lemon juice together slightly in a medium-sized basin. Add the icing sugar gradually, beating well after each addition. Keep adding icing sugar until the mixture stands in firm peaks. Add the glycerine and beat well again. Use immediately, or keep in a covered container until ready to use.

For piping trellis work the icing can be thinned a little with a few drops of water until it is of the correct consistency.

Confectionery and Drinks

Although you can find plenty of sweets and soft drinks in a supermarket, they are seldom as good as the products that you make yourself.

Sweets have always been special-occasion treats in our household. They signify birthdays, school holiday activity, Mother's and Father's Days, Christmas parties, and so on.

My pleasure and satisfaction in turning out a 'good batch' has been considerable, especially in the days when I was starting to cook, as a child, and I can still remember the friends of my mother who had perfected their sweet-making skills and who would produce a sample when we visited them!

I hope that you will try the drinks at the end of this chapter. Some can be made very inexpensively, with surplus fruit, and although economical, taste much more natural than many of their commercially made counterparts.

If you like to know exactly what ingredients are in the foods and drinks that your child consumes, you will enjoy making your own sweets and drinks.

If you are a beginner, start with the easy sweet recipes that do not require the skills of sugar cookery. There are many to choose from. You can graduate to the other recipes later.

C M Best Ever Chocolates

(See photograph on page 244.)

These wonderful chocolates have a texture similar to the most expensive Swiss chocolates. You can make them your own specialty, with a little practice. New chocolate products make the process relatively easy.

½ cup double cream
180–200 g dark chocolate
50 g butter, cubed
½ cup coconut cream
¼ tsp rum (or other) essence
200 g cooking chocolate

Heat, but do not boil, the cream. Stir in chocolate and room-temperature butter until mixture is smooth. Add coconut cream and essence. For fruit-flavoured fillings, dissolve ⅛ teaspoon citric acid in ¼ teaspoon water. Add a few drops of this with fruit-flavoured essence.

Transfer to a 15–20 cm shallow container and refrigerate for several hours, until firm. Shape into small squares or balls, etc., using teaspoons. Work fast or return shapes to refrigerator. They must be very cold when you dip them.

Melt second measure of chocolate for coating. Dip cold filling into melted chocolate, on a fork. Push off fork on to a plastic bag. When set, decorate with a thin stream of chocolate. Refrigerate for up to 1 month.

M Chocolate Fudge

Rich and smooth, this foolproof fudge is nearly as good as well-made traditional fudge.

100 g butter, cubed
¼ cup milk
2 tsp vanilla
4 cups sifted icing sugar
½ cup cocoa
½–1 cup chopped nuts (optional)

Measure butter, milk and vanilla into a microwave-proof bowl. Add sifted icing sugar and cocoa. Microwave at Full power for 2 minutes then remove and beat until smooth. Stir in nuts if used.

Pour into a loaf tin lined with sprayed greaseproof paper. Refrigerate for several hours or freeze. Leave overnight for easiest cutting.
Variation:
Replace 1 teaspoon vanilla with 1 teaspoon rum essence.

M Fabulous Fudge

This is such delicious soft, smooth

fudge that you should experiment with the cooking time until you get it exactly right. If you have to beat the fudge for too long, increase the cooking time by 30 seconds next time.

100 g butter
1 cup sugar
¼ cup golden syrup
1 can (400 g) sweetened condensed milk
1 tsp vanilla

Mix all ingredients except vanilla in a 22 cm flat-bottomed casserole or a batter bowl resistant to high heat. Microwave at Full power for 7–9 minutes, stirring after 2, 4, 6 and 7 minutes. At end point all sugar should have dissolved, mixture should have bubbled vigorously all over surface, and formed a soft ball in cold water.

Add vanilla (or other essence). Do not worry if mixture looks slightly curdled or buttery. Beat with a wooden spoon for about 5 minutes or until mixture loses its gloss and keeps its shape without flattening when poured onto a buttered metal surface.

Let stand about an hour and then cut into squares. Mixture should be creamy, with melting texture. Fudge will be a little firmer the next day.
Note:
If fudge will not set, reheat until whole mixture bubbles, stirring often. Cook 30 seconds longer, then beat again.

C Marshmallows

Economical marshmallow requires a strong arm or an electric beater!

2 Tbsp gelatine
½ cup cold water
2 cups sugar
¾ cup hot water
1 tsp vanilla
pinch salt
1 cup toasted coconut

Soften gelatine in cold water. Over moderate heat, boil sugar and hot water until a little, dropped in cold water, forms a ball which can be flattened when squeezed (about 15 minutes) then stir in the softened gelatine.

Stand pot in cold water until you can rest your hand on saucepan bottom. Add vanilla and salt and beat until thick and white. Pour into buttered or sprayed 20 cm cake tin.

Refrigerate several hours, until firm, then warm tin and lift marshmallow on to board sprinkled with coconut. Cut in squares and shake in plain or toasted coconut, dampening cubes with water if coconut does not stick.
Variation:
Colour half the mixture pink.

Flavour with raspberry or strawberry essence.

C M Hazelnut Chocolates

When you make these chocolates, you have several options.

1 (70 g) pkt hazelnuts
200 g cooking chocolate
50 g soft butter
1 egg yolk
2 Tbsp hazelnut liqueur

Toast hazelnuts at 180°C for 10 minutes. Chop, reserving some for garnish. Melt chocolate in microwave at Medium (50% power) for 2–4 minutes. Stir in butter, egg yolk, liqueur and nuts. Spoon into small paper or foil cups and top with reserved nuts.

To Melt Chocolate
Break chocolate into squares. Heat in the microwave at Medium (50% power) until chocolate softens and can be stirred until it is completely smooth. Do not heat longer than necessary.

Guide times for heating
25 g — about 30 seconds–2 mins.
50 g — about 1–3 mins.
100 g — about 2–4 mins.
200 g — about 3–5 mins.

For ease, use easy-to-melt chocolate and easy-to-dip chocolate, if available, following melting instructions on packets.

U Cherry Truffles or Squares

Shape this mixture into balls or cut into small squares and ice with chocolate icing, if desired.

1 (200 g) pkt wine biscuits, crumbed
2 cups coconut
12–20 glacé cherries
100 g butter, melted
½–1 tsp almond essence
¾ cup (½ tin) sweetened condensed milk
1–3 Tbsp sherry, brandy or kirsch

Crumb biscuits. Add coconut, cherries and melted butter, then the essence and condensed milk. Mix well, adding enough liquid to form a workable dough. Roll into balls or press into tin, 2 cm thick.

If desired, ice with chocolate icing. When cold, cut into 2 cm squares.

U Chocolate Truffles

My favourite truffle recipe!

From left: Marzipan Fruits, Chocolate Truffles, Hazelnut Chocolates, Bulls' Eyes and Cherry Squares

½ pkt (125 g) wine biscuits
100 g soft butter
¼ cup cocoa
1 cup icing sugar
½ cup coconut
¼ cup chopped walnuts
¼–½ tsp essence*
1–2 Tbsp sherry or fruit juice

Crumb biscuits in a food processor. Add soft (not melted) butter, cocoa, icing sugar and coconut. Add walnuts, if desired, and whatever essence you like.

Mix, adding a little liquid if dry. Form mixture into about 30 small balls. Roll in extra coconut and chill until firm. Refrigerate or freeze in airtight container for up to 2 months.
*e.g. vanilla, almond, peppermint, raspberry, orange, rum, caramel, brandy or coconut.

Bulls' Eyes

The texture of these nutty bulls' eyes is unpredictable. You need to add enough liquid to form an easily-rolled mixture.

1 cup freshly roasted hulled
  peanuts
50 g soft butter
¾ cup icing sugar
½ tsp almond or vanilla essence

1–3 Tbsp orange juice or sherry
100 g cooking chocolate

Process peanuts in food processor until very finely chopped. Drop in soft butter, then add the icing sugar and essence. When well mixed, add orange juice or sherry to make rolling consistency. Form 20–30 balls, then chill.

Melt 100 g cooking chocolate. Put bulls' eyes one at a time on a fork, and nearly submerge each in melted chocolate, leaving a circle on each uncovered. Chill on a plastic-covered tray until set. Store in one layer in refrigerator.

Marzipan Fruit

Use this ground almond mixture to make realistic fruit.

100 g ground almonds
1 cup icing sugar
½ cup castor sugar
1 egg yolk
½ tsp almond essence
2–3 tsp lemon juice
food colourings and cloves

Combine the first five ingredients in a bowl or food processor. Add just enough lemon juice to make a firm dough. Divide mixture into four parts. Leave one plain, and colour

the rest pale yellow, green and orange, mixing colours as necessary.

Shape fruits, using cloves to make stems. Mix a few drops of food colouring on a plate and paint deeper colours on fruit.

Easy Peppermint Creams

Although these may be served plain, they are especially good when chocolate-dipped.

25 g butter
¼ cup sweetened condensed milk
½ tsp peppermint essence
about 2 cups icing sugar
green food colouring (optional)

Have butter soft but not melted. Mix first four ingredients in medium-sized bowl or food processor, adding enough icing sugar to form a firm paste.

Colour half green, if desired.

Form one or two rolls, press then roll together for green/white roll, wrap in plastic then chill until firm. Cut in slices or roll in balls.
Variation:
Dip in melted chocolate (see page 246) if desired. Store chocolate-coated peppermints at room temperature, but uncoated creams in refrigerator.

C Pulled Taffy

Popular with all age groups, this is my favourite toffee recipe. I like to pull the partly cooled toffee into a pearly rope, but it may be left to set as ordinary toffee, then broken into pieces, if preferred.

½ cup sugar
2 Tbsp water
2 Tbsp honey
25 g butter
½ tsp rum or vanilla essence

Boil sugar, water, honey and butter over moderate heat, without stirring, until it forms a ball which cracks when bitten, when dropped into cold water. Remove from heat, add essence and swirl mixture in pan to mix.

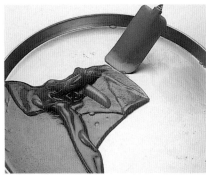

Pour into well buttered, preferably non-stick, pan to cool. When mixture is firm enough, lift edges towards centre.

As soon as it can be handled, lift with buttered hands and stretch and twist several times to form a rope. Keep stretching and twisting mixture as it cools.

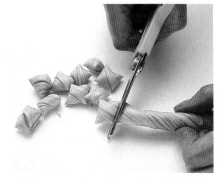

When nearly cold, cut in short lengths with a heavy knife or kitchen scissors. Store in airtight container when cold.

C Hokey Pokey

Small quantities go a long way in this old-fashioned recipe!

½ cup sugar
1 Tbsp water
2 tsp vinegar
¼ cup golden syrup
½ tsp baking soda

Butter a metal baking sheet or sponge roll pan. Heat sugar, water and vinegar in a medium-sized pot or frying pan until the sugar dissolves, over moderate heat. Add the golden syrup and cook slowly over low heat or the mixture may darken and burn before it has cooked long enough. Heat until mixture forms a hard ball which breaks when bitten after being dropped in cold water, then remove from heat and sprinkle with sieved baking soda. Stir just enough to mix in soda thoroughly. While mixture is still puffy, pour on to buttered sheet.

When cold, break into pieces and store in airtight jars, since hokey pokey softens on contact with air.

Variation:
Dip in chocolate to prevent softening if desired.

C Toffee Apples and Lollipops

1 cup sugar
¼ cup water
1 Tbsp vinegar
½ tsp red food colouring
4 small apples
12 wooden sticks

Spray an oven slide with non-stick spray or butter it well.

Boil the sugar, water and vinegar in a small saucepan over moderate heat until mixture forms a hard ball which breaks when bitten, when dropped into cold water. Add enough red food colouring to make toffee brightly coloured. (Add ¼ teaspoon raspberry essence if desired.) While toffee cooks, polish small apples and push sticks into them. Turn one apple at a time in the toffee, holding the pot on an angle. Once coated, leave to drip then stand on buttered oven-slide.

Spoon toffee round stick-end of apple when level of toffee in pot drops.

For lollipops, pour circles of toffee on buttered oven-slide. Turn end of stick in toffee pot then place on circle. Wrap apples and lollipops promptly.

Note:
Add 1 tablespoon liquid glucose with sugar, if available.

U Fizzing Sherbet

Old-fashioned fizz-on-your-tongue sherbet powder is a remarkably popular novelty for 6–12 year olds! Easy and economical to make, it may be kept for weeks in an airtight jar.

1 cup icing sugar
1 tsp baking soda
1 tsp powdered citric acid
1 tsp powdered tartaric acid
½ tsp lemon or other essence
Or
2 Tbsp fruit drink powder

Combine all ingredients so they are well mixed, using a food processor or a fine sieve.

Notes:
If either acid is crystalline, convert it to powder in a pestle and mortar or with the back of a spoon.

For easier mixing, use liquid essence only if food processing.

Traditional sherbet flavours are lemon, orange and raspberry. Use more acids and flavouring, if desired.

Presentation suggestions:
In small cellophane paper or plastic (or zip-lock) bags, with a short length of straw or licorice tube for sucking, *or* in teaspoon lots on the palm of a hand for touching with tongue tip!

U Uncooked Coconut Ice

This recipe is good for beginners! It always sets, never hardens too much, and may be eaten soon after making.

½ can sweetened condensed milk
2 cups coconut
2 cups icing sugar
1 tsp vanilla
¼ tsp raspberry essence
4–6 drops red food colouring

Warm can of condensed milk if cold. Measure into fairly large bowl (or food processor bowl). Add coconut, icing sugar and vanilla. Mix with rubber scraper or metal cutting blade until combined.

Remove half mixture and press out 1 cm thick on extra coconut on board. To remaining mixture, add raspberry essence (if desired) and enough colouring to make a medium pink. Press this over the white layer. Chill until firm for 15–30 minutes, then cut in squares.

Variation:
Use trimmings, or unset mixture, to stuff dessert dates.

M Cream-Cheese Chocolate Fudge

This rich fudge should be cut in very small squares.

½ cup (125 g) cream cheese
200 g cooking chocolate
1 tsp vanilla
2½ cups sifted icing sugar

Soften cream cheese for 2 minutes at Defrost (30% power). Microwave chocolate in fairly large dish at Medium (50% power), for about 3 minutes, or until evenly soft.

Stir until smooth, add cream cheese, vanilla and icing sugar and mix until evenly combined, using a rubber spatula. Mixture will be thick. Work quickly before chocolate or cream cheese cools. Spread in a well-sprayed container about 12 × 15 cm.

Refrigerate until firm. Cut in small pieces.

Variations:
Add ½–1 cup chopped nuts.
Replace ½ teaspoon vanilla with rum essence.

C M Russian Fudge

Condensed milk gives this fudge extra richness.

3 cups sugar
½ cup milk
½ × 200 g can condensed milk
2 Tbsp golden syrup
125 g butter, cubed
1 tsp vanilla
½–1 cup chopped walnuts (optional)

Combine first five ingredients in a high heat-resistant microwave (12-cup-capacity) bowl or large saucepan.

Microwave at Full power, stirring every 2 minutes or cook over moderate heat, stirring continuously, for about 15 minutes, until mixture forms a soft ball.

Remove from microwave oven or stovetop. Add vanilla and walnuts and beat for 4–5 minutes until mixture starts to thicken. Pour quickly into 20 cm pan lined with a strip of baking paper. Leave until firm, tip from pan then cut into squares.

M Candied Peel

This is a firm-textured confection, rather than a cooking ingredient.

4 mandarins
1 cup water
2 Tbsp water
¼ cup sugar
¼ cup castor sugar

Quarter mandarins. Peel away skins. (Use flesh for another purpose.) Cut each quarter skin lengthwise into two thinner strips. Put pieces in a heat-resistant measuring cup with 1 cup of the water. Cover and boil for 15 minutes. Drain and pat dry.

Put peel, sugar and remaining water into a high heat-resistant casserole dish. Boil, uncovered for 3–4 minutes until sugar dissolves and forms a syrup which almost evaporates. Stop cooking before syrup turns golden. Lift hot pieces of peel out, one by one and turn them in castor sugar.

Cool on a rack. Store in an airtight jar for up to 2 weeks. Eat as a confection, plain or dipped in chocolate.

U Apricot Balls

These little balls will brighten any collection of confections.

250 g dried apricots
¼ cup sugar
rind of 1 orange or tangelo
1 Tbsp orange or tangelo juice
about ½ cup coconut

Chop dried apricots roughly and put aside. Put sugar in food processor with thinly peeled citrus rind. Process until chopped, then add apricots and liquid and process until finely cut. Add enough coconut to make a firm mixture.

Shape into 20–30 balls, roll lightly in extra coconut and refrigerate, uncovered, until firm.

Without a food processor, mince apricots with remaining ingredients several times.

C Fruity Nut Balls

Home made fruit and nut mixtures taste very fresh and interesting.

½ cup dried apricots
¼ cup orange or lemon juice
½ cup roasted peanuts
½ cup washed sultanas
½ cup washed currants or raisins
¼ cup toasted sesame seeds
about ¼ cup coconut

Boil chopped apricots in juice until liquid has disappeared.

Chop nuts roughly in food processor. Add apricots, sultanas, currants and sesame seeds, and process until finely chopped. Add

enough coconut to form a rollable mixture.

Form into bars or small balls. Roll in extra coconut.

D Dehydrated Confections

It is possible to make sweet, chewy, candy-like foods with little or no added sugar using a dehydrator.

When foods which are naturally slightly sweet are dried, their sweetness and flavour is intensified.

Sometimes foods are dried to preserve them and are reconstituted later by simmering in water, but often the dried foods are eaten exactly as they are, as snacks — as are commercially dried apricots, sultanas, etc.

In hot, dry climates some food may be sun-dried but a dehydrator gives good results all year round. With moving air at a low temperature, it produces better results than an oven.

D Candied Kiwifruit Slices

Peel sweet, well-flavoured kiwifruit. Cut into 5 mm slices. Add 500 g fruit to a plastic bag containing a syrup made from ¼ cup sugar dissolved in ½ cup warm water. Squeeze air from bag and leave to stand for 4–8 hours.

Arrange drained fruit on rack of dehydrator (sprayed with non-stick spray) and dry at 60–70°C for 6–8 hours or until leathery. Store in airtight containers when cold. For long storage, keep in freezer.

Eat as is or dip in melted chocolate for an after-dinner confection.
Variation:
For bright green colour (and slightly modified flavour) add 2 tablespoons crème de menthe to syrup.

D Candied Mandarin or Tangelo Slices

Use sweet ripe fruit with unblemished skins. Marinate 5 mm slices in sugar syrup, as for kiwifruit. Dry at 60–70°C until skin cracks when bent. Eat plain or chocolate-dipped.

D Chewy Yoghurt Candy

Pour 500–600 g apricot-flavoured yoghurt on to a solid dehydrator tray sprayed with non-stick spray. Dry at 55°C for about 10 hours or until you can lift the leather from the tray.

Roll up tightly, wrap in plastic film to keep airtight and cut into sections with a knife or kitchen scissors, as required.

Experiment with different brands and flavours until you find your favourites.

D Apricot Banana Leather

This unbelievably delicious fruit 'leather', made in a dehydrator is a wonderful snack for any time of the day.

1 cup whole-grain oats
2 cups apricot yoghurt
2 cups mashed ripe bananas
¼–½ cup sultanas, raisins or chopped nuts

Stir all ingredients together, by hand, then spread the mixture evenly on to two solid (35 cm) dehydrator sheets which have been lightly sprayed or oiled.

Dehydrate at 55°C for 12–18 hours, turning once, when mixture is dry enough to lift in one piece. When ready, leather should be quite crisp. Cut or break into pieces, then store in airtight containers.

D Fruit Leathers

Simmer, then purée fruit which discolours on standing or purée raw fruit. Make mixtures if desired. Sieve berry fruit with large seeds. Add 1 tablespoon honey per 3–4 cups fruit purée if desired, or if fruit is tart. Purée should be thick enough to spread with a spatula.

Spread on solid tray sprayed with non-stick spray so purée is about 5 mm thick. Dry at 50–60°C for 6–8 hours or until leather is dry enough to lift from tray and feels pliable and leatherlike.

Roll up while warm, cut in lengths as desired and wrap in plastic. Store in a cool dark place until required. For long storage (more than several weeks) keep in freezer.

D Dried Sliced Fruit

Slice sweet, ripe fruit, e.g. bananas, tamarillos, about 5 mm thick. If necessary, dip in citrus fruit juice to prevent browning. Dry at 60–70°C until crisp. Store in airtight containers to prevent fruit softening and losing its crispness.
Note:
Turn dehydrator containing partly dried food off at night, if desired.

Dehydrated Confections: Dried Sliced Fruit and Fruit Leathers

Caramel Walnuts, Caramel Peanuts and Caramel Popcorn

C Caramel for Coating

Heat ¹/₂ cup sugar in a 20–25 cm clean dry saucepan or frying pan, or ¹/₄ cup in a small pan, without stirring it at all.

Shake and tilt pan, with heat low enough to melt sugar evenly, without letting it darken unevenly. Caramel is ready to use when it is an even light golden-brown. Dark caramel develops a bitter flavour.

C Caramel Popcorn

Caramelise ¹/₄ cup sugar in a fairly large saucepan. Use to coat warm, freshly popped popcorn (made from ¹/₄ cup unpopped corn). Sprinkle lightly with salt, mix well, then spread on well-sprayed or buttered surface to cool. Wrap when cold.

C Caramel Walnuts

Impale walnut halves, one at a time on a fine skewer. Dip in hot caramel, drip off excess and cool on well-sprayed or buttered surface, twisting skewer to remove it as soon as possible. Wrap as soon as cold.

C M Caramel Peanuts

Tip ¹/₄–1 cup hot, freshly roasted peanuts (about 3–5 minutes at Full power in microwave) into hot caramel, made from ¹/₂ cup sugar, stir to coat, separate into bars or blocks and cool on well-sprayed or buttered surface. Press nut toffee into more definite shapes when a little cooler. Wrap when cold.

U Ginger Beer

What I like best about home-made ginger beer is that is has such a good flavour — quite unlike anything bought. The element of chance, as each batch will differ slightly, and the satisfaction from the savings made on each bottle, add to the enjoyment.

For 4 × 1.25 litre bottles:
1 tsp dried yeast granules
2 tsp sugar
¹/₂ cup warm water
2 cups sugar
1 Tbsp ground ginger
1 tsp lemon essence
1 tsp tartaric acid
2 litres hot water
2 litres cold water

Stir the first three ingredients together in a glass and leave to stand in a warm place.

Measure the remaining sugar, ginger, lemon essence and tartaric acid into a clean plastic bucket. Pour on the hot water and stir to dissolve the sugar. Add the cold water to cool the liquid down.

When you are sure the mixture is no hotter than lukewarm, add the bubbling yeast. Leave in the lightly covered bucket for 24–36 hours, then strain into four thoroughly clean 1.25 litre plastic soft-drink bottles. Fill each bottle up to within 3 cm of the top with extra cold water. Put 1 teaspoon of sugar in each bottle, and screw on the washed tops. Shake to dissolve sugar.

Leave to stand in a warm place until the bottles feel absolutely rigid when you squeeze them. This should take from 1–5 days, depending on the temperature, type of yeast, etc.

Refrigerate bottles for at least 2 hours before removing the lids. If the bottles are very fizzy, loosen then tighten the lids several times, so that the gas is released slowly.

Plan to drink all of the brew within 3–4 weeks.

Note:
In hot weather, or if previous batches are very bubbly, use less yeast, and add less sugar to each bottle, when bottling.

Grape Drink

If you make this juice, you might like to experiment with the amount of acid used, and the variety. I drink a lot of the drink made by this recipe, but for young children it might be rather strong. I use tartaric acid, because this comes from grapes, but citric acid, from citrus fruit, is milder in flavour.

2 cups grape juice
2 cups sugar
1½–2 tsp tartaric acid

Combine the three ingredients in a saucepan, using the smaller amount of acid for a less tart drink.

If the drink is to be consumed quickly, heat it only until the sugar dissolves. If you want to keep it for some months, bring it to the boil before straining it into small clean bottles. Screw on tops straight away. When cold, dip the tops of the bottles in melted wax for an added precaution, if desired.

Dilute the more acid juice using 5–6 parts of water to 1 part cordial. The other drink requries slightly less water.

Iced Lemon Tea

This refreshing hot-weather drink can be made with a small amount of hot liquid.

For 2 servings:
1½ cups water
1 tea bag
3 slices of lemon
juice of remaining lemon
ice
mint sprigs

Heat ½ cup water in a measuring cup until it boils rapidly (about 2 minutes). Immediately drop in tea bag and one slice of lemon.

Leave for 2 minutes and then remove (and squeeze) tea bag. Add juice squeezed from lemon after removing 3 slices. Add sugar to taste (2–3 teaspoons). Add remaining water.

Pour over ice cubes and mint sprigs in two glasses topping up with extra water if necessary. Garnish with remaining lemon slices.

Tangelo Cooler

Tangelos give this drink a very definite colour and flavour, but you can use oranges instead, if you like.

For 4–6 servings:
2 tangelos, rind and juice
½ cup sugar
½ tsp citric acid
¼ cup water

Grate or peel the coloured skin from the tangelos. Put into a 1 litre jug with the sugar, citric acid and water. Microwave at Full power for about 2 minutes or until mixture boils. Stir until sugar dissolves. Add tangelo juice and fill to 1 litre level with cold water. Pour over ice cubes.
Variation:
Measure equal portions of recipe and white wine.

Raspberry Soda

This brightly coloured drink may be made using whatever berries are in season.

For 6–8 servings:
2 cups fresh or frozen raspberries
¼ cup water
¼ cup sugar
½ tsp citric acid

Crush the berries with the water using a potato masher, fork or food processor. Microwave in a wide-bottomed bowl at Full power for 2 minutes. Add sugar and citric acid and microwave for 2 minutes longer or until hot enough to dissolve sugar. Stir once or twice.

Strain to remove berries, shaking strainer. Pour ¼ cup syrup over ice in tall glasses. Fill glasses with ¼–1 cup soda water (or water). Refrigerate remaining syrup for up to 2 weeks.

Fresh Lemonade

Quickly made, this drink is deliciously refreshing. Make it fizzy or not.

For 2 servings:
1 lemon, rind and juice
2 Tbsp sugar
½ cup water
ice
extra water or soda water

Peel lemon, removing only coloured rind. In a measuring cup microwave lemon rind, juice and sugar at Full power for 2 minutes or until sugar dissolves when stirred.

Stir in ½ cup cold water. Pour liquid over ice in two tall glasses. Top up with extra water or soda water. Stir, garnish and serve.

Home-Brewed Beer

Home brewing is fun, and can save you a considerable amount of money. The most important and time-consuming aspect of successful beer making is hygiene, but with a little care the rewards are great! Always clean and rinse your brewing equipment and bottles before and after use, and you should have few problems.

For about 40 × 750 ml bottles:
1 kg white sugar
1 kg soft brown sugar
about 1.5 kg light malt extract
1 tsp Epsom salts
1 tsp common salt
150 g dried hops
1 (about 5 g) pkt Lager beer yeast or 2 tsp Active Yeast (dried yeast granules)
2 tsp extra sugar
brewers finings (optional)
sodium metabisulphate to clean bottles

Combine the sugars, malt and salts with 2 litres of boiling water. Strain into a 10–20 litre plastic container, then add 4 more litres of boiling water.

Simmer the hops in 5 litres of water for 30 minutes, then strain the liquid into the plastic container, too. Leave to cool to 30°C.

Mix the yeast with a cup of blood-temperature water and 2 teaspoons sugar, and leave to start working while the hot liquid cools.

Add the bubbling yeast mixture to the 30°C brew, cover the container loosely or fit with a water lock, and leave to ferment at a warm room temperature for about 10–14 days (longer in colder weather).

If desired, add finings, following the manufacturers' instructions. I don't usually bother and find that the beer is usually quite clear anyway.

While the beer ferments, organise your bottles (screw-top plastic soft-drink bottles are fine). Wash thoroughly, then dip into a mixture of 1 tablespoon of sodium metabisulphate dissolved in 10 litres of water, and leave to drain. If you are working in advance, cover the openings with lids or pieces of foil.

When the beer is clear, siphon off the clear liquid into a clean container. Pour 1 cupful into each 750 ml bottle, and a proportionate amount into bottles of other sizes, add ½ teaspoon sugar to each bottle, then nearly fill the bottles with cold water. Top with crown tops, or screw on the tops of the plastic bottles.

Leave for about 2 weeks before drinking. You can judge when the beer in plastic bottles is bubbly by squeezing. They are hard when ready. Refrigerate bottles before opening, taking care not to disturb any sediment in the bottom. When pouring, it is a good idea to decant the beer from the bottle into a glass jug, and to fill glasses from this.

For best results, drink your beer 1–3 months after making it.

Hot Mocha

Irish Coffee

Hot Egg Nog

M Hot Mocha

Mixtures of chocolate and coffee are popular and interesting. This is a good winter drink for children or adults. Alter the proportion of ingredients if you like.

For 1 large serving:
1½ Tbsp drinking chocolate
1–2 tsp instant coffee
1 cup milk
whipped cream
cinnamon or chocolate curls

Mix drinking chocolate, instant coffee, sugar and milk in a mug. Microwave at Full power until steaming (1½ minutes). Top with lightly whipped cream and add a pinch of cinnamon or chocolate curls.
Note:
Use other chocolate-flavoured drinks instead of drinking chocolate, if preferred.

> To make chocolate curls, warm a potato peeler under the hot tap, then run it along the edge of a cake of chocolate. Experiment with the chocolate at different temperatures, until you get the curl the shape and size you want it.

M Irish Coffee

These days almost any whisky-coffee mixture is called Irish coffee, so please yourself when you make it, using strong, freshly made coffee or instant granules. Sweeten the coffee, the cream, or both.

For 1 serving:
½ cup freshly made strong coffee
Or 2 tsp instant coffee dissolved in
* ½ cup hot water*
1–2 tsp sugar
1–2 Tbsp whisky
lightly whipped cream

Mix all ingredients except cream in a microwave-proof mug or glass. Microwave at Full power for 45 seconds to 1 minute, until very hot. Stir to mix sugar. Then carefully pour cold cream on to the surface. Drink without stirring, so the layer of cold cream remains on top of the hot, whisky-flavoured coffee. Alter proportions to suit your taste.

M Hot Egg Nog

For a pick-me-up or a meal in a glass, this is hard to beat.

For 1 large or 2 small servings:
1 egg, separated
1 cup milk
3–4 tsp brown or white sugar
few drops of vanilla
¼ tsp freshly grated nutmeg

Separate egg into two small bowls. To the yolk add milk, 1½ teaspoons sugar, vanilla, and most of the nutmeg. Mix with a rotary beater and microwave at Full power for 2½–3 minutes, until bubbling around the edges. Beat the mixture again briefly, and then microwave for a few seconds until it bubbles again.

In the meantime rinse beater and beat egg white until foamy. Add remaining sugar and beat until peaks turn over. Tip most of the egg white into the hot mixture and beat briefly.

Pour mixture into one or two mugs or glasses, top with remaining egg white and sprinkle with nutmeg. Serve hot.
Variation:
For adults, replace vanilla with 1 tablespoon rum, whisky or brandy if desired.

Hot Buttered Rum

Blackcurrant Cup

Hot Toddy

Ⓜ Hot Buttered Rum

This is a welcoming drink for a cold winter evening. The butter is an essential flavouring. If you leave it out you will get a quite different drink.

For 1 large serving:
1 cup apple juice
cinnamon stick (optional)
2–3 cloves (optional)
curl of lemon or orange rind (optional)
2–4 Tbsp rum
¹/₂–1 tsp butter

In a microwave-proof mug combine juice, spices and rind (if used). Microwave at Full power for 2 minutes or until hot but not boiling. Add rum and butter. Stir and serve with a cinnamon stick.

Variation:
If you are planning to make this for a large group, increase amounts using the proportions given here. Make spiced apple juice ahead of time, by microwaving the apple juice and spices and rind until boiling, and leaving it to cool. Strain, and add more spices for appearance. Use clear, well-flavoured apple juice for best results.

Ⓜ Blackcurrant Cup

Although blackcurrant and wine mixtures are often served cold, they are delicious when hot, too. Sweeten to taste.

For 2 servings:
1 cup white wine
1 Tbsp blackcurrant cordial (or cassis)
1 strip orange peel
sugar (optional)

Combine ingredients in one or two heat-proof mugs. Heat at Full power for 2 minutes or until hot but not boiling. Taste, add a little sugar if desired, and serve with orange wedges, slices or curls of orange peel.

Ⓜ Hot Toddy

This makes a wonderful nightcap and is widely acclaimed as a cold cure. Whatever its medicinal properties, it is sure to make you feel better! Alter proportions to suit your mood and need!

For 1 serving:
1 Tbsp brown sugar
thinly peeled rind and juice from ¹/₂ lemon
¹/₂ cup (125 ml) water
1–2 slices root ginger (optional)
1–2 Tbsp whisky (optional)

Measure sugar, lemon rind, juice and water into a microwave-proof glass or mug. Add ginger if desired. Heat at Full power for 45 seconds or until hot but not boiling. Stir and then add whisky to taste.

Variation:
Replace lemon, ginger and sugar with suitable quantities of commercially made lemon cordials.

Keep a piece of root ginger (wrapped in plastic) in your freezer door.
You can grate it without thawing it, to add a good ginger flavour to many foods.
Replace it in the freezer before it thaws.

Storecupboard

Jams and Jellies

It is very satisfying to turn a basket of fresh fruit, picked from your own garden or bought cheaply at the height of the season, into a few jars of sparkling jam or jelly.

For most of us, jam and jelly making does not mean a huge production line. We don't have to get out a giant jam pan, or spend all of a hot summer day stirring huge bubbling mixtures while everybody else enjoys the sunshine. Nowadays we can buy good fresh fruit all the year round, and if we have gardens where we produce large fruit crops, we probably choose to preserve much of this by quick methods such as freezing, so we don't need to think of jam making as a basic method of fruit preservation.

There are some jams and jellies which you just can't buy. For example, I like to make glazes and sauces for meat with redcurrant jelly or, if I don't have this, with guava or crabapple jelly. The only redcurrant jelly I have been able to buy was very expensive and was made in Scotland!

If you want unusual, personalised gifts, consider developing your own jam or jelly specialities. To get ideas for possible combinations, and to check prices, look at some of the more interesting jams in a good delicatessen. Look, too, at the way these are bottled and labelled — who knows, you may decide to make your fortune as a jam maker!

I hope these recipes will inspire you to make a few jars of jam and jelly. It doesn't take long, and your family and friends are sure to be appreciative. This, to most of us, is reward enough!

From left to right: Dark Red Jelly, Peach Conserve, Apricot Jam, Strawberry Jam, Rhubarb Conserve.

C Jam Making

In a large, uncovered saucepan boil prepared fruit briskly until soft, adding a little water to stop fruit sticking if necessary. Measure cooked fruit pulp. Add 1 cup sugar and 1 tablespoon lemon juice to each cup of pulp.

Boil briskly, stirring regularly. If you have a jam thermometer, use it to check setting point, at about 222°F, but use wrinkling-skin test as well.

Near final setting point, pour about 2 teaspoons jam on a dry saucer. Stand it by an open window until it cools. When jam forms a skin which wrinkles when finger is drawn over it, remove pan from heat.

Pour hot jam into clean jars previously heated at 140°C oven for 15 minutes. Top immediately with metal lacquered tops which have been soaked in boiling water for 5 minutes.

Alternatively, pour hot jam into clean, hot preserving jars. Top immediately with preserving seals which have been soaked in boiling water for 5 minutes. Screw on bands tightly.

Or pour into clean jars as for other methods. Cool jam until quite firm. Top with a thin layer of paraffin wax melted in an old teapot or other container. Tilt jar so paraffin sticks to dry edge above jam. Cover with dampened cellophane top, stretched tightly.

M Jam

Small amounts of jam cook well in microwave ovens. The jam never sticks or burns on the bottom and has a good fruit flavour and bright colour.

Because jams get very hot, it is important to use containers which will not soften or melt at high heat. Use larger bowls or casserole dishes, since small amounts of jam can bubble up surprisingly high. Bubbling stops as soon as oven door is opened and is more manageable if lower power levels are used. Lower the power level to Medium-High (70% power) or Medium (50% power) and increase times, if necessary.

Do not seal before end point is reached or jam may form mould on top during storage.

To test for setting, pour about 2 teaspoons of jam on to a cold, dry saucer. Stand in a cool place for 2–3 minutes. When the jam is ready, its surface should wrinkle when you draw your finger over it. Modify your own jam recipes, using these as a guide.

If jam and pickles are to be eaten within a few weeks, do not seal the jars but keep them in the refrigerator. For longer storage or for gifts, seal the preserves in clean jars which have been heated thoroughly and have laquered metal screw-on lids.

Wash jars thoroughly then:
• Heat in conventional oven at 140°C for 15 minutes *or*
• Boil in a large bowl or saucepan in water to cover *or*
• Quarter fill jars with water and microwave until water boils for 1 minute.

To sterilise metal lids, drop them in a container of boiling water. Do not microwave.

Pour hot jams and pickles into hot jars to within 1 cm of top. Screw on hot lid immediately.

C Apricot Jam

Follow general method for jam. Use 500 g–1 kg of slightly under-ripe apricots. Add 1–2 tablespoons water to the quartered fruit to stop it sticking while it starts cooking. Boil the kernels from the cracked apricot stones with the fruit if you like an almondy flavour.

M Apricot Jam

500 g apricots
2 Tbsp lemon juice
sugar

Halve apricots, then cut each half into four quarters. Place in a large high-heat-resistant bowl or high-sided casserole. Add the lemon juice.

Microwave at Full power for 5–8 minutes, stirring when fruit bubbles around the edge of the dish, and heating again until whole surface boils vigorously.

Measure the volume of fruit, and add ³/₄ cup sugar to each cup of fruit. Stir thoroughly. Cook for 5–10 minutes, until a little jam sets.

Pour into prepared jars and seal. (Do not increase the quantities given.)

M Kiwifruit Jam

Serve this for breakfast, instead of marmalade.

500 g prepared kiwifruit
¹/₄ cup lemon juice
2 cups sugar

Remove skins of kiwifruit, either by peeling or by halving and scooping out centres. Cut lengthwise and remove central core and the area close to it containing most seeds. Weigh fruit after this preparation. Mash with potato masher.

Microwave fruit and lemon juice in a large, high-heat-resistant bowl until mixture boils vigorously, about 6 minutes. Stir in sugar, dissolving it as much as possible. Cook about 8 minutes longer until a little jam sets.

Add enough green food colouring to produce a pleasing green colour. Pour into prepared jars and seal.

C Strawberry Jam

This jam has a clear, bright colour and sets well.

500 g strawberries
1 Tbsp water
2 cups sugar
¹/₂ tsp tartaric acid

Heat clean strawberries with the water in a large saucepan, mashing with a potato masher to break them slightly.

When soft, add sugar and stir over moderate heat until it dissolves. Boil briskly for 3 minutes, then stir in the acid.

Boil briskly for 4 minutes longer, then pour into hot jars and seal.

M Strawberry Jam

Ever popular, with adults and children alike.

500 g strawberries
3 cups sugar
1 tsp tartaric acid

Halve or quarter large berries. In a large high-heat-resistant microwave bowl or high-sided casserole dish heat at Full power until berries bubble around edge of container. Add sugar and heat again for 6 minutes, stirring after 2 and 4 minutes. Add tartaric acid and heat again for 6–10 minutes or until a little jam sets. Pour into prepared jars and seal.

Kiwifruit Jam

Metric Marmalade

 Raspberry Jam

Raspberry jam is best made in small quantities. Its bright colour and excellent flavour makes it popular both for table use and cooking.

This method produces jam which sets better than usual, with a short cooking time which produces jam with a particularly bright colour.

500g (4 cups) raspberries
500g (2¼ cups) sugar

Put raspberries in a large saucepan and bring to the boil. Add sugar immediately and stir over moderate heat until the sugar dissolves. Protecting your hands with rubber gloves, break up the fruit while the jam boils by beating with a rotary egg-beater.

Let jam boil briskly for 3 minutes, then turn off heat. Beat several times during the next 5 minutes, then pour into hot jars. Seal as for other jams.

It is not just an old wives' tale! Jams and jellies do set more readily on a clear bright day. High humidity slows setting — make sure you work in a well-ventilated situation.

Raspberry Jam

For best flavour make small batches of this jam at regular intervals.

500 g raspberries, fresh or frozen
500 g sugar

In a large, uncovered high-heat-resistant bowl or casserole dish microwave the raspberries at Full power until they boil vigorously, about 5 minutes. Add sugar and stir until most of it dissolves. Heat for 6–8 minutes, stirring every 2 minutes until a little jam sets on a cold saucer.

Remove from oven. Beat with a rotary beater for about 1 minute. Pour into prepared jars and seal.

Rhubarb Conserve

Jams made from fruit mixtures are called conserves. This particular conserve is good on toast, for breakfast.

3 cups finely sliced rhubarb
1 Tbsp grated fresh root ginger
1 lemon, rind and juice
1 orange, rind and juice
2 cups sugar
½ cup walnut pieces

Trim rhubarb and slice thinly (5 mm slices). Tip the measured rhubarb into a large saucepan. Grate peeled ginger and measure without packing into spoon. Add to rhubarb.

Grate coloured rind (no white pith) from lemon and orange. (Or peel citrus fruit thinly with a potato peeler, then chop finely in a food processor with the sugar.) Add squeezed juice and sugar to saucepan, so all ingredients but walnuts are combined.

Bring to boil over low heat, stirring often, then boil until thick and clear (about 5 minutes).

While jam is cooking, pour boiling water over walnuts. Leave for 2 minutes, then drain. Chop nuts or leave in pieces. Stir nuts into jam just before it is removed from heat. Bottle as for other jams.

C Red Plum Jam

Follow the general method for jam, but do not add extra water, since most plums form liquid quickly as they cook. For plum jam made with small sour plums, add about ½ cup water for each 500 g fruit, or jam may set firmer than desired.

To remove skins and stones from plums, push the cooked plums through a coarse colander before measuring and adding sugar.

C Peach Conserve

Peaches alone, make rather bland, runny jam. In this delicious mixture, citrus fruit adds acid and pectin, so the jam sets better and tastes tangier. It tastes good on anything, at any time of day, and makes an unusual gift.

Use slightly under-ripe peaches from preference.

1 kg peaches
1 orange, rind and juice
1 lemon, rind and juice
½ cup water
½ cup sultanas or currants
2 cups sugar
¼ cup chopped crystallised cherries
(optional)
½ cup blanched almond halves
(optional)

Peel and slice peaches into a large saucepan. Add extra fruit if you have discarded much skin, bad spots, etc.

Grate rinds. (See Rhubarb Conserve method, page 260.) Add all ingredients except cherries and almonds to peaches in saucepan. Add sugar, heat gently until it dissolves, then boil conserve over moderate heat until clear and thick.

Stir in cherries and almonds just before conserve is removed from heat. (These add colour and crunch but are not important for setting the jam. Leave them out, if preferred.) Bottle as for other jams.

C Mandarin Marmalade

Marmalade made from mandarins alone doesn't set as readily as marmalade made from a mixture of immature grapefruit and mandarins. The more immature the fruit, the better the marmalade will be. Use marmalade grapefruit which are as green as possible, and use whichever mandarins are the later maturing type. To explain this — Satsuma mandarins mature first, Clementine mandarins next, and Burgess Scarlett after this. If both Satsuma and Clementine mandarins are in the store, Clementine would be your best choice for marmalade, because they would probably be less mature than the Satsuma mandarins.

500 g marmalade grapefruit
250 g mandarins
8 cups (2 litres) water
1½ kg and 1 cup sugar

Halve, then quarter the grapefruit and remove any seeds. Mince or blend or process the grapefruit, then the mandarins, so all the fruit is in very small pieces.

Add the water to the pulverised fruit and leave it to stand for 24 hours. Boil it briskly for about 30 minutes, until the skin is very tender, then add the sugar. Use 1½ kg bag, then the extra cup.

Boil briskly in a jam pan, until the mixture jells. (See jelly making, general method, page 263.)

Bottle and seal as for jam.

C Metric Marmalade

It is very hard to produce a foolproof marmalade recipe because the citrus fruit used for marmalade changes during the 'marmalade season'. Marmalade made from early fruit (i.e. in May) is usually light in colour. It sets with little trouble and will be sour, but not bitter. Riper fruit, picked later in the season, will make brighter marmalade. It will not set as easily and may require longer boiling. It will not be so sour, but may have a bitterness not noticeable in marmalade from early fruit.

This recipe is the one I use for early grapefruit. As the season goes on I use more fruit — up to 1½ kg, with the same quantity of sugar and water. Really late in the season I add citric acid as well, using about 2 teaspoons for the amounts above, from August onwards.

1 kg marmalade grapefruit (immature goldfruit)
12 cups (3 litres) water
3 kg sugar

Halve fruit and remove and discard the seeds. Slice very finely or mince the fruit, or pulverise it in a blender with part of the measured water. (Blenders and food processors work better with small rather than large quantities.)

Add the water to the prepared fruit, cover the container and leave it to stand for 12–24 hours. Immature fruit which has been pulverised in a blender does not need this standing time, although it will reduce the cooking time later.

Boil the fruit and water briskly in a large uncovered pan for 30–60 minutes, until the pieces break when squeezed between the fingers.

Add the sugar and stir until the mixture returns to the boil. Adjust the heat so the mixture boils in the centre, and the froth collects at the edge of the pan. Remove this froth when it is solid enough. Start testing the marmalade as soon as it boils.

The cooking time required is unpredictable. Test and bottle and seal as for jam and jelly.
Note:
For freezing, mince or blend fruit with 1 litre of water. Add 1½ litres water after thawing (i.e. ½ litre less than usual).

C Lime Marmalade

This recipe makes economical marmalade with an excellent lime flavour.

200 g limes
4 cups (1 litre) water
½ pkt (40 g) jam setting mix
1½ tsp citric acid
5 cups (1 kg) sugar

Quarter the limes, then chop them to pulp using the metal chopping blade of a food processor, a fine-bladed mincer, or a very sharp knife.

In a large saucepan or smallish jam pan boil the lime pulp with the water for 10 minutes. Add the jam setting mix and the citric acid and boil for 5 minutes longer, stirring frequently. Add the sugar and return the mixture to the boil, stirring until the sugar dissolves. Boil briskly until setting consistency is reached.

While the marmalade boils you can indulge in a little cosmetic treatment, if you like. Skim off the froth and quite a lot of the chopped fruit, using a sieve. Add a drop of yellow food colouring and dip the end of a bamboo skewer first in green food colouring, then in the marmalade so you finish up with a realistic lime-green coloured, fairly clear product.

Which Fruits Make Good Jellies?

Fruits which are rich in acid and pectin make good jellies (and jams which set easily).

Fruits which are low in acid and/or pectin but which have interesting flavours may often be used with bland pectin- and acid-rich fruit to make good jellies.

Fruits rich in acid and pectin
Sour apples and crabapples,
sour (under-ripe) blackberries,
redcurrants and blackcurrants,
green gooseberries,
grapefruit (goldfruit) and lemons
sour plums
guavas and grapes

Fruit low in acid but rich in pectin
Sweet apples and ripe quinces

Fruit rich in acid and low in pectin
Under-ripe apricots, cherries, pineapple and strawberries

Fruit with low acid and low pectin
Peaches, raspberries, most over-ripe fruits

Fruits which are high in liquid, e.g. redcurrants, grapes, berries, require no water.

Fruits which are high in pectin, but are hard and dryish, need 1–2 cups water per 500 g fruit.

Jelly Making

Choose fruit (or mixtures) high in pectin and acid. Do not peel or core. Chop fruit, add water and boil, uncovered, until tender. Do not overcook. Pour through sieve or colander. Discard sediment.

Pour sieved liquid through a medium-weave cloth, without squeezing or stirring, for clear, sparkling juice.

Test for pectin by adding 1 tablespoon methylated spirits to 1 tablespoon jelly juice. Mix briefly, leave for 30 seconds, then tip gently on to flat surface. Pectin-rich juice forms a definite clot. Juice with lower levels of pectin forms several small clots. Do not eat clots. Throw mixture out.

For juices rich in pectin, add ³/₄ cup sugar and 1 tablespoon lemon juice to each cup. (Use ¹/₂–³/₄ cup sugar for juices lower in pectin.) Boil jelly in small batches (1–4 cups juice) for best results.

Boil briskly, stirring until sugar dissolves, and skimming froth from edge as it forms, until a tablespoonful on a cold dry saucer

A selection of jellies

forms a skin which wrinkles after standing for a few minutes.

Pour into clean jars, previously heated in low oven for 15 minutes. Use jelly jars (wider at top) if jelly is to be unmoulded for serving. When set, seal with melted paraffin wax and top with dampened cellophane seals.

Redcurrant Jelly

Redcurrant jelly is a good accompaniment for hot roast lamb and hogget. Boiled with orange juice, it makes an interesting sweet-sour sauce for rich meat.

It is not necessary to remove all the stems for currants used for jelly. It is very easy to pull frozen currants off their large stalks while they are stil frozen, so freeze them without removing any stalks.

Put frozen or fresh currants (and small stems) in large saucepan. Bring to boil, mashing frequently with a potato masher to remove all juice from berries. Do not add any water. When stems look light-coloured, strain.

Follow general method for jelly making, adding ¹/₄ cup sugar to each cup of redcurrant juice.
Note:
Add currant juice to raspberry jam to increase the yield and make it set better. Measure cooked raspberry and redcurrant juice volumes, and add sugar as for general jam method.

Apple Jelly

Follow the jelly-making general recipe, using slightly under-ripe apples which do not turn mushy when boiled. Add enough water to cover the chopped fruit.

Apple and Blackberry Jelly

Mix tart apples and preferably slightly under-ripe blackberries in any proportions you like. Even 1 cup blackberries to 4 cups chopped apple gives a good blackberry flavour. Add enough water to almost cover the fruit in the large saucepan. Follow general method.

Apple and Rhubarb Jelly

For best results, boil the apples and rhubarb separately. For apples, follow apple jelly method. For rhubarb, chop stalks without stringing. Add only enough water to start juices running, and boil until

tender. Strain juice. Mix with apple juice, using 1 cup rhubarb juice to 1 or more cups apple juice. Follow general method.

Crabapple Jelly

Chop brightly coloured crabapples (with brown or black seeds), using a food processor if available. Barely cover prepared fruit with water. Follow general method.

Mint Jelly

Pour 1 cup boiling water over 1 cup packed mint leaves in food processor bowl. Finely chop mixture, then drain. Add 2 tablespoons of this mint extract and 2 tablespoons white wine vinegar to every cup of juice from strained tart apples. Follow general method, adding a little green colouring after sugar has been added, if desired.

Herb Jellies

Add fresh herb sprigs, e.g. thyme, marjoram, sage, bay leaves, scented geranium, lemon verbena, to tart apple juice, allowing ³/₄ cup sugar and 2 tablespoons lemon juice to 1 cup apple juice (see general method).

Lift out sprigs before bottling, but lay a leaf or small sprig of the fresh herb on the bottom of each jar. Follow general method.

Red Pepper Jelly

A few years ago a Californian friend introduced me to green pepper jelly and later in Toronto I tasted red pepper jelly (or more strictly, red pepper jam) for the first time. It looked and tasted delicious.

1¹/₂ cups minced or finely chopped red peppers
1 cup cider vinegar
¹/₂ pkt powdered pectin
¹/₄ cup water
2¹/₄ cups sugar

Remove the seeds, pith and stems from 2–3 large red peppers, and mince them, or chop them finely in a blender or food processor.

Measure the solids and juice into a large saucepan. Add the vinegar, and the pectin mixed with the water. Boil, stirring frequently, for five minutes. Add the sugar, bring mixture back to the boil and boil briskly until setting consistency is reached.

Pour into clean heated jars and seal.
Note:
A 70 g packet of King jam setting mix, pectin base, was used.

Pickles

For our grandmothers and great grandmothers late summer and autumn were busy times. As garden produce ripened, surpluses were 'put away' for use at less fruitful times of the year.

Vegetables were often preserved in vinegary mixtures, since they could not be safely bottled without pressure cooking.

Pickles, soured with vinegar, sweetened by sugar, with flavours emphasised by spices and herbs, brightened tables all year round.

Served with cold meat and hot potatoes, they are invaluable, moistening the (sometimes dry) meat and boosting the bland flavours. Pickles served with bread and cheese served much the same purpose, preventing dryness and adding zest.

Today, if we are gardeners we can freeze our surplus vegetables. We do not need to stock our shelves with jars to ensure our winter food is not boring.

We can buy very interesting (if expensive) pickles, especially at delicatessens, where such jars arrive from many different parts of the world. Yet, in many houses around the country, homemade pickles are tucked away in pantries year after year. Not dozens and dozens of jars but a few of each variety.

Why? Because everybody likes them. They are an indication of the cook's skill and imagination. They cost very little to make, and even though we have a wide range of food available, a small amount of pickle still serves the same purpose that it used to, 'livening up' plain, quickly prepared food.

This selection, my family's favourite pickles, are more American than English. I loved the different-tasting pickles served by my American friends when I lived in California and modified my collection of pickle recipes.

I hope you try several of my pickles, and that you enjoy them!

Tips for Good Pickles

• For good pickles you should follow the recipes precisely. In many pickles vegetables are either sprinkled with salt or left to stand in salty water. These processes remove water. The vegetable is firmer, less likely to mush on cooking and will absorb vinegar more readily later in the pickling process.

• Iodised salt is not used in pickling because it darkens the pickled food and sometimes toughens the vegetables.

• Some pickles are surrounded by unthickened liquid. Usually only the food itself is eaten. Since the liquid has been diluted by juice from the pickle it should not be used again for pickling but can be used for other cooking purposes.

• Often the liquid is thickened. Too much thickening spoils pickles. Liquid which seems runny when hot will thicken much more on cooling and standing.

• Good seals on pickles are very important. The type of seal needed varies with the type of pickle.

• Onions and cucumbers which have been salted then surrounded by strong vinegar do not need to be sealed at all, but may just be lightly covered to keep out dust.

• Pickles in diluted vinegar, however, spoil if they are not airtight. Once most homemade pickles are opened they should be kept in the refrigerator until used.

• For long storage, use preserving jars and seals. Pour the very hot mixture into thoroughly cleaned, very hot jars to within a few millimetres of the top. Top with a hot, boiled seal and screw on the band tightly. The next day, remove the band and wipe down the jar.

• Jars previously used for commercially made jams and pickles make good containers, too. Thoroughly clean and heat the jar. Boil the lacquer-coated lid with its composition inner rim for a few minutes. Fill the jar almost to the top and screw the top on tightly, working quickly while everything is hot. Do not open the jar until the pickle is to be used or the seal will be broken.

• If you cannot use either of these methods, pour the hot pickle into clean, lidless jars keeping the inside of the jar, above the pickle, as clean as possible. Pour melted paraffin wax over the pickle surface so that it adheres to the inside of the jar, making a good seal. Cover the jar with a cellophane top.

• When bottling liquids I use soft drink bottles with screw-on lids with rubbery inserts wherever possible, using much the same procedure as for commercially used lacquered lids. As an added precaution I dip the lids and the tops of the bottles in melted wax to make sure no air can get in. This step is essential if you use corks to seal bottles, or tops which do not fit tightly.

• Although well-sealed pickles may be kept for several years, most are best used within a year for maximum flavour and best texture.

M Parliament Pickle

A good all-purpose pickle, a cross between mustard pickle and tomato relish.

250 g firm red tomatoes
1 medium cucumber (250 g)
1 small onion
¾ cup finely sliced celery
1 Tbsp salt
¾ cup sugar
2 tsp dry mustard
2 tsp turmeric
2 Tbsp flour
½ cup white vinegar

Blanch tomatoes by pouring boiling water over them, leaving them to stand for 1 minute, draining them and covering with cold water.

Halve, peel, discard seeds and cube flesh finely.

Peel cucumber only if skin is tough. Halve, scoop out, discard seeds, and cube, like tomatoes.

Mix cucumber, onion and celery in a plastic or glass bowl and the tomatoes in another. Sprinkle both with the salt and leave to stand for an hour, stirring occasionally.

Mix sugar, mustard, turmeric and flour in a large microwave-proof bowl. Add vinegar and stir until smooth. Microwave at Full power for 3 minutes or until mixture thickens and boils.

Drain and rinse both lots of vegetables. Add to thickened vinegar, heat again for 3–4 minutes, or until boiling again. Pour into prepared jars and seal.

C Christmas Pickle

I named this pickle because of its festive colour. I often give it to friends at Christmas time, not only because it tastes so good with any cold meat, but because it turns a simple snack of bread and cheese into something special and is very useful when you have unexpected guests.

8 cups diced cucumber
¼ cup plain salt
4 onions, diced
2–3 red peppers, diced
3 cups sugar
1 tsp celery seed
1 tsp mustard seed
2 cups wine vinegar
2–3 Tbsp cornflour

Use long, thin-skinned cucumbers. Halve lengthwise then scoop out central, seedy part using a teaspoon. Without removing peel (unless it is very tough) cut cucumber flesh into small, evenly shaped cubes.

Measure cucumber into a glass, plastic, china or stainless steel container. Sprinkle with salt and leave to stand for 30 minutes, stirring several times. Drain and

Christmas Pickle

rinse, discarding liquid.

Put cucumber, onion, peppers, sugar, seeds and vinegar in a large saucepan. Bring to the boil, stirring constantly. Mix cornflour with a little extra vinegar and stir into cucumber mixture. Bottle and top using metal lids or preserving seals.

C Pickled Onions

500 g small, round onions
1 Tbsp plain salt
1¹/₂ cups wine vinegar
¹/₄ cup honey
bay leaf (optional)
peppercorns (optional)

To skin onions easily, pour boiling water over them and leave to stand for 30 seconds. Drain then cut off roots and tops. Peel off outer skins. Put onions in bowl, sprinkle with salt and leave to stand for an hour, shaking occasionally.

Bring vinegar and honey to the boil then cool to room temperature. Pack onions into jar with bay leaf and peppercorns for extra flavour if desired.

Cover generously with cool vinegar, cover jar (an airtight seal is not necessary) and leave for 2–3 weeks before using.

C Bread and Butter Pickles

2 litres sliced cucumbers
¹/₂–1 litre sliced onions
¹/₂ cup plain salt

3 cups wine vinegar
2¹/₂ cups sugar
1 Tbsp mustard seeds
1 Tbsp celery seeds
1 tsp turmeric

Halve cucumbers lengthwise and remove seeds if watery. Slice cucumbers and onions by hand or with food processor. (Use ice-cream containers for measures.) Mix with plain salt, leave to stand for 30–60 minutes, then drain and rinse well.

In a large saucepan bring remaining ingredients to the boil. Add vegetables and return to the boil.

Fill hot, sterilised bottles almost to overflowing. Seal immediately with lacquered metal lids or preserving seals.

Refrigerate after opening.

Cucumber and Pineapple Pickle

M Tamarillo Chutney

Deep in colour with an interesting flavour, this is a good all-purpose chutney.

For 1 medium-sized jar:
3 large or 4 small tamarillos
1 apple, chopped
1 onion, finely chopped
³/₄ cup brown sugar
¹/₄ tsp mixed spice
¹/₄ tsp salt
¹/₄ cup vinegar

Cut stems from tamarillos and halve lengthwise. Place, cut surface down, on flat-bottomed high-sided casserole or high-heat-resistant bowl.

Microwave at Full power for 4 minutes or until skins may be lifted off fruit easily. Mash fruit with potato masher. Add finely chopped apple and onion, sugar, spice, salt and vinegar. Cover and cook for 10 minutes. Uncover and cook for 6 minutes longer until fairly thick. Pour into prepared jars and seal.

C Sweetcorn Pickle

1 cup chopped celery
1 cup chopped onion
1 red pepper, chopped
1 green pepper, chopped
1 tsp celery seed
1 tsp turmeric
1¹/₂ cups wine vinegar
4 cups canned corn kernels
³/₄ cup sugar

1 Tbsp cornflour
2 tsp dry mustard
2 tsp salt

Measure the first seven ingredients into a large saucepan. Boil for 5 minutes then add the corn. Bring back to the boil.

Mix the sugar, cornflour, mustard and salt to a thin cream with more vinegar, stir in and bring back to the boil again. Simmer for 2 minutes, stirring constantly, then bottle. Top with metal lids or preserving seals.

C Cucumber and Pineapple Pickle

This popular pickle blends the flavours and textures of cucumbers, onions and pineapple. Sometimes I cube these ingredients, and at other times, I slice the cucumber and onion thinly and mix them with crushed pineapple. Both versions are good.

1 × 25 cm cucumber
1 cup drained cubed or crushed pineapple
2 large onions
³/₄ cup sugar
1 cup wine vinegar
2 tsp salt
1 tsp curry powder
1 tsp turmeric
¹/₂ tsp celery seed
2 tsp cornflour

Halve, seed and cut up cucumber. Do not salt cucumber.

Cut pineapple in small cubes (or use crushed pineapple).

Remove top and bottoms of onions. Halve lengthwise then remove skins. Cut lengthwise parallel cuts, leaving just enough to hold onion together, then cut crosswise into small cubes.

Put all the ingredients except cornflour in a large saucepan. Stirring frequently bring to the boil then simmer, uncovered, for 15 minutes.

Mix cornflour to a paste with extra vinegar. Stir into pickle, simmer for 2–3 minutes longer. Bottle.

C Pretty Pickle

This pickle is easy to make and turns the plainest snack into something special. Try it with bread and cheese, or in a baked potato. It makes a nice gift, too.

Use long, thin-skinned cucumbers.

8 cups diced cucumber
¹/₄ cup plain salt
4 onions, diced
2–3 red peppers, diced
1–2 green or gold peppers, diced
1 cup drained whole-kernel corn
3 cups sugar
1 tsp celery seed
1 tsp mustard seed
2 cups wine vinegar
2–3 Tbsp cornflour

Halve lengthwise then scoop out central, seedy part using a teaspoon.

Without removing peel (unless it is very tough) cut cucumber flesh into small, evenly shaped cubes.

Measure cucumber into a glass or plastic container. Sprinkle with salt and leave to stand for 30 minutes, stirring several times. Drain and rinse, discarding liquid.

Put cucumber, onion, peppers, corn, sugar, seeds and vinegar in a large saucepan. Bring to the boil, stirring constantly. Mix cornflour with a little extra vinegar and stir into cucumber mixture.

Ladle into bottles with metal screw-topped lids. Seal immediately.

C Sweet and Sour Pickled Gherkins

Many recipes for pickling gherkins call for several steps, often with hours, or even days, between the different stages. It doesn't pay to change these recipes, nor to try to speed them up — if you do, you may finish up with shrivelled pickles.

This is a very quick pickled gherkin recipe. You should use small, freshly picked, immature gherkins. If they are fairly big, cut them into chunks or strips before starting to work with them.

2 kg small, freshly picked gherkins
* (5–8 cm long)*
½ cup plain salt
2 cups sugar
4 cups water
3 Tbsp (45 ml) glacial acetic acid
pickling spice or mustard and celery
* seeds*

Wash and scrub the gherkins, if necessary. Sprinkle the salt over the damp gherkins, mix gently so they are coated with it and leave them to stand for 2–3 hours, stirring occasionally. As they stand, the salt will turn to brine. Drain off the brine, then pour enough boiling water over them to cover them. Bring the sugar, water and acetic acid to the boil. Simmer for 2–3 minutes then turn off the heat.

Drain the boiling water from the gherkins and pack them into clean jars, preferably jars which have plastic screw tops. To each litre add 1 teaspoon of pickling spice, or a teaspoon each of mustard seeds and celery seeds. Pour the very hot sweetened acid mixture over the still hot gherkins so they are covered. Screw on plastic tops, and try to leave gherkins for at least two weeks before using them.

C Dill Pickles

Mildly flavoured dill pickles (unlike gherkins) may be eaten whole. Select small, freshly picked cucumbers or gherkins up to 10 cm

long. Scrub well. Soak overnight in cold water. Drain and pack loosely in cleaned preserving jars.

Add to each litre jar:
1 or 2 dill sprigs
½ tsp mustard seed
6 peppercorns

For each five jars:
½ cup plain salt
¼–½ cup sugar
7 cups hot water
3 cups wine vinegar

Stir salt, sugar (according to taste) and hot water together until dissolved. Add vinegar. Pour over cucumbers, leaving 1 cm at top of jars. Top with boiled seals and screw-bands.

Place jars in a rack in a boiler with water 2 cm over tops of jars. Bring to the boil for 5 minutes. Remove, cool, check seals. Store for 6 weeks before using.

U Sauerkraut

If you've eaten and enjoyed sauerkraut in Europe or America, you may like to make your own — especially if you have a good supply of cabbages. With a food processor you can shred buckets of cabbage in a very short time. Be warned — sauerkraut makes awful smells around the house while it ferments and cooks — but it doesn't taste the way it smells!

2 kg drumhead cabbage
50 g plain salt
(or multiples of this ratio)

Quarter and trim the cabbages. Discard outer leaves and cores. Weigh after trimming, then cut in pieces to fit feed tube. Shred cabbage using the metal slicing disc. (This is a good time to practise shredding techniques. You can produce fine shreds if the cabbage fits tightly in the feed tube and you press gently on the food pusher. Coarse shreds result from a loose fit and firm pressure. For kraut, fine shreds are desirable but not essential.)

Put the sliced cabbage in very clean plastic buckets. Sprinkle with salt (using plain, not iodised salt) then mix gently but evenly. Do not bruise the cabbage but press it firmly so it wilts and is covered by salty liquid formed by the cabbage juice and salt.

Transfer cabbage and brine to large jars, crocks, etc. or whatever you intend to use for the fermenting process. Press it in firmly so there are no air bubbles and the juice covers the cabbage.

Press the mixture with a clean weight that prevents air coming in contact with the cabbage. To do this

take three large, good quality unpunctured plastic bags. Put them inside each other and partly fill the inner-most one with water. Sit the bags on the surface of the cabbage adding more water if necessary to weigh the cabbage down and press against the edge of the container. Tie a twist tie around the inner bag or all the bags, to keep the water in place. Place in a warm room (but not direct sun) and leave to ferment.

Bubbles start forming in a few days and finish after one to two weeks by which time the sauerkraut is strongly flavoured and acid. You can stop the fermentation at any time, by refrigerating it or processing it, so taste it regularly and stop when it suits you.

Sauerkraut packed in liquid in lidded jars in the refrigerator will keep for months. If not refrigerated, it must be processed for safe storage. Pack into sterilised jars and cover with brine to within 1 cm of top. Screw on boiled seals, cover jars with water and bring to boil. Boil for 20 minutes for small jars, or 30 minutes for large jars.

Always boil bottled sauerkraut for at least 15 minutes before eating it. Refrigerated sauerkraut may be eaten raw as a salad or boiled. For milder flavour, reheat in water.
Note:
If extra brine is needed at any time, dissolve 2 teaspoons salt in 1 cup boiled water.

C Capers

'Proper' capers are made from the pickled buds of a small flowering shrub which grows wild in some Mediterranean countries. My 'substitute' capers are made from very small nasturtium buds and immature nasturtium seeds.

1 cup white vinegar
1 Tbsp salt
½ bayleaf
4 peppercorns
4 cloves

Bring the vinegar, salt and flavourings to the boil, then remove from heat and leave to stand until cool. Transfer liquid to small jar with a plastic screw-top.

Gather nasturtium buds and seeds as they are ready (or whenever you have time). Leave them to stand in the warm kitchen for several hours, until they are wilted, then drop them into the seasoned vinegar. Both seeds and buds may be added over a period of several weeks. They will stay at the top of the vinegar for a day or two, but will gradually drop. Buds develop the caper flavour more quickly than seeds do. Capers will be ready for use about a month after the last seeds/buds are added.

Tomatoes

Tomatoes are called for in many recipes because of their flavour, colour and acidity.

There are plenty of good ready-prepared tomato products around, and I use many of them, finding the following products especially useful.

- tomato juice
- tomato purée
- tomato paste (concentrate)
- whole peeled tomatoes in juice
- diced tomatoes
- savoury tomatoes

If you grow, or have access to, a good supply of ripe red tomatoes, you may want to preserve some of them to use during the winter. Try these recipes if you want to put aside a few kilograms at a time.

For the following recipes you will need carefully prepared, completely clean jars. Thoroughly wash, then bring to the boil in a large pot, covered with water, the preserving jars or empty jars with metal screw tops which you will use. Boil gently for at least 5 minutes, with the preserving seals, or the screw-topped metal lids (with composition inserts).

The lids should be concave when the jars are cold. If any gas forms during storage, or if any off-flavours or odours develop, do not taste or eat the contents.

Any of the bottled recipes may be frozen in plastic bags or covered containers, if preferred.

C 'Overflow' Bottled Tomatoes

Quarter or cube firm, ripe, red tomatoes, cutting off the white core at the stem end, and squeezing and shaking the tomatoes to remove extra juice and seeds. When you feel you have enough to fill the jar(s), bring to the boil, stirring often, pressing the tomatoes until liquid forms.

Add about ¼ teaspoon of salt and sugar and 1 tablespoon lemon juice for each cupful.

When the tomato mixture has been boiling fast for 3–4 minutes, spoon or ladle the very hot tomato pieces into the hot jar which has been removed from the pot in which it boiled. Work fast, and make sure that there are no pockets of air in the jars. Fill to the top of the jar, wipe around the rim with a clean paper towel, and top with the hot seal, then screw on the band, or top with the cleaned metal lid, screwing it on tightly.

C Thick Tomato Savoury

Prepare Tomato Purée (see recipe this page) using tomatoes only, and boil down to about half its original volume. Measure it and put it aside.

For two cups of purée, cut in small cubes 1 medium-sized onion, 1 red pepper, and 1 green pepper. Sauté these in 2 tablespoons oil (not butter) without browning, until onion is transparent, then add the tomato purée, ½ teaspoon each of dried basil, oreganum, and mustard seed and ¼ teaspoon celery seed. Cook over moderate heat for 5–10 minutes, until thick enough to spread on pizza, etc., add salt to taste, then spoon into small jars with metal screw tops heated as above. Fill jars to overflowing and seal as above.

C Tomato Purée

5 kg tomatoes, quartered
2–4 large onions
2 tsp dry basil (optional)
2 tsp dry marjoram (optional)
2 tsp celery seed (optional)
1 Tbsp salt
2 Tbsp sugar
1 tsp pepper

Boil all together, stirring frequently, until half of its original volume.

Put through a food mill, blender or food processor, and sieve if desired to remove seeds, skins etc. Bring mixture back to the boil, then pour into clean sterilised jars, to overflowing. Top with pre-boiled seals and screw on bands.

C M Tomato Paste

Chop ripe tomatoes into a microwave dish or saucepan. Add some finely chopped onion and red pepper, and fresh or dried oreganum and basil if you like. Microwave at Full power, or boil until everything is soft, then push through a coarse sieve, discarding seeds and skin, etc.

Microwave or cook uncovered until boiled down to half or less of its original volume. Stir occasionally in the microwave oven, and stir frequently on the stovetop, until mixture is as thick as you want it. Season with salt and sugar to taste at this stage. Spoon into smaller jars which have been cleaned and boiled, and seal.

D Dehydrated Tomatoes

The easiest way to preserve tomatoes is to dry slices or 1 cm cubes, using a dehydrator. Spread the prepared tomatoes on the dehydrator trays and dry according to the instructions until they are crisp. Store in screw-topped jars, or chop to powder in the food processor, alone or mixed with dehydrated chopped peppers, onions and herbs, to use for salad and pizza toppings.

Use dried tomato cubes and slices as snacks (they are remarkably sweet) or add them to simmered mixtures, or microwave or simmer them in water, for 5–15 minutes.

D Tomato Leather

Make Tomato Purée (see recipe this page) and pour it on to the solid dehydrator trays to make tomato leather. When you want it, rip pieces off the discs of dried tomato and reconstitute to instant juice, purée or paste in a food processor according to the amount of hot water you add. The discs of tomato leather may well all get eaten dry, as snacks! They are very light to carry, if tramping.

You can also make tomato leather from food-processed uncooked tomatoes, if you like.

C Tomato Ketchup

4 kg red tomatoes, chopped
2 onions, sliced
2 cloves garlic, sliced
2 Tbps pickling spice
1 tsp celery seed
1 tsp dried basil
1 tsp dried oreganum
4 cups wine vinegar
4–5 cups sugar
3 Tbsp plain salt

Chop tomatoes roughly into a large saucepan. Add finely chopped onions and garlic. Tie spice, seed and herbs loosely in muslin. Add half the vinegar and boil, uncovered, for an hour. Push through holes of a food mill, discarding skin and seeds. Add remaining vinegar, sugar and salt and boil for 15 minutes longer.

Pour hot sauce into clean hot bottles. Screw on boiled tops tightly. When cold, dip tops in melted wax. Refrigerate after opening.

Notes:
Larger amounts of sugar make a sweet sauce, very popular with children.

Sauce will be thin unless most of the pulp is forced through the food mill.

From top: finely chopped Tomato Leather, Tomato Purée, dehydrated onions and red and green peppers, Overflow Bottled Tomatoes (quartered), Thick Tomato Savoury, Tomato Paste (2), Tomato Leather.

Microwave Menus

These microwave menus have been planned to fit in with different family situations. Each menu is made up of several recipes, all of which can be cooked in a microwave oven.

You will not always want to prepare each menu exactly as I have, but seeing a complete menu can help to remind you of the different ways you can use your microwave, to help you get a meal on the table with less time, fuss and bother — and less washing up!

It is relatively easy to cook an isolated recipe, but the hardest thing for any cook to learn is how to cook several foods, and get them together on the table at the right time, to form a tasty, attractive and nutritionally well-balanced meal.

For each menu, a 'Plan of Attack' is given, telling you where to start and how to proceed, and all the recipes are included in the pages following each menu.

Most family cooks, when they prepare a meal, cook part of it by conventional methods, and part in their microwave oven. I usually do, too. You can modify these menus, cooking some of the recipes conventionally, if you like. My intention is to show that it *is* possible to cook delicious and attractive complete meals in a microwave oven.

What's for Breakfast?

How can your microwave help you cope with that difficult time of the day — after you crawl out of bed in the morning, and before you leave the house for the day?

It is important to have something to eat before you start on your day's activities. You will feel better, do a better morning's work, and you won't need to dash out to buy food halfway through the morning.

Unless you have a very active morning ahead you will probably find that a shortened version of this menu is all that you need.

A bowl of muesli with fruit, served with milk or yoghurt, is a good breakfast in itself.

Or, you may settle for scrambled egg piled on a warmed, halved roll, and a piece of fruit.

Perhaps a bacon-filled roll and a cup of tea is exactly what you feel like for breakfast.

Or, you may thaw and warm a roll, spread it with butter and marmalade and swallow a quick glass of milk with it.

BREAKFAST

Crunchy Muesli

Stewed Fruit
or
Raw Fruit

Scrambled Eggs

Bacon

Bread Rolls
Butter/Marmalade/
Jam

Tea/Instant Coffee/
Milk

Plan of Attack

Before you start cooking work out the order in which you should prepare and cook this meal.

1. Make Crunchy Muesli. You can make muesli whenever it suits you, because you can keep it in an airtight jar for several weeks, if necessary. (If it loses its crunch you can re-crisp it by spreading it on paper towels and microwaving it until it feels hot.)
2. Stew fruit (up to 2 days ahead). Cover, cool, and refrigerate stewed fruit until you need it. In cold weather, you can take the chill off the fruit by microwaving it before serving it.
3. Soften butter to spreading consistency, if necessary.
4. 'Freshen' marmalade or other jam, if necessary.
5. Cook the bacon and mix the scrambled eggs.
6. Cook the scrambled eggs during the bacon standing time.
7. Heat the bread rolls while the eggs stand.
8. Boil water for tea or instant coffee.

Crunchy Muesli

Microwaved muesli is easier to make, and less messy, than muesli made any other way. This recipe makes 7–8 cups of economical family muesli.

½ cup sugar
¼ cup brown sugar
¼ cup milk or water or fruit juice
¼ cup corn or soya oil
1 tsp cinnamon
1 tsp mixed spice
½ tsp salt
4 cups whole-grain flaked oats
1 cup wheat bran or oat bran
½–1 cup wheatgerm

Measure the first seven ingredients into a microwave-proof bowl.

Cook at Full power for 3 minutes, stirring after 1 and 2 minutes for most even cooking.

While syrup cooks, measure the flaked oats, bran and wheatgerm into a large (about 25 cm) round, flat-bottomed microwave-proof pan which will not melt in contact with hot sugar. (If you do not have a large pan, cook mixture in two lots, in a smaller pan.)

Combine cereal and hot syrup (in either container) mixing to ensure all grains are coated and free from large, sugary lumps (which may burn).

Spread mixture evenly, so it is not more than 3 cm thick.

Microwave at Full power for 6 minutes, then cook longer, stirring every minute, until the mixture looks browner, the grains appear drier and more separate, and the muesli has a nice cooked smell.

When cold, store in an airtight container.

Note:
Undercooked muesli will be sticky, and light in colour. Overcooked muesli will be dark in colour, and slightly bitter in flavour.

Variations:
Replace 1 cup flaked oats with any other flaked cereal. Replace white sugar with ¼ cup honey; add ½ cup coconut to cereal; add ¼ cup toasted sesame seeds to cereal; stir in lightly roasted nuts and/or (chopped) dried or candied fruit to the hot, cooked muesli.

Stewed Fruit

• Fruit stewed in the microwave oven has very good flavour, texture and colour, when cooked to the right stage.
• Because they do not need to be surrounded by water, or syrup to cook evenly, the pieces of fruit may be cooked using very little, or no extra liquid, intensifying flavour and colour.
• For most even cooking, cover the containers used for cooking fruit.
• When cooking fairly small quantities, put the pieces of fruit in a ring pan, or a pan with a central cone insert, for even cooking.
• When cooking large amounts (in large round covered containers) stir the pieces gently during cooking so that the slower cooking pieces in the centre are moved to fast cooking areas near the sides of the container.
• To stop delicate fruits from mushing, cook them at Defrost (30% power) or Medium (50% power) for about two to three times as long as they take at Full power.
• Many fruits cook well prepared as for conventional stewing, sprinkled with sugar (or layers of fruit sprinkled with layers of sugar covered and cooked with no added liquid).
• When cooking fruit which discolours quickly, cook a small amount of sugar and water first, to form a syrup, add a little lemon juice if desired, then add the pieces of fruit, turning them to coat them with syrup.
• To cook tamarillos without peeling them, cut off the stem ends, then halve them lengthwise. Arrange the halves, cut side down on a mixture of brown or white sugar, and any citrus fruit juice. Cook at Full power until the skins rise and may be lifted away from the fruit.

Scrambled Eggs

Scrambled eggs are easier to microwave than most other egg dishes. Microwaved scrambled eggs

do not stick or burn on the bottom, and do not have to be stirred all the time, as they cook. Scrambled eggs cook most evenly in a container which is not too wide or too deep. For example, a two-egg mixture cooks well in a 2-cup glass measure.

To cut dishwashing to a minimum, cook an individual (1–2 eggs) serving of scrambled eggs in a small bowl with fairly low sides, in which the eggs may be mixed, cooked and served.

If you like, melt a teaspoon of butter, or bacon fat, in the container in which you will cook your egg(s), or you may use no added fat at all.

For 1 serving:
1 egg
2 Tbsp milk
pinch salt (if no butter or bacon fat used)
finely chopped fresh herbs (optional)
¹/₂ tomato, finely cubed (optional)

Break the egg (into the melted butter if used) into the glass measuring cup (or other container).

Add the milk and beat with a fork, only long enough to combine. Add any other desired additions and stir to mix.

Cook at Full power for 30 seconds, stir, then cook for 30–45 seconds more until you see the volume increase. Stir gently, then leave to stand for 1 minute to finish cooking, to become firmer. If egg is not firm enough, cook for a little longer.

For larger quantities:
• 2 eggs and ¹/₄ cup milk cook in

2–3 minutes.
• 4 eggs and ¹/₂ cup milk cook in about 4 minutes.

Bacon

It is very convenient to microwave bacon. It cooks very well, in a short time.

Allow 1–1¹/₂ minutes per slice of bacon, at Full power.

The exact time depends on the thickness, size, and leanness of the bacon.

Bacon becomes browner in the 2 minutes after it has cooked (standing time).

Plate Method
Cook 1 or 2 slices of bacon on the plate (without metal trim) on which you will eat it. Cover the bacon and plate loosely with a paper towel to spread the heat and absorb any fat splatters.

Ridged Plate or Rack Method
Lie several slices of bacon on a ridged roasting rack so that fat can drip away from bacon as it cooks. Cover lightly with a paper towel, as above.

Bacon which is hard to separate from other slices will pull away much more easily if the pack of bacon (with no metal trim) is microwaved briefly, until bacon is slightly warmed. Bacon which is not to be cooked may be replaced in refrigerator.

Warming Bread Rolls

Bread rolls have a nicer aroma and texture if they are served warm.

Rolls should be heated at Full power until they feel only slightly warm, since they will be warmer inside, when broken open.
• 6 bread rolls warm at Full power in about 15 seconds.
• 10 bread rolls warm at Full power in about 30 seconds.

Wrap single rolls in a paper towel or serviette to warm them. You can warm several rolls in a basket (with no metal fasteners or staples) which has been lined with a paper serviette or towel. For best results cover rolls in basket with another serviette or towel.

Tea and Instant Coffee

It is considerably quicker to heat the water for one cup of tea or instant coffee in the microwave oven than it is to heat it in an electric jug.

Fill the cup or mug with tap water and heat it at Full power until the water boils. This will take from 30 seconds to 3 minutes, depending on the size of the mug, and the initial temperature of the water.

Remove from the oven and add the teabag or instant coffee.
Note:
Finely powdered instant coffee may froth when stirred into very hot water. It pays to be prepared for this.

Weekend Breakfast

For many of us, the weekend brings a change in our normal weekday routine.

It's a good feeling to be able to wake up, look at the clock, then roll over and go back to sleep again.

When we decide that it is time to get up, most of us are feeling decidedly hungry. Because there isn't a deadline for our weekend breakfast, we have time to potter around in the kitchen, preparing food that there isn't time to make on weekdays.

I make the foods on this menu because I like their flavours and textures, but it is nice to know that these are foods that are high in fibre and vitamins as well.

You may decide that you would like to make yourself a glass of juice and a quick plate of porridge as soon as you 'hit the kitchen', then make the muffins to eat with a mid-morning coffee.

Or, you may choose to prepare only juice and muffins, or muffins and a hot drink especially if you have stayed in bed for rather a long time!

WEEKEND BREAKFAST

Tomato Juice
or
Mixed Vegetable Juice

Plain Porridge
or
Mixed Grain Porridge

Fruited Bran Muffins

Cream Cheese/Honey

Coffee/Hot Milky Drink

Plan of Attack

1. Make the Tomato Juice or Mixed Vegetable Juice first (preferably the day before) because you want to serve it cold.
2. Make and cook the Fruited Bran Muffins at least five minutes before you eat them because they need this time to firm up, and for their outsides to dry out nicely.
3. While your muffins cook, think about a suitable spread for them. Soften cream cheese to spreading consistency in the microwave, or whip in a food processor with a little milk. If you like it light and fluffy.
4. Soften honey, if necessary.
5. Put out the ingredients so that anyone who wants porridge can make it for themselves when they are ready. Mix and make your own porridge. Squeeze juice if this has not been done in between other steps.
6. Assemble drink-making ingredients, putting what you want for your own drink into a mug ready for microwaving, and leaving things ready for other people to help themselves.

Tomato Juice

During the tomato season I use ripe red, but less than perfect, tomatoes from my garden to make this tomato juice.

For about 1 litre:
about 1 kg tomatoes, quartered
1 onion or 2 spring onions, finely chopped
2 tsp sugar
1 tsp salt
½ tsp celery salt (optional)
fresh or dried basil and/or parsley to taste
¼–½ slice white or wholegrain bread

Put the prepared tomatoes and onions in a covered 2 litre microwave dish. Add the seasonings, altering the herbs, and adding pepper if you like. Break the bread (or toast) into small pieces and add.

Cook at Full power for 10 minutes, or until tomatoes are pulpy.

For greatest yield, purée in a food processor.

Shake mixture through a sieve, discarding the solids.

Chill, taste and sharpen with a little lemon juice or wine vinegar if necessary. Add Worcestershire or Tabasco sauce if desired. Chill, or pour over ice-cubes to cool it down quickly.
Note:
Refrigerate juice for 2–3 days if desired. This mixture is not suitable for bottling, but may be frozen or dehydrated.

Mixed Vegetable Juice

You can count the number of vegetables you use in the preparation of this juice, and name it accordingly — V7, V8, V9, V10, etc! The beetroot gives it a wonderful bright red colour. However, the main vegetables used for this juice are tomatoes and carrots.

Use this recipe as a guide, changing vegetables and amounts to suit yourself.

For about 1½ litres:
1 kg tomatoes, quartered
1–2 cups grated carrots
½–1 cup finely sliced celery
1 small beetroot, grated
1 red or green pepper, chopped
1 cup thinly sliced greens (e.g. silverbeet, lettuce, parsley, watercress)
1½ tsp salt.
¼–½ slice white or wholemeal bread

Combine all ingredients in a covered 2–3 litre microwave dish (as for tomato juice).

Cover and microwave at Full power for 20 minutes, or until all vegetables are mushy.

Purée mixture in a food processor, if possible. Shake through sieve, then season and serve as for tomato juice.

Hot Breakfast Cereals

If you like porridge but hate soaking and washing a porridge pot, you'll find that your worries are over with microwaved porridge.

Make and serve the porridge in the same bowl.

Choose a bowl that will be only half-filled by the quantity of cereal you mix. This leaves room for bubbling during cooking. Choose a fairly deep bowl rather than a wide shallow one.

If the porridge in your favourite plate boils over in the microwave oven, add boiling water to the uncooked cereal, then cook it at Medium (50% power), until the cereal in the middle of the plate has heated through and changed colour.

Unless you have a large family, all wanting their cereal at the same time, make the porridge in separate plates. Different types of porridge require slightly different amounts of liquid.

Start with these proportions and change them until you have your porridge exactly the way you like it.

Plain Porridge

For 1 serving:
4 Tbsp rolled oats
pinch of salt
8 Tbsp water

Measure the rolled oats into the plate and add the salt.

Add hot water if available (for a shorter cooking time).

Microwave at Full power for 1–1½ minutes, then stir and cook until the porridge in the middle of the plate looks cooked, for another ½–2 minutes, depending on the temperature of the added water.

Mixed Grain Porridge

Use whatever proportions of different cereals you like.

For 1 large serving:
3 Tbsp rolled oats
1 Tbsp wheat or oat bran
1 Tbsp wheatgerm
1 Tbsp kibbled rye
pinch of salt
12 Tbsp (¾ cup) water

Use the same method as for plain porridge. If there is a possibility of porridge boiling over, add boiling water, and cook at Medium (50% power) for 2 minutes, then stir and cook for 2 minutes longer.
Note:
Add extra hot water near the end of the cooking time if porridge looks too thick.

Fruited Bran Muffins

The fruit in these muffins keeps them moist. Unlike most microwaved muffins they do not dry out and are good served even a couple of days later.

I make eight large muffins in individual glass ramekins which have been lightly brushed or rubbed with any type of butter, e.g. unsalted, cultured, standary creamy or semi-soft.

If preferred, make about 12 smaller muffins in solid-bottomed microwave muffin pans.

For 8–12 muffins:
25 g butter
¼ cup treacle
1 egg
½ cup milk
1 cup bran
¼ cup wheatgerm
¼ cup rolled oats
½ cup flour
½ tsp baking soda
1 chopped or grated apple, banana, pear or 2 feijoas (unpeeled)

Melt the butter until just liquid in a fairly large microwave-proof mixing bowl.

Add the treacle, heat until the treacle is liquid, then stir to mix the butter and treacle.

Break in the egg, add the milk, and stir together with a fork.

Without mixing, tip in the bran, wheatgerm, rolled oats, and the flour and soda which have been sieved together. Add the finely chopped or grated fruit (unpeeled if possible).

Fold ingredients together, just enough to combine. Depending on fruit texture, add a little flour or milk to get a fairly firm muffin texture if necessary.

Spoon into ramekins, so each is half to three-quarters full and each muffin has a rounded top.

Stand ramekins on an upturned plate so they are elevated. Cook muffins, four at a time at Full power, for about 2–2½ minutes, or until the muffins spring back when touched in the middle and they look dry around the edges.

Leave to stand for 1 minute, turn out and stand for 3–4 minutes longer. During this time they become firmer around the edges. Serve warm or reheated.

Hot Milky Drinks

Everybody in the family can mix their own milky drink, exactly as he/she likes it, then reheat it at Full power to drinking temperature.

A Picnic in the Sun

When the sun shines, and the air is balmy, nobody wants to sit around inside.

This is the time to think about family food which can be prepared ahead, and eaten outdoors, casually.

Of course you don't have to take a picnic a long distance to enjoy it.

Depending on the time and transport available, you can enjoy a picnic meal in the privacy of your own garden, in the nearest park, or on a beach or riverbank.

Picnic food should be relaxed and easy, so that the cook hasn't had to spend hours in the kitchen getting food ready.

Your microwave oven does not heat up the kitchen the way conventional stoves do. You can prepare food quickly without getting hot and bothered and without attracting all the flies in the vicinity because the cooking odours are reduced.

Try to plan a menu of food which doesn't have to be eaten while it is hot, and which is easy to eat and serve in an informal way.

If you prepare the food for a picnic, instead of relying on bought ready-prepared food, you will save a lot of money.

It is a good idea to build up an assortment of disposable picnic containers: buy paper plates, and serviettes and save containers in which you buy some foods.

So, let your microwave oven help you to get outside more quickly and easily to enjoy your picnic.

PACK A PICNIC

**Scotch Eggs
or
Confetti Meat Loaf**

Potato Salad

**Green Salad with
Italian Dressing**

Tomatoes

Bread Rolls

American Brownies

Fresh Lemonade

Fresh Fruit

Plan of Attack

Since all of this picnic food will be eaten cold, you don't have to worry about keeping anything hot.

Some foods spoil easily, if they sit around while they are warm. Make spoilable foods early, so you can cool them down before transporting them in an insulated container with cooler pads if you have them.

The perishable foods in this menu are Scotch Eggs, Confetti Meat Loaf and Potato Salad.

1. Make Savoury Crumbs first. These give Confetti Meat Loaf and Scotch Eggs a nicely browned surface. Any which are left over may be stored for a few days, for further use.
2. Make Confetti Meat Loaf next, because it is fairly large and solid and needs time to cool down.
3. Make Scotch Eggs so that they also have time to cool down. Do not try to hard-boil eggs in your microwave oven.
4. Make the dressing for Potato Salad next. Coat the potatoes after they have been cooked. You save time and trouble if you slice the potatoes before cooking them.
5. Prepare the Italian Dressing for the salad, but don't add it to the washed, crisp salad greens until you are going to serve it.
6. Make American Brownies, and carry them to your picnic in their baking pan, if you like.
7. Prepare and heat the Lemonade concentrate last. Carry it to the picnic in a small container and dilute it with cold water or soda water just before you serve it.

Savoury Crumbs

(See recipe on page 122.)

Easy Mayonnaise

This dressing is a cross between old-fashioned boiled dressing and mayonnaise.

2 Tbsp flour
½ tsp salt
½ tsp sugar
½ tsp dry mustard
*   or 1 tsp mixed mustard*
½ cup cold water
1 egg yolk
2 Tbsp vinegar
½ cup corn or soya oil

Measure the first four ingredients into a 2 cup measuring jug or a bowl of about the same size.

Stir well, then add the water.

Microwave at Full power for 2 minutes or until thick and clear.

Add remaining ingredients and beat with a rotary beater for a few seconds, until smooth and thick, or tip into a food processor containing the remaining ingredients, and process until smooth and thick.

Store in refrigerator in a screw-topped jar, thinning with milk before use, if too thick.

Scotch Eggs

(See recipe on page 39.)

Confetti Meat Loaf

(See recipe on page 122.)

Potato Salad

Make Easy Mayonnaise, as above.

Scrub new or waxy potatoes, allowing 1 large or 2 smaller potatoes per serving. Slice 5 mm thick or cut in 1 cm cubes.

Place in oven bag allowing 1 teaspoon oil and 1 teaspoon water per potato then shake to coat potatoes. Secure top of bag loosely with a rubber band, leaving a finger-sized hole.

Cook at Full power until potatoes are barely tender, allowing 2–4 minutes per potato. Leave to stand for 2–3 minutes, so potatoes finish cooking.

Cool potatoes by holding bag under a cold tap.

When cool, add chopped spring onions, parsley, capers, anchovies, chopped hard-boiled eggs and enough Easy Mayonnaise to coat. Adjust seasoning only if necessary.

Store in cool place until serving in lettuce cups, or in a bowl lined with lettuce leaves. Garnish if desired.
Note:
Hard pieces of potato have not been cooked long enough. Shrunken pieces of potato have been overcooked.

Italian Dressing

(See recipe on page 297.)

Green Salad

Break a mixture of washed, dried salad greens into tablespoon-sized pieces, in a plastic bag.

Add other salad ingredients for added flavour, colour or texture.

Close bag tightly with a rubber band, enclosing some air, so vegetables are not squashed together.

Chill until required. Just before serving add enough dressing to coat leaves when they are shaken gently (with some air enclosed in bag during shaking).

Tip into serving bowl or place with tongs on to individual (paper) plates.

American Brownies

Brownies are an American favourite. A chocolate slice with a dense fudgy texture, they may appear soft soon after cooking, but become firmer on standing.

Brownies microwave best in a straight-sided, flat-bottomed ring pan, without a cover.

100 g butter
2 eggs
1 cup sugar
1 tsp vanilla
³/₄ cup flour
¹/₄ cup cocoa
1 tsp baking powder
¹/₄–¹/₂ cup nuts (optional)

In a medium-sized bowl melt the butter at Full power, for 1¹/₂ minutes, or until liquid.

Beat in eggs, sugar and vanilla, using a fork or rubber scraper.

Fold in sifted dry ingredients and the nuts, if used. Do not overmix.

Spoon and spread mixture into a flat-bottomed, straight-sided ring pan which has been lined with a Teflon ring liner or baking paper.

Microwave uncovered, without raising the dish, at Full power, for 4–7 minutes, until the mixture beside the ring feels dry. Check every 30 seconds after 4 minutes, to make sure brownies do not overcook (the mixture will rise up during cooking and will then sink again).

Cool in pan, turn out, remove liner, dust surface with icing sugar, and cut into pieces.

Note:
Brownies which are dry and hard have been overcooked. Use them for crumbs for truffles, etc.

Variations:
Sprinkle ¹/₂ cup chocolate chips over surface before baking. These sink through brownies during cooking.

For firmer, drier brownies add up to ¹/₄ cup more flour.

Fresh Lemonade

This drink is quickly made and deliciously refreshing. For instant use, make it in a 1 litre jug, then add iceblocks and cold water or soda.

For later use, keep and transport in a screw-topped bottle, diluting when required. Increase quantities to suit your needs.

For 4 servings:
2 lemons
¹/₄ cup sugar
1 cup water
ice
extra water or soda water

Peel lemons thinly with a potato peeler, into a 1 litre jug. Add juice and sugar.

Microwave rind, juice and sugar at Full power for 2 minutes, or until sugar dissolves when stirred.

Stir in the cold water. Lift out lemon peel, then fill jug with ice and water.

or Pour liquid over ice in four glasses, and top with water or soda water.

or Pour liquid into a screw-topped bottle for diluting later.

Snacks for Friends

The foods which are cooked and served in this menu are some of the many foods suitable for quick preparation for informal meals.

They are foods which can be organised and partly prepared before they are needed, so that when a group of hungry young people arrive, the food can be put out to eat with the minimum of preparation by the young host or hostess.

Although the microwaved fresh Corn on the Cob has a seaon of only a few months, the Cheese Fondue and Barbecued Beef filled rolls are especially good in cold weather, for example, served after Saturday sports.

Half the fun of a cheese fondue is that it is placed in the centre of the table, so everybody can help themselves. A coffee table is a good serving venue. Another advantage of microwaving cheese fondue is that the dish can be readily reheated if necessary.

SNACKS FOR FRIENDS

Easy Cheese Fondue

Barbecued Beef on French Bread with Salad Vegetables

Corn on the Cob

Peanut Butter Squares

Coffee or Hot Mocha

Fresh Fruit

Note:
If you would like a group of young people entertained in one part of the house, remember that a microwave oven is portable, and may be plugged into a power outlet in a rumpus or games room. The semi-prepared food may be left beside it, ready to cook, since the messier preparation has been done ahead.

Plan of Attack

1. For a meal like this, a plan of attack is not really necessary. because the food need not all be served at the same time.
2. So that you have time to relax with your friends, assemble the ingredients you need and do most of the preparation ahead. Only the cooking needs to be done at the last minute.
3. Prepare the Peanut Butter Squares and leave to cool in the refrigerator before icing them. You may find they disappear. Hide them if you make them the day before!

Easy Cheese Fondue

I am sure that no self-respecting Swiss would lay claim to this microwaved cheese fondue!

I make two versions — the first uses a fairly dry white wine and Gruyère cheese, while the second uses beer and Cheddar. Both are good. Try them both when you have the right ingredients to hand.

Cook the fondue in a microwavable dish, 17–20 cm in diameter, shallow enough for chunks of French bread to be dipped into.

If you are not a traditionalist, try dipping pieces of apple, pear, cauliflower, etc. into the fondue as well as bread.

2 cups (150 g) grated Cheddar or
  Gruyère cheese
2 Tbsp flour
1 clove garlic, chopped
¹/₂ tsp nutmeg
1 cup flat or fresh beer or dry white
  wine

Mix grated cheese and flour in a bowl or flat-bottomed casserole dish.

Add garlic and nutmeg. Stir to mix.

Cover bowl and put aside, adding the liquid just before you are going to cook it.

Heat at Full power for 2 minutes, then stir (with a whisk, if possible).

Heat for another 2 minutes or until whole surface bubbles, stirring after each minute.

Serve hot, reheating fondue when it becomes cool.

To serve, dip crusty bread, apple or pear wedges or raw cauliflower into the hot fondue.

Barbecued Beef on French Bread

You can make barbecued beef with cooked or raw beef. Whichever you use, it should be sliced very thinly, against the grain of the muscle.

The best cooked beef to use is that from a lean roast which has been cooked to the rare or medium stage.

If you are using raw beef, choose rump steak, cross-cut blade (from which the central line of the gristle has been removed), flank skirt or schnitzel. Take great care not to overcook any of these.

For 2 servings:
2 hamburger buns or lengths of
  French bread
1 onion, very finely chopped
1 Tbsp oil
2 Tbsp tomato or chilli sauce
2 tsp tomato paste
1 Tbsp brown sugar
2 tsp Worcestershire sauce
1 tsp mixed mustard
200 g thinly sliced raw or cooked beef

Split bread and toast lightly, if desired.

Cook onion in oil in covered microwave dish, at Full power for 3 minutes. Add next five ingredients.

Heat for 3 minutes or until sauce bubbles.

Stir in beef, coating well with sauce.

Cover. If using raw beef, microwave at Full power for 3–4 minutes, until beef loses its pink colour. Heat cooked beef for 1–2 minutes or until hot. Spoon meat and sauce on to buns or lengths of French bread. Reheat if desired. Serve with salad vegetables.

Corn on the Cob

Sweetcorn is best cooked no more than 2–3 cobs at a time. Select freshly picked young corn cobs.

Put corn cobs (exactly as picked) in microwave oven with no wrapping, coating or additions.

Microwave at Full power for about 2–3 minutes per cob. Leave to stand for 1 minute

Cut through stem end to detach all outer layers. Peel away outer layers and silk.

Add butter and eat immediately.

Peanut Butter Squares

Peanut Butter Squares always disappear with great speed!

Make them ahead and keep them in the refrigerator so they are cold and firm when eaten.

Because the squares are rich, cut them into small pieces. The people who don't care about calories can always have several small pieces.

100 g butter
¹/₂ cup peanut butter
1 cup biscuit crumbs
1 cup icing sugar
about 6 drops almond essence
¹/₄ tsp vanilla
¹/₂ cup white chocolate pieces
2 tsp butter

In a large microwave bowl put the
butter (cut into cubes) and the
peanut butter (in 4–5 blobs) and
microwave at Full power for 2
minutes, or until you can blend them
easily.

Stir in crumbs, icing sugar and
essences. Mix well.

Press the mixture into a square
pan.

In another dish, melt chocolate
and second measure of butter in the
microwave at Full power for 1–2
minutes, or until the two can be
mixed together smoothly.

Spread on top of peanut butter
mixture.

Cool before cutting into small
pieces.

Coffee from Ground Beans

Make up the quantity of coffee you
require, using your favourite
method. Reheat a cup of the coffee
in the microwave at Full power for
about 1¹/₂ minutes, when you want
hot coffee. Two- or three-cup
quantities can be heated in a glass or
china jug as long as the container
has no metal decoration or screws,
etc. is not too tall and narrow or is
not constricted at the top.

Do not let the coffee boil as the
pressure of bubbling liquid can
break tall, narrow-necked
containers.

Hot Mocha

This is an interesting winter drink
for children or adults. Alter the
proportion of ingredients if you like.

For 1 large serving:
1¹/₂ Tbsp drinking chocolate
1–2 tsp instant coffee
sugar to taste
1 cup milk

whipped cream
cinnamon or chocolate curls

Mix drinking chocolate, instant
coffee, sugar and milk in a mug.
Microwave at Full power until
steaming (1¹/₂ minutes). Top with
lightly whipped cream and add a
pinch of cinnamon or chocolate
curls.

Microwave Drinks

Use microwave-proof mugs or
cups for warming up drinks. Here
are some examples of possible
combinations.

For easiest reheating, heat 1
mug or cup at a time, at Full
power. Stand it on a paper
serviette or towel to prevent
spills or boil-overs.

The time will vary from 30
seconds to 3 minutes, depending
on the size of cup or mug, initial
temperature of liquid, proportion
of milk, the amount of cream in
the milk, etc.

For best flavour, and to prevent
boil-overs, do not reheat to
boiling point (you cannot drink it
this hot, anyway).

Weekend Snacks

This menu is a little different from the other menus.

It is the sort of list that the 'food buyer and organiser' of the family might fasten on the refrigerator door, so that everyone who wants to make a snack knows what is available.

Assembling and cooking snacks like these for yourself really saves money.

Remember these important facts.
• For most even cooking, wrap or cover foods.
• Food heated from room temperature takes a shorter time than cold food does.
• For greatest speed, it often pays to use your microwave alongside other appliances, such as an electric jug or toaster.
• Overheating and overcooking cause:
— boil-overs
— cheese 'disappearing' — that is, melting and running off food
— bread and baked foods drying out and toughening.

WEEKEND SNACKS

**Soup
with
Croutons or
Crisp Bread**

**Cheesy Snacks and
Savouries**

**Spaghetti
or
Baked Beans on Toast**

Hot Dogs

Pita Bread Pockets

Hot Meat Sandwiches

Plan of Attack

For snack foods like those listed here you do not need a definite working timetable because you are not likely to be preparing all of them to serve at once.

You are more likely to choose one or two of these foods, which you will probably heat just before you need them.

Common sense and basic rules apply.

Get out all the ingredients you are likely to need before you start.

If you are preparing two things such as soup and a bread-based snack, decide whether you will have time to prepare the second while the first is heating, or whether it is better to prepare them both before you heat the first, which is often a good idea. You can then keep an eye on the microwave oven while your food heats, putting away the ingredients you have used, and cleaning up, so by the time you start to eat, the kitchen is cleared and you can leave it more or less as you found it.

Hot Soup

Reheating soup from the refrigerator
Soup from a covered container in the refrigerator may be reheated easily and quickly. Stir the soup well.

Fill a mug or soup bowl so that it is no more than two-thirds full. (Don't use a very wide shallow soup bowl.) Stand it on a folded paper towel or serviette, on a plate if you like, and heat, not until boiling, but until soup is drinking temperature, stirring it several times for most even heating. It should take about 3 minutes per 250 ml cup.

Making soup from a can
Read the can instructions for diluting the soup. Pour into your mug about a third of a can of (well stirred or shaken) soup, then dilute it with hot or cold tap water, as instructed. Heat to drinking temperature, add milk if required, and heat again. Heating time will be shorter than for refrigerated soup, and will depend on the temperature of the water you used.

For '1 serving' packet soups
Read the packet instructions. Pour the required amount of hot (tap) water over the soup and heat it in the microwave until it is at the required temperature, stirring several times. The soup will not need to boil in its container.

For packet soups for several servings
It is usually easiest to make up the whole packet in a microwave-proof casserole bowl, or wide measuring jug, then serve what you need. With experience you may use part of the powder only, and cook this in a small container, but this can be a bit fiddly. These packet soups must be boiled, not just heated to drinking temperature.

Croutons

(See recipe on page 297.)

Crisp Bread Slices

1 Tbsp soft butter
1/8 tsp garlic salt
1/8 tsp paprika
1/8 tsp curry powder
*about 6 thin slices French bread
or 2 slices bread*

For ease and no mess, make the spread on a paper plate with a rubber spatula.

Soften but don't melt the butter and mash with the seasonings.

Spread mixture thinly, covering the whole surface of thin slices cut diagonally from bread rolls or French bread; or spread on sliced bread, then cut each slice in quarters.

Place the buttered bread on a folded paper serviette or towel, or on a ridged microwave dish.

Microwave at Full power until the bread starts to darken slightly, about 15 seconds per slice (or quarter). Leave to stand for 1–2 minutes.

Cheese Savouries

These are wonderful microwave standbys. Most cheeses microwave very well, softening deliciously and developing even more flavour. It is worth trying different cheese varieties after you become an expert cooking with Cheddar.
e.g. Edam — which is low in fat
Gruyère — which is low in salt
Gouda — which has a very mild flavour
Mozzarella — which has a special stringy texture when heated, and which is also low in fat.

For savouries made with minimum of mess and maximum convenience, cook with cheese which you buy pre-grated, e.g. mild or tasty Cheddar, and Mozzarella.

Cheese on Crackers

Arrange a ring of crackers on a round plate, on which you will serve them, or in a circle on a paper towel.

Top each cracker with the cheese of your choice, and a garnish. Put on the garnish before or after the cheese, depending on its texture and appearance.

For example:

tomato slices	paprika
green/red pepper	chopped parsley
chutney etc.	fresh/dry herbs
spring onions	mushrooms
olives	onion rings
salami/bacon	creamed corn

Microwave at Full power, just until the cheese starts to soften. Allow 1/2–3 minutes depending on amount of food.

Important:
If you overheat the savouries, the cheese will disappear off the crackers completely.

Stand for 1–2 minutes before serving.

Hot Bubbly Cheese Savouries

(See recipe on page 47.)

Spaghetti or Baked Beans on Toast

You can heat spaghetti or baked beans on the plate on which you will eat it.

Make and butter a piece of toast, and place it on a plate.

Top with beans or spaghetti straight from the can.

Cover loosely with a paper towel to prevent splattering.

Microwave at Full power for about 1 1/2 minutes. Time depends on amount and initial temperature. When fairly hot, top with grated cheese if desired. Reheat until cheese melts.

Hot Dogs

(See recipe on page 124.)

Pita Bread Pockets

Pita or pocket breads make excellent edible containers for mixtures of raw or cooked foods.

Halve pocket breads and sprinkle each with a few drops of water if they appear to be dry. Wrap in a paper towel or slip into an oven bag. Microwave briefly to warm bread (so they split open more easily) but do not let them dry out.

Make any filling mixture you like, adding finely chopped or grated cheese for extra flavour and to hold filling together when heated. Pile into pockets.

Prop several paper serviette-wrapped pockets so they are upright, in a basket or deep plate.

Microwave at Full power, until cheese softens.

Filling suggestions
Cooked mince or dried bean mixtures, cooked rice, macaroni or cracked wheat, mushrooms, onions, tomatoes, beansprouts, carrot, cabbage, green/red pepper, corn, relishes, herbs, luncheon sausage.

Hot Meat Sandwiches

A sandwich like this is a delicious way to serve leftover cold meat or poultry. With a salad, one of these makes a complete meal.

For 1 serving:
1 crusty bread roll or bagel
mayonnaise or butter
1–2 slices roast or corned beef, chicken
  or other cold meat
gravy (optional)
1 Tbsp mild mixed mustard
1 Tbsp relish or tomato sauce

Split the bread roll (not quite all the way through) and spread the cut surface with mayonnaise or butter.

Slice, chop or fold the meat, adding a little leftover gravy if desired. Place the meat in the roll.

Add mustard and relish, tomato sauce, etc. Fold a paper towel around the roll.

Heat at Full power for 30 seconds or until meat is hot and roll is warm.

Note:
If meat is dry, spread with relish before placing in roll.

Homemade Takeaways

This menu is made up of homemade versions of three foods that you often buy as takeaways.

When you realise how easy and how quick it is to prepare these foods in a microwave oven, you may decide that you will sometimes make them yourself, rather than buying them.

Certainly, if you work out how much the ingredients cost you, then compare this with the price of the takeaway, you will find that it really pays you to make your own.

What's more, you can make sure that the quality of the ingredients is high and the fillings generous. You can include plenty of freshly prepared fruit and vegetables so your homemade takeaways are well balanced nutritionally.

Each of these hamburgers contains a juicy, generous-sized meat patty with cheese for extra flavour, and vitamin C-rich vegetables. The pizza has plenty of cheese with a variety of vegetables and other ingredients. The muesli bars have an especially good flavour and extra crunch because they are so fresh.

HOMEMADE TAKEAWAYS

Hasty Hamburgers

Pronto Pizza

Salad or Raw Vegetable Strips

Munchy Muesli Bars

Yoghurt, Milk or Fruit Juice

Raw Fruit

Plan of Attack

If you are making only one of these foods you won't need a workplan — just
• read through the recipe
• get out all the ingredients
• start mixing and cooking.
It pays to get out all the ingredients first, because it is disappointing to find that you don't have something vital when you are halfway through mixing.

If you are going to make all these foods, follow this order:

1. Start with the muesli bars, as these are served cold and need a few minutes to cool and harden.
2. Next make the pizza, because it can be reheated easily.
3. Make the hamburgers last. You can warm the bread rolls and assemble relishes etc. during their standing time.

In between 1, 2 and 3 you can cut up vegetables or make a salad, get drinks ready, polish and arrange raw fruit, and assemble the things you will need to serve your food.

Pronto Pizza

This pizza is made in a doughnut shape for faster, even cooking.

Its base is made from a quick cheese- and herb-flavoured dough and it browns nicely as it cooks because it is placed on a special microwave crisping wrap material which acts like a browning dish.

For 2 servings:
½ cup self-raising flour
2 Tbsp Parmesan cheese
¼ Tbsp dried basil
¼ tsp dried oreganum
about 3 Tbsp milk
2 Tbsp pasta tomato sauce mix
about 1 Tbsp hot water
1 cup grated Cheddar or Mozzarella cheese
1–2 cups vegetables, e.g. sliced peppers, spring or mild onions, tomatoes, mushrooms
1 Tbsp oil

In a medium to large mixing bowl combine the flour, Parmesan cheese and dried herbs with enough milk to mix to a firm dough.

Roll into a sausage about 40 cm long, then join ends to form a circle.

Place this on a square of microwave crisping wrap, and pat out until it forms a neat flattened doughnut shape about 20 cm across.

Mix dried tomato sauce mix with enough hot water to make a spreadable paste. Paint this over the surface and outer edges of the uncooked dough.

Cook on a ridged surface or flat plate at Full power for 2–3 minutes, until the dough near the centre is no longer spongy. Base will brown as dough cooks.

Sprinkle half the grated cheese over the cooked base. Cut, chop or slice the vegetables, toss in the oil, then arrange on the cheese. Sprinkle with remaining cheese. Add garnishes of olives, anchovies, bacon, luncheon sausage, salami or anything you have and like.

Cook at Full power for 2–4 minutes until cheese melts. Reheat, if necessary, before serving.
Variations:
Brush base with water-thinned tomato paste or concentrate, with tomato purée, canned spaghetti and tomato, or other suitable tomato-flavoured mixtures.

Salad Vegetables

Serve finger-food salad vegetables, e.g. whole tomatoes, young carrots, radishes, peas in pods, crisp inner lettuce leaves, celery strips, cauliflower florets, etc.

Hasty Hamburgers

This amount of mixture makes two large hamburger patties, each containing 125 g of minced beef. You can make three smaller (about 85 g) patties from the same amount of mixture if you like.

½ slice toast bread
½ tsp dark soya sauce
1½ tsp tomato ketchup
1 spring onion, chopped
½ tsp instant beef stock
250g minced beef

If a food processor or blender is available, break the bread into small pieces and process until evenly crumbed, then add all other ingredients and combine until evenly mixed.

Without a food processor, break the bread into small pieces and leave them to stand in the soya sauce and ketchup for a few minutes. Add the chopped onion and powdered stock, and mash everything together with a fork. Lastly add the meat broken into smaller pieces. Mix again until well mixed.

Shape into two or three pattties with wet hands.

Brush the top and sides of each patty with a little extra soya sauce. Cover prepared patties and refrigerate until required, if desired.

To cook, place patties so they are

equidistant (on a paper towel if desired). Cover loosely with a paper towel (for even cooking). Cook at Full power for 2 minutes. Turn patties over, and cook for 2 minutes longer, or to desired stage. Leave to stand for 2 minutes before serving in warmed bun.

To cook in a browning dish, heat empty browning dish for 6 minutes at Full power, or according to manufacturer's instructions. Cook burgers for 2 minutes then turn and cook for 1–2 minutes longer until they are no longer red in the centre.

While your burgers stand, halve 2–3 rolls, wrap in paper towels and heat for 20–30 seconds, or until bread is warm.

Spread bread with chutney, tomato ketchup, relish or mild mustard according to taste. Next put on a lettuce leaf or other salad greens. Add sliced green and red pepper rings and/or tomato. Put the hot patty on this and top with a square of cheese. Garnish with cucumber, pickle, gherkin, etc., if desired.

Just before eating, heat up each assembled hamburger briefly, if it has cooled down since it has been made. (The meat patty and cheese will become hot before the bread and other garnishes.)

Notes:
Frozen patties: Patties may be made ahead, wrapped and frozen until required. For fast thawing, thaw each patty wrapped in greaseproof paper at Defrost (30% power) until patty has thawed in centre.
Frozen hamburger buns: Wrap each hamburger bun in a paper towel and thaw at Defrost (30% power) for about 1 minute, or until thawed in the centre. Halve with a serrated knife before thawing, so you can see how the centre is warming. Do not overheat or bread will toughen.

Munchy Muesli Bars

Muesli bars are made in three separate steps. It is important to cook each stage for the right amount of time, since the finished bars may be too chewy if they are not cooked enough, or too hard and crunchy if they are cooked too long.

The times given here are exactly what I use for my 650 watt oven, at Full power.

For 12 gem-iron bars:
about ¼ cup chopped dried apricots (or other dried fruit)
2 Tbsp orange juice or water
2 Tbsp honey
¼ cup brown sugar
3 Tbsp butter
1½ cups rolled oats
½ cup coconut
pinch of salt
¼ cup chopped nuts

Chop the dried apricots (or other dried fruit) into pieces the size of currants, in a small bowl or measuring cup.

Add the liquid, toss to coat, cover the container and cook at Full power for 1–2 minutes or until the fruit is hot and steamy, and most of the liquid has disappeared. Leave to stand. The remaining liquid should disappear during this time.

Measure slighty rounded measuring spoons of (softened) honey, the brown sugar, and the butter into a flat-bottomed, 20–23 cm casserole.

Heat for 1 minute, stir well then heat for another minute until butter and sugar have melted.

Tip in the rolled oats, coconut, salt and nuts.

Heat for 2 minutes then stir well, and heat for 2–3 minutes longer, stirring well every minute. When mixture is cooked it will have lost its raw smell and will not stick together as readily as it did initially.

Stir the softened dried fruit into the hot cereal mixture

Working quickly with the hot mixture, press it together into small lightly buttered moulds, such as patty tins or gem irons.

When nearly cold, remove from moulds. Wrap each bar in (airtight) plastic film, or put in an airtight jar.
Notes:
If preferred, mix and heat the honey, sugar and butter in a bowl or measuring cup, then stir it into the cereal in the large flat-bottomed container.

If bars are crumbly and hard to press together, the mixture has been cooked for too long.

A Posh Picnic

A microwave does much more than save you time and effort. In this menu, it will help you in additional ways.

You will save time cooking your terrine and bread, and this is important when the weather is pleasant and you don't want to spend unnecessary time in your kitchen. However you do still get the irresistible smell of home-baked bread!

Microwaved bread tends to be heavy, a quality I like in this firm 'grainy' brown bread. The precooked kibbled wheat adds texture to this loaf and ensures it will stay moist and fresh for longer.

As you prepare the bread and dip for this menu, you will see some of the ways your microwave oven will help to streamline the steps in your food preparation.

It is very convenient being able to use the microwave oven to warm bread dough while it rises, without overheating it. You can take advantage of this, even if you intend to bake light textured, crusty bread in your conventional oven.

A POSH PICNIC

Blue Cheese Ball or Dip with Fresh Vegetables

Clare's Terrine

Homemade Brown Bread

Bread and Butter Pickles

Fresh Fruit

Similarly, when you are making Blue Cheese Ball (or Dip), the job is so much easier if you can bring the cream cheese to a warm creaming temperature in a short time.

Plan of Attack

1. Prepare the terrine. Put all the ingredients out on your workbench before you start, so you can put everything together fast. The terrine, which needs to cool before you serve it, can be made first or after you have mixed the bread and left it to rise.
2. Start the bread at least an hour and a half before you want to eat it. It doesn't take long to prepare, but its rising time will be about 1 hour if given 1 minute bursts at Defrost (30% power) every 10 minutes, i.e. until the loaf has risen to almost double its size.
3. While the bread rises and then cooks for 15–16 minutes, prepare the Blue Cheese Ball or Dip, and slice the vegetables to serve with the dip.

Blue Cheese Ball or Dip

The Blue Cheese Ball or Dip is one of my favourites — I've made it for 25 years. It isn't cooked in the microwave, but I use the microwave to soften the cream cheese so it blends easily with the other ingredients.

1 carton (250 g) cream cheese
1 Tbsp onion pulp and juice
1 tsp Worcestershire sauce
¼–½ cup grated blue vein cheese (e.g. Bleu de Montagne or Blue Supreme)
1 Tbsp sherry or brandy

Put the cream cheese in the microwave oven. Depending on the initial temperature of the cream cheese and whether it was a firm or soft cream cheese, it will take 1–2 minutes at Medium (50% power) to soften to a consistency where it will blend quickly and easily with the other ingredients. Take care to remove all the foil from the container before putting it into the microwave.

To the softened cream cheese add the onion pulp and juice made by scraping the cut surface of the onion with a teaspoon.

Stir in the Worcestershire sauce, grated cheese and sherry or brandy.

The firm mixture can be coated in fresh herbs or nuts to serve as a ball.

Variation:
To thin the mixture down for a dip, add buttermilk, yoghurt or sour cream.

Both mixtures can be potted for serving later with crisp sticks of celery and carrots, young beans, asparagus or cauliflower florets. If kept for a long time this dip will probably need thinning down occasionally.

Clare's Terrine

This terrine cooks quickly and tastes excellent, but it is not an exciting mixture when it is raw!

300 g cubed lamb's liver
1 egg
¼ cup sherry
1–2 cloves garlic
½ tsp salt
1 tsp fresh thyme
¼ tsp grated nutmeg
¼ tsp dried sage
⅛ tsp ground cloves
300 g sausage meat
2–4 thin rashers of bacon

Trim and cut liver into small cubes.

Purée in a food processor or blender, then add the egg, sherry and seasonings.

Add sausage meat in several pieces; process until mixed.

Line a microwave loaf pan with loaf pan Teflon liners or a strip of oven bag down its long sides and bottom. Arrange thin bacon strips on bottom or on the bottom and sides. Pour the mixture evenly over this. Fold ends of ovenbag or liner over meat. Cover with clingwrap or a lid.

Stand loaf pan on an inverted plate. Microwave at Medium-High (70% power) for 6–7 minutes or until loaf springs back when pressed and juices from centre do not run pink. Cooking time will be longer if terrine is small and deep.

Invert the lid of the container so it pushes down on the surface of the terrine, or lay something flat on the terrine and weigh down with cans, or anything heavy, until cold.

Unmould and slice as required.

Homemade Brown Bread

This makes a well-flavoured, heavy-textured, unkneaded brown loaf, which will remain moist for days. The top of the loaf tends to be flat rather than rounded. The dough is kept close to body temperature, as it rises, by brief 'bursts' in the microwave oven at Defrost (30% power).

1 tsp dried yeast granules
1 tsp sugar
½ cup warm water
½ cup kibbled wheat
1 cup cold water
2 Tbsp treacle
½ cup rolled oats

1½ cups wholemeal flour
¾ cup flour
1½ tsp salt
1 Tbsp oil
½ cup milk
toasted sesame or sunflower seeds

In a small container mix the yeast, sugar and lukewarm water. Leave to stand in a warm place until the surface bubbles.

Measure the kibbled wheat into a fairly large plastic mixing bowl.

Add the water and bring to the boil, about 4 minutes at Full power.

Leave to stand for 1 minute, then drain off the liquid, leaving the wheat in the bowl.

Stir in the treacle.

Without mixing, add the rolled oats, flours, salt, oil and milk into the kibbled wheat.

Tip in the bubbly yeast mixture and beat well to mix everything thoroughly. Heat in the microwave oven at Defrost (30% power) for 1 minute. Stir and feel temperature of dough. If quite cool, heat again until dough has warmed to body temperature. *Do not overheat.*

Spoon dough into a loaf tin lined along the bottom and long sides with a strip of cling wrap or Teflon liner. Moisten top and sprinkle with toasted sesame or sunflower seeds. Leave to rise in a warm, steamy place or stand in microwave oven.

Microwave at Defrost (30% power) for 1 minute every 10 minutes. When dough has risen to double its bulk after about 1 hour, stand loaf tin on an inverted dinner plate. Cook, uncovered, at Medium (50% power) for 16 minutes or until firm in the middle and cooked on the bottom.

Remove bread from the pan, turning in extra kibbled wheat, toasted sesame or sunflower seeds, if desired.

Bread and Butter Pickles

This pickle seems to be everybody's favourite, in sandwiches, on crackers, with cheese and cold meat. It looks and tastes very good when used as a garnish on terrine or brown bread.

2 cups sliced cucumber
1 cup sliced onion
2 Tbsp plain salt
¾ cup white vinegar
¾ cup sugar
1 tsp mustard seeds
1 tsp celery seeds
¼ tsp turmeric

Slice cucumber(s) to fill a 2 cup measure. Slice onions thinly and measure.

Combine vegetables, sprinkle with salt and leave 30 minutes. Drain and rinse well.

In a large, deep heat-resistant bowl or casserole, combine white vinegar, sugar and flavourings. Microwave at Full power for 2 minutes. Stir to dissolve sugar. Heat again until boiling rapidly.

Add vegetables, stir well, and heat until bubbling around the edge.

Seal for long storage, or pour into large jar without sealing and refrigerate, if it is to be used within several weeks.

Fish for Dinner

In this menu, fish is used in the main course. Fish microwaves wonderfully, and very fast. I usually serve the fish on long-grain white rice. Instead of serving cooked vegetables with this, I usually make Quick Minestone Soup, which includes many vegetables, to serve before it, or I make a salad which can be eaten before or after the fish, or at the same time.

You may decide that soup, fish on rice, and salad is enough for you for dinner. On the other hand, if you are cooking for active, hungry people, or have friends coming to share your meal, you may want to do some quick baking in your microwave. Orange Snacking Cake is a good, quick microwave cake/slice. For people who don't feel they need a slice of this, you can serve fruit, with a wedge of special cheese. Your microwave can make all the difference to soft cheeses with white, mould-ripened surfaces. If you warm these cheeses before serving, their texture will be soft and creamy. In your microwave, this takes only a matter of seconds.

Plan of Attack

1. Make the Orange Snacking Cake first. It needs about 5 minutes'

FISH FOR DINNER

Quick Minestrone Soup

Creamy Paprika Fish
on
Rice

Mixed Salad

Orange Snacking Cake and/or
Fresh Fruit and Camembert

standing to cool, before you ice it. Mix, cook it, and leave it to stand.

2. Make the soup next. Because this soup uses a lot of ingredients it is not worth making in small quantities. Refrigerate the soup, using it over several days, if necessary.

As the flavour improves on keeping, if you are making it for a special occasion, try to make it early enough to leave standing for several hours.

3. Ice the cake after making the soup.

4. Put the rice on to cook after the cake and soup. You can set the table and prepare the salad while it cooks.

(If you know you are going to be short of preparation time, cook the rice earlier in the day, just before you go out of the house, or before you do something in another part of the house.)

5. Cook the onion and butter for the fish mixture.

6. Reheat the soup, just before you want to serve it.

7. Cook the fish (with the cooked onion) while you are eating your soup. Warm plates during the fish standing time.

8. Put the cheese in the microwave oven to warm through, while you are eating the fish. This allows standing time before you serve and eat it.

Quick Minestrone Soup

This recipe makes a brightly coloured, well-flavoured soup in a short time.

For about 8 servings:
2 Tbsp butter
1 onion, chopped
2 carrots, cubed
2 rashers bacon, chopped
3 cups boiling water
1 potato, cubed
¼ cup perciacelli
½–1 cup chopped zucchini
½–1 cup chopped green beans
1 cup chopped cabbage
1 (420 g) can tomatoes in juice
1 can (any size) of white, kidney, or
*   mixed cooked beans*
2 tsp instant beef stock
1 tsp sugar

Combine first four ingredients in a large covered bowl or casserole which holds at least 10–12 cups.

Cover and microwave at Full power for 4 minutes, stirring after 2 minutes.

Add 1 cup boiling water, the potato and perciacelli.

Stir, cover, and cook for 5 minutes longer, or until potato is tender.

Add zucchini, beans, cabbage and the tomato juice.

Cover and cook for 5 minutes longer.

Add chopped canned tomatoes, the canned beans and their liquid, and the remaining 2 cups boiling water in which are dissolved the instant stock and sugar.

Heat until the soup is very hot, stirring several times for even heating. Leave to stand until needed.

Reheat just before serving. Serve with Parmesan cheese if desired.

Creamy Paprika Fish

This is a delicious recipe, and may be made with any fresh or frozen, skinless, boneless fish fillets. Try some of the less expensive varieties, experimenting until you find your favourite.

You can cube fish while it is frozen or partly thawed, but if you combine it with the other ingredients while it is partly frozen, you will need to allow a longer cooking time.

For 3–4 servings:
1 large onion, chopped
1 Tbsp butter
500 g boneless fish fillets, cubed
½ tsp celery salt
2 tsp cornflour

1 tsp paprika
½ cup evaporated milk, sour cream or
*   dairy cream*
2 spring onions, chopped

Put chopped onion and butter into a 20–22 cm microwave cooking/ serving dish.

Cover and microwave at Full power for 3 minutes, stirring once.

Add fish cut into 1 cm cubes.

Sprinkle with celery salt, cornflour and paprika and turn to mix.

Add evaporated milk, or cream, and mix again.

Cover and cook for 3 minutes, stirring once after 2 minutes. Stand for 1 minute before uncovering. Fish is cooked when the pieces are opaque. Cook for 1 minute longer if necessary.

Before serving sprinkle with extra paprika if desired and top with spring onions.

Variation:
After cooking sprinkle with grated cheese before added extra paprika. Microwave until cheese melts.
Note:
If cooked onion is cold when fish and other ingredients are added, the cooking time should be increased by about a minute.

Plain Rice

When you microwave rice you save little time but you finish up with well-flavoured rice, which does not need draining, which has not burnt on the bottom or dried out, and which is easy to reheat.

It is worth experimenting with the rice you usually buy and the dish you want to cook in and serve from, using lower power levels and slightly longer times if the rice has a tendency to boil over.

You can avoid the boiling over problem even at high power levels, if you use a big enough (lidded) container, i.e. about 23 cm in diameter, with fairly straight sides, and a 3–4 litre capacity. In this case, transfer the cooked rice to a smaller container, if you want to serve it at the table. The easiest rice I have cooked is par-boiled or heat-treated rice, which is long-grained, and yellowish in colour.

The rice with the best flavour is Basmati rice. This rice spoils you for other rices, even though it costs a little more.

For 4 servings:
1 cup long-grained rice
2 tsp butter or oil
¹/₂ tsp salt or 1 tsp instant stock
2¹/₄ cups very hot water

Put rice in a fairly deep, 2 litre casserole dish, since it boils up during cooking.

Add the butter or oil, the salt or instant stock (any suitable flavour) then pour in the hot water.

Stir, cover loosely, leaving lid ajar, and cook at Full power for 12 minutes.

Stand for 5–8 minutes, then toss with a fork. To cook ahead, cook as above, then reheat for about 3 minutes.

Variations:

If you have trouble with rice boiling over, cook for longer at a lower power level. Using boiling water, then cook at Defrost (30% power) for 20 minutes, or at Medium (50% power) for 15 minutes.

For 2 cups of rice double everything, use boiling water, and cook for 20 minutes. Stand for 10 minutes.

Orange Snacking Cake

(See recipe on page 241.)

Warming Soft Cheese

Brie, Camembert and other white-mould-covered cheeses which have soft, almost runny interiors when ready to eat at room temperature are too firm and do not have their full flavour when cold, straight from the refrigerator.

If you want to serve any of these cheese before they have had time to warm up slowly, unwrap then microwave them for a short time, on their serving plate or board (as long as it has no metal components).

Heat a 125 g cheese at Medium-High (70% power) for 30–45 seconds, until slightly warmed right through.

Leave to stand for at least 5 minutes before serving.

Look, No Pots!

This menu is made up of a selection of plainly cooked foods.

This is the sort of meal that an inexperienced cook could make fairly easily.

It could also be made and left for a babysitter to warm up for a child too young to cook for itself.

The chicken and vegetables served here are all cooked in disposable containers — paper plates, oven bags, or greaseproof paper packages. The Chocolate Peanut Sauce may be prepared and cooked in the jug from which it is served, if you want a meal without any cooking containers to wash.

Fresh corn on the cob microwaves superbly and is well worth serving as a course by itself. When it is not available it can be replaced with frozen, halved cobs of corn. This cannot compare with the fresh product, and if used should be served *with* the chicken and other vegetables.

Chicken drumsticks (and thighs) cook so quickly that they do not brown. The coating gives them colour and extra flavour.

Small new potatoes microwave very quickly and tomatoes with their high water content heat very quickly in microwave ovens. Frozen peas for one or two servings may be thawed and reheated in greaseproof paper packages.

Chocolate Peanut Sauce is child's play in a microwave oven. Use crunchy or smooth peanut butter.

CHILD'S CHICKEN DINNER

Corn on the Cob

Paprika Chicken Drumsticks

New Potatoes

Tomatoes

Frozen Peas

Chocolate Peanut and Banana Sundae

Plan of Attack

If you are leaving everything to be reheated later, it doesn't matter what you cook first. I tend to cook the foods as if I was going to serve them straight away, following the basic rules!
a) Cook foods to be served cold first
b) Cook easily reheatable foods next.
c) Cook dense foods which keep hot longest, next.
d) Cook foods with short cooking and standing times last.

Here are these rules put into practice:
1. If you serve stewed fruit instead of raw banana, cook it first, and leave it to cool.
2. Prepare and cook the Chocolate Peanut Sauce next, and leave it to be reheated later.
3. Cook the corn on the cob.
4. Cook the Paprika Chicken Drumsticks next.
5. Next, cook the new potatoes.
6. Prepare and cook the peas.
7. Last, cook the tomato which can be put on the serving plate straight away, without waiting for standing time.
8. If the corn is served and eaten first, reheat the plate of chicken, potatoes, peas and tomatoes.
9. If you are serving ice-cream from a 2 litre pack, soften it in the microwave then leave it to stand until scooping it out, a few minutes later.

Fresh Corn on the Cob

(See recipe on page 278.)

Frozen Corn Cobs

Unthawed corn cobs require about 4–5 minutes per 100 g (i.e. per half cob). Wrap in a greaseproof paper parcel, or put in an oven bag, fastened loosely with a rubber band. Add 1 tablespoon water per half cob. Allow 2 minutes' standing time before unwrapping and adding butter (and salt if desired).

Neither the flavour nor texture of this corn compares with that of fresh corn.

Paprika Chicken Drumsticks

This chicken is good served hot, warm, or cold, as finger food. Make the dry coating mixture in fairly large quantities and keep it in an airtight jar, so you can sprinkle it evenly over lightly buttered chicken drumsticks or thighs whenever you want to cook chicken pieces quickly.

2 chicken drumsticks or thighs
2 tsp butter, melted
¼ cup flour
1 Tbsp paprika
1 tsp curry powder
1 tsp garlic salt
1 tsp celery salt
2 Tsp castor sugar

Melt the butter on a paper plate for about 30 seconds at Full power, then brush it thinly and evenly over the thawed, dried chicken pieces.

Using a paper towel, remove any leftover butter from the paper plate.

Combine the dry ingredients by shaking them together in a small lidded jar (or mix them in a food processor if you want the mixture to keep, without separating, for some time).

Using a sieve to ensure even coating, sprinkle the buttered chicken pieces evenly with the paprika mixture.

Place pieces on opposite sides of the paper plate, with the thinner ends of the drumstick nearer the centre, and cover loosely with a paper towel.

Cook at Full power for 2–3 minutes per piece (2 minutes per 100 g).

Leave to stand for 2 minutes, then check to see whether chicken is cooked by piercing the flesh almost to the bone, at the thickest part. If juice runs pink, a little more cooking is needed. If juice is clear and yellowish, chicken is cooked.

New Potatoes

(See recipe on page 292.)

Tomatoes

Tomatoes cook very quickly and well. Always pierce skin of whole tomatoes by cutting a cross in the end opposite the stem. This prevents whole tomatoes bursting during cooking. Halve or cut in thick slices if preferred. Cooking times vary with temperature, ripeness and size of tomatoes.

firm red tomatoes
butter
sugar
salt
basil, thyme, spring onions or parsley

Halve tomatoes. Place close together, cut side up, in shallow baking dish.

Dot each half with ¹/₈ teaspoon butter. Sprinkle with sugar, salt and herbs, if desired.

Bake uncovered at Full power, allowing about 30 seconds per tomato, or for 2–4 minutes per 500 g tomatoes, depending on size, ripeness and initial temperature.

Frozen Peas

Microwaved frozen peas have very good flavour. Small amounts of frozen peas require less time per serving than large amounts.

Cook quantities for one or two servings in a square, flattish steam-proof parcel made using a double layer of greaseproof paper, or in an oven bag fastened loosely with a rubber band which has been rolled down so that it is close to the peas which lie evenly in one layer.

For each serving allow:
¹/₂ cup frozen peas

¹/₂ tsp butter
¹/₂ tsp water
sprig of mint
pinch of sugar

Allow 1–1¹/₂ minutes per serving for one or two servings, and 1¹/₂–2 minutes per serving for larger amounts.

Shake the container once or twice during cooking time then allow about 1–3 minutes' standing time, increasing this with larger quantities.

Chocolate Peanut Sauce

This sauce is very popular with children. After cooking, thin it to the thickness you like with extra milk, remembering that it will thicken as it cools.

³/₄ cup cooking chocolate pieces
¹/₄ cup smooth or crunchy peanut
*   butter*
¹/₄ cup milk

Combine all ingredients in a small bowl or jug. (If crunchy peanut butter is used, sauce has a slightly crunchy texture.)

Microwave at Medium (50% power) for 2 minutes, then stir until

all ingredients are evenly blended.

Thin as desired with extra milk.

Reheat, if desired, just before use.

Softening Ice-Cream

Containers of ice-cream which have been stored in a freezer may freeze very hard, so the ice-cream is too hard to scoop easily.

Loosen top of a (2 litre) container, and microwave at Medium (50% power) for 45–60 seconds, depending on hardness.

Chocolate Peanut and Banana Sundae

Serve two scoops of ice-cream on a flattish plate or oval sundae dish.

Halve a peeled banana lengthwise and arrange on either side of ice-cream.

Pour warm chocolate peanut sauce over ice-cream and banana halves.

Garnish with chopped roasted peanuts, or with other small colourful fruits or with ice-cream wafers.

Chicken Fricassee Dinner

I have planned this menu to show you that it is a good idea to think ahead at times when you are cooking — to cook twice as much as you need for one meal.

For this meal, the main course, Chicken Fricassee, is made with cooked chicken, and the dessert with crêpes from the freezer and apples dried in the autumn.

When I have decided to cook chicken, I often choose a bird big enough to serve for two meals. My Chicken Fricassee is the second half of a Grand Poulet which has been cooked in an oven bag.

If you want to make Chicken Fricassee and you haven't leftover cooked chicken, you have another option — buy a chicken that has been cooked for you. Chicken Fricassee made from cooked, smoked chicken has a slightly different (pinkish) colour and an exciting flavour.

In our house, I nearly always mix up a double batch of crêpe batter. The food processor makes light work of the task, and the batter does not spoil on standing. The crêpes not needed immediately are frozen in a stack with a piece of plastic film between each for easy removal later.

CHICKEN FRICASSEE DINNER

Chicken Fricassee

Mashed Potato or Rice

Spiced Apple Crêpes

These crêpes thaw very quickly at a low power level and make elegant containers for different fruit mixtures.

You can make a spiced apple filling in a very short time in the microwave oven, whether you use apples which you have dried yourself (in a dehydrator) or which you have bought.

This filling keeps for several days in the refrigerator, or for several weeks in the freezer. Again, the microwave makes short work of heating it.

Plan of Attack

1. In conjunction with the preparation of meals on previous days:
   a) Cook the bagged roast chicken.
   b) Prepare, cook and freeze the crêpes.
   c) Dry the apples (or buy dried apple).
   d) Prepare pastry shapes from pie trimmings.
2. Remove crêpes from freezer and thaw them in microwave oven.
3. Prepare and cook the spiced apple filling.
4. Assemble the filled crêpes ready for reheating later.
5. Prepare and cook the potatoes or cook the rice.
6. Make and cook the Chicken Fricassee.
7. While it cooks, mash the potatoes.
8. Freshen the pastry garnish if desired.
9. Warm the crêpes in the microwave or pan while eating the first course.

Bagged Roast Chicken

(See recipe on page 65.)

Chicken Fricassee

Chicken Fricassee is made by cooking a good selection of vegetables in a buttery cooking liquid, then adding thickening and liquid to produce a smooth creamy sauce. When the sauce is cooked, cooked chicken is stirred in and the fricassee is reheated.

For 4 servings:
200 g carrots, thinly sliced
1 cup sliced celery
4 small onions, quartered
50 g butter
³/₄ cup water
2 Tbsp flour
1 tsp instant green herb stock
1 cup milk
¹/₂–1 cup peas
2 cups cubed chicken, cooked or smoked

Put carrots, celery, onions, butter and ¹/₄ cup water in a covered casserole.

Cook at Full power for 8 minutes until vegetables are tender.

Stir in flour, instant stock, milk

and remaining water. Add the peas.

Cook, uncovered, until sauce boils and thickens, stirring every minute. Add chicken and heat for 2 minutes longer, taking care not to boil it.

Serve with mashed potatoes and garnish with pastry shapes.

Pastry Garnish

When you are making a pie, save the pastry trimmings. Roll them out thinly, brush lightly with beaten egg and cut them into interesting shapes with small cutters, or into diamonds with a sharp knife.

Cook in a conventional oven at 190–200°C until they are golden brown and quite crisp.

Cool, then store in an airtight container, up to several weeks. Use as a garnish.

If necessary, refresh by standing the decorations on a folded paper towel and heating at Medium (50% power) until warmed through. Cool on a rack.

Mashed Potato

There are several important points to remember when you are microwaving potatoes for mashing.

• Cut the peeled potatoes into evenly sized pieces.
• Use a cooking container with a central insert (the potatoes in the centre of a solid dish cook more slowly).
• Cook until potatoes are just tender then leave them to stand before you mash them.
• Do not overcook them. Overcooked potatoes are shrunken and will not mash well.
• Mash with a potato masher, then beat the potatoes with a fork, until they are creamy.

For 4 servings:
4 medium-to-large potatoes
¹/₄ cup water
1 Tbsp butter
milk
salt and pepper

Select a bowl in which the potatoes can be cooked, mashed and served. Half fill bowl with cold water.

Peel potatoes, cut them in half lengthwise, then cut each half into 4–6 fairly even, fairly square pieces. Drop potatoes into bowl of water and, as soon as all are prepared, drain off water.

Add the measured water and butter.

Cover and microwave at Full power for 7–10 minutes. Shake after

4–5 minutes, to coat potatoes with melted butter and to reposition.

Test with sharp knife removing potatoes as soon as centre cubes are tender.

Leave to stand, covered, for 4–5 minutes, or until potatoes are required. Don't drain off water or butter.

Mash, adding milk, salt and pepper to taste. Beat potatoes with a fork, after mashing.

Spiced Apple Crêpes

Use freshly made, or thawed frozen crêpes. Place one crêpe at a time on a board.

Either spread several spoonfuls of filling evenly over the whole surface, or place it in a line down the centre.

Roll up the filled crêpe, and place on a lightly buttered shallow microwave dish.

Cover with plastic film and microwave until warmed through.

Serve warm, with a sprinkling of lightly toasted slivered almonds or a dusting of icing sugar, and whipped cream if desired.

Crêpes

The recipe may be doubled so that you can have some extra frozen crêpes on hand.

These thin, delicate, tender pancakes may be made ahead and refrigerated or frozen till required. Allowing for a few experimental failures, this recipe makes 8 crêpes, using 2 tablespoons ($\frac{1}{8}$ cup) of batter for each crêpe.

2 eggs
$\frac{3}{4}$ cup milk
$\frac{1}{2}$ cup flour
$\frac{1}{2}$ tsp salt

Combine ingredients in order given, in a food processor or blender. If mixing in a bowl, add egg then milk to dry ingredients and beat till smooth.

Pour a meausred quantity (e.g. 2 tablespoons) into a smooth, sprayed or buttered, preheated pan.

Immediately tilt the pan so the batter covers the bottom in a thin film. If the batter does not spread thinly, add more milk to thin batter down before making the next crêpe. Do not worry if crêpes are not evenly shaped circles.

When the batter no longer looks wet in the centre, ease the edges of the crêpe from the pan. Turn carefully. Dry the second side, without necessarily browning it.

Stack the crêpes until required. Place them on a plate in a plastic bag to prevent drying out.

Spiced Apple Filling

This filling keeps for some days in the refrigerator, and is delicious used in pastry slices and pies, or as a filling for crêpes. Commercially dried apple or dried pears can be used if you do not have your own dried apples available.

100 g dried apple
$\frac{1}{2}$ cup sultanas or currants
1 cup wine or orange juice or water
2–3 Tbsp brown sugar
$1\frac{1}{2}$ tsp cornflour
1 tsp cinnamon
about 1 tsp grated nutmeg
$\frac{1}{4}$ tsp ground cloves
2 Tbsp butter

Put the dried apple and sultanas or currants in a microwave dish.

Measure the liquid, using wine, juice or water, or a mixture of two or three of them. (Diluted bottled concentrated orange juice mixtures give a good flavour.) Add to dried fruit.

Cover and microwave for 3–5 minutes, at Full power, or until the fruit is tender.

Mix all the ingredients together, stirring well so that there are no lumps. Sprinkle over the plumped, cooked fruit, then stir evenly through it.

Add the butter.

Cover and microwave mixture again until it boils and thickens.

Store in a covered container in the refrigerator, thinning the mixture, if it looks dry, with more fruit juice, wine, sherry, brandy or rum.

To Freeze Crêpes

Stack crêpes with plastic film between for easy removal later. Slide the crêpes into a plastic bag, and seal with a rubber band.

These crêpes thaw very quickly when required. Microwave at Full power for 4–5 seconds per crêpe or until soft enough to roll easily.

Spring Chicken Breast Dinner

When you have a microwave oven in your kitchen, you will find that you can cook delicate, tender foods evenly, so they do not dry out. The Stuffed Chicken Breasts in this menu illustrate this point very well. It is hard to cook them as evenly by any other method.

New potatoes and asparagus are wonderful spring vegetables. They will be full of flavour when microwaved.

If there are no fresh raspberries available when you are preparing this meal, make the sauce with frozen ones. The colour and flavour will be very good, whichever you use.

When you cook beaten egg whites and sugar in a conventional oven, you get a pavlova with a crisp outside and, hopefully, a marshmallow centre. In the microwave oven, no crisp crust forms, but the marshmallow centre is so fast and easy to cook, you can make and serve it at times when you would not dream of making a

SPRING CHICKEN BREAST DINNER

Stuffed Chicken Breasts

New Potatoes

Asparagus and Hollandaise Sauce

Marshmallow Pavlova

or

Ice-Cream and Raspberry Sauce

conventional pavlova.

If you can't accept this modification, serve the sauce over ice-cream instead — it will still be good.

Plan of Attack

1. Start by preparing the dessert. The Raspberry Sauce is served at room temperature and the Pavlova cold, so make these first.
2. Prepare the Savoury Crumbs for the Stuffed Chicken Breasts and stuff and coat the chicken breasts so they are ready to cook. Prepare them ahead if you like. Put them on to cook 25 minutes before you want to eat.
3. Prepare the new potatoes while the chicken cooks. Put them on to cook as soon as the chicken comes out of the oven.
4. When the potatoes are cooked, put the Hollandaise Sauce on to cook.
5. Prepare and cook the asparagus. If you feel that you have too tight a timetable, cook the new potatoes or asparagus on your cook top.

Savoury Crumbs

(See recipe on page 122.)

Stuffed Chicken Breasts

Tender chicken breast meat microwaves very well. The tasty stuffing keeps the meat very moist, as well as adding flavour. The crumb coating disguises the fact that chicken breasts cook so quickly that they do not brown.

For family service you can leave each breast whole. For more elegant service, slice each breast, and overlap the slices on each plate.

For 4 servings:
4 boneless and skinless chicken breasts
50 g butter
1 rasher bacon, chopped
1/2 cup finely chopped mushrooms
1 Tbsp soft breadcrumbs
1/4 cup flour
1 egg, beaten

Make Savoury Crumbs.

Put each boneless, skinless breast between two pieces of plastic (or two plastic bags). Using a rolling pin, bang evenly and gently until each breast is double its original length and width. Lift carefully from the plastic.

Melt butter in a small container.

Add 1 tablespoon of the melted butter to the bacon, mushrooms and soft breadcrumbs, and mix.

Cover and cook at Full power for 3 minutes, stirring or shaking after 1 minute.

Put a pile of stuffing on the inner side of each breast. Roll up and secure with toothpicks.

Dust lightly with flour, then turn, first in beaten egg to coat, then in the Savoury Crumbs.

Arrange breasts in a circle on a flat dish. Pour remaining melted butter over them and bake, uncovered, at Full power for 8 minutes. Stand for 2–3 minutes before serving or slicing.

New Potatoes

New potatoes cook beautifully in a microwave oven.

Scrub potatoes, scraping them if desired. Halve or quarter large potatoes, or peel a ring of skin from around the middle of small whole potatoes to stop them splitting as they cook.

Drop into cold water as they are prepared, to stop them browning.

Just before cooking, transfer to a microwave casserole or oven bag.

For each serving add 1 tablespoon water, a mint sprig and 1/2 teaspoon butter.

Cover or close bag loosely with a rubber band.
Approximate cookings times at Full power:
1 serving (100–125 g) — 2 1/2 minutes
2 servings (200–250 g) —

3 1/2–4 minutes
4 servings (about 500 g) —
6–7 minutes

Shake casserole or turn bag half way through cooking time.

Potatoes are cooked when barely tender. Allow standing time of 3–4 minutes.

Asparagus

Choose good quality spears of asparagus of even thickness. Fat spears cook better than very thin ones. Snap off and discard the bottoms of the stems. For best results and most even cooking, peel the outside skin off the lower part of the stems using a potato peeler or sharp knife.

Use an oven bag for a few servings, or a covered casserole for more. The asparagus should almost fill the cooking container.

Add 1–2 teaspoons water per serving.

Fold or fasten bag with rubber band, leaving a finger-sized hole for steam to escape.

Microwave at Full power. Ten medium stalks take about 2 minutes. 500 g asparagus takes 4–5 minutes.

Allow about 2 minutes' standing time.
Note:
Do not overcook. Asparagus should be bright green and slightly crunchy. Serve plain or with butter or Hollandaise Sauce.

Hollandaise Sauce

For 4 servings:
100 g butter
2 egg yolks
1 Tbsp lemon juice

Heat the butter in a 2 cup measuring cup, covered with a saucer to stop spatters, at Full power for 3 minutes.

In a fairly small bowl with a rounded bottom beat the egg yolks with a whisk until well mixed.

Add the hot butter to the egg yolks in a thin stream, whisking all the time. (Do not add the butter sediment, i.e. stop after about ¹/₄ of the butter is added.) The sauce should thicken as the hot butter is added.

Whisk the lemon juice into the thickened sauce. This may thin the sauce considerably. If sauce needs further thickening microwave at Defrost (30% power) for 1–1¹/₂ minutes, whisking after each 30 seconds. Stop as soon as sauce thickens around edge.

Whisk to make sauce smooth.

Serve sauce warm, not hot, warming carefully atn Defrost (30% power) for short intervals if necessary.

Marshmallow Pavlova

This does not have the crisp crust of an oven-baked pavlova, but it has the advantage of being beaten, shaped and cooked in ten minutes.

I like to top my pavlova with plenty of lightly toasted slivered almonds. These add colour and crunch and taste good with fruit.

4 egg whites
¹/₄ tsp salt
1 cup castor sugar
1 tsp wine vinegar
1 tsp vanilla
¹/₄–¹/₂ cup toasted slivered almonds

In electric mixer, beat egg whites with salt until soft peaks form.

Add the sugar gradually and continue beating for 2–3 minutes.

Fold in the vinegar and vanilla.

Pile meringue on to a flat plate and stand this on an inverted plate in the microwave oven.

Cook at Full power for 3 minutes.

Leave to cool in the oven with the door ajar.

Serve in wedges, with Raspberry Sauce.

Note:
(a) Pavlova may split while baking. Splits close on standing.
(b) Some syrup will leak from pavlova on standing.

Raspberry Sauce

This is a brightly coloured sauce with a sharpness that goes well with pavlova or with ice-cream. You can use free-flow frozen raspberries without thawing them first. If you have berries which are frozen in a block, thaw them enough to cut as much as you need, then cut or break this into smaller pieces.

¹/₂ cup sugar
1 Tbsp custard powder or cornflour
¹/₂ cup water or white wine
2 cups fresh or frozen raspberries
2–3 Tbsp rum or brandy (optional)

In a small bowl or jug mix the sugar with the custard powder or cornflour.

Stir in the liquid and microwave at Full power for 2 minutes until it boils and has thickened.

Stir, then leave to stand for 1–2 minutes. Stir in the thawed or fresh raspberries. Add flavouring, if desired, and cover while sauce cools.

Serve warm or cold, with ice-cream or marshmallow pavlova.

Dinner for One, Please James

This menu is specially planned to help you on days when you walk in the door and feel that you just don't have enough energy to go into the kitchen, let alone to cook.

If you cook for a family, you will find it invaluable for occasions when somebody has to have a meal before everybody else, because of sports practice, swimming or music lessons — or any one of many activities.

You can prepare this menu with the absolute minimum amount of mess and dishwashing, because you can prepare, cook and serve each of the two courses in only one container. It is especially geared to one person, but you can, of course, multiply quantities and cook in larger containers for more people.

I think it is worth investing in a small casserole — deep enough to cook in and shallow enough to eat from. I use a 'snack plate with lid' made by Willow. If you don't have something with a lid, cover the container with plastic cling wrap while the food cooks.

As far as the pudding goes, I use a tough stemmed glass, in which I can serve fruit juice, beer, wine and ice-

DINNER FOR ONE, PLEASE JAMES

Cook-in-the-Plate Easy Dinner

Optional Salad

Optional Bread Roll

Chocolate Pudding (plain or fancy)

cream, and make a microwave-cooked pudding as well. You may find a tough plastic container that will serve the same purposes. If you don't have a suitable container just make the pudding in a glass or plastic measuring cup, or in a mug.

Use the two main recipes as guides to formulate your own 'lazy day' specialties.

As a final note — if you know that you are likely to cook the main dish often, buy a kilo of mince, divide it into 100 g (or 125 g) portions, and freeze these, individually wrapped. You can thaw one of these in a few minutes at Defrost, while you are assembling the other ingredients.

Plan of Attack

1. For this menu, I usually cook the Chocolate Pudding first to give it time to cool down.
2. Make the Cook-in-the-Plate Easy Dinner next. The potato version will take 6 minutes to cook, and the pasta recipe will take 10 minutes, but both require 3–4 minutes' standing time.
3. Prepare a salad if you are not too weary, and heat a bread roll.

Cook-in-the-Plate Easy Dinner

While this recipe is, basically, the easiest and quickest meat and vegetable mixture you can prepare, it is still very good nutritionally.

You can choose to make the potato version for one, or the pasta version for one.

Cook-in-the-Plate Easy Dinner with Potato

100 g lean minced beef (or lamb)
1 or 2 cloves garlic, crushed, or
*   ¼ onion, finely chopped*
1 cup fresh vegetables, e.g. carrot,
*   corn, peas, beans, broccoli or celery*
1 (100 g) potato
1 Tbsp tomato soup powder
¼ tsp dark soya sauce
paprika, oreganum, marjoram or
*   thyme, if desired*
½ cup boiling water

In a lidded dish mix together the mince, garlic or onion and the prepared vegetables, which should be cut the same size as the corn or peas.

Scrub the potato, cut into cubes the size of the other vegetables and add to dish.

Add the soup powder, soya sauce

and paprika or herbs, as desired.

Pour the boiling water over.

Cover the dish and put in the microwave oven, on a paper towel in case it boils over.

Cook at Full power for 6 minutes.

Stand for 3–4 minutes before serving.

Cook-in-the-Plate Easy Dinner with Pasta

100 g lean minced beef (or lamb)
1 or 2 cloves garlic, chopped, or
*   ¼ onion, chopped*
¾ cup frozen mixed vegetables
1 Tbsp tomato soup powder
¼ tsp dark soya sauce
paprika, oreganum, marjoram or
*   thyme, if desired*
¼ cup pasta, e.g. perciacelli, small
*   shells, risone or a little less*
*   alphabet noodles*
1 cup boiling water

In a small, lidded dish mix together the mince, garlic or onion, and the frozen vegetables.

Sprinkle the tomato soup powder, add soya sauce, flavourings and the pasta.

Pour the boiling water over and stir to mix.

Cook, covered, at Full power for 10 minutes.

Stand for 3–4 minutes before serving.

Chocolate Pudding for One

2 Tbsp chocolate chips
2 tsp sugar
2 tsp cornflour
½ cup milk

Into the dish or container you have chosen measure the chocolate chips.

Add the sugar and cornflour and stir to mix.

Add the milk and stir well.

Cook at Full power for 2 minutes. (The time it takes to cook will depend on the temperature of the milk when you take it from the refrigerator. The warmer it is the faster it will boil. If you replace some of the milk with a higher fat mixture it will cook even faster).

After 1 minute, take out the pudding, stir and return to the oven. Don't worry if it doesn't look chocolatey at this stage. Just watch it carefully till it starts to bubble on top — before it starts to boil vigorously — then take it out and stir. The mixture gets smoother, thicker and darker as the chocolate finishes melting through the mixture.

You can serve the pudding as it is,

or top with cream and chopped nuts, e.g. walnuts.

Variation:
When the pudding is cool, but before it is cold, fold in half a chopped banana. Decorate as desired.

Peanutty Chocolate Pudding for One

2 Tbsp chocolate chips
2 tsp sugar
2 tsp cornflour
1 Tbsp peanut butter
¹/₂ cup milk
whipped cream
roasted peanuts, finely chopped

Mix together the chocolate chips, sugar and cornflour in a container.

Add the peanut butter and milk and stir to combine.

Cook at Full power for 2 minutes, stiring after 1 minute.

Leave to cool.

Top with whipped cream and chopped roasted peanuts.

Chocolate Cheesecake Pudding for One

2 Tbsp chocolate chips
2 tsp sugar
2 tsp cornflour
¹/₄ cup milk
¹/₄ cup cream cheese
raspberry purée (optional)

Mix together the chocolate chips, sugar and cornflour, stirring well.

Add the milk and cream cheese and stir well.

Cook at Full power for 1¹/₂–2 minutes, stirring well after 1 minute.

Leave to cool and top with fresh raspberry purée and whipped cream.

To make raspberry purée, mash ¹/₄ cup fresh raspberries with a fork, but keep one or two whole to decorate the top of the pudding.

Garnishes and Decorations

You can make all the difference to a plain pudding-in-a-glass, by decorating it. It is worth taking a little time to make a pudding look more special.

Keep a supply of garnishes which can be sprinkled on to dessert toppings:

• Hundreds and thousands — use with restraint for small children
• Chopped roasted nuts — peanuts, almonds, cashew nuts, etc. Roast, toast or microwave your own and keep in airtight containers for crispness.
• Toasted sesame seeds, ground with sugar, make a delicious topping. Grind them in a coffee and spice grinder attachment for a food processor or beater, or use a pestle and mortar.

Raw fruit or drained cooked fruit is always popular with pudding. Keep pieces small enough to be picked up with a spoonful of pudding.

Suggestions include: peaches, pears, nectarines, raspberries, strawberries, passionfruit.

Casual Weekend Meal for Friends

When you ask friends in for a meal, you don't want to spend a lot of time doing last minute cooking, while everyone else is sitting around talking and laughing in another part of the house.

It's a good idea to plan a meal which doesn't have too many small bits and pieces to think about.

Choose a main dish which can be made ahead so that you can get the 'fiddly parts' out of the way when you have no distractions, then reheat it when it suits you.

One of the great advantages of microwave ovens is the way that they reheat food when you want it — in a remarkably short time, without the food drying up or having a 'reheated' appearance or flavour.

This meal is based on lasagne, which is easy to prepare, serve and eat. My version of this popular recipe calls for no precooking of sauces, or precooking of pasta, so it is not nearly as messy or time-consuming as many lasagne recipes.

Plan of Attack

If you are cooking this meal at a time when stores are shut, make sure you have all the ingredients you need, ahead of time.

Most of the ingredients in the Lazy Lasagne and Carrot Cake are staples which you should always keep on hand.

If you keep packets of minced beef in your freezer, you can thaw one (in the microwave) and make lasagne whenever you want it.

CASUAL WEEKEND MEAL

Lazy Lasagne

Green Leafy Salad with Italian Dressing and Croutons

Carrot Cake with Cream Cheese Icing

Fresh Fruit

If you like to cook ahead, you can make both the cake and the lasagne the day before you want to eat them. The cake will not dry out in this time, but you may find it has greenish flecks in it, since the carrot sometimes discolours on standing. Its flavour is not affected, however.

If you are cooking closer to serving time, plan your work more carefully.

1. Mix, then cook the Carrot Cake, 1½–2 hours before serving time.
2. While the cake cooks measure out the icing ingredients so you can warm them before the lasagne goes in to cook, and ice the cake later, when it has cooled.
3. Next make the Lazy Lasagne. Its total cooking time is about 45 minutes, then it needs to stand for about half an hour before it is served.
4. Once the lasagne base is cooking, mix the topping ingredients.
5. Mix the dressing while the lasagne cooks, so it is ready to heat briefly when the lasagne topping is firm.
6. Prepare the croutons so they are ready to cook after the other foods.
7. Prepare and chill salad vegetables.
8. Clean up and organise serving and eating area.
9. Reheat lasagne before serving, if necessary, covering it, and using Medium (50% power) for even heating. Feel the centre of the bottom of the dish to judge hotness.
Note:
For faster, easier reheating, microwave individual portions on plates.

Lazy Lasagne

This lasagne requires no precooking of ingredients, so it is very easy to make.

It is important to start cooking it as soon as you have assembled it, otherwise the noodles may soften.

Lasagne is best made in a square or rectangular container, so it can be served in brick-shaped pieces, but if you only have a round container, use it! This recipe is best made in a 20 cm square, or 17 × 23 cm dish, with sides at least 3 cm high.

For about 4 servings:
300–400 g minced beef or lamb
1–2 cloves garlic, crushed
½ tsp dried basil
1 tsp oreganum or marjoram
1 (450 g) can tomato purée
2 Tbsp tomato paste
½ packet (3–4 serving size) tomato soup mix

1 tsp instant beef stock
1¼ cups hot water
100 g lasagne noodles
2 cups grated cheese
2 tsp cornflour
1 or 2 eggs
¾ cup milk
paprika

Mix the first nine ingredients in a bowl or food processor, until evenly combined.

Spray or butter the cooking container (see above) and pour a third of the meat mixture into it. (Meat should be sloppy enough to spread easily with a rubber scraper). Add a little extra hot water if necessary.

Cover with half the lasagne noodles, laid in rows, broken into lengths so they cover the meat evenly (use a few more or less noodles, if necessary).

Sprinkle ½ cup cheese over the noodles.

Repeat these layers using half the remaining meat, the rest of the noodles and another ½ cup of cheese.

Top with the remaining meat, adding a few tablespoons of extra liquid if it needs to be runnier to spread evenly.

Cover container and microwave at Full power for 30 minutes.

Mix the remaining cheese, cornflour, egg(s) and milk (the mixture will set better if extra egg is used). Pour this over cooked mixture, sprinkle with paprika, cover again, and microwave at Medium (50% power) for 15 minutes or until topping sets.

Leave to stand for 30 minutes before cutting into rectangles for serving. (If cut earlier, the layers may collapse as served).

Note:
Reheat whole lasagne, covered, in dish at Medium (50%) or Medium-High (70% power), or reheat individual servings at Full power.

Green Leafy Salad

Wash, dry and chill salad greens.

Make Italian Dressing (or use any other dressing you like).

Make croutons.

Toss vegetables with dressing, and sprinkle with croutons, just before serving.

Choose a mixture of leaves for the salad, if possible. Wash them, shake or blot them dry, and break into bite-sized pieces. Put them in a plastic bag, tie with a rubber band (leaving some air in the bag so leaves are not flattened) and refrigerate to become crisp and cold.

Italian Dressing

This dressing coats all salad ingredients well because it is thicker than a plain oil and vinegar dressing.

2 Tbsp cornflour
1/2 cup cold water
1/4 small onion, chopped
1 clove garlic
1/4 cup wine vinegar
2 Tbsp tomato sauce
2 tsp sugar
1 tsp salt
1/2 tsp paprika
1/2 tsp oreganum or marjoram
1/4–1/2 cup corn or soya oil

Mix the cornflour and cold water to a smooth paste in a small bowl or measuring cup.

Microwave at Full power for 1 1/2 minutes or until mixture boils and thickens.

While it cooks combine all remaining ingredients, except oil, in a food processor or mixing bowl.

Process to combine or beat with a whisk.

Add oil in a thin stream, while processing or whisking.

Store in a cool place, in a bottle with a screw top, shaking before each use.

Crisp Croutons

Croutons add interest and flavour contrast to salad and soups.

Although you can make them ahead, storing them in an airtight jar and warming them up 15 minutes before serving, they are best when made within 24 hours of use.

2 Tbsp butter
1 cup small cubes of bread
1/4 tsp garlic salt
paprika (optional)
curry powder (optional)

Melt the butter in a flat-bottomed dish, 20–23 cm in diameter, at Full power, for about 45 seconds.

Cut bread (with crusts on) into 5 mm cubes, using a sharp or serrated knife.

Toss the cubes in the butter to coat them as evenly as possible.

Sprinkle bread with garlic salt, paprika and curry powder for extra flavour and colour, if desired, then spread cubes evenly around the dish.

Microwave at Full power for 3–4 minutes, or until lightly browned, stirring after 2 minutes. Remove well-browned cubes before others finish cooking, if desired.

Store in an airtight container if not using within 30 minutes.

Carrot Cake

(See recipe on page 238.)

Cream Cheese Icing

2 Tbsp cream cheese
1 Tbsp butter
1/2 tsp vanilla
1 1/2 cups sifted icing sugar

Put cream cheese, butter and vanilla in a medium-sized bowl.

Microwave at Full power for 20–30 seconds until cream cheese and butter are very soft.

Add icing sugar and mix with a knife until smooth and creamy. Add a little milk or icing sugar if mixture is too thick or thin. Spread on slightly warm cake.

Sprinkle chopped walnuts over icing before it sets.

Note:
This cake is best stored, loosely covered, at room temperature or refrigerated in an airtight container. It may sweat if tightly enclosed at room temperature.

'Grilled' Steak, Tipsy Cake

Most of us, when we come into the kitchen to prepare a meal, have one idea uppermost in our minds. How can we prepare and cook the food efficiently, well and as quickly as possible, so that we can get on with the rest of our lives?

I seldom say to myself, 'Tonight I will cook everything in the microwave oven'. Instead, I work out what I will save most time microwaving, and what else will cook on the cooktop while the microwave oven is in use. I'm sure you will want to do the same with this menu — cooking either the steak or potatoes on the cooktop.

You get best results microwaving steak if you use a browning dish, which works efficiently and well. It is important to watch the timing carefully.

Golden Potatoes are the closest things to chips that I microwave.

Mushrooms microwave very fast. In their slightly thickened sauce they make a good accompaniment to the steak.

You can cook the pepper mixture to the stage you like it.

Tipsy Cake is based on a cake made from a packet mix.

Although there is no reason why you can't serve your freshly made cake exactly as it is, you will make it look as if you have spent all day in the kitchen if you leave the cake to macerate (or soak) in a fruit-and-rum-flavoured syrup.

'GRILLED' STEAK, TIPSY CAKE

Tender Beef Steak

Garlic Mushrooms

Golden Potatoes

Sesame Peppers

Tipsy Cake

Plan of Attack

1. Make the Tipsy Cake first. It needs time to soak in its rum-flavoured syrup. The cake may be made not long before serving but the syrup soaks through more evenly if left to stand for several hours.
2. Prepare and soak the Sesame Peppers. They can be reheated just before serving.
3. The Garlic Mushrooms may be prepared and cooked next and also reheated just before taking to the table.
4. Prepare the marinade for the steaks. Leave steaks to marinate for at least 10 minutes.
5. Scrub or peel the potatoes and cut into cubes. Coat with the dry ingredients.
6. Decide whether to cook the steak or the potatoes in the microwave oven then, following the manufacturer's instructions, heat the browning dish in the oven.
7. Add either the steak or the potatoes to the browning dish and while this cooks, cook either the potatoes or the steak on the cooktop.
8. Should you choose to cook both in the microwave oven, cook the potatoes first, reheat the browning dish and then cook the steak. It takes tight timing and some juggling to cook both, one after another, in the microwave. Remember to reheat the peppers and mushrooms before serving.

Tender Beef Steak

Steak browned on a microwave browning dish looks just like steak cooked in a hot pan. For even better colour (also flavour and tenderness), marinate it first. Even if the steak is left to marinate only while the browning dish is heating up, you will notice the difference.

It is really important to put the steak in the preheated dish before it cools down, so you should make a point of getting your timing just right!

For 2 servings:
2 fillet steaks or 1 ribeye or 1 sirloin steak

Marinade
1–2 cloves garlic, crushed
equal parts of dark soya sauce, oil and orange or lemon juice

Prepare marinade, turn steaks in it and leave for 5–60 minutes.

Heat the browning dish following the manufacturer's instructions.

Have the meat at room temperature. Lay the steaks on the hot browning dish.

Microwave at Full power for 1 minute. Turn and cook for another minute.

Leave to stand for 2–3 minutes.

Take the steak out of the browning dish, then add 1–2 tablespoons wine or vegetable oil, scrape the bits from the dish and heat for 1–2 minutes until the volume is reduced to half. Swirl in ½ teaspoon butter and pour the sauce over the steak.

Note:
For 2 larger steaks, you need to cook them for about 2 minutes on each side. The precise times will depend on your own preference, but just like steaks cooked by other methods, if you overcook them you toughen them.

Garlic Mushrooms

Mushrooms microwave very fast. If you overcook them they will be shrunken and soft, and produce a lot of extra liquid — so take care with your timing. Use a lightly thickened glaze for extra colour and flavour.

For 2 servings:
200 g mushrooms
1 clove garlic, finely chopped
1½ tsp butter
½ tsp light soya sauce
½ tsp cornflour
1 Tbsp chopped parsley or spring onion
pepper

Wipe mushrooms and halve, or slice if large.

Put garlic and butter in a casserole just large enough to hold mushrooms.

Heat at Full power for 30 seconds or until butter has melted.

Stir in soya sauce and cornflour then sprinkle with parsley or spring onion. Toss mushrooms in this mixture, coating them evenly and lightly.

Cover loosely and microwave at Full power for 3–4 minutes or until mushrooms have softened to the desired degree and are coated with lightly thickened sauce. Sprinkle with pepper.

Serve with steak.

Golden Potatoes

(See recipe on page 154.)

Sesame Peppers

Peppers add colour and crunch to
this menu.

Cut them into strips or slices and
cook them to the degree you like
them. Red and golden-yellow
peppers tend to have a sweeter
flavour than green peppers, so
include them in pepper dishes for
extra flavour, as well as colour.

For 2–4 servings:
1 Tbsp corn or soya oil
1 clove garlic, chopped
¹/₂ tsp sesame oil
¹/₂ tsp light soya sauce
1 green pepper, sliced
1 red or yellow pepper, sliced
¹/₂ tsp cornflour (optional)
pinch sugar
1 Tbsp toasted sesame seeds

Combine the first six ingredients in
a medium-sized covered casserole.

Microwave at Full Power for 3–4
minutes, until tender-crisp.

Thicken liquid with cornflour if
desired, add sugar and cook for 1
minute longer.

Sprinkle with sesame seeds before
serving.

Toasted Sesame Seeds

1 Tbsp butter
¹/₄ cup sesame seeds

Microwave butter in a small dish at
Full power for 40 seconds or until
melted.

Add sesame seeds, microwave,
stirring each minute until the seeds
are light brown. Seeds in the centre
of dish brown first.

Drain on a paper towel.

Tipsy Cake

This cake is based on a microwave
cake mix.

You can use any brand of cake
mix, of any flavour that you feel
would be suitable.

My favourite is a light chocolate
ring cake. If I use a mix which has a
packet of icing enclosed, I save this
to use on another (non-packet) cake
at a later time.

Although the amount of syrup
may seem too much for your cake to
absorb, you will find that it is
soaked up surprisingly fast. I often
serve this cake very soon after
making it — but the syrup soaks
through more evenly if the cake is
left to stand for several hours, or
even days.

1 pkt microwave cake mix (any
flavour)

Syrup
³/₄ cup jam — raspberry, strawberry or
blackcurrant
³/₄ cup liquid (¹/₂ cup water and ¹/₄ cup
orange concentrate)
¹/₄ cup rum (or a few drops of rum
essence)
fresh or frozen fruit

Make the cake first. Read the
instructions on the packet and
follow them to the letter. I put a
paper towel over the surface of the
cake as it seems to make the cake
cook more evenly with a drier top
(no wet patches).

Cook at Full power for 6–7
minutes. The cake is cooked when it
looks cooked near the ring and
starts to come away from the edges.
Stand for a few minutes before
turning out.

In a microwave-proof bowl or jug,
put the jam and orange juice and stir
to combine. Heat at Full power until
the liquid boils.

Add the rum, or rum essence.

Spoon the hot syrup over the hot
cake. Keep spooning it over the top
until most of it is absorbed. If it will
soak up more, heat a little extra
syrup.

Decorate the cake with fresh fruit
to serve.

Traditional Corned Beef Dinner

Your microwave oven can be used to cook a traditional corned beef dinner. You can produce juicy, tender, lean, pink slices of lightly salted meat, potatoes which have been cooked to just the right stage, then mashed to a smooth purée, carrots that are tender but not soggy, and cabbage which is bright green and tender-crisp.

You can also make delicious, tangy mustard sauce using some of the cooking stock, adding cream to soften the flavour.

And, to finish off your meal, what about old fashioned crumble, made with whatever fruit is most readily available — or what fruit you like best?

The crust on a microwaved fruit crumble does not brown quite as much as the crust of a conventionally baked crumble, but it has a very good flavour and texture, and can be made in a fraction of the time.

Plan of Attack

What foods do you cook first?

When you are cooking for four or six, follow this order:

TRADITIONAL CORNED BEEF DINNER

**Corned Silverside of Beef
with
Mustard Cream Sauce**

Mashed Potatoes

Carrots

Buttered Cabbage

**Fruit Crumble
with
Ice-Cream or Cream**

1. Soak the corned beef in a large container of plain cold water, an hour before you are to cook it.
2. Make and cook the fruit crumble.
3. Put the meat on to cook next. A 1½ kg piece is a good size to cook, since leftover corned beef is delicious. It needs 30 minutes at Defrost (30% power) per 500 g. Time the meat cooking, making sure you leave 30–60 minutes' standing time after the meat finishes cooking. Put the meat on to cook 2–2½ hours before you plan to eat dinner
Meat timetable:
— Soak meat 1 hour (in case it is salty)
— Cook 1½ kg piece 1½ hours (1 kg piece 1 hour)
— Standing time ½–1 hour.
4. Cook potatoes, so that there will be time to mash them after their standing time.
5. Prepare and cook the carrots next.
6. Shred and cook the cabbage next.
7. Make the sauce last — or as soon as the meat comes out of the microwave oven, before the potatoes cook.

If you are cooking this dinner for only two people, put the meat to cook first, cook the fruit crumble next, then make the sauce and cook the vegetables.

Corned Silverside of Beef

When you microwave corned beef, you save time and reduce cooking smells and steam.
For best results:
• use silverside rather than brisket
• buy a piece at least 1½ kg
• trim off all visible fat before cooking.

1–1½ kg corned silverside
optional seasonings (see below)
2 cups boiling water

Soak the meat in cold water for an hour, if you think there is any chance of it being too salty.

Place drained beef in a covered casserole with whatever seasonings you like, or with no seasonings.

Pour boiling water over meat (and seasonings).

Cover and microwave at Defrost (30% power) for 25–30 minutes per 500 g, turning once or twice, during cooking.

Leave to stand in hot cooking liquid for at least half an hour, preferably an hour, before slicing.

If you are serving meat cold, refrigerate it in a plastic or oven bag, with about ½ cup cooking liquid, and with all the air squeezed

out of the bag.

Slice across the grain of the muscles.

Optional seasonings
Bayleaf, celery, celery seed, cloves, coriander seeds, dill, dill seeds, garlic, lemon rind, mustard seeds, orange rind, onion, parsley, peppercorns.

Mustard Cream Sauce

This is one of the sauces traditionally served with corned beef.

2 Tbsp butter
2 Tbsp flour
1 Tbsp mixed mustard
1 cup liquid from meat (diluted if necessary)
2 tsp wine vinegar
2–4 Tbsp sour cream or top milk

Heat the butter and flour together at Full power for about 1 minute.

Stir in the mixed mustard, then ½ cup of strained, skimmed cooking liquid from the beef.

Heat until mixture bubbles and thickens. Stir until smooth, then taste.

Add another ½ cup of cooking

stock or water, depending on saltiness.

Stir in the wine vinegar, then add the cream, tasting after adding 2 tablespoons, and adding extra if you want it to be more bland.

Mashed Potatoes

(See recipe on page 290.)

Carrots

Young carrots may be cooked whole, but as carrots mature they are best cut into smaller pieces.

Mature carrots usually microwave best if they are cut into strips thinner than pencils, in slices the thickness of a large coin, or if they are shredded coarsely.

For 4 servings:
250–300 g carrots, as above
2–4 Tbsp water or corned beef cooking liquid

Prepare carrots as above. Place in dish which carrots almost fill.

Add water, using larger quantity if carrots are mature.

Cover tightly and cook at Full power, for 5–10 minutes, depending on size of pieces and age of carrots,

until carrots are barely tender.

Leave to stand for 3–4 minutes, adding a little butter, grated orange rind and/or juice, chopped parsley, honey or whatever you like with your carrots.

Buttered Cabbage

Cabbage microwaves well, with good colour and flavour retention.

Cabbage cooked without any added water may be too crisp for some people.

Cabbage cooked with a little water (which turns into steam during cooking) has a softer texture.

For 4 servings:
about 300 g cabbage
2–3 tsp water or corned beef cooking liquid
about 1 tsp butter

Shred cabbage, discarding coarse ribs, but using some of the well-coloured outer leaves.

Place in a casserole dish just big enough to hold cabbage or an oven bag, with water or cooking liquid, and butter.

Cover casserole, or fasten bag with a rubber band as close to the cabbage as possible, leaving a finger-sized hole so that steam can escape during cooking.

Cook at Full power for 4–5 minutes, until cabbage is wilted and tender, but still bright green.

Leave to stand for about 2 minutes, then serve.

Alternative method
1–2 tsp butter
1–2 garlic cloves, chopped
1 Tbsp water or corned beef cooking liquid
about 300 g shredded cabbage

Put butter and garlic cloves together in a casserole just big enough to hold the cabbage.

Cook at Full power for 30 seconds, then add the (hot) liquid and the cabbage and toss to coat leaves.

Cover tightly and microwave as above.

Fruit Crumble

Microwaved fruit crumble does not have a browned topping, but it will be crisp, and well flavoured.

When you make a crumble you can choose whatever fruit is in season, e.g.
spring — rhubarb
summer — peaches, nectarines
autumn and winter — pears, apples, tamarillos, feijoas, mixtures of above
If the fruit is really tart, put a little sugar with it, or if desired add sugar and cornflour to thicken the fruit.

For 4–6 servings:
Base
4–5 cups sliced raw fruit or 3 cups drained cold stewed fruit
sugar and cornflour (optional)

Topping
½ cup rolled oats
½ cup white or brown sugar
¼ cup wholemeal or plain flour
1 tsp mixed spice
50 g cold butter
ground cloves, etc. (optional)

Prepare the base first.

Lightly spray or grease a 20–23 cm microwave dish with a flat bottom and fairly straight sides.

Prepare and slice the fruit thinly and arrange it in the dish, with sugar, or a sugar and cornflour mixture between the layers of fruit if desired. (The fruit always sinks during cooking).

Prepare the topping. Combine all the dry ingredients except the cloves in a bowl or food processor. Cut or rub the cold butter into it, until the mixture looks like breadcrumbs.

Sprinkle topping over the cold fruit, and sprinkle the surface with the ground cloves (or any other spice you like) for extra colour, if desired.

Microwave uncovered, at Full power, for 10–12 minutes, or until the fruit base is cooked, and the top is crunchy.

Serve warm or reheat before serving.
Hint:
Reheat individual servings rather than whole crumble.

Lamb Dinner for Someone Special

This menu is one which may be served when you want a meal which is extra-special.

It looks spectacular, and tastes wonderful, but takes only a short time to prepare and cook, when you use your microwave oven.

A dinner like this may be prepared ahead, then cooked and served with the minimum of time spent in the kitchen just before the meal. Or it may be prepared and cooked just before it is eaten, by two people working happily together, in an even shorter time!

The rack of lamb, one of the most tender cuts on the lamb carcase, is cooked to perfection in an amazingly short time, in the microwave.

The selection of vegetables shows, yet again, what wonderful colour, flavour, and vitamin retention you get when you microwave them.

When new potatoes are in season, I microwave these, very successfully, instead of baking mature potatoes.

Even seasoned microwave cooks are confounded by the individual cheesecakes which cook unbelievably fast, and look and taste so good.

And to finish off on a high note, there is Irish Coffee! What more could you ask?

LAMB DINNER FOR SOMEONE SPECIAL

Herbed Rack of Lamb

Jacket Baked Potatoes

Creamy Pumpkin Cubes

Broccoli

Cheesecake Tarts

Irish Coffee

Plan of Attack

Although I have not included a starter course in this menu, you could easily make one.

Especially if you have not entertained a great deal, you are best to choose something which can be cooked ahead, and served cold, either informally, or at the table, e.g. Chicken Liver Pâté.

1. Make the Cheesecake Tarts. You can start work on them half an hour before you want to eat, or you can make them the night before.
2. Cook the jacket potatoes next. As long as you sit them in a folded cloth, or in a tea-cosy, or wrap them in foil, you should have no problem keeping them hot for ten minutes after they come out of the microwave oven.
3. Next, cook the rack of lamb. Prepare it while the potatoes cook.
4. While the lamb cooks, prepare the pumpkin. Cook it as soon as the lamb comes out of the oven.
5. Prepare the broccoli while the pumpkin cooks, and cook it while you get the other things ready for serving.
6. It only takes a few minutes to get the Irish Coffee ready, but if you prefer to, get it ready for later reheating at any time when you have something cooking in the microwave oven.

Herbed Rack of Lamb

A rack of lamb is one of the nicest things you can cook in your microwave oven.

A rack of lamb is cut from the front end of the loin. It is made up of rib chops, joined together. You can usually count about eight ribs in a rack.

If you are asking for a rack which you want to cook without trimming at all yourself, ask for a chined, frenched rack, with the fell and all the fat coating above the rib-eye muscle removed.

You will frequently see racks like this displayed in butchers' shops and supermarkets.

For 2 servings:
1 frenched, chined, 6–8 chop rack
1 Tbsp dry or smooth mixed mustard
2–3 tsp dark soya sauce
finely chopped fresh herbs

Place rack, bone side down, on a microwave roasting rack or on a makeshift roasting dish made by inverting a bread and butter plate on a dinner plate.

Mixed the mustard with enough soya sauce to make a spreadable paste, and brush or rub this evenly over all the meaty surfaces of the rack.

Sprinkle the finely chopped herbs evenly over the mustard mixture.

Microwave, uncovered, or lightly covered with a paper towel tent, at Full power for 4–4½ minutes, or until the meat in the middle of the rack springs back when pressed.

The cooking time varies with the size and age of the lamb from which the rack was cut, the initial temperature of the uncooked meat, and the number of chops on the rack.

Cover the rack with foil, and leave to stand for 5–10 minutes before carving it. Pour over the pan juices when serving.

Jacket Baked Potatoes

Potatoes which are baked in your microwave oven are especially quick and easy to prepare.

You should experiment until you become an expert at judging exactly when potatoes are perfectly baked. Potatoes which are hard have not been cooked long enough, and potatoes which are shrunken have been overcooked.

Remember the proverb about the carpenter who blames his tools. Do not blame the microwave oven or the potatoes!

Select and scrub evenly shaped, preferably unblemished potatoes.

Pierce each potato deeply, in several places.

Arrange potatoes so they are equidistant, and the same distance from the centre.

Microwave at Full power, allowing 3–5 minutes per potato, turning over once, about half way through the estimated cooking time. The potatoes should 'give' slightly all over, when pressed.

Leave to stand in a warm place, for at least 3–4 minutes. The potatoes will continue to cook during this time.

1 small potato (100 g) 3 minutes
2 medium potatoes (300 g)
    7–8 minutes
3 medium potatoes (400 g)
    10 minutes
4 large potatoes (600–800 g)
    12–14 minutes

Creamy Pumpkin Cubes

In a microwave oven, you can cook raw pumpkin and the sauce surrounding it together, without the worry of either burning.

For 2 servings:
200 g cubed pumpkin
1 tsp flour
1 garlic clove, chopped
¼ tsp curry powder (optional)
pinch salt
2–3 Tbsp cream or creamy milk

Cut pumpkin into 1 cm cubes.

Place in oven bag with the flour, garlic, and curry powder, and toss to coat.

Add salt and liquid, and fasten bag with a rubber band, leaving a finger-sized hole for steam and air to escape. (Because vegetables cook best in a small, confined space, push the rubber band down, close to the pumpkin.)

Microwave at Full power for 2–4 minutes, or until the pumpkin feels tender when the bag is squeezed. Move the pumpkin around in the bag half way through the cooking time, for best results

Leave to stand for 1–2 minutes, before serving.

Broccoli

(See recipe on page 304.)

Cheesecake Tarts

These are small, rich individual tarts which are cooked in paper cases, and are removed from them before serving.

Don't worry if the little tarts look rather odd before you top them with cream. The whipped cream can hide a multitude of sins!

For 8–10 cheesecakes:
2 tsp butter, melted
¼ cup malt biscuit crumbs
1 egg, lightly beaten
½ can sweetened condensed milk
3 Tbsp lemon juice
grated rind of ½ lemon

Melt the butter in a small bowl, at Full power for about 15 seconds, then stir in crumbs.

Press a rounded household teaspoon of crumbs into the bottom of 8–10 paper cupcake liners (large size) standing in microwave cupcake pans, or in cups.

In a larger bowl beat the egg, add the condensed milk, juice and rind, and beat to combine.

Pour about 3 tablespoons filling on to the crumbs in each case.

Microwave at Medium (50% power) for 2–3 minutes for 5–6 tarts, until the filling is set in the centre.

Leave to stand in the paper cups for about 5 minutes, then carefully pull away the paper.

Decorate with whipped cream and seasonal fruit just before serving.

Irish Coffee

These days almost any whisky-coffee mixture is called Irish Coffee, so please yourself when you make it, using strong, freshly made coffee or instant granules. Sweeten the coffee, the cream, or both.

For each cup:
½ cup freshly made strong coffee (or 2 tsp instant coffee dissolved in ½ cup hot water)
1–2 tsp sugar
1–2 Tbsp whisky
lightly whipped cream

Mix all ingredients except cream in microwave-safe mugs or glasses.

Microwave at Full power for 45 seconds to 1 minute or until very hot. Stir to dissolve sugar.

Just before serving, carefully pour whipped cream on to the surface of each cup. Drink without stirring.

Winter Lamb Casserole Dinner

There are times when it is nice to be able to make a casserole which will not need any last minute fuss or additions. Lamb is my favourite meat for microwaved casseroles.

Once it is underway, you can go out, knowing that the microwave will turn itself off at the time you have set. The casserole can be reheated when you want it.

Use the microwave oven to bake kumara (or cook rice) and to cook broccoli. Just before you sit down to dinner, you can put the Steamed Carrot Pudding, a spicy, popular cold-weather dessert, in to cook.

If you feel that it is complicated cooking everything in the mcirowave oven, you can cook broccoli or beans in a pan on the cooktop.

For speed and ease, I like to serve an uncooked sauce with the carrot pudding.

WINTER LAMB CASSEROLE DINNER

Winter Lamb Casserole

Rice or Baked Kumara

Broccoli or Beans

Steamed Carrot Pudding with Apricot Cream Sauce

Plan of Attack

1. Prepare the Winter Lamb Casserole at least an hour and a half before you want to serve it. The flavour will be even better if it is cooked before it is needed and left to stand.
2. Scrub the kumara, prick and bake, or prepare and cook the rice.
3. If you are serving beans with this meal, prepare and put into a pan of salted boiling water on the cooktop. (Beans take longer than expected to cook in the microwave). Or prepare and cook broccoli in the microwave oven.
4. While vegetables are cooking and the casserole standing, prepare the Steamed Carrot Pudding and Apricot Cream Sauce. The pudding can be put into the microwave just before you sit down to eat the main course. It will be cooked and will have stood long enough to serve straight away.

Winter Lamb Casserole

In this casserole the additions to the lamb add flavour and colour as well as thickening the sauce. Cubes of tender lamb in this sauce make it one of the nicest casseroles I make.

Make sure that the meat is trimmed of nearly all visible fat before combining it with the other ingredients.

For 4–6 servings:
750 g cubed shoulder lamb
¼ cup flour
2 tsp instant beef stock
1 tsp dry mustard
1 Tbsp Worcestershire sauce
2 tsp dark soya sauce
1 onion, chopped
1 green pepper, chopped
1 red pepper, chopped
*2 cups chopped tomatoes (or 1 cup
    tomato purée and 1 cup water)*
about 10 drops hot pepper sauce

Trim lamb, removing fat.
Toss meat with dry ingredients, then add remaining ingredients.
Cook in large, covered microwave dish at Full power for 10 minutes, then stir and cook on Defrost (30% power) for 45 mintues or until meat is tender.

Rice

You don't save much time by cooking rice in a microwave oven, but you get an excellent product without any rinsing, draining, or scraping the bottom of the container. For best results, choose Basmati rice — it is well worth the extra price because it has such a delicious flavour.

1 cup Basmati or other long-grain rice
2 tsp oil or butter
½ tsp salt
2¼ cups hot water

Put all the ingredients into a microwave dish and microwave, covered at Full power for 12 minutes.
Leave to stand for 5–10 minutes. During this time the rice will soak up the rest of the water and finish cooking.
Fluff up with a fork. The rice doesn't need draining and never burns on the bottom.
Reheat if necessary.
Note:
You can avoid the boiling-over problem, even at Full power, if you use a big enough, lidded container — i.e. about 23 cm in diameter, with fairly straight sides, and a 3–4 litre capacity — and you leave the lid ajar. Or you can use boiling water and cook the rice at Medium (50% power) for 15 minutes, or Defrost (30% power) for longer — about 20 minutes.

Baked Kumara

Kumara microwave very well, with times similar to those of potatoes the same weight.

If you cannot find small kumara, cook larger ones and slice them before serving.

For a special treat, try whole split kumara or kumara slices topped with sour cream, reduced cream or yoghurt and a sprinkling of brown sugar.

Scrub evenly shaped kumara well. Cut off any stringy ends
Prick in several places.
Microwave at Full power, allowing 3 minutes per 100 g, turning over after half the estimated cooking time. Cook until kumara give when pressed.
Leave to stand for 3–4 minutes.
Cut a cross in the tops and press between the cuts. Serve with sour cream and chives, or with sour cream mixed with brown sugar in proportions to taste, e.g. 1 teaspoon brown sugar to 2 tablespoons sour cream.

To Warm Plates

Hot plates are important, especially for lamb. Between plates put wet paper towels and heat at Full power for ½–1 minute per plate, or until plates are hot.

Broccoli

Broccoli is one of my favourite microwaved vegetables. Allow 125–150 g per serving.

For best results, cut the flowerbud heads into even pieces, peel off and discard the tough skin on the stalk, starting at the base of the stem, then cut the stems into pieces the same size as the tops. (Unpeeled broccoli overcooks before stems become tender).

Add 2 teaspoons water per serving.

Cook at Full power. Allow:
1 serving — 1½ minutes
2 servings — 2½ minutes
4 servings — 4 minutes.
Allow 2 minutes' standing time.
Toss with butter.

Green Beans

If you choose to cook beans in the microwave, add ½ cup water to 500 g sliced beans. Cook at Full power for 8–15 minutes, depending on their age. Stir at intervals.

Steamed Carrot Pudding

If by any chance all your Steamed Carrot Pudding does not get eaten while it is hot, slice it and butter it as you would a fruit loaf.

The grated carrot added to the mixture keeps it nice and moist for some time after it is cooked. Because the mixture is soft, the pudding tends to break when turned out of its ring pan unless you take extra precautions. The best precaution is to spray the ring pan lightly with non-stick spray, then to line the bottom with a Teflon liner especially shaped for ring pans.

Note:
Remember to retrieve the Teflon liner after use. It can be used many times, but it is easy for someone who doesn't know this to throw it out when clearing up after the meal.

For 6 servings:
100 g butter
2 cups finely grated carrot
1 egg
1 cup brown sugar
1 cup flour
¾ tsp baking soda
1 tsp cinnamon
1 tsp mixed spice
½ cup sultanas

Melt butter in a mixing bowl at Full power for about 1½ minutes.

Stir in carrots, egg and sugar.

Sift in dry ingredients and add sultanas. Stir until just mixed. The thickness of the mixture depends on the carrots. If very thin, stir in ¼ cup flour. The final mixture should be thinner than butter cake mixture.

Pour into a small ring mould that has been lightly sprayed with non-stick spray and the bottom lined with a Teflon liner. Cover with a lid or plastic cling wrap.

Microwave at Full power for 7 minutes. Leave to stand for 2 minutes, then unmould.

Apricot Cream Sauce

This sauce seems deliciously rich although it is made from a low-fat cream, mixed with low-fat yoghurt. If you find it too thick, thin it down with milk.

A little orange rind, grated over it, looks pretty if you are serving the pudding for a special occasion.

I use equal parts of reduced fat cream and apricot-flavoured yoghurt — use proportions to suit yourself.

Tangy Pork Fillet Dinner

It is a good feeling to know that you have some special recipes in your cooking repertoire, so that you can cook an impressively tasty and attractive meal for a friend.

You can serve the main course of this meal, from scratch, less than half an hour after you come in the door. Or, if you want to spend as little time in the kitchen as possible, you can plan ahead and impress your guests by producing this meal after spending only 10 minutes or so popping things in and out of your microwave oven.

The recipes used in the main course are modifications of Chinese favourites of mine. The microwave oven ensures that the rice is beautifully light and fluffy, the pork fillet is amazingly tender and the sauce colourful, tangy and of good consistency. The vegetables may be cooked just as you like them, but I hope you will try them while they are tender-crisp, with maximum colour.

One of the reasons that all the food in the main course tastes so good is that no cooking or marinating liquids are thrown out — so no flavour or nutrients are lost.

If you like a slice of cake to serve with tea or coffee, you will find this banana cake, made with a mixture of wholemeal and plain flour, is easy and popular. Make different icings for it on different occasions.

TANGY PORK FILLET DINNER

Marinated Pork Fillet in Tangy Plum Sauce

Rice

Stir-Fried Green Vegetables

Iced Banana Cake

Coffee

Plan of Attack

1. Make the Iced Banana Cake first. It will need 3-4 minutes' standing time before it is turned out to cool, and once cold it can be iced. Mix, cook and leave it to stand.
2. While the banana cake is cooking, prepare the pork fillet so it can marinate for at least 10 minutes for extra flavour.
3. Put the rice on to cook as soon as the cake comes out of the microwave oven. Rice needs standing time and is easy to reheat when it suits you.
4. Next, make the chocolate icing for your banana cake.
5. Measure the Tangy Plum Sauce ingredients in a separate bowl.
6. Prepare the vegetables. (When you have got to this stage, you have everything organised and can sit and relax!)
7. Then, back to the kitchen. Reheat the rice for a few minutes and while it reheats, put the cake on its serving plate and ice it.
8. Cook the marinated pork fillet. When it is cooked, cook the sauce and stir the cooked meat into the cooked sauce.
9. Put the vegetables in to cook while you serve the meat and rice.

Marinated Pork Fillet in Tangy Plum Sauce

This recipe is one of my favourites. The meat is very tender and in its sweet and sour sauce everyone seems to like it.

For 2–3 servings:
1 pork fillet (250–350 g)
1 tsp dark soya sauce
1 tsp sesame oil
1 tsp sherry
1 clove garlic, finely chopped

Sauce
2 tsp cornflour
1 tsp instant green herb stock
2 tsp dark soya sauce
¼ cup plum jam
¼ cup dry sherry
½ cup water
1 clove garlic, finely chopped

Cut fillet into pieces about 5 mm thick.

Mix with soya sauce, sesame oil, sherry and garlic. Leave to stand for at least 10 minutes.

Cover and microwave at Full power for 2-4 minutes, stirring after each minute until meat loses its pinkness (fillet can overcook in a very short time).

In another bowl combine sauce ingredients.

Microwave, covered, at Full power for about 2 minutes, stirring occasionally, until smooth and clear.

Stir meat into cooked sauce and spoon over rice. The meat will be best if you cook it just before you need it, and stir it into the hot sauce just before serving.

Rice

1 cup Basmati or other long-grain rice
2 tsp oil or butter
½ tsp salt
2¼ cups hot water

Put all the ingredients into a microwave dish and microwave, covered, at Full power for 12 minutes.

Leave to stand for 5-10 minutes. During this time the rice will soak up the rest of the water and finish cooking.

Fluff up with a fork. The rice doesn't need draining and never burns on the bottom.

Reheat if necessary.

Note:
If you find the rice boiling over, leave the lid ajar or add boiling water and cook at Medium (50% power) for 15 minutes or Defrost (30% power) for longer — about 20 minutes.

Stir-Fried Green Vegetables

I like a mixture of green vegetables cooked this way, but you can choose any vegetable you like. Serve them tender-crisp.

For 2–3 servings:
1½ Tbsp oil
1 clove garlic, finely chopped
300 g prepared vegetables (e.g. zucchini, green peppers, celery, pea pods, etc.)
1 tsp cornflour
½ tsp instant chicken stock
¼ tsp salt
2 tsp brown sugar

1 Tbsp dry sherry
1 tsp light soya sauce

Prepare green vegetables. Slice diagonally or into evenly thin slices.

In a covered microwave dish cook the garlic in the oil at Full power for 1–2 minutes.

Add the vegetables and cook for 2 minutes.

While the vegetables cook, mix together the remaining ingredients.

Stir into the hot vegetables and cook for 1 minute longer so vegetables are lightly coated with the glaze.

Iced Banana Cake

Banana cake is a favourite with most. I sometimes top it with cream cheese icing or lemon butter icing. This time I have chosen an easy chocolate icing.

125 g butter, melted
1 cup brown sugar
1 Tbsp wine vinegar
2 eggs
2–3 very ripe bananas, mashed
1 cup wholemeal flour
¾ cup flour
1 tsp baking soda
¼ cup milk

In a fairly large mixing bowl, melt the butter at Full power for 1½ minutes.

Add sugar, vinegar and eggs, then beat with a fork or rotary beater until well mixed.

Stir in the mashed bananas.

Sprinkle the wholemeal flour over the surface.

Add the flour and baking soda, sifted together, and the milk.

Fold everything together, using a rubber scraper.

Turn into a baking paper or Teflon-lined 20 cm square pan or ring pan.

Microwave at Medium-High (70% power) for 12 minutes, or until centre is firm.

Notes:
Your cake is done when you start to smell it, when the surface springs back, when you can't see uncooked dough and when it is starting to come away from the sides of the pan. As an extra precaution with soft cakes, use a thin film of non-stick spray. A paper towel on top of the cake pan means more even rising and no sticky uncooked cake on top.

Chocolate Sour Cream Icing

½ cup cooking chocolate pieces
¼ cup sour cream

Microwave the chocolate at Full power for 1½–2 minutes or until melted.

Stir in the sour cream.

Spread on the cold cake and refrigerate until the icing has set, if you want it firm.

Or try these alternative icings:

Cream Cheese Icing

2 Tbsp cream cheese
1 Tbsp butter
1 tsp vanilla
1½ cups sifted icing sugar

Put cream cheese, butter and vanilla in a medium-sized bowl. Microwave at Full power for 20–30 seconds until cream cheese and butter are very soft.

Add icing sugar and mix with a knife until smooth and creamy.

Add a little milk or icing sugar if mixture is too thick or thin. Spread on slightly warm cake.

Lemon Butter Icing

1 Tbsp butter
1½ Tbsp lemon juice
½ tsp finely grated lemon rind (optional)
1½ cups sifted icing sugar

Put butter, lemon juice and rind in a medium-sized bowl. Microwave at Full power for 20 seconds or until butter is soft.

Add icing sugar and mix with a knife until smooth and creamy. Spread on slightly warm cake.

Pork Stir-Fry Dinner

This is a bright, colourful dinner which you could serve to a group of your friends, without having to spend a lot of time in the kitchen while everybody else is having a good time.

Although the tomato soup has the name 'fresh' attached to it, you can make it using good quality canned tomatoes in juice.

The stir-fried pork and vegetables makes a good main course. It may be prepared the night before, and left to marinate in the refrigerator, in the bag in which it will be cooked. Microwave 'stir-fries' are worth perfecting if you do not have an efficient gas burner and wok.

Microwaved brown rice cooks in about half the time it takes to cook conventionally.

Upside-down Cake looks so pretty when you turn it out of its ring pan that nobody notices the light-coloured bottom surface.

PORK STIR-FRY DINNER

**Fresh Tomato Soup
with
Croutons**

**Stir-Fried Pork
with
Vegetables and
Cashew Nuts**

Brown Rice

Upside-Down Cake

Plan of Attack

1. Start by marinating the pork.
2. Prepare and cook the cake next. It can be served cold, but is nicer if warmed up.
3. Make the soup next.
4. Cook the rice. While it cooks, tidy up, and set the table, etc.
5. Prepare the vegetables, and put them in a casserole dish, ready to cook.
6. When you are ready to eat, reheat the rice, then reheat and serve the soup.
7. Put the vegetables on to cook while you are eating the soup, or just after it. While the vegetables stand, cook the pork, watching it carefully so it cooks for exactly the right time, then combine the vegetables and pork, and serve them on the rice.
8. Warm up the cake while the main course is eaten.

Fresh Tomato Soup

It's nice to come across chunky pieces of skinned tomato when you eat this slightly thickened soup.

For 3–4 servings:
*1 medium-sized onion, very finely
    chopped
1 clove garlic, chopped
2 Tbsp butter
2 tsp cornflour
1 tsp salt
2 tsp sugar
¼ tsp paprika
½ cup hot water
500 g ripe tomatoes, skinned and
    chopped*

In a large covered bowl or casserole dish cook the onion and garlic in the butter at Full power for 4 minutes, stirring after 2 minutes.

Stir in cornflour, then the next four ingredients.

To skin the tomatoes, dip them in boiling water for 20–30 seconds, then run them under a cold tap. Pull off skins. Halve the peeled tomatoes and shake them over the sink to remove any watery juice and seeds, before cutting them into cubes. (Use extra tomatoes if you discard too much liquid and seeds).

Add them to other ingredients, then cook until mixture is clear red, and slightly thickened, stirring several times. This will probably take 6–8 minutes.

Variation:
Replace fresh tomatoes with a 425 g can of peeled tomatoes in juice and an extra ½ cup of water. Drain the juice into the other ingredients with the water then chop up, and add the

tomatoes. Because the canned tomatoes may have been seasoned, use half the salt and sugar listed, adding more after tasting, at the end of cooking time, if necessary.

Croutons

(See recipe on page 297.)

Stir-Fried Pork with Vegetables and Cashew Nuts

Use lean, thinly sliced pork schnitzels for this recipe. Marinate them first, then take care not to undercook or overcook them, for best texture and tenderness.

For 4 servings:
*500 g pork schnitzel
2 cloves garlic, chopped
2 Tbsp corn or soya oil
1½ Tbsp light soya sauce
1 Tbsp sherry
2 tsp brown sugar
1 tsp instant chicken stock
1 Tbsp cornflour
500 g sliced quick-cooking vegetables
¼–½ cup whole cashew nuts*

At least half an hour before you intend to serve this stir-fried pork, trim all visible fat and membrane from the schnitzels and cut them into strips no wider than 1 cm.

Place the strips in an oven bag with the garlic, 2 teaspoons of the oil, the soya sauce, sherry, sugar, instant stock and cornflour.

Knead the bag well to mix the

marinade through the meat, squeeze all air from bag, fasten it tightly with a rubber band, and put it aside.

Refrigerate bag of marinated pork if it is to stand for longer than four hours.

Remove from refrigerator so meat comes to room temperature before cooking. Knead bag again, spread meat so that it forms a doughnut shape, about 20 cm in diameter, and loosen rubber band, so bag has a finger-sized hole for air and steam to escape.

If cashew nuts have not been toasted, coat them with a teaspoon of the corn or soya oil and microwave them at Full power until they brown, watching them carefully, removing nuts as they brown. Nuts sometimes do not brown readily, and you may find it faster to brown them in a frying pan or under a grill.

A short time before cooking, slice vegetables such as red and green peppers, celery, spring onions, snow peas, broccoli, cauliflower, cabbage, spinach, mushrooms, etc. into strips about the same size as schnitzels. Place in a lidded microwave dish 20–23 cm in diameter, then toss in remaining oil.

Assemble marinated pork, toasted cashew nuts, and oiled vegetables.

Microwave covered dish of vegetables at Full power for 3–4 minutes, or until tender-crisp, shaking once or twice at intervals. Remove from oven, and leave to stand without removing the lid, while you cook the pork.

Cook pork in loosely fastened oven bag at Full power, turning bag

and repositioning pork after 2–3 minutes. Cook pork until it loses its pinkness, and take care to remove it from the oven before it overcooks and toughens.

Tip the contents of the bag, and cashew nuts into casserole with cooked vegetables, toss to mix, and to coat vegetables, then serve immediately.

Brown Rice

Brown rice has a nutty flavour, a chewier texture and more B vitamins than polished white rice. The microwave cooks it in half the time of conventional cooking, producing a tender result.

For 4 servings:
1 cup brown rice
1 tsp butter
¹/₂ tsp salt
*   or 1 tsp instant stock*
2¹/₄ cups very hot water.

Combine rice with remaining ingredients in a lidded casserole of about 3 litre capacity. Cover and cook at Full power for about 20 minutes, then leave to stand for 10 minutes before uncovering and serving.
Note:
Exact cooking times, standing times, and amounts of cooking liquid vary with different brown rices. Experiment, using longer cooking times and more liquid for softer rice. If rice boils over, lower power level to Medium or Medium-High (50%–70%) after rice boils.

Upside-Down Cake

Choose a pan about 20 cm in diameter with fairly straight sides and a flat bottom, if possible. If it does not have a central cone (i.e. if it is not a ring pan), invert a glass in the centre of the pan after lining the pan, since this helps the cake cook more evenly.

Line the bottom and lower sides of the pan with:
a Teflon liner made for a ring or round pan
or a round or ring of baking paper with snipped edges
or an oven bag, cut open flat, trimmed to be square or round, to cover the sides and bottom of a round pan. (Put a glass in pan after lining it).

Topping
2 Tbsp butter
2–3 Tbsp golden syrup
peaches, etc.
cherries

In measuring cup or in oven bag-lined pan melt the butter at Full power, then stir in syrup, warming mixture if syrup is very cold and hard.

Spread evenly over bottom of pan then arrange the fruit of your choice and the cherries over it, remembering that the side of the fruit touching the liner will be uppermost later.

75–100 g butter
¹/₂ cup brown sugar
1 tsp vanilla
¹/₂ tsp cinnamon
1 egg
1–1¹/₄ cups flour
1–2 tsp baking powder
about ¹/₂ cup cooking liquid from fruit,
*   or fruit juice, or milk*

Melt the butter in a mixing bowl, using larger amount for a richer cake.

Add the sugar, vanilla, cinnamon and egg and beat with a rotary beater until light.

Sift the flour and baking powder into the mixture (using the smaller amount for a richer cake). Pour in ¹/₄ cup of the liquid, for smaller amount of flour, and ¹/₂ cup liquid for the larger amount of flour, and fold dry ingredients and liquid together, to form a batter which will drop easily off a spoon. Use a little extra liquid if necessary. Take care not to overmix.

Pour or spoon the batter over the prepared fruit topping. Cover pan with a paper towel and cook at Full power for 4–6 minutes or until the batter nearest the centre of the dish is set.

Leave to stand for 5 minutes, or, if reheating, leave until just before serving, before turning upside down and removing liner etc.
Note:
If syrup has soaked into fruit, drizzle over a little more before serving.

Roast Pork Loin — Celebration Dinner

This is a menu for a special-occasion dinner at any time of the year.

I sit down beforehand and work out at what precise time I should put the different foods on to cook and to reheat.

When I make this meal in the summer, I always enjoy the fact that the kitchen does not heat up as it would if I cooked the pork roast in the conventional oven.

I cook the beans on my cooktop — partly because the microwave oven is being fully utilised with other foods, and partly because I don't think that green beans microwave very well.

When I make the Prune and Apple Sauce (or another fruit sauce), I usually reconstitute fruit leather. It is possible to make a similar sauce using fresh fruit, but the convenience and speed of sauce made from the dehydrated fruit always impresses me.

The time spent cleaning up dishes is always much shorter when a microwave oven is used. In this menu, there will be no messy roasting pan to worry about, and several of the foods may be served from the dishes they are cooked in.

ROAST PORK LOIN — CELEBRATION DINNER

Stuffed Loin of Pork with Prune and Apple Sauce

Baked Potatoes

Red Cabbage

Green Beans

Ice-Cream with Spiced Fruity Sauce

Note:
Trim Pork loin roasts are pre-trimmed to remove outer layers of fat and skin, which means they are not coated with the skin that forms crackling. If you like crackling, ask your butcher for a sheet of skin with 5 mm or less fat under it.

Some people cook crackling in a microwave oven, but I prefer it cooked under the grill.

Plan of Attack

1. Prepare the Spiced Fruity Sauce, to serve with the ice-cream, first. It should be left to stand for an hour or more after cooking so the fruit can plump up nicely. If you intend serving it hot, it can be reheated before serving.
2. While the sauce cooks, prepare and cook the onion for the pork stuffing. Blanch the spinach leaves for the stuffing also.
3. Prepare the red cabbage and put in to cook while you stuff the meat and get it ready to cook. The meat takes nearly an hour to cook in the microwave oven.
4. While the pork cooks, scrub the potatoes ready for baking.
5. The potatoes should be cooked allowing 3 minutes per potato plus standing time, so they should be put into the oven towards the end of the the standing time for the pork.
6. Prepare and cook the beans on the cooktop.
7. Prepare the Prune and Apple Sauce, using the drained meat cooking liquid.

Note:
An alternative to this work plan is to prepare the Spiced Fruity Sauce, the Red Cabbage and the Prune and Apple Sauce earlier, especially if you like to get preparation out of the way, and reheat before serving. Add water or wine instead of the meat liquid to the Prune and Apple Sauce.

Stuffed Loin of Pork

The tender juicy roast of lean pork is stuffed with a colourful and well-flavoured mixture, making it suitable to serve for a special family occasion. Order a 1.5 kg loin of Trim Pork. Depending on how long you cook it and the size of the servings, it will make six or more servings.

For 6 servings:
1.5 kg loin Trim Pork
mixed mustard
Stuffing:
1 onion, finely chopped
2 tsp butter
a small can of pimentos, slices of tamarillo, fresh cherries or soaked dried apricots
spinach leaves
fresh basil leaves

Cook the onion and butter in a covered dish at Full power for 4–5 minutes, until tender.

Open out Trim Pork and cut a pocket in the large muscle. Brush mustard over the pork. Spread the onion evenly down the pocket.

For the next layer use either a small can of drained pimentos, or slices of tamarillo, fresh cherries or soaked dried apricots.

Blanch spinach leaves briefly in a little water in a loosely tied oven bag, or covered microwave dish. Spread spinach leaves over meat for colour and fresh basil leaves for flavour.

Roll up pork, starting with the leanest, most tender section inside. Run small skewers or strong toothpicks down the join and criss-cross strong string to hold it in place.

If desired, score the outside of the meat.

Rub with a coating of 1 tablespoon dry mustard mixed with 2–3 teaspoons dark soya sauce and a sprinkling of paprika, if desired.

Put in a ridged dish, cover with a lid or plastic film, or put in an oven bag that is loosely closed. Place dish, elevated 2–3 cm, in microwave oven.

Cook at 40% power for 16–17 minutes per 500 g for medium well done. (If you allow 20 minutes per

500 g it may be a bit overcooked.)

Leave roast to stand, covered, for at least 30 minutes after cooking.

Crackling

I prefer to cook crackling under the grill.

The sheet of pork skin should have 5 mm or less fat on its under-surface. Make sure that the whole surface is scored with lines about 5 mm apart.

Sprinkle the surface with salt, and rub it into the cuts. Next, rub oil evenly over the whole surface.

Lay the crackling on a rack or flat pan. You can cut it into strips, about 5–6 cm wide, if this suits you. Tuck the ends under the rungs of the rack, so they do not curl up as they cook.

Grill crackling 10 cm from the heat, for about 10 minutes, until it bubbles and turns golden brown. (Take care it does not burn). Turn and grill another 10 minutes on the underside.

Gravy

Drain off from roast the liquid which should have a good flavour and colour. Thicken it with a small amount of cornflour paste.

Prune and Apple Sauce

I like to make a fruit purée from dried fruit. I dry raw or cooked puréed fruit in a dehydrator for about 10 hours or until it is flexible. The fruit leathers can be reconstituted in the microwave oven.

fruit leather (made with 1 cup cooked apple and ¹/₂ cup cooked prunes)
1 cup water
pork cooking liquid
dash of sherry (optional)
¹/₂ tsp sugar
1 tsp butter

Break leather into small pieces, add water and microwave at Full power for 3–4 minutes.

To the thick purée add some of the drained meat cooking liquid and stir.

Serve with the pork as is, or add sherry, sugar and butter if desired.

Variation:
If you don't have fruit leather to make the sauce, replace with 1 cup of puréed cooked apples and ¹/₂ cup of cooked prunes.

Baked Potatoes

(See recipe on page 157.)

Red Cabbage

(See recipe on page 167.)

Green Beans

To cook in the microwave, add ¹/₂ cup of water to 500 g sliced beans. Cook at Full power for 8–15 minutes depending on the age of the beans.

Because the microwave is used to cook everything else for this menu, I prefer to cook the beans with a little garlic, butter and water in a covered saucepan on the stove.

My personal opinion is that beans aren't as good microwaved as they are cooked this way.

Spiced Fruity Sauce

This is a simplified version of a Christmas Sauce I make. It can be served hot in winter and at room temperature in summer. Spoon it over ice-cream and top with wafer.

Allowing the sauce to stand for an hour or so gives the fruit time to plump up.

1 cup mixed dried fruit
1 Tbsp cornflour
2 Tbsp sugar
1 tsp cinnamon
1 tsp mixed spice
¹/₄ tsp ground cloves
1 cup water
1 Tbsp wine vinegar
1 tsp butter
1–2 Tbsp concentrated orange juice
rum (optional)

In a covered microwave dish measure the dried fruit and the next eight ingredients.

Cook at Full power for 8 minutes or until the fruit is plump.

Stir in the orange juice and a dash of rum, if desired.

Leave to stand for an hour or so if you can.

Serve, rewarmed slightly, over ice-cream, with pieces of fruit, or in brandy snap baskets.

Softening Ice-Cream

Containers of ice cream which have been stored in a freezer may freeze very hard, so the ice cream is too hard to scoop easily. Loosen top of a (2 litre) container, and microwave at Medium (50% power) for 45–60 seconds, depending on hardness.

PARSLEY
Use raw or cooked
flat and curly leaf
plant annually
hardy

MINT
Use raw or cooked
several varieties
perennial
hardy

THYME
Usually cooked
many varieties
perennial
hardy

CHIVES
Use raw or cooked
several varieties
perennial
hardy

Fresh Herbs

Fresh herbs can made a tremendous difference to your cooking! Whether you prepare inexpensive family meals, assemble quick and easy convenience foods, or are willing to spend quite a lot of time and energy preparing 'gourmet' meals, fresh herbs can prove a valuable asset for you.

I've noticed a growing interest in fresh herb cookery lately. First came herb books, then a wider range of seeds and plants for keen gardeners, and, more recently, their wider use in good restaurants, and packs of fresh herbs at produce counters.

For centuries, herbs have been used to flavour food, to help make it more digestible and sometimes to preserve it, amongst other uses. In general, herbs are quite hardy small plants that grow in temperate climates. Especially if you grow

them yourself, you can use them, in small quantities, to add different flavours to your cooking.

Don't hesitate to experiment with herb additions to your favourite basic recipes. Sometimes you will find herbs listed in recipes, sometimes not. I use fresh herbs regularly but do not always list them in my recipes in case inexperienced cooks, without the herbs available, feel they cannot make those particular foods. Especially if you are introducing herbs to your family, take care not to be heavy-handed, or to add herbs to everything. Too much can be worse than none! If you are replacing dried herbs with fresh, use two to three times as much as a rough guide. For fleshy leaves, use the larger amount; for leathery leaves, use the small quantity.

If you intend growing only a few herbs, choose herbs that lose most of their character and flavour when dried, e.g. parsley, chives, basil, dill

leaves, tarragon, coriander leaf, and chervil.

In warm places, grow herbs outside in the garden for preference. In cooler places pamper herbs such as basil, coriander and chervil in large pots on a window sill, but plant others outside in a sunny sheltered open spot, preferably close to the kitchen.

Listed and photographed, are the fresh herbs I use most.

1. PARSLEY: Leaves and stalks flavour and colour many cooked and raw savoury foods. Flat-leafed parsley has a stronger flavour. For a continuous supply, plant parsley every spring.

2. MINT: Spreads rapidly in damp conditions. Although to many it is associated only with lamb, peas and new potatoes, it is widely used in many cuisines.

LOVAGE
Usually cooked
perennial
hardy

CORIANDER
Use raw or cooked
annual
needs warmth

CHERVIL
Use raw or cooked
annual
needs warmth

**SUMMER
SAVORY**
Usually cooked
several varieties
annual

MARJORAM
Use raw or cooked
several varieties
annual
fairly hardy

BASIL
Use raw or cooked
several varieties
annual
needs warmth

OREGANUM
Usually cooked
several varieties
perennial
hardy

BAY
Usually cooked
perennial (tree)
hardy

3. THYME: Has strongly flavoured leaves which are usually cooked. Different varieties have interesting scents and flavours. It is hardy if not overgrown by other plants. Use sparingly in most savoury cooking.

4. CHIVES: Have a mild onion flavour and are used cooked or raw. Grow several clumps and pick one at a time. It is especially nice with egg and creamy mixtures.

5. KNOTTED (OR SWEET) MARJORAM: Has a milder flavour and is used in many cooked mixtures. It needs replacing annually. It is not always easy to distinguish between different marjoram varieties.

6. BASIL: Used sparingly with tomatoes, pasta, eggs and salads, it has a strong, distinctive, exciting flavour, most of which is lost when dried. Pinch out and use the tips of stems to encourage bushy growth. Grow in large pots kept handy for frequent use.

7. OREGANUM (WILD MARJORAM): Strongly flavoured, easy to grow, and especially good with cooked tomato and mince mixtures.

8. BAY: Grows to a large, bushy tree if not constrained. Use leaves in stocks, sauces, pickles, stews and casseroles, discarding before serving.

9. LOVAGE: Has a strong celery flavour and is used sparingly in cooked stocks, casseroles, soups and sauces.

10. CORIANDER: Seeds have an orange-curry flavour, especially good with lamb and used in curry mixtures. The young leaves (Chinese parsley) are widely used in Asian cooking.

11. CHERVIL: Has a delicate flavour and very pretty leaves. Use raw, as garnish, and in quickly cooked dishes, especially with eggs and cream.

12. SUMMER SAVORY: Used with vegetables (especially beans), eggs, sauces and salad dressings. Winter and prostrate savory are perennials with similar, less delicate flavours.

13. DILL: After one seeding, will appear in your garden every year. Its feathery, delicate leaves are much nicer than its seeds. Use in dressings, creamy mixtures, with fish, and in salads and pickles.

14. SAGE: Strongly flavoured, especially in hot weather. Use sparingly with rich foods such as pork, liver, cheese, and as a drink.

15. ROSEMARY: An easily grown shrub with leathery leaves. Chop them very finely and use sparingly with tomato, lamb and fish.

16. FRENCH TARRAGON: Has a distinct flavour important in French cookery, in sauces, butters and meat dishes.

DILL
Use raw or cooked
annual
hardy

SAGE
Usually cooked
several varieties
perennial
hardy

ROSEMARY
Usually cooked
several varieties
perennial
hardy

FRENCH TARRAGON
Use raw or cooked
several varieties
perennial

Spices

Spices are special. They have been used in small quantities for thousands of years to add zip, zing and zest to food.

Cooking with spices is easy. You can use ground or whole spices. Sometimes it is an advantage to have ground spices which mix quickly with other ingredients, and can be eaten. At other times, when you don't want food darkened by ground spices, it is·a good idea to use whole spices, and to remove them before the food is served.

Spices which you grind yourself just before use have a strong, interesting, fresh flavour. Do not spice food so heavily that you can no longer taste the original food. Experiment by adding small amounts of spices to recipes which do not have them, keeping an open mind about combinations.

Don't make the mistake of spicing everything you cook. You need the contrast of spiced and plain foods to enjoy both.

How many of the spices photographed do you recognise and use?

1. CAYENNE PEPPER: A type of chilli pepper, ground.

2. BLACK PEPPER: Peppercorns are dried berries which grow on a vine. Unrelated to chilli peppers. Most aromatic when freshly ground. For black pepper, berries are picked green and sun dried. For white pepper, ripe berries are fermented and hulled.

3. YELLOW MUSTARD SEED: Most pungent when mixed with water. Much less pungent when heated.

4. SMALL CHILLIES: Chillies come in different sizes and colours, and can vary in hotness. Always use chillies with care. Chop finely or remove from food before eating.

5. TURMERIC: Ground root of a ginger-like plant. It has a distinctive flavour as well as a bright yellow colour.

6. CLOVES: The dried unopened buds of an evergreen tree have a strong flavour.

7. MIXED SPICE: A widely used, ground mixture of, e.g., coriander, cinnamon, cassia, allspice, nutmeg, caraway seed.

8. FIVE SPICES: A ground mixture used in Chinese cooking. It may contain star anise, fennel, cloves, cinnamon, cassia, nutmeg, bay leaves.

9. LARGE CHILLIES: Hot. Use with care, to judge hotness.

10. SESAME SEED: An oily seed with a nutty flavour when roasted. May be used in sweet and savoury mixtures.

11. PIMENTO (ALLSPICE): A pungent (not hot) berry, with a flavour rather like mixed spices.

12. ROOT GINGER: Well known and widely used, fresh, ground, dried, crystallised, etc.

13. GARAM MASALA: A mixture of spices, sweeter and milder than curry powder, often added near the end of cooking. May contain cinnamon, black pepper, cloves, cumin, mace, cardamom, bay leaves, coriander.

14. CASSIA: Thick slices of bark with a strong, pungent cinnamom flavour. A very ancient spice.

15. FENNEL SEED: Has a strong aniseed flavour. Used to aid digestion, and in spice mixtures.

16. POPPY SEEDS: Have a nutty flavour. Used as decoration on breads, etc.

17. CINNAMON: Widely used, finely rolled thin bark, ground for powdered cinnamon. More delicate flavour than cassia.

18. STAR ANISE: Star-shaped seed with a very strong aniseed flavour, used in Chinese cooking.

19. BAY LEAVES: Tough, strongly scented leaves. Used fresh or dried in Mediterranean cooking.

20. MACE: The outer net-like layer of the nutmeg seed. Orange in colour, with a delicate nutmeg-like flavour.

21. PICKLING SPICE: A mixture of whole spices used to flavour pickles, e.g., allspice, cloves, chillies, coriander, ginger, mace, mustard seed and peppercorns.

22. FENUGREEK; Yellowish seed used in curry powder.

23. CURRY POWDER: A spice mixture, e.g., cumin, coriander, fenugreek, turmeric, nutmeg, bay leaf, black pepper, mace. Its hotness depend on the amount of chilli included.

24. NUTMEG: The seed of a tropical tree. Grate it straight into sweet or savoury mixtures, since it loses flavour on standing.

25. CARDAMOM PODS: Contain eucalyptus-flavoured seed, used in sweet and savoury foods.

26. HOT INDIAN CURRY POWDER: Different flavour, colour and hotness result from grinding different spice mixtures (see 23).

27. SAFFRON: Very expensive, dried crocus stamens, with a bright yellow colour and mild flavour.

28. CARAWAY SEEDS: Strong flavoured, used in baking and savoury food, in German and Austrian cooking.

29. JUNIPER BERRIES: Have a pine-like flavour. Used in European cooking and to flavour gin.

30. CORIANDER: The seed of the plant of which the leaf is Chinese parsley. It has an orange, curry-like flavour.

31. PAPRIKA: The bright red ground seed of a sweet, mild red pepper.

32. CUMIN SEED: Often used in spice mixtures, e.g., curries. It has a distinctive, but not hot flavour.

33. BLACK MUSTARD SEED: Smaller and hotter than yellow mustard seed, and often used with it. When fried in Indian recipes, it loses much of its hotness.

34. CHILLI POWDER: May be ground hot chilli, or a much milder mixture of chilli with oreganum, cumin, etc.

35. CELERY SEED: Is the seed of a wild celery. Strong, sometimes ground with salt. Widely used for flavouring stews, etc.

QUATRE ÉPICE: A mixture of four or more spices used in French cooking. It may contain allspice, cloves, cinnamon, ginger, mace, nutmeg and white pepper.

Index